Africa on the Cheap

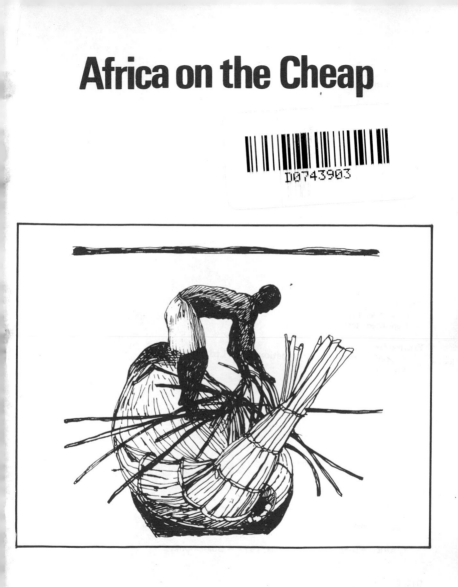

Africa on the Cheap

Published by
Lonely Planet Publications
PO Box 88, South Yarra
Victoria 3141, Australia

Produced by
Graphic Consultants International
Singapore

Typeset by
Lonely Planet Productions

Illustrations by
Peter Campbell

Design by
Andrena Millen

This edition
November 1980
Reprinted October 1981

Printed by
Graphic Consultants International Pte Ltd
Singapore

National Library of Australia
Cataloguing in Publication data
Crowther, Geoffrey
Africa on the Cheap

2nd ed.
Bibliography.
ISBN 0 908086 19 9

1. Africa — Description and travel, 1977 — Guide-books.
I. Title

916'.04328

Lonely Planet Guides

Across Asia on the Cheap
Africa on the Cheap
Australia — a travel survival kit
Burma — a travel survival kit
Europe — a travel survival kit*
Hong Kong & Macau
Kathmandu & the Kingdom
of Nepal
New Zealand — a travel survival kit
Papua New Guinea — a travel
survival kit
South America on a Shoestring
South-East Asia on a Shoestring
Sri Lanka — a travel survival kit
Trekking in the Himalayas
USA West

* this book is available only in Australasia

We'll soon have a new guide titled
Kashmir, Ladakh & Zanskar and we
have a half dozen other new guides
currently underway.

Lonely Planet travel guides are available around the world. If you can't find them, ask your bookshop to order them from one of the distributors listed below. For countries not listed write to Lonely Planet in Australia.

Australia — Lonely Planet Publications, PO Box 88, South Yarra, Victoria 3141.
Canada — Milestone Publications, Box 445, Victoria, British Colombia, V8W 2N8.
Hong Kong — Hong Kong University Press, 139 Pokfulam Rd, Hong Kong.
India — UBS Distributors, 5 Ansari Rd, New Delhi, 110002.
Japan — Intercontinental Marketing Corp, IPO Box 5056, Tokyo 100-31.
Malasia — see Singapore
Nepal — see India
Netherlands — Nilsson & Lamm bv, Post bus 195, Pampuslaan 212, 1680 AD Weesp.
New Zealand — Caveman Press, PO Box 1458, Dunedin.
Papua New Guinea — Gordon & Gotch (PNG), PO Box 3395, Port Moresby.
Singapore — MPH Distributors (S) Pte Ltd, 116-D JTC Factory Bldg, Lorong 3, Geylang Square, Singapore 1438
Thailand — Chalermnit, 1-2 Erawan Arcade, Bangkok.
UK — Roger Lascelles, 16 Holland Park Gardens, London, W14 8DY.
USA (West) — Bookpeople, 2940 Seventh St, Berkeley, CA 94710.
USA (East) — Hippocrene Books, 171 Madison Ave, New York, NY 10016.
West Germany — Versandhaus Sud-West, PO Box 3680, D-7900 Ulm.

Geoff was born in Yorkshire, England and started his travelling days as a teenage hitch-hiker. Later, after many short trips around Europe, two years 'on the road' in Asia and Africa, spells in the overgrown fishing village of Hull and on the bleak and beautiful Cumberland fells with a happy band of long-haired lunatics and mystics, Geoff got involved with the London underground information centre BIT. He helped put together their first, tatty, duplicated *Overland to India guide* and later their *Overland through Africa* guide. Geoff's first guide for Lonely Planet was the first edition of *Africa on the Cheap* which he followed up with *South America on a Shoestring*. Having travelled Africa once again to produce this completely updated new edition he now lives on an old banana plantation near the New South Wales/Queensland border in Australia — between spells on the road working on other new Lonely Planet guidebooks.

MANY THANKS.........

Unlike the previous edition which was written under impossible odds in the seedy basement flats of North London, England, this guide was put together in the company of pythons, red-backs, leeches and kookaburras in the infinitely more conducive surroundings of the northern New South Wales rainforest, Australia. However, this vastly improved edition owes its inspiration not only to the beautiful surroundings but also to the following people whose help was invaluable:

Eileen Mills: For love, an easy smile and endless pots of tea.

Bob Bathie: For spiritual inspiration and companionship.

John & Lyssa Hagen: For hospitality, encouragement and the loan of the typewriter on which the guide was put together (my own spent many months rusting away on the Brisbane docks).

Jane Siegel: Who proved that out of sight was not out of mind and for assistance with the Kenyan section.

Tony & Maureen Wheeler: For hospitality and a seemingly endless fund of energy.

And to the following travellers who sent in some excellent and gratefully received feedback:

Rod Mackichan, Barbara Konig & Brian Bolton, Rob Condon, Sharon Murray, Jo & Brian Hanson, Peter Waldorf, Walter Hegnanes, David Plavcan, John Jackson, Warren Tyson, Dan Glimne, Eke van Batenburg, Lane Parker, Myra Hauben, Roos & Annik Engelhard and Marjorie Richardson.

AND A REQUEST

Travel guides are only kept up to date by people who travel. It's impossible to retrace every step for each new edition but you can help us, and your fellow travellers, by writing and telling us what you've found along the way. This request particularly applies to Africa — where changes are often so immense! The best letters score a free copy of the next edition — or any other Lonely Planet guide.

Contents

Introduction

Most places are far easier and cheaper to get to than packaged tour travel agents and discouraging consular officials would have you believe. The hardest part is making the decision to go. The rest is easy and will quickly turn into one of the best buzzes you've ever experienced. Remember that wherever there are people, there will be food, company, shelter and transport no matter how primitive and, the further off the beaten track you go, generally the more interesting it becomes. If at all possible, avoid making hard and fast plans or having rigid deadlines. Instead, be open to suggestions from other travellers about which route to take and what to see and leave yourself enough time to stay as long as the interest holds you. Things don't work like they do in the western world as a rule. Transport rarely runs on schedule or in a manner that you're familiar with and if you expect them to you'll drive yourself to distraction. In many parts of Africa it's impossible to predict anything, especially during the rainy season when roads turn into rivers and bridges get washed away. Allow plenty of time and try to see delays or forced changes of plan as new opportunities rather than set-backs. Most Africans will stare in blank disbelief and amazement at a westerner who starts kicking up dust because something isn't on time or is taking a long time. It's an accepted way of life and, in many cases, if you make a fuss, things simply take even longer.

There are few well-established routes like those across Asia, not just because there are any number of ways you can criss-cross the continent but because sudden political upheavals or antagonism between neighbouring nations can wipe a route off the overland map virtually overnight. There are also countries which it is very difficult to get into or even impossible because of reconstruction campaigns following wars of liberation or guerilla activities. Nevertheless, there are at present only two routes south from the African Mediterranean coast to Central Africa. These are either through the Saharan desert from Algiers to Mali or Niger or down the Nile valley from Egypt to Kenya.

Outside the capital cities — which are much the same everywhere in many respects — the continent is still very uncommercialised and undeveloped. Many places are still very self-sufficient, agriculturally based and village orientated, and if you really want to get the feel of a country you should get off the beaten track as much as possible and into the culture, religion, politics and day-to-day life of people outside the cities. It's in these villages you're most likely to come across the greatest degree of hospitality and interest. We receive letters from travellers all the time which rave on about the welcome they've received especially, though not exclusively, in these small villages.

Many African countries have only very recently emerged from the colonial era — often after long and bitter struggles against their colonial overlords — and, as a result, are still going through profound political and social changes in their search for a national identity. This obviously cannot be achieved overnight and there will doubtless be many more upheavals to come. Boundaries imposed by the colonial powers often bore no resemblance to those related to African kingdoms or tribal regions with the result that many of its people were artificially divided or lumped together according to the whim of the colonisers. These unnatural divisions have, to some extent, been rigidified by the Organisation of African Unity (OAU) one of whose cardinal principles is the non-interference in the internal affairs of other African countries. While no doubt praiseworthy in intent as a means of containing what otherwise might be explosive political tensions between neighbouring countries, this principle has prevented a more natural re-integration of related peoples and tribes following the departure of the colonisers. Colonial agricultural and industrial policies also hindered more broad-based development by concentrating on monoculture and cash crops to the detriment of local and national needs. Despite some noteworthy achievements, many African countries are still desperately poor and subject to the vagaries of the climate and the price-fixing which goes on in the financial capitals of the world. The Sahel drought several years ago, for instance, had a disastrous effect on the southern Saharan countries and spelt the end of a way of life for many desert nomads. In South Africa there's still the revolting spectacle of apartheid and white supremacy which is likely to continue poisoning racial relations for quite some time though, with a bit of luck and a large helping of give and take, this has happily been brought to a close in Zimbabwe-Rhodesia. It is with legacies such as these that Africa is struggling.

You might easily get the impression from reading newspapers that Africa is just a dangerous miasma of political instability, coups, military dictators and guerilla warfare. It isn't — but then this sort of stuff is the bread and butter of the press and good news is no news. Don't let it put you off going there. There are countries in which all this is going on (and we warn you about them) but remember that most ordinary people are open, friendly and eager to talk to you especially if it's clear you have at least a little time to pass with them. Most power struggles take place in the capital and rarely percolate down to village level — though there are obvious exceptions to this general rule. It's a very colourful continent with many different traditions and ways of life and the friendliness and hospitality which awaits you there is second to none. I once had hospitality lavished on me by Algerian freedom fighters during the war with France despite posters all around the room denouncing the Brits and the Balfour Declaration (which led to the creation of the state of Israel). Another time I was befriended by Eritrean Liberation guerilas while heading towards the Sudanese border from Asmara in Ethiopia despite western military and financial support for Hailie Selassie's regime which was doing its best to annihilate the guerillas. Other travellers will tell you similar stories.

Many people find that two is the ideal number for travelling but there are quite a few who go as threesomes and sometimes even more. If you do go as more than a couple, make sure you know your companions well before setting off. Travelling can bring out the best and worst in people. There are, of course, many others who prefer to travel alone and link up from time to time with others they meet along the way. There are plenty of cross-roads you'll come across where you can link up with others if that is what you're looking for. The most important of these 'crossroads' include both main routes south from the Mediterranean as well as the cities of Dakar (Senegal), Lagos (Nigeria), Nairobi (Kenya), Dar es Salaam (Tanzania), Blantyre (Malawi) and any of the Moroccan cities.

Travel as light as possible. An overweight bag will quickly become a nightmare. Be willing to adjust to local customs and food. Don't worry about your health. Eat a balanced diet and your health will look after itself. Diarrhoea you'll almost certainly get once if not several times but hepatitis can generally be avoided if you're reasonably fastidious and lay off un-boiled water and green salads. Remember that diarrhoea isn't always the result of an infection and is often due simply to a sudden change of food. The slower you go, the more immunity you'll build up against this sort of a stomach rumble. It's a harsh way to treat your body and can result in serious vitamin imbalance and weaken you for further digestive problems.

The main languages in Africa are English, French, Arabic and Swahili. If you don't already know some, learn some French before you go and, if possible, a smattering of Arabic or Swahili. Presumably if you want to see a country you also want to meet its people, talk with them and spend some time with them as well as mingle with fellow travellers and go sight-seeing. On the other hand, don't let language deter you from going. Local people will always warm to any effort you make to speak their language however botched the effort. It's one sure way of making friends. If you know only a little, they'll delight in teaching you more. And non-verbal communication goes a long way. Remember that even if all you want to know is the time, a greeting, a joke, a few minutes conversation before making your request makes all the difference. Otherwise you're just another tourist. Seems obvious until you realise how many travellers don't, apparently, give it a thought and go around with their heads inside guide books talking only to people from their own country. Ease up. You're among friends. A country is only foreign if you treat it that way.

You'll occasionally meet arrogant people while travelling. Avoid becoming one of them. These sort of people leave behind them a legacy of resentment and bitterness which other travellers coming after them have to deal with. It can be a heavy task trying to convince local people that you're not a leaf out of the same book. Prejudice and notions of cultural superiority don't belong in a traveller's rucksack. Beware of equating a strange culture, a different life-style, a more 'primitive' existence or the inability to speak your language as stupidity. There are a lot of people throughout Africa who've had quite enough of this contemptible rubbish already but are still having it rammed down their throats. In some countries, where one tribe has gained political dominance over another or others, they even do it to themselves.

Despite the title of this book, travel in Africa is not 'cheap'. The faster you travel and the more comforts you demand, the more it will cost. Inflation hits African countries just like anywhere else and for those countries which have no oil reserves of their own every hike in price of this commodity pushes up the prices of others across a broad spectrum. The further off the beaten track you go and the slower you travel, the longer your money will last and the more hospitality you'll run into. Transport is often erratic. Don't expect to be able to hitch free everywhere you go. In many places, hitching is a recognised form of public transport and you'll be expected to pay like everyone else. On main routes 'fares' are more or less fixed but on lesser routes you'll have to bargain. Some journeys — even short ones — can take days and, in the wet season, you'll be expected to lend a hand when the trucks get bogged down in dust, sand or mud.

Africa is one of the few remaining continents where there are substantial wildlife parks and reserves where the variety of animal life is still breath-taking. Nevertheless, a lot of poaching and indiscriminate killing goes on where there is a demand for animal products — often only one small part of an animal like rhinoceros horn or ivory, the rest being discarded as useless. It doesn't take long with modern weapons and traps to push a species to the brink of extinction. If you don't care, carry on buying those skins and furs. If you do, refuse to buy them.

We wish you luck for an amazing journey. Have a good time!

PAPERWORK

The essential things to have are a passport and an International Vaccination Card to cover smallpox, cholera and yellow fever. It's also useful to have an International Student Card, a Youth Hostel Card and an International Driving Permit. If you're taking your own transport you also need a Carnet de Passage (Triptique) and Motor Insurance.

International Driving Permits can be obtained from any national motoring organisation on production of your national driving licence. A small fee is charged and you need two passport-size photos.

A Youth Hostel Card is obtainable from your national Youth Hostels Association or from the UK YHA at 14 Southampton St, London WC2 (tel 01-836 8541). They are useful in Kenya, Morocco, Tunisia, Egypt, Rhodesia and South Africa although in many places it makes no odds whether you have a card or not. The national YHA will also have international handbooks listing all the hostels around the world.

International Student Cards are very useful, money-saving documents well worth the trouble of acquiring. Many airlines have student discounts of 25% though most Middle East airlines offer 50% reductions to anyone 26 years old or under regardless of whether they have an International Student Card or not. They include MEA (Middle East Airlines) and Egyptair. Air Afrique and UTA, however, only grant reductions if you're studying in the country you wish to fly in or from or are a national of that country. Note that it's often essential to have, in addition to the International Card, a letter on headed notepaper confirming that you are a student at the university/college/institute mentioned on your student card. Some airlines insist on such a letter before granting you student concessions. If you have a student card and are not a student, make sure you have the word 'student' in the occupation section of your passport. All the same, don't worry too much if you have no confirmatory letter. You might miss out here and there but a little back-hander and/or the eagerness of travel agents to sell you a ticket goes a long way to make this unnecessary. Other concessions you can get with a student card include shipping companies which offer 15% reductions (eg Turkish Maritime Lines and Adriatica), the national railways systems of Senegal, Mali, Egypt, Sudan and western European nations and museums all over the continent (generally free with a card). In Egypt you have to be a student of archaeology or history to get into the antiquities free of charge. All the concessions which are possible are noted in the main text under the appropriate country.

How to get a student card:
If you are, or recently were, a student you can get them either from your local student travel bureau or from one of the many foreign student travel centres to be found in most capital cities on production of your university/college union card or a letter on headed notepaper confirming that you are a student there. A small fee is charged and you need a passport-size photo.

If you are not a student, try one or more of the following:
Ask someone who has access to cards to get you one.

Try applying for one at a nearby university or college saying, if they ask, that you haven't got your union card with you or you lost it. The success or failure of this ruse often depends on how busy they are or what side of the bed they got out of that morning.

Enrol at a local technical college for some course (usually only possible at the beginning of the academic year) and you will automatically get a local union card which you can then use to get an International Card in the normal way. If course fees are payable at the time of registration, say you're still in the process of arranging your grant/bank overdraft/any other plausible excuse.

Many travel agents will supply you with one if you're booking through them. Likely places at present include London (UK), Amsterdam (Holland) and Athens (Greece). Some of these agents will charge you for the privilege. Make sure you're happy with the deal. The ones in Athens will sell you one regardless of whether you're booking through them or not.

CTG, via Nazionale 51, Rome, Italy, dispense cards with very little fuss. They charge 1000 Lire. Don't buy travel tickets here though as their prices are inflated.

The Communist bloc countries of East Europe dispense cards like confetti. Any reasonable evidence which suggests you are a student suffices. The fee is generally US$1 and two photos. Some good places include International Student Travel Bureau, Prague 2, Naplavni II, Czechoslovakia and Skopje University, Skopje, Yugoslavia. Tell them you've lost your card and they'll gladly provide you with another — free.

In many northern African cities you'll come across people touting student cards — either fellow travellers or local hustlers. They cost between US$5-10 and they vary in quality between the genuine article and a joke. Some are even the obsolete type which used to be issued in the '60s. Make sure you know what a genuine card looks like.

VISAS
Visas, where needed, are stamped into blank pages of your passport and are obtained from the embassy or consulate of the appropriate country either before you set out or along the way. It's often best, and frequently cheaper, to get visas along the way especially if you're not sure when you'll be arriving but note that many African countries have little overseas representation. Where you need to be warned about this in advance a note has been included under 'Visas' in the appropriate country section as well as under the same section of neighbouring countries.

Embassies and consulates vary widely in their concern about your appearance, the amount of money you have (either as travellers' cheques or cash) and whether you have an 'onward ticket'. These differences have been noted in the main text together with suggestions as to where it's best to get necessary visas. Don't turn up on borders without a visa if one is required otherwise you'll be sent back to the nearest consulate which can often be a *long* way back. Carry plenty of passport-size photos with you for visa applications — two dozen should suffice.

The location of embassies and consulates abroad are given, where known, in the main text. Remember that in all Moslem countries there is a public holiday to celebrate the end of the Ramadan fast. The festival lasts about four days during which all embassies, post offices and banks are closed so if you plan to cross a border at this time make sure you get hold of any necessary visa beforehand. (Ramadan is a kind of Moslem Lent during which no eating or drinking is permitted between sunrise and sunset but because Moslems use the lunar calendar, which is 11 days shorter than the solar year Gregorian calendar used in the west, the festival moves back 11 days every year. Find out when it is before you leave.)

If you're thinking of visiting a lot of countries in Africa you should bear in mind that visas are required for a large number of them. Very few of them are free and some of them are really expensive. If you're on a tight budget, these visa fees will eat into your resources so before you leave it would be a good idea to make a rough calculation of how much these fees are going to come to. Also you should make sure you have sufficient blank pages in your passport to accommodate all the visas you're going to need. Consular officials sometimes refuse point-blank to stamp a visa onto anything other than a completely blank page. I once persuaded a Sudanese consulate to stamp a visa onto the printed back cover of my passport but it took all day and my back ached after endless genuflection.

You'll occasionally come across some obstreperous, petty power freaks in embassies and consulates whose only pleasure in life seems to be making as much nuisance of themselves and causing as much delay as possible. If you display frustration or anger with these creeps they simply take twice as long. There's one born every minute. However, if you want that visa, just grin and bear it.

You normally don't have to show how much money you're carrying when you apply for a visa. The hassle, if any, comes at the border or airport where you may be asked to show how much you have. If the official who's dealing with you decides that you haven't 'sufficient' then your permitted length of stay may be limited. This is generally no sweat, since if you want to stay longer you can always renew the visa at immigration inside the country by showing, if necessary, your own and someone else's travellers' cheques artfull combined. The signatures on the cheques are never scrutinised. If you have an international credit card then you won't encounter any hassles here.

The biggest bugbear is when entry is dependent on you having an 'onward ticket' — in other words, they won't let you in without an air, bus, rail or boat ticket out of the country. Luckily in Africa you'll encounter few of these hassles if you're going overland except possibly in Kenya and South Africa. The best way to get round this hassle is to buy a Miscellaneous Charges Order for, say, US$100 from an airline which operates flights between Europe and the African country in question. MCOs are generally accepted by border/airport officials as 'onward tickets'.

CARNETS/TAKING YOUR OWN VEHICLE

A carnet is required for the majority of countries in Africa with the exception of Morocco, Algeria and Tunisia. Most carnets at present exclude Ghana and there are some customs posts in Upper Volta which won't accept carnets for some reason or another. Nigerian customs officials can also be very difficult about accepting your carnet.

Taking a vehicle through Africa requires plenty of forethought. Red lines on maps can be little more than a cartographer's fantasy and denote nothing more than a pot-holed dirt-track or a few tyre marks in the sand. At certain times of the year, parts of Africa are simply impassable due to heat (in the Sahara) or rain (Central Africa). If you're only planning on travelling around North Africa then almost any reasonable car will do as the roads along the northern coast are generally in very good repair and metalled. Anywhere south of here demands four-wheel drive, especially if you're heading for Zaire, though many travellers do make it in VW Kombis and even Beetles. Other non-four-wheel drive vehicles which have been recommended are Peugeot 404s and Citroen 2CVs since spares for these are very easy to find. Whatever you take, make sure it's in excellent mechanical condition and that

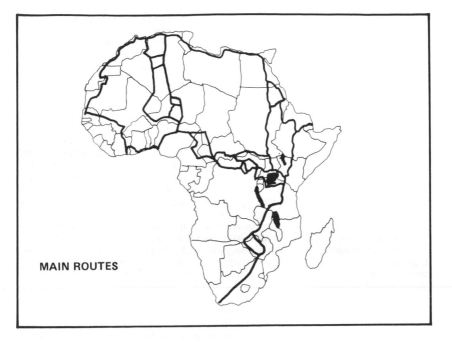

MAIN ROUTES

you're well stocked with spares before setting off.

The purpose of a carnet is to allow an individual to take a vehicle into a country where duties would normally be payable without the necessity of having to pay those duties. It's a document which guarantees that if a vehicle is taken into a country but not exported then the organisation which issued it will accept responsibility for payment of import duties. Carnets can only be issued by one of the national motoring organisations (in the UK, this is the AA or RAC, in Australia the AAA) and obviously before they will issue such a document they need to be absolutely sure that if the need to pay duties ever arises they would be reimbursed by the individual to whom the document is issued.

The amount of import duty can vary considerably but generally speaking it's between one and 1½ times the new value of the vehicle. There are exceptions to this where duty can be as high as three times the new value.

The motoring organisation will calculate the highest duty payable of all the countries that it is intended to visit and arrive at what is known as an 'Indemnity Figure'. This amount must be guaranteed to the motoring organisation by the individual before carnet documents are issued. The indemnity or guarantee can be of two types:

(i) A bank can provide the indemnity but they require an equal amount of cash or other collateral to be deposited with them.

(ii) An insurance company will put up the necessary bond in return for a non-refundable premium. In the UK, for AA carnets, the premium required is calculated at 3% of the indemnity figure subject to a minimum premium of £25. Indemnity figures in excess of £5000 qualify for a slightly lower premium. For RAC carnets, the premium is calculated at 10% of the indemnity figure though half of this is refunded when the carnet is eventually discharged.

If duties ever become payable — for example if you take the vehicle into a country but don't export it again — then the authorities of that country will demand payment of duties from the motoring organisation. They in turn would surrender the indemnity they were holding and if this were a bank indemnity then the bankers would hand over the deposit they were holding. In the case of an insurance indemnity the insurance company would have to settle the claim. If the latter, then the company have the right of recovery from an individual of the amount they have had to pay out though it is possible to take out a double indemnity with some insurance companies whereby they'll not only make funds available for the issue of a carnet but will also waive the right of recovery from an individual. If you want this kind of cover, the premium you pay will be exactly double that normally required.

To get a carnet you first need to make an application to one of the motoring organisations. They will issue an indemnity form for completion either by a bank or an insurance company. Once this is completed and a bond deposited with a bank or a premium paid to an insurance company then the motoring organisation issue a carnet. The carnets themselves cost approximately £7. The whole process takes about a week to complete.

Important points to remember about carnets
(a) Insurance companies designate certain countries as 'War Zones' and no insurance company will insure against the risks of war. This means that the only way of getting a carnet for such countries is either with a bank deposit or to go without a carnet and make transit arrangements at the border. At present, Egypt is regarded as a 'War Zone'.

(b) If you intend to sell the vehicle at some point arrangements have to be made with the customs' people for the carnet entry to be cancelled. This means surrendering the vehicle into a customs' compound from which it will not be released until duties have been paid by the prospective buyer. In some places (eg Niamey, Niger) the buyer has to bribe a minister before a vehicle can change hands. It's fairly easy to sell a car in Ouagadougou (Upper Volta) but you must sell it within three days of arrival otherwise you run into complications. It's legal to sell cars in Togo and the Ivory Coast without going through customs but the price you get for them is correspondingly lower because of this. Generally, the older a car, the less duty is payable and therefore the easier it is to sell. Note that in Bamako (Mali) cars under five years old carry prohibitive duty.

(c) Indemnity insurance is issued for a minimum period of one year. You cannot get a reduction in premium or a refund for shorter trips.

The addresses of various motoring organisations are:
UK   Automobile Association, Overseas Operations Dept, Leicester Sq, London WC1.

Royal Automobile Club, PO Box 92, Croydon CR9 6HN (tel 01-686 2314).

West Germany   ADAC, 11 Konigstrasse, Munchen.

ADAC, Bundersalle 9-30, Berlin 31.

France   Automobile Club de France, 6 Place de la Concorde, Paris 8e (tel 265 3470).

Bank indemnities can be arranged through Agence Sports de Tourisme, 1 rue Bourdaloue, Paris 75009 (tel TRU 34620).

The above organisations can be very fussy if you're a foreign national or have a vehicle with foreign registration plates. Some of them insist that you must first be a member of one of your own national motoring organisations before they'll issue a carnet. In Germany you also need to have good references.

CAR INSURANCE

Whilst it's true in the EEC countries of Europe that if you have a national motor insurance policy to cover you for driving in your own country you no longer need a Green Card to cover you for driving in other EEC countries, you should know that the cover which this gives you is restricted to bodily injury claims only. So, if you crash into another vehicle or shop front, for instance, the cost of the repairs to your vehicle and to the other property damaged may not be covered by your insurance. In addition, many British insurers have a 'claw-back' clause which comes into effect if you take a vehicle to Europe without a Green Card being issued. This means that the insurers will immediately reclaim from the policyholder any amount they may be forced to pay out under EEC legislation. A Green Card will extend your national insurance to provide identical cover to that which applies in your own country whilst you travel in Europe. The cost of a Green Card is minimal. Get one.

A Green Card will cover you for most of Europe including Greece. Outside this area no single comprehensive policy is available due to varying legislation in different parts of the world in respect of third party cover so you must buy insurance on the borders. Where compulsory this generally costs about US$5-6 for 15 days' cover but note that the liability limits can be absurdly low by western standards. Also you can often only guess whether or not the premium is passed onto the company. There must be many instances where the premium is simply pocketed by the person collecting it. If this concerns you, or you want more realistic cover, then arrange it before you set off. As for carnets, we recommend the following people for motor insurance: Campbell Irvine Ltd, 48 Earls Court Road, London, W8 6EJ, (tel 01-937 9903). Note that no insurance company will touch you at present as far as Egypt or Zimbabwe Rhodesia as they're designated 'War Zones'. If you would like a very comprehensive leaflet explaining all the points about Carnets and Motor Insurance, write to Campbell Irvine Ltd, and ask them for a copy of their *Overland Insurance* leaflet. They are a very friendly small firm and have been doing this kind of business for years.

A policy covering all ex-French colonies is obtainable in France and is much cheaper than in Britain.

HEALTH

Useful books to study are *The Traveller's Health Guide* by Dr A C Turner (Roger Lascelles) or *The Preservation of Personal Health in Warm Climates* put out by the Ross Institute of Tropical Hygiene, London. Both tell you all you need to know.

Vaccinations & International Vaccination Cards

Before you're allowed to enter most African countries you are required to have a valid International Vaccination Card as proof that you're not the carrier of some new and wonderful plague. The essential vaccinations are: Smallpox (vaccination valid for three years), Cholera (valid for six months), Yellow Fever (valid for 10 years).

In addition to the above, you are strongly advised to be vaccinated against: Typhoid and Paratyphoid (vaccination valid for one year), Tetanus (valid for one year), Tuberculosis (valid for life), Polio (valid for life).

Opinion divides roughly down the middle regarding the efficacy of having a gamma globulin shot against hepatitis. The trouble with liver diseases is that the organ is so central to your body's well being and its functions and structure so complicated that not a great deal is known about it and even less about its malfunctions. Some doctors will tell you that gamma globulin will provide about six months protection against certain types of hepatitis though one thing is certain — the vaccination will not give you absolute protection. It's up to you.

You need to plan ahead for vaccinations since they cannot all be given at once and typhoid requires a second injection about two weeks to one month after the first. The effect of the vaccines vary from one person to the next and the skill of the doctor/nurse who makes the injection. Cholera and typhoid generally leave you with a stiff arm for a couple of days if you've never had them before. The others have no effect.

If your vaccination card expires whilst you're away there are many Health centres where you can be re-vaccinated, often free of charge. Such centres that we know of are listed under the main country headings.

Your local practitioner will arrange a course of injections for you if you live outside of a large city otherwise there are generally vaccination centres which you can find in the telephone directory. Generally a standard fee is charged for each injection which ranges from US$2-3. In London you can get them from any of the following centres:

(a) Hospital for Tropical Diseases, 4 St Pancras Way, London, NW1 (tel 01-387 4411). All injections are free of charge but they're often booked up at least one month ahead.
(b) West London Designated Vaccination Centre, 53 Great Cumberland Place, London W1 (tel 01-262 6456). No appointment necessary, just turn up. Fees vary from £1 to £1.50 though a gamma globulin shot will cost you £3.50.
(c) British Ariways Terminal, Buckingham Palace Road, London, SW1 (tel 01-834 2323). Try to book about two days in advance if possible otherwise you might have to wait around for hours until they can fit you in. Similar charges to the West London Centre.

Avoid turning up at borders with expired vaccination cards as they may insist on you having the relevant injection before allowing you in. The needles they use for this on borders are often retrieved from filthy old tobacco tins and have been used on umpteen successive travellers without any sterilisation and you stand a fair chance of contracting serum hepatitis (the variety junkies get from the use of dirty needles).

Medical Insurance

Get some before you leave home. You may never need it but if you do it can save you a fortune. Most countries do not have free medical facilities. Policies for medical insurance as well as baggage insurance and personal money insurance can be bought from most insurance brokers and many travel agents but premiums vary considerably between one company and another. Some are very fussy about your mode of travel and others have maximum liability clauses for fragile or valuable objects included in your baggage insurance which are totally unrealistic. Others are tardy about paying up in the event of a claim. Read the small print and make sure you are buying the cover you want. It pays to shop around. In the UK probably the best deal is offered by Thomas Cook. At any one of their branches you can buy medical, baggage and personal money insurance over the counter without any fuss. They aren't interested in your appearance or your mode of travel and, as far as baggage is concerned, they'll insure individual items (even fragile ones such as musical instruments) for any sum you care to name so long as you declare it/ them on the proposal form you have to fill in. Their policies are done through the Prudential Assurance Company who are OK when it comes to paying up on a claim. Note that we've never come across any insurance company which will insure you against loss of documents — passports, airline tickets, etc, so if you lose these or have them stolen the cost of their replacement and the expenses involved will come directly out of your pocket. This can be expensive.

Diseases you can definitely avoid catching

Malaria This is caused by a blood parasite which is spread by certain species of

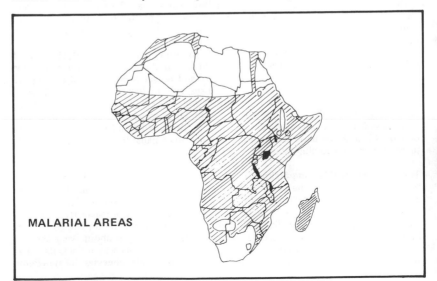

MALARIAL AREAS

night-flying mosquito (Anopheles). Only the female insects spread the disease but you only need to be bitten by one insect carrying the parasite to contract the disease. Start on a course of anti-malarial drugs before you set off and keep it up as you travel. The drugs are fairly cheap and any pharmacy will advise you about which kind to buy. There are basically two types: (i) proguanil (or paludrine) which you take once daily (ii) chloroquine, which you take once per week. Both are marketed under various trade names. In some areas of Africa the parasite is beginning to acquire immunity against some of the drugs. In the southern Sudan, for instance it is said that only chloroquine-based drugs are now effective.

Other than the malaria hazard, mosquito bites can be troublesome and although it's probably useless to say this, *don't scratch the bites*. If you do, and they don't heal quickly, there's a chance of them being infected with something else. You'll come across people in Africa pock-marked with angry sores which started out as insignificant mosquito bites whose owners couldn't resist the urge to scratch them. Don't join them. Will power works wonders, as does anti-histamine cream. If you want to keep them off at night, use an insect repellant on your skin or sleep under a fan at night. Mosquitos don't like swift-moving currents of air and will stay on the walls of the room in these circumstances.

No vaccination is possible against malaria. Take those pills.

Bilharzia This is caused by blood flukes (minute worms) which live in the veins of the bladder or the large intestine. The eggs which the adult worms produce are discharged in urine or faeces. If they reach water, they hatch out and enter the bodies of a certain species of fresh-water snail where they multiply for four or more weeks and then are discharged into the surrounding water. If they are to live they must find and invade the body of a human being where they develop, mate and then make their way to the veins of their choice. Here they start to lay eggs and the cycle repeats itself. The snail favours shallow water near the shores of lakes and streams and they are more abundant in water which is polluted by human excrement. Generally speaking, moving water contains less risk than stagnant water but you can never tell.

It's quite a common disease in Africa. If you don't want to catch it, stay out of rivers and lakes and if you drink water from any of these places boil it or sterilize it with chlorine tablets. It's a painful disease and causes persistent and cumulative damage by repeated deposits of eggs. If you suspect you have it, seek medical attention as soon as possible — look for blood in your urine or faeces that isn't associated with diarrhoea. The only body of water in Africa which is largely free of bilharzia is Lake Malawi. Keep out of Lakes Victoria, Tanganyika and Kiva and the Rivers Congo, Nile and Zambesi. As the intermediate hosts (snails) live only in fresh water, there's no risk of catching bilharzia in the sea.

Trypanosomiasis (Sleeping Sickness) This is another disease transmitted by biting insects, in this case by the tsetse fly. Like malaria, it's caused by minute parasites which live in the blood. The risk of infection is very small and confined to areas which are only a fraction of the total area inhabited by the tsetse fly. The flies are found only south of the Sahara but the disease is responsible for the absence of horses and cattle from large tracts of central Africa. The fly is about twice the size of a common housefly and recogniseable from the scissor-like way it folds its wings while at rest. The disease is characterised by irregular fevers, abcesses, local oedema

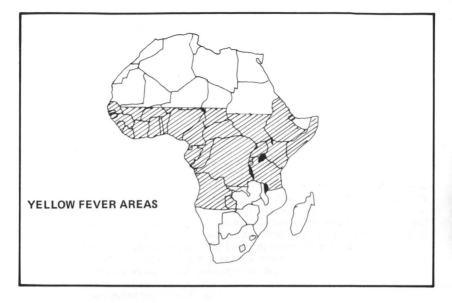

YELLOW FEVER AREAS

(puffy swellings caused by excess water being retained in body tissues), inflammation of the glands and physical and mental lethargy. It responds well to treatment.

Diseases you can probably avoid catching.
Hepatitis This is a liver disease caused by a virus and although there are several varieties the one you're most likely to pick up is infectious hepatitis. It's a very contagious disease and you pick it up somewhere along the oral-faecal route by drinking water or eating food that's been contaminated by the mucous, piss or shit of an infected person. It's also possible to pick it up by sharing the towel, toothbrush or chillum of an infected person. Foods to avoid are salads (unless you know they have been washed in purified water) and un-peeled fruits. Other things to watch for are dirty crockery and cutlery (take your own?).

Symptons appear 15-50 days after infection and consist of loss of appetite, nausea, complete lack of energy, dull pains around the bottom of your rib cage and jaundice. Some people also get a bad bout of depression. The simplest way of keeping a check on the situation is to watch the colour of your eyes and urine. If the whites of your eyes become yellow and your urine turns a deep orange no matter how much liquid you've drunk, then you've probably got it. If it's just your urine which turns orange don't immediately jump to conclusions. You lose a lot of water in hot climates and it's bound to be more concentrated. Check it out by drinking a lot of fluid all at once. If it still comes through orange, start making preparations for a long rest in an easy-going place. The severity of the disease varies considerably most people get over it within a few weeks; in others it takes months. A lot depends on the state of your health at the time.

There's no 'cure' as such for the disease except plenty of rest and nourishing food. Fat-free diets have gone out of medical fashion though you may find you can't take grease at all for a while. If this is the case, simply cut it out. Alcohol and tobacco are right off the menu. Don't give your liver extra work de-toxifying that lot.

There's no need to panic like some people do and start rushing around to your embassy demanding repatriation on your medical insurance or their good will (or lack of it) unless it gets really bad. Give rest and good food a chance first. Remember that you will be infectious from about one week before the onset of symptoms to about one week after so, if someone is looking after you, warn them about this.

Every traveller has his/her favourite shock-horror story about hepatitis but you can generally avoid catching it by being reasonably fastidious about what you eat and where. Having your own cutlery helps a little bit but food and water are the main sources of infection.

Diseases & ailments you will probably catch

Diarrhoea Sooner or later, unless you're a very exceptional person, you'll get diarrhoea so you may as well accept the inevitable. You can't really expect to travel half way around the world without succumbing to this at least once or twice but it doesn't always mean you've caught a bug. Depending on how much travelling you've done and what your guts are used to, it can be merely the result of a change of food. If you've spent all your life living out of sterilized, cellophane-wrapped packets and tins from the local supermarket then you're going to have a hard time of it at first until you adjust.

There are lots of flies in Africa. Flies which live on the various wastes produced by humans and other animals. In most places local people shit fairly indiscriminately wherever the urge takes them. Public toilet facilities are rare or non-existent and that goes for sewerage treatment systems too. Some places are notorious for their open sewers and in very few places is the connection ever made between food, flies and shit. This is the source of most gut infections which afflict both travellers and local people alike. It is changing — but slowly — and travellers are helping to spread the concepts of hygiene in many places.

If and when you get a gut infection, avoid rushing off to the chemist and filling yourself with antibiotics. It's a harsh way to treat your system and you can build up a tolerance to them with over-use. Try to starve the bugs out first. Eat nothing and rest. Avoid travelling. Drink tea with no milk or sugar or lime/lemon juice into which a small amount of salt has been dissolved and drink plenty of it. Diarrhoea will dehydrate you and may result in painful muscular cramps in your guts. The cramps are due to a bad salt balance in your blood hence the idea of taking small amounts of salt with your tea or fruit juice. Chewing a small pellet of opium or taking a tincture of opium (known as 'Paregoric' and often mixed with kaolin — sort of Milk of Magnesia) will also relieve the pain of cramps. Something else you may come across, called RD Sol also helps to maintain a correct salt balance and so prevent cramps. It's a mixture of common salt, sodium bicarbonate, potassium chloride and dextrose and although somewhat unpalatable itself is OK when mixed with a fruit juice. Two days of this regime should clear you out.

If you simply can't hack starving, keep to a *small* diet of curd, yogurt, lime/lemon juice, boiled vegetables and tea. Stay away from butter, milk, sugar, cakes and non-citrus fruits.

If starving doesn't work or you really have to move on and can't rest for a couple of days try 'Pesulin' (or Pesulin-O' which is the same but with the addition of a tincture of opium). Dosage is two teaspoons four times daily for five days. Or Lomotil, the dosage is two tabs three times daily for two days.

If no luck with either of these, change to antibiotics or see a doctor. There are many varieties of antibiotics and you almost need to be a biochemist to know what the differences between them are. They include Tetracyclin, Chlorostrep, Typhstrep, Sulphatriad, Streptomagma, Thalazole.

If possible have a word with the chemist about their differences. Avoid 'Enterovioform' which used to be sold widely in Europe and is next to useless for treating gut ailments in Africa, and, anyway, is now suspected of causing optic nerve damage. With antibiotics, keep to the correct dosage. Over-use will do you more harm than good.

Dysentery This is, unfortunately, quite prevalent in some places. It's characterised by diarrhoea containing blood and lots of mucus and painful gut cramps. (Ah, travellers' toilet tales!) There are two types: (i) bacillary dysentery which is short, sharp and nasty but rarely persistent — the most common variety; (ii) amoebic dysentery which, as its name suggests, is caused by amoebic parasites. This variety is much more difficult to treat and often persistent.

Bacillic dysentery comes on suddenly and lays you out with fever, nausea, painful cramps and diarrhoea but, because it's caused by bacteria, it responds well to antibiotics. The one most often prescribed is 'Fladgyl' which is available from chemists without prescription. Amoebic dysentery builds up more slowly but is more dangerous. You cannot starve it out and, if untreated, it will get worse and permanently damage your intestines. If you see blood in your faeces persistently over a couple or three days, seek medical attention as soon as possible. If you're a long way from such help and have antibiotics available, start on a course of them. You may be lucky and only have the bacillic variety.

General points about health

Teeth Get them checked and treated, if necessary, before you set off. Dentists are few and far between in many places.

Food Bought in cheap cafes and street stalls food tends to be overcooked and lacking in protein, vitamins and calcium. Eat sufficient milk, curd or yoghurt, peeled or washed fresh fruit and give your gums some exercise by chewing sticks of liquorice or any twig. Avoid unboiled/unpasteurised milk. There is very little inspection of dairy herds in much of Africa and milk may contain brucellosis or tuberculosis. Whenever possible, try to put your own food together from the wide variety of fruit and vegetables available in local markets. Some people take their own cooking utensils, crockery and cutlery but if you prefer travelling light this can be impractical.

Heat In hot climates you sweat a great deal and so lose a lot of water and salt. Make sure you drink enough liquid and have enough salt in your food to make good these losses (one teaspoon of salt per day is sufficient). If you don't, you run the risk of heat exhaustion and cramps. Heat can make you impatient and irritable. Try to slow down; live a less structured life and don't try to get too many things together at once.

Heat and dryness will make your hair brittle and may thin it out. To counteract this, oil it when necessary with something like refined coconut or mustard oil. Similarly your skin will benefit from the occasional oiling. A pair of sunglasses is a good idea to minimise the effect of glare on your eyes.

Skin infections/grazes,cuts Treat them immediately. Clean them up and cover them otherwise they'll attract flies and African flies are very persistent (or maybe it's just because there are more of them?). Change bandages daily and, if the skin is badly broken use an antiseptic cream.

Something you might come across if you're from a temperate climate is 'prickly heat' which comes up as many tiny, itchy blisters on various parts of your body — often on your hands. These are little beads of sweat that have been trapped under the top layer of skin, usually because your pores haven't opened up sufficiently to cope with the greater volume of sweat you put out in a hot climate. They are nothing to worry about and will disappear as your skin adjusts. Anything which promotes sweating such as exercise, tea or coffee, will make it worse. Keep your skin aerated and wear loose-fitting clothes. Hog the fan where there is one and take frequent showers. Use calamine lotion or a zinc-oxide-based talcum powder to soothe your skin. The condition often looks alarming, but it's harmless.

Don't walk around in bare feet except on beaches. It's a nice idea but you can pick up hookworm which is widespread in Africa. The larvae can bore through the thickest feet. Should you pick it up by accident, get medical attention. It's easily got rid of.

Drinking Water Avoid drinking unboiled water (or using ice) anywhere it's not chlorinated unless you're taking it from a spring on a mountainside. Obviously this is easier said than done, especially in the desert and in parts of Zaire and it may well be that you'll have to take a drink no matter what source it comes from. This is part of travelling. There's no way you can eliminate all risks. The only thing you can do is minimise them as far as your health is concerned. Remember that carbonated drinks (fizzy drinks) are only as safe as the water they are made from. The same goes for ice. There are preparations you can buy which will purify unboiled water but they often impart a disagreeable taste to the water and take some getting used to. They are useless against amoebic dysentery. One of the most commonly used preparations is 'Halzone'. Another is 'Potable Aqua' though this latter is not widely available in Europe and, as far as we know, only available in the USA or from the manufacturers — Frost Labs, Inc, 430 Lexington Street, Auburndale, Boston 66, Mass. Some travellers use a simpler iodine solution calibrated to the right strength — any chemist will make this up for you.

Mental Health Adjustments to the outlook, habits, social customs and religious practices of different peoples can be a strain on your ability to adapt, especially if you're trying to get from A to B quickly or have never spent much time out of your own country. Many people suffer from some degree of cultural shock (which is something you can get too on returning to your own country if you stay away a long time). Heat tends to exaggerate petty irritations which might pass unnoticed in a more temperate climate. It can take a long time to get simple things together like buying a ticket or getting a visa. Things are often cancelled at a moment's notice without any forewarning. Life starts at dawn on the streets of Africa and you'll have to get used to an 'early to bed, early to rise' regime because you'll be lucky to catch any sleep through the row outside once a day gets moving. Night owls may well have a hard time at first.

Fellow travellers (the insect variety)
Fleas You'll find these in many places — or, more likely, they'll find you. Numbers vary considerably with the season. Some places seem to have a lot, others none at

all. Naturally, the cheaper your sleeping and eating habits, the more likely you are to encounter them. They're one of the facts of life and there isn't much you can do about them. As with mosquitos, don't scratch the bites if you can summon the will-power.

Lice You could well avoid these completely by washing yourself (including hair) and clothes frequently. They thrive on dirt. The places where you're most likely to pick them up are in crowded situations — buses, trains, very cheap hotels. You'll occasionally meet tribes-people whose hair is so matted and which hasn't seen water for so long that it's literally crawling with them. Many's the time I've shared a lift on the back of a truck with people like this and had to spend the bulk of the time fighting back the advancing army of lice. However, it takes a while for them to get stuck into you so you should get a companion to look through your hair about once a week to see if you've acquired any eggs near the base of the hairs. If you do get infested you can either pick the eggs out one by one (very laborious) or blitz them with an insecticide shampoo like 'Lorexane' or 'Suleo'. We've had letters from people who've doused their hair in petrol or DDT before now and although we'd readily concede such methods ensure total wipe-out we dread to think what condition it leaves your hair and scalp in. It does seem mildly hysterical to say the least!

Bed Bugs These evil little bastards live in the crevices of walls and the framework of beds where they hide during the day. They look like lice but move like greased lightning when you become aware of their presence and the light goes on in the middle of the night. They tend to be localised in certain areas and in certain hotels. In budget hotels look for tell-tale bloodstains on the wall near the beds. This is where previous occupants have squashed them. If you see these stains, choose a different hotel. They're not that common.

On the Road

MONEY
How much will it cost?
This is a question which everyone asks. It's also the hardest to answer. So much depends on how fast you want to travel; what degree of comfort you consider desirable; the standard of cafe you're prepared to eat in and hotel you're prepared to stay in; how much sight-seeing you want to do; how many diversions from the main routes you're thinking of making; whether you're travelling alone or in a group, and a host of other things. Some travellers cover the most amazing distances for next to nothing and have a fantastic time, staying with tribal people every evening and making do with whatever is available. It's unlikely, however, that you'll immediately become one of these people unless you've already done a lot of travelling. It takes a lot of effort, initiative and time. Many people simply don't have this amount of time available for one reason or another. Also, if you are totally dependent on those rare free lifts, travelling *can* degenerate into a succession of endless, boring waits at the side of the road. A certain degree of financial independence tends to ensure a more interesting trip. You should bear in mind too that many African people are too poor to be able to lavish hospitality on anyone who comes along so be wary of making sweeping assumptions about this.

What can be done is to make a shrewd guess about average daily living and travelling expenses based on a variety of different peoples' experiences. At present you would get by on about US$7 per day. This includes the cost of budget hotel accommodation, food, transport, visas and the occasional purchase of something small in a market. It excludes the cost of getting to Africa and any major purchases in markets. If you're going to hitch as much as possible, sleep on floors, in hammams and on beaches rather than in budget hotels and eat from street stalls wherever possible then you could get by on US$5 per day and less. If your time is limited however and you're going to have to take a number of flights to see all the places you have in mind then US$10-12 would be a more realistic figure. Some countries, notably Ivory Coast, Nigeria, Cameroon, Kenya, Zambia, Zimbabwe and South Africa, are relatively expensive and so if you're going to spend any length of time in these places your US$7 a day average is going to quickly float up to US$10-12. The only way you can effectively reduce your expenses on a US$7 a day average with its associated assumptions is to make a number of long stays in a few places. This way, there's the chance of finding cheaper accommodation on a long-term basis and of putting your own food together. Your transport expenses will also be minimal while you stay in one place.

If you have little time at your disposal or you want to spend the bulk of your time in central or southern Africa but don't want to completely miss parts of the north, then it could well be cheaper in the end to buy a return air ticket to a convenient destination (such as Nairobi) with stop-overs en route. Such tickets are comparatively cheap especially in London. The best place to find out what is on offer at any particular time is the weekly publication *Time Out*, available from most news-stands, newsagents and booksellers.

Which currency to take & how to take it
You need to take a mixture of £ sterling, French francs and US dollars. Francs are

the most useful currency in the ex-French colonies, £ sterling in the ex-British colonies and £ sterling and US dollars in the western-orientated countries such as those of the west coast, Zaire, Kenya and southern Africa. If you take currencies other than these you may experience difficulties changing them and will certainly find it difficult, if not impossible, to ascertain the exact exchange rate on any particular day. Since fellow travellers are your most important source of current information and as most of them will be carrying one or more of the above currencies, this is worth bearing in mind.

Most people prefer to take a mixture of travellers' cheques and cash — the former making up the larger component. This gives you the greatest flexibility and a high degree of security. On the other hand, some people prefer to take their money entirely in the form of cash and others entirely as travellers' cheques. Cash undoubtedly has the edge on travellers' cheques in terms of convenience and for street deals (only in a very few places can you change travellers' cheques on the black-market) but in terms of rectifying a loss or rip-off it's a dead duck. Travellers' cheques have the advantage of security and immediate replacement in case of loss or theft (immediately, that is, in theory) but there will be times when you can't always change travellers' cheques, especially in small places. Even if you don't like the idea of carrying cash around with you, we suggest you take a small amount since there are times when a dollar bill here and there can make all the difference between getting something moving and sitting around all day waiting. A small backhander, discreetly offered, is an integral part of the bureaucracy of many African countries.

Whichever form you decide to take your money in have it made up out of a combination of various denominations such as US$1, $5, $10, $20 and $50 (or the equivalent in £ or francs). Have a sufficient number of small bills/cheques and not too many large ones otherwise you might find yourself having to change, say, $50 in a country you're only going to spend a few days in and so being left with a wad of local currency which you have to convert into another at a relatively bad exchange rate. The only exception to this concerns the ex-French colonies. Most of these use the same currency unit — the CFA (Communite Financielle Africaine) or AFR which is the same thing. Officially these all have the same value vis-a-vis the French franc and are freely inter-changeable in all the countries which use this unit. They are also inter-changeable with the Mali Franc. Sometimes, however, there are slight differences in the exchange rate between the CFAs of one country and those of another and at times like this you won't be able to exchange them on a one-for-one basis or use the CFAs of one country as legal tender in another.

American Express Travellers' cheques are the most widely used and their offices operate a poste restante service for clients but others which are widely recognised include First National City Bank, Bank of America and Cooks. Avoid taking travellers' cheques issued by small banks or you'll have difficulty in persuading African banks to change them. Most banks charge 1% commission for issuing these cheques and when you cash them you will more than likely have to pay a further 1% on the transaction. With cash you avoid these commission charges. Keep your original bill of sale for travellers' cheques in a safe place and separate from the cheques since if you have to have the cheques replaced they'll demand to see this receipt. It's also a good idea to keep a record of the cheque numbers in a safe place and separate from the cheques. That way, you can tell them exactly which cheques have been lost or stolen.

An alternative way of having secure funds to hand is to carry a credit card and personal cheque book and to withdraw money when and where you need it against your home account. The normal limit is about US$200 in travellers' cheques and US$50 in cash every seven days but unlimited credit as far as purchases in shops and airline tickets are concerned. In this way you avoid having to carry large amounts of cash or travellers' cheques. The one major disadvantage of this system is that you might not always be able to take out the cash or cheques in the currency that you want it in.

If you have to have money sent out to you whilst you're away, have it cabled out to the local branch of an international bank and make sure you know exactly whether you will be able to have it as hard currency (cheques or cash) or only in local currency. Many people have been caught out this way in the past. American Express certainly allow you to have it in US dollar cheques or £sterling. All the same, money can take weeks to arrive and be cleared for collection even through international banks. Don't rely on it being there within a few days. It doesn't always happen that way. Lastly, don't have money sent out to you via your embassy — they often make swingeing charges for the so-called privilege.

Note that it's virtually impossible to get British banks to transfer funds to banks in ex-French colonies except Barclays. The Libyan Bank in Niamey, Niger and the SIC bank in Abidjan, Ivory Coast, will cash UK bank cheques — the latter with little or no commission.

If you're carrying your total worldly funds with you and run out completely or, if carrying cash and have it stolen, then unless you can find a benefactor or someone who is prepared to lend you some there are few options open to you. Most embassies and consulates offer the facility of repatriation though one notable exception are French embassies and consulates. If you're British, they'll take your passport off you and fly you back to the UK on the first available flight. You don't get your passport back until you pay them off. Also you'll not only find yourself paying for the flight at the full retail price but also 'consular fees' and the like.

Exchange rates & what your money is worth

No matter how many times we put these words into towering block capitals underlined and surrounded by stars and exclamation marks we still get people writing in to complain that our exchange rates and prices are out-of-date. Thanks for your letters — they're invaluable — and so once again

CHECK OUT ALL PRICES AND EXCHANGE RATES CONSTANTLY WITH YOUR FELLOW TRAVELLERS ALONG THE WAY. THEY ARE YOUR BEST SOURCE OF CURRENT INFORMATION.

The exchange rates which we quote at the beginning of each country chapter are for guidance only and correct only at the time of going to press. It's easy enough to find out the current rates for various currencies from the financial pages of newspapers in industrialised countries but when you're out in the sticks you have to rely on the travellers' grapevine. This applies particularly where there is a blackmarket. A few words of advice about the blackmarket. Avoid pulling out large wads of notes only some of which you intend to change. Have the amount you want to change separate from the rest. Flashing large wads of notes encourages hit-and-run merchants. If possible, have a companion with you unless you are fully confident about the situation. Never let your money 'walk around the corner' even if one of the dealers stays with you 'until the other returns'. You won't see it again. Always count out, note by note, the money that is handed to you — don't let anyone do this for you. Some dealers came out of the womb practicing sleight-of-hand tricks. Sometimes the blackmarket rates are better outside the country than inside but this isn't always the case. More details under appropriate country chapters. The main countries where a blackmarket exists at present are Algeria, Ghana, Nigeria, Rwanda, Tanzania, Zaire and Zambia. Changing money in these places on the street market makes a hell of a lot of difference to your costs. One traveller recently sent us this comparison:-

Money spent in country		% changed on blackmarket	Additional cost if all money had been changed at official rate
Ghana	US$157	100%	US$574
Nigeria	US$ 86	100%	US$ 55
Zaire	US$135	100%	US$272
Tanzania	US$250	24%	US$ 40

The exchange rate of all currencies, including hard ones, varies from day to day. If there's a serious run on the hard currency you're carrying its purchasing power may drop considerably. If you're travelling on a breadline budget this could be serious. Another thing which can affect your finances if you're away a long time is inflation. In many places, it runs in double figures and oil price hikes can send it spiralling, making a mockery of transport prices in this guide. It may make little difference to you if the cost of overland transport from Algiers to Tangier rises by, say, 15% as you'll still be able to make that ferry back across to Spain, but if you're down in Zambia and have to make it back to the Mediterranean that 15% rise could be serious. Bear this in mind if you want to be sure of getting back.

Some countries have two official exchange rates — a lower one for business and international financial transactions and a higher one called the Tourist Exchange Rate. As a tourist you're entitled to the higher rate which is generally a lot nearer to, if not equal to, the currency's real value vis-a-vis the 'hard' currencies. The idea is to encourage tourism and attempt to stamp out the blackmarket. Egypt is one such country with two rates.

Currency Declaration Forms

Quite a few African countries have you fill in one of these on entry stating how much cash and travellers' cheques you have and demand that you produce it for customs' examination on exit. The idea is to theoretically force you to change money at the official rate in banks since you have to account for the difference between what you brought in and what you're taking out. If you'll be using the blackmarket whilst in the country, declare less than you have and hide the rest. The thoroughness with which these forms are checked on exit varies. In some they're very strict, in others it's just a formality. We warn you about this if necessary under the appropriate country chapters.

How to carry money

There is no 'safe place' to keep your money whilst you're travelling but the best place is in contact with your skin where, hopefully, you'll be aware of an alien hand before it disappears. The usual method is in a leather pouch which is hung around your neck and kept under cover of a shirt or dress. It's an excellent idea to incorporate a length of old guitar string (the D string should be thick enough) into the thong which goes around your neck. This will make it extremely difficult to cut whilst you're asleep. Few thieves carry a pair of wire cutters with them but quite a few carry scissors. Another method is to sew an extra pocket (s) onto the inside of your trousers invisibly. Ideally, you should have your passport in the same place too though sometimes they're too large or stiff. Wherever you put your money, it's a good idea to enclose it in a plastic bag. Under a hot sun that pouch or pocket can get soaked through with sweat — repeatedly — and your cash or cheques will end up looking like they have been to the launderette.

Last word!
Never leave cash or cheques lying around and don't assume that because you locked the door to your hotel room before you went for a shower that non-one else can get in. If you have the slightest doubt, take it with you for a shower. Better wet than gone.

Some African cities are unfortunately getting notorious for muggings. We warn you about them where necessary and let you know which areas to avoid.

BARGAINING
Most purchases involve some degree of bargaining. This includes hotels, transport, food, cigarettes, etc, but the prices of most basic commodities are settled within minutes. It's a way of life in many parts of the world where commodities are looked on as being worth what their owners can get for them. The concept of a fixed price would invoke laughter. If you cop out and pay the first price asked you'll not only be considered a half-wit but you will be doing your fellow travellers a disservice since this will create the impression that all travellers are willing to pay outrageous prices (and all are equally as stupid). You are expected to bargain. It's part of the fun of going to Africa. All the same, no matter how good you are at it, you'll never get things quite as cheaply as local people do. To traders, hotel and cafe owners you represent wealth — whatever your appearance (you couldn't have got there without it) — and it's of little consequence that you consider yourself to be a 'traveller' rather than a 'tourist'. In the eyes of a trader, you're the latter.

Bargaining is conducted in a friendly, sometimes exaggeratedly extrovert manner in most cases though there are occasions when it degenerates into a bleak exchange of numbers and leaden head-shakes. Decide what you want to pay or what others have told you they've paid and start off at a price about 50% less than this. The seller will inevitably start off at a price about 50% higher than what he's prepared to accept. This way you can both end up having appeared to be generous. For larger purchases in souks, bazaars and markets, especially in Moslem countries, you may well be served tea as part of the bargaining ritual. Accepting it places you under no obligation to buy but helps you to get to know each other better and anyway your throat gets dry with all that talking. There will be times when you simply cannot get a shopkeeper to lower his prices to anywhere near what you know his product should be selling for. This probably means that a lot of tourists are passing through and if you won't pay his outrageous prices he knows some mug on an overland tour bus or package tour will. Don't lose your temper bargaining. If you get fed up, go home and come back the next day.

BAGGAGE
Take the minimum possible. An overweight bag will become a nightmare. A rucksack is preferable to an overnight bag since it will stand up to more hammering and doesn't screw up your posture by putting unequal weight on one side of your

body. Choose a pack which will take some rough handling — overland travel destroys packs rapidly. Make sure the straps and buckles are well sewn on and strengthen if necessary before you set off. Whether you take a pack with or without a frame is up to you but there are some excellent packs on the market with internal frames (eg Berghaus). Probably the best stockists in Britain are the YHA Adventure Centre, 14 Southampton Street, London WC2 (tel 01-836 8541). Take a strong plastic bag with you that will completely enclose the pack. Use it on dusty journeys whether your pack is in the luggage compartment of a bus or strapped on to the roof. If you don't you'll be shaking dust out of your pack for the next week.

A sleeping bag is more or less essential. It gets very cold in the desert at night and, if you'll be visiting mountainous areas you'll need one there as well. You'll also be glad of it on long bus or train journeys as a supplement to wooden seats or sacks of potatoes. A sheet sleeping bag — similar to the ones used in Youth Hostels — is also useful when it is too hot to use a normal bag. It's cool and keeps the mosquitos off your body.

Take clothes for both hot and cold climates and include at least one good sweater for use at night in the mountains or in the desert. You needn't go overboard, however, and take everything in your wardrobe. Things like T-shirts, cotton pants and sandals are very cheap in most places and it's usually more interesting and economical to buy these things along the way. It's prohibited to wear clothes that reveal large areas of your body in some places like Tanzania. This includes shorts, short skirts, see-though stuff and even flared trousers are frowned on (who dreamt that one up!? What about sailors?). These sort of clothes apparently offend the local sense of propriety. Apart from silly things like this, it's inadvisable for women to wear short anything in Moslem countries otherwise they will be hassled endlessly by local men/youths. Most women in these countries are veiled from head to toe so if you go around with little on they will assume you are sexually available. Long skirts and a resilient nature can allay this kind of attention but doesn't guarantee success. On the other hand, being sexually hassled is by no means an exclusively female complaint.

Some people take a small tent and portable stove. These can be very useful and save you a small fortune but they do add considerably to the weight of your pack. Many local people carry portable stoves around with them. If you take a stove make sure it's leakproof! Don't forget the small essentials: a combination pocket knife or Swiss Army knife; needle and cotton and a small pair of scissors; pair of sunglasses; towel, tooth brushes and paste; oral contraceptives (if used); tampons; a supply of anti-malarial pills; one or two good long novels. Most toiletries — toilet paper, tooth paste, shaving cream, shampoo, etc — are available in the capital cities and large towns. A water bottle (fabric covered) is very useful where it's hot or for walking in the mountains. It also enables you to give those dubious water holes a miss and so cut down your chances of getting hepatitis.

MAIL

Have letters sent to you c/o Poste Restante, GPO, in whatever city/town you will be passing through. Alternatively use the mail-holding service operated by American Express offices and their agents if you're a client (ie if you have their cheques or one of their credit cards). Most embassies no longer hold mail and will forward it to the nearest Post Restante. Plan ahead. It *can* take up to two weeks for a letter to arrive even in capital cities and sometimes much longer in smaller places.

Most Poste Restantes are pretty reliable and will hold mail for one month — sometimes longer, sometimes shorter — after which they'll return uncollected letters to the sender. The service is free in most places but in others there's a small charge for each letter (never more than a few cents). As a rule, you need your passport as proof of identity to collect letters. In large places, where there's a lot of traffic, letters are generally sorted into alphabetical order. In small places they may all be lumped together in the same box. Sometimes you're allowed to sort through them yourself. In other places a post office employee will do the sorting for you. If you're not receiving expected letters ask them to check under every conceivable combination of your Christian name, surname, any other initials and even under 'M' (for Mr Mrs Ms Miss). This sort of confusion isn't as widespread as many people believe though most travellers have a crazy story to tell about letters. Confusion is usually the result of indistinct handwriting. It may also be related to the fact that English (or French) is not the first language of many postal clerks so one person's handwriting may look like a completley different language compared with another's even if they're in the same language. Avoid this confusion by telling your friends before you leave to print your name in block capitals and to underline your surname on the envelope.

It's inadvisable to send currency notes by mail. They'll often be stolen by post office employees no matter how cleverly the contents are disguised. Every trick in the book is used to see if the letter is worth opening up. On the other hand many people do receive money this way.

When sending letters yourself, try to use aerogrammes (air letters) rather than ordinary letters but if you do send the latter make sure that the stamps are franked in front of you otherwise there's a fair chance they will be steamed off, re-sold and the letter thrown away.

There's little point in having any letter sent by Express Delivery (called Special Delivery in the UK) as they won't get there any quicker on average than an air letter.

CUSTOMS

These vary considerably from one country to the next and between different entry points in any one particular country. Some are really obstreperous, others hardly look at you. A great deal depends on your appearance and whether they get that feeling that you're hiding something. A lifetime spent as a customs official often gives a person a high degree of intuition so it's dangerous to assume they're idiots if you are hiding something. Equally it can depend on what time of day you go through, which side of the bed they got out of that morning and because bribes can be extracted from people caught with contraband. Some places are highly bureaucratic and crossing the border can take hours. If you kick up the dust about this, it takes even longer. South African stamps in your passport will ensure you a heavy time on the borders of most Moslem countries except Egypt and may result in them refusing you entry altogether.

Borders where many people cross daily are usually OK — they can't possible check everyone — but don't take this an invitation to be careless. Arrivals and departures by air are usually checked more thoroughly if only because of hijackings. If X-rays are being used to screen people keep your camera and films well out of the way otherwise the films will fade. X-ray baggage checks are relatively harmless, however.

Watch out in Mauritania and Tanzania if you have blackmarket money as the police many stop and search you (anywhere in the former, in game parks in the latter). If they discover money that isn't accounted for on your currency declaration form they'll either confiscate it or cart you off. Whatever you do, don't bring drugs back with you from Morocco to Spain. The search is super-heavy and there are hundreds of people languishing in Spanish jails as a result of trying to smuggle hashish. The same goes for Algeria, Libya and France.

HITCHHIKING
It's possible to hitch free all the way through Africa and sometimes this is an excellent way to get involved in a country and its people since you'll often have to spend a lot of time in small rural villages. Its only major drawback is that it often involves a lot of inescapably boring and tedious waiting at the side of the road. Some travellers have written to us in the past to suggest that trying to hitch for free is an abuse of the hospitality/respect that is accorded to visitors (who are usually relatively affluent) since taking passengers is one way in which truck drivers supplement their income. We feel that is only one side of the coin. Other than expatriate volunteers (Peace Corps, VSO, etc) hitchhikers are the only westerners which many African people come into contact with. They bring with them news of the outside world, a different outlook and set of assumptions and give villagers a chance to exchange views and make friends. This is important in a country where newspapers are few and far between outside of capital cities and where many people are, in any case, illiterate. Also hitch-hiking involves a lot of effort.

The most likely places for free lifts are Morocco, Algeria, Tunisa, Libya, Ghana, Nigeria, and Kenya. As for the rest of Africa expect to pay for lifts. Hitching is a recognised form of public transport in much of Africa. Most of the lifts you will get will be on the top of lorries though it's sometimes possible to travel in the cab for about twice the price it costs to travel on top. For the bulk of regular runs between towns and cities the 'fare' is more or less fixed and you'll be paying what the locals pay — but check this out before you agree to a price. Sometimes it's possible to bargain, especially if there are a few of you (form an impromptu group). Trucks are generally a little cheaper than buses over the same distance.

There are trucks to most places on main routes every day but in the more remote areas they may only run once or twice a week. Many lifts are arranged the night before departure at the 'truck park' — a compound/dust patch that you'll find in almost every African town of any size. Just go there and ask around for a truck which is going the way you want to go. If the journey is going to take more than one night or one day, ask whether the price includes food and/or water. Remember that the roads are in many places atrocious and break-downs/getting stuck are a regular feature of the journey. Don't look too closely at the tyres or the springs. When you see the state of many of the roads you'll know why nothing lasts very long. In some places like Zaire, Sudan, Rwanda, Burundi, Tanzania, Zambia, and Mozambique the 'roads' have to be seen to be believed — pot holes as high as a man, bridges washed away, etc. Desert roads in places like Sudan, Chad, Mali, Niger and Mauritania are just a set of tyre tracks left in the sand or dust by previous trucks. Don't pay any attention to red lines drawn on maps in places like this. Many roads are impassable in the wet season.

In the more developed countries of the West Coast there are taxis (often Peugeot 404s) as an alternative to trucks. They cost on average about twice as much as trucks but are much quicker. Regular scheduled buses where these exist, cost midway between the two. Many of the taxis also pick up fares from the truck parks.

Don't expect much in the way of lifts from expatriate workers. As a rule they are the very people who detest 'bums' (ie anyone not dressed in crisp, clean clothes ready for a day at the office). They tend to be very status conscious. On the other hand, teachers and volunteer workers in the more remote areas often welcome new faces and the opportunity to talk about what's happening 'back home'. If you are offered this kind of hospitality please don't abuse it. Try to contribute towards your keep — most volunteers have to get by on next to nothing. Peace Corps Volunteers and VSOs are often welcoming and will pass you on to other volunteers further along the line, if they like you. Check out Peace Corps offices in capital cities along the way or try British Council Libraries, American Information Centres and so on.

Hitching through Europe on the way to Africa is good in Holland, Germany, Belgium and Italy. It's less good in Switzerland and Austria and can be very slow in France, Spain, Yugoslavia and Greece. In Spain, it often works out cheaper in the end to use public transport.

Remember that sticking out your thumb in many African countries is the equivalent of saying 'up yours' although some allowances are made for foreigners. Wave your hand up and down vertically instead.

LOOKING FOR SOMEONE TO TRAVEL WITH

It's a fact of travelling life that overlanding is rarely a solo activity. Even if you start out by yourself you'll inevitably meet people along the way who are heading in the same direction. This is especially true on the two main routes south from the Mediterranean coast — south from Algiers to Mali//Niger and south from Alexandria to Nairobi. On these routes you will be very lucky not to become part of a larger group.

If on the other hand, you would prefer to start out with someone, check out notice boards in Youth Hostels and at Universities and Colleges. In London, the best place to look is in the weekly publication *Time Out* which you can get from any news-stand, newsagent or bookseller. Otherwise try newsagent noticeboards around Earls Court and the one at 'Trail Finders' at 48 Earls Court Road, London W8. If you can't find anyone, put an advertisement in a suitable publication yourself and see what turns up.

Cross-roads where travellers congregate are good places to meet companions. The best are Athens, Cairo, Nairobi, Lamu, Dar es Salaam, Lagos, Dakar and any of the Moroccan cities.

ORGANISED OVERLAND TOURS

The purpose of this book is to help you get there under your own steam but if you don't have this kind of initiative or would prefer to go on an organised overland tour then we recommend you get in touch with 'Trailfinders', 48 Earls Court Road, London W8 UK (tel 01-937 9631). They've had many years' experience of recommending and booking various organised tours throughout the world as well as knowing the ins and outs of the budget air fares jungle. They print a quarterly magazine called *Trailfinder* which you can pick up free if you call in at their office or have sent to you by mail for an annual subscription of £1.50 (UK & Eire addresses) or £4 (addresses elsewhere around the world). It's packed full of details about overland tours, cheap flights, books and maps of relevance to overland travel and chatty

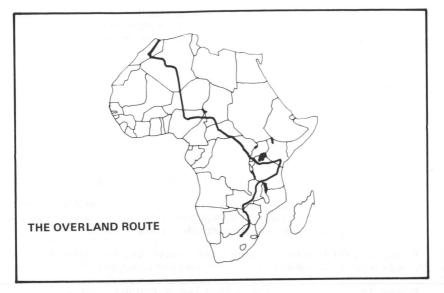

THE OVERLAND ROUTE

articles from people who are travelling/have been travelling in various parts of the world. A friendly bunch of people who will work hard to get you what you're looking for.

Other addresses to write to for promotional literature include:

Treasure Treks, 3rd Floor, Panton House, 25 Haymarket, London SW1, UK.
   40-42 Willis St, Wellington, New Zealand.
   15 Hunter St, Sydney 2000, Australia.
   3, Manchester Lane, Melbourne 3000, Australia.
Aardvark, 14 Coleridge Rd, London N8 UK.
   516 Rathdowne St, North Carlton, Vic 3054, Australia.
   Adventure Centre, 5540 College Ave, Oakland, CA 94618, USA.
Pennworld, 122 Knightsbridge, London SW1, UK.
   Tower Building, Australia Square, Sydney 2000, Australia.
   177 Collins St, Melbourne, 3000, Australia.
Encounter Overland, 271 Old Brompton Road, London SW5, UK.
   369 Pine St, San Francisco, CA 94104, USA.
Capricorn, 21 Ebury Bridge Rd, London SW1, UK.

LANGUAGE
The main languages used are English, French, Arabic and Swahili, though of course, there are many more localised languages like Amharic, Galla, Tigre (all in Ethiopia), Sesotho (in Lesotho), Shona (in Zimbabwe) and Africaans (in South Africa). We've included short vocabularies for some of these localised languages under appropriate country chapters.

It's more or less essential to have a working knowledge of French which is spoken in all ex-French colonies. A smattering of Arabic and Swahili would repay itself over and over again, though we'll readily concede that they are not easy languages for westerners to learn. Local people will always warm to any attempt to speak their language no matter how botched the effort. It's also an excellent way of making friends.

Even if you don't learn Arabic, it's essential to know the numerals from one to 11. They are:

0	٠	sevr	3	٣	talata	6	٧	sitta	9	٩	'ashara
1	١	wahad	4	٤	arba'a	7	٧	sab'a	10	١٠	hidaashara
2	٢	thneen	5	٥	khamsa	8	٨	thamanya	11	١١	

GENERAL INFORMATION
Some books for background information and the spirit of travelling:

With Love, Siri & Ebba (Nicholas Saunders) A beautifully illustrated book written by two women who hitched and walked through the remoter parts of Ethiopia, Sudan and Egypt and lived with nomadic tribes. Available from Lonely Planet.

In Ethiopia with a Mule Dervla Murphy (John Murray) A journey through Ethiopia's remote highlands. Written by the same woman who cycled from Ireland to India.

Penguin Africa Handbook edited by Colin Legum (Penguin) Useful for basic geographical, historical and economic information but a little out of date.

Power in Africa Ruth First (Penguin Books) Describes three major coups in Sudan, Nigeria and Ghana and briefly refers to others.

The Africans: An Entry to Cultural History Basil Davidson (Longmans) A general study of African civilisations. Examines what is known about the ideas, politics, social systems, religions, philosophies and moral values, magical beliefs and arts of a wide range of African people and shows that, far from being fragmentary or primitive, they formed a variant of a peculiarly African civilisation.

Africa in Modern History Basil Davidson (Allen Lane) Very readable, interesting new angles and conclusions from the perspective of African society and politics. It's incredibly well researched and quite up to date (1978).

False Start in Africa R Dumont (Andre Deutsch) A paperback about the necessity of agricultural reforms, economics and education.

The White Nile Alan Moorehead (Penguin) An extremely readable book on the search for the source of the Nile and the exploration of central Africa.

The Man Died Wole Soyinka A novel by one of Nigeria's most outspoken writers about the Biafra war and his own imprisonment.

Blame me on History Bloke Modisane (Pan) About a young African growing up in South Africa under apartheid.

GUIDES

For those who are looking for more specialised guides, especially if taking their own transport, these are some of the best:

Guide du Sahara Available only in French but it's excellent.

Sahara Handbook Simon & Jan Glen (Roger Lascelles) A brand new (1980) and comprehensive guide to the Sahara with sections on vehicle selection and equipment, on the main routes and with many route maps and town plans. Available from Lonely Planet.

Trans-Africa Motoring Colin McElduff (Wilton House Gentry) A book by the head of the foreign routes section of the British RAC. Costings, routes, documents, health, equipment, how to cope with ferries, sand storms, deserts, petrol stations and maps. Practical and easily digested information but somewhat expensive and the routes are now dated.

Guide to Land-Rover Expeditions A useful free guide from the British Leyland public relations department.

Trans-Sahara Klaus & Erika Darr (Globetrotter) An excellent book written in German by a young couple who've made many crossings of the desert by vehicle and run one of the best places in Europe for expedition and desert crossing equipment.

Backpacker's Africa Hilary & George Bradt (Bradt Enterprises) Subtitled '17 walks off the Cape to Cairo route', a bit short on maps but otherwise good suggestions for African walking trips. Available from Lonely Planet.

Some other guides worth looking at are *Game Sanctuaries of Southern Africa*, *Africa A to Z* and *Africa on Wheels*.

PERIODICALS

Africa A monthly political, social and economic magazine covering the whole of Africa. Some excellent articles, news, features, etc, which give a balanced view of events and issued from all sides. Subscription office is Africa Journal Ltd, Kirkman House, 54A Tottenham Court Rd, London W1, UK. It costs 60p per issue in the UK, $2 in the USA and Canada.

New Africa Similar to *Africa* magazine and just as informative but leans more heavily on the political news and analysis and less on the business news. In this respect it's perhaps better for the general reader than *Africa* magazine. The subscription office is 63 Long Acre, London WC2, UK or IC Publications Ltd, Room 1121, 122 East 42nd Street, New York, NY 10017, USA. It costs 60p in the UK, $2 in the USA.

ABC Guide to World Shipping Published quarterly by ABC Travel Guides Ltd, 40 Bowling Green Lane, London EC1, UK and at 3-13 Queen Street, Chippendale, NSW 2008, Australia. It's useful if you're trying to work out unusual sea routes and boat passages to Africa from anywhere in the world.

MAPS

Bartholomew's World Travel Series covers Africa in three sheets — North-West, North-East and Central & Southern. The detail on these is quite adequate for most travellers. If you want less, they also publish one map for the entire continent. Michelin maps are perhaps better than Bartholomew's as they indicate rainfall, temperatures, important ruins, water holes and petrol stations. There are three sheets covering the whole continent, as with Bartholomew's, as well as more detailed sheets for Morocco, Algeria & Tunisia and the Ivory Coast.

Getting There

AUSTRALIA TO AFRICA

There is no cheap way of getting from Australia to Africa — there are no shipping services and flights are expensive. Only South African Airways are now operating on this route (Qantas withdrew a few years back, supposedly for political reasons) and their twice weekly flights are heavily booked. The one-way economy fare from Sydney or Melbourne is A$1041 — this permits stopovers at Perth and/or Mauritius on the way to Johannesburg. There is also an 18 day (minimum) 90 day (maximum) excursion fare which costs A$1339 return and you can add in the stopovers for another $25 each. From Perth the equivalent fares are A$949 one-way or A$1019 return-excursion. From Sydney or Melbourne to London via Johannesburg costs A$1476 — this permits unlimited stopovers at no extra cost but since Australia-Johannesburg-London is already close to the maximum permitted mileage for a regular Australia-London ticket you'll probably have to pay more if you start hopping across Africa from the south.

The only other alternatives would be to fly to Africa via Asia. British Airways fly Hong Kong-Colombo (Sri Lanka)-Seychelles and then to a number of African cities including Johannesburg, Dar es Salaam, Mauritius, Nairobi and Khartoum. The Colombo-Seychelles-Johannesburg sector costs A$724 so you could hook that on to a Sydney or Melbourne-Singapore APEX ticket (about A$360 in the low season) plus a Singapore-Colombo ticket bought in Singapore (about A$160) and get to South Africa by a rather interesting route for around A$1250. Note that there are just two British Airways flights to the Seychelles a week out of Colombo and they tend to be heavily booked. South African Airways do the same route but direct from Hong Kong to the Seychelles. You can also fly from Bombay, India to a number of East African cities since India has strong trade links with that region. This route could also be included in a straightforward Sydney (Melbourne) to London economy ticket. You could be routed on a multi-stop ticket from Australia through South-East Asia then Colombo-Seychelles-Nairobi-Cairo and on (with a number of European stops if you wished) to London for A$1549 — that's 5% over the regular Sydney-London full economy fare since it exceeds the Maximum Permitted Mileage by 5%.

NORTH AMERICA TO AFRICA

The cheapest way of getting there is first to take a standby (or other cheap fare scheme) flight from San Francisco, Los Angeles, Houston or New York to London and then make your way through Europe to North Africa from there. The main flight possibilities are:-

Los Angeles/San Francisco-London

(1) Laker 'Supersaver Fares' vary from US$365 to $540 depending on the season. Fares are identical for Los Angeles and San Francisco but you must add another $22 for weekend departures. Flights to London are usually on Wednesdays and Saturdays (return Tuesdays and Saturdays) from LA and on Mondays (return Sundays) from San Francisco.

(2) Jetsave 'Latesave' fares vary from US$422 to $530 return and are generally similar to Laker Supersaver fares.

(3)   Laker Skytrain standby fares cost US$199 (return from London costs $180). In LA you can either buy tickets at the airport or from a number of Laker sales desks in the city.

(4)   Standby on other airlines is a little more expensive than on Laker ($10-15 more) and the fares vary with the season. Pan Am, British Airways, TWA all operate this route.

(5)   Other special deals include Budget, ABC and APEX fares which must be booked in advance. See New York-London for details.

Houston-London
(1)   The cheapest standby fares on this route are offered by British Caledonian Airways. From London they cost between US$150 and $195. Ring the airline the night before departure to check seat availability. These flights operate out of London Gatwick — not Heathrow.

(2)   Pan Am standby fares vary from US$165 to $185 depending on the season. Daily departures.

(3)   Braniff International also do standby fares to London at similar prices to Pan Am but the flights involve a change of aircraft — and a six hour wait — at Dallas. Daily departures. Like British Caledonian, these flights operate into and out of London Gatwick.

New York-London
(1)   Laker 'Supersaver Fares' vary from US$195 to $355 return depending on your outward and return dates. There's an additional charge of $12 if you want a weekend rather than a weekday flight. Flights must be booked through a travel agent or through Laker Air Travel on the 23rd, 22nd or 21st day prior to departure. There's a one week minimum, one year maximum stay period. Once you're booked (bookings can be heavy) you're guaranteed a seat and there are about 17 flights per month. Laker operates in and out of London Gatwick.

(2)   Jetsave 'Latesave' scheme varies from US$210 to $355 return. Basically a similar scheme to Laker Supersaver and must be booked through a travel agent.

(3)   Laker Skytrain costs US$135 from New York to London and $127 from London to New York. Flights depart daily and tickets can be bought only on the day of departure but if that day's flight should already be sold out you can purchase a ticket for the next available flight so there's no need to queue more than once. Once you've bought a ticket your seat is guaranteed. In New York the main Laker office is at 95-25 Queens Blvd, Rego Park, where tickets go on sale at 4 am. They're also available at the World Trade Centre, 1 East 59th St (at 5th Ave), at Newark airport and at the Laker desk in the United Airlines Terminal at JFK airport. They go on sale at 7 am at JFK. In London tickets go on sale at 6.30 am at the Laker office at Victoria station or at Gatwick airport from 4 am. Going either way you may buy tickets for yourself and immediate family or for one friend who is travelling with you provided you have their valid passport and visa (if required).

Laker have a phone number in London and New York with a recorded message advising you of the latest seat availability news.

(4)   Standby on other airlines costs US$150. British Airways, Pan Am, TWA, Air India, El Al, Iran Air and National all operate standby fares. Tickets are sold at JFK airport in New York and at the airlines' town terminal in London on the day of departure only. There are plenty of flights daily but you only get on if there are seats available after full fare paying passengers have been accommodated and there are a maximum number of standby seats per week. For Pan Am, BA and TWA the weekly maximum is 1050 seats. In London it's best to phone around the airlines on the night before departure to check seat availability then get to the airline you choose in time for their terminal to open in the morning. In New York it's probably quicker to do the rounds of the ticket counters at JFK. Standby ticket sales stop three hours before flight departure time. Standby fares are higher during the peak summer season.

(5)   Budget fares cost US$320 return and must be booked 21 days before your intended week of departure. Your flight date is notified 10 days before departure. Once you've booked you're guaranteed a seat but, as for standby, there are a limited number of seats per week.

(6)   ABC fares (Advance Booking Charter) vary from US$270 to $300 in the low season and from $460 and $475 in the high season. You must book the flight 45 days before departure and there is 14 day minimum, 45 day maximum stay period, but 'long-stop' holidays are also available. The flights operate in and out of London Gatwick.

(7)   APEX fares (Advance Purchase Excursions) vary from US$330 to $415 plus a US$14 weekend supplement. Tickets must be booked and paid for 50 days in advance. Once booked your seat is guaranteed but at peak times the flights may be heavily booked.

As we go to press in mid-1980, the Atlantic carriers are about to engage in another price-war over standby, Apex and Budget fares.

LONDON TO AFRICA DIRECT
Some recent fares from *Time Out* to London include Nairobi £270, Accra £355, Lagos £360, Dar es Salaam £330, Lusaka £360, Seychelles £410, Mauritius £500, Tunis £135, Salisbury £440 and Khartoum £310.

LONDON TO NORTH AFRICA
Whether you're hitching, taking a bus, train or flight across Europe you should decide which of the two routes south from the African Mediterranean coast you are going to take before you leave since once you get there your choice will have been made for you. The border between Libya and Egypt is, at present, closed due to Libyan antipathy over the Egyptian-Israeli peace settlement. This means that you can't land in Morocco, Algeria or Tunisia and then cross over to Egypt in order to go down the Nile. The same applies if you land in Egypt and want to cross over to Algeria in order to go through the Sahara desert.

The only routes south which are open are either through the Sahara desert from Algiers to Mali/Niger or down the Nile Valley from Egypt though the one from Algeria to Mauritania (Route du Mauritaine) may re-open soon due to the Mauritanian withdrawal from the Western Sahara (formerly Spanish Sahara). If you're taking the route through the Sahara desert you need to take one of the ferries from Spain, France or Italy to the North African coast. If you're heading down the Nile you need to take one of the ferries from Greece. It's also useful to know that the only land crossing between Morocco and Algeria (Oujda-Tlemcen) which is allowed at present is occasionally closed when relations between Morocco and Algeria get particularly vitriolic. (Morocco has occupied the whole of Western Sahara and is fighting a war there with the Saouarhis who are supported by Algeria).

Direct Buses across Europe

There are many companies which operate direct buses across Europe from London to such places as Algeciras, Madrid, Barcelona (Spain); Milan, Rome, Naples (Italy); Thessaloniki, Athens (Greece). These buses are the cheapest way of getting across Europe, other than hitching, but only marginally cheaper than a direct train *if* you have an International Student Card and are 26 years old or under. If you'd prefer to go by train, contact British Rail in the UK and ask about current offers. If you're looking for a bus, buy a copy of *Time Out* (published weekly on Thursdays and available from any newsagents or bookseller in the London area). It's full of advertisements for direct buses to points all over Europe as well as flight ticket bargains. Alternatively, go along to 'Trailfinders', 48 Earls Court Road, London W8. They'll be able to recommend a reliable company and book you a ticket. It's suggested you avoid Magic Bus. We get letters from travellers all the time explaining in graphic detail how very un-magical they are.

MAKING YOUR OWN WAY ACROSS EUROPE

The cheapest way of getting from London to the Continent if you're 26 years old or under is to take one of the daily trains from London to any one of the following destinations. Since the fares include the cost of the cross Channel ferry, this makes it cheaper than hitching *unless* you manage to get a free passage across the Channel on the hovercraft from Ramsgate to Calais. Even if you're over 26, it's still pretty competitive.

	single	return
Calais	£ 9.85	£19.40
Boulogne	£ 9.85	£19.40
Dunkerque	£ 9.85	£19.40
Hook of Holland	£11.00	£21.90
Amsterdam or any station in Holland	£13.85	£27.65
Paris	£14.60	£25.80
Cologne	£16.00	£31.70
Rome	£32.70	£65.00
Barcelona	£34.00	£67.70
Any station in Belgium	£11.55	£23.15

These discount tickets are available from 'Transalpino'. Their London offices are at 71-75 Buckingham Palace Road, London SW1 (tel 01-834- 9656/6283) and 214

Shaftesbury Avenue, London WC2 (tel 01-836 0087/8). They also have offices in Liverpool, Birmingham, Dublin and many cities throughout Europe. The above discounts are only a few of the many available.

If you decide to hitch and are starting from London, catch the Underground train to either New Cross or New Cross Gate on the Metropolitan line and then either choose the A2 or A20 roads to Dover or Folkestone respectively. Initially you will probably have to walk and hitch as the roads are very congested with local traffic until you get a few miles out. Carry a sign with 'Dover' or 'Folkestone' on it.

Ferries across the English Channel

There are many daily ferries throughout the year from Dover, Folkestone, and Ramsgate to the Belgian ports of Zeebrugge and Ostend and the French ports of Calais, Dunkirk and Boulogne. The cheapest is the hovercraft service from Ramsgate to Calais which costs £7.90 (under 18 it's £6.70) but there are reductions of 15% for student card holders. This is also the only ferry on which it's still possible to get a free passage across the Channel. Each car/van is allowed up to six passengers without further charge so try standing a few hundred metres back from the terminal building with a sign saying 'You're allowed six passengers FREE — please take me'. Be careful not to let the officials at the terminal see you. They can be very stroppy and refuse you on board unless you buy a ticket. One of the advantages of sussing out a free passage at Ramsgate is that you stand a good chance of securing a lift into the heart of Europe with the person who takes you on and so avoid the scramble for lifts at the other side.

All the other boat ferries from Dover and Folkestone charge a standard £8.60 each and there are no student concessions. If you're thinking of hitching across Europe then the best place to start from is Ostend (trying to hitch out of Calais will discourage you for life which is why the hovercraft is a mixed blessing unless you get a free passage across the Channel and a lift into the heart of Europe). Whilst you're on the boat ferry, try to find a lift into Europe with someone who is travelling by car on the ferry. Once a ferry has docked at Ostend it takes about two to three hours to clear all the hitch-hikers from the beginning of the motorway to Brussels. The ferry crossings to the Belgian ports take longer than the ones to the French ports but they have the advantage that Belgium is much better for hitching than France.

THROUGH EUROPE

There are obviously any number of different ways you can travel through Europe to end up in southern Spain, France, Italy or Greece. Any map of Europe will indicate the possibilities. If you are hitching, the only constraints on which route you take will be how easy or difficult it is to hitch through the various countries. Most people find France and Spain very slow; Switzerland, Austria, Yugoslavia, and Greece not too bad, and Belgium, Germany and Italy very good. It is possible to get to southern Italy or Greece in four or five days. On the other hand, getting to southern Spain via France could take you at least eight days.

The ferries across the Mediterranean to the North African coast are, in order of cheapness, Spain-Morocco; Italy-Tunisia; Greece-Egypt (if you have a student card) and France-Algeria.

To Southern Spain

Since hitching is very slow in France and Spain it might be quicker (though longer) to go through Belgium, Germany and Switzerland to Turin or Milan in Italy and then head west across southern France. In Spain it may well prove cheaper in the long run to take a train to the port of your choice. The cheapest accommodation available in both countries are the youth hostels. You will need a YH membership card to use them. In Spain they cost 100 pesetas/night. If you don't want to stay in hostels the cheapest alternative accommodation is in either Casa de Huespedes or Pensaos for which you can expect to pay 250 pesetas a night. These places often have cheap evening meals for about 150 pesetas including wine. In Paris there's a sort of student hostel at 46 rue de Vangirard just off Boulevard St Michel in the Quartier Latin which has dormitories and double rooms. For good cheap food try the student HQ (CROUS) at 39 Avenue Georges Bernanos — ask a student in the meal queue to sell you a spare ticket otherwise you pay double for the meal.

To Southern Italy
The quickest way to get there is through Belgium, Germany and Switzerland. Hitching is fast in Northern Italy down as far as Rome. After that it slows up quite considerably. The ferries to Tunis depart from Naples, Palermo and Trapani. If you're heading for either of the latter two in Sicily there are ferries to Messina from both Reggio di Calabria and Villa San Giovanni on the mainland. The ferries depart once every 20 minutes in either direction throughout the night and day and cost 300 lire (US$0.40) and 200 lire ($0.30) respectively.

To Greece
There are two main routes to Greece:

(1) Along the motorway system as follows: Ostend - Brussels - Liege (Belgium)-Aachen - Cologne - Frankfurt - Munich (Germany) - Salzburg - Vienna -Graz (Austria) - Maribor - Zagreb - Belgrade - Nis - Skopje (Yugoslavia) - Thessaloniki - Larisa - Athens (Greece). The real motorways finish at Graz (despite what maps sometimes show as motorways through Yugoslavia) but the central road through Yugoslavia is just as fast — and very monotonous between Zagreb and Belgrade, though it has the compensation that when you get a lift it's generally going a long way. If you prefer to travel through the more interesting part of Yugoslavia, take the coastal route along the Adriatic Sea. Mountains, fjords and ancient Roman cities make this route very beautiful and you can sleep on the beaches at night. The road is motorway standard most of the way. To join the main route again, turn off the coast road at Titograd and head for Skopje through Kosova Mitorvici. If you decide to by-pass Vienna and go directly through the mountains from Salzburg to Graz but get stuck, take the train through to Villach or Klagenfurt and try again. From either of these two towns you can pick up lifts going through the Ljobl Tunnel to Ljubljana in Yugoslavia.
(2) Along the motorway system through Belgium, Germany, Switzerland and Italy to either Brindisi or Otranto at the tip of Italy. From either of these places there are ferries across the Adriatic to Corfu, Igoumenitsa and Patras and from there buses to Athens. For full details of these ferries, see later under 'Mediterranean Ferries.'

Transport & Accommodation in Greece
The train from Thessaloniki to Athens costs 380 Drachmas (US$10) and takes 8½ hours. A bus costs 380 Drachmas and takes nine hours.

Student discounts are available on Greek trains but are hard to get. It's suggested you have a confirmatory letter on headed notepaper with your photo and student ID number attached. Have the photo rubber-stamped. If you haven't got such a letter make one. Use a button and ink for the rubber stamp. Take this and bitch like hell at the ticket office. Some people have hassled for hours and got precisely no-where.

The areas for cheap accommodation in Athens are Plaka and Syntagma. Average price is between 50 and 60 Drachmas. Many cheap student hostels in the Plaka area for about 60 Drachs but it's generally dormitory accommodation with up to 10 people per room. Some which have been recommended are: *Jimmy's Student House*, 40 Drachs; *Student Inn*, 80 Drachs; *Funny Trompets*, 60 Drachs; *Plaka Inn*, Lussukratous St, 50 Drachs on the roof, 80 Drachs in the dormitory.

In addition to these there are *Ilon House*, 48 Nikis Street, just behind American Express. Costs 65 Drachs with showers extra at 20 Drachs. *Hotel Lefkas*, Wleou Street, opposite the Grand Hotel and not far from Omonia Square. Costs 65 Drachs. Clean and comfortable but no shower. Manager speaks English.

For places to eat, drink and meet other travellers try 24 Kidathineon Street, two doors down from the 'Magic Bus' office. Many travellers come here for breakfast. *Sintrivani*, 5 Fisellinon, just off Syntagma Square. Cheap little caff. *Peter's English Fireside Pub*, just around the corner from Plaka Square, this is a hang out for travellers in the evenings.

If you're looking for travelling companions/info/lifts, most of the student hostels have useful noticeboards. There's also a page of ads in the English-language

Athens News.

If hitching out of Athens, take bus No. 150 from Eletherias Square to Daphni if going to the Peloponnese; bus No 25 from Kelfinia to National Road or bus No 6 from Omonia Square if going to Thessaloniki; bus No 184 from Syntagma Square if going to the airport. If you need any vaccinations you can get them free from the Health Centre on Abelokipi Square.

International Student Cards are available from the following places:

STS Travel, 1 Filellion Street, off Syntagma Square. At this place you must have a letter from the college which must be rubber stamped. They charge 90 Drachs. Good notice board here.

Antonio Student Centre. This place used to be excellent for student cards and involved actual enrolment in the Athens Ballet School though they were expensive at 575 Drachs! However, 'Antonio' isn't as free and easy with them anymore and may refuse unless you're buying a long-distance air ticket (in which case you get the card free).

Condor Travel, 41 Voulis (tel 32 34 407). Manager is called Nikitas Kypridemos. One traveller was ecstatic about this place and said Nikitos could do anything and even at short notice. Very helpful and persistent. The business is owned by an English guy who's also very resourceful. Some of the cheapest tickets available in Athens from here.

Some tips if you're hitching through Europe

(1) If you get stuck in Frankfurt, catch tram No 15 to the last stop and then walk a short distance (about two km) to the slip road for the autobahn going south.

(2) If you get stuck in Munich, take tram No 33 to Pilsensee Strasse from where it's a short walk to the autobahn slip road. Alternatively, take the Underground to Bahnhof Ost from where it's a few minutes walk to the autobahn slip road going to Salzburg. Munich is a good place to pick lifts going south or north. The best place to look for these is in *Ziggy's* which is a truckies' cafe on Arnulfstrasse. It's also possible to pick up lifts from the Youth Hostel here — usually with other travellers who have their own transport.

MEDITERRANEAN FERRIES

The list which follows starts from Spain and moves east to finish with Greece. The list is not exhaustive but includes all the ferries you're most likely to use. Note that many of the ferries from Greece actually start from Venice but would, of course, be much more expensive from there.

Spain-Canary Islands

Compania Transmediterranea operates a drive-on drive-off car ferry on the route Cadiz-Tenerife-Las Palmas-Cadiz. The 1½ day service operates every four or five days and one-way fares start from 4280 Pesetas (US$60).

Spain-Morocco

(1) Algeciras-Tangier Compania Transmediterranea operates a drive-on drive-off car ferry which departs Algeciras daily at 9 am, 12.30 and 5.30 pm except on Monday and Thursday. From Tangier departures are at 8 am, 12.30 and 3.30 pm, again except Monday and Thursday. Minimum fare for the 2½ hour service is 670 Pesetas

(US$10) one-way.

Transtour have a four times daily (except Sunday) hydrofoil service which takes one hour and costs 850 Pesetas or 50 Dirhams (US$12.50).

(2) Algeciras-Ceuta Compania Transmediterranea have a five times daily car ferry except on Sundays when it only operates once. Minimum fare for the 1½ hour journey is 250 Pesetas (US$3.60). This is the cheapest and quickest ferry across the Mediterranean.

There is another drive-on drive-off car ferry operated by Isnasa (Islena de Navegacion SA). This service operates four times daily except Sunday when there are only two services. Minimum fare for the 1¼ hour journey is 345 Pesetas (US$5).

(3) Malaga-Melilla Compania Transmediterranea have a drive-on drive-off car ferry which departs Malaga at 12 noon daily except Sundays and at 11.30 pm on Wednesdays. From Melilla it departs at 11.59 pm daily except Sundays and at 11.30 am on Fridays. Minimum fare for the eight to nine hour journey is 530 Pesetas (US$7.50).

(4) Almeria-Melilla Compania Transmediterranea have a drive-on drive-off car ferry which departs Almeria at 11.30 pm on Monday, Wednesday, Thursday and Saturday and departs Melilla at 11.30 pm on Tuesday, Thursday, Sunday and at 11.30 am on Thursday. Minimum fare for the seven to nine hour journey is 530 Pesetas (US$7.50).

There are also other ferries which operate between Ceuta and Melilla, calling at Penon de Velez, Alhucemas Island and Chafarinas Island (these are all Spanish islands just off the north Moroccan coast).

Gibraltar-Morocco
The border between Spain and Gibraltar is closed so the only way you can get into the latter is either on the ferry from Tangier or to fly in from northern Europe. These ferry services will, therefore, only be of use to you if you particularly want to visit Gibraltar (it's worth a visit!).

Transtour have a hydrofoil which departs Gibraltar daily at 4 pm except Sundays and Tangier daily at 9 am except Sundays. Minimum fare for the one hour journey is £8.50, 70 Dirhams or 1200 Pesetas one-way.

Bland Line have a drive-on drive-off car ferry which departs Gibraltar at 9 am on Tuesday and Sunday and at 6 pm on Thursday and Friday. It departs Tangier at 11.30 am on Tuesday, 8 am and 8 pm on Friday and 5 pm on Sunday. Minimum fare for the 2¼ hour trip is £10 one-way but the same fare round trip if you return on the same day.

Spain-Algeria
(1) Alicante-Oran Compagnie Nationale Algerienne de Navigation has a car ferry with five departures (in each direction) per month. Minimum fare for the 34 hour journey is 194 French francs (US$43.50)

(2) Palma (Balearic Islands)-Algiers Compagnie Nationale Algerienne de Navigation have a car ferry which costs 137 French francs (US$31). To get to Palma on

Majorca there are daily ferries from Barcelona, Valencia and Alicante one mainland Spain. Minimum fares for these ferries all start at 760 Pesetas (US$11).

France-Algeria

All these ferries are operated jointly by Compagnie Nationale Algerienne de Navigation and Societe Nationale Maritime Corse Mediterranee. All are car ferries.

(1) Marseilles-Algiers Virtually daily services, some via Palma (Balearic Islands) in which case they take longer although the cost is the same. Minimum fare for the 24 hour journey is French francs 301 (US$68).

(2) Marseilles-Annaba There are three ferries per month and minimum fare for the 22 to 24 hour trip is 301 French francs (US$68).

(3) Marseilles-Bejaia There are two to three ferries per month with a minimum fare for the 24 hour journey of 301 French francs (US$68).

France-Tunisia

A joint car ferry service is operated by the Societe Nationale Maritime Corse Mediterranee and Compagnie Tunisienne de Navigation. There are five or six departures month and minimum fare for the 23 to 25 hour journey is 301 French francs.

France-Senegal

Paquet Cruises operate a car ferry from Toulon to Dakar calling at various Spanish and Moroccan ports along the way but it's expensive and no current schedules are available. Minimum fare is 1435 French francs (US$322) and you can also pick up this ferry from Casablanca (Morocco) in which case the minimum fare is 1100 French francs (US$247).

Italy-Greece

(1) Otranto-Corfu-Igoumenitsa 'R Line' (Redalis Shipping Company) have a daily (except Sunday) car ferry in the summer only. Minimum fare is US$24 and cars cost the same. Student card holders can get a further 30% reduction on these fares. This is the cheapest ferry between Italy and Greece.

(2) Brindisi-Corfu-Igoumenitsa & Patras Adriatica Line/Hellenic Mediterranean Lines have a car ferry operating daily in either direction. If you're coming by train from Rome note that the train arrives in Brindisi at 9.45 pm and the boat leaves at 10 or 10.30 pm — and it's over a km from the train station to the docks! From Brindisi at 10 pm the ferry arrives Corfu at 7 am the next morning, Igoumenitsa at 9 am and Patras at 6 pm.

Buses for Athens meet the boat at Patras and you get to Athens at 10 pm the same day. From Patras departures are at 10 pm, arriving Igoumenitsa at 7 am the next day, Corfu at 9 am and Brindisi at 5 pm. The bus from Athens to connect with the departing boat leaves at 1.30 pm.

Minimum fares are Brindisi-Corfu/Igoumenitsa US$48.50, Brindisi-Patras US$59, Patras-Athens (by bus) US$8. Student Card holders, holders of International YH Cards and people up to the age of 26 are entitled to a 30% reduction. Note that there are cheaper local buses from Patras to Athens for 193 Drachmas, half the price of the shipping line coaches. There are also cheap trains available.

On this same route Fragoudakis Line have 12 to 14 sailings monthly except for one month in winter when the ship is dry-docked. From Brindisi at 10 pm the boat arrives Corfu at 6.45 am the next morning then Igoumenitsa at 8.15 am and Patras at 5 pm. The connecting bus to Athens arrives there at 9 pm. From Patras the ship leaves at 9.30 pm, arrives Igoumenitsa at 6 am the next day and continues on to Corfu at 8 am and Brindisi at 3.30 pm. The connecting bus from Athens to Patras leaves at 1.30 pm.

Italy-Tunisia
(1) **Naples-Palermo-Tunis** Tirrenia Lines have a car ferry once weekly in each direction. It departs Naples at 11 am on Thursday and arrives Palermo at 11.59 on the same day and Tunis at 2 pm on Friday. From Tunis at 7.30 pm on Friday it arrives Palermo at 10 am on Saturday and Naples at 7.15 pm on Saturday. Minimum fares are Naples-Tunis US$64, Palermo-Tunis US$40.50.

(2) **Trapani (Sicily)-Tunis** Tirrenia Lines have a once weekly car ferry which departs Trapani at 11.30 am on Tuesday and arrives Tunis at 9 pm on the same day. It departs Tunis at 8 am on Wednesdays and arrives Trapani at 7 pm on the same day. Minimum fare is US$24.

Greece-Egypt
(1) **Piraeus-Alexandria** Adriatica Line have a once weekly car ferry which leaves Piraeus on Sundays and Alexandria on Tuesdays. It takes 35 hours and the minimum fare is US$110. The minimum fare is for deck class seats and these are not available between 15 October and 31 March, at that time you have to go C class cabin which costs US$197 minimum. Young people aged 26 or under, holders of FIYTO, International Youth Hostel Cards and International Student Cards as well as anyone holding a Eurail or Eurail Youthpass card is entitled to a 30% reduction on the above fares.

(2) **Piraeus-Larnaca-Alexandria-Latakia-Piraeus** The Black Sea Shipping Company have a once monthly service with minimum fare for Piraeus-Alexandria of US$82.

(3) **Alexandria-Corfu-Venice-Corfu-Piraeus-Alexandria** Federal Arab Maritime Company have a car ferry which departs from each end once every 10 days. The trip takes 35 hours and minimum fares Alexandria-Corfu or Piraeus-Alexandria are US$90. From Greece to Egypt you can board the ship either at Corfu or Piraeus but from Egypt to Greece it does not stop at Piraeus and you have to get off at Corfu. The fares are the same between Alexandria and Piraeus or Corfu.

(4) **Piraeus-Alexandria** The Egyptian Navigation Company operates the same route but we have no details of their schedule or fares.

Addresses of the Ferry Operators
Compania Transmediterranea
HQ: Zurbano 73, Apartado de Correos 982, Madrid 3, Spain
   Throughout the rest of Spain they are represented by AUCONA
AUCONA, Marina 59, Santa Cruz de Tenerife, Canary Islands
AUCONA, Muelle Santa Catalina, Las Palmas, Canary Islands
INTERCONA, 31 rue Quevedo, Tangier, Morocco
Melia Travel, 12 Dover St, London W1, UK

Transtour
   Tourafrica, Estacion Maritima, Algeciras, Spain
   Smith Imossi & Co Ltd, 47 Irish Town, Gibraltar
   54 Boulevard Pasteur (1st floor), Tangier, Morocco

Bland Line
   Cloister Building, Gibraltar
   Gibmar Travel SA, 22 Ave Mohamed V, Tangier, Morocco
   Cadogan Travel Ltd, 159 Sloane St, London SW1, UK

Compagnie Nationale Algerienne de Navigation
   HQ: 2 Quai No 9, Nouvelle Gare Maritime, Algiers, Algeria
   Agencies Passages, 6 Boulevard Khemisti, Algiers, Algeria
   SNCM, 61 Boulevard des Dames, Marseilles 13222, France
   CNAN, 29 Boulevard des Dames, Marseilles 13002, France
   Bureaux Passages, Gare Maritime, Alicante, Spain
   Agencia Schembri, Plaza Lonja 2-4, PO Box 71, Palma, Balearic Islands

Societe Nationale Maritime Corse Mediterranee
   HQ: 61 Boulevard des Dames, Marseilles 13222, France
   CNAN, Quai No 9, Nouvelle Gare Maritime, Algiers, Algieria
   Navitour, 8 rue d'Alger, Tunis, Tunisia
   P&O Normandy Ferries, Arundel Towers, Portland Terrace, Southampton, UK

Compagnie Tunisienne de Navigation
   HQ: 8 rue d'Alger, Tunis, Tunisia

Paquet Cruises (Compagnie des Croisieres Paquet)
   72 rue de la Republique, 13002 Marseilles, France
   Agence Maritime Gaillard 'Le Cygne V', Ave Franklin Roosevelt, 83100 Toulon, France
   Voyages Paquet, 65 Avenue de l'Armee Royale, Casablanca, Morocco
   Voyages Paquet, 21 Avenue d'Espagne, Tangier, Morocco
   Senegal Tours, 5 Place de l'Independence, Dakar, Senegal

'R Line' (Redalis Shipping Company Ltd)
   HQ: PO Box 9, Corfu, Greece
   Stazione Marittima, 73028 Otranto, Italy
   CIT, 10 Charles II St, London SW1, UK

Adriatica Line
   Sealink Car Ferry Centre, 52 Grosvenor Gardens, London SW1, UK
   De Castro & Co, 33 Sharia Salah Salem, Alexandria, Egypt
   Adriamare Transporti Marittimi, Akti Miaouli 19, Piraeus, Greece

Fragoudakis Line
   Inomena Praktoria, 6 Astingos St, Piraeus, Greece
   Il Globo, Corso Garibaldi 24, Brindisi, Italy

Tirrenia Line
   HQ: Rione Sirignano 2, 81021 Naples, Italy
   Stazione Marittima Molo Angioino, Naples, Italy
   Via Roma 385, Palermo, Italy
   Sealink Car Ferry Centre, 52 Grosvenor Gardens, London SW1, UK
   126 rue de Yougoslavie, Tunis, Tunisia

Federal Arab Maritime Company
HQ: 5 Gabarti St, Alexandria, Egypt
Mena Shipping Company Ltd, Stoaloumou Building, 81 Akti Miaoli, Piraeus, Greece
The Universal Travel Service, 132 Johan Theotokis St, New Port, Corfu, Greece

Egyptian Navigation Company
2 El Nasr St, Alexandria, Egypt
20 Talaat Harb, Cairo, Egypt

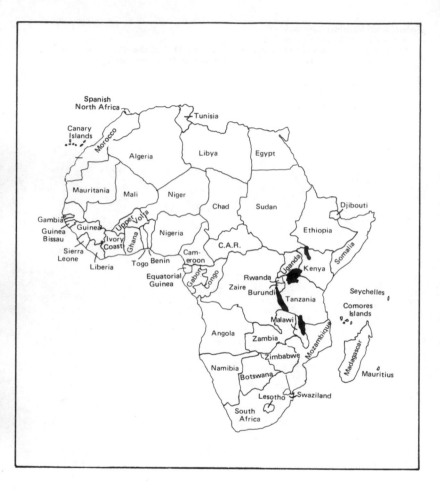

Algeria

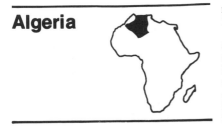

A French colony since 1830, Algeria became independent in 1962 after eight years of guerilla warfare in which one million Algerians died. A brief struggle for power followed between 'moderates' and 'militants' before Colonel Boumedienne led the Armee de Liberation to victory with the 'Front de Liberation National'. Ben Bella was elected Prime Minister, pledged to a 'revolutionary Arab-Islamic state based on the principles of socialism and collective leadership at home and anti-imperialism abroad'.

Landless peasants quickly put these ideals into practice and moved in on land vacated by the French, setting up co-operative farms to be run by peasant councils. However, with the French common enemy gone, there was rapid polarisation between the advocates of real socialism and those for whom the expulsion of the French meant their chance to become rich. Nationalisation of major industries was carried out but the re-distribution of land was limited to that previously owned by the French, leaving large estates privately owned by rich Algerians. These conservative landowners were frightened by the call for liberation of women in particular. Armed revolts, based on the slogan 'Islam is not compatible with socialism' broke out in 1963 and 1964 but with the people tiring of civil disorder and economic stagnation and impatient for the prosperity and progress for which they'd sacrificed a whole generation, most were relieved when Colonel Bou-

medienne staged a bloodless coup in 1965.

Boumedienne was a competent, if authoritarian, pragmatist who made economic reconstruction his first priority. Economic growth was boosted by the exploitation of vast deposits of natural gas in the Sahara but unemployment remained high and large numbers of Algerians were forced to go to France to find work, despite a vicious climate of racism there. In Algeria itself 70% of the working population are employed on the land but concentration on the industrial sector has meant that productivity is no greater, and in some instances much less, than what was achieved under the French. Since 1971, nearly one million hectares have been distributed on the condition that the land is farmed collectively. Agricultural machinery and expertise has been made available for this and efforts are being made to improve literacy and increase understanding of agricultural technology.

Algeria is very conscious of its role as a model for less well endowed Third World countries. It earns a great deal of respect for the intelligence and integrity of its regime and supports a number of liberation struggles around the world. At present Algeria is deeply committed to supporting the POLISARIO guerila army of the Western Sahara in their liberation struggle against the Moroccans who have now occupied the whole of what was formerly the Spanish Sahara, following the withdrawal of the Mauritanians. This support has brought Algeria and Morocco to the brink of war on several occasions. Tension between the two remain high. Since Boumedienne's death Chadli has been the country's new leader.

The new socialist government declared the equality of women and tried to encourage education for women as well as the re-education of male attitudes in what is essentially an exclusively male-dominated society. They have been relatively successful in the north, especially in the urban areas, but in the south a women remains a chattel, locked away from the age of 12 and never appearing in public unless veiled and suitably chaperoned. As a result, there's a popular myth that any women more than 12 years old who is not locked up and veiled is obviously a whore. This attitude is less prevalent in the north and among the well-educated and the peasants but it is at its worst with the newly-literate middle class in the towns. Real problems generally only arise out of a difference of culture and consequent misunderstandings, rather than from any real ill intentions as Algerians are both generous and hospitable.

FACTS

The population is estimated at over 12 million most of whom live in the north. One third of the population is concentrated in the cities with Algiers, the capital, having about one million. The least densely populated area is, of course, the Sahara with less than one person per square km. Of the ethnic groups, the largest is the Berbers most of whom are farmers living in small towns and villages. Other groups include the Kabyles — a tribe living in the central coastal mountain range — which has a long history of popular education and many of whose members hold high administrative positions in the government. The Chaouias and Mozabites tend to live around the Saharan oases and especially in Ghardaia. They are largely a merchant group, many owning business and land in France and whose politics are fiercely reactionary. The Tuaregs are nomads who travel throughout the Sahara herding goats and camels. They were very severely affected by the Sahel drought and, for many, this spelt the end of that way of life. Thousands became destitute and flocked to the various towns and cities on the fringe of the desert.

There are many important Roman ruins in excellent shape due to the dryness of the desert, the most important being Djemila (near Setif), Timgad (again near Setif but nearer to the desert) and Tipasa (on the coast near Mostaganem). For further details see the tourist literature available from the Algerian National Tourist Organisation who have a good collection of brochures and leaflets on this and other subjects.

Algeria is Africa's second largest country. The mountain range to the north — the Saharan Atlas — runs roughly parallel to the coast and is interspersed with valleys and plateaux. The altitude varies from less than 1000 metres in the southern Sahara to over 3000 metres in the Hoggar Mountains near Tamanrasset. There is an important string of oases along the southern foot of the Atlas Mountains.

The temperature and rainfall vary considerably with altitude and position relative to the coast and mountains. Average coastal temperature is between 10 and 12°C in winter and between 24 and 25°C in summer. Inland the temperatures are much higher, varying from 12°C in winter to over 33°C in summer. Rainfall varies from 70 to 100 cm to zero. Heavy rains in April may make some roads impassable or very difficult. Local people are usually very helpful about alternatives.

VISAS

Required by all except nationals of most West European countries excluding Belgium, Eire, Germany (West), Luxembourg, Netherlands, Portugal and Austria. Nationals of Israel, Malawi, South Africa, South Korea and Taiwan not admitted. You cannot get a visa at the border — it must be obtained beforehand. Visas cost 15 Dinar for a one month stay and are valid for five weeks from the date of issue.

Note that visas can be a real hassle for West Germans. They need a letter

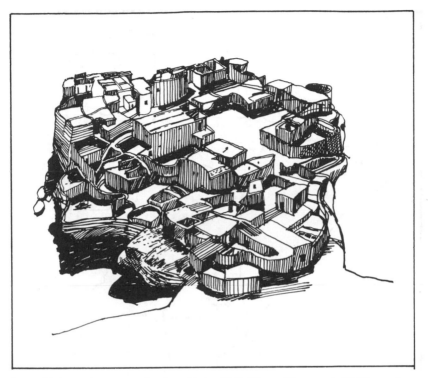

from their embassy confirming that they are not on any 'terrorist' list back in Germany and must take this letter with their passport to the nearest Algerian Embassy who send the whole lot off to Algiers for approval.

Niger Visas In Algiers these cost 27 Dinar, three photos and take 24 hours, although they can take up to three days. They are valid for one month from the date of issue and allow a one month stay. The embassy is at 127 Boulevard Salah Bouakouir, Gallini, Algiers. *There is no consulate further south.*

Nigerian Visas You can wait up to one week for a Nigerian visa. They cost 16 Dinar. The embassy is at 27 rue Blaise Pascal (otherwise known as Ali Boufelgued), Gallini, Algiers.

Mali Visas These cost 42 Dinars, two photos and are issued while-you-wait. Visas are valid for a one week stay. Embassy is at Villa No 14, Cite DNC/ANP, Chemin du Kaddous, Hydra, Algiers.

Upper Volta Visas Obtainable from the French Embassy.

CURRENCY

The unit of currency is the Dinar = 100 centimes. Import/export of local currency is allowed up to 50 Dinar.

Exchange rate:

£1	=	8.81 Dinar
US$1	=	3.83 Dinar
A$1	=	4.41 Dinar

Blackmarket exchange rates are US$1 =

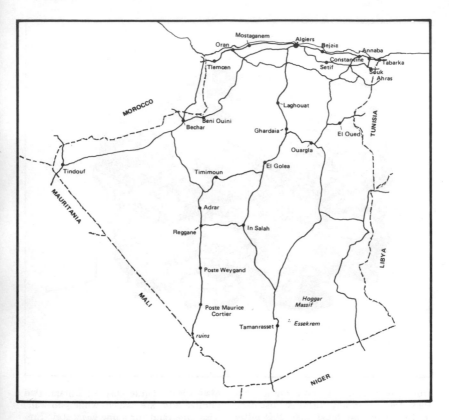

8 Dinar and 25 Dirhams = 35 Dinar. The above blackmarket rates are available in Oujda (Morocco) and Ceuta and Melilla (Spanish Morocco). Inside Algeria the rate is US$1 = 6 Dinar.

Currency declaration forms must be filled in on arrival but experiences differ as to the strictness with which they're checked on departure. Some times they are lax, sometimes very strict. At Tamanrasset they're very strict. Make sure your currency form is in order before attempting to leave as people have been turned back at In Guezzam for discrepancies. It is suggested you list all non-money valuables (camera, jewellery, etc)

on the currency declaration form to avoid hassles about importation of goods. Note that banks are closed on Thursdays and Fridays. There is a bank at El Golea but none at In Salah. The best currency to have in Algeria is the French Franc.

LANGUAGE
Arabic, French and some English.

ACCOMMODATION
Hotels Hotel accommodation is generally expensive in the cities — around 16-30 Dinar a double and often full though there are cheaper beds to be found in the back streets if you look hard. The

cheapest and most convenient places to stay and the ones that most travellers use are the bath houses ('hammam' in Arabic or 'bain maure' in French). In these places you get a mattress on the floor in a dormitory for 3-4 Dinar and a bath for 2 Dinar. They are safe and warm though often damp (not surprisingly!) and you often have to be out quite early in the morning (around 6.30-7 am). You find them in just about every city, town and village.

Youth Hostels It's rumoured these are now defunct so check with the Tourist Office first before turning up. Recommended, if still functional, are the ones in Djelfa and Constantine.

Camping If you inform the police or local authorities you can camp legally and free on common land and beaches.

There are also a large number of organised camp sites with facilities. Guard your belongings at these sites as quite a bit of pilfering goes on.

Other If you're stuck for accommodation the local scout troop huts are worth trying. Also the Foyer de Jeune in Saharan towns for 3-6 Dinar.

Algiers
Cheap hotels are situated around the train station but note that the ones labelled 'hotel' in Roman script are more expensive. The cheaper ones are labelled in Arabic although even these can be as much as 20 Dinar/double.

Hotel Britannique costs 15 Dinar, and is 'dirty'. *Hammam* on the edge of the Casbah between Port Said Square and Place des Martyrs costs 3 Dinar.

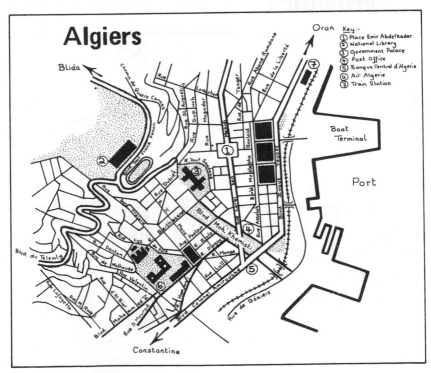

Hotel Rose at 3 rue Debbih Cherif costs 24 Dinar/double. *Hotel Michelet*, near the University costs 24 Dinar/double, 'clean and comfortable'. *Hotel d'Isly* costs 25 Dinar/double and 14 Dinar/single including breakfast, recommended.

For Food try the *Restaurant Amirouch*, near central police station and PTT. A three course meal costs 2.40 Dinar with a student card. Also try the *Foyer de Cheminots* (for railway workers) where a three course meal costs 3.50 Dinar.

Annaba (Bône)
Dormitoire at 12 rue de St Nicholas, costs 5 Dinar for a shared room.

Bejaia
Hotel de l'Etoile, costs 15 Dinar/single with breakfast.

Blida
Hotel Bindi costs 16 Dinar/double.

Constantine
Cross the bridge over the gorge opposite the station and turn left. There are many cheap hotels in this area especially at the top end of the hill. *Hotel El Hana* costs 11 Dinar/single. *Hotel Dardamel*, 37 rue Hamlacui. Costs 5 Dinar. If it says 'Complet' in the window, ask anyway. They usually find somewhere for you to stay.

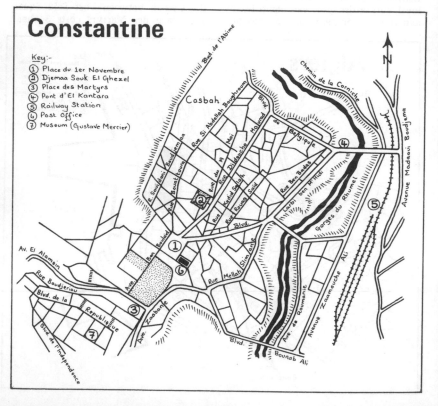

Constantine

Key:-
1. Place du 1er Novembre
2. Djemaa Souk El Ghezel
3. Place des Martyrs
4. Pont d'El Kantara
5. Railway Station
6. Post Office
7. Museum (Gustave Mercier)

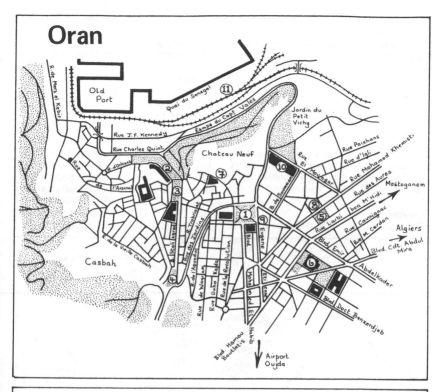

Oran

Old Port

R. de Mers el Kebir

Quai du Senegal

Jardin du Petit Vichy

Rue J. F. Kennedy

Rampe du Cap't Vales

Rue Charles Quint

Chateau Neuf

R. d'Orleans

Rue Paixhans

Rue d'Igli

Rue Mohamed Khemisti

Rue El Moungar

Rue des Aures

Mostaganem

Rue de l'Arsenal

B. de Soummam

ben M' Hidi

Rue Larbi

Rue Cavaignac

Rue M. Cerdan

Algiers

Rue de la Vieille Casbah

Casbah

Rue des Jardins

R. Trobmdt

R. del Haouedd

Rue de Mostpzan

Rue Doho Kdda

Rue de la Revolution

Blvd. Eugene

Mohamed El

Blvd Emir

Blvd. Cdt. Abdul Mira

Abdelkader

Blvd. Doct. Benzerdjeb

Bled Hamou Boudlets

Habib

Airport Oujda

1 Place de 1er Novembre	7 Mosque du Pacha
2 Place de la Republique	8 Post Office
3 Place Klebe	9 Air Algerie
4 Place des Quincances	10 Banque Central d'Algerie
5 Place du Maghreb	11 Railway Station
6 Cathedral & Place Jean d'Arc	

Djelfa

If it's still in existence, the *Youth Hostel* is 8 Dinar/double.

El Golea

Very good campsite about a km from the centre, costs 5 Dinar/night. The SNTL truck park is opposite so it's a good place to stay if you're trying to find a lift.

Ghardaia

Youth Hostel (Maison Jeunesse) on the main street is free. There are two camp sites which cost 5 Dinar per person per night. One of them is eight km from the centre and has rush huts and hot showers. There are many tourists here and the demand for blue jeans and watches is heavy so it's worth selling anything you don't want at this oasis town. The *Hammam* near the bus station costs 12 Dinar/double.

In Salah

There's only one hotel here which costs

55 Dinar!! Free camping at the Palmerie just outside town on the Reggane road. The *Hammam* costs 6 Dinar without bath but is 'sweaty and uncomfortable'.

Maghria
Town on the Moroccan border. Only three hotels, the cheapest being 20 Dinar/double.

Oran
Hotel de la Gare, right next to the train station, costs 20 Dinar/single. *Hotel Marhaba* costs 25 Dinar/double. You can camp free at Ein Turk beach.

Ouargla
Hotel du Sahara is the cheapest hotel.

Situated five minutes from the market.

Souk Ahras
Hotel Terminus costs 6 Dinar/single.

Tamanrasset
There are two camp sites, one for 15 Dinar and the other for 6 Dinar though both are of the same standard. They're good places for picking up lifts. It's officially forbidden to camp anywhere other than the camp sites but plenty of Tuaregs do so perhaps you could stay with them. The *Bain Maure* costs 6 Dinar. Note that the 15 Dinar camp site is in town but may be closed from time to time. The 6 Dinar camp site is 12 km from town on the Assekram road.

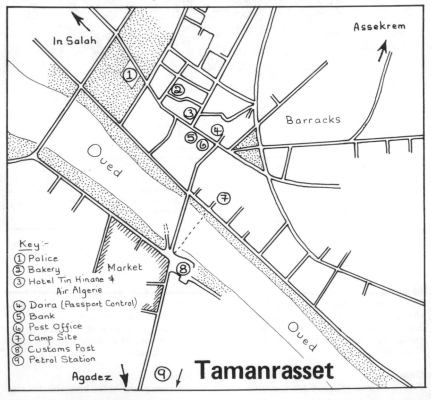

In Salah

Assekrem

Barracks

Oued

Key:-
1 Police
2 Bakery   Market
3 Hotel Tin Hinane &
     Air Algerie
4 Daira (Passport Control)
5 Bank
6 Post Office
7 Camp Site
8 Customs Post
9 Petrol Station

Agadez

Oued

Tamanrasset

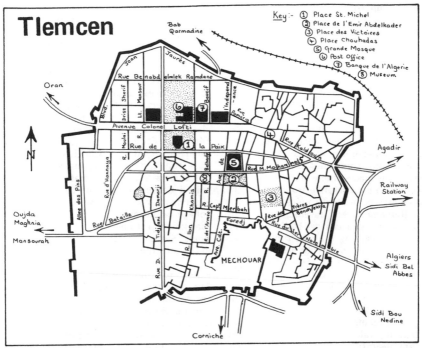

Tlemcen

Key :-
① Place St. Michel
② Place de l'Emir Abdelkader
③ Place des Victoires
④ Place Chouhadas
⑤ Grande Mosque
⑥ Post Office
⑦ Banque de l'Algerie
⑧ Museum

It's possible to visit the Ermitage at Essekrem up in the Hoggar Mountains from Tamanrasset but unless you walk (!) you'll probably have to find a rich tourist willing to take you there or hire a land-Rover with a bunch of other travellers at 400 Dinars and split the cost.

Note that the poste restante in Tam only keeps letters for 14 days. Tam is the last place to stock up with food, water and petrol. No more until you get to Agadez (Niger). A good place for making contacts for lifts in Tam is the *Restaurant des Amis* on the main street. They also do fairly cheap meals (eg cous-cous for 3 Dinar). A beer in Tam will set you back 12 Dinar!

Tindouf
The workers' hostel, run by the government is the cheapest in town and costs 10 Dinar/bed and 3 Dinar/breakfast. It's sometimes possible to sleep on the floor for next to nothing. The hostel is situated next to the gendarmerie.

Tlemcen
Free camp site at the Roman ruins at Mansourah just outside town. The *Hammam* in town costs 2 Dinar. The *Hotel El Menreh* costs 15 Dinar/double.

TRANSPORT
Hitch-hiking is very easy even for groups of two and three. Most Algerians have no qualms about packing their cars to the roof. Many people manage to hitch free as far south as Tamanrasset. The only difficult stretch seems to be the Algerian/Tunisian border via Souk Ahras where there are no villages between the border posts and so very little traffic. Even so, it's more a question of being

slowed up than actually stuck. In the north free lifts are the rule rather than the exception but don't try hitching at night — you won't get anywhere. South of the mountainous coastal area (ie from Ghardaia and Bechar south) you will generally have to pay for lifts. Most of them will be on the top of trucks and the 'fare' works out at about half the cost of the bus. Always bargain over the price asked unless you have a very good idea what local people pay. It's supposedly forbidden for drivers working for the national companies to carry passengers so in places where traffic control is known to be strict, like around In Salah, they may be hesitant to pick you up.

Remember that travelling on the top of a truck you can get badly sunburnt without realising it at the time because of the breeze. Cover your head and neck with a turban/towel/piece of clothing. Also remember that, depending on the season, the desert can be extremely cold at night and even during the day on occasions. Take a sweater with you.

If hitching out of Algiers to Constantine, take the Sidi-bel-Abbez bus from near the railway station and get off at the turn-off.

Buses The long-distance, orange buses run by the National Bus Company (SNTV) are modern, comfortable, reliable and expensive (Algiers enquiries tel 63 72 80). There are regular buses every day between most large centres of population. They cost around 8 Dinar per 100 km. There are, in addition, a large number of local buses which are cheaper but less reliable and involve varying degrees of discomfort. On the other hand they're far more interesting. Triple check departure times and fares. Some examples of bus fares include: Algiers-Ghardaia: 40 Dinar, Ghardaia-El Golea: 20 Dinar, Ghardaia-Adrar: 60 Dinar. Note that baggage charges can be high — as much as 10 Dinar for a rucksack on long distances.

Trains There's a fairly extensive network of lines linking all the main centres in the north. Going south, you can get as far as Bechar in the west and Touggourt in the east. The main east-west service runs from Souk Ahras on the Tunisian border through Constantine, Algiers and Oran to Tlemcen on the Moroccan border. Fares are: 1st class: 0.13 Dinar/km, 2nd class: 0.11 Dinar/km, 3rd class: 0.09 Dinar/km.

Flights Air Algerie will give the usual 25% student discount for internal flights but there's a big bureaucratic hassle involved which requires you to produce a letter from your embassy or university/college on headed notepaper confirming that you're a student.

Boats See under 'Mediterranean Ferries' in the introduction.

Routes to/from Morocco

The only land crossing possible at present is the Oujda-Tlemcen route in the north and even this is closed from time to time when diplomatic relations between Morocco and Algeria break down. Algeria supports the POLISARIO guerilla fighters of the Western Sahara in their struggle against Moroccan military occupation of that area and there are occasional border skirmishes between Moroccan and Algerian regular forces as a result.

There are daily buses to the border from both directions. Tlemcen to the border costs 4.80 Dinar; Oujda to the border costs 1-2 Dirhams. There used to be a daily train in either direction between the two places for 7.40 Dirhams but the service is presently suspended. It's easy to hitch. The customs check on the Algerian border is very strict and you may well get searched for money and drugs.

The crossings between Ben Ounif and Figuig and between Tindouf and Tantan are currently closed.

Routes to/from Tunisia

(a) Coast route: El Khala (Le Calle)-Tabarka Get to the border well before 6 pm otherwise you'll miss the last bus to Tabarka and have to walk 25 km across the mountains. People living in this area are not exactly friendly according to several letters we've received.

(b) Souk Ahras-Ghardimaou The most popular route. It's difficult to hitch this stretch, but not impossible. Starting from Souk Ahras there's a 20 km walk between the two customs posts if you can't get a lift. There's a daily train in either direction between Souk Ahras and Jendouba which costs 1.64 Dinar. If you need to change cash the Tunisians will only change Algerian Dinars until you get to Ghardimaou. On the Algerian side, Algerian customs officials will offer to change your Tunisian currency for you (Algerian banks won't change Tunisian currency) but they offer you a very poor rate. If you're forced by circumstances into this exchange, remember to change *before* you fill in the currency declaration form, otherwise they'll have to change them at the official rate.

(c) Gafsa-Nefta-El Oued This is a little-used route but convenient if you came across on the ferry from Italy and want to go directly onto one of the trans-Saharan routes. There is a bus twice weekly. It's difficult to hitch as there's very little traffic.

Trans-Saharan Routes

The eastern (Algeria-Niger) and middle (Algeria-Mali) routes south begin at Ghardaia — a beautiful town surrounded by small oases and villages built on their own hills around Ghardaia. It's the last well-stocked place for food before you get to Tamanrasset, so stock up. If you need to change money, do it here — there is no bank in Tamanrasset. Don't forget to take a cheche (a scarf to wrap around your head to protect you from the sun). Sunglasses and skin cream and a sweater and sleeping bag for night time are useful. The road is surfaced as far as Tamanrasset if you're heading for Niger, after which it's 'piste' (corrugated earth road). If you're heading for Mali via Adrar it's 'piste' all the way and in poor repair.

If you have your own transport you have to get authorisation from the wilayate, police, gendarmerie or dairate before each stage of the journey and show this to traffic control officers along the way. Between April and November this is sometimes refused, depending on conditions. Single vehicles have to join a convoy of not less than two other vehicles.

You need a sturdy vehicle in perfect working order and fitted with special track tyres called 'Saharan Specials' as well as an oil filter to keep sand out of the engine. Car springs should be reinforced and you should carry plenty of spares and a full tool kit as well as medical kit. Two days' reserve of food should be carried and 10 litres of drinking water per person. If you break down, stay with your vehicle. In a sand storm park your vehicle so it faces in the opposite direction to that of the wind to avoid getting the engine sanded up. Water holes are few and far between in the deep south. The Algerian tourist literature contains a section on taking transport across the Sahara — get hold of a copy if you need more details. The best time to cross the desert is between January and March. By May it's too hot and you'll meet with complications in West Africa due to the rainy season there. It's almost essential to be able to speak French and/or Arabic.

Minimum car insurance (Civil Liabilities Insurance) is compulsory at the border. The premium depends on the length of stay and the capacity of the engine. Three days cover costs 36-55 Dinar; 10 days costs 47-99 Dinar; 20 days costs 76-169 Dinar and 30 days costs 101-231 Dinar.

(a) Route du Mauritaine The most westerly route via Bechar and Tindouf to Nouakchott is presently closed due to the war in the Western Sahara but it may re-open soon due to the recent withdrawal of Mauritania from that part of the former Spanish territory which they took over following the departure of the Spanish.

(b) Route du Tanezrouft The middle route via El Golea, Timimoun and Adrar (all in Algeria) to Gao and Timbuktu (Mali). The route is less well-used than that further east through Tamanrasset to Zinder in Niger. South of Adrar there are virtually no supplies so stock up well on essentials — food, water and petrol if you're driving. Adrar is the last place where you'll find a hotel or repair facilities for a vehicle. The road is metalled as far as Adrar after which it's 'piste'. 'Piste' are vehicle killers so carry spare springs and shock absorbers and go slowly.

Adrar to Gao takes about one week averaging 200 km per day. Carry plenty of water. The road is marked by beacons every five km or so. It's a flat desert track to Reggane where there's a military post and a Sous Prefecture to which you have to report. After that there are beacons every five km for the next 250 km to Poste Waygande. From here it's about 250 km to Bidon Cinq (Post Maurice Cortier). Note that both Poste Weygande and Bidon Cinq are derelict and there is no water. The road is poor with sandy stretches and rocky outcrops. The last 120 km to the border requires extreme caution. The border is at Borj Moktar (an oasis). The route is often closed between May and September. During the rest of the year there are about a dozen vehicles per day taking this route. If you're hitching, Adrar to Gao will cost about 200 Dinar.

About 27 km south of Borj Moktar you come across the first Mali beacon (red and white checks). At Tessalit, the first Malian town, there's an airport and the Mali Immigration Post but hardly any other facilites. After Tessalit the route is marked every two km with beacons though some have fallen down. Anefis, 285 km south of Tessalit, is the next village. If you're looking for water you can find this at Tabonkort, 40 km south of Anefis. The road here is poor in parts, good in others and includes dry water course crossings. Bourem on the River Niger is 194 km south of Anefis and has a dispensary, post office and repair facilites. There's also an airfield and sometimes petrol is available.

From Bourem to Gao the track runs along the River Niger through scrub and dunes — there are plenty of camel thorns along this stretch which will plague you with punctures. Extreme caution is needed crossing open gullies some of which are signposted. Bourem to Gao is 93 km. At Gao there is accommodation, food, petrol, repair facilities and a ferry across the Niger. From Gao the all-weather road continues further south along the Niger River to Niamey (capital of Niger) via Labezanga but barriers may be erected during the rainy season if there are floods (June to October). If you want to visit Timbuktu, you branch off at Bourem and follow the track along the River Niger, but it's only passable in the dry season and four-wheel drive is advisable. Bourem to Timbuktu takes about two days.

(c) Route du Hoggar The most easterly route via El Golea, In Salah, Tamanrasset to Agadez in Niger and Kano in Nigeria. This is the most popular route and possibly the most picturesque. The road is surfaced as far as Tamanrasset. It is possible to hitch free as far south as Tam and even as far as Agadez if you're really lucky. Free lifts as far as El Golea and In Salah are not all that uncommon. Note that the authorities sometimes have a purge on truck drivers taking passengers (officially they're not allowed to if they work for a national company) so you might have difficulty finding a lift but they don't do this very often. If you can't find a free lift, some common lift and bus prices include Algiers-Ghardaia: bus for 62 Dinar; Ghardaia-El Golea: bus for 20 Dinar; Ghardaia-Adrar: bus for 20 Dinar (if you're heading for Mali).

From Ghardaia to Tamanrasset the bus costs 120 Dinar. During the summer there is a bus in either direction, daily by SNTV. They run only at night to avoid the heat. During the rest of the year the buses leave Ghardaia on the 1st, 11th and 21st of each month and Tamanrasset on the 4th, 14th and 24th of each month. It's often difficult to get on a bus after Ghardaia as they frequently leave full and you have to rely on cancellations. If you're lucky, the bus from El Golea to Tam costs 95 Dinar and from In Salah to Tam costs 60 Dinar.

El Golea-Tamanrasset by truck will be 50 Dinar; In Salah-Tamanrasset by truck should be 30 Dinar (but can cost 100 Dinar!) and takes about 24 hours.

You have to complete passport formalities with the police in Tamanrasset (you'll be sent back from the border if you have no exit stamp) but they won't give you one of these until you've fixed up a lift. If you're hitching it is possible to be stuck in Tam for a week. The best place to find lifts is at the customs post where all trucks have to stop. The petrol station is another good bet as is the Restaurant des Amis on the main street. A lift on a truck from Tamanrasset to Agadez costs between 150 and 200 Dinar but truck drivers prefer CFA in which case the charge will be around 10,000 CFA. The journey normally takes about three days but can take up to five. There are no buses on this route and the trucks stop for about three hours during the hottest part of the day. There is no Niger consulate in Tamanrasset — if you need a visa you must get it in Algiers. The border is at In Guezzam and this is the only place where water is obtainable between Tam and Agadez. Make sure your Algerian currency declaration form is in order when leaving through In Guezzam — they are very strict about it and people have been sent back to Tam for discrepancies. Note that if you want to move between Tam and Agadez, avoid small heavy trucks. Try to take Peugeots and Berliets instead, much faster.

OTHER INFORMATION
Things to Sell Buy whisky in either Ceuta or Melilla (Spanish Morocco) for 275 pesetas (just over US$4) and re-sell in Algeria for 120 Dinars (US$30) in the north and 150 Dinar (US$37.50) in the south. In Algiers try around the main post office. In Tamanrasset you'll have no trouble selling it at the prices quoted above. The best brand to buy is Johnny Walker Red Label. You're only allowed one bottle of spirits duty free on entry.

Angola

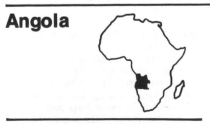

The Portuguese first arrived in this part of Africa in the 16th century and in later years attempted to run the colony as an 'Overseas Province of Metropolitan Portugal'. Resistance was strong from the first but not until the 1930s was it organised on a national rather than a tribal scale. 1956 saw the fusion of the various cultural and political groups into the single Popular Movement for the Liberation of Angola (MPLA). This was the only movement to retain effective control of the areas liberated before the coup in Portugal itself precipitated the abrupt dismemberment of the remaining Portuguese Empire.

There were, however, three other liberation movements — the National Front for the Liberation of Angola (FNLA), the National Union for the Total Independence of Angola (UNITA) and the small Front for the Liberation of the Enclave of Cabinda (FLEC). The latter was a separatist movement prompted partly by the discovery of large oil deposits just off the coast of the enclave. The three other Angolan liberation movements were committed to maintaining Cabinda within Angola.

On 15 January 1975, Portugal and the three liberation movements drew up an agreement setting out the mechanics of the transition to independence, set for 11 November of the same year. Deep seated differences remained and the country rapidly slid into civil war as the independence date drew closer. There was a massive flight of white settlers back to Portugal as the intensified fighting created major problems in Angola and Portugal. At this time FNLA controlled the extreme north and various urban centres down to Luanda, the capital. The MPLA controlled the bulk of the centre while UNITA held the south and east. The better-equipped MPLA rapidly gained the upper hand and FNLA and UNITA formed a united command opposed to MPLA. World powers were soon drawn (or jumped) into the conflict.

At the height of the struggle FNLA were supported with American arms from Zaire, the MPLA by 14,000 Cuban troops and Russian arms and UNITA by regular South African troops and armour plus white mercenaries from Britain and northern Europe. The South Africans, who had previously occupied the territory around the Kunene hydro-electric scheme (a South Africa-Portuguese joint project), staged a very hush-hush invasion of southern Angola, which very soon embroiled Vorster in a major political row and destroyed what detente he'd established with a few African states, as word got out. South African prisoners were displayed as proof at the OAU meeting in Kampala. Gulf Oil, who were working the Cabindan oil deposits, froze payments to Angola but later resumed them.

More people were killed in the few months following the Portuguese withdrawal than in the many years of guerrilla struggle and thousands of people lost everything they owned. The war will inevitably leave a legacy of bitterness.

Although the MPLA, with their Cuban support, emerged victorious and has been recognised by most countries, the Marxist-oriented regime still has much internal fighting to contend with. The Cabindan separatists are still active and remnants of UNITA occasionally stir up conflict in the southern part of the country. There still remains a lot of tension between Angola and Zaire.

FACTS

Angola is about 14 times the size of Portugal and has a slightly smaller population. Until the 20th century there were seldom more than a thousand Portuguese lving there. After their early successes in the Congo they found the warm, humid climate and cannibal tribes of the north too unhealthy for comfort and confined their settlements to the coast, particularly Luanda, although urban settlements later grew up alongside the railways. The population is now estimated at 5½ million, there were 400,000 Portuguese before the mass exodus. In the remote parts of the interior it's very sparsely populated (less than a person per square km). About a

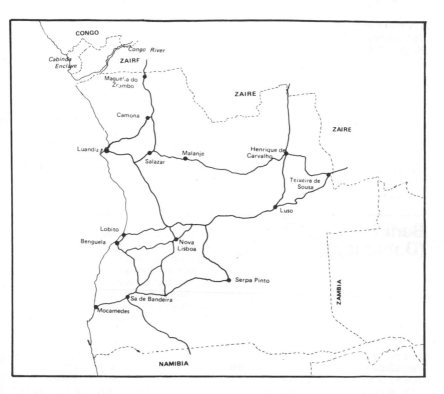

hundred ethnic groups are represented, mostly Bantu speaking with a few surviving bushmen in the south.

The country consists of a narrow coastal plain between 50 and 200 km wide and a mountain chain parallel to the coast with a vast plateau in the centre averaging 1500 metres in height. It includes many major river systems. The climate varies with altitude, latitude and on the coast it depends on the hot Benguela current in the Atlantic. The coast is hottest between March and April, the plateau between September and October. Best time to travel is between May and August though it can be very dry at this time. There is a desert climate in the south. The interior and mountain regions are subject to frequent torrent-ial rains during the October to May wet season.

Mining (especially iron ore and diamonds), oil, fishing and plantation farming are the four pillars of the economy. Coffee accounts for 35% of current exports and Angola is third amongst world coffee producers. Before independence most profits and earnings were transferred out of the territory.

VISAS

Required by everyone. Visas are only issued by the Ministry of Foreign Affairs in Luanda, Angola or through the Angolan Embassy in Lisbon, Portugal. It's unlikely you'll be allowed in at present unless you have a very good reason.

LANGUAGES
Portuguese, Spanish, French and a little English. Many local languages.

CURRENCY
The unit of currency is the Kwanza = 100 centavos. Import of local currency is allowed up to 1000 Kwanza, export is prohibited. If you manage to get into the country you're required to spend at least 500 Kwanza per day of your stay.

Exchange rate:

£1   =   64 Kwanza

US$1   =   27 Kwanza
A$1   =   32 Kwanza

There is a 30 Kwanza airport tax on domestic flights.

ACCOMMODATION & TRANSPORT
We haven't heard of anyone going to Angola for years now. Perhaps this is because it's extremely difficult to get a visa. As a result we have no details of accommodation or transport in the country. If you do manage to get in, let us know how things are.

Benin (Dahomey)

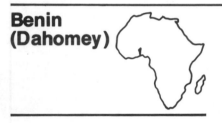

If any country has been ruined by the colonisation and subsequent Balkanisation of West Africa it is Benin and yet this densely populated country — 25 people per square km, the highest in Africa — once supported a series of states whose civilisations were amongst the most brilliant in Africa. Colonisation brought economic and political instability, breaking 26 French governors in 50 years. This reputation has been maintained over the 18 years since independence. Coups come and go with monotonous regularity.

There are frequent interruptions in communications caused by Beninois emergencies (seen by outsiders as largely imaginary) and a continual failure to form a viable ruling party. The combination of extreme left-wing political rhetoric with the whole-hearted neo-colonialism in the economic sphere must lend some credence to the sniping

of the increasing band of exiled diplomats, civil servants and businessmen. There is constant tension with Togo due to border closures when trucks are held up for days on end, preventing access to the Lagos markets and adversely affecting Togo's export markets. In retaliation Togo holds up Beninois traffic going west.

In view of the close tribal links with Nigeria a union might be logical but the attempted secession of Biafra in 1967 left a great deal of scepticism about such a possibility. Civil service salaries take 70% of all public revenue — under the French the people showed a great eagerness for education and made up the clerical class of French West Africa. When the various countries became independent these Beninois had to return home where they form an unemployed, grumbling intelligentsia.

FACTS
The country consists of a low, sandy coastal region, the plateau of Akatora in the north-west (about 800 metres high), and the plains of the Niger in the north-east. The land of the plateau is fertile agricultural land with many plantations; mostly oil palms, which provide 85% of the country's exports. The climate of the south is equatorial with high humid-

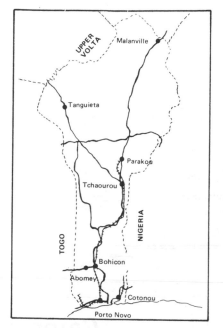

to get a visa at the Malanville border on the River Niger where the Niger steamer from Niamey calls on the way to Nigeria.

On arrival you must get a 'Permit de Circulation' from the Chef du District in the first town — Natitingou, Kandi, or Parakou. This lasts for either 24 or 48 hours and carries more weight than a stamp in your passport and is always asked for by police and customs. You need to renew it if you're staying longer.

You must report to the police and Chef du District in each and every town you stay for the night. If you neglect to do this you're likely to spend several days in jail. If you can keep abreast of the bureaucracy in Benin you'll have a good time.

Before you can leave Benin you must have an Exit stamp. These are obtainable from Surete in Cotonou which is on the main road near the embassies and ministries. The stamp takes half a day and is free.

ity and high constant temperatures (between 20 and 30°C). The north is less humid and has a tropical climate. One rainy season in the north from March to November and two in the south — March to mid-July and mid-September to November.

VISAS
Required by all except nationals of Denmark, France, Germany (West) and Italy. Nationals of South Africa not admitted. Even if you have a visa (where necessary) it doesn't guarantee you entry especially if you have a backpack.
Visas at the embassy in Niamey (Niger) cost 300 CFA, two photos and are issued while-you-wait. They allow for a three day stay only. Visas from the embassy in Accra, Ghana, cost 5 Cedi, two photos and take 24 hours to issue. Visas are also obtainable from the Ivory Coast Embassy in Freetown, Sierra Leone, here they cost 3 Leones. It's not possible

CURRENCY
The unit of currency is the CFA. There is no restriction on the import or export of local currency.

Exchange rate:

£1	=	473 CFA
US$1	=	205 CFA
A$1	=	236 CFA

LANGUAGES
Mainly French, some English and some local dialects.

ACCOMMODATION
The State-owned Resthouses in the larger towns are expensive. It's suggested you don't camp out or take photos as it is not worth the risk. Official paranoia of coups, spies and subversion borders on the hysterical. In the smaller villages, just ask around for somewhere to stay.

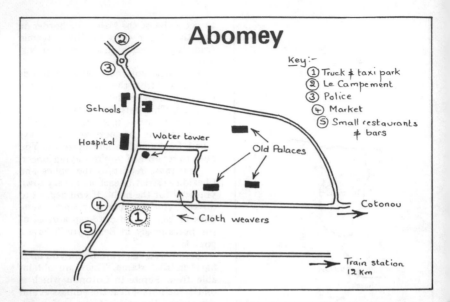

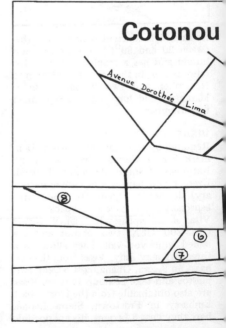

Abomey

Le Campement costs 1200 CFA/double and is quiet. There's an excellent museum here covering the history of the Abomey kingdoms as well as the Fun Palace and the Fetish Temple. The throne of the Abomey kings is made of human skulls. Abomey was the centre of the Fon Kingdom. Next to the museum is the Centre des Artisanants where you can buy crafts at a price lower than anywhere else in the region. They'll even make swaps for unwanted personal effects.

Cotonou

Hotel Babo is the most popular with travellers and is well known in the African quarter. It costs 800 CFA per person; 1400 CFA for two people and 1700 CFA for three people in a room. Showers and mosquito coils are provided free and it's clean. There is an excellent restaurant next door where you can get prawn salads, omelettes, steak and chips — average cost of a good meal is

100 CFA. It's also possible to sleep on the beach in fishermens' huts which they use only during the day. Chambres a Louer (Rooms to Let) opposite the Benin Cinema.

The Dan Tokpa market is held every four days. The museum in Cotonou is well worth a visit.

Natitingou
Le Campement costs 800 CFA for a double.

TRANSPORT
There are good/fairly good roads linking Benin with its three neighbours. The northern route to Niamey is part dirt, part pot-holed tarmac and can be hitched in three-five days (1070 km). The road down the centre of the country is good. Some travellers say hitching is easy but others say it's very slow. There are regular bus services if you don't want to hitch. Otherwise there are taxis, pick-ups and lorries. Some examples of truck charges are — Abomey-Cotonou: 500 CFA, Cotonou-Parakou: 1500 CFA, Tanguieta-Natitingou: 250 CFA, Cotonou-Lagos: 1000 CFA by taxi.

If you arrive in Nigeria after the banks have closed you can change at the border on the blackmarket quite openly. Customs officials will show you where the money-changers are.

1 Tourist Office	6 French Embassy
2 Main Post Office (PTT)	7 US Embassy
3 Market	8 Ghanian Embassy
4 Banque Central	9 Railway Station
5 Transcap Travel Agency	

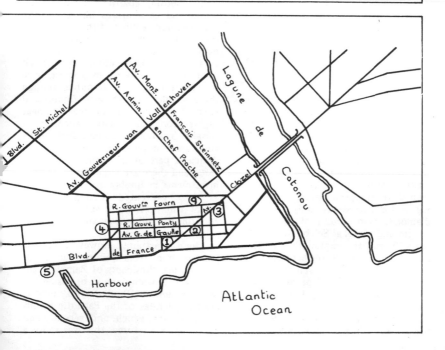

If you're coming from Nigeria, Idoroko to Cotonou costs 400 CFA in a taxi. If you are heading for Togo, Cotonou, to Lome costs 600 CFA for a direct taxi or 500 CFA for a 'pada'.

Trains The main line runs north-south linking Cotonou with Porto Novo, Save and Parakou. There's also a coast line linking Cotonou with Lome (Togo) and various other coastal towns. Some examples of the fares are — Cotonou-Parakou: 1500 CFA, (twice daily), Bomicon-Tehaourou: 1050 CFA.

PLACES TO SEE/THINGS TO DO
Abomey has already been mentioned.
Porto Novo Good museum here with a fine collection of masks, weapons and musical instruments. It's also possible to get a free ride with the fishermen around the lagoon. Well worth the effort!

Somba People A tribe in the north-west who live in fortified houses which look like fairy-tale mud castles. The women go naked, decorate their bodies and have an animal tooth through their lower lip. The market at Boukombe on Saturdays where these people come to sell their wares is very interesting.

Ganvie A village on stilts out in the lagoon near Cotonou. From Cotonou go to Calavi from where you can hire canoes to visit the place.

Botswana

Botswana, formerly Bechuanaland, was a British Protectorate until 1966 when it gained its independence under the leadership of Sir Seretse Khama, paramount chief of the Tswana. At independence the country's main money-earner was cattle raising and its associated industries. Many of the larger ranches are owned by European farmers. Crop raising is for subsistence only. Although diamonds were found at Orapa and copper and nickel at Selebi-Pikwe in the late '60s and the exploitation of these minerals has changed the economic outlook of the country as well as to give it new political and social problems, Botswana remains a poor, but peaceful, country.

Khama, who died in mid-1980, refused to exchange ambassadors with South Africa and insisted on keeping relations to a minimum while consistently opposing apartheid at various international conventions like the OAU, the Commonwealth and the UN. Nevertheless, his country remains very much dependent on South Africa for both trade and communications. Virtually all of Botswana's imports and exports have to pass through the Republic though there is some trade through Zambia and a small amount on the weekly meat flights from the Lobatse abbatoir to Lusaka. In addition, about a fifth of the adult male population works in South Africa as part of the immigrant labour force and there are large South African investments in Bhotswana. Factors such as these prevented Khama, and no doubt will prevent his successor, from adopting too militant an approach to his southern neighbour.

These constraints, however, did not prevent him from joining the other 'Front Line' Presidents of Zambia, Tanzania and Mozambique in opposing the Smith regime in Rhodesia and supporting the guerillas of the Patriotic Front. For Botswana, which, until recently had no army or air force, this was quite a brave stand to take and resulted in Rhodesian Army 'hot pursuit' raids on its territory and the bombing of the Kazangula ferry across the Zambesi River — Botswana's only land link with Zambia (the country is almost completely surrounded by Rhodesia, South Africa and South African-occupied territory). With this ferry inoperative and the possibility of military action in the north-east, few travellers have been able to visit Botswana for some time though with the settlement in Rhodesia — at least as far as an internationally accepted black majority government is concerned — it should soon again become one of southern Africa's favourite countries for the traveller.

The all-weather BOTZAM road from Francistown to Kazangula, which for many years was the major single item in the country's budget, is now complete and getting from the Zambian border to Gaberone, the capital, should no longer be the trial of strength it used to be.

FACTS

Like Lesotho and Swaziland, Botswana is a single tribe country although there are a few non-Tswana groups, notably the bushmen, squeezed out of the rest of southern-Africa into the Kalahari by migrating Bantu speaking people since 1600. The tone of life is peaceful, friendly, 'like a scoutmaster's dream'. People live in large villages (Serowe with 35,000 people is still a village) so those who want to live in African villages will enjoy themselves here. The larger places have secondary schools which often have British and American volunteer teachers who are usually friendly to visitors. The population is less than ¾ of a million (about one person per square km) — very sparsely populated. Most of the people live along the railway line, in the main centres and on the northern and southern edges. Europeans comprise less than 1% of the population — mostly cattle ranchers, teachers and technical experts.

Botswana covers an area the size of France and Belgium combined and for the most part is a broad tableland averaging 1000 metres in altitude with hill tracts rising in the west and south-east. The east is more prosperous with good grazing lands, reasonable supplies of water (underground) and an average rainfall of 50 cm per annum. This is the most populated area. The Kalahari is dry grassland merging into desert and living off the dew with as little as 20 cm rain per annum. The third area is the Okavango Swamps — formed by a river which fans out into a vast inland delta. The area floods yearly creating thousands of waterways and islands — one of the best places in Africa for seeing wild game. January is the hottest month, July the coldest. There's often severe frost in the north. Rainy season is between late October and April, the rest of the year being very dry.

VISAS

Not required by nationals of any West European nation (except Spain and Portugal), any Commonwealth nation, South Africa or USA. Stay permits are generally issued for 30 days. If you want to extend your stay for longer than this you have to apply in advance from the Immigration and Passport Control Officer, PO Box 942, Gaberone. Officially no visitor is allowed to work or look for work.

CURRENCY

The unit of currency is the Pula = 100 Thebe. No limit on import of local currency, export is allowed up to 50 Pula.

Exchange rate:

£1	=	1.84 Pula (fluctuates)
US$1	=	0.81 Pula
A$1	=	0.92 Pula

HEALTH

Beware of tsetse fly in the Okavango Swamps. Try not to wear dark-coloured clothing as this seems to attract them. You can get a check up for sleeping sickness at Maun hospital if you get badly bitten. Use a fly-whisk to keep them off you. The water in the Swamps is bilharzia-free and generally safe to drink too.

LANGUAGES

Tswana, Afrikaans and English.

ACCOMMODATION

Most hotels, as such, are expensive and will cost you around 10 Pula/night, though you'll only find them in Gaberone, Francistown, Serowe, Palapye, Maun and Mahalapye. Most travellers either stay with local people in the villages or with various expatriate volunteers (Peace Corps, VSO, etc). It's easy to sleep out in the villages — with or without a tent — and you'll often be invited to stay with a family. People are very friendly and hospitable and, if you ask politely, they're usually more than happy to help out with accommodation. There's no problem with thieves except perhaps in Gaberone and Francistown. Otherwise, there are many volunteers throughout the country who, if they like you and you're willing to contribute to your keep, are welcoming and will pass you on to others further along your route. In Gaberone the best place to contact them is on the balcony of the *President Hotel* overlooking the Mall. In Maun they can be found either at *Riley's Hotel* or at Okavango Island camp, eight km from the town, especially at weekends. In Ghanzi you'll find them in the front bar of the *Kalahari Arms Hotel* which is situated at the Maun end of the main road into town. In Mochudi, Serowe and Tonota, try the schools.

If you are coming from Zimbabwe or heading towards there, Alakanani Nghakazhogwe has a small cafe in Tshesebe just inside the Botswana Frontier with Plumtree on the railway line where you can eat and get a bed for 1 Pula. He's a really friendly guy.

At Kalkfontein there's an elderly South African called Mr Sharp who runs a chain of stores along the road who will give you a bed and a meal as he enjoys company. Another very friendly soul.

Other accommodation possibilities are covered in the 'Transport' section as, and when, they crop up.

TRANSPORT

Trains The Zimbabwean-owned railway from Bulawayo to Mafeking (South Africa) runs through Botswana via Francistown, Lobatse and Gaberone. Both passenger and freight trains use the line and there are at least two passenger trains every day in either direction as well as several freight trains. The latter are usually easy to hitch (the drivers and guards are often white Zimbabweans) and very useful if they're stopping where you want to get off. They are also generally faster than the passenger trains.

Passenger trains have four classes of accommodation: 1st (compartment to yourself); 2nd (compartment shared with one or two others); 3rd (compartment shared with several others including their various domestic animals) and 4th (rows of benches). Avoid travelling at the end of the month on trains as Botswana miners from Johannesburg pack them to capacity. Also, as wages are frequently paid at the end of the month, there's a migration of people into the towns for shopping and entertainment at this time. During the rest of the month there's plenty of space on the trains. There is very little difference between 3rd and 4th classes and 4th is sometimes preferable if you're travelling overnight as there's more room to relax and more room to breathe even though the compartments are generally more crowded. All passenger trains have a buffet car. There's no racial disharmony (which is amazing considering its proximity to South Africa) so there's no need to be apprehensive about travelling in 3rd or 4th class.

Lobatse-Francistown: Costs 9 Pula in 1st class, Gaberone-Francistown: Costs 4 Pula in 4th class and 12 Pula in 2nd class.

Roads There is now an all-weather gravel road all the way from the South African border at Mafeking to Kasane on the Botswana-Zambia border via Lobatse, Gaberone and Francistown. For a little while yet, however, there may be difficulties and hold-ups getting across the Zambesi River at Kazangula as Zimbabwe-Rhodesian forces blew up the ferry during Bishop Muzorewa's brief tenure as Prime Minister. With the recent victory of Robert Mugabe in the Zimbabwean elections and the long-awaited international recognition of the black majority government in that country communications should improve and the journey from Lusaka (Zambia) to Gaberone no longer be fraught with the dangers of military action.

Hitching is easy from Mafeking to Gaberone and fairly easy from there to Francistown and on to Bulawayo. All the same, you should allow three days for the Gaberone-Francistown hitch (and more in the rainy season) though it can be done in half a day if you get the right lift. From Francistown to Kasane and Kazangula hitching is more difficult as there's little traffic but this should improve as trade grows with Zambia following the settlement in Zimbabwe. Government coaches ply along this main route — they're painted blue with one black and two white stripes (the same as the national flag— and to catch them you simply get out on the road and flag them down. Some examples of fares are — Lobatse-Gaberone; 1.20 Pula, Gaberone-Francistown; 6 Pula, Francistown-Maun; 5.90 Pula, and takes 10-14 hours.

In addition to the government buses

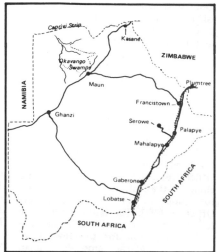

there are Volkswagen mini-buses run by private individuals and firms (usually called 'Kombis') which charge about 1½ cents/km and which connect the main centres of population between Lobatse and Serowe/Palapye. On the Gaberone-Lobatse road there is one of these Kombis every 20 minutes or so. Try to travel early in the day as fares tend to rise later on.

As the Lobatse-Gaberone-Francistown-Kasane road (known as the BOT-ZAM road) is the only all-weather in the country, getting to other parts of Botswana demands four-wheel drive or a flight. Because of this, hitching demands a fair bit of initiative and can be slow but is very rewarding. You will have to rely on a mixture of Land-Rovers, trucks, mail vans and planes. Many travellers get around by fixing up lifts with farmers and mail trucks delivering goods to and from Lobatse/Gaberone and Maun/Ghanzi as well as on planes. Hitching rides on planes is not all that difficult. There are quite a few UN, bank and private planes operating in the more remote areas which are willing to take hitchers if they have room. Just hang around the airport and ask everyone who comes along where they're going and if they can take you. As for road transport, we heard that the government passed some kind of legislation about hitch-hikers not being allowed on government transport (mail and other trucks) but most truckies don't seem to know about it or turn a blind eye. If you're stuck for a lift anywhere try any of the following places: (a) District Council Office, (b) local trading store (for farmer's trucks), (c) local volunteer workers, (d) Post Office, (e) Police Station, (f) hospital/clinic — they often go to the capital for supplies, (g) Central Transport Office — CTO. The latter is the place to pick up lifts on mail trucks but note that competition for the few places available is intense. Most Botswanan government officials are very helpful about finding lifts especially in .the remoter areas of the country.

Apart from luck and the results of your own initiative with the above, there exist the following definite possibilities:

Lobatse-Maun/Ghanzi There are beef runs, usually twice a week, from both Maun and Ghanzi to Lobatse. To find a lift in Lobatse, check out the registration numbers of the trucks there or ask at the Botswana Meat Corporation. In Ghanzi, the best person to ask is the store keeper near the Kalahari Arms. The trucks leave Ghanzi on Sundays and Mondays. It's possible to get free rides all the way to Ghanzi with white farmers though you can expect to pay 2-25 Pula with black drivers over the same route.

'Bank day' in Ghanzi is on Thursday and on that day a Standard Bank official flies in from Lobatse in a chartered plane. The pilot is usually willing to give travellers a lift from Ghanzi to Lobatse.

Francistown-Maun In Francistown check with the Botswana Game Indus-

tries (BGI) for trucks going west and north-west. Otherwise ask around for Willie Phillips who does the run to Maun twice weekly though there are usually about 20 people waiting for a lift and it can be crowded sitting on top of four or five dozen oil drums. It's also very hot during the day and freezing cold at night so bear this in mind.

Maun-Ghanzi The most reliable possibility here is the mail truck. It leaves Maun on Tuesdays and Ghanzi on Thursdays. The journey takes all day and part of the evening and there's stiff competition for the five places available. Ask at the Central Transport Office in either place. For lifts on planes, contact Albert Smith at Winnella Airways in Maun.

For lifts further west into Namibia you will have to rely on the three or four trucks which do this run every week. There's only one entry/exit point along the whole 1600 km border which is marked by a high barbed wire fence. The trucks stop overnight at Kuke and continue on the next day to Gobabis in Namibia. The road between Ghanzi and Gobabis is slow due to soft sand and areas of limestone. In the wet season everything gets bogged-down for days on end and flash-floods can bring this about within a matter of hours.

Maun-Kasane Before trying to hitch this stretch you need permission from either the DC in Francistown or Maun or from the local police. It's very difficult even in the dry season and impossible in the wet. Ask at the various government offices opposite Barclays Bank in Maun for trucks going in that direction. There is an agricultural truck which does the run usually once per week but try to tie them down to something definite as they'll sometimes make promises in order to appear helpful when in fact they can not help you.

Barclays Bank have a plane which goes from Maun to Kasane every Tuesday and sometimes has room for hitch-hikers. Ask at the bank or the airport.

To the Caprivi Strip It's possible to get rides with trucks from Shakawe. These trucks call at all the NTC stores in each village. From Shakawe it's also possible to visit the Tsodilo Hills where there are rock paintings and scattered tribes of Bushmen. The main area of interest is about 30 km from Shakawe Fishing Lodge on the banks of the River Okavango. The Lodge is expensive but you can camp there for 2 Pula/night/person. From here the track runs alongside the river. If you're walking, try to do as much as possible at dawn and dusk and take plenty of water with you (at least three litres per person). Water is available in the hills but you should take your own food. It's possible to hire donkeys and a guide in Shakawe to take you to the Hills. Two donkeys and a guide will cost you about 30 Pula.

GAME RESERVES/PLACES TO VISIT

Okavango Swamps The Swamps start about 14 km outside of Maun. If you're looking for accommodation in Maun there are three hotels — Tati, Grand and Riley's — but most travellers manage to find a Peace Corps Volunteer or UN worker to put them up. There are only two streets in Maun so you can't go wrong. It's possible to hire a canoe (called a 'makuru') in Maun to explore the swamps but you may have to haggle over the price for hours. If you take one of these, make sure there are no 'hidden extras' like providing all the poler's food which can double the price on mealy meal alone. If possible, get in touch with a black guy called Allen at Crocodile Camp who hires out a makuru and poler for about 4 Pula/day.

There are three camp sites at the swamps all situated in the same area. Opinions differ as to which is the best but they all charge the same — 1 Pula/night — and all provide fairly cheap meals though it's a good idea to stock up on provisions in Maun. Consensus

favours *Island Camp* which is about five minutes by makuru from the other two camps. It's a beautiful spot and there are hippos to be seen at night. *Crocodile Camp* is described as a 'barren patch of earth' but it does provide wood for a fire. The third is known as *Okavango Camp*. There's usually transport to and from Maun every day in Land-Rovers. The whole area is really beautiful and peaceful with amazing jungle scenes and noises. There are few mosquitoes and tsetse flies around the camps but they can get unbearable further into the swamps. A lot of overlanders work in the camps cooking and doing general management. All three camps have their own smaller camps further into the swamps where they take visitors on safari. These safaris can be expensive as you need four to five days to really see the swamps and makurus cost around 5 Pula/day plus the cost of the poler's food. The only way to avoid these charges is to ask if any of the camps are moving their overnight stops (possibly because the water is getting low at a particular point) in which case they often appreciate help and will take you there just for the cost of your food.

The swamps are amazing and are one of the 'musts' of any visit to Botswana. Game can be sighted all the way up to Moremi National Park. Birdlife is prolific and it's a good idea to have someone along who knows about them. The only drawback to these safaris are the tsetse flies. Their bite is painful but doesn't itch afterwards — take a fly swat to keep them at bay. Remember too that reflection of the sun off the water of the swamps can make the boats very hot during the day. Take some protection. The Moremi Game Reserve north of Maun is the only tribally-run game reserve in Africa and is well worth a visit. It's completely unspoilt.

Tsodilo Hills These are situated northwest of Maun and are well worth a visit if you have the time. It's a tough journey getting there — takes two weeks there and back and you have to take your own food and water — but there are some beautiful examples of Bushman cave paintings and scattered tribes of Bushmen.

Lentswe-La-Udi weavers If you're interested in indigenous weaving they are well worth a visit. It's situated 15 km north of Gaberone.

OTHER INFORMATION
Teaching jobs are readily available in the main centres of population. Wages are approximately 2700 Pula per year. You don't normally have to sign a contract but three months' notice is expected on either side.

Burundi

A little-known mountainous country, Burundi has a stormy past filled with factional struggles and tribal warfare complicated by attempts at colonisation first by the Germans and later by the Belgians. The country gained its independence from Belgium in 1962, since independence there has been continuous strife between the ruling Tutsi tribe, comprising about 15% of the population and the Hutu who are the peasant tribe making up the remainder of the population. There were large-scale Hutu risings in both 1972 and 1973 both of which were fiercely repressed and many thousands systematically wiped out including the whole of the educated Hutu elite. Inevitably there is still a great deal of tension. In addition to the above two tribes there is a small pygmy population and about 5000 assorted Europeans, mostly Belgians. It's a largely rural country with only about 2% of the population living in the urban centres. Communications are relatively primitive.

If you'd like to know more about its people and the tribal tensions between the two tribes read the Minority Rights Group publication, *Selective Genocide in Burundi* from Benjamin Franklin House, 36 Craven Street, London, WC2, England.

FACTS
It's a beautiful country with magnificent views over Lake Tanganyika. The capital, Bujumbura, is a very pleasant town with a population of approximately 100,000. The land varies in altitude between 800 and 1000 metres in the lowlands to about 2500 metres in the highest mountain regions with the central plateau varying between 1500 and 2000 metres. The climate varies from tropical along Lake Tanganyika to cold in the central mountains. There is a heavy rainy season from February to May and again in December. The dry season stretches from June until September.

VISAS
Required by all. South African nationals are not admitted unless they are regular residents of Burundi.

Officially, if you arrive at Bujumbura airport without a visa you may be deported on the next international flight regardless of destination. In practice you receive an Entry Permit and, within 48 hours, a visa. This also applies if you arrive overland. Nevertheless, it's strongly recommended that you get your visa before arrival as the situation may change.

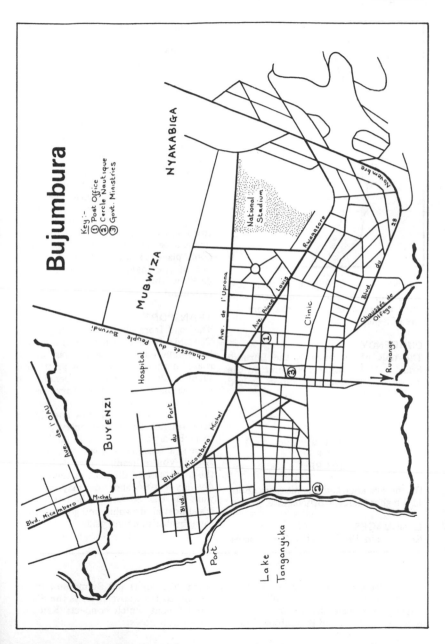

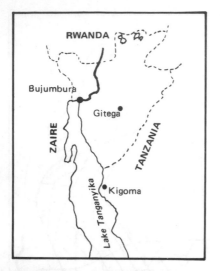

Rwanda Visas In Bujumbura these cost 1000 BFr and take 48 hours to issue. They are valid for two weeks from the day of issue.

CURRENCY
The unit of currency is the Burundi Franc = 100 centimes. No limit on the import of local currency, export limited to 2000 BFr.

Exchange rate:

$$£1 = 208 \text{ BFr (fluctuates)}$$
$$US\$1 = 91 \text{ BFr}$$
$$A\$1 = 104 \text{ BFr}$$

On the blackmarket, the rates are about 11% higher than the official rate.

LANGUAGES
Kirundi and French. All official correspondence is in French.

ACCOMMODATION
Except in Bujumbura, the capital, there are neither hotels nor resthouses of any kind so you must either camp or ask around in the villages for somewhere to stay.

Bujumbura Most of the hotels in the centre are expensive and geared towards businessmen and the like. The *Protestant Mission* at Vigosi is free if you help out. The people who run it are very pleasant. *Hotel Paradis*, near Place de l' Independence costs 350 BFr/single. *Hotel Tanganyika* 20 minutes from town allows camping for 200 BFr. Hippos can be seen in the mornings here. A good place to watch the hippos come out of the lake, in the evening, after dark, is the Cercle Nautique bar and restaurant.

TRANSPORT
The road from Bujumbura to Kigoma in Tanzania is being surfaced and should be completed soon but the rest of the roads in the country are in pretty bad shape — dusty or muddy depending on the season and pot-holed. There are no railways or public transport systems. Movement can be very slow and there's little traffic. The easiest entry point is from Bukavu in Zaire to Bujumbura as there's a reasonable road between the two. If you're heading towards Rwanda the hitch can be difficult as there's hardly any traffic and you may have to walk the last 30 km to the border but it's almost all downhill and goes through some beautiful countryside.

Boats There is a ferry service between Kigoma (Tanzania) and Bujumbura which goes most days and costs 1200 BFr. In addition to the above there is the SNCZ (Societe Nationale des Chemins de Fer Zairois) boat which connects Kalemie, Kigoma, Kalundu and Bujumbura. The schedule is as follows:

Kalemie	Kigoma	Kalundu	Bujumbura
dep 4 pm Wed	arr 7 am Thur dep 2 pm Thur	arr 7 am Fri dep 9 am Fri	arr 10 am Fri
Bujumbura	Kalundu	Kigoma	Kalemie
dep 12 noon Fri	arr 1 pm Fri dep 4 pm Fri	arr 7 am Sat dep 4 pm Sat	arr 7 am Sun

	1st class	2nd class
Fares: Bujumbura-Kalundu	297 BFr	118 BFr
Bujumbura-Kigoma	952 BFr	347 BFr
Bujumbura-Kalemie	1436 BFr	514 BFr

Cameroon

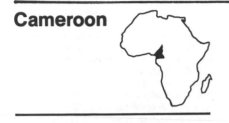

The Cameroons became a German colony towards the end of the 19th century and was later divided between the French and British after the First World War.

The French speaking areas of south and east Cameroons became independent as the Republic of Cameroons in 1960 followed by the English speaking areas of the north and west in 1961. The two formed a unified state at that time. There is a single ruling party under President Ahmadou Ahidjou, described as a very astute leader. The Federal Republic is divided into eight states, six in the French speaking area and two in the English speaking area.

80% of the population is engaged in subsistence agriculture, the bulk of any surplus is bought up by businessmen in Douala and transported to Libreville (Gabon) where high prices are fetched — this despite near famine conditions in northern Cameroon. A famine was recently averted only by massive imports of grain from America. Efforts are being made to provide greater self-sufficiency

and a large area of irrigated and non-irrigated land in Yagoua, Mbo and Ndop has been planted with rice — a staple food of most Cameroonians. There is some heavy industry — mostly concerned with aluminium — and some manufacturing of consumer goods. Cameroon has considerable trade with Common Market countries. The government is encouraging investment in industry and has used overseas aid to begin a modern communications network.

The country is remarkable for the success with which it has formed a single unified state out of so many separate and vastly differing cultural and ethnic backgrounds. The population is composed of over 130 different tribes speaking over 100 dialects. There are groups of Bantu in the south and north-west while in the highlands the most important groups are the tenaciously independent and commercially successful Bamileke and the Tikar. The former, organised in the Union des Population du Cameroon, were ruthlessly suppressed by government forces with French military aid, after independence. In the north, the population falls into two main groups — the Moslem Semites and the non-Moslem people known as Kirdi.

The peoples of the Cameroon have a rich cultural heritage of all forms, particularly in their varied and abundant musical forms and the many exotic sculptures which can be seen on display throughout the country. There's a certain amount of tension between the French and English speaking parts due generally to unequal development although so far an uneasy equilibrium has been maintained and prospects for the future look promising.

FACTS

There are great differences in climate and geography in this long wedge shaped country — near desert in the north through dense tropical vegetation in the east and centre to upland savannah in the west. A chain of mountains in the north-west rises to about 2000 metres and gradually falls away to the depression of Lake Chad on the plain of Maroua. Some of the most beautiful country is in the inland north-west of Douala-Bamileke country. There are volcanic hills rising to 2000 metres and more, with bamboo forests on the higher peaks, fine waterfalls and attractive villages.

The cool freshness of the atmosphere is a great attraction to Europeans tired of the heavy humidity of the coast (Cameroon has a large European population). Many go to stay at Bamenda and Dschang. There's a fine monkey-filled forest near Douala worth visiting and the famous Wasa Game Park — though this latter is well touristed and expensive (1000 francs entry fee). There are spectacular waterfalls along the Sanagi and Nyong Rivers. Lots of festivals and feast days — celebrated with music and dancing. In the south Foumban is worth visiting — major centre of the Bamoun culture — native art and sculpture and a good museum. Travel in the north is best in November to February. Many roads are impassable during July-August due to flooding. Moslem influence governs the life style and tradition is very much alive. An almost European climate and very friendly people.

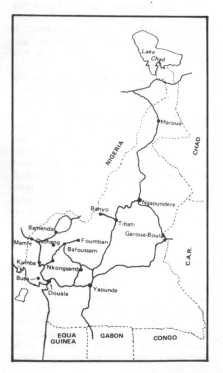

VISAS

Required by all. If you're entering overland without a visa you'll be given a 10-day visa at the border free of charge. They demand to see that you have 'sufficient' funds but otherwise there are no problems. Arriving by air at Douala airport you'll be given a 20-day visa free of charge. No hassles about 'onward tickets' or money.

Visa extensions can be obtained in Douala for a further 20 days and in Yaounde for 30 days. They are difficult to obtain outside these two cities. In Yaounde they're available from the Department of Immigration up the hill near the USA Embassy. When you get there ask for the Commissaire and have a plausible explanation ready as to why you need to stay longer. Extensions cost between 1500 and 2000 CFA depending on who processes your passport.

Central African Republic Visas The embassy is situated in the Bastos district of Yaounde close to the Greek Cathedral and not far from the centre of town. Visas cost 2500 CFA, one photo and are issued while you wait. Visas allow for a 10-day stay.

Zaire Visas These cost 2000 CFA and take 24 hours to issue. They allow for a stay of one month with one entry/exit. Before a visa will be issued you must· have a letter of recommendation from your embassy. At the British Embassy these letters cost 2500 CFA and take two days to issue.

The British Embassy in Yaounde is situated in the IBM Tower near the Post Office and Tourist Bureau. They're very helpful with the letter of recommendation needed for the Zaire visa and have information about the Bangui-Zongo ferries (between the CAR and Zaire), the. border situation between Kenya and Tanzania and about Equatorial Guinea.

CURRENCY

The unit of currency is the CFA. Import/export of local currency is allowed up to 25,000 CFA.

Exchange rate:

£1	=	474 CFA
US$1	=	208 CFA
A$1	=	237 CFA

Note there are no banks in Banyo, Tibati, Kalaldi or Lokiti. The nearest bank to these places is at N'Gaoundere. There are no banks between N'Gaoundere and Bangui, capital of the Central African Republic. Plan ahead. The Societe Cameroun de Banque is recommended for money-changing. Domestic airport tax is 450 CFA.

LANGUAGES

French in the south and east and English in the north and west. There are many local dialects.

MAIL

Note that no air letters (aerogrammes) are 'available' but when they are they cost 80 CFA! Douala poste restante is better than Yaounde. Sending parcels from Cameroon is easy so long as they are under one kg in which case they cost 400 CFA. Between one kg and two kg send the parcel as a 'letter' for 1700 CFA. Registration of the parcel costs 150 CFA.

ACCOMMODATION

Most missions no longer welcome travellers (they've been abused). Others have gone in the opposite direction and offer purpose-built accommodation at standard hotel rates.

Bafousam

Foyer Evangelique offer accommodation for 500 CFA/night including shower. *Federal Hotel* costs 1500 CFA/double. Accommodation can also be arranged at the *Restaurant Populaire* which also serves good food. Other cafes which are recommended include the *Restaurant Familiare* at the top of the hill and the *Riz Restaurant* near the market and taxi rank. Bafousam is a good place to buy chevron beads.

Bamenda

Mezam National Hotel Commercial Street, costs 1050 CFA for bed and breakfast and 1550 CFA for bed, breakfast and a bath. Pretty dirty place. Another similar hotel is the *Savannah* off the main street. The *Presbyterian Mission* offers dormitory accommodation for 600-750 CFA/night, or you can camp for 250 CFA, good value. *Ideal Park Hotel* near the market costs 2250 CFA/single. *Ring Way Hotel* costs 2500

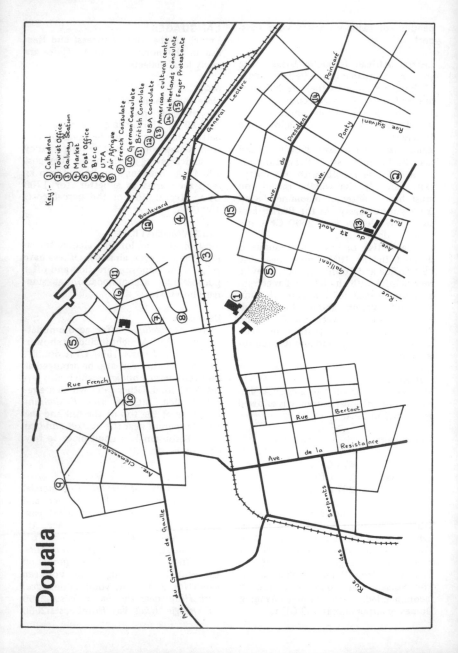

Douala

Key:- ① Cathedral
② Tourist Office
③ Railway Station
④ Market
⑤ Post Office
⑥ BICIC
⑦ UTA
⑧ Air Afrique
⑦ French Consulate
⑩ German Consulate
⑪ British Consulate
⑫ USA Consulate
⑬ American cultural centre
⑭ Netherlands Consulate
⑮ Foyer Protestante

CFA/single or married couple and 3500/ double with own bathroom. Another possible place to camp is at the rear of the *Restaurant de Ville*.

Excellent meals are available from the street stalls around the car park where a combination of cocos, yam, vegies, meat and plantain will cost you 25-100 CFA. The museum and artisans' co-op 'up station' is well worth a visit and there are some good bargains to be found. A taxi there costs 50 CFA.

Bafang

For accommodation here ask for M Michel Djimai (tailor) opposite the BICIC Banque. He offers simple but comfortable rooms for 1000 CFA for three nights.

Banso (also known as Nsu, Kumbo and Kinbo)

Baptist Mission Rest House costs 500 CFA. Very comfortable with kitchen facilities, meals by arrangement. *Tobin Tourist Home* costs 1000 CFA per room meals by arrangement. *Kilo's Rest House* costs 1500 CFA/single.

The Banso tribes which live in this area are worth a visit. The local ruler, the Fon of Banso, is a friendly chief who speaks English. If you go there remember not to cross your legs in front of these people or shake their hand. These are considered to be insults.

Buea

Hotel Mermoz is 1500 CFA/single and 2500 CFA/double. *Parliamentarian Flat* has rooms to rent for between 1500 and 3000 CFA. If you're thinking of staying in the area for a while it might be best to find a house in the country nearby to rent on a long-term basis. These can be found for 1000 CFA/day and upwards.

From Buea it's possible to climb Mt Cameroon — the highest mountain in West Africa. You're supposed to take a guide with you but it's possible to get around this by talking to the proprietor

of the Fonchas Restaurant or to a Peace Corps volunteer. There are huts to stay in at various points on the ascent but as it's over 4000 metres high you'll need a good sleeping bag and warm clothes.

Douala

The *Foyer des Marines* (Seaman's Mission) which used to be popular with travellers costs 2500 CFA/double but they will only take people who have proof that they're seamen or connected with them these days. They have a swimming pool, library and bar so it's well worth a try. *Mission Protestante* situated near the port has accommodation at 1200 CFA/single and 1800 CFA/double. They'll allow several people to share a double. *Evangelical Eglise* near the port in the centre of town will rent you a basic room for 1400 CFA if they have the space and if they want to take you. *Hotel de Douala* is 1200 CFA/double. Most of the other hotels in Douala will cost you 4000 CFA/single upwards. It's possible to camp in the grounds of the Catholic Cathedral.

For food try the street vendors who come out after 10 pm — you can get coffee, chocolate, sandwiches, or kebabs for around 250 CFA. Also the cafe opposite the railway station does good omelettes and coffee for 150 CFA. Otherwise try the *Moritz Cafe*, three blocks up from the Seamen's Mission — steak and salad for 250 CFA — or the *Miami Bar*. The latter puts on good wooden xylophone music but beware of paying more than 200 CFA for a beer (the price of admission).

For crafts go to the Artisanal National on the corner of Avenue President and the rue des Ecoles where there is a group of about a dozen outdoor stalls. Most of what they have for sale is 'tourist art' but you might find something worthwhile.

Note there are no buses to or from the airport so you'll have to get a taxi. A 'remassage' taxi (shared taxi) around town costs 70 CFA. To or from the airport a 'remassage' taxi should theoretically cost each individual 350 CFA but as a foreigner you won't get it for that price and will end up paying 750-1000 CFA (the cost of the whole car) — Douala is a busy modern seaport with all the usual facilities, distractions, expense and rip-off merchants.

If you need to change money, *Novotel*, the fanciest hotel in town, 10-15 minutes walk from the centre, has a bank which is open daily including Sundays from 3 pm to 7 pm. Make sure you change money in the bank itself and not at the reception desk where the rates are 5-10% less than in the bank. American Express is at 'Camboyages', 15 Ave de la Liberte, PO Box 4070.

Foumban

Catholic Mission has the occasional bed (take your own bedding). A contribution is asked. The cheapest hotels are at the southern end of the town and will cost you around 1200 CFA/single 'if you play it poor'. Most of the main hotels charge an outrageous US$22 and upwards for a single or double but they are quite basic for the price and most do fixed price dinners which you're obliged to have. Minimum cost of a meal is around 1300 CFA. For food there's a good inexpensive market where you can get things like bread, tomatoes and bananas. There are many interesting traditional houses in the countryside around Foumban and the Old Palace and two museums are well worth a visit.

Garoua-Boulai

This is the commercial capital of the north with a market on Saturdays and many foreign residents. *Relais de St Hubert* has air-conditioned rooms for 1500 CFA/single and 3000 CFA/double or non air-conditioned rooms for 1500 CFA/double. This place has the best menu in town with wine for 1000 CFA and Chinese food on Sundays. *Relais*

Korman used to be known as Chez Odette. Air-conditioned rooms for a little less than the St Hubert. *Hotel Boulai* has rooms for 2500 CFA. It's possible to camp in the grounds of the American Hospital.

Kumba

The hotels *Playfair, Authentique, Monte Carlo* and *Congo* all have rooms for 1500 CFA/single. *Harlem City Hotel* has rooms for 1000 CFA/double. *Meme Central* has basic rooms for 750 CFA.

Mamfe

Alvenow Guest House costs 1500 CFA/double.

Maroua

It's sometimes possible to stay at the Missions but the Catholic Mission is only 'barely friendly' these days. If no luck here, try the *Chez Pierrot* which is mainly a restaurant but sometimes has rooms for between 800 and 1000 CFA.

Plenty of interesting excursions can be made from this town. Also there are very primitive people who come down from the hills to the market every Sunday at Mora, a short distance from Moroua.

N'Gaoundere

Hotel Haut Plateau located in the centre of town. Costs 1500 CFA/single and 2000 CFA/double, no restaurant. During vacation time it's worth trying the College Mazenot as they may well provide you with a bed.

N'Gaoundere has a cool mountain climate, it's a volcanic area and there are crater lakes in the vicinity but don't swim in them as bilharzia is rife.

N'Kongsamba

Central Hotel costs 1000 CFA per person.

Yaounde

Foyer Internationale costs 750 CFA but

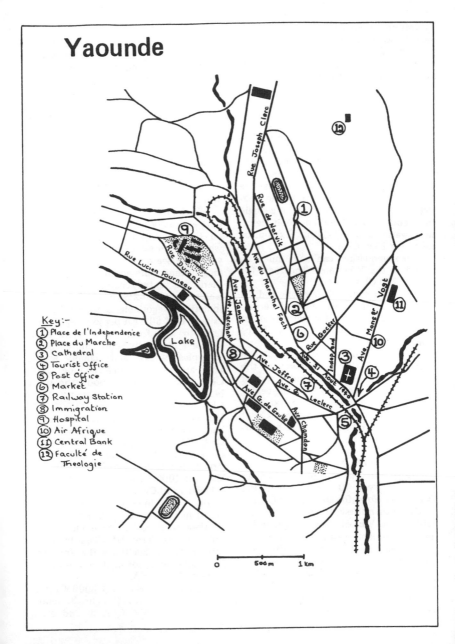

Yaounde

Key:-
1. Place de l'Independence
2. Place du Marche
3. Cathedral
4. Tourist Office
5. Post Office
6. Market
7. Railway Station
8. Immigration
9. Hospital
10. Air Afrique
11. Central Bank
12. Faculté de Theologie

Lake

0   500 m   1 km

is unfriendly. *Presbyterian Mission* costs 600 CFA/single. *Mission Protestante* has accommodation available but you need a letter of introduction from your embassy. Bus No 4 from town. You can camp here for 300 CFA. *Hotel Aurore* in the African part of town, costs 1000 CFA/single and 2000 CFA/double. *Hotel Nations* a fair way out of town (get a taxi if you're going there), costs 2000 CFA/double and is clean. *Hotel Flamenco* has rooms for 2000 CFA. They allow several people to stay in a double room. *Hotel Le Progress* near the Mokolo taxi park across from the market place, charges 3500 CFA for a single or a double. The hotel has good views, hot water and is clean. Fixed-price menu for 1500 CFA.

Accommodation can sometimes be found in the Faculte de Theologie for around 750 CFA.

American nationals are allowed to camp in the grounds of the International School — ask for permission at the school (special rates for Peace Corps volunteers).

For food you can get a stew in the market for 50 CFA. Otherwise try the *Club L'Ani 2000* in the African part of town but it's a long way from the centre and you'll have to take a taxi. Excellent food. The *American Recreation Camp Club* has good but expensive hamburgers and salads.

Victoria & Kribi

Mansion Hotel is one of the cheaper places to stay at 700 CFA a single. Eat at the *City Hotel* for around 100 CFA.

Other than these, food and accommodation in Victoria can be expensive and the tourist season stretches from November until February but there are some beautiful white sand beaches where you could camp or sleep out. If the ones nearer town are crowded go further down the coast where you will be able to find one all to yourself.

TRANSPORT

Hitching can be slow and involve long waits especially in the rainy season when bridges and roads get washed away or damaged. You'll generally have to pay for lifts. Hitching is much harder in the north and you'd be well advised to arrange lifts the night before at the lorry park. The journey from Garoua-Boulai to Bangui in the Central African Republic can be really slow and, in the rainy season, you may have to wait at the border for days if the bridges to Bangui have been washed away or damaged.

There are few buses and public transport is usually by taxi or 'mammy wagon' (bush taxis). Taxis have fixed prices which are posted up at the taxi parks. If you can't see one — ask. Taxi fares over long distances are about 5 CFA/km but there are extra charges for luggage which run at 20-25% of the fare but are sometimes negotiable. In the cities, taxis usually cost 50 CFA per journey though fares to and from airports and night journeys naturally cost more. Some examples of taxi and mammy wagon fares are — Bamenda-Yaounde: 3000 CFA, takes 10 hours, book the night before. Bamenda-Bafoussam: 1000 CFA, Bafoussam-Yaounde: 2000 CFA, Banyo-Tibati: 800 CFA, Kumbo-Foumban: 700 CFA, Foumban-Banyo: 1500 CFA, Tibati-N'Gaoundere: 1500 CFA, N'Gaoundere-Garoua-Boulai: 1500 CFA (trucks for 1000 CFA), Garoua-Boulai-Maroua: 1000 CFA, Maroua-N'Djamena (Chad): 1500 CFA.

Trains The lines run from N'Kongsamba in the west to Victoria and Douala then north-east to Yaounde, Belabo and N'Gaoundere. 1st Class fares are approximately 2¼ times the 2nd class fare. Couchettes for night journeys cost an extra 1000 CFA.

Yaounde-Douala costs 3000 CFA in 2nd class and takes all night. Yaounde-Belabo costs 1830 CFA in 2nd class.

Yaounde-N'Gaoundere costs 3875 CFA in 2nd class and takes 12 hours. There are two trains daily which depart Yaounde at 7.10 am and 4.20 pm. Yaounde-Garoua-Boulai costs 3000 CFA in 2nd class.

Boats A Nigerian boat and a Cameroon boat ply between Victoria and Idua Oron in Nigeria (Oron is across the river from Calabar). Quite a few travellers take this boat as an alternative to hitching into Cameroon via Ikom and Mamfe. The boat costs 2500 CFA one-way. If you're coming from Nigeria, the customs people are not interested in the Currency Declaration Form. You're supposed to go to Immigration in Calabar for an exit stamp before boarding the boat. The Cameroon-crewed boat is said to be 'best for theft', ie the worst!

Flights There is a network of internal flights but they're all pretty expensive. If you're heading for the Central African Republic in the rainy season, however, it might be cheaper in the long run to take one of the three times weekly UTA/Air Afrique flights from Douala or Yaounde to Bangui.

Route to/from Nigeria

The most popular overland crossing between the two countries is via Ikom and Mamfe. From the Nigerian/Cameroon border to Mamfe by taxi costs 1000 CFA. Mamfe to Bamenda by taxi costs 1500 CFA. Mamfe-Kumba costs 1000 CFA by Peugeot car. There are also direct taxis from the border to Victoria for 2500 CFA. It's a fairly easy hitch along this route as there's plenty of traffic. Note there are several police checkpoints along the way and you'll more than likely get searched at each.

Route to/from Central African Republic

If you're heading this way you're advised to arrange a lift in Yaounde as hitching for free is very difficult. It's sometimes possible to get lifts with drivers taking new cars through to Bouar. If you do decide to hitch, allow a week to get to Bangui as it's particularly difficult from the border onwards and you might have to wait there for several days. If you get stuck at the border you can stay either at the American Mission which charges 500 CFA for a bed and shower or with local people who will offer you rooms for around 400 CFA. It is a friendly border even if your visa has expired! There is a bus from Bertoua to Garoua-Boulai which costs 1350 CFA (bad road) and a bus from Garoua-Boulai to Baboua for 800 CFA. By truck the journey from Garoua-Boulai to Baboua costs about 400 CFA or 3000 CFA direct from Garoua-Boulai to Bangui. The road from Bouar to Bangui is pretty good and it's possible to hitch the stretch in a day with the right lift(s) but this would be exceptional.

PLACES TO VISIT

Kimbi River Game Reserve Accommodation here for 300 CFA/night. Game sighting fees are 500 CFA per day.

Mt Cameroon If you'd like to climb this mountain it's best to start from Buea. Guides cost 3000 CFA/day and with Tourist Office authorisation you can camp free at the prison farm. There is not much point in going during the wet season — November to March — as it's shrouded in cloud.

OTHER INFORMATION

The Peace Corps may still be producing their excellent guide, *A Revised Guide to Cameroon*, which is distributed free to their volunteers but it's possible for travellers to get hold of a copy. The guide contains very detailed information. Enquire at their office in Yaounde (BP 817, Yaounde, tel 22 25 34). The office is open Monday through Friday from 8.30 am to 12.30 pm and from 2.30 pm to 5.30 pm and on Saturday mornings between 9 am and 12 noon. They also have an office in Bamenda (PMB 45, Mankon Town, Bamenda, tel 36 12 97) which has similar opening times except in the afternoons.

There are Cameroon Tourist Offices in Yaounde, Douala, Kribi, Garoua-Boulai, Maroua and N'Gaoundere.

Canary Islands

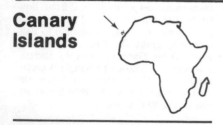

These are a group of Spanish islands just off the coast of Morocco/Western Sahara and therefore have the same visa and currency regulations as mainland Spain. The main islands of Gran Canaria and Tenerife are very much geared to package tour holidaymakers from northern Europe and are therefore pretty expensive and not exactly what the average overland traveller might be looking for but the other, smaller, islands are still very unspoilt and rural. Of late, there has been some agitation for greater autonomy from Spain along the Basque and Catalan models but it's still fairly low-key.

Before the Spanish handed over Western Sahara to the Moroccans and Mauritanians, quite a few travellers used to use this route to get to either the Western Sahara or Mauritania as an alternative to coming through the desert from either southern Morocco or along the Route du Mauritaine from Algeria. Neither of the desert routes are currently open because of the war between Morocco and the guerilla fighters of the Western Sahara. (Morocco occupied the whole of the Western Sahara following the withdrawal of the Mauritanians from the southern half of the country but their hold is relatively tenuous and the war is likely to continue for a long time yet). Since the overland routes were closed very few travellers have been going to Mauritania if only because of the inconvenience of getting there either from Europe direct or by coming up from West Africa but if you want to make a complete sweep all the way round West Africa it's still possible to get to Mauritania from Spain via the Canary Islands and so we're including details of the route.

VISAS

As for Spain. Required by nationals of Australia, Israel, New Zealand and South Africa.

CURRENCY

The unit of currency is the Peseta = 100 centimos. Import/export of local currency is allowed up to 50,000 Pesetas.

Exchange rate:

£1	=	164 Pesetas
US$1	=	71 Pesetas
A$1	=	82 Pesetas

LANGUAGE

Spanish.

ACCOMMODATION

La Palma is probably the greenest island with flowers and meadows but, as we said, it is an expensive tourist island. Hierno is very rocky with 13 volcanic craters and some lakes. Very tranquil. The island which is recommended most is Gomera where there are very few, if any tourists.

In Las Palmas you'll be lucky to find anything 'cheap' but try the San Nicholas and Tekor areas though they're pretty rough. The cheapest places we know of are *Hotel Savoy*, Calle 29 Avril, *Santa Catalina Pension* and *Jermiah's Pension*, Calle Secretario Artiles. There is also the *Hotel Buenos Aires* on the street of the same name. Near to the Pension there's a cafe of the same name which is the cheapest in town and serves excellent fish, chicken and salads.

The Tourist Office in Las Palmas (Parque Santa Catalina) has free maps, bus timetables, addresses of consulates, etc. In Tenerife the Tourist Office is on Plaza de Espagne.

If you need any vaccinations for West Africa get them at Sanidad Exterior on the road just in front of the docks facing Santa Catalina in La Palmas. They cost between 100 and 150 Pesetas depending on the shot.

If you're heading for Mauritania, Senegal or Mali buy a bottle or two of whisky or, even better, Courvoisier Cognac here for re-sale in those countries. On whisky it's possible to make 100% profit with no fuss and much more on the Cognac especially in Bamako, Mali.

TRANSPORT

(a) Spain-Canary Islands Compania Transmediterranea has a drive on-drive off car ferry service operating Cadiz-Tenerife-Las Palmas-Cadiz. It departs once every five days (approximately and takes 39 hours to Tenerife and 43 hours to Las Palmas. Minimum fares — Cadiz-Tenerife/Las Palmas: 4280 Pesetas (US$74), Tenerife-Las Palmas: 630

Pesetas (US$11).

(b) Tenerife (Los Cristianos)-Gomera (San Sebastian) Ferry Gomera SA is a car ferry operating three times daily in either direction. Departs Tenerife at 9.30 am, 2 pm and 8 pm. Departs Gomera at 7 am, 12 noon and 6 pm. Minimum fare is 295 Pesetas (US$5).

(c) Canary Islands-West Africa The only regular possibility at present is with Polish Ocean Lines who operate a service once every two weeks along the following route: Las Palmas/Tenerife-Nouadhibou (Mauritania)-Dakar (Senegal)-Banjul (Gambia)-Freetown (Sierra Leone)-Monrovia (Liberia)-Abidjan (Ivory Coast)-Tema (Ghana)-Lome (Togo)-Cotonou (Benin)-Douala (Cameroon)-Owendo (Gabon)-Pointe Noire (Congo). We have no details of their schedule or fares so if you're heading this way write to their British agents for details. The address is Stelp & Leighton Agencies Ltd, 238 City Road, London EC1 (tel 01-251 3389).

There are no ferries any more between the Canary Islands and the Western Sahara or between the Canary Islands and Morocco. If you're heading for Mauritania from the Canaries and need a visa it's possible to get these from the Mauritanian Vice-Consul in Las Palmas. The office is located at 'Pecheurs Mauritaine' a poorly marked office in Calle Raffael Cabrera. The only trouble with applying for a visa here is that your passport has to be sent to the embassy in Madrid and this takes about one month so it is much better to have your visa beforehand. The nearest Mauritanian consulates/embassies are in Madrid and Rabat.

Central African Republic

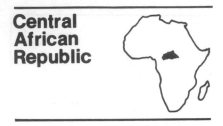

Formerly a French colony, this country was once part of an attempt to create a federation of the central African states of Gabon, Congo (Brazzaville) and the CAR though only the name survives following the withdrawal of the richest state — Gabon — from the negotiations. It is one of the poorest states in Africa and one of its most land-locked.

From 1965 until 1979 the country was ruled with an iron fist by a pretentious, brutal, megalomaniac, military dictator — Colonel Bokassa — who came to power following a military coup in 1965. His sordid and brutal regime was outmatched only by that of Amin in Uganda. Opponents and even mere critics of his regime, students and petty thieves were frequently clubbed to death in public often with the participation of Bokassa himself. Though he was an embarrassment to his clients, the French, he was, for many years, tolerated and supported with aid and arms because of the coveted uranium deposits at Bakouma and the exclusive big game hunting grounds near the Sudanese border, patronised by the French President, Giscard d'Estaing. He also received a good deal of support from the South Africans, desperate for trade links with black Africa, who negotiated a 250 million Rand loan for Ivory Coast, Gabon and the CAR as well as helping to develop the CAR's tourist potential for the exclusive rich. Part of the latter's programme involved building a 4 million Rand, 500-bedroom luxury hotel in the capital, Bangui, despite the fact that Bangui's other hotels are rarely more than half-full.

Following in the footsteps of his declared hero, Napoleon, Bokassa progressively took over virtually all the important government portfolios such as agriculture, commerce and industry, transport, information, civil service and social security, national defence and civil and military aviation until he embarked on his final and, for one of Africa's poorest countries, disgustingly extravagant and indulgent fantasy which was to be crowned Emperor of the renamed Central African Empire. Virtually all of the GNP of the CAR for a whole year — just over US$18 million — was spent on his coronation with the unstinting support of the French Government which provided many of the services and props and underwrote a large part of the finance. Few world leaders, including those from Africa, accepted invitations to his coronation.

The charade was maintained for a year or so longer until news leaked out about the murder of scores of young schoolchildren in Bangui who were boycotting classes. Bokassa was directly implicated if not directly involved in these murders and, though he denied any knowledge of them at the time, the truth was soon established. International protests followed and the French, tiring of this continuous embarrassment, engineered and supported with French troops a coup which toppled Bokassa and forced him to flee to France. The new regime set about restoring some degree of democracry in the country while making demands for Bokassa to be extradited for trial on charges of murder. The French were caught in a double-bind since no other country in the world was prepared to offer asylum to Bokassa and for weeks he was confined to his luxury jet on the tarmac of Paris airport. The most recent development is that the French have agreed to extradition and it seems likely that Bo-

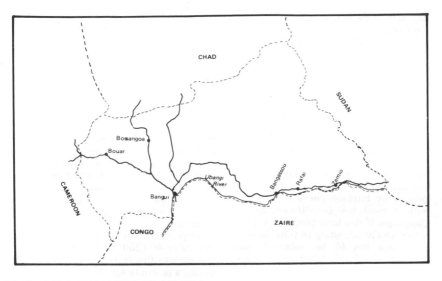

kassa will be returned to the CAR to stand trial. Time is running out for Bokassa and none too soon.

French influence in the Republic remains dominant and is likely to for some time if only because of continued interest in the uranium deposits in the country on which France depends for its nuclear war programme. At present some 60% of CAR exports have to travel along 1100 km of the Ubangui and Zaire Rivers merely to get to Brazzaville from where they have to be transported another 500 km to Pointe Noire on the Atlantic Ocean by rail. At the best of times the CAR has difficulty maintaining a flow of trade with the outside world and when the river is low at Bangui it is completely cut off from the outside world except by air. Lack of communications remains the CAR's major problem in trying to do something about the grinding poverty suffered by most of its inhabitants.

FACTS
CAR has a population of around two million, many of whom still live a 'primitive' lifestyle in the bush and forest. Letters we've had from the occasional traveller who has explored the CAR outside of the urban areas suggests that it's well worth the effort. They had an amazing time. There's still lots of wild life around Rafai and Zemio in the east and people can still remember cannabilism in these parts.

The country is one immense plateau varying in altitude between 600 and 700 metres. There are three main climatic belts, the south with a humid, tropical climate; the centre with a 'Sudan-Guinea' type climate with abundant rainfall and the north with a Sahelian climate which is very dry. Average temperature for the country is 26°C. The rainy season in the south is between May and November.

VISAS
Required by all except nationals of France, Germany (West), Israel and Switzerland.

In Yaounde (Cameroon), visas cost 2500 CFA, one photo and are issued while you wait. The visas allow for a 10-

day stay. This is the best place to get your visa.

Visa extensions for a further 10 days in Bangui cost 2000 CFA and take 48 hours. You need both entry and exit stamps for Bangui itself and an exit stamp for the country before you'll be allowed to leave — don't try to leave without these stamps or they'll send you back to Bangui. The stamps are free and obtainable 24 hours a day from the Immigration Office in Bangui.

Sudan Visas If you're thinking of crossing the Sudan border by public transport or by hitching you can get a visa without much fuss from the embassy in Bangui but if you have your own vehicle which you're intending to travel in then permission has to be obtained from Khartoum and this takes, on average, 2½ months!

Zaire Visas These cost 2000 CFA, three photos and take 24 hours to issue. Before a visa will be issued you must have a letter of recommendation from your embassy though we have had reports that they will issue visas without such a letter. Note that there is no British Embassy in Bangui (except for a representative in the UTA building in the Place de la Republique) and that letters of recommendation can be obtained from the USA Embassy — applies to other Commonwealth citizens too. Remember to specify on the visa application form that you want a three month visa with two entry/exits otherwise they'll issue you with a one month, one entry/exit visa. The price is the same for either visa.

CURRENCY
The unit of currency is the CFA. Import/export of local currency is limited to 75,000 CFA.

Exchange rate:

£1	=	474 CFA
US$1	=	208 CFA
A$1	=	237 CFA

There is a good blackmarket for Zaires (the currency of Zaire) in Bangui in the Marche Bokassa where the latest rate is US$1 = 2.90 Zaires or 1000 CFA=9.40 Zaires. The rate in Zongo across the river in Zaire is nowhere near as good.

Note that the only banks are in Bangui. Here the BIAC Bank is very efficient and you can buy travellers' cheques and US dollars. There are no banks between N'Gaoundere (Cameroon) and Bangui but if you're stuck the Maison Murat in Bouar will change money for you at good rates (cash or travellers cheques).

Airport tax for West Africa, Sudan and Zaire is 1200 CFA but for other destinations this is 3500 CFA. If you're buying a return ticket they'll charge you *double* this amount. In view of the above charges you're well advised to buy airline tickets elsewhere.

LANGUAGES
French and local languages. Very little English is spoken.

ACCOMMODATION
Baboua
The *Lutheran Mission* offers accommodation for 1000 CFA per person.

Bambari
Hotel Restaurant des Chasses very comfortable rooms for 1000 CFA per person and meals for 750 CFA. The hotel has only eight rooms.

Bangassou
You can either camp free at the *Mission Protestante* or for 250 CFA in the grounds of the *Tourist Hotel*. Other than these there is the very exclusive and expensive *Hunting Hotel-Restaurant* where you could rub shoulders with French Cabinet Ministers, possibly even Giscard d'Estaing though it's unlikely he has a copy of this guide.

Bangui

The capital — a pleasant, shady town quite unlike the rest of the country. *Centre Protestante pour la Jeunessee* is near the bus station, about five km from the centre — 200 CFA to camp or 500 CFA for a bed inside. Clean, mosquito nets provided, showers and car repair facilities — run by a friendly guy. Many travellers and students stay here. They have a dining room where you can get a meal for 100 CFA but you must give advance notice.

ONAF within walking distance of town has accommodation for 300 CFA/person. It's possible to camp free on the river banks below the *Hotel Roc* but be wary of the hippos! The *Hotel Roc* will cost you 4000 CFA/single and 5000 CFA/double minimum though it is air-conditioned and has a swimming pool, restaurant, dancing room and bowling green if you're looking for a little luxury after crossing the Sahara desert.

Less expensive than the Hotel Roc are the *Minerva Hotel* (rooms for 3000 CFA/single and 3500 CFA/double, (partially air-conditioned); and the *Palace Hotel* (rooms for 1500 CFA/single and 2600 CFA/double. Partially air-conditioned with a bar and restaurant with meals for 775 CFA).

Eats: *Restaurant des Militants* is about a km down the road from the Centre Protestante. It has good food for 250 CFA. *Restaurant Moderne* in the African quarter, which runs past the Centre Protestante has very good food. *Kitkat Restaurant* is further down the same road as the Moderne. Run by a Lebanese person who does good yogurt and cookies. *Chez Hussan* is in the centre of town. Serves good food.

The museum is very well organised and worth a visit. Admission costs 200 CFA but you get a guide with that.

In the artisans market there are malachite necklaces for sale which some travellers report being worth US$200-300 back in the west. Most of the prices in this market are more or less fixed. Hippopotami can be seen near the *Hotel Safari* which is the most expensive hotel in Bangui.

Bossambele

There are two Missions in town both of which you can stay at but the best one is a few kilometres out of town on the road to Chad.

Bouar

It might be possible to stay with the Peace Corps here about six km east of the town centre on the road to Bangui. Otherwise there is the *Hotel des Relais* which has five comfortable rooms.

Carnot *ONAF* in the market place offers accommodation for 300 CFA per person.

Elsewhere in the CAR there are no hostels or hotels and you'll have to ask around for accommodation. The villages between Bangui and Bangassou are very friendly and again in the remote areas around Rafai and Zemio.

In the remoter areas the police may be helpful in finding you accommodation. Very few travellers go to eastern CAR and so Missions are usually only too pleased to put you up for a small charge as they very rarely see another westerner and are glad of the company.

During times of political tension within the country you're advised not to sleep out and stay clear of the military and the police otherwise they may arrest you, though with the departure of Bokassa this may no longer be true.

TRANSPORT

There are no railways but one of Africa's best road systems outside the more developed countries and one which is fairly well maintained though, as elsewhere in Africa, there can be long delays in the rainy season when bridges and roads get washed away. Hitching can be very slow if you're waiting for one of those rare free lifts especially along the Garoua-Boulai to Bangui road from Cameroon. It's quite normal to get stuck at the border for four or five days and then for it to take another four or five days to get from there to Bangui. The non-stop journey from Garoua-Boulai to Bangui takes 1½ to two days which is, of course, how long it will take you if you're prepared to pay for a lift or if you take a combination of trucks and buses or taxis. Hitching further east the journey from Bangui to Bangassou can take three to five days. If you're heading for Chad it's possible to pick up lifts from Bossangoa in the north of the CAR to Gore in Chad for 1000-1500 CFA.

Buses These cost on average 6 CFA/km. There are daily services between Bangui, Bossangoa and Bangassou. Some examples of bus prices are — Bangui-Bangassou: 4000 CFA, Cameroon/CAR border-Bouar: 1500 CFA, Bouar-Bossembele: 2500 CFA (takes one day), Bossembele-Bangui: 1250 CFA, baggage under 30 kg is carried free.

Paying for a lift on a truck from Garoua-Boulai costs approximately 3000 CFA. Or there are trucks: Garoua-Boulai-Bouar: 1000 CFA, Baboua-Bouar: Bouar-Baoro: 500 CFA. If you're told in Garoua-Boulai there is no transport going east it's a nine km walk to the customs post and another 50 km to Baboua in CAR which is where Immigration is located. Other than delays at the border due to lack of transport, there's usually a delay of 24 hours caused by the customs people there.

Boats & Ferries

(a) Bangui-Zongo Ferry This ferry across the Ubangui River is the way most travellers cross over into Zaire. When it's running (it breaks down occasionally) it costs 50 CFA (2000 CFA for a car). If it's not running there are motor boats and piroques for hire though beware of the latter as they tend to want a lot of money. The Zaire customs post at Zongo is very easy going though you may be stuck there for days waiting for a lift — there is no regular scheduled transport from Zongo to Lisala on the River Zaire. Stock up with sufficient Zairois currency in Bangui as banks are very few and far between.

(b) Ubangui River Service Boats are operated by ONATRA, a Zaire government owned company. Very few travellers use the boat if only because the service is poor and very slow. The route is — Mbandaka-Buburu-Imese-Zongo and return. Officially the service operates once every two weeks taking four days upstream and five days downstream.

Flights
Aeroflot flies between Bangui and Khartoum. The fare is US$240.

Chad

Like its other Sahelian neighbours, Niger and Mali, Chad was carved out of the vast colony of French West Africa and gained its independence in 1960 though it still relies heavily on French aid and military assistance. The country straddles the boundary between Arab and Black Africa and relations between the proud nomads of the north and the more settled negro population of the south have traditionally been uneasy. This tension has so far thwarted all attempts at creating any sense of national unity and frequently leads to violence.

From independence until 1975 the landlocked, half-desert country was ruled by Ngata Tombalbaye whose eccentricities did little to foster harmony between the various ethnic groups. While he was President, Tombalbaye sought to erase the memory of French colonialism by having all French street and place names changed in favour of tribal names. He also insisted that all government officials, civil servants and ranking military officers of his own tribe undergo the manhood initiation rites of 'yondo' which included beatings, trials of strength such as fasting and crawling through termites' nest, scarring of the face, drinking concoctions to induce vomiting and taking oaths of secrecy and loyalty broken only on pain of death. His control of the country, like that of his successor was limited to the south and west, the remainder being controlled by various factions of the Chadian National Liberation Front (FROLINAT) which made international headlines some years ago by their kidnap of the French archeologist Mme Claustre (and subsequently her husband too).

FROLINAT was founded in Khartoum in 1966 and immediately set about organising an armed struggle against Tombalbaye's government by channelling discontent among the people of the north, known as the Toubou. The discontent stemmed from the abuses perpetrated by the Sara tribe of the south who dominated the civil service and administration. Support for the revolt also came from Libya where the Derdei, the traditional spiritual and temporal leader of the Toubou, lived in exile. Indeed Libya, in mid-1973, occupied a sizeable slice of northern Chad though the reasons for this still remain vague.

In an attempt to control the revolt, Tombalbaye was forced to call in French troops on three separate occasions but this merely drove the movement underground. In 1975, Tombalbaye was assassinated in a coup led by supporters of the former Army Chief of Staff, General Malloum, whom Tombalbaye had imprisoned two years earlier on charges of plotting against the Government. Though FROLINAT were suspicious of a man who had once led Tombalbaye's troops against them, it did seem for a while that the differences between the various ethnic groups might be settled and a civilian administration was set up with key posts being held by the leaders of the various contending groups. In 1980, however, the fragile truce broke down and led to fighting between the three main factions headed by the President, Goukouni, the Defence Minister, Hissen Habre, and the Vice-President, Abdelkader Wadal Kamougue. Hundreds of people lost their lives, the expatriate community was evacuated in French military aircraft and the capital, N'Djamena, devastated. Vain attempts were made by various African leaders to bring the warring sides together — notably by the President of Togo who rafted across the Logone River to N'Djamena — but the fighting continues. It seems that the logical step to take would be dismember the country along ethnic lines though it's unlikely this will happen. Because of the fighting, the country will remain effectively closed to travellers for quite some time thus eliminating the possibility of travelling from Maiduguri in northern Nigeria to Bossangoa in the CAR via N'Djamena and Sarh.

FACTS
The population of Chad is about 4 million with a growth of about 1.5% per annum. It stands at an ethnic crossroads where Arab Africa meets Black Africa and in this respect is similar to Sudan, Mauritania and, to a lesser extent, Mali and Niger. In Chad it is the black Africans who are in the majority and, unlike in neighbouring Sudan, it is they who dominate the government and the civil service. Its main export crop is cotton.

The Sahelian drought probably affected Chad more than any other country bordering the Sahara. It is one of the world's most isolated countries — landlocked and with very primitive communications.

There are three main zones to the country: (a) the south with a semi-tropical climate and between 50 and 120 cm of rain per year, (b) the centre which is a dry zone ranging from tropical to sub-desert, (c) the north which includes the Tibesti Mountains in the heart of the Sahara desert. The rainy season is from November to May though very little, if any, rain falls in the Saharan regions. Temperatures average 20-25°C but can rise to 40°C just before the rains.

VISAS

Required by all except nationals of Andorra, France, Germany (West) and Monaco.

Note that excluding N'Djamena, you require special authorisation from the Ministry of the Interior to travel anywhere in Chad. You can only apply for this on arrival and it can take a *long* time to obtain.

CURRENCY

The unit of currency is the CFA. Import/export of local currency is allowed up to 10,000 CFA.

Exchange rate:

£1	=	474 CFA
US$1	=	207 CFA
A$1	=	237 CFA

The BIAO Bank in N'Djamena charges no commission for exchanges. There are no banks between N'Djamena and Bangui in the CAR. Airport taxes for destinations in West Africa, Sudan and Zaire are 1200 CFA, all other destinations cost 3500 CFA. Airport charges on return tickets are double the above.

LANGUAGES

French and local languages.

ACCOMMODATION

There is very little accommodation and most travellers have to camp. It's not possible to stay at the Peace Corps hostel in N'Djamena but there is an unofficial camp site on the outskirts of town but without facilities. The cheapest hotel in N'Djamena is the *Hotel Grand* on the Place de l'Independence which charges 4400 CFA/double. Note that Chad is generally more expensive than either Nigeria or Cameroon for foreigners so bring supplies with you if possible.

TRANSPORT

The best time to travel is between November and May. Communications are rudimentary and at times some parts of the country are completely cut off from the capital, N'Djamena, especially during the rainy season when roads get flooded/washed away. There's no public transport system — rail or bus. Presently the best route from N'Djamena to Bangui (CAR) goes via Bongor, Lai, Doba, Gore (border) and Bossangoa rather than through Sarh. It's possible to enter Chad either by this route or from Maiduguri in Nigeria via a sliver of northern Cameroon. If you go the latter way you are issued an automatic free transit visa for Cameroon at the border. Trucks from Maiduguri to the Cameroon border cost about 500 CFA. The border between Cameroon and Chad is the River Logone which flows into Lake Chad. Boats across the river cost about 50 CFA — there's no bridge.

Apart from the above two routes, travel in the rest of Chad is limited by the following climatic and political restrictions:
(a) A combination of uncertain security conditions and a lack of housing, food, gasoline, and vehicle repair facilities

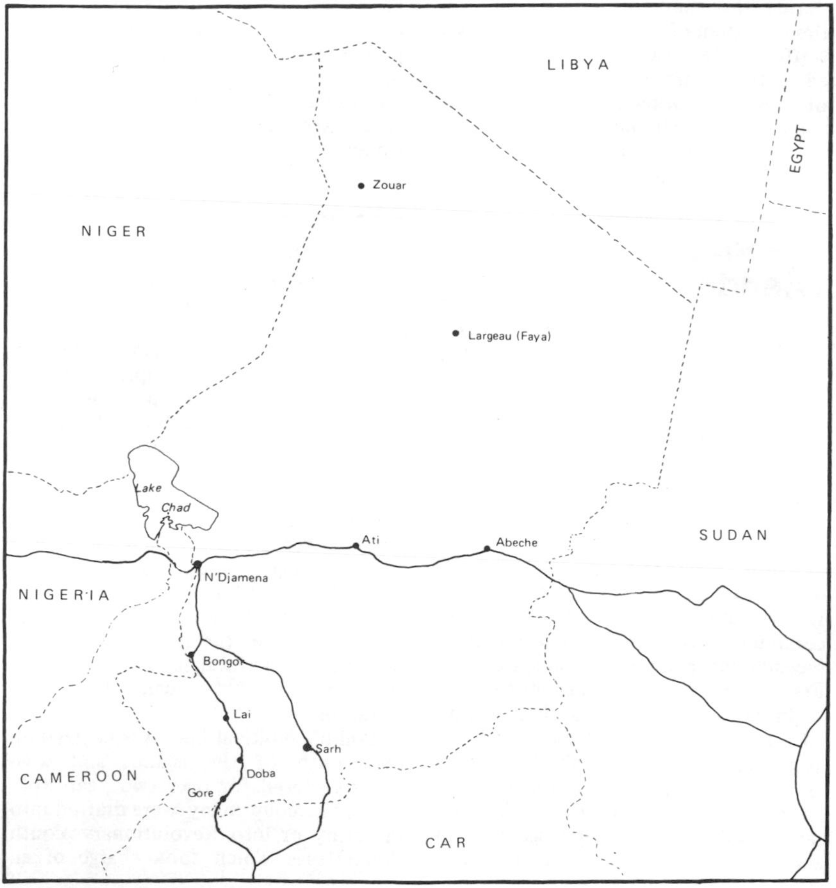
LIBYA
EGYPT
Zouar
NIGER
Largeau (Faya)
Lake
Chad
Ati
Abeche
SUDAN
N'Djamena
NIGERIA
Bongor
Lai
Sarh
CAMEROON
Doba
Gore
CAR

have resulted in the government prohibiting travel especially in the central and northern areas of the country. This applies even to convoys of vehicles and covers routes from Libya via Zouar and Faya-Largeau to N'Djamena and the road from N'Djamena via Ati and Abeche to the Sudanese border.

(b) If you want to go to the CAR via Sarh you need government authorization.

(c) Much of Chad is flat and the soils are not very porous. Roads quickly become impassable due to flooding and mud during the rainy season. During this time a system of rain barricades controls traffic on the roads. You may be delayed at these barriers for varying periods of time and during June, July, August some roads, including principal routes, are simply closed completely.

(d) The unpaved road running from Maiduguri in Nigeria through Cameroon to N'Djamena is a major trucking route into Chad. Its condition varies according to the maintenance it receives and the weather. The rains often render it impassable most of the time from the last week of July to the first week of September, even in a Land-Rover. The Cameroon road from N'Gaoundere through Garoua, Maroua and the Wazza Game Reserve to N'Djamena has paved all-weather sections but the unimproved sections make this road difficult in the rainy season.

(e) Note that even if, by some stroke of extraordinary luck, you managed to get permission to travel overland to the Sudanese border you will need a Sudanese visa endorsed specifically for overland entry via the Chad/Sudan border at Geneina.

Comores Islands

This group of four islands off the northwest coast of Madagascar unilaterally declared independence from France in 1975 though, at the time, the island of Mayotte dissociated itself from the others with encouragement from Paris. It subsequently joined the Comoran community for a short while but later seceded and reverted to the status of a French colony which it remains today.

In January 1976 the National Council for the Revolution elected Ali Soilih as president and Abdallah Mohammed as prime minister. A month later Soilih executed a coup against Abdallah and sent a military expedition against him and most of his ministers who had withdrawn to their island stronghold of Anjouan. Following the coup, Soilih pushed ahead with a radical programme of reform which included the dismissal of a large number of civil servants (the civil service was the largest employer on the islands and often took up the whole of the public expenditure budget), banned the wearing of veils by women thus inciting the wrath of the older generation in these Moslem islands and started a land reform programme, based on giving every citizen a piece of land which they would be legally bound to farm. At the time, although 90% of Comorans owned at least a small amount of land, more than 30% of all the fertile land was in the hands of foreign companies and the remaining 70% owned by feudal landlords.

Soilih's political base was centred on the youth of the islands and with schools closed for over two years following the coup many were drafted into the army or into Revolutionary Youth Committees which took charge of all political, economic and social organisation at village level. The excessive and sometimes high-handed manner in which the Youth Committees attempted to institute Soilih's ideas and particularly the reforms of the Moslem religion alienated many people and Soilih was eventually overthrown in an invasion and coup by a bunch of white mercenaries led by a Frenchman. This escapade highlighted for many other small African countries how easy it was for a small band of well-armed mercenaries to take over a country. The mercenaries ruled the country for about a year but were eventually forced to withdraw mainly as a result of international pressure. The new leaders have taken a turn to the right and reversed many of Soilih's socialist reforms.

The main exports of the islands are cloves, allspice, pepper, vanilla and ylang-ylang (a perfume similar to patchuli). People in the rural areas are poor and prices are high though most will offer accommodation to travellers — very few come here. Roads are generally primitive but hitching is reported to be easy.

VISAS
Required by all. Visas are issued on arrival to everyone. If you're staying 48 hours or less they are free. Up to 72 hours visas cost 500 CFA up to one month they cost 1150 CFA, up to three months 1250 CFA and for six months they cost 2500 CFA. You must get an Exit Permit before you leave. Also, you must have an 'onward ticket' before they will allow you into the islands.

CURRENCY
The unit of currency is the CFA.

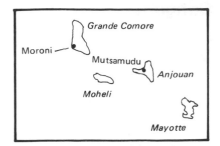

Exchange rate:

£1	=	473 CFA
US$1	=	207 CFA
A$1	=	237 CFA

Airport tax for domestic flights is 200 CFA, for Madagascar, Reunion, Tanzania and Kenya it is 500 CFA and for other international destinations 1500 CFA.

LANGUAGES
French and Swahili.

ACCOMMODATION
In Moroni on Grande Comore one of the cheapest places is the *Hotel Al Madad* which has rooms for 500 CFA per night. They will allow several people to share a room.

TRANSPORT
Shipping services to the islands are infrequent. Enquire at Mitchell Cotts Ltd in Mombasa, Kenya, to see if they still run their monthly service to the islands. The crossing takes five days. There are occasional boats to Madagascar from Moroni. Probably the best way to get there is by air with Air Madagascar from either Nairobi or Dar es Salaam or from Tanarive on Madagascar itself.

Congo

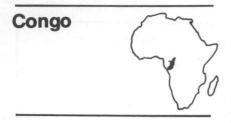

Since independence from France in 1960 the Congo was, for a long time, the only unreservedly Marxist-Leninist state in Africa with its closest neighbours — Zaire, Gabon, CAR and Cameroon — all more or less ideologically opposed to the regime. Since then, however, it has been joined by Mozambique, Angola, Guinea-Bissau (all former Portuguese colonies) and Ethiopia. Nevertheless, it maintained a strictly neutral foreign policy and insisted on non-alignment while supporting African struggles for national self-determination and independence. During the civil war in Zaire from 1960 until 1965 the Congo, under the leadership of Abbe Fulbert Youlou, effectively supported Tshombe and his attempted Katangan secession in return for promises of economic aid.

Youlou was deposed in 1963 by a general strike and replaced by Alphonse Massemba Debat who headed a new revolutionary government. Debat struggled to establish a personal dictatorship until in 1968 a combined military and youth force replaced his corrupt rule with a People's Republic. The new Republic was headed by Marien Ngouabi who pushed ahead with the revolutionary process and attempted to eliminate reactionary elements in the government and civil service but was assassinated in mid-March 1977 by a small group of soldiers including a member of his own body-guard who were led by a former French and later Congolese intelligence agent. Retribution was swift and those responsible were executed along with

the former President Massemba Debat who was accused of masterminding the plot. Following Ngouabi's assassination, the Catholic Archbishop of Brazzaville was murdered precipitating the arrest of three members of Ngouabi's family who were thought to have killed him in revenge as he had met with Ngouabi shortly before the assassination and was accused of having known something about the coup plot.

Sassou-Nguesso took over as President and set about establishing himself as a linear successor to Ngouabi. In Ngouabi's government he had held the Ministry of Defence.

FACTS
The narrow coastal plain is low-lying and dry with grassland vegetation. Further inland there are the Mayombe and Chailou highlands which are forested and deeply dissected with gorges and valleys. The northern part of the country is equatorial rain forest with an average rainfall of 110 cm. The rainy season is from October to May with a brief dry spell around the end of December. Average temperatures are around 24°C.

Road conditions are very poor and there are no sealed roads outside of Brazzaville. It's pretty hopeless to try to use the roads in the rainy season as they're all closed for the first six hours after rain to protect the surfaces. The main overland route into the country is from Lambarene in Gabon via Dolisie to Brazzaville. The road from Cameroon is only passable in the dry season.

VISAS
Required by all except nationals of France, Germany (West) and Romania. Transit Visas obtainable on arrival (72 hours maximum stay) for 1250 CFA.

CURRENCY
The unit of currency is the CFA. Import/Export of local currency is limited to 10,000 CFA.

Exchange rate:

£1 = 473 CFA
US$1 = 207 CFA
A$1 = 237 CFA

LANGUAGE
French, Lingala and Mounoukoutouba.

ACCOMMODATION & TRANSPORT
The Congolese Government does not encourage tourism and we've never heard of any travellers going there and so have no details.

The only railways are from Pointe Noire on the Atlantic coast to Brazzaville and Mbinda. There is a train daily between Brazzaville and Pointe Noire with dining and sleeping carriages. There's also a once weekly service between Mbinda and Pointe Noire.

There is a half-hourly ferry operating across the Zaire river between Brazzaville and Kinshasha (Zaire) but it often gets suspended because of political tension between the two countries.

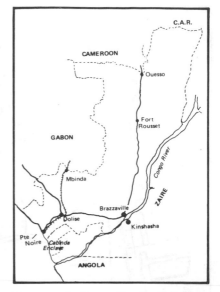

If you go to Brazzaville, the Poto Poto Arts Centre there is worth a visit for displays of modern Congolese art.

Djibouti

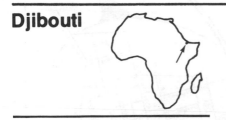

As the French Territory of the Afars and Issas, this was the last French colony on the African mainland and gained its independence from France in 1977. It is one of Africa's smallest states and consists of little more than the port of Djibouti and a sliver of semi-desert hinterland. Ethnically it is a part of Somalia and the most logical step for it to take would be to merge with that country though continuing French economic interests make this unlikely at present.

Most of its income comes from the port — one of the few deep-water ports on the Horn of Africa — and from the railway which connects Djibouti to Dire Dawa and Addis Ababa in Ethiopia. This line is of vital importance to the Ethiopians as 60% of their imports and exports pass along it. The existence of the rail line explains Djibouti's importance to both the Ethiopians and the Somalis who, for many years, have been fighting for control of the Ogaden desert in southern Ethiopia. If Djibouti merged with Somalia the Somalis would largely be able to dictate terms to Ethiopia by closing the rail link. The Ethiopians take this threat very seriously and probably would, in the event of a merger or obstacles erected by the Djibouti government, invade the tiny state.

Before independence the French used Djibouti for years as a training

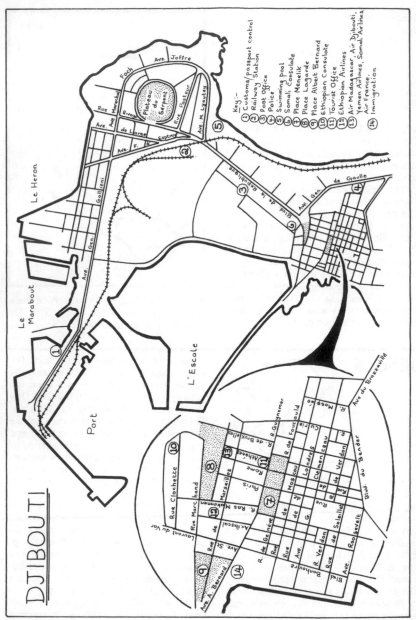

ground for their Foreign Legion and it was the wages of these soldiers — spent in the bars and brothels of the port — which constituted a large part of the income of the colony.

Like many people in Ethiopia and Somalia, Djiboutians spend a large part of their income on 'qat' which is a mildly narcotic leaf whose effect falls about half-way between that of coca leaves and amphetamine. It allays hunger and allows the user to work long hours in the fields. It's said to be flown in at the rate of seven tonnes per day though most of it is for re-export.

VISAS

Required by all except nationals of France. A three-day 'visa d'escale' is given free of charge on arrival to nationals of Belgium, Denmark, Finland, West Germany, Italy, Japan, Luxembourg, Netherlands, Norway, Sweden, the UK and the USA provided they have an onward or return ticket. The same nationalities are granted a 10-day visa on request on arrival for 1500 Djibouti Francs, provided they have onward tickets. No extensions to the 10-day visa are possible. Nationals of South Africa and Israel are not admitted.

A Djibouti visa in San'a, North Yemen costs 24 Rials and is issued while you wait. It allows for a stay of 10 days only.

Note that the onward ticket requirement is strictly enforced. If you haven't got one they'll jail you and later allow you into town to buy one, holding your baggage until you return. If you arrived by dhow they also detain the captain of the dhow until you come back from town with an onward ticket.

CURRENCY

The unit of currency is the Djibouti Franc. There are no restrictions on the import or export of local currency.

Exchange rate:

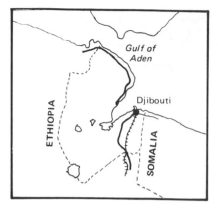

£1	=	391 DjFr
US$1	=	170 DjFr
A$1	=	196 DjFr

LANGUAGES

French, Arabic and some English.

ACCOMMODATION

Djibouti survives mainly by being a glorified truck-stop for tourists and travellers en route to somewhere else. As you might expect, with a function like this, everything is geared to taking as much money from tourists in transit as possible and it's a *very* expensive place. The only cheap hotels you will find are those bar-hotels which double as brothels. Other than this you could sleep out on the beach near the tennis courts in the French quarter or ask around the owners of yachts in the harbour — you may be offered a bed on a boat.

There are many bars and restaurants, mainly French but including some Vietnamese and Chinese, though in the French part of the city prepared food is expensive. Cheaper possibilities exist in the African quarter and there is a street market with a wide variety of fruit and vegetables.

USEFUL ADDRESSES

Tourist Office: Place Menelik.

Bureaux de Change: At the airport and in Place Menelik. There are banks in the Place Lagarde (Banque de l'Indochine and Banque Nationale pour le Commerce et l'Industrie) and the rue de Ras-Makonnen (Commercial Bank of Ethiopia).

Post Office: Boulevard de la Republique.

Immigration: Avenue Administrateur-Bernard.

Airlines: Air Djibouti, Messageries Maritimes, Place Lagarde. Ethiopian Airlines, 16 rue de Marseilles. Yemen Airlines and Somali Airlines, at the airport. Alitalia and Air India, L Savon et Ries, Ave Saint Laurant-du-Var.·

TRANSPORT

It's impossible to hitch to Dire Dawa in Ethiopia as there is no road (red lines on maps are a pure figment of the cartographer's imagination) and there is the danger of being ambushed by Eritrean Liberation Front guerillas. All traffic to Ethiopia goes on the railway from Djibouti to Addis via Dire Dawa and even this is occasionally sabotaged by the ELF. It may be possible to arrange a lift with trucks going to Hargeisa and Berbera in Somalia but don't count on it.

Trains There are two categories of trains: 'Express' (1st and 2nd class only) and 3rd class only trains. Both types depart for Addis three times weekly. The 'Express' train takes 21 hours to reach Addis. Fares are Djibouti-Addis Ababa: 3404 DjFr in 2nd class, 1363 DjFr in 3rd class. Djibouti-Dire Dawa: 1384 DjFr in 2nd class, 552 DjFr in 3rd class.

Boats Most of the boats which call at Djibouti are expensive round-the-world liners and long distance cargo boats and would be of little interest to you. If you are heading for Kenya it's sometimes possible to get jobs on boats going from Djibouti to Mombasa with Mitchell Coutts whose office is on the Avenue de la Republique. Perhaps worth a try.

Arab dhows ply between Djibouti and Mokha (North Yemen) and Aden (South Yemen) and it's possible to get rides with them. From Djibouti to Mokha will cost you approximately 70 Rials (US$17.50), the trip takes two days. Check them out at the port.

Flights Djibouti-Ta'izz (North Yemen): US$46, Djibouti-Addis Ababa: US$68, Addis Ababa-Nairobi: US$130. If you buy a Djibouti to Nairobi ticket with Ethiopian Airways and there is no connecting flight from Addis on arrival, the airline will pay your hotel bills in Addis overnight.

Egypt

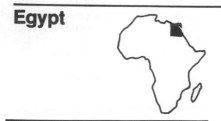

Egypt, along with Mesopatamia and the Indus Valley, was one of the very first centres of civilization in the world and has a recorded history which stretches back 6000 years to the time of the Pharoanic Kingdoms which waxed and waned over a period of about 3000 years. The ruined cities and monuments which these kingdoms left — Memphis, Karnak, the pyramids, the funerary temples and burial chambers in the Valley of the Kings, Abu Simbel, Philae and many others — still stand today and are some of the oldest and best-preserved monuments in the world thanks to the dry desert climate. They are undoubtedly the highlight of any visit to Egypt. Almost any book on archaeology will contain a wealth of information about them and it's worth reading up about them before you go.

Until fairly recently the Egyptian civilization was regarded by most archaeologists and historians as part of the Middle Eastern cultural genesis rather than one of African origin. Though Middle Eastern influences were obviously absorbed as a result of trade with various empires in that area and invasions by the Assyrians, Persians and Macedonians, recent research strongly suggests that the early Egyptian kingdoms had far more contact with Africa than was previously supposed. It's now known that they frequently sent trading missions and expeditions to West Africa and as far south as the Congo rain forest and, in their turn, influenced civilisations which were to spring up there later.

Egypt lapsed into obscurity following its conquest by the Romans and was to remain that way until taken by the forces of Islam after the death of the prophet Mohammed many hundreds of years later. Shortly after this, Cairo became one of the great centres of Islamic culture and learning where scholars from all over West and Central Africa came to study. Later on it became part of the Turkish Empire which, at its height, included the whole of the North African coast, Saudi Arabia, the Middle East, Greece and a large part of Eastern Europe but as the power of the empire waned and the Sultans took to being virtual recluses inside the palace at Istanbul, Egypt became autonomous under the rule of the Janissaries — eunuch mercenary troops of the Turks. Corruption, misgovernment and cultural decline set in and was to continue until the government was effectively taken over by the British in the 20th century following the Egyptian Government's inability to finance its foreign debt. Throughout the 19th century the British and French vied with each other for control and trade advantages in the country and it was during this century that de Lesseps conceived of and built the Suez Canal.

The founder of the modern nation was Colonel Nasser who overthrew the corrupt and degenerate monarchy in a military coup in the 1950's. He was a politician of international standing who made skilful use of the rivalries between the Americans and the Russians to attract aid and military hardware with which to finance the building of the Aswan Dam and to encourage the various Arab wars against the state of Israel. He was instrumental in attempting to form a united Arab state to include Egypt, Syria and Iraq but this fell through and only the name survives as the official name of Egypt — the United Arab Republic. Similar mergers have been proposed since with Libya on the one hand and Sudan on the other but disagreements have always surfaced and prevented anything coming to fruition. In the mid-70's, relations with Libya were so tense that thousands of Egyptians who worked there were expelled, the border closed and war very nearly declared. Though they eased up for a while they are now firmly back to square one and the border again closed as a result of the American-inspired Camp David peace treaty with Israel. Libyan-inspired coup plots against the regime are unearthed with monotonous regularity and go a long way to explaining the tension between the two nations.

The wars with Israel have had a devastating effect on the country's economy by diverting much-needed funds for development into the arms race. They also resulted in the closure of the Suez Canal for many years with its consequent loss of income as well as the occupation of Sinai (where Egypt's only oil wells are situated) by the Israelis. President Sadat, who succeeded Nasser on his death, was involved in protracted negotiations for the gradual withdrawal of the Israeli Army from Sinai — a process which is going ahead at present, though slowly and with great Israeli reluctance. In order to achieve this, Sadat

expelled all Russian military advisors and engineers, accepted an American aid and arms package and signed a unilateral peace treaty with Israel in the teeth of opposition from virtually every other Arab state in the Middle East and North Africa. Egypt is now in the unusual position of having an open border and trade links with Israel and a closed border and no trade links with Libya. Whether Sadat can survive and see the process through to completion will depend largely on the American's ability to control their Israeli allies and Sadat's ability to pass the economic fruits of this settlement onto his people in the form of a better standard of living and more employment.

As with the ancient civilizations which sprung up alongside the Rivers Euphrates, Tigris and Indus further east, life is still centred around the River Nile whose annual flood used to provide a rich fertile soil. The rest of the land area — about 95% of the total — is an almost completely barren, flat plateau broken only by a few scattered oases In view of its capacity to grow food, Egypt is a very overpopulated country with over 38 million people and a growth rate of around 30% per decade.

The building of the Aswan Dam — built largely with Russian aid and technical assistance — has stopped this annual flood and it may be that over a period of time the fertility of the lower Nile Valley will deteriorate though the Dam now allows the irrigation of a far larger area of land than was previously possible as well as the growing of two and sometimes even three crops per year. It's other major benefit is, of course, hydro-electric power.

Lake Nasser, created by the Aswan Dam, stretches back almost 400 km right over the border into Sudan and has made possible the beginnings of a small fishing industry though it has also brought problems such as an alarming increase in the incidence of bilharzia and, because it traps the mud and silt brought down from the Ethiopian highlands and prevents it reaching the sea, has resulted in the virtual extinction of the rich sardine shoals which used to be plentiful off the Mediterranean coast. Dams are not always the panaceas they are made out to be as many countries have discovered. The temples of Abu Simbel were rescued from the rising waters of the lake with international help and now stand on high ground above the lake. As the only way to get to them is by boat and they're an internationally famous tourist attraction visiting them is now quite expensive. If you're heading for Sudan on the Lake Nasser boat you might be lucky and see them from a distance.

VISAS

Required by all. Nationals of South Africa are not admitted unless they hold a student card which proves that they are studying at an Egyptian university.

At the embassy in Athens, visas cost 170 Drachmas (approximately US$4.50) one photo and take two days to issue. They allow for a stay of 30 days. At present there are no hassles and they don't ask to see money.

Visas can be issued on arrival if you are flying into the country but this is at the discretion of the immigration official if you're coming from a country which has an Egyptian embassy or consulate. If you're coming from one which hasn't — no problems. Visas issued on arrival cost US$2.

Officially anyone coming to Egypt on a Transit Visa (valid up to seven days) or on an Entry Visa/Tourist Visa (valid for 30 days) without an 'onward ticket' is required to change US$150 or the equivalent into Egyptian currency before they will be allowed to leave the airport/port. In practice this problem is faced by all travellers regardless of the type of visa they hold or whether they have or haven't got an 'onward ticket' except those entering from Sudan on the Lake Nasser Ferry in which case none of this applies. The amount you are forced to change varies depending on the official who deals with you, how you arrive, who you are and just pure luck. Arriving by boat from Athens, the customs people board the boat before anyone gets off. Some people are required to change US$150, others US$100, yet others US$50 and some none at all. There's no way of predict-

ing whether you'll be the unlucky one. The only loophole in all this is that if you tell them you're staying no more than three days then (officially) you're not obliged to change any money. If you get through this hassle using this excuse, it's possible to have a three day Transit Visa renewed up to seven days. This might be worth a try if you're short on funds. Other, tried, methods include reconversion of Egyptian currency into US dollars the next day at one of the airport banks. Tell them you are leaving the next day. Alternatively try the manager of the Golden Hotel, Cairo who at present is willing to convert Egyptian currency into US dollars at a much better rate than offered by the banks — if you ask *discreetly*.

If your stay in Egypt is less than seven days then you're allowed to reconvert Egyptian currency into hard currency up to the amount you have changed legally. If you stay more than seven days you are allowed to reconvert up to the amount you changed *less US$25* for each day you have stayed. You're advised not to leave any reconversion you want to do until you get to Aswan. It can be impossible. On the other hand, you can buy Sudanese currency with Egyptian currency there so if you only have a small amount left it's not going to make any odds.

Sudanese Visas The embassy in Cairo is situated opposite the Canadian Embassy and near the British Embassy in Shari Latin America, Garden City. The visa costs E£5.10 though for some nationalities (eg Dutch) it can cost E£10.20 and is issued the same day. No problems but you need a 'letter of introduction' from your embassy before the visa will be issued. Two photos needed.

Ethiopian Visas Visas can be issued the same day if you have an onward ticket from Ethiopia and 'sufficient funds' — the required amount can be quite high. There is a war on in Ethiopia at present and overland entry is not permitted. Probably the most you would be allowed to do (and the only thing involving any degree of safety) would be to see Addis Adaba. Visas are hard to get unless you are flying in and right out again with an overnight stop in between.

Student Cards
You need one of these to get concessions (50%) on Egyptian Railways but it doesn't matter if it's out of date or a fake — they merely glance at it. Some travellers have even got concession by showing a YH Card. Note that students of anything other than archaeology or history can no longer get authorisation for free entry to all the antiquities. The entry fees to the antiquities are quite steep and if you're thinking of visiting a lot of them it's well worth the hassle of getting a free ticket. In order to do this you need a letter from your embassy stating that you're a student of the above categories (or, possibly, art too). Take this to the Antiquities Office near Abbassaia Square, Cairo (bus No 500 from Tahrir Square). Fake Egyptian Student Cards are available from 97 Al Gumhuriya opposite the Victoria Hotel Cairo. They're acceptable for student concessions in Egypt but useless outside.

HEALTH
Keep out of the Nile and Lake Nasser and don't drink the water unless it has been boiled. There's an alarming incidence of bilharzia especially around Aswan. If you need a Yellow Fever vaccination these can be obtained cheaply in the lobby of the Continental Hotel, Cairo.

CURRENCY
The unit of currency is the Egyptian Pound (E£) = 100 piastres. Import/export of local currency is allowed up to E£20.

Exchange rate:

Official rate		Tourist rate	
£1	= E£0.67	£1	= E£1.53
US$1	= E£0.30	US$1	= E£0.67
A$1	= E£0.34	A$1	= E£0.77

There is a thriving blackmarket and the Nile Hilton and other large hotels in Cairo are worth checking out. US$1 = E£0.74-0.77 for travellers cheques. A little more for cash. Egyptian currency can be bought at considerable discounts in Europe especially Greece and Switzerland. Note that if you're thinking of reconverting back into hard currency you need a bank receipt to cover you. Banks will not reconvert it otherwise.

Airport tax for international flights is E£3. Egypt is a good place for buying airline tickets since you can pay for them with money obtained on the blackmarket making them relatively cheap. If you fly into Egypt, buy a bottle of Johnny Walker whisky duty-free at the airport as well as 200 cigarettes. They can be sold easily at kiosks in Cairo for US$8/litre (whisky) and US-$10 (cigs).

LANGUAGES
Arabic, French, English and some Greek.

MAIL
The poste restante in Cairo is notorious. Avoid having mail sent here. Letters take forever to get through — if they get through at all — and the 'sorting' is chaotic. There's a small fee for letter collection.

FOOD
Standard fare in most cheap cafes is 'foul' (beans in sauce), 'falafels' (meat balls) and unleavened bread similar to the Greek 'pita', 'Tahina' is sometimes served as a bread dip and is similar to the Greek taramasalata but more spicy. Fresh fruit juices are widely available —

mango, lemon, carrot, orange and 'carcady' (a sweet red drink made from fushca leaves). There is also 'zaglib' (made from herbs and coconut milk and dressed with chopped nuts). There are many varieties of sticky cakes, nuts and dates like you will find all over the Middle East and the usual vegetables found in this area — courgettes (zuccini), aubergines (egg-plant), tomatoes, etc. Meat is usually mutton with some veal.

The prices of a few basics are — tea: 4 pt, coffee: 6 pt, orange juice: 10 pt, carrot juice: 8 pt, sugar cane juice: 3 pt, bread: 1 pt, oranges: 10 pt/kilo, dates: 25 pt/kilo, white cheese: E£1/kilo, tomatoes: 12 pt/kilo, nuts: 70 pt/kilo.

In Cairo there are plenty of Greek and Italian restaurants if you'd like that sort of food and most larger hotels offer three or four-course meals for around E£1.50. The Nile Hilton does amazing breakfasts for E£2 plus 10% tax. You don't have to be a resident.

ACCOMMODATION

Probably the cheapest places to stay are the Youth Hostels which you'll find in Alexandria, Cairo, Luxor and Aswan. They cost 40 pt if you're under 21, 60 pt if you're over 21 and 75 pt if you have no YH Card. They are generally pretty good value and many travellers stay in them but you should keep an eye on your gear.

Alexandria

The *Youth Hostel* is on Port Said Street and costs 60 pt. The staff is none too friendly and there's nowhere to leave packs safely but they do offer basic meals. The *Luxor Hotel* costs E£1/double. Other hotels along the boulevard cost, on average, E£2-3/double. Note that Alexandria hotels can be awkward about unmarried couples sharing a room.

For food try the *Restaurant Foul* which serves, as you might expect, 'foul'

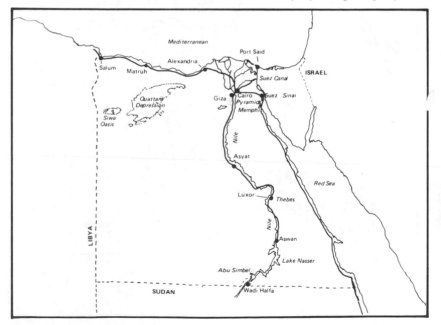

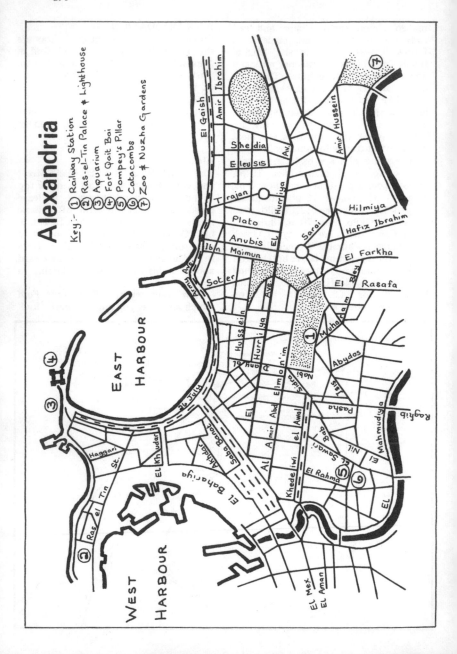

Alexandria

Key:-
① Railway Station
② Ras-el-Tin Palace & Lighthouse
③ Aquarium
④ Fort Qait Bai
⑤ Pompey's Pillar
⑥ Catacombs
⑦ Zoo & Nuzha Gardens

with four to five side dishes for 25 pt. 'Famous even in Cairo'. Ask anyone for directions.

Aswan

The *Youth Hostel* is three minutes walk from the station on Abtal Al Tahrir Street. Turn right coming out of the station and it's the second street on the left. The Hostel is signposted. Nice people, good showers and toilets, lounge, TV and it doesn't close during the day. No prepared food available but there are cooking facilities. You cannot stay here without a YH card and if you haven't got one they'll sell you one for E£3. Staff will arrange trips to Abu Simbel.

The *Aswan Palace Hotel* is quite a long walk from the station. Costs 55 pt for a bed in the dormitory and 97 pt/double with cold shower. The *Hotel Continental* is situated by river and has a lot of character. Costs 50 pt for a bed in the dormitory but it's none too clean. There is a camping ground with toilets, showers and an armed (!) guard 24 hours a day which costs 12 pt. The *Amer Hotel* first street on the left, coming out of the station, costs 40 pt for a bed in the dormitory and 70 pt/double. The *Hotel El Saffa* is just right, then first left coming out of the railway station. Costs E£2.20/double, clean, new building, big rooms.

The swimming pool by the main post office costs 50 pt. It's possible to hire a felucca (small sail boat) for the trip along the Nile to Elephantine Island, the tomb of the Aga Khan. Costs about E£3 shared between eight people and takes all afternoon. A shared taxi to the Aswan Dam should not cost more than 40 pt each.

Cairo

The *Youth Hostel* is situated by El Gamas Bridge (University Bridge) opposite Salah el Din Mosque facing the river in Shari Abdel Aziz. It's a fairly new hostel with friendly staff and snacks available. There are good facilities but watch your gear. It closes between 10 am and 2 pm and after 11 pm at night. It's suggested you eat out.

Most of the hotels are located on or near Talaat Harb. They include:
Pension Oxford 32 Talaat Harb, run by a friendly Greek woman and very popular with travellers. Costs E£1.60/double including tax. *Hotel Select* Adli Pasha Street, costs E£2/double. *Pension Roma* Adli Pasha Street, costs E£2/double. *Hotel Viennoise* first street on the right hand side of Tahrir Square, costs E£11.80 for a double without own bath. *Hotel Everest* opposite the railway station, costs 70 pt in the dormitory and E£1.50 double. *Golden Hotel* Talaat Harb near Tahrir Square is popular with travellers. Costs E£3.30/double with toilet, shower and hot water. The manager is friendly speaks English, and is a mine of information. Dorm costs E£1. *Grand Hotel* corner of 26 July Street and Talaat Harb, is also popular with travellers. An excellent hotel with all the usual comforts. Costs E£4.50/double including breakfast (served between 7 am and 12 noon). *Pension Olympic* Near Olympic Airways (Greek national airline), costs 75 pt in dormitory. Hot showers available. *Hotel Suisse* of Shari Bassiuni, near Tahrir Square, costs E£5.50/double. Fairly average hotel.

For food try the *Koshari* shop near the Youth Hostel. Filling meal for 10 pt. Otherwise try *Roy's Bar and Restaurant*, 42 Talaat Harb. Very large meals for 70-80 pt. Also *Felfela Village* near Talaat Harb — very good Egyptian food, cheap. *Groppi* (Shari Qasar El Nil) and *Estorial* are also recommended.

Tourist Office: 5 Adli Street.
American Express: 15 Sharia Ksar El Nil PO Box 2160, (tel: 970138). Branch offices at the Nile Hilton Hotel, the Meridien Hotel and at the airport.
Useful buses: — No 70 or 95 from Tah-

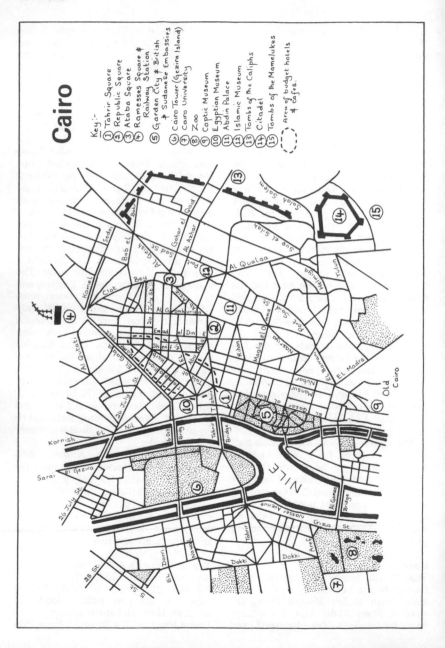

Cairo

Key:-
1. Tahrir Square
2. Republic Square
3. Ataba Square
4. Ramesses Square & Railway Station
5. Garden City – British & Sudanese Embassies
6. Cairo Tower (Gezira Island)
7. Cairo University
8. Zoo
9. Coptic Museum
10. Egyptian Museum
11. Abdin Palace
12. Islamic Museum
13. Tombs of the Caliphs
14. Citadel
15. Tombs of the Mamelukes
Area of budget hotels & cafes.

rir Square to Ramses Square.

No 8 from Tahrir Square to the Youth hostel.

No 400 from Tahrir Square to the airport. Run day and night and costs 10 pt.

No 900 from Tahrir Square to Gizeh (for the pyramids).

No 18 from Tahrir Square to the GPO.

Note: Bus numbers are usually in Arabic numerals.

Luxor

The *Youth Hostel* is about eight·minutes' walk from the railway station and is signposted. Friendly staff and reasonable facilities but recently described as 'small, grubby and stinks'. Only serves breakfast. Hires out push-bikes for visiting the Valley of the Kings, etc.

New Karnak Hotel, near the station costs 50 pt in dormitory and 95 pt/ double. Clean and has hot showers, will hire out push-bikes for 75 pt/day. *Mahata Hotel*, near the railway station, costs 80 pt/double. Ask for a room with a balcony. *Venus Hotel*, costs E£2/double, clean but be careful about your bill. *Horous Hotel*, costs 96/pt single and E£2-4/double, comfortable, friendly management and hot showers. The *Seti Gordon Hotel* costs E£2.50/double including breakfast. Clean and hot showers.

For food try the Mensa on the main street on the right hand side as you leave the railway station. Vegetable dishes for 10-15 pt. Boulis Bicycles on main street rent bikes for 50 pt/day — open at 7 am, must return it by 5 pm. Boats across the Nile go when full and cost 2 pt or 10 pt if you have a bike.

If you haven't already got authorisation for a free student ticket to the antiquities you can get one from the Antiquities Office which is part of the Savoy Hotel. Closed on Fridays. Remember you have to be a student of archaeology, history, or art — see under 'Visas'.

TRANSPORT

Hitch-hiking is officially forbidden but with the peace treaty with Israel this regulation might be relaxed in the near future.

Buses These are dirt-cheap but very crowded and few travellers use them. Bus from Asyout to the oasis of El Kharga costs E£1.25. Takes four hours and goes through beautiful desert countryside.

Trains The most popular form of transport in the country. Even without a student card they are very cheap. With student concessions (50%) they make even thinking about hitching redundant. Student concession forms are no longer necessary — just show your IS card to get the concession. The officials merely glance at it so it doesn't really matter whether it's out of date or even a fake one so long as it has a number on it. Some travellers have even got the concessions by showing their YH card. Student concessions are only available in 2nd and 3rd classes.

Only 1st and 2nd classes can be reserved though 2nd class is often booked up days in advance so plan ahead. 3rd class tickets can only be bought on the day of departure. Some examples of the fares are —Alexandria-Cairo: 95 pt in 2nd class with student reduction. Cairo-Luxor: E£1.75 in 2nd class with student reduction, 75 pt in 3rd class (with student reduction). The train takes 12½ hours. The 1st and 2nd class train departs Cairo every day at 7.30 am. There is also a 3rd class only train which departs every day 8 pm.

Cairo-Girga: E£2.06 in 2nd class with student reduction. El Balyana-Luxor: 77 pt in 2nd class with student reduction. Luxor-Aswan: E£1 in 2nd class with student reduction, 65½ pt in 3rd class with student reduction. The journey takes four hours. Trains every day at

8 am and 6 pm. Aswan-Saad el Ali: 6 pt in 3rd class with student reduction and takes half an hour. There are departures from Saad el Ali for Cairo everyday at 6.30 pm.

Boats

(a) **Feluccas** There are many of these which ply up and down the Nile at various points. One of them has already been mentioned under Aswan in the accommodation section. Another which is worth considering is the one from Luxor to Armant which costs 8 pt and takes 2½ hours. Many of the boats are really beautiful.

(b) **Nile Steamer** This plies between Luxor and Aswan. The boats depart at 4 pm on Mondays and Thursdays and take two nights to get there. Tickets can be bought from Nile Navigation Co, 8 Qsar el Nil, Luxor, which is an alley off the main street. The boat jetty in Aswan is a half hour train ride from the centre. 'Foul' and tea are available on the boat.

(c) **Lake Nasser Steamer — Aswan-Wadi Halfa (Sudan)** Boats depart Aswan and Wadi Halfa on Mondays and Thursdays and take two days for the trip so take your own food and water if possible — water available for drinking on the boats is often taken directly from the lake and not boiled, though tea and soft drinks are also available. The boats depart Aswan at about 2 pm but you need to be there by 12 noon for customs clearance. Customs is generally totally chaotic but otherwise no hassle. If you're late, there is a train from Aswan to Saad el Ali (boat jetty) at 1 pm which will just get you there in time to catch the boat though by that time it will be pretty full. The railway station at Wadi Halfa is just over the brow of the hill from the boat jetty (about a kilometre). Trains from Wadi Halfa to Khartoum wait for arriving boat passengers before setting off. There are taxis and Land-Rovers from the Wadi Halfa boat jetty to the railway station for S£0.50. In Aswan you can change Egyptian currency into Sudanese currency on a one-for-one basis. Don't change too much as the rates for hard currency are better inside Sudan.

Fares — Deck class: E£2.89, 2nd class: E£7.19 (Cabin), 1st class: E£9.67 (Cabin). Deck class is fine so long as you arrive at least two hours before departure as you have to stake out a patch of deck. It's pretty crowded. Tickets can be bought either at the boat jetties at either end or from the Sudanese Railway Offices: Cleopatra Tours, 4 Talaat Harb, Cairo; or the Nile Navigation Company, Aswan, (near the Tourist Office).

The Sudanese boats are considered best as they're more modern. Food, ('foul') and hot sweet tea are available on the boat but take your own bread and fruit.

Flights It's cheaper to fly between Cairo and Athens if you're 26 years old or under than to take the Mediterranean ferry. The Adriatica ferry between Alexandria and Piraeus will cost you US$77 deck class with a student reduction or US$110 without. Youth fares are available on the airlines for anyone 26 or under regardless of whether they are a student. The fare between Cairo and Athens is presently E£37.50 (Youth Fare) with Egyptian Olympic Airways, Alitalia, TWA, Swissair and Malev (Hungarian airways). There are two or three flights per day. If you have any trouble getting the Youth Fare or you're over 26, go to Malev and ask for the manager. Give him a few E£ as a backhander and he'll sell you a ticket for E£38.

PLACES TO VISIT/ANTIQUITIES

Alexandria A fading coastal resort (have you read the *Alexandria Quartet*?) which sprawls along the coast as far as Abukir where Nelson had his famous beach battle in the Napoleonic Wars. Bikinis are not allowed on the beaches and Saudi ladies swim fully clothed and bedecked with jewels. Montazza Palace, the one-time home of King Farouk, is worth a visit as are the beautiful gardens surrounding it. There are a few ancient sites worth visiting such as Pompey's Pillar, the catacombs and the only surviving Roman theatre in Egypt. The museums are also worth a visit. The market area is busy and interesting.

Aswan Once the frontier of ancient Egypt but Aswan is a modern town these days. The main attractions are the Aswan High Dam, Philae Temple, Elephantine Island and the tombs on the west bank. You need a permit to visit the high dam and Philae Island as they're restricted military areas. Both the YH and the tourist office will arrange these permits. A guide is compulsory and the trip to the Dam and Philae Island will cost you about E£3. If you can't afford this or haven't got the time go and see Elephantine Island. Catch the ferry down by the river but watch what the locals pay otherwise they'll attempt to charge you three times as much. Access free via the Hotel Oberoi Launch, if you walk on as though you are staying at the hotel. There's a good bazaar in Aswan where you can pick up bargains in baskets, djellabahs and musical instruments. Nubian dancing most evenings for E£1 — arrange through the Youth Hostel.

Cairo An enormous and fascinating place that would take you months to get around properly. Contains relics and monuments from all the important eras in its history. The centre of modern Cairo is full of tall, new buildings, 18th and 19th century mansions and palaces, graceful palms, dhows and feluccas on the River Nile, noise, people, life and continuous activity especially around Tahrir Square — the centre of the city. The Egyptian Museum, just off Tahrir Square, contains one of the best selections of exhibits from the time of the Pharoahs you'll find anwhere in the world and is worth at least two visits.

The Mummy room costs extra and there are no student reductions for this section. Tutankhaman is back there after a world-wide tour and just as impressive. The Museum opens at 8.30 am and closes at 1 pm (earlier on Fridays). The Citadel in Old Cairo is worth seeing — fair walk from Tahrir Square. You have to show your passport to get in as its a military camp. In addition to these there are the Sultan Hasan Mosque, Abdin Palace, the Coptic Museum, Islamic Museum and the tombs of the Caliphs and Mamelukes. The tourist office will provide you with plenty of literature about these places.

Giza Situated about 10 km from Cairo at the end of the No 900 bus route from Tahrir Square and site of the pyramids and the sphinx. One of the most visited sites in the world. Admission costs 50 pt (unless you have a concession ticket) from the hut about 100 metres from the entrance to the pyramids. You're allowed to climb up inside the pyramid of Cheops to the Funerary Chamber in the middle. Tickets for the Son et Lumiere can be bought for E£1 (no student reductions available) but it's possible to see and hear everything from outside the area. The English-language production is on Mondays.

Luxor, Karnak and the Valley of the Kings Luxor itself is full of ruins and has the very impressive and interesting Karnak Temple, the Sacred Lake and the Avenue of the Sphinxes nearby. Don't miss them! The Valleys of the Kings and Queens, the Nobles' Tombs, Hatshepsut's Temple, the Ramasseum, Colossi of Memnon, etc. are on the other side of the Nile about 10 km from Luxor. To visit them you need to hire a bicycle, donkey or taxi. A bike will cost you 50-75 pt depending on where you hire it. If you want to hire a donkey you can pick them up on the far side of the Nile where the muleteers wait for tourists. They cost 75 pt plus the cost of the guide (compulsory). If you're going by bicycle or donkey you need to start as early as possible during the day as it gets very hot later on. If there are four of you it's just as cheap to hire a taxi. There are two ferries across the Nile — the tourist ferry which costs 10 pt, and the local ferry a little further north which costs 2 pt. Bikes are carried free on the local ferry though it may be difficult for you, as a foreigner, to get it free and most people end up paying around 10 pt for themselves and bicycle.

Without a special student permit, visiting the antiquities can be expensive. The entrance fees are — Luxor Temple (E£1), Museum (75 pt), Karnak (75 pt), Deir-el-Bahari (50 pt), Valley of the Kings (E£2), Valley of the Nobles (E£1). **Memphis & Sakkara** Situated about 20 km from Giza, Memphis was once the capital of ancient Egypt. There are several ways of getting there but be warned of the profiteers who offer camel or horse trips there as they'll charge E£6 for the five-hour trip to Sakkara and

back though some people say it's worth it. If you take a horse, wear long boots otherwise you'll rub the skin off your legs. Beautiful scenery along the way. Another way to get there is to take the half-hourly train to El Badrshein and from there the local bus to Sakkara village (5 pt) then a 1½ km walk alongside the irrigation channel to the main road. There's also the possibility of a bus from Giza to Sakkara costing 7 pt. Admission to Sakkara costs 85 pt. A taxi from Cairo to Memphis will cost you about E£4 shared between four people though you'll probably have to add another E£1 as 'baksheesh'. The site is in the middle of nowhere.

Abu Simbel The hydrofoil is out of action at present and the only way to get there is by plane from Aswan. This costs E£23.60. Admission to the site costs a further E£2.

OTHER INFORMATION
Film is expensive and you're advised to bring a supply with you. Slides tend to be slightly less expensive.

Equatorial Guinea

This ex-Spanish colony is made up of the islands of Fernando Poo and Annabon and the mainland of Rio Muni. It was ruled for 11 years by Francisco Macias Nguema whose brutal regime rivalled those of Amin in Uganda and Bokassa in the CAR. Only a third of the 300,000 Guineans who lived there at independence were still there by 1979. Tens of thousands fled to Spain and to neighbouring African countries, leaving

over 28,000 political prisoners in forced labour camps inside the country. Nguema's dictatorship made an economic shambles of the country whose main crops of cocoa and coffee failed badly under cultivation by prisoners, and arbitrary arrests became common with his assassins claiming 50 to 60 victims each day for imaginary plots against his regime. Unable to command the loyalty let alone support of his people, he found it necessary to bring in expatriate labour, mainly from Nigeria, but conditions were so bad that they led to riots which were crushed with much bloodshed by the army and police. This action against Nigerian expatriate workers precipitated demands by some politicians in Nigeria for Equatorial Guinea's annexation and, had Nguema re-

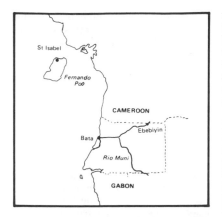

mained in power much longer, this might well have happened.

However, in late 1979 Macias Nguema was toppled in a coup led by his nephew, Colonel Teodoro Nguema. The news prompted crowds of exiles in Gabon to demonstrate in favour of the new regime though the leaders of the Equatorial Guinea Opposition described the overthrow as a cosmetic operation aimed at gaining international help for the country. It remains to be seen what will happen though the new head of state pledged to defend human rights, declare a general amnesty and free all political prisoners. Spain immediately recognised the new regime and despatched a three man mission to the capital, Malabo (Santa Isabel). Colonel Teodoro Nguema was educated in Spain and is considered to be a pro-western nationalist which doubtless explains their enthusiasm for the new regime.

Macias Nguema fled to his home town of Mengomo along with his personal bodyguards following the coup reportedly with every asset he could lay his hands on in the national bank vaults. He was last heard of in the Equatorial Guinea/Gabon border town of Ebebiyin though his eventual capture seems inevitable as the Gabonese would be loathe to offer him asylum. His overthrow is undoubtedly a step in the right direction and it may be that with Spanish collaboration in the reconstruction of the former colony that the country will become a part of the overland route once again. Let us know if you get there as we never heard of anyone going there during Macias Nguema's reign of terror.

FACTS

On the mainland the country rises gently from the coast to the Cristal Mountains and is thickly forested except for the coastal plain where there are plantations of cocoa and coffee. The main island, Fernando Poo, is volcanic and less fertile and, in the south, very rugged and uninviting. Rainfall averages around 1000 cm per year. Temperatures remain fairly constant at 27°C. Humidity is high at all times.

On the mainland, wildlife is abundant and the traditional life of the small villages is well worth seeing. Magic still has a powerful grip and the unique religious ceremonies and costumes of their festivals survive unspoilt by European influence in most rural areas.

VISAS

Required by all. Just about the only embassy in existence is the one in Madrid, Spain (Alonso Cano 27) so if you want to go there you must first get your visa in Spain. Visas take, on average, two months to come through. Exit permits are required by all. These can usually be arranged at the airport.

CURRENCY

The unit of currency is the Ekuele = 100 centimos. Import of local currency is prohibited. Export is limited to 3000 Ekuele. The currency is on a par with the Spanish peseta.
Exchange rate:

£1	=	164 Ekuele
US$1	=	77 Ekuele
A$1	=	82 Ekuele

Airport tax is 100 Ekuele for international flights.

LANGUAGE
Spanish and local languages.

ACCOMMODATION & TRANSPORT
We've never heard of any travellers going there so we have no details. All that is known as far as transport is concerned is that there are no sealed roads on the mainland and the only way you can enter overland is via Ebebiyin on the Cameroon border. Please let us know if you go there.

Ethiopia

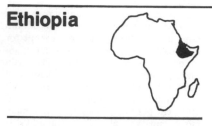

Ethiopia is unique among African countries in that it avoided colonisation except for a brief Italian occupation shortly before WW II and has a home-grown Christian Church going back to the 4th century AD which has successfully resisted the onslaughts of Islam right through to the present day. Unfortunately it has recently become a Russian vassal state wracked by internal revolt and unfinished wars with the Eritreans of the Red Sea coast and the Somalis of the Ogaden Desert. Thus, if only because of the amount of military activity going on, it is effectively a closed country at present which is a great pity since it's one of Africa's most beautiful and interesting areas. Probably the most you'll be allowed to do is stay overnight in Addis en route to somewhere else.

The first recorded kingdom in Ethiopia grew up around Axum in the northern highlands during the 3rd century BC at the time when the Egyptian influenced state of Meroe was flourishing near the site of modern-day Atbara in Sudan. It was an offshoot of the Semitic Sabean kingdoms of southern Arabia and soon became the greatest ivory market in north-east Africa whose king traded with the Greeks and spoke their language. Over the next few centuries Axum gradually encroached more and more on Meroe until in the 4th century AD, when Christianity became the state religion, it finally conquered that declining kingdom and forced its rulers to flee to the western Sudan. Axum went on to conquer parts of the Yemen and southern Arabia and was to remain the dominant power in this region until the eve of the Prophet Mohammed's birth. Even when the armies of Islam began their northwards expansion, Axum remained in control of the western Red Sea coast down as far as Zeila in Somalia though the Moslems were able to take advantage of a temporary weakness in the kingdom to take Massawa and the neighbouring Dahlak Islands.

As Islam expanded, Ethiopia was cut off from its former Mediterranean allies and Moslem traders gradually replaced the Egyptians, Greeks and Jews in the Red Sea ports yet this was not to result in hostilities between the two religions for some six to seven centuries. Part of the reason for this remarkable co-existence when compared with European relations with Islam is to be found in the fact that Ethiopia had followed the Syrian and Egyptian leads in adopting the Monophysite heresy — condemned by orthodox Christianity in 451 AD — and so benefited from the live-and-let-live arrangement between Islam and the Egyptian Copts. Thus, throughout the Middle Ages, Ethiopian bishops were consecrated in Cairo and thousands of Christian pilgrims were able to make the journey to Jerusalem in safety without any restrictions being placed on their religious rites and ceremonies. Even Saladin, one of the greatest opponents of the Crusaders, gave the Ethiopian Christians their own church in Jerusalem to use as a religious centre.

In this way Ethiopia's first major challenge to its existence came not from Islam but from the pagan tribes of the south living in the area around the bend in the Blue Nile. Pressure from these tribes forced the rulers of Axum to adopt the life of military commanders living in temporary tented cities and its priests to become monks and hermits in order to keep the religion alive. Gradually however, the kingdom recovered and went on to incorporate the provinces of Amhara, Lasta, Gojjam and Damot with Amhara becoming the centre of the resurgent state.

Moslem expansion into Ethiopia began to take place in the 12th century as a number of independent trading kingdoms grew up along the coast and gradually moved down the Awash Valley following the line of the present day railway between Djibouti and Addis Ababa. Their wealth was based principally on slaves, ivory and gold which they acquired from the pagan tribes and kingdoms to the south of the highlands. They didn't, however, remain independent for too long and were made into Ethiopian vassal states during the 13th and 14th centuries. The largest of the Muslim states — Ifat — was eclipsed in 1415 and its people forced to flee to the Yemen after the king was killed in battle at the capital, Zeila.

Ethiopian fortunes were reversed in the 16th century as the Ottoman Turks, who succeeded the Mamelukes in Egypt, began to bring firearms and artillery down the Red Sea and into Arabia where they used them to support various Muslim kingdoms in their struggles with the Ethiopians. The latter were only saved from invasion at the last minute by the intervention of the Portuguese in 1542. Thereafter, for a hundred years, Portuguese missionaries were to unsuccessfully try to get the Ethiopians to accept the Pope in Rome as head of the Church.

The Empire fell apart in the 18th century into its constituent provinces with rival emperors being a common feature but in 1855, Ras Kassa, a local warlord and robber baron, managed to have himself crowned emperor at Axum under the name of Theodore. He went on to build something approaching a modern army and managed to unite Tigre, Amhara and Shoa after turning the tide against the pagan Gallas who had been troublesome since the end of the 16th century but his arrogant treatment of British envoys was to lead to his downfall. A military expedition was mounted in 1867 under the command of Napier which blockaded the fortress of Magdala. Abandoned by many of his vassals, Theodore shot himself. His successor John IV, fought his way to the throne using British arms which he had acquired in exchange for help at Magdala. Meanwhile a young vassal king from Shoa — Menelik — who had taken note of the efficacy of European arms used at Magdala, made himself so powerful that John IV was forced to acknowledge him as his successor. Whilst waiting for the throne Menelik built up stocks of European weapons and was to use these in 1896 to defeat the Italians at Adowa and to expand his empire at the expense of the Afars and the Somalis of Harrar and the Ogaden Desert in the south-east and the Gallas and other tribes in the south-west.

After WW I, Ethiopia became a member of the League of Nations but this didn't prevent the country being overrun by Mussolini's Italy in 1936. Though the other Western nations, somewhat hypocritically in view of their

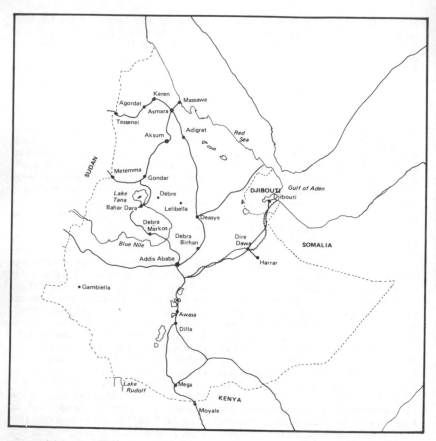

own activities in Africa, condemned the Italian invasion and though the Emperor Haile Selassie, made many impassioned speeches pleading for assistance, nothing was done until the Italians were thrown out in 1941 during WW II. Following this, Ethiopia resumed its course as an independent country though the province of Eritrea bordering the Red Sea remained under British military administration until 1952 when it was federated with Ethiopia. The federation did not take into account the wishes of the Eritreans themselves and when the federation was dissolved and the province annexed by Haile Selassie in 1962 this led to the outbreak of guerilla warfare. The Moslem Eritreans who were not a part of Ethiopia for the past four or five centuries and who, under the federation, had their own government, flag and security forces, regard themselves as having been colonised by another African country and want independence from Ethiopia. By the mid-70s, the Eritrean liberation fighters were becoming so successful that the northern cities of Asmara and Massawa were totally cut off from the rest of the country. Without the intervention of the Russians they might well have achieved their objective but other events were to intervene to prevent this.

Though Haile Selassie had established himself as a national hero in the campaigns against the Italians and had become a respected African statesman being instrumental in the creation of the Organisation of African Unity, dissatisfaction with his regime grew rapidly throughout the '60s. The constant accumulation of wealth by the nobility and the Church, the hardships experienced by millions of land-less peasants, student protests, serious famines in the south of the country in which hundreds of thousands died and discontent within the armed forces over the conduct and progress of the war in Eritrea all combined to precipitate a revolution in which Haile Selassie was deposed and held under armed guard in his palace until his death a few months later. The running of the country was taken over by a clique of Marxist military officers of whom Major Mengistu Haile Mariem soon emerged as the leader. Mengistu threw out the Americans, who had previously been responsible for training and equipping the armed forces; instituted a number of far-reaching reforms particularly in respect of land-tenure and the economy, and, sought economic aid from the USSR. Nevertheless, the country rapidly fell apart into its constituent provinces, neighbourhood vigilante groups alienated many people with their violent excesses, the war in Eritrea intensified rather than abated and the Somalis began to make threatening noises about taking back the Ogaden Desert. In the capital there have been several massacres of opponents and demonstrations in which hundreds of people have lost their lives.

The dispute over the Ogaden finally came to a head in the late '70s as the Somalis poured troops into the area in support of the liberation fighters there. They over-ran Jijiga and very nearly captured the regional capital, Harrar. Mengistu's regime tottered on the brink of collapse for several weeks and was rescued only by a massive airlift of Soviet and Cuban arms and troops. Having thrown the Somalis back across the border these troops went on to attack the Eritrean liberation fighters.

Though many of the Russian and Cuban troops are still in the country, the situation remains tense and chaotic with little prospect of an early resolution. Neither the Eritreans nor the Somalis are likely to accept anything less than, on the one hand, independence from Ethiopia, and, on the other hand, the return of the Ogaden. Mengistu, for his part, with Russian backing, is unwilling to compromise over either issue.

VISAS
Required by all. White nationals of South Africa not admitted. Transit visas can be issued on arrival at Addis Ababa airport to those waiting for a connecting flight who have to stay overnight. Tourist visas (validity 30 days) cost US$6.50 or equivalent, two photos and take at least four weeks to issue. They're difficult to get hold of.

You can only enter and leave Ethiopia via Addis Ababa airport. Entry through any other point needs special permission. Onward tickets must be held and at least US$50 per day of stay. If you're given a transit visa on arrival they keep your passport at the airport so you cannot use it to get other visas whilst you're there.

CURRENCY
The unit of currency is the Birr = 100 cents. Import of local currency is allowed up to 50 Birr. Export is prohibited.

Exchange rate:

£1	=	4.68 Birr
US$1	=	2.03 Birr
A$1	=	2.34 Birr

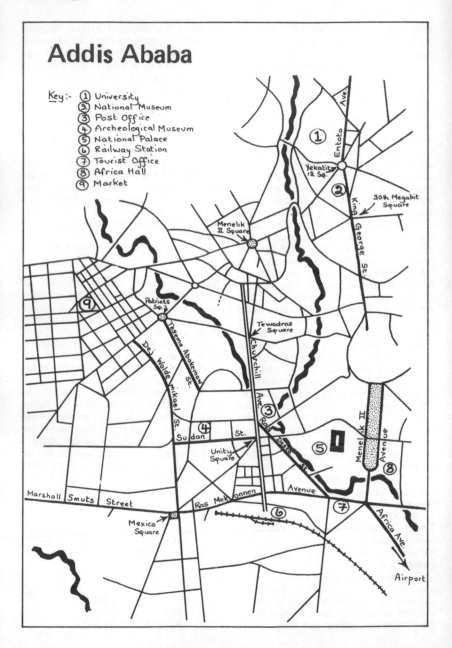

Addis Ababa

Key:-
1. University
2. National Museum
3. Post Office
4. Archeological Museum
5. National Palace
6. Railway Station
7. Tourist Office
8. Africa Hall
9. Market

Airport tax on domestic flights is 2 Birr, on international flights it is 8 Birr.

LANGUAGES
Amharic, Gallegna, Arabic, Italian, English and French. Amharic is the official language but Gallegna is more useful in the countryside in the south. Italian speakers are located mainly in and around Addis Ababa and Asmara. Old people and civil servants often speak academic French. Arabic speakers live mostly along the Red Sea coast and in the north of the country (Eritrea).

Some Amharic
Numerals: 1-ant, 2-hulet, 3-sost, 4-arat, 5-amst, 6-sidist, 7-sabat, 8-simnut, 9-zutang, 10-assr, 20-hya, 30-salasa, 40-arba, 50-hamsa, 100-moto.
Water-ooha, tea-shai, milk-wa'tat, coffee-buna, bread-dabhu, sour-dough bread-injera, banana-mooz, meat & vegetabh, sauce-wat, mincemeat and onion-kufto, egg-uncolal.
Please-bakh, thank you-amasagunalhu, yes-ow (very breathy), no-idełem, OK-ishi, hello-tenastele.
How much does that cost?-sintenow wagow? expensive-zerzer, cheap-santim, road-mungat, right-keing, left-graa, car-machina. Which is the road to?-yet-mungat now? Where are you going?-wa'dit tehedalhe?

FOOD
In the countryside and most small Ethiopian towns the only thing there is to eat as a rule is 'wat' (also sometimes called 'zegeni') and 'injera'. 'Wat' is a fiery-hot sauce sometimes containing bits of chicken, beans or lentils and 'injera' is the national foam-rubber bread made with millet flour mixed with yeast and left to go sour for about three days before being cooked on a clay board heated by a log fire. Quite tasty depending on how you take to hot food. It's very cheap. Stay clear of salads as there's a good chance of contracting liver fluke

and DDT is used like rain water in some parts. Local markets are excellent for fruit but peel before eating. In the larger towns there's a variety of different food styles available (Italian, Indian, and Chinese in Addis and Italian in Asmara and Massawa).

ACCOMMODATION
Since there has been so much fighting and destruction of buildings all over the country especially around Asmara and Massawa in Eritrea, Gondar in the west and Harrar and Dire Dawa in the east it is likely that many of the places we recommended in the last edition no longer exist. Add to this the fact that it's almost impossible to visit any place except Addis Ababa on an overnight transit stop so there's little point in putting anything in this section until the country opens up again and travellers start sending back reports.

If you have to stay overnight in Addis, the cheapest hotels are located in the market (Mercado) area of town and up the hill around Menelik II Square. Most of these hotels used to double as brothels though it may be that the Marxist regime has put an end to this. If you want something more salubrious for an overnight stop, try the *Hotel Suisse* which used to cost 10 Birr/double and has friendly management. It's located nearer the centre of town.

TRANSPORT
The same applies to this section. Also it's very difficult to get permission to go anywhere other than Addis Ababa.

Ethiopian Airlines used to offer 50% student reductions for a three-month period every year (usually around March/April). It might be worth checking out whether they still do this especially for the Addis-Nairobi route. We had one report recently which said that if you fly from Djibouti to Nairobi via Addis, Ethiopian Airlines may pay your hotel bill in Addis.

Gabon

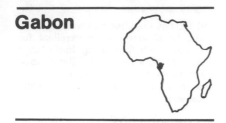

An ex-French colony which achieved independence in 1960, Gabon is one of Africa's richest and fastest developing countries though much of the population live in poverty, relying on subsistence farming. President Bongo, who was converted recently to Islam, is the Head of State and also holds almost all the departmental portfolios.

The economy depends chiefly on timber, oil, manganese and uranium with exports exceeding imports by a substantial margin of approximately 15 billion CFA francs, oil exports representing two fifths of export earnings. France remains overwhelmingly Gabon's main trading partner. Industrial production is mainly a question of processing timber and minerals. This includes the oil refinery at Libreville, 17 sawmills and a uranium enrichment plant (which greatly increases the value of the uranium exported). Manufacturing is confined to small factories making soap, textiles, clothing, paint, food products and furniture. Government policy is to take a minority shareholding in big foreign companies. Gabon has also formed its own national company (PIZO) for the distribution of petroleum products. The state holds 50% of the company's capital with the remaining shares being held by an international consortium of Shell, Elf and Agip.

Of the less than one million population approximately 49% are Catholic with a small 3,000 strong Moslem community. The main tribal group is the Fang, many of whose young men are attracted or forced into the timber industry, staying away from their homes for months or years at a time. About 20% of the population is urbanised. The pygmies, said to be original inhabitants of Gabon, have dwindled to a few thousand living in the remote parts of the forest.

FACTS
Most of the country is high with peaks rising to over 1500 metres. Over three quarters of the country is still covered with impenetrable forest with deep river valleys dividing the country into small units. The climate is tropical with a long dry season from May to September, a short wet season from October to mid-December, another short dry season from mid-December to January and a long wet season from January to May. The average rainfall is about 400 cm per annum and the average temperature is 27°C.

VISAS
Required by all except nationals of

France and Germany (West). Visas cost US$13, three photos and take 14 days to issue but since visa applications have to be referred to Libreville you also have to pay for the telex charges. They are not easy to get.

CURRENCY
The unit of currency is the CFA. Import/export of local currency is allowed up to 200,000 CFA.

Exchange rate:

£1	=	473 CFA
US$1	=	207 CFA
A$1	=	237 CFA

Airport tax for domestic flights is 400 CFA.

LANGUAGES
French is the official language.

ACCOMMODATION & TRANSPORT
We've never heard from any travellers who have been to Gabon and very few tourists go there. Accommodation is expensive in Libreville. Both the climate and the terrain create major obstacles to travel in Gabon and roads are only passable in the dry season. Hitching is incredibly slow and buses, where they exist, are some of the most expensive in Africa.

Gambia

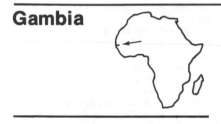

Consisting of only a narrow strip of territory on either side of the River Gambia and surrounded on all sides by Senegal, Gambia is perhaps Africa's most artificial legacy of colonialism. Other than foreign aid, it exists on the 'unofficial re-export' (ie smuggling) of British imports into Senegal. Its only other industry, a groundnut oil refining factory owned by a Lebanese merchant family, has, like most other commercial enterprises, been taken over by the government though strictly on the basis of a gentleman's agreement.

It attained independence from Britain in 1965 and is a member of the Commonwealth. Since independence, British aid has amounted to around £10 million and other aid programmes have been negotiated notably with the People's Republic of China which gave

Gambia an interest-free, long-term loan of £7 million. Other benefits have included a scholarship scheme with the USSR and, because of Gambia's Muslim majority, a Libyan technical and cultural aid programme. Libya has also provided 40% of the capital for a joint project to improve low-cost passenger transport services.

The modernisation of the harbour and river facilities has been high on the list of government priorities for many years with Britain providing a loan for the replacement of the veteran river steamer and the West German government a loan for a new ferry and ferry terminals at Banjul and Barra.

Rapid population expansion and a relatively stagnant economy has encouraged many young Gambians to leave for France and Britain where, without previously arranged scholarships and finance, they eke out a meagre existence under the constant threat of deportation for illegal residence.

FACTS
Gambia is one of Africa's tiniest states. The land is flat with a tropical climate and the rainy season lasts from May to

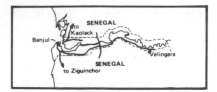

October with intermittent dry spells.

VISAS

Required by all except nationals of the Commonwealth countries and most West European countries (the exceptions being Austria, France, Portugal and Switzerland). Officially, all visitors must have an 'onward ticket'.

Banjul is a good place to apply for visas for neighbouring countries — Senegal, Liberia, Guinea, Guinea-Bissau and Sierra Leone.

Guinea-Bissau visas cost 10 Dalasi, three photos and take a day to issue. Note that the Secretary at the Sierra Leone High Commission is a real bolshie bastard and that unless you grovel and scrape he'll tell you the visa will take up to two weeks.

CURRENCY

The unit of currency is the Dalasi = 100 batut. There are no restrictions on the import/export of local currency.

Exchange rate:

£1	=	3.86 Dalasi
US$1	=	1.68 Dalasi
A$1	=	1.93 Dalasi

The currencies of Algeria, Ghana, Guinea, Mali, Morocco, Nigeria, Sierra Leone and Tunisia are not accepted in Gambia and cannot be exchanged in the banks. Airport taxes for international flights is 5 Dalasi.

LANGUAGE

English, French and several local languages.

ACCOMMODATION

Banjul

The *Government Rest House* behind the Catholic Cathedral costs 5 Dalasi/bed but it is often full. Slightly scruffy but the cheapest in town. *All City Travellers' Lodge*, Dobson Street, costs 10 Dalasi/single. *Uncle Joe's Rest House*, Clarkson Street, costs 15 Dalasi/single. Other budget hotels which have been recommended include the *Brikamaba Hotel*, Buckle Street and the *Teranga Hotel* around the corner from the Brikamaba.

There are possibilities of staying with VSO and Peace Corps volunteers if they have room. Enquire at 9 Mardi Flats, Wellington Street for VSO (in the same building as the British High Commission) and at 31 Leman Street for Peace Corps.

For eats try the *Apollo Hotel*. English-style breakfasts for 2 Dalasi. The *Faraja Club*, mainly for expatriates, has no entrance fee and sells good cheap beers. To get there you have to take a taxi to Bakau (about eight miles) then change to a Serracunda taxi and get off half way or walk about one and a half miles from Bakau — take the left-hand turn at the T-junction there.

There's a good map of Banjul and the rest of the country for 4 Dalasi from the tourist kiosk in front of the Craft Market. If you're arriving at Banjul airport don't take a taxi direct to Banjul unless you have money to burn. Walk to the main road and then take a taxi to Serracunda. From there change to a taxi for Banjul.

TRANSPORT

You can enter Gambia either by the Trans-Gambia Highway which goes across the middle of Gambia and connects Kaolack with Ziguinchor or by the direct road from Kaolack to Banjul. If you take the latter you end up at Barra on the opposite side of the River Gambia to Banjul and have to take the car

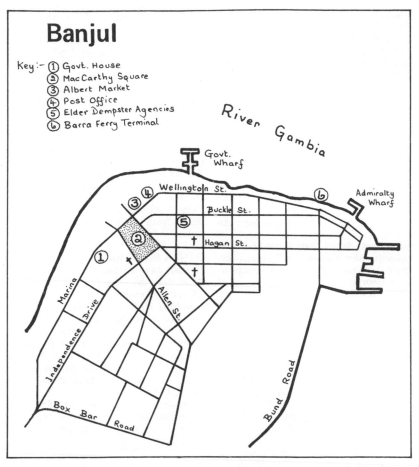

Banjul

Key :-
1. Govt. House
2. MacCarthy Square
3. Albert Market
4. Post Office
5. Elder Dempster Agencies
6. Barra Ferry Terminal

River Gambia

Govt. Wharf

Wellington St.

Buckle St.

Hagan St.

Admiralty Wharf

Marina

Independence Drive

Allen St.

Box Bar Road

Bund Road

ferry across to Banjul (50 batut).

Road Transport

Banjul-Basse Santa Su by taxi costs 8 Dalasi and takes seven hours. If you are heading for Ziguinchor there are three possibilities —

(a) **Banjul-Brikama**; taxi costs 75 batut. Brikama-Ziguinchor; taxis leave every morning early and take a direct but very rough road. They cost 900 CFA.

(b) **Banjul-Soma** (at the intersection of the Banjul-Basse road with the Trans-Gambia Highway); taxi costs 4 Dalasi along a sealed road. From Soma to Ziguinchor by taxi costs 5 Dalasi.

(c) **Banjul-Serracunda**; taxi costs 50 batut. From Serracunda to Ziguinchor by truck along a rough road costs 4 Dalasi or 900 CFA.

If Heading for Dakar — First take the ferry across the River Gambia to Barra (50 batut) then a truck from there to

Kaolack for 500 CFA (taxis also available). From Kaolack to Dakar by minibus costs 500 CFA or by taxi 600 CFA. There's also the possibility of direct taxis from Barra to Dakar for 1200 CFA.

If you're heading for Tambacounda there are taxis from Basse Santa Su to Velingara for 6 Dalasi and from there to Tambacounda for 700 CFA. The journey from Basse to Velingara takes two hours.

Boats

Ferry: Banjul-Barra Point Departs once every two hours in either direction and takes 20 minutes. The last ferry departs about 5.30 pm. Costs 50 batut per passenger.

River boat: Banjul-Basse Santa Su Route is Banjul-Albreda-Kerewan-Tendaba-Balingho-Yellitenda-Sankwia-Kaur-Kuntaur-Sapu-Georgetown-Bansang-Basse. Departs Banjul every Tuesday at 6 pm and arrives at Basse on Wednesday at 9 pm but can be up to three hours late depending on cargo traffic.

Fares: two-berth cabin 85 Dalasi, four berth cabin 75 Dalasi or deck class 13 Dalasi. The boat is called the *Lady Chilel Jawara* and tickets can be bought from the Gambia Ports Authority, Wellington Street, Banjul. Cheap food available on board and the crew are friendly.

Other boats If you're looking for a boat to places like Dakar (Senegal) or Freetown (Sierra Leone) you might well be in for a long wait but if you want to do this check out with Elder Dempster and GPMB, Wellington Street (next to Customs & Excise building). Deck Class to Freetown costs 52 Dalasi. For boats to further afield you may be taken at the captain's discretion for £5-10 per day.

Flights 40% student discounts are available with British Caledonian and Nigerian Air to both Freetown (Sierra Leone) and Accra (Ghana). Concession forms are available from the Education Offices (without proof of student status). Mali Air also does similar deals. With the student reduction the flight from Banjul to Freetown costs approximately 80 Dalasi (without costs 152 Dalasi). The flight from Banjul to Accra costs 60 Dalasi.

OTHER INFORMATION

If you want to visit Juffore of *Roots* fame, take the ferry to Barra from Banjul in the morning and then a van to Juffore for 1.50 Dalasi. To get back to Banjul, wait at nearby Port Albreda for the *Lady Chilel* to come down the river about 3 pm on Fridays. There have been numerous reports about people being screwed for 30 Dalasi to get back from Juffore to Banjul (it's become a heavily-subscribed tourist spot).

Beware of 'friendly people' who offer you joints of grass then turn you in to the police. They can sometimes be foreigners.

Ghana

The first recognisable signs of civilization among the Negro tribes of Guinea — the geographical area south of the Sahara stretching from present day Guinea to Nigeria — took place during the 13th century. They were strongly influenced by the Sahelian trading kingdoms such as those of ancient Ghana (present day Senegal and western Mali), Songhai,

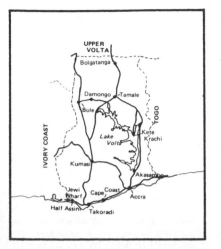

Kanem-Bornu and Hausa from which they took their patterns of social and political organisation. The earliest known states of Bono and Banda were located in the orchard bush of the northern Gold Coast from where they gradually swept south following the line of the Volta River to the coastal grasslands. The rain forests were not penetrated until the 15th century.

The Ashanti, who were to rule Ghana for two centuries until conquered by the British, arose in the late 17th century and quickly took over the northern states of Bono, Banda, Gonja and Dagomba after which they turned south to secure the trade routes with the Europeans on the coast. For centuries the focus of trade in West Africa had been away from the coast inland towards the kingdoms which held sway along the Niger River and the edge of the Sahara Desert which is why the cities of Gao, Timbuktu and Djenne were so rich and powerful until the 17th century. The thing which was to cause their decline and move the focus of wealth and power southwards to Guinea was the slave trade to the Americas. Though slaves had been traded along the Sa-

haran routes previously the numbers involved were small in comparison to the vast scale on which the European nations carried it out. Nevertheless, the European share in the political power of the Guinean states was very limited until the 19th century even though the Portuguese had built their first forts along the West African coast in the late 1400's. Islam, too, continued to be the major religious force throughout this period and there was very little Christian missionary work until recently though the Portuguese tried unsuccessfully for a hundred years to implant their own hell-and-damnation variety as they did more successfully in their Latin American colony. Even the forts which the Europeans built along the coast were there on a rental basis from the local rulers and there were times when even these were over-run and handed back only when a substantial ransom was forthcoming.

The Ashanti were a highly organised nation with a capital, Kumasi, whose planning and services were the equal of most European cities at the time. The ruler, who was known as the Asantehene, employed literate Muslim secretaries from the north to look after the trade with the Saharan kingdoms and others to oversee distant provinces and help draw up treaties and maintain records. Later on they began to employ Christian Europeans as advisors. When the British invaded in the 1870's, the Asantehene engaged a German to raise and train an army composed of Hausa troops. Other adventurers who became involved included a Frenchman who became governor of a province and a Scots American who supplied economic advice.

As the slave trade was gradually suppressed in the 19th century and thus became unprofitable, the Danish and Dutch forts on the Gold Coast were handed over to the British who were becoming more and more involved in the interior. A war was fought with the Ashanti in 1824 though it was confined to the coastal area and it was not until the middle of the 1870's that Kumasi was taken and the Gold Coast declared a colony. Following this plantations were established and a railway and deepwater port built.

It was the experience of WW II, during ing which African soldiers fought alongside British soldiers on terms of equality which helped to generate a renascent nationality among Ghanaians together with the frustrations of those who had acquired new skills and outlooks. Fired by the resurgence of Negro consciousness in America and the West Indies, expressed by men like DuBois and Marcus Garvey, the early nationalist leaders became converts to the intellectual socialism current among university students at the time and, on returning to Ghana, helped focus pressure on the colonial authorities. The man who was most successful in galvanising African opinion and aspirations and who was instrumental in making Ghana the first African country to achieve independence was Dr Kwame Nkrumah.

After independence was granted in 1957, Nkrumah became famous for his intense commitment to African liberation and although he provided inspiration for many nationalist movements all over the continent his regime's flamboyant public spendng on prestige projects, which were often unrelated and inappropriate to the country's needs, provoked increasing disillusion and he was overthrown in 1966 by the army. In 1969 they handed over to a more conservative civilian government headed by Dr Busia but his administration was crippled from the start by the empty treasury and the debts which Nkrumah had left behind so in 1972 the army again intervened. Nevertheless, corruption and mismanagement continued to plague any progress toward economic stability and continued civilian exclusion from political power generated widespread resentment. Changes of regime came to be regarded with cynical detachment by the Ghanaian intelligentsia who were fond of repeating the slogan, 'The driver is different but the lorry is the same.'

Colonel Achaempong, the leader of the 1972 coup, was overthrown in the late '70s and, after a court martial on charges of corruption, executed. The aftermath of his trial saw many of his supporters removed from power and others placed on trial. All the same, these changes made no inroads on civilian confidence or support until the nation was inflamed by the passionate speech of a junior army officer who had attempted to engineer a coup and been condemned to death by a court martial. Public support for his ideas rose quickly to a crescendo and forced his release and the resignation of the then military government. Progress of a sort is now being made towards a sharing of power between civilians and the military though it remains to be seen how successful this will be. Certainly there seems to be an atmosphere of reckless and indiscriminate fraud in almost every kind of transaction though much of this may be simply due to the very high inflation rate which makes the Cedi one of the weakest currencies in Africa. Just about the only productive members of the community are the cocoa labourers and the peasants.

FACTS

The geography of the country features a sandy foreshore studded with palms reaching back to wooded hills and the close Ashanti forest of silk-cottons and hardwoods. Northwards again the forest thins until it becomes pleasant orchard country. Across the northern end of Lake Volta — an artificial lake created by a dam built across the River Volta — the country becomes harsh and barren until further north along the Ghana/

Upper Volta border open grasslands are reached. There are a range of mountains in the east which form part of the Togo range with peaks of 1000 metres or so. Humidity is high except in the north. Rainy seasons are April to July and September to October. The Harmatten, a dry and dusty north-east wind, blows in January and February.

VISAS

Required by all. Nationals of Commonwealth countries require entry permits before being allowed in though some travellers have managed to cross the border without a permit. Don't count on this however, as it depends largely on the customs officer who deals with you. If you do manage to get across without a permit, your passport will be stamped for a 14-day stay renewable at the Immigration Department in the Ministry of the Interior, Accra.

Usually before a visa or entry permit is issued you are required to buy with hard currency 'Cedi Vouchers' on the basis of 70 Cedis for the first day of your stay and 20 Cedis for each additional day. The Ghanaian embassy where they don't enforce this is the one in Ouagadougou, Upper Volta. At the embassies in Abidjan, Ivory Coast, and Lome, Togo, you have to buy vouchers. If you're extending your Ghanaian visa/Entry Permit try to do it at Cape Coast where they're not too heavy on Cedi Vouchers. Avoid Accra and Takoradi.

Nigerian Visas/Entry Permits In Accra these cost 2.55 Cedi, are valid for three months and allow for a 14-day stay. They take *at least* one week to issue unless you are prepared to pay a 20 Cedi bribe. The High Commission is just off Liberation Road.

Mali Visas In Accra these cost US$13 or 3000 CFA. The embassy won't take Cedis in payment for visa fees.

Zaire Visas The embassy will only take visa applications on Monday and Tuesday mornings. Passports are handed back on Thursdays.

Upper Volta Visas In Accra these cost 11.50 Cedi for a multiple entry 90-day visa. The visas are valid indefinitely.

CURRENCY

The unit of currency is the Cedi=100 pesawas. Import/export of local currency is prohibited.

Exchange rate: (official)

£1	=	6.60 Cedi
US$1	=	2.85 Cedi
A$1	=	3.30 Cedi

There is a thriving currency blackmarket whose exchange rates are much higher than those in the banks. The best rates are obtainable outside the country. Depending on where and with whom you change you could get:

£1	=	19-20 Cedi
US$1	=	10 Cedi
1000 CFA	=	43-48 Cedi.

In Accra try outside the GPO or, better still, with traders from Niger or Upper Volta or with Lebanese businessmen. Avoid changing on the High Street as it is too well known and a tourist trap. Note that if changing in Tamale, CFAs are preferred to US dollars but in Kumasi US dollars are preferred to CFAs. If you're coming from Togo, change your money in Lome which is the currency blackmarket centre of West Africa. In Lagos, Nigeria, try around the Bristol Hotel.

If you had to buy Cedi Vouchers to get your visa/entry permit these can be exchanged at the official rate in the banks. You can change unused Cedis back into hard currency through local banks or at the Bank of Ghana so long as your currency declaration form (known as Form T5) shows that you acquired them officially. The trouble is that overland travellers are rarely given one of these forms at the border and they're generally restricted to entry by air. If you think you'll have officially obtained Cedi left over at the end of your intended stay in Chana, ask for one of these forms at the border.

The International Trade Fair on Labadi Road, Accra, is like a duty free shop but you can't use Cedis to buy things. If you use travellers cheques here you can get change in any other hard currency ($, £, CFA). Useful if you need quick cash.

Note that market 'mammas' still talk in terms of pre-decimal English coinage (£ s d) so one shilling = 10c, sixpence = 5 c and threepence = 2½c.

Airport tax on domestic flights is 1 Cedi, international flights it's 5 Cedis.

LANGUAGES
English and many local languages.

MAIL
The Poste Restante in Accra has a good reputation. Also postage rates in Ghana are very cheap and it's one of the best places to send back parcels from.

ACCOMMODATION
Accra
Mary's House, 49 Farrar Avenue, opposite the Hotel President. A favourite haunt of travellers and very friendly. Rooms cost from 8 to 12 Cedi and good food is available. The *YMCA* and *YWCA* both on Castle Road, cost 5 Cedi/night without breakfast. Weekly rates are available and work out cheaper than paying by the day but as they're used by Ghanaian students it may be difficult to find a room during term time. They allow camping in the grounds for 1 Cedi/night including use of showers. The *Methodist Rest House*, Barnes Road across from Mobil House, has pleasant rooms for 5 Cedi/night. The *Ghana*

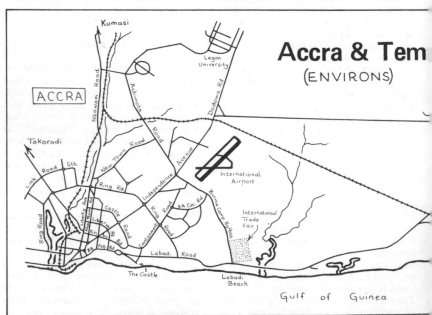

Labour College, 7th Avenue across from the Ridge Hospital, costs 5 Cedi/night but there are no meals available and you should keep an eye on your baggage. Nearby on the same road is the *Ghana National Association of Teachers Hostel* which sometimes has beds for 5 Cedi/night but it's not very clean.

Other fairly cheap hotels which have been recommended include the *California Hotel* and the *Prince Royal Hotel* which are adjacent to each other on Kojo Thompson Road.

Fawzy's Restaurant, at the intersection of Kojo Thompson and Kinbu Roads opposite the main lorry park, is the favourite Peace Corps hang-out. Run by a Lebanese proprietor who serves more or less standard western food. Sandwiches and meals for between 2 and 6 Cedi. *Avenue Hotel*, Farrar Avenue, serves pints of cold beer. Open to non-residents. For sweets try *Dan's Milk Bar* on Liberty Avenue near the Ring Road which serves expensive milk shakes and ice cream. On the opposite side of the road to Dan's is the *Glyco Confectionery Co* which has sweet, gooey cakes to either eat there or take away. Good hot bread from the bakery at the intersection of South Liberia Road and Liberty Avenue (South Liberia Road is a continuation of Liberia Road towards Liberty Avenue). If you want a meal on Sunday when everywhere else is closed try the *Crown Prince Hotel* on Kojo Thompson Road opposite Castle Road where you can get a meal for around 6 Cedi. The *Palm Court Chinese Restaurant* has also been recommended — meals for around 6 Cedi including a beer. The Labadi Free Beach has a cafe called *Tourist Rendezvous* which sells cheap sandwiches and hamburgers. It's also a good place to go swimming.

Tourist Office: Kojo Thompson Road, Free maps of Accra and plenty of other information.

American Express: Scantravel Ltd, High Street, PO Box 1705, Accra (tel 63134/64204).

Both the British and American Embassies have movie nights. Free at the former, small charge at the latter. Also the American Ambassador's residence on Independence Avenue has a swimming pool which is open for use by any American from 10 am to 5 pm, Monday to Saturday. It's free and has dressing rooms, showers and toilets. The British Council on Liberia Road has an air-conditioned library and reading room with current British newspapers and magazines.

The University of Accra at Legon, 13 km from Accra, is a nice peaceful place where you can meet academic Ghanaians if your interests lie in that direction. The university bookshop has an excellent selection of reasonably priced books and there's a canteen which

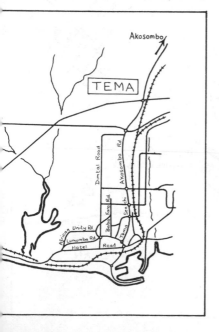

Akosombo

TEMA

Dmtal Road

Akosombo Rd

Babatfang Rd

Tema Stn

African Unity Rd

Lumumba Rd

Hotel

Road

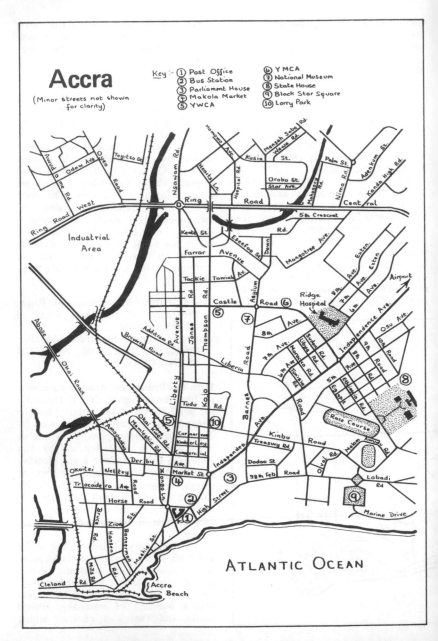

Accra

(Minor streets not shown for clarity)

Key :-
① Post Office
② Bus Station
③ Parliament House
④ Makola Market
⑤ YWCA
⑥ YMCA
⑦ National Museum
⑧ State House
⑨ Black Star Square
⑩ Lorry Park

ATLANTIC OCEAN

serves very good, cheap food — rice, plantain and stew for 1.20 Cedi.

Hitch-hiking around Accra is OK and enables you to meet Ghanaians who are often very friendly and hospitable.

Cape Coast

Travellers' Inn near Mfantsipim School costs 6 Cedi/double. The University of Cape Coast, a few km out of town on the Takoradi road, has accommodation for 3 Cedi/night during vacations. Good bookstore and cafe. If no luck at the above, try St Augustine's Secondary School though accommodation is only likely during vacations.

If you want to stay in any of the old colonial forts along the coast — Dixcove, Elmina and Pampam — all of which have now been converted into *Rest Houses*, you have to make reservations at the West African Musuem in Cape Coast, Monday through Friday. Dixcove is often full but Elmina has fantastic facilities for 5 Cedi per person per night. There are no meals available but the caretaker will cook up something for you if you buy food. Good shrimps, lobster and tuna fish can be got from the fishermen at Dixcove. Also just around the headland from Dixcove at Busua is a beautiful beach where you can sleep under the coco palms or rent rooms in the village. There are a few tourists at weekends. The old forts are very popular with travellers.

Kete Krachi

This is stop-off point on the Lake Volta steamer route. A *Rest House* bungalow is available for 3 Cedi per night. Ask directions from the police.

Kumasi

This is the old Ashanti capital and a major cultural centre. *Abuanaba Rest House*, Accra Rd, costs 10 Cedi/double. *Ayigya Rest House*, also on Accra Rd near the University Hotel, costs 6 Cedi per night. *Hotel Montana* costs 20 Cedi

a double. *Catering Rest House* has accommodation for 27 Cedi/double.

You might also like to try the University of Science and Technology where you might strike up a friendship with one of the students and be offered accommodation. There's also a swimming pool for 1 Cedi which is a Peace Corps hangout. The *YMCA* costs 5 Cedi a night without breakfast though, like the one in Accra, it's often full of students.

For food try *Afua's Cold Store and Patisserie* across from the railway tracks near the Central Market. Serves 'American' food and is a good place to sit and relax. Otherwise try the *Ashante Chicken Bar*, the *Kingsway Hotel* and local chop houses.

The Ashanti Museum is well worth a visit, there's a small entrance charge.

Navrongo

A small town near the Upper Volta border. The Catholic Mission here offers accommodation for 4 Cedi/night.

Tamale

The *Workers' College* has accommodation during holidays for 4 Cedi/person. The *Catering Rest House* costs 24 Cedi a double. Other possibilities include the Catholic Mission and the Government *Rest House*.

The Bole National Park is worth a visit. From Tamale get a bus or truck to Damongo. When you get there look for one of the park Land-Rovers and ask if they'll give you a lift there. The *Bole Hotel* inside the park is quite cheap even for budget travellers. You can also stay at *Lovi Camp* but you'll need a sleeping bag and your own food as there are no facilities on the site.

Ghana is a friendly place and you may well be offered hospitality by local people, especially out in the countryside. If you really get stuck, ask the police who will doubtless put you up for the night. The Tourist Office in Accra has a list of non-catering Rest Houses which are cheap places to stay whereas the Catering Rest Houses are expensive.

TRANSPORT

Roads are generally good and hitching can be as fast as taking the bus though you'll have to pay for most lifts. Between the major towns there is a regular and expensive bus service which runs on schedule with 'mammy wagons' in the more remote areas. Note that in common with several other West African countries there is a charge for luggage on trucks and buses. Sometimes this can be quite high though it is negotiable up to a point. If there are three or four of you it's often cheaper to hire a taxi between the main towns than to go by bus.

Some examples of fares are — Accra-Takoradi by bus for 7 Cedi, Takoradi-Half Assini (Ghana/Ivory Coast border) by bus for 10 Cedi. Note that crossing the border from Ghana to Ivory Coast can take *hours* (one traveller reported nine hours!) but the ferry has to wait until all passengers have gone through border formalities. A direct bus from Accra to Abidjan will cost around US$14. Accra-Lome (Togo) costs 6 Cedi in the government bus or 10 Cedi by mini-bus. These fares do not include baggage charges.

Trains These cost about a Cedi per 100 km but they're very slow, even by West African standards. There are regular services between Accra, Kumasi and Takoradi.

Boats on Lake Volta The *Akasombo Queen* operates between Akasombo (at the southern end of the lake), Kete Krachi (about half-way up the lake) and Yapei (near Tamale at the northern end of the lake). The schedule is as follows:

(a) Departs Akasombo Monday at 8 am, arrives Kete Krachi same day at 8 pm. Returns to Akasombo overnight, arriving mid-Tuesday morning.

(b) Departs Akasombo Tuesday at 12 noon, arrives Yapei on Wednesday at 6 pm. Departs Yapei Thursday at 8 am and arrives Akasombo on Friday afternoon. From Yapei there is a connecting bus to Tamale and Damango.

In addition to the *Akasombo Queen* there is the *Yapei Queen* which is a cargo boat. It leaves Yapei on Tuesdays and goes direct to Akasombo. Much cheaper than the *Akasombo Queen* though there are, of course, no facilities.

OTHER INFORMATION

There are severe food shortages in Ghana, especially in the north between Tamale and Gambaga where it occasionally reaches famine proportions. As a result there's a lot of seasonal hoarding which pushes up prices. Even the cheapest 'meal' available — cocoa and a piece of bread — now costs at least 1 Cedi.

Kumasi market is an experience not to be missed. You need several days to see the market properly — it's vast. Goods are cheaper here than in Accra but somewhat more expensive than in Upper Volta.

Guinea

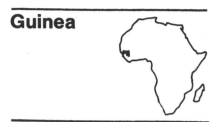

Guinea remains one of Africa's most reclusive and isolated states despite moves by President Sekou Toure to re-establish relations with western countries. Toure has never been a man to surrender political objectives for economic considerations. In 1958 he stood on the same platform as President de Gaulle who was touring French colonies trying to sell his idea of a French Commonwealth as an alternative to total independence. Toure replied that 'we prefer poverty in liberty to riches in slavery'. The result was immediate independence but the penalty was stiff. French capital ceased to flow to Guinea and the new republic's exports were subjected to the same tariffs as those of other foreign countries. All French public servants, technicians and army units were withdrawn within three months.

Since then there have been recurrent allegations of plots to overthrow the government, show trials, imprisonments, executions of dissidents and suspects as well as Guinea's virtual isolation from the rest of the world. There are 250,000 Guineans living in exile abroad. Toure has never been short of would-be counter-revolutionaries nor have his methods of dealing with them altered very much. At various times in the past few years he has accused many African countries and countries in the rest of the world (east and west) of plotting to overthrow him. the two incidents which have had the most effect on his xenophobia were the overthrow of Nkrumah in Ghana in 1966 and the Portuguese backed invasion of Guinea in 1970. A series of executions followed, the 100-man West German technical mission was expelled and Bonn accused of massing a 500-man force for another invasion. All this was part of a prolonged witch-hunt which has never really ended.

FACTS

The main physical characteristics of Guinea are its meandering rivers and wide estuaries where it's difficult to distinguish mud, mangrove and water from solid land. Rich vegetation, tropical climate and high rainfall in the summer months between June and October. Hot with very high humidity.

VISAS

Required by all. White nationals of South Africa are not admitted. Journalists of any nationality are prohibited except on invitation of the government. If you want to go there you have to have a very good reason. Visas are not issued for 'tourism'. Officially, visitors from Belgium, France, Irish Republic, Luxembourg, Netherlands, Norway, Spain, Switzerland and the UK must apply for visas through the Paris Embassy (24 rue Emile-Meurnier). Those from Denmark, Italy and Sweden must apply through the Rome Embassy (via Luigi Luciani 41). Other nationals must apply through the embassies in New York, Tokyo or Washington. As authorisation must be

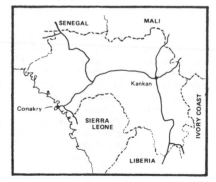

137

obtained from the Ministry of Foreign Affairs, Conakry, five to six weeks should be allowed for visa applications. In practice, the Guinean authorities are easing up a little so if you'd like to visit the country it's suggested that you apply at one of the following African embassies: Accra, Banjul, Freetown, Lagos or Monrovia. Recent reports from travellers suggest that it's not that difficult to get a visa especially in Banjul for travel between October and January.

CURRENCY
The unit of currency is the Sily = 100 Couris. Import/export of local currency is prohibited.

Exchange rate:

£1	=	42.12 Sily
US$1	=	18.31 Sily
A$1	=	21.06 Sily

Airport tax on domestic flights is 100 Sily, international flights (Africa) 150 Sily, other international destinations 200 Sily.

LANGUAGES
French, English and Arabic.

ACCOMMODATION & TRANSPORT
No details available. All that we know is that with visa issue easing up there is a twice-weekly bus service between Conakry and Freetown (Sierra Leone).

Guinea – Bissau & Cape Verde

Guinea-Bissau and the Cape Verde Islands are in the process of rebuilding their countries after a long and bitter liberation struggle against Portuguese colonialism. Almost everything was destroyed during the war and the countries are desperately poor after centuries of colonial exploitation. Roads and bridges will have to be repaired and replaced, international communications restored, agricultural output boosted (food production is barely half of what is required to feed the population) and port facilities modernised. At present the port of Bissau is only capable of handling one ship at a time.

Greatest priority is being given to agriculture and people are being aided to return to their villages and fields to res-

ume cultivation. 40,000 former refugees are now back in their villages and helping with this programme while seed and other aid has been provided by a number of African countries. In addition a great deal of effort is being put into health and education.

Cape Verde, 11 islands scattered in the Atlantic Ocean 500 km off the Senegalese coast, achieved independence a little later though for a time, despite the revolution in Portugal, the Lisbon government continued to talk of Cape Verde as 'more Portuguese than African' Cape Verde's history is a tragic story. In the past 200 years more of its

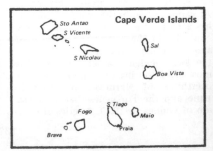

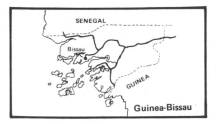

people have emigrated, perished in the Portuguese plantations of Sao Tome and Angola as contract labourers or died of starvation and dysentry at home than today make up the islands' population of about 280,000. Those who have managed to survive the past seven years' drought are desperately poor.

Agriculture is the main employer yet it only provides 10% of the GNP and on most of the islands the long drought has ended almost all plant life. Two of the islands — Santiago and Sal — are like stony deserts but the windward islands are more fertile.

VISAS
Officially visas can only be obtained from either the embassy in Lisbon or direct from the Commission of National Security in Bissau. At least three weeks should be allowed for application. In practice visas can be issued on the day of application in Banjul (Gambia) for 10 Dalasi and three photos. If you desperately want to go there and want to arrange your visa beforehand, apply to PAIGC, Hotel Altis, Lisbon, Portugal.

CURRENCY
Guinea-Bissau: the unit of currency is the Peso da Guine-Bissau = 100 centavos. Import/export of local currency is prohibited.

Exchange rate:

£1	=	76 Pesos
US$1	=	33 Pesos
A$1	=	38 Pesos

Cape Verde: the unit of currency is the Cape Verde Escudo = 100 centavos. There is no restriction on the import of local currency but export is limited to 6000 Escudos.

Exchange rate:

£1	=	81 Escudos
US$1	=	36 Escudos
A$1	=	41 Escudos

Airport taxes in Guinea-Bissau for domestic flights 85 Pesos, for international flights to West African countries 210 Pesos, for other international destinations 350 Pesos. There are no airport taxes in Cape Verde Islands.

LANGUAGES
Portuguese and some French and English.

ACCOMMODATION & TRANSPORT
No details.

Ivory Coast

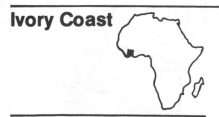

The Ivory Coast is a classic example of the worst excesses of neo-colonialism. It was created and developed in the image of its President, Felix Houphouet-Boigny. After his entry into politics in 1944 he worked with leaders of neighbouring countries and with the French Communist Party in the radical African Democratic Union. Soon, however, his liking for things French led him to declare his support for co-operation with France in all fields, for 'evolution' as opposed to 'revolution' and the rejection of class struggle on the grounds that classes did not exist in the Ivory Coast. He also went in for unrestricted reliance on foreign and local private enterprise.

The result was rapid development of Abidjan, the capital, with luxurious suburbs, large central slums and an urban freeway system dividing the two. If indeed he was correct in saying that classes did not exist, they certainly do now, even if the top classes consist of both black and white elements. National sovereignty it seems is best consolidated in Paris where the president, his cabinet and the directors of the companies which plunder the Ivory Coast for lumber, oil palms and rubber are to be found. Franz Fanon accurately captioned Houphouet-Boigny as 'an enemy of national independence who has never ceased in his efforts to convince the African people that the position of the native was the one most worthy of emulation — a straw man and fellow traveller of French colonialism'.

Not content with this sell out, Houphouet-Boigny's principal role in modern times is that of advocate of detente and trade with South Africa. Any other attitude, he maintains, could lead to war and the interference of foreign powers in internal African affairs. This opinion is hard to take seriously when the outflow of private funds from the Ivory Coast is approximately double that which flows in as foreign aid and investment.

FACTS
The geography of the country is characterised by coastal lagoons, large coffee and cocoa plantations with an equatorial climate in the south and a tropical to sub-tropical climate in the north. The wet season is between May and July (when it's at its heaviest) and between October and November (when it is lightest). Humidity is high in the coastal regions.

If you'd like to know more about the politics and economics of the Ivory Coast, there is a good section in the book *Neo-colonialism in West Africa* by Samir Amin (Penguin Books).

VISAS
Required by all except nationals of Denmark, Finland, France, West Germany, Italy, Norway, Sweden and the UK.

If you are entering overland, crossing the border can take a whole morning or afternoon as the commissioner has to sign your passport and he's only in attendance for one hour in the morning and one in the afternoon. If you are driving your own transport ask for 'Vignette' at the border post. Police inside the country may demand to see it.

Mali Visas In Abidjan these cost 2500 CFA, two photos and are issued the same day.

Liberian Visas These cost 1200 CFA, two photos and take 24 hours to issue.

Ghanaian Visas/Entry Permits These cost 1000 CFA and can take up to five days to come through. The people who work in the embassy there are a miserable pack of bastards according to letters we've received.

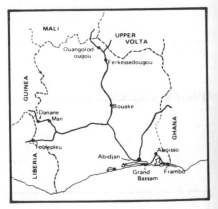

CURRENCY
The unit of currency is the CFA. There is no restriction on the import of local currency. Export is limited to 10,000 CFA.

Exchange rate:

£1	=	473 CFA
US$1	=	207 CFA
A$1	=	237 CFA

Ivory Coast CFAs are accepted as legal tender in Mali. The SIC bank in Abidjan (on the main street) will cash. UK bank cheques for very little, if any, commission. A useful source of instant money if you run short and have your cheque book with you.

LANGUAGE
French, very little English is spoken.

ACCOMMODATION
Abidjan
One of the most expensive cities in the world — the American Embassy rates it close to Tokyo! Though its setting is undoubtedly beautiful, it's being developed into an anonymous consumer town for tourists, with sophisticated night clubs and flash cinemas. Many of the villages in the interior have suffered a similar fate though the area around Man is relatively unspoilt. The city is divided into roughly five parts — the Plateau (the modern French quarter), Treichville (the African quarter with plenty of colourful night life, cheap hotels and cafes), Cocody (a residential suburb), Adjame (another African quarter) and Marcory (a residential suburb). The cheapest places to stay are located in Treichville and cost, on average, 2000 CFA including own shower.

The *Catholic Mission*, rue 25 and Ave 14-15 takes men only, and has the cheapest dormitory accommodation in town. You pay 2000 CFA on arrival and for every night you stay 250 CFA is de-

ducted. What remains is refunded to you when you leave — they're honest but their maths are poor so it's best to work out how much they owe you. There's usually a 15-day maximum stay if there's pressure for space. Cheap rolls and coffee available in the market nearby.

For women the cheapest places are the *Eglise St Terese* in Marcory for 250 CFA; the *Foyer de Jeunes Filles*, Ave Bachalme for 2000 CFA and the *Mission Biblique* in Cocody. To get to the latter, take the Bingerville Road and turn right before the Ecole Gendarmerie. They only have rooms during vacations but at other times you can camp in the grounds free.

Maison Protestante Etudiante, behind the Catholic Hospital in Cocody, sometimes has space during vacations for 300 CFA but there are no cheap cafes nearby.

Hotel Haddad, Ave de la Reine Pokou, is often used by travellers but is dirty. It costs 2000 CFA/double, and is in Treichville.

Hotel Palmyre, Ave de la Reine Pokou is very near to the Haddad. Costs 2000 CFA and is better value than the Haddad, also in Treichville.

Hotel Fraternite, is near the cinema in Treichville and costs 600 CFA/double. The hotel doubles as a brothel and accommodation is basic.

Hotel de la Paix, also in Treichville, costs 2000 CFA/double.

Hotel Silva, near the cemetery in Adjame, costs 1500 CFA/double for clean and airy rooms.

Hotel du Nord, in quartier 220, costs 3500 CFA/double minimum.

Relais d'Adjame, next to the lorry park, costs 1500 CFA and is ideal for those who want to study open sewers, bus horns and the nocturnal habits of cockroaches.

Hotel Passer-Voir, near the Hotel Flamboyant in quartier Braccodibar, Ad-

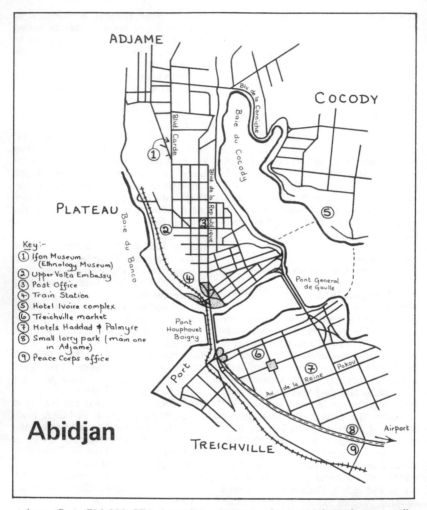

Key:-
1. Ifan Museum (Ethnology Museum)
2. Upper Volta Embassy
3. Post Office
4. Train Station
5. Hotel Ivoire complex
6. Treichville market
7. Hotels Haddad & Palmyre
8. Small lorry park (main one in Adjame)
9. Peace Corps office

jame. Costs 700-900 CFA depending on whether you want your own shower.

Hotel Continental, near the railway station on Dabour Rd, Plateau, costs 3000 CFA/double.

Cheap cafes are few and far between and if you're on a tight budget you'll have to rely on snacks and street stalls. The US embassy has a snack bar with coffees for 40 CFA. Street stalls in the Adjame lorry park do 'riz gras' for 75 CFA. The street stalls in the vegetable market near the BICIC building in Plateau offer similar snacks. 'Plat de Jour' cafe near the Mali Embassy has good sandwiches — a beer and sausage sandwich will cost you 175 CFA. A good cafe in the Plateau area is *Cafe Central*, rue Franchal d'Esperey.

The Tourist Office has plenty of glossy information in glorious technicolour plus a map of the city. American Express is at Socopao-Cote d'Ivoire, 14 Boulevard de la Republique, Boite Postale 1297, Abidjan (tel 32 02 11).

The Ifon Museum (Ethnological Museum) in Adjame is well worth a visit. It is situated about 200 metres from the Commissariat de Police Centrale and Bibliotheque. Buses to Adjame pass the museum and there's a stop called 'Musee Ifon' so you're unlikely to miss it but few people in the centre of town (Plateau) know how to get there.

The bus from the airport to Plateau costs 80 CFA. Taxis in Abidjan have two tariff rates, one from 6 am to 12 midnight and another from midnight to 6 am. The latter costs twice the former.

Bouake
Ram Koko Hotel costs 1000 CFA per room. *Hotel Bakary*, close to the railway station and lorry park, costs 1000 CFA double.

Danane
Le Campement has accommodation for 1000 CFA/double. The *Mission Catholique* sometimes has rooms but don't count on it.

Grand Bassam
43 km from Abidjan, this is where the nearest beaches to Abidjan are situated. They are virtually deserted and you could sleep on the beach. A taxi from Abidjan would cost you much less than paying for overnight accommodation there. If you want somewhere to stay off the beach try *Chez Antoinette* which costs 1500 CFA.

Katiola
Hotel Makawa costs 1500 CFA.

Korhogo
Hotel Gon costs 1500 CFA but has no water. *Hotel Anorme* costs 1500 CFA, it is situated near the hill. *Hotel Syndicat* costs 2500 CFA. *Hotel Dakrou* costs 2500 CFA and is very pleasant. Avoid the *Hotel Normandie* as it has a very bad reputation.

The artisans market here is very interesting and well worth spending time to see.

Man
The *Mission Catholique Guest House* has plenty of rooms for 500 CFA. The *Catholic College* (Seminaire) sometimes has space for 200 CFA. Both these places, however, require a 400 CFA taxi ride. *Hotel Mont Dent* has rooms at 700, 1000 and 1500 CFA depending on what you are looking for.

Tiebissou
Hotel de Providence has rooms for 1000 CFA/double but there are no fans.

Toulepleu
There is a *Government Rest House* at this Liberian/Ivory Coast border town, where you can stay free but you first have to collect the key from the Sous-Prefecture.

TRANSPORT
Hitching is OK on the main routes, which are in good shape, but not really worth it along minor routes. In Abidjan, hitching is simplicity itself — just ask drivers at traffic lights. On the main routes there are daily scheduled buses and taxis. The former leave when full. Note that on public transport you will have to pay for any piece of luggage larger than a weekend bag. For the average back-pack this will amount to about 10% of the fare.

Some examples of road transport costs are — Abidjan-Man; costs 2750 CFA by regular bus and 3000 CFA by de-luxe bus. Both buses leave from the Gare Routiere in Adjame in the early morning. Abidjan-Bouake; costs 2200 CFA by Peugeot taxi.

Route to Liberia You can either go via Danane or Toulepleu. The latter crossing is very quiet and you'll have to hire a taxi from Toulepleu to Tappi, the first Liberian town. There is more transport along the former route — Abidjan-Man; regular bus for 2750 CFA or de-luxe bus for 3000 CFA. Abidjan-Danane costs 2600 CFA by truck from the lorry park in Adjame and takes 10 hours. Man-Danane costs 500 CFA by taxi. Danane-Liberian border; costs 400 CFA by taxi.
Route to Mali You can either go via Man, Odienne and Bougouni to Bamako or take the train from Abidjan as far as Ferkessedougou and hitch the rest of the way from there via Sikasso. It's also possible to hitch all the way from Abidjan. On the main road north from Ferkessedougou to the Malian frontier there are police checkpoints every five to 10 km where the police will help you get lifts if you are stuck.

Going via Man and Odienne — Man-Odienne costs 1750 CFA by taxi. Odienne-Malian border costs 1500 CFA by taxi. Note that between Odienne and Bougouni in Mali there are no buses and hitching is very difficult as there are very few cars. Also the bridge at Manankaro in Mali is under water throughout August.
Route to Ghana The normal route is via the coastal towns of Frambo, Jewi Wharf and Half Assini. Try to get to Frambo by early afternoon as the last ferry leaves at 4 pm. The border here can be particularly slow (at its worst it can take up to nine hours but this would be exceptional). The ferry has to wait until all passengers have gone through border formalities. The water in the estuary should keep you amused, if you have to wait, with its remarkable purple/mauve phosphorescence.

Abidjan-Accra costs 6500 CFA by taxi. They leave from the Total petrol station. Several companies cover the route. Abidjan-Aboisso by daily bus for 500 CFA. Aboisso-Frambo by daily bus for 500 CFA. Frambo-Jewi Wharf daily ferries for 500 CFA. If you have a pack this will cost you an extra 100 CFA on average. From Jewi Wharf to Half Assini there are daily buses for a few cents.

Trains The only railway line in the country runs from Abidjan via Ferkessedougou and Bobo Dioulasso to Ouagadougou, the capital of Upper Volta. This is also the main route to Upper Volta though it's also possible to go by road. The road follows more or less the same route as the railway line. There is a daily train in either direction from Abidjan and Ouagadougou but sleeping berths are only available on Mondays, Wednesdays and Saturdays. If you want a seat on the train you should get there at least two hours before the train leaves. The schedule is as follows:

Abidjan	16.55		
Bouake	24.00		
Ferkessedougou	08.00 (next day)		
Bobo Dioulasso	11.45	05.50	16.25
Ougadougou	18.30	12.05	22.35

Ougadougou	06.50	
Bobo Dioulasso	14.00	08.00
Bouake	01.25 (next day)	
Abidjan	11.45	21.30

Fares in 2nd class:
    Abidjan-Ferkessedougou 1650 CFA
    Abidjan-Bobo Dioulasso 2700 CFA
    Bobo-Ougadoughou 1140 CFA

OTHER INFORMATION
You can pick up jobs easily if you speak fairly fluent French and plug in to the US circuit. Hang around the embassy or ask the desk clerk for a list of US firms operating in the country then go around their Abidjan headquarters to see what's available.

Kenya

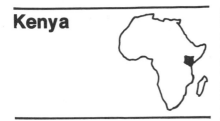

Kenya became a British Protectorate in 1895 as part of the last-minute scramble by the European nations to partition what was left of independent Africa. Previously the British had had little interest in the area since there were no minerals or economic crops which justified the expense of setting up a colonial administration backed by a military force. Communications too were primitive and so it was not until the first decade of the 20th century when a railway was built from Mombasa to Lake Victoria and a couple of steamers put onto the lake that the products of the area became marketable. The first products to come out of the area were hides and skins, wild rubber and beeswax but these soon gave way to coffee and cotton which are still the two major crops in the region.

In the process of establishing a plantation economy many Africans lost the lands they had previously cultivated and were forced to move to new and often inferior land. Others, though left in possession of the lands they were cultivating at the time of colonisation, lost the surrounding uncultivated land which in a sense was their 'fallow' and so when they moved in the course of shifting cultivation found themselves rent-paying 'squatters' on expropriated land. The present government is still trying to sort out the legacy of all this and since independence some 60,000 families have been resettled on land formerly owned by expatriates. Nevertheless, a large proportion of the large-scale mixed farms are still owned by expatriates and polit-

icians and much still needs to be done in this direction. Many of the country's employment problems stem from the fact that there is little access to the land and in any case only 7% of the total area receives adequate rainfall to support viable agriculture. Though the reconciliation of black and white around the time of independence was a major political feat, the white farmers have ever since been prone to assume that no further gestures are necessary — an attitude which may very soon have to change.

Not all the various tribes of Kenya were equally affected by European settlement. Most of the land taken for plantations came from the pastoral tribes — the Masai, Nandi and Kipsigis — while the numerically larger Luo and Baluyia tribes remained virtually untouched. Even the Kikuyu, who later came to nurse a particular grievance on the question of land expropriation in the Mau Mau rebellion, were only marginally affected. The main effect of white settlement on these agricultural people was to block their natural expansion into land previously held at spear point by the pastoralists.

In the early part of the 20th century the British held onto their colony by discouraging inter-tribal contacts, maintaining conflicts between them and putting down rebellions with a fair amount of brutality — the old policy of divide and rule. Political consciousness and its organisation in the form of nationalism began to grow among the Kikuyu peasants in the 1920s and was eventually to lead to the Mau Mau revolt in the '50s. Despite the outcry in the western press at the time, far more Africans were killed than European settlers and although the fighting was virtually over by. 1956 the state of emergency was not lifted until 1960. The intervening years to independence were almost as important as the years of armed conflict in subduing African resistance and grooming a relatively tame and agreeable generation of politicians who were not going to rock the boat when independence came. It was during these years that Jomo Kenyatta became transformed from the hunted and feared leader of black nationalism into the grand old man of the settlers.

Kenyatta ruled Kenya from 1964 until his death recently in a more or less dictatorial fashion through the KANU party. There is opposition to KANU's strong economic and political links with western nations which comes to the surface from time to time but it's rarely allowed to develop very far. In 1966, Kenyatta outlawed the opposition Kenya People's Union and imprisoned its leader, Oginga Odinga, who was only released when he agreed to rejoin KANU. More recently two critics of KANU's policies were arrested on Kenyatta's instructions in the parliament buildings while they were taking part in a debate. Neither of the two — Shikuku and Seroney — have yet been charged or brought to trial. On Kenyatta's death, Daniel arap Moi succeeded to the Presidency.

In recent years there's been a lot of tension between Kenya and Tanzania. The cause was the unilateral seizure of the assets of the East African Community (an economic union between Kenya, Tanzania and Uganda) by Kenya. It included the railways, the ships on Lake Victoria, the airlines and the Post and Telecommunications. As a result, the border between the two countries has been effectively closed for years though it's still possible to get across with police passes and permits. Negotiations were begun recently with a view to normalising relations between the two countries so the border may soon be reopened.

VISAS
Required by all except nations of Commonwealth countries (except Australia), Denmark, West Germany, Irish Republic, Italy, Norway, Spain and Sweden.

If you're flying in via Nairobi airport you have to have an 'onward ticket' before they'll allow you in. If you haven't got one they may require you to deposit a bond of US$500 which is refundable on departure. Immigration authorities are pretty strict about this. On the other hand, entry overland involves none of these hassles.

Visa/entry permit extensions up to three months can be obtained from the BIMA building near the new Post Office in Nairobi.

Sudanese Visas These cost 100 Shillings (Sh) and are valid for a one-month stay but before they'll issue you with a visa you need to show an air ticket into the country or the papers of a vehicle that's going to take you there.

Egyptian Visas Cost 25 Sh for a one-month visa and take 24 hours to issue.

Zaire Visas Cost 38 Sh for a three-month, single entry visa. Take two days to issue.

Chad Visas & Central African Republic Visas These are both obtainable from the French Embassy (Embassy House, Harambee Ave, Nairobi). They cost 25 Sh and take a day to issue. The Chad visa is for one month and the CAR visa for two weeks. With the present trouble in Chad, however, it's unlikely that they're issuing visas for that country.

Ethiopian Visas These cost US$6.50 or the equivalent, two photos and take at least four weeks to come through. They are very difficult to acquire at present. Since you can't enter overland and since there's a war on anyway, it's unlikely you'll be doing anything other than stopping overnight in Addis Ababa en route to somewhere else in which case transit visas are issued on arrival at the airport. If you need a visa for the country you are heading for after Ethiopia, get it in Kenya as your passport will be

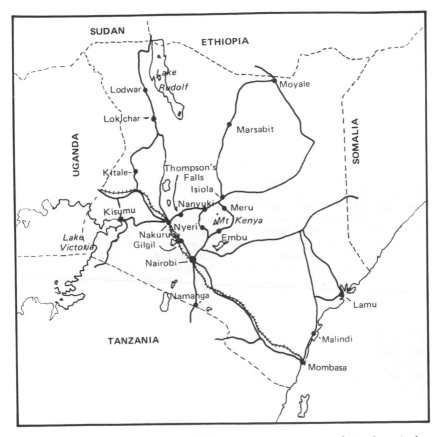

retained by the airport authorities in Addis so you can't get any visas there. Ethiopian Embassy address: State House Ave, Nairobi.

Somali Visas Since the Somalis kicked out the Russians and turned to the west, tourist visas are now obtainable in Nairobi from the embassy on Mama Ngina St. So far we haven't heard of anyone going that way.

Malagasy Visas There is no Malagasy Embassy in Nairobi (it closed about two years ago) but you can apply for the visa through Air Madagascar which is in the Hilton Hotel, Nairobi. You must apply on Monday as forms have to be sent to Madagascar via the Seychelles but you get it back on Wednesday of the same week. Costs 65 Sh, four photos and four forms. Visa valid for a month, no hassles.

Rwanda Visas The embassy is in the International House, Nairobi. Visas cost 100 Sh, two photos and take 24 hours to issue. On the form you have to sign a declaration saying you will spend at least US$20 a day and only stay in government approved hotels but there's no check on this once you get there so feel free to sign it and keep them happy.

CURRENCY

The unit of currency is the Kenyan Shilling = 100 cents. Import/export of local currency is prohibited.

Exchange rate:

£1	=	16.20 Sh
US$1	=	7.04 Sh
A$1	=	8.10 Sh
DM1	=	4.05 Sh
French Fr 1	=	2.13 Sh
Swiss Fr 1	=	4.40 Sh

There is a currency blackmarket where you can, if you're very lucky, get double the official rate (US$1 = 16Sh) but you're strongly advised to avoid street deals as there are a lot of rip-offs and even muggings. Try the C&A Camera shop in Nairobi where it's safe.

Note that there are strict baggage and body searches at Kenyan borders.

All banks in Kenya close at 1 pm except for the Commerical Bank of Africa in the lobby of the Hilton Hotel, Nairobi, which is open from 1 pm to 4 pm, Monday through Friday. The Standard Bank charges a flat rate of 15 Sh commission for cashing travellers cheques. Barclays Bank will sell you cash US dollars at 2% commission. Ugandan and Tanzanian Shillings cannot be exchanged in Kenya.

Airport tax for international flights is 80 Sh.

HEALTH

Vaccinations for cholera, smallpox and yellow fever are free from the Public Health Department, Msanifu Kombo Street, off Haile Selassie Road, Mombasa and cost 5 Sh from the City Hall Clinic, Nairobi. Malaria treatment is free in Lamu hospital. Note that Nivoquine doesn't always guarantee immunity. We've had letters from travellers who said they took it and still got the disease. Don't go around barefoot or you might pick up jiggers and watch out for 'Nairobi fly' which, if squashed on your skin can cause nasty blistering and a rash.

LANGUAGE

English and Swahili.

Basic Swahili

pronounce   A as in father
            E as in better
            I as in bee
            O as in law
            U as in too

Double vowels are long, there are no diphthongs, consonants are as in English. Swahili is a prefixed language: adjectives change prefix according to the number and class of the noun. Thus mzuri, wazuri, vizuri and kizuri are different forms of the word 'good'. Verbs use a prefix noun:

I	Ni	we	Tu
you	U	you	M
he/she	A	they	Wa

and a tense prefix:

present	Na
past	Li
future	Ta
infinitive	Ku

Thus you get:

We will go to Moshi
                    Tutakwenda Moshi
I can take a picture?
                    Ninaweza Kupiga Picha
Juma spoke much
                    Juma Alisema Sarfa

Some useful words in Swahili:

hello*	Jambo or Salamu
welcome	Karibu

thank you	Asante	fish	Samaki
how are you?	Habari?	egg(s)	(Ma)yai
goodbye	Kwa Heri	milk	Maziwa
food	Chakula	yes	Ndiyo
rice	Wali	no	Hapana
bananas	Ndizi	how much/how many?	Ngapi
bread	Mkati	where?	Wapi
spinach	Mboga	toilet	Choo (Yvoo)
water	Maji	today	Leo
salt	Chumvi	tomorrow	Kesho
meat	Nyama	guest house	Nyumba ya wageni
goat	Mbuzi	eat	Kula
beef	Ngombe	sleep	Lala
chicken	Kuku		

want	Taka
come from	Toka
is	Ni
there is	Kuna
there isn't	Hakuna
white people	Wazungi

*There is also a respectful greeting used for elders — Shikamoo. The reply is Marahaba.

1	Moja	11	Kumi Na Moja
2	Mbili	20	Ishirini
3	Tatu	30	Thelathini
4	Nne	40	Arobaini
5	Tano	50	Hamsini
6	Sita	60	Sitini
7	Saba	70	Sabini
8	Nane	80	Themanini
9	Tisa	90	Tisini
10	Kumi	100	Mia
		½	Nusu

MAIL
Sending parcels from Kenyan post offices can be a real hassle. Two hour waits are normal.

ACCOMMODATION
Amboseli National Park
There are several camp sites in the Park but the one with the most beautiful surroundings is at Oltukai. Either camp for 5 Sh or rent a bush house for 20 Sh per bed. Excellent English breakfasts as well as lunches and evening meals are available. No prior reservations are necessary contrary to what the tourist literature would have you believe. The gates to the Park close at 7 pm and, because of lions, you must go by car.

Kanamai
The *Youth Hostel* costs 12.50 Sh plus 2 Sh extra for gas in the kitchen with an International YH Card. Camping in the grounds costs 5 Sh. If you're coming from Mombasa, get off the bus at 'Whispering Palms' if the conductor doesn't know where the Youth Hostel is situated.

20 km north of Kanamai is the 'Pole Pole' — an old house overlooking the sea where you can stay for 10 Sh. Just take a mattress and sleep where you like, popular with travellers. It's possible to get a lift there from Andy Diaz Camera shop near the junction of Nkrumah Road and Digo Road, Mombasa. Go there before 4 pm, the lift costs 2 Sh.

Kitale
You can stay at the Sikh Temple here free but please give them a donation. The *Youth Hostel* (where you can also camp) is 10 km from Kitale on the main road to Eldoret. Excellent facilities but bring your own food. This YH is the main place for information on climbing and camping the Mt Elgon region and for trips to Lake Rudolph, ask the warden.

Kisumu
The Sikh Temple still welcomes travellers. Otherwise try *Sam's Hotel* which costs 15 Sh/bed.

Lamu
This is a very popular place with travellers and many years ago became the Kathmandu of Africa which resulted in a lot of government paranoia about 'hippies' and their activities. All that blew over a long time ago but if you use grass keep it out of sight. People still get busted. It's a very beautiful place.

Castle Lodge is just behind and to the left of the prison in the market square. Costs 5.50 Sh on the roof with a mattress, 11 Sh for a bed inside and 33 Sh/ double.

New Century: very popular with travellers. Costs 5 Sh on the roof or 11.50 Sh for a bed inside.

Karibuni Lodge: costs 2.50 Sh on the roof or 6 Sh for a bed inside. Very clean with showers and friendly management (owner called Francis).

Bahari Lodge: Costs 10 Sh per person, quiet.

New Maharus: Costs 47 Sh/double.

Amu Lodging: Costs 5 Sh on the roof, 7.50 Sh for a bed inside (goes up to 11 Sh in the tourist season).

Other places which have been recommended and which cost between 4-5 Sh on the roof include *Kenya Lodging* (behind the police station) and the *Kandaras*.

Yogurt Inn just behind the Bahari serves excellent banana pancakes, fruit salads and yogurt. Friendly atmosphere, cheap. The roof restaurant of the *New Maharus Hotel* is worth a try. Large helpings though the food varies in quality. If you want sea food, try *Ghais* (also known as 'Guy's'). Also *Suli-Suli Restaurant*.Serves pancakes and wild honey for 2 Sh and good yogurt.

The museum in Lamu is worth a visit for its interesting collections of tribal crafts, etc. It's possible to walk across the island in about 1½ hours to the village of Matandoni where dhows are built. There's no hotel accommodation or cafes as such but if you ask around someone generally offers accommodation. There are 14th and 15th century Arab ruins on the nearby islands of Manda and Pate which you can visit either by motor boat or dhow but note that the latter are not at all cheap unless you can get a group of four or five people together.

Lamu beach (white sandy beach) is a 45 minute walk from the town itself. Lamu is particularly good to visit on the Prophet's birthday (most of the inhabitants are Swahili Muslims) when there's a week long festival for which Lamu is famed throughout the Indian Ocean region.

Malindi

Similar to Lamu — white sand beaches, coral reefs, surfing, scuba diving, old ruins, etc — but more commercialised as you might expect being nearer to Mombasa.

Youth Hostel is probably the cheapest place to stay at 12.50 Sh per person. They have cooking facilities and also more expensive double rooms. If you are not a member of the YHA you can join on the spot.

New Kenya Hotel costs 10-11 Sh for a bed in the dorm and 29 Sh/double. It's unwise to leave baggage there.

New Safari Hotel is next to the bus station. Costs 11 Sh for a bed in the dorm and 35 Sh/double. Doubles as a brothel.

Malindi Rest House is opposite the market and owned by the bakery two doors up. Costs 10 Sh/bed in dorm.

Metro Hotel costs 40 Sh/double.

Other cheapies include the *Guji Guest House* (10 Sh/bed in dorm); *Lucky Lodge* (25 Sh/double) and the *Coronation Guest House* (10 Sh/bed in dorm). two km from town on the coast road south is the popular *Silver Sands* campsite. If you have your own tent it costs 18.50 Sh for two people. If you have to hire a tent it will cost you 35 Sh for two. They also have bandas which cost 40 Sh/double and a few larger ones which will take more than two people for a slightly higher charge. There's a small restaurant and bar with showers and cooking facilities.

Excellent Indian meals at the Hindu restaurant off Kikoi Street near the Coronation Guest House and at *Chagga's* on the road leading down to the coast. The *Matinga* bar behind the hotels is well worth a visit. They sell very cheap palm wine.

At Gedi, 16 km south of Malindi, lie the ruins of an old city dating back to the 13th century. Tracks have been cleared through the forest and excavations have unearthed several mosques, a palace, many large houses and wells. Very interesting if you're into history or

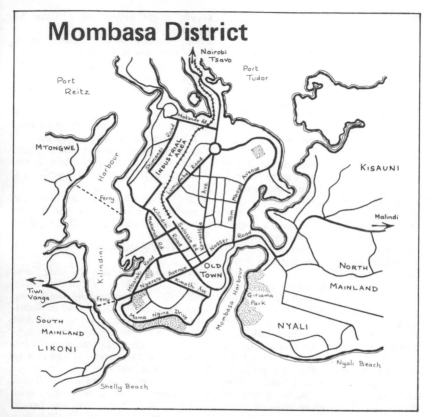

Mombasa District

archaeology.

Mombasa

One of the most interesting cities along the East African Coast.

Hydro Hotel: Digo Rd near the market, costs 13 Sh for a bed in the dorm, or to sleep on the roof; 35 Sh/double. There are no single rooms. Popular with travellers and a good place to meet people going to or coming from Lamu.

Savoy Hotel, Digo Rd. Costs 13.50 Sh for a bed in the dorm. Another popular place with travellers.

Mrs Lobo's, corner of Archbishop Mak-

arios and Kisumu Streets, costs 12 Sh for bed in dorm. The place is dirty but luggage is safe.

Hotel Splendid Digo Rd, costs 35 Sh/ double.

Hotel New Bristol near the Post Office, costs 25 Sh/double.

Hotel M Vita, Turkanas Street, costs 30 Sh, for a bed in dorm.

The Sikh Temple on Munju Rd won't put people up anymore but if you're genuinely very short of money the Sikh School nearby is friendly and might help find somewhere for you to sleep free of charge. The *YMCA* and *YWCA* (combined) cost 40 Sh per person for full board (four meals per day).

The popular *Twiga Lodge*, is 25 km south of Mombasa at Tiwi. The place has showers, toilets, a bar and cafe. Nearer to Mombasa at Likoni Beach is the *Timbwani Camp* site which costs 5 Sh per night plus 30 Sh if you need to hire a tent but watch out for thieves as it's very poorly guarded.

Blue Fin Fish serves excellent fish, chips and salad for 6 Sh. The *Central Tea Rooms* on Digo Rd has cheap fruit juices and curries for 6-9 Sh. There's another good Indian restaurant opposite the large Hindu temple on Haile Selassie Road. *Ashur's* on Jomo Kenyatta Ave has also been recommended. If you're looking for a cheap night club try the *Sunshine Club* which costs 6 Sh entrance.

Note that Kilindini Rd has been renamed Moi Avenue. Both names are in current use.

Warning Robbery with violence is becoming quite common in Mombasa. Don't walk the streets or along the beaches alone at night. Avoid, if possible, carrying bags which can be snatched by hit and run merchants. Especially don't try to sleep out on the beaches. Even Tiwi Beach isn't free of this sort of thing.

American Express: Express Kenya Ltd, Nkrumah Rd, PO Box 90631, Mombasa (tel 24461)

Tourist Office: Kilindini Road next to the giant tusks. Open 8 am-12 noon and 2 pm-4.30 pm Monday through Friday. 8 am-12 noon on Saturdays. Closed on Sundays.

Bus offices: All the bus lines — Coast Bus Services, Goldline Ltd and Kenya Bus Services — are located on Mwembe Tayari Rd. Taxis operating to Malindi are located on Jomo Kenyatta Ave, ('Malindi Taxis'). The other taxi agents — Mombasa Peugeot Services — are located in Haile Selassie Rd.

Ferry: The Likoni Ferry runs at frequent intervals throughout the night and day — on average every 20 mins between 5 am and 12.30 am and less frequently between 12.30 am and 5 am.

Things to see:

Fort Jesus Built by the Portuguese in 1593 and taken by the Omani Arabs in 1698 after a 33 month seige. It's now a museum with displays of historical relics going back to its foundations as well as things from other sites along the coast. Open every day of the year from 8.30 am to 6.30 pm.

The Old Harbour Fascinating place where dhows from Arabia, Persia and India dock.

Dhow Careening Beach Further along from the Old Harbour. Large oceangoing dhows are careened and repaired here between December and April. When the tide is out you can walk right up to them.

The Bazaar Centred around Biashara St. Particularly good for fabrics but plenty of other things from the countries bordering the Indian Ocean and the African interior.

The Ivory Room Just off Treasury Square behind the Kenya Commerical Bank, Mvita Rd. Open from 8 am to 12 noon.

Hindu Temple Situated on Haile Selassie Rd and worth a visit if only to see its brilliantly painted door.

Mount Kenya

The usual centre for exploring/climbing Mt Kenya is Naro Moru. Within a few km of this village there are several places where you can find accommodation. One of the most popular with travellers is *Mrs Kenealy's* whose stone built farmhouse is situated four km off the main road to Mt Kenya. She is an old time settler and offers accommodation for 10 Sh/room and camping for 5 Sh.

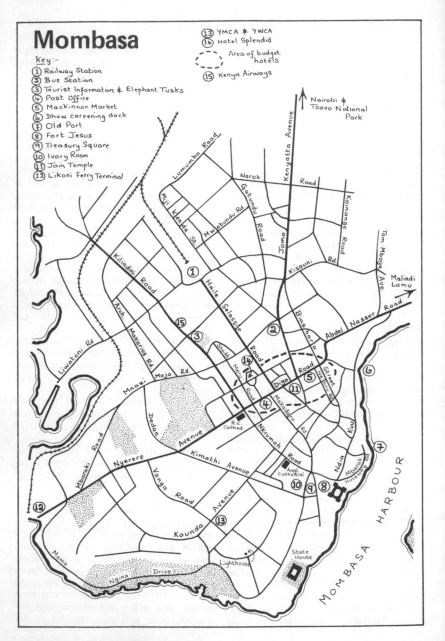

Mombasa

Key:-
1. Railway Station
2. Bus Station
3. Tourist Information & Elephant Tusks
4. Post Office
5. MacKinnon Market
6. Dhow careening dock
7. Old Port
8. Fort Jesus
9. Treasury Square
10. Ivory Room
11. Jain Temple
12. Likoni Ferry Terminal
13. YMCA & YWCA
14. Hotel Splendid
    Area of budget hotels
15. Kenya Airways

Wood stoves and kerosene lamps provided. Horses can be hired at 15 Sh/hour. Take your own food with you (available in Naro Moru). In addition to these places there's the *Youth Hostel* for 12.50 Sh per person about six km past Mrs Kenealy's; *Naro Moru Lodge* which has six bunk-bed houses (two beds per house) at 10 Sh per bed though full board and camping are also available, and climbing equipment for hire. *Minto's Safaris* again past Mrs Kenealy's which has bunk-bed houses for 10 Sh per person and climbing equipment for hire (they also have bunk houses on the far side of Mt Kenya).

In Naro Moru itself there is *River Lodge* where you can either rent a room or camp. Food is available there.

Nairobi

The place to head for if you're looking for budget accommodation is River Rd though two of the most popular travellers' hotels are not located on this road (*Iqbal Hotel* and *Mrs Roche's*). You'll pass the Iqbal on the way to River Rd but Mrs Roche's is located in Westlands which is quite a way from the centre of town.

Iqbal Hotel, Tom Mboya Street, costs 13.75 Sh/bed in dorm; 16.50 Sh/bed in double room; 6 Sh on the floor. Hot showers, clean, central and baggage is safe. Very popular with travellers.

Mrs Roche's, 3 Parklands Ave opposite the Aga Khan Hospital, costs 12 Sh to camp; 15-20 Sh per bed and 27 Sh for bed and breakfast but you may have to sleep on the floor for the first night as it's very popular. Nice place with trees and flowers and you will be pleased to know that her notorious dogs, which used to eat clothes put on the line to dry, are now too old for antics like that. Bus Nos 11 and 12.

Youth Hostel, Race Course Rd, costs 12.50 Sh per person with an official four-day maximum stay. They have a store where you can leave baggage safely and free of charge. The hostel is highly recommended.

Al Mansura Hotel, Munyu Street, costs 12.50 Sh for a bed (two to four beds per room) or 30 Sh/double room. Clean and a good restaurant downstairs but it can be noisy from time to time.

City Lodge, River Rd, costs 12.50 Sh for a bed in the dorm.

New Kenya Lodge, corner of River Rd and Latema Rd, costs 30 Sh/single and 45 Sh/double.

Zahra Hotel, River Rd, costs 20 Sh per person in double room.

Forest Lodge, near the museum and snake farm, costs 16 Sh per person in double room but you must supply your own bedding.

There are three *YMCAs* and one *YWCA*. The YMCAs are situated on State House Rd and the YWCA on Nyerere Rd. They cost 65 Sh per person for full board (dormitory accommodation). The meals are excellent value and include a smorgasbord lunch, substantial breakfast, high tea and an English-style dinner. Non-residents can eat there too and there is a swimming pool. Note that gear left in rooms will be ripped off and the reception won't accept money or passports for safe-keeping as the safe is regularly broken into. The YWCA is more expensive than the YMCA but married couples are allowed to stay there.

Salvation Army Hostel, near Kanakore Market, a 25 cent bus ride from the centre, has dormitory accommodation for 10 Sh (mixed dorms) but you have to watch your baggage carefully as there's very little supervision.

Other cheapies which have been recommended include the *New Flora Hotel* round the corner from the Iqbal

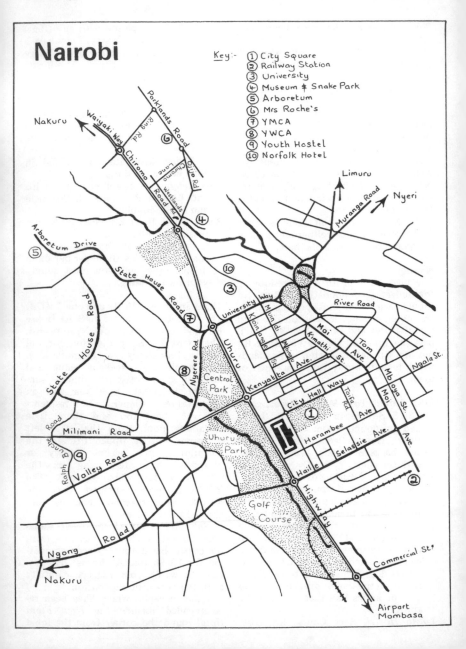

Nairobi

Key:-
1. City Square
2. Railway Station
3. University
4. Museum & Snake Park
5. Arboretum
6. Mrs Roche's
7. YMCA
8. YWCA
9. Youth Hostel
10. Norfolk Hotel

and the *Hill Top Lodge*, Raeta Road near the bus depots. If you're looking for somewhere to camp try the *Jamhuri Park Scout Ground* which costs 5 Sh but is quite a long way from the centre through a pleasant place. There's also the *Westward Park Country Club*, 25 km from the town, where you can camp free. Swimming pools, bar and restaurant.

Indian restaurants at the end of Tom Mboya Street have set evening meals for 15 Sh. The *Super Hotel*, River Road, offers as-much-as-you-can-eat South Indian vegetarian meals for 18 Sh. The *Curry Pot*, Government Rd (also known as Moi Avenue) offers steak, egg and chips for 15 Sh. As-much-as-you-can-eat-meals from both the *Ambassador Hotel* and the *YMCA* for 10 Sh. The *Thorn Tree Cafe*, under the New Stanley Hotel, is a good place to meet other travellers. It's somewhat touristy but it's where people hang out and has the best notice board in the city. Also recommended are the *Red Rock Restaurant*, *Cafe de Paris* and the *Moonflower-Sunflower Restaurant*. There are cheap fish and chip places at the back of the GPO and if you're short on money you can get a bowl of beans and potatoes from the food shacks at the bottom of Latema Road for a couple of Shillings. If you're looking for a good place to have a beer, try the old English pub in the *Intercontinental Hotel*. It looks flash but the beers are cheap.

Note that Government Rd has been re-named Moi Ave but both names are in current use.

Warning It is dangerous to wander the streets alone at night especially around the River Road area. Armed robbery and mugging is common.

American Express: Express Kenya Ltd, Consolidated House, Standard Street, PO Box 40433, Nairobi (tel 334-7277/8).

Tourist Office: Situated at the corner of Moi Ave and City Hall Way. Have free copies of the weekly magazine 'What's On' which is full of useful information but the street map which it contains is pretty useless — better to buy a decent one from a bookshop for 15 Sh.

British Council Library, opposite the Norfolk Hotel, is open 9 am-12.30 pm and 1.45 pm-5 pm Monday through Friday and 9 am-12.15 pm on Saturdays.

Nairobi National Museum: Open everyday from 9.30 am to 6 pm.

Embassies:
Australia: Development House, Moi Ave (tel 334666).
Britain: Bruce House, Standard St (tel-335944).
Canada: Comcraft House, 6th Floor, Haile Selassie Ave (tel 334033).
Ethiopia: State House Rd (tel 23941).
France: Embassy House, Harambee Ave (tel 28373).
Germany: Embassy House, Harambee Ave (tel 26661/2/3).
Italy: Prudential Assurance Bldg, Wabera St (tel 21615).
Japan: Bank of India Bldg, Kenyatta Ave (tel 332955).
Malagasy Republic: Waiyaki Way (tel 48063).
Somalia: Mama Ngina St (tel 24301).
Sudan: (tel 20770).
Netherlands: Uchumi House, 6th Floor, (tel 27111).
UAR (Egypt): (tel 22991).
USA: Cotts House, Wabera St (tel 334-141).

Seychelles Tourist Information Office: 3rd Floor, Esso House, Mama Ngina St.

Bus to the airport: No 34 from outside the Ambassador Hotel, costs 2 Sh. If hitching to Mombasa take bus No 13 to the airport turn off and start from

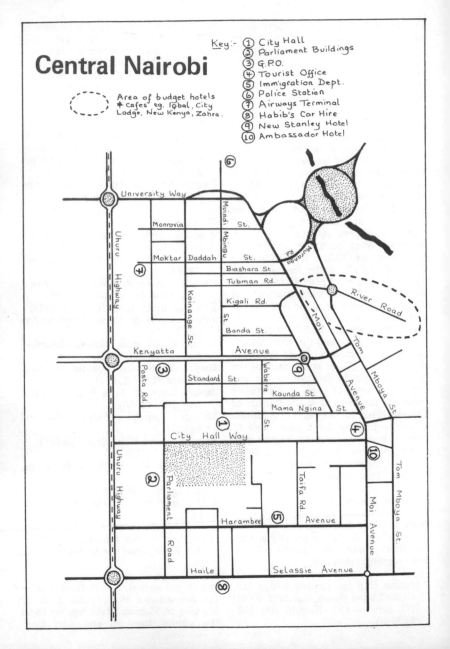

Central Nairobi

Key:-
1. City Hall
2. Parliament Buildings
3. G.P.O.
4. Tourist Office
5. Immigration Dept.
6. Police Station
7. Airways Terminal
8. Habib's Car Hire
9. New Stanley Hotel
10. Ambassador Hotel

Area of budget hotels & cafes eg. Iqbal, City Lodge, New Kenya, Zahra.

there. If heading for Uganda take bus No 23 from the Hilton to the end of its route. Hitch from there. Going to Naro Moru, Nyeri, Nanyuki, Embu or Mt Meru take bus No 5 from the Central Bus Station up Thika Rd to Kenyatta College and hitch from there.

Naivasha Lake

Youth Hostel and Camp site ('Fisherman's Camp') on Lake Hotel Road, 12 km beyond the Lake Hotel itself. Costs 5 Sh to camp or 8.50 Sh for bed in a banda. Bookings through General Sec, YMCA, Box 30330, Nairobi.

Nakuru

The *Anglican Youth Centre* costs 15 Sh per night. It's quite a long way out of town going west and down at the end of a dirt road. See Stephen about accommodation. There's no food there so take your own. Free accommodation in the Sikh Temple 400 metres behind the market on the left. Two relatively cheap hotels are the *Top Lodge* and the *Stag's Head Hotel.* Good food at the *Railway Hotel* and at the coffee house at the Kisumu end of the main street run by the Kenya Coffee Board. There's a camp site at the Agricultural Society of Kenya show ground except during shows, costs 5 Sh.

Namanga

Camp site at *Namanga River Hotel*, right on the Tanzanian border at the entrance to the Amboseli Game Reserve, costs 10 Sh.

Nanyuki

Many people who come this way stay at the popular *Chololo Ranch* which is 45 miles north west of Nanyuki. To get there, take the Thomsons Falls road out of Nanyuki for about a mile and then turn right on Naibor Road then right again on Doldol Road. Chololo is the last ranch on the left before you get to the police barrier of the Mukogodo.

From there you drive three miles through Ol Jogi ranch to Chololo gate where the owner, Florence Schieren, will meet you. If you'd like to book in advance the address is: Box 236, Nanyuki. Banbas for rent here for 20 Sh which includes everything bedding and food — bring your own. The ranch is full of all the game you're likely to see in any of the game parks elsewhere. Florence runs safaris and is a very amusing person. Recommended by many people. There's a *Youth Hostel* at Emmanuel Parish Centre near the post office on Market Rd.

Nyahururu

Rooms anywhere cost 22 Sh. Food is scarce and there's no running water. There's an entrance fee of 4 Sh to see the waterfall.

Nyeri

Camp site at the Hindu Temple, Temple Rd.

Thomson's Falls

Camp site at the Thomson's Falls Lodge for 10 Sh. It's a beautiful site with all the firewood you want. Often no-one comes to collect the money.

Wajir

On the Nairobi-Moyale road. *Corner Hotel* costs 11 Sh per person. There is very little variety as far as food goes but there's one cafe which does egg and chips.

TRANSPORT

Hitching on the main roads, which are sealed and well-maintained, is easy and generally free but on the minor roads you can wait all day for a lift and still end up paying, so it's probably worth getting a bus or matutu (a shared taxi or van). Matutus cost about half the price of buses. They stop and honk along most roads and drive like maniacs. Hitching to the game parks is very difficult because most people either go in organised tours or get a group together to rent a car/camper van but you could try the notice boards at the New Stanley Hotel, Nairobi, or the Automobile Club of East Africa, Nairobi.

Renting Vehicles This is the best way to see the game parks especially if you can get a group together to share the cost otherwise you're at the mercy of the far more expensive organised tour people. You can hire camper vans, Land-Rovers and Suzuki four wheel drives. The latter are more economical than Land-Rovers but popular and therefore heavily booked. You need to make prior reservation if you want to be sure of getting one. A four wheel drive vehicle will cost you about 400 Sh per day to hire but they take up to six people. Two of the best places to rent vehicles from in Nairobi are Kimbla on Market Street and Habib's Cars, Agip House, Haile Selassie Ave. The latter also have a branch in Mombasa in the New Carlton Hotel, Kilindini Rd (also called Moi Avenue). Kimbla is also a good place to buy flight tickets and for advice.

Taxis There are basically three types of taxis: (a) matutus — shared vans or small trucks which act as feeders to the main bus lines. You can find them almost everywhere. They cost about half the price of the buses. (b) conventional taxis and 'speed taxis' which work out pretty expensive. The so-called speed taxis are actually something of a con as no vehicle is officially allowed to exceed 100 km/hr though some companies have a reputation for turning a blind eye to the clock. Also note that since car owners no longer require a licence to carry fare-paying passengers, many of the so-called taxis you'll come across are simply private car owners who are out to make a few shillings since they're going in that direction anyway. (c) Peugeot taxis, these run on fixed routes with fares about 50% higher than the buses. They operate a bus-style service and you generally have to book a seat· in advance. Like matutus, they're shared.

Mombasa Peugeot Taxi Service (booking office on Haile Selassie Rd, Mombasa), operate the following service: Mombasa-Nairobi daily at 7.30 am, 10.30 am, 1.30 pm and 4.30 pm. Nairobi-Mombasa daily at 2.30 pm, 5.30 pm 8.30 pm and 11 pm.

Malindi Taxi Service (booking office on Jomo Kenyatta Rd, Mombasa) operate the following service — Mombasa-Nairobi daily at 1 and 8 pm. Nairobi-Mombasa daily at 9 pm and 6 am.

Buses On the main routes there are express luxury buses and ordinary buses. They often travel at night to avoid the heat. Kenya Bus Services operate the following schedule — Mombasa-Nairobi daily at 7.30 am, 12 noon and 8.30 pm. The first and last take 10½ hours approximately and the noon bus eight hours (express). Mombasa-Malindi is daily at 8 am and 2 pm. The first takes six hours and the last four hours. Mombasa-Wundanya (Taita Hills near Voi) daily at 7 am and 2 pm. Takes approximately five hours.

Coast Bus Service (booking office on Mwembe Tayari Rd, Mombasa) operate the following schedules — Mombasa-Nairobi daily at 7.30 pm takes 10½ hours. Nairobi-Mombasa daily at 1 pm takes seven hours. Mombasa-Malindi daily at 6 am and 12.30 pm takes four hours. Malindi-Mombasa daily at 6 am and 12.30 pm, takes four hours.

Goldline Bus service (booking offices at Mwembe Tayari Rd, Mombasa and corner of Cross Rd and Riata Rd, Nairobi) operate the following luxury coach services — Mombasa-Nairobi daily at 1 pm and 8 pm. Nairobi-Mombasa daily at 1.30 and 8 pm. Nairobi-Kisumu daily at 9 pm. Kisumu-Nairobi daily at 9 pm.

Some other bus fares and journey times include — Malindi-Lamu costs 35 Sh plus 3 Sh for the ferry to Lamu Island and takes seven hours if there are no hassles. The road is liable to flooding and accidents and if you encounter anything like this the daily journey can take twice as long. Nairobi-Namanga (Tanzanian border) daily buses for 20 Sh. Nairobi-Naro Moru daily buses for 24 Sh. Nyahururu-Nanyuki daily at about noon and takes 2½ hours, costs 13 Sh. Gilgil-Thomson Falls Ford Transit which goes when full, costs 12 Sh.

Trains Railway timetables are available free at Nairobi Railway Station. There are no trains to Tanzania because of the long-standing dispute over the East African Economic Community but trains are running again to Kampala, Uganda though departure times are still pretty erratic. If you're heading that way, make prior enquiries at the railway station. Note that trains are invariable late arriving but very comfortable for travelling overnight if you book a sleeper.

Nairobi-Mombasa/Mombasa-Nairobi daily in either direction at 6.30 pm takes 14 hours, costs 34 Sh in 2nd class without a sleeper and 60 Sh in 2nd class with a sleeper. Dinner on board the train costs 24 Sh.

Boats

Dhows These ply regularly between Mombasa and Lamu when the winds are favourable. The journey takes one to two days (exceptionally three) and costs 60 Sh. There are also regular dhows between Mombasa and Zanzibar/Dar es Salaam which cost between 100 and 300 Sh depending on the captain and your luck. It's possible to find a dhow which will take you all the way from Mombasa to the Persian Gulf and even India and since there are no longer any regular ships between Kenya and India/Pakistan this is the only way you can get there other than flying. For all dhows, enquire down at the Old Port, Mombasa.

Lake Victoria Steamers The Kenyan Lake Victoria services are rarely used by travellers these days since they serve only the tiny Kenyan part of the lake. The boats are the *Kamongo* and *Alestes*. There are no services between Kenya and Uganda and between Kenya and Tanzania. The schedule is as follows:-

	Mon	Mon	Tues	Tues	Wed	Wed	Thur	Fri	Sat	Sat
Kisumu	9.10	14.40	10.00	12.15	9.10	14.40	12.15		9.10	14.40
Kendu Bay	11.10			14.15	11.10		14.15		11.10	
Homa Bay		18.55	16.00			18.55				18.55
Homa Bay			7.00 (Wed)					7.00		
Mbita			10.00					10.00		
Mfangano			12.00					12.00		
Karungu			18.30					18.30		
Karungu			7.00					7.00		
Mfangano			13.00					13.00		
Mbita			15.00					15.00		
Homa Bay			18.30					18.30		
Homa Bay		7.00 (Tues)				7.00 (Thur)		23.59		7.00 (Sun)
Kendu Bay	11.40		14.45	11.40 (Wed)		14.45 (Thur)		11.40 (Sat)		
Kisumu	13.40	11.15	16.45	13.40 (Wed)	11.15	16.45 (Thur)		13.40 (Sat)	6.00 (Sun)	11.15

Fares:

		2nd class	3rd class
Kisumu to	Homa Bay	14.90 Sh	9.90 Sh
	Mbita	22.90 Sh	15.30 Sh
	Mfangano	27.00 Sh	18.00 Sh
	Karungu	34.50 Sh	21.50 Sh

River trips It's possible to find canoes in Lamu which will take you up the Tana River to Garissa. Plenty of wild life to be seen including hippos and crocodiles but take insect repellant as the mosquitos are really heavy. When you get to Garissa there are two hotels where you can stay — *Blue Nile Hotel* (15 Sh) and the *Safari Hotel* (15 Sh). There's a bus back to Lamu from Garissa for 42 Sh.

Note There are no longer any regular scheduled passenger ships between Kenya or Tanzania and India/Pakistan. If that's the way you want to go, you'll either have to fly or find a dhow to take you.

Flights There are two private aviation companies which operate flights between Nairobi, Mombasa, Malindi and Lamu. They are Sunbird Aviation Ltd (booking office in New Stanley House, Nairobi) and Ticair (Ticair Charters Ltd Box 146, Malindi, tel Malindi 153). Sunbird operate a daily flight from Nairobi to Lamu and a once weekly (sometimes twice weekly) service from Nairobi to Juba in Sudan. Nairobi to Lamu costs 700 Sh and Malindi to Lamu costs 220 Sh. Nairobi to Juba costs US$130.

If you're looking for flights back to the Mediterranean or Northern Europe the cheapest are Air Egypt (Youth Fares at 50% of the normal price if you are 26 years old or under) and Aeroflot. Nairobi to Athens presently costs 2600 Sh (US$316). Buy your tickets from one of the following places: (a) Crocodile Travel — address from the Al Mansura Hotel, Nairobi, reputedly the cheap-est in town. (b) Kimbla Travel, Market Street, Nairobi. (c) Tamana Tours, Nairobi.

If you're heading for Tanzania you can either take the Air Comores (Kilindini Rd, Mombasa) twice weekly flight on Tuesdays and Wednesdays from Mombasa to Dar es Salaam for 280 Sh or enquire at the YMCA in Nairobi about a charter flight which operates between Nairobi and Dar es Salaam via Arusha and which costs 1200 Sh.

Routes out of Kenya
You cannot go overland from Kenya to Ethiopia at present (there's a war on and entry through any point other than Addis Ababa airport requires special permission from the government). Overland travel to Uganda and Somalia is now possible but we have no details at present. Enquire at the relevant embassy in Nairobi.

Kenya-Tanzania
The possibilities by dhow and 'plane have been mentioned previously. The land border between the two countries has been officially closed for several years now but that doesn't mean you can't cross by land transport. If you intend to do this you have to obtain a sura Hotel, Nairobi, reputedly the cheap-in Nairobi. This is more or less a formality these days (many people do it every day) but you *may* have to shell out up to 100 Sh in back-handers to the border guards though things are easing up considerably now as a result of talks between the Kenyans and Tanzanians aimed at normalising relations between the two countries and the land crossing at Namanga, south of Nairobi, is no hassle anymore. If the talks are a success, then the border will again be normally open.

Kenya-Sudan

You can either fly there with Sunbird Aviation Ltd (see under 'Flights') or take one of the overland routes. You should allow two weeks for the latter trip and remember that it's pretty rough but beautiful and a superb adventure. The trucks only go in the dry season. Take plenty of food. There is no official border post with Sudan so get your passport stamped in Nairobi. Trucks normally go in convoys on average once every two weeks. There are two routes: (a) Nairobi-Nakuru-Lokichar-Lodwar-Lokichoggio-Kapoeta-Torit-Juba; (b) Nairobi-Nakuru-Tororo-Gulu-Nimule-Juba. The second route is the preferred route being less arduous but during the latter part of the Amin regime in Uganda and during the Tanzanian intervention this was not possible. It's now being opened up again and shouldn't take the two weeks that the other route can take. If you're coming from Sudan, initial passport formalities take place at Lokichoggio but you must take your passport to be stamped at the police station in Kitale or at Immigration in Nairobi. Currency declaration forms have to be filled out at Kitale Post Office otherwise banks won't entertain you.

GAME PARKS/NATIONAL PARKS

Student entry fees and reduced residents' fees have been abolished. Entrance to the reserves and game parks now costs a standard 20 Sh plus 20 Sh for a vehicle. The only exceptions to this are the Marine Park at Malindi and Nairobi National Park and Animal Orphanage which are cheaper. If you plan on visiting quite a few game parks these fees can make a sizeable hole in your budget and you're advised to go along to the Wildlife Club HQ at the National Museum, Nairobi and become a club member. This costs 60 Sh for Kenyan residents (more for overseas members) — just say you're a resident; they don't ask for proof. Membership entitles you to free entry into all game parks and sometimes free camping if the gate attendant is cool. You only need one Wildlife Membership ID per group.

However you choose to do it, visiting the game parks is an expensive business. The cheapest way is to get a group together and rent a vehicle and camping gear. If you're not able to do this for some reason you'll have to count on finding a share-expenses lift on the notice-board of the Thorn Tree Cafe under the New Stanley Hotel, Nairobi, or from the one at the Automobile Club of East Africa. There are buses which go through the game reserves but they stick to the major roads and often travel by night so you see very little. If you're renting a vehicle, try to get a Suzuki four wheel drive as they're more economical than Land-Rovers but are in heavy demand so you need to plan ahead. Some of the cheapest places to rent from in Nairobi are: Kimbla Tours, Market Street; Habib's Cars, Agip House, Haile Selassie Avenue, and Oddjobs. Hertz charge 420 Sh per week plus 1.20 Sh per km to hire a Suzuki four wheel drive. Use this as a guide. Hire camping gear from Ahamed Bros, 22 Kenyatta Ave, Nairobi, if you need it — again it is not exactly 'cheap'. If you have to patronise a tour firm, you're going to need a lot of money. Here are some sample prices:

Nairobi National Park & Animal Orphanage (four hours) 80 Sh (US$10).

Nakuru Flamingo Park (one day) 320 Sh (US$39).

Amboseli Game Reserve (1½ days), 800 Sh (US$97)

Amboseli & Tsavo East (four days) 2000 Sh (US$243).

Masai Mara, Lake Naivasha, Nakuru, Amboseli, Tsavo East (six days) 3500 Sh (US$425)

Kimbla and Safari Camp Services (Koinage Street) do slightly cheaper tours such as the Masai Mara Game Reserve (five days for US$200) and Lake Turkana (seven days for US$225). Their tours are all inclusive but you have to bring your own sleeping bag.

Some of the more important game reserves include:

Amboseli National Park At the foot of Mt Kilimanjaro. This Masai reserve is noted for its elephant, lion, leopard, buffalo, antelope and rhino. There are lodges and a tented safari camp to stay at in the park if you need accommodation.

Lake Nakuru National Park Kenya's largest bird sanctuary. Its flamingo flocks can number up to two million birds at certain times of the year! There are also sizeable flocks of wild duck and other water birds.

Marsabit Game Reserve Off the beaten track in the north of the country situated in a lush volcanic rain forest. Elephant and the rare kudu, colourful nomadic tribes also inhabit the area.

Mt Kenya National Park One of the highest mountains in Africa at 5200 metres. Parts of the park are famous for leopard. A favourite place for climbers and walkers. If you need a guide or to hire equipment these can be found at any of the lodges around the village of Naro Moru which is the centre for this park. At the right time of day there are some superb views from this mountain.

Meru National Park North of Mt Kenya and home of lions and Kenya's only herd of white rhino.

Nairobi National Park Only 10 minutes by car from the centre of Nairobi and remarkable for the large concentration of game in a small area. The only one which is missing is the elephant. At the entrance to the park is the Animal Orphanage where young animals which have lost their parents or been abandoned are brought. Where possible, these are released when able to take care of themselves.

Tsavo East National Park & Tsavo West National Park The largest game park in East Africa. It abounds with game of all kinds but is particularly famous for its large herds of elephant. In Tsavo West are the Mzima Springs inhabited by hippopotamus and crocodile which can be seen either from the surface or from the sides of a glass-panelled tank.

The more popular game parks are being over-exploited by the tourist industry as a result of which many animals are hard to find. If possible, talk to someone who knows the game parks well before you go and find out where the best locations are and the best times of the day to find them.

OTHER INFORMATION

Jobs If you're thinking of finding some work here and staying for a while but haven't arranged any contract from your home country note that work permits can cost up to US$200 in bribes. Unemployment is high in Kenya.

The dreaded weed Bush costs 30-45 Sh an 'arm' depending on how near you are to Kisumu near the Ugandan border where most of it is grown. It's illegal (of course) so be careful. A natural stimulant which is legal is 'khat' (also known as 'murangi' or 'mirah'). It's also popular in Ethiopia and Yemen and has an effect not unlike mild amphetamine. A small bunch of leaves (a day's chewing supply) should cost around 5 Sh. Easiest place to find it is around River Rd, Nairobi.

Cottage Crafts A good place offering these is NCCK shop in Phoenix Arcade Standard Street, Nairobi. They have basketry, jewellery, pottery, leather and sisal work, chairs, educational toys, banana fibre work and books by African authors. The centre is run as a Co-operative and there are no middle men. It's designed to encourage craftspeople to produce high quality products while at the same time ensuring them a fair price for their work.

Film Kenya is one of the few countries in Africa where you can buy relatively cheap film. Processing of Kodachrome 135-36 costs about 75 Sh. Ebrahim's Camera House, Government Rd (Moi Ave), Nairobi has been recommended.

Lesotho

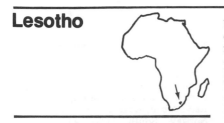

Formerly one of the British High Commission Territories which also included Botswana and Swaziland, Lesotho became independent in 1966. Although the country has taken an increasingly strong stand against South Africa's apartheid policies, it remains very much an economic and geographical hostage of its powerful neighbour. In its search for allies in southern Africa, Lesotho has exchanged ambassadors with Mozambique though the prime minister remains opposed to communism as an ideology.

The country has been ruled since independence by Chief Leabua Jonathon, the prime minister, who was assisted in his election campaign at the time by Verwoerd who provided helicopters, jeeps and other assistance. Jonathon in his turn abstained from voting against South Africa in the UN and is one of those few African leaders who is in favour of a dialogue with that country. He has little choice. When he lost the 1970 elections to the Basutoland Congress Party, Jonathon cancelled the results and declared the party illegal, arresting many of its members. The leader of the party Ntsu Mokhehle, fled the country and ever since there has

been a steady stream of exilés from Lesotho to Botswana in the wake of police repression in response to opposition to Jonathon's regime. Even school children have not escaped his dragnet. Soon after he cancelled the elections, Jonathon suspended the constitution, made the King into a constitutional monarch and banned Mokhehle from ever returning to Lesotho. Lately, however, he has been forced to include two opposition politicians in his cabinet to shore up the flagging credibility of his regime.

The creation of the so-called independent state of Transkei caused difficulties for Lesotho a little while back since the government was loathe to afford it diplomatic recognition in view of its obvious puppet status. In an effort to force them to do so, the leaders of the Transkei closed their common borders with Lesotho making it very difficult for its people to use the traditional short route to Matatiele to trade their goods and obtain supplies. The matter has still not been resolved though the border closures do not affect non-Lesotho citizens.

Lesotho's main export is about half its able-bodied men to work in South Africa under a pernicious migrant labour system which has wreaked havoc with the social stability of the country. Cash income comes from the sale of cattle, wool and mohair to South Africa and diamonds are being mined around Letseng by the South African company De Beers who spent 23 million Rand on the project. Other mineralogical surveys have produced evidence of deposits of iron, coal and possibly uranium. Canada supplied the services and equipment for the mineral surveys while Britain and the USA have supplied other aid.

One of the country's chief aims is to become self-sufficient in food but it suffers from erosion stemming from overgrazing. The lowlands remain infertile because the lack of trees has meant that animal manure is used for fuel instead of being returned to the soil. Lesotho's most valuable resource — water — is not tapped at all though there is an old scheme, shelved many times, for damming the Orange River. If this were ever built it would allow Lesotho to sell electricity and water to South Africa.

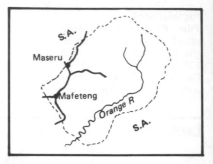

FACTS
The Lesotho people are some of the most friendly and generous in Africa though they remain very poor. Most of the population live in the lowlands at about 1500 metres though much of the land is above 3000 metres. It's excellent walking country with some amazing mountain scenery but can be hard going with changeable weather. Don't go out, even for an afternoon, without a sleeping bag and tent and take sufficient food in case you get fogged in. It's generally clear from May to September but cold and windy higher up with often 10-15 degrees of frost at night. Even in summer it can freeze and there are often thunderstorms in the afternoons. There is no trouble finding clean drinking water in the mountains even in the dry season but if you take water from below a village you must boil it before drinking it.

VISAS
Required by all except nationals of Commonwealth countries, Belgium, Denmark, Finland, Irish Republic, Israel Italy, Japan, Luxembourg, Netherlands, Norway, South Africa and Sweden. Visas for Lesotho can be issued by British Embassies where there is no Lesotho Embassy. They are issued free to citizens of the USA.

CURRENCY
The unit of currency is the South African Rand = 100 cents. There are no restrictions on the import or export of local currency.

Exchange rate:

£1	=	Rand 1.74
US$1	=	Rand 0.76
A$1	=	Rand 0.87

LANGUAGES
Sesotho and English. Greetings are an important social ritual in Lesotho. Here are a few phrases with male and (female) variations:

when meeting	pronunciation	meaning
lumela (khotso) ntate	du-may-lah (ko-tso) n-tah-tah	greetings sir (madam)
lumelang (khotsong) bontate		....sirs (ladies)
O phela (tsuele) joang	pay-la (tswee-lay) zhwawng	how are you?
ke pehla (tsuele) hantle	kee pay-la (tswee-lay) han-clay	I'm fine
le kae? ke teng	look eye	how are you? I'm fine

O ya kae?		where are you going?
O tsoa kae?	tswa	where do you come from?
ke leboha	kee-ya le-bow-ah	thank you

when parting

tsamae [ng] hantle	tsa-my-ah [ng] han-clay	go well
sala [ng] natle		stay well

[ng] for plural

HEALTH

Lesotho is a very healthy country, mainly because of the altitude. There's no malaria or bilharzia but you should guard against frostbite when walking in the mountains.

ACCOMMODATION

There's very little purpose-built accommodation for travellers outside of the capital, Maseru. There is a Youth Hostels organisation (Secretary, Lesotho YHA, PO Box 660, Maseru) with a Youth Hostel at Lancer's Gap, four km from Maseru, and the government also maintain rest houses in the mountains which range from 50 cents to 2.50 Rand. Details from the Ministry of Tourism, PO Box 52, Maseru. When planning on camping near villages always first ask permission from the village chief. He will often offer you a rondoval to sleep in for the night.

Maseru

The town is a playground for South African and Zimbabwean businessmen and holidaymakers who come here looking for all the things which are banned in the Republic itself — certain films, prostitutes, casinos, etc. Consquently much of the town is geared to catering for their wants. There are several cheap places to stay near the market otherwise the Lancer's Inn is the cheapest. A shared room, costs 2.65 Rand per person. If you're prepared to contribute toward your keep, it's worth checking out with the Peace Corps Office on Constitution Road or with the IVS and United Nations volunteers behind the Lancer's Inn. They're generally welcoming and will provide a floor for you to crash on or space for camping. If they like you, they may well direct you to other volunteers working in other parts of the country.

TRANSPORT

You need plenty of time in this country. Life goes on at a very steady pace and nothing happens in a hurry. Hitching is easy in the 'lowlands' though lifts to the remoter parts, often by store trucks, are difficult to find. All the roads are incredibly rough except the ones connecting Maseru with Mafeteng and Leribe which are tarred. The Basotho travel almost exclusively on horseback but buying a horse tends to be expensive in the towns and very difficult in the countryside as they're too valuable for their owners to part with. It's superb walking country with endless interest along the way. There's no danger of robberies or anything of that nature. There are a few buses to some of the larger towns and they all leave from the bus station near the market in Maseru. Lesotho National Buses are the best bargain. Maseru to Butha Buthe costs 1.55 Rand. If you're heading for South Africa from there, it's a 20 km hitch to Fouriesburg.

There's a three km rail link from Maseru to the South African border from where there are connections to the rest of the Republic.

If you're going walking in the mountains, maps (1:50,000) can be bought for 1 Rand each from the Department of Survey behind the Department of Mines which in turn is behind Barclays Bank in Maseru. David Amrose's *Guide to Lesotho* (Winchester Press) is also a very useful companion. Here are some walking suggestions:

Thaba Bosiu This is a flat-topped hill where the Basotho made their stand against the Boers. The graves of the chiefs who were killed are located here. To get there, take the bus from Maseru and ask for the official guide.

Ha Khotso Rock Paintings The best examples of bushmen paintings in the country. From St Michael's at the start of the mountain road near Roma, which can be reached by bus from Maseru, take the mountain road for 12 km and watch for the sign. From there the paintings are situated six km down a minor road to the left.

Semon Kong This is the nearest place to the Maletsunyane Falls (also known as Lebihan Falls) which is about 15 km distant. You can either fly from Maseru for about 10 Rand or take a bus to Ramabanta and walk from there (takes about a day). The Falls are 200 metres high and particularly spectacular in summer. There's a lodge at the falls where you can stay for 3 Rand and a shop where you can buy provisions.

Qacha's Nek & the Sani Pass You can either fly from Maseru for 18 Rand to Qacha's Nek or come by road from Matatiele in the Transkei. There is an hotel and store at Qacha's Nek. From here you walk along a bridle path to Ramatseliso's Gate where there is a store (takes about 1½ days) and then on to Schabathebe National Park where there is a lodge for 2.50 Rand and a store (takes about a day). From here it takes another two days to climb and walk along the escarpment to Sani Pass. There are no villages along the way. Spectacular views all the way if the weather is clear. At Sani there is a shop and chalet with cooking facilities for 3.50 Rand.

Sani to Butha Buthe A road connects the two and it's fairly easy to get a ride on a truck. Total cost between the two places would be about 5 Rand. From Sani it's about four hours' walk to the top of Thabana Ntlunyana, the highest point in Southern Africa though the views are not particularly spectacular. It's possible to continue along a ridge from here to Mokhotlong where there are shops but no accommodation. The walk will take one strenuous day or two easy-going days. It's a very rugged part of Lesotho. At Letseng-la-Terae there is a diamond mine and an expensive lodge at Oxbow for 10 Rand. From here you get to Butha Buthe via the Moteng Pass — trucks ply along this route. Have warm clothing with you as the mountain air is cold. 12 km north of Letseng is a bridle path to Mont-aux-Sources where the views are fantastic. A flight is possible from Maseru to Mokhotlong for 18 Rand.

Liberia

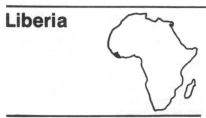

Liberia began as a venture of American philanthropists in 1821 the idea being to resettle freed slaves in Africa. It was not a particularly successful venture and by 1847, when it was formally declared an independent republic, it consisted of only a few thousand Negro settlers who had to strive to maintain themselves and their ideals against the hostility of native tribes. Even its foster parent, the United States, did not formally recognise it until 1862 though it managed to maintain its independence from all but European money-lenders throughout the scramble for colonies in the late 19th century.

Though, on the surface, one of Africa's most stable states, animosity between the descendants of the settlers and the indigenous Krios (various tribes constituting 97% of the country's population) continued to poison relations between the two groups. Power was hogged by the settler descendants and although Dr William Tolbert, the president since 1971, attempted to conjure up a sense of national unity he failed to convince the Krios that they had any part in the running of the country or a reasonable slice of the cake. In an attempt to hang onto power, harsh laws were passed against 'sedition' and any sort of activity considered to be an incitement to unrest. The resentment boiled over in April 1980 when a coup, led by Master Sergeant Samuel Doe, overthrew Tolbert's government and placed the Krios in control. Tolbert and many of his ministers as well as high-ranking members of the armed forces and security police were killed during the coup and dumped into common graves. Those who were left were briefly 'tried' and then publicly shot tied to stakes on the beach. Since the coup, most African leaders have snubbed Doe and his fellow officers.

Before Tolbert was assassinated, the country was a gold-mine for overseas companies interested in exploiting the mineral wealth (mainly iron ore), the rubber and oil and providing technical assistance and advice. A very high percentage of the profits which these companies made were exported abroad and the government seemed happy to keep things that way, but with the Krios now in power this may all change. In addition, Tolbert was one of the strongest supporters of South Africa's attempt to maintain economic and diplomatic relations with the rest of black Africa.

Though it has one of Africa's largest Peace Corps contingents, it's not a country which attracts many travellers and those who go there are generally only in transit between Sierra Leone and the Ivory Coast. It has a monsoon climate with an average temperature of 26°C but is drier and cooler in the interior.

VISAS

Required by all. White South Africans not admitted. If you're thinking of going there, get your visa beforehand since, although they can be issued on arrival they will cost you US$20!! Obtained beforehand they cost less but are still expensive (for British passports holders they cost US$9.50). Visas are generally valid for a 30-day stay. Those obtained on arrival cannot be renewed. An exit visa is necessary — obtainable from Immigration in Monrovia. We've had reports from travellers in the past saying that it's possible to get in through the Liberia/Ivory Coast border at Toulepleu without a visa and leave via the Sierra Leone without a fuss

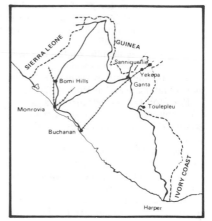

by telling the customs people that no-one was on duty at the border of entry—often true. This might still apply.

CURRENCY

The unit of currency is the Liberian Dollar = 100 cents. The bank notes are, in fact, US Dollars but the coins are Liberian. There is no restriction on the import/export of local currency. The exchange rate is on a par with the American Dollar.

LANGUAGES

English and many local languages.

ACCOMMODATION
Monrovia

The *Lutheran Mission*, 13th Street on the beach, costs $3 for Lutherans, $6 for Peace Corps volunteers and $8 for others. Very comfortable double rooms with hot water. To get there, take a poda or taxi (25 cents) to the Sinkor Shopping Centre. The *United Methodist Mission*, 12th Street on the beach, costs $10 for an apartment with washer and spin drier! Peace Corps not welcome.

Hotel Plaza near the waterside, costs $10 per room (sleeps three). *Hotel Victoria*, costs $10 though it's sometimes possible to talk the manager into letting you have a room for $5 if the hotel is empty. The *YMCA* is at the opposite end of Broad Street to the Duncor Hotel, no recent details.

Forget about sleeping on the beaches in Monrovia. They're covered in oil. Beware of pickpockets and gangsters down by the waterside and at Roberts Port.

For food try the restaurants and rice chop houses on Gurly Street, off Broad Street, which is in the middle of the bar area.

Taxis in Monrovia cost 25 cents per person and a zoning system is in force. The truck and taxi park for upcountry lifts is in Walter Street.

American Express is at Morgan Travel Agency, 80 Broad Street, PO Box 1260, CDB King Building, Monrovia (tel 22149).

Yekepa

A modern town with incredible facilities right out in the sticks. One of the cheapest places to stay is the *Humble Inn* which costs $4 per room and you're allowed to have as many people as you like sleep in a room. Alternatively, try the bars where expatriate workers congregate (especially British). You might well get invited back. Most of them are bored stiff.

TRANSPORT

To Sierra Leone From Monrovia to the border (Bombom) costs $3 by poda or $5 by taxi. The route goes through the Bomi Hills. From the border you can get a poda direct to Kenema via Zimi for 3 Leone. Kenema is the railhead in Sierra Leone from where you can get a train to Freetown. It's also possible to take the much longer route through northern Liberia to Kailahun in Sierra Leone and from there to Kenema.

To the Ivory Coast You can either take the route from Monrovia direct to Abidjan via Ganta and Toulepleu (not much traffic between Tappi and Toulepleu so this route may involve long waits for lifts) or from Monrovia to Man via Sanniquellie and Danane. Both routes initially take the train from Buchanan.

Monrovia-Buchanan by taxi costs $3.50. Buchanan-Yekepa/Sanniquellie: train departs daily at 4.50 pm except Sundays when it departs at 6.30 pm, costs $7 to Yekepa. If you have a word with the driver before departure he'll stop for you at Sanniquellie. British Rail cars!!

If you're heading for Man you take a taxi from Yekepa to the border for $1.50 and from there another taxi to Danane for 400 CFA. From Danane to Man costs a further 500 CFA by taxi.

If you're heading for Abidjan via Toulepleu get off the train at Sanniquellie and take a taxi to Ganta. From there you can pick up a taxi to Toulepleu for $2.50. From Toulepleu there are occasional buses to Abidjan but the best bet is a lift with a truck for around 2500 CFA.

There are no buses across the border between the two countries. If you don't want to take the train from Buchanan to Yekepa or Sanniquellie there are taxis direct from Monrovia.

Libya

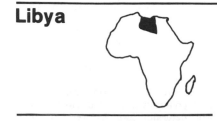

Libya has been conquered and settled at one time or another by the Garamantes, Greeks, Romans, Berbers, Arabs and Turks. The remains of these various periods can still be seen today in the ruined cities along the coast, the Greek remains at Leptis Magna being particularly interesting and some of the best preserved in the world. From the middle of the 16th century until 1911, Libya was part of the empire of the Ottoman Turks and was that empire's last possession along the North African coast. It was taken from them by the Italians in that country's last-minute bid for colonies but following WW II was placed under United Nations trusteeship until 1951 when it became an independent nation.

In 1969 the old King Idris was deposed in a military coup led by Colonel Muammar Qadafi, a man then in his early 30s, deeply religious and inspired by a vision of Pan-Arabism. Qadafi has succeeded in placing the country in the forefront of Middle Eastern and even world politics and drastically changing Libya's former status as a UK-USA client state. His regime is pledged to the equitable distribution of Libya's enormous income from the sale of oil and is currently spending thousands of millions of dollars on roads, schools, houses

hospitals and agriculture. Soon after he came to power the British and Americans were ordered to leave their bases occupied since WW II and the 25,000 descendants of the Italian colonists forced to pack their bags and leave promptly.

Some promising moves are being made in the devolution and sharing of political power stemming from Qadafi's 'Green Book'. In it he states that the parliamentary system practised in the west is undemocratic since it is used by politicians to take power away from the people and that a multi-party system is detrimental to political progress, encouraging sterile opposition for opposition's sake while in reality the parties in power pursue much the same policies. Though the book contains some refreshing insights and promising new directions which have revolutionised Libyan society, a fair amount of it is pure eccentric eye-wash.

From being almost wholly foreign-owned and controlled at the time of King Idris' overthrow, Libya's vast oil deposits have gradually been taken over by a government determined to return control of the country's natural resources to the people. Despite an attempt to form a cartel to resist such a development, by 1973 all the oil companies had been forced to accept a minimum 51% Libyan participation. The National Oil Corporation began independent operations in 1971 and by 1973, with its own operations and the participation agreements it had wrung from the foreign oil companies, it controlled 70% of oil production. Soon after that it embarked on its own refining, distribution of refined products and the direct export of crude to state concerns. Before these events took place, Libya, despite being one of the world's largest producers of crude oil, was forced to import all of its refined requirements since none of the foreign oil companies had built refineries in Libya. Refined oil is now being exported, often in Libyan-owned tankers and the natural gas which had been flared in the past is being harnessed to fuel power stations.

Ambitious plans to make Libya self-sufficient in food have brought agriculture into a dominant position in the country with forestry and fishing following closely behind. Vast areas of land are in the process of reclamation and the government is encouraging farmers to adopt co-operative methods. Dams have been constructed to catch what little water falls and many novel methods of turning desert back into arable land utilised. In Roman times this area and that in adjacent Algeria were known as the 'granary of the empire' but because of overgrazing, neglect of irrigation systems, lack of planning and wars the desert has expanded over the centuries leaving precious little of the country which was suitable for agriculture.

Libya is well known for its support (in both money and arms) of liberation movements around the world though its support for some regimes — like that of Idi Amin in Uganda before his downfall — stretches the concept of liberation beyond belief and has helped to cast serious doubts on Qadafi's idealism. Recent interviews Qadafi has given to selected press correspondents suggest that power has gone to his head in recent years and that he has become something of an egotist. Movements presently receiving Libyan support include the IRA, the Polisario of Western Sahara, the Popular Front for the Liberation of Oman, the Eritrean Liberation Front and even the Mindanao rebels in the far away Philippines. Libya is also heavily involved in the war in Chad and indeed several years ago took over a section of the northern part of that country for reasons which still remain unclear. Though Libya and Egypt were, at one time, involved in negotiations to create a unified republic, they have since then been on the brink of war at least twice, once as a result of the treatment of Egyptian workers in Libya all of whom were subsequently expelled, and again in 1979 following the Camp David peace settlement between Egypt and Israel. The border between the two countries is again closed and likely to remain so for a long time which means that your arrival point in North Africa will determine which overland route you can take south.

Though the income from oil has given Libya the opportunity to vastly improve the quality of life of its relatively few citizens, the extremely rapid transition from a largely nomadic to a modern consumer society has resulted in many problems. Travellers write of the streets full of discarded trash, the rampant inflation, expensive food and accommodation and the same old neuroses to be found on the streets of any western capital city. Fresh fruit and vegetables are scarce and over 90% of food is imported, most of it as canned produce.

VISAS

Required by all. Nationals of Israel and South Africa are not admitted. If your passport contains a current or expired visa for Israel, regardless of your nationality, you will be refused entry. If you hold a German passport you must get your visa in Bonn (you'll be refused entry unless you get it from there). Single women under 35 years of age are not allowed into Libya!

Before applying for a visa you must have pages one and two of your passport translated into Arabic and endorsed in your passport. If travelling on a

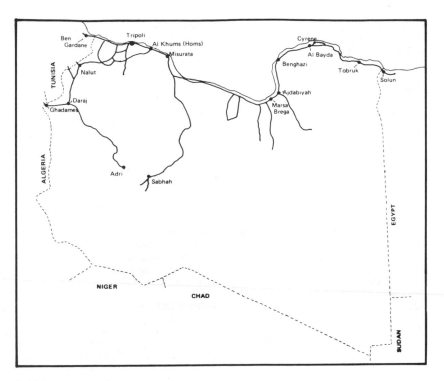

British passport you can have this done free at the Passport Office in London or at the British or American Embassies in Tunis or Cairo. You're also supposed to have this done with your international Vaccination Card though they're more concerned with your passport. In London visas cost £4, two photos and take 48 hours. In Tunis they cost 3 Dinar, two photos and take five days to issue.

If you arrive at Sebha in southern Libya from Niger by air without a visa you will be given a seven day transit visa.

CURRENCY
The unit of currency is the Dinar = 100 dirham. Import/export of local currency is allowed up to 20 Dinar. Currency Declaration Forms are issued on arrival.

Exchange rate:

£1	=	0.65 Dinar
US$1	=	0.29 Dinar
A$1	=	0.33 Dinar

Customs regulations prohibit the import of alcoholic drinks, goods manufactured in Israel and goods manufactured by firms trading with Israel (tear off those St Michael labels from your underpants folks!).

LANGUAGE
Arabic with some English and Italian. All correspondence with government departments must be in Arabic.

ACCOMMODATION
Many travellers sleep on the beaches at

the archaeological sites such as Sabrantha, Leptis Magna, Tocra (Tukrah), Tolemaida (Tulmaythah) and Cyrene (Shahhat).

Tripoli
There's no such thing as a 'cheap' hotel in Tripoli. The places around the large bus station outside the old city will cost you at least 2 Dinar for a bed in a dormitory. Probably the best place to stay is the *Youth Hostel* situated about 500 metres outside the old city on Sharia Omar Ibn El As (otherwise known as Omar Ben Alas). It's just past the cinema on the opposite side of the road. Beds cost 0.35 Dinar (there are 120 beds). Most of the rooms are double ones and it's spacious and comfortable with clean linen, TV lounge, hot and cold showers and sometimes they even have movies. Friendly place. The cafe next door offers macaroni for 0.40 Dinar.

Tobruk
The *Hotel Benghazi* has double rooms for 2 Dinar.

TRANSPORT
The Egyptian-Libyan border is presently closed so the only way you can get in is from Tunisia. Hitching is easy and lifts are often for long distances especially between Tripoli and Benghazi between which there's very little habitation. Lifts are often with foreign travellers/employees of oil companies and most often free. If you're heading down to Sabha in the desert, however, expect to pay something for the lift.

There are daily buses between the main Libyan coastal towns. Buy your ticket at least a day in advance as they are usually heavily booked. We have no further details as very few travellers go there any more because of the border closure between Libya and Egypt. A visit to Libya would mean doubling back from Tunisia at present. It's also a very expensive place.

OTHER INFORMATION
Avoid taking photos of anything other than the ruins on the coast. Libyan officials are phobic about spies and you can get yourself into a lot of aggravation unless you're very discreet.

Madagascar

Madagascar is an enigma in Africa since the majority of its 6½ million population are descended from Indonesians who began to arrive there from the 9th century onwards when the powerful Hindu Sumatran empire of Sri Vijaya controlled much of the maritime trade in the Indian Ocean. They brought with them the South-East Asian food crops like the banana and coconut so that, even today, the agriculture of the island resembles that of the area of their origin rather than that of the mainland. It has been suggested that the spread of these crops to the mainland in the centuries which followed assisted the migration of the Bantu tribes from the interior to the Kenyan and Tanzanian coasts. None of the mainland apes, lions, elephants, antelopes or poisonous snakes are to be found on the island. It is also the descendants of these Indonesian colonisers who control agriculture on the island while the rest of the population (composed of Europeans, Chinese and Indians) control the services sector.

Madagascar became a French colony

in the 19th century though French rule was never accepted without resistance and after a series of rebellions in the 20th century the island gained its independence in 1960 under the presidency of Philibert Tsiranana, a moderate Francophile noted for his rigging of elections. He was overthrown in 1972 by the military. Under the military regime French influence began to wane and there was a revival of the collective work system practised in the rural areas which is comparable with the Ujaama movement in Tanzania. Nevertheless, the military government inherited a stagnant economy which was so geared to French interests that even basic foodstuffs had to be imported while 85% of the country's external trade remained in the hands of foreign companies.

The new regime was cautious at first in acting against French interests but in 1973 the two banks which were the pillars of French influence were taken over. This was followed up by bringing a number of other areas under state control and pursuing a vigorous foreign policy. Links were cut with South Africa, Rhodesia and Caetano's Portugal and others established, notably with Russia and China. The struggle to shake off French dependence was not easy and negotiations for the evacuation of the French base at Diego Suarez dragged on for years. The French tried to bargain for keeping the bases in return for a large measure of monetary independence for the country coupled with continued French guarantees of support for the country's currency but in the end the French were forced to quit and Madagascar withdrew from the franc zone. This precipitated the departure of several thousand members of the French farming community which resulted in a painful reminder of how dependent the Madagascans still were on French capital and know-how. The Americans, too, were evicted from their satellite tracking station at Imerintsitosika.

Despite these moves unrest continued to surface, fomented by French businessmen and firms which wanted to perpetuate the colonial hold, and General Ramanantsoa was forced to step down in an abortive coup and was replaced by Lt Colonel Ratsimandrava. Though pledged to follow the progressive line of his predecessor but with more vigour, Ratsimandrava was shot to death in his car within a week of taking office and a rebel group of army officers promptly announced a military takeover. They were routed by those officers loyal to the former president and a new government headed by the former Foreign Minister, Didier Ratsiraka, set up. Since coming to power Ratsiraka has been following similar socialist policies to those of Ramanantsoa and there are encouraging signs that foreign powers are coming to terms with the new nationalist currents on the island.

FACTS

Madagascar is set almost entirely in the tropics though there is a dramatic difference in the geography and climate from one area to the next. Tropical rain forests dominate the east coast while savannah and dry forests cover the west coast with cacti-like vegetation in the west. There is a rugged mountain chain down the centre with deep valleys and lush grasslands. Cyclones are common on the east coast. The dry season is from November to March.

VISAS

Required by all. Note there is no Malagasy Embassy in Nairobi any longer, but you can apply for the visa through Air Madagascar in the Hilton Hotel, Nairobi. You must apply on the Monday as the forms have to be sent to Madagascar for approval but you get them back on Wednesday of the same week. Visas cost 65 Sh, four photos, four forms and are

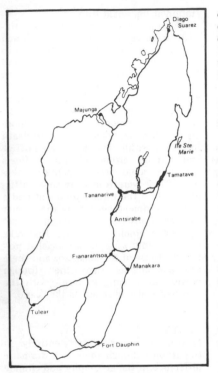

valid for a stay of one month. No hassles about money or onward tickets. In Port Louis, Mauritius, visas cost 42.50 Rupees.

CURRENCY
The unit of currency is the Malagache Franc = 100 centimes. Import/export of local currency is allowed up to 5000 Fr.

Exchange rate:

£1	=	473 Fr
US$1	=	207 Fr
A$1	=	237 Fr

There is a very strict currency control on arrival. All your cash is checked thoroughly down to the last cent both on arrival and on departure. Currency declaration forms are issued. Don't change too much money into Malagache Francs as they can't be changed outside the country. Airport tax for international flights is 1500 Fr.

LANGUAGES
French and Malagasy, very little English is spoken.

HEALTH
If you arrive from a country where cholera is endemic (eg Tanzania) your International Vaccination Card is taken by the authorities and you have to go back five days later to collect it — a nuisance if you want to go travelling around the island.

ACCOMMODATION
Antsirabe
Hotel Baobao costs 800 Fr and is clean and comfortable.

A'tondrazaka
Hotel Boahirana costs 1000 Fr and is highly recommended.

Fort Dauphin
Accommodation here is cheaper than in Tananarive but expect to pay at least 800 Fr for anywhere reasonable. For less than that the accommodation you get will be very dirty and uncomfortable. It's sometimes possible to get houses either for free or for rent through the Mission if they like you.

Isle St Marie
A beautiful island of cloves and other spice crops off the east coast. Bungalows at Petty Plage for around 600 Fr. There's only one cafe on the island.

Majunga
Hotel Boira costs 800 Fr.

Tamatave
Hotel Plage costs 1800 Fr. It's also poss-

ible to sleep on the beach or in the soccer stadium opposite the Hotel Plage. For eats, try the *Restaurant Vietnamien* rue Aviateur Goulette 16, off Boulevard Joffre. There are also plenty of 'Soupe Chinoise' restaurants where you can get soup for 150 Fr.

Tananarive

Decent accommodation is expensive. Many of the cheaper places are located to the right of the railway station but are often full. They cost on average about 800 Fr/single and 1200 Fr/double. One of the cheapest is *Hotel Lapan' ny Vaniny*, near Avenue de la Liberation and the Indonesian Embassy. It costs 850 Fr and although alright for a night is very dirty and can't really be recommended. Another is the *Hotel Ivarivo* — similar charge.

Hotel Select, Avenue 18 de Juin, next door to Alitalia, a small room costs 1320 Fr. Very clean and conveniently situated. *Hotel Terminus*, Avenue de la Liberation, just by the railway station, costs the same as the Select, is very clean and comfortable and you can change money there if you arrive after the banks have closed. *Glacier Hotel*, near the train station, costs 1400 Fr/double.

Food is plentiful and relatively cheap. If you're into street stall food try the Central Market. Otherwise the *Restaurant Fiadanana*, 12 Avenue Adrianampoinimerina — first street left from the station — it is recommended for good food.

The Tourist Office opposite Aeroflot is not particularly helpful. The GPO is also nearby. A taxi from the airport costs 2000 Fr, the bus costs 350 Fr.

TRANSPORT

Hitching is difficult and you usually have to pay for lifts. During the wet season everything takes much longer and some roads are impasable. All the minor country roads in the central highlands are very beautiful and it's well worth spending some time there. Try going to Lac Aloatra (accessible by either road or rail) but don't swim in the lake as there's bilharzia. The cheapest form of public transport is the 'taxi-brousse' — shared minibuses which cost about 6 centimes/km and are amazingly uncomfortable. Normal buses cost about 25 centimes/km and are slow but not quite so uncomfortable. The best form of transport between the towns is the 'taxi-be' — shared taxis costing about 35 centimes/km which are quick and fairly comfortable. Getting down to Fort Dauphin in the south is difficult and expensive because of bad roads. A taxi-be will cost you 10,000 Fr from Tananarive and take 24 hours. They go once every four days and you're advised to book a seat in advance.

Trains The main line between Tamatave and Tananarive is very comfortable, slow and cheap. Trains depart Tamatave daily at 6 am and arrive at Tananarive at 6.20 pm. Cost is 1800 Fr in 2nd class.

There are also several trains per day to Antsirabe which take four hours and cost 400 Fr. The carriages are old and dirty. You can also get a train to A'tondrazaka near Lac Alaotra for 981 Fr but the journey can be very slow.

Boats There's a possibility of picking up a boat from Tamatave to Fort Dauphin. Ask at Auximad opposite the beach or chat with the sailors at the Hotel Plage bar. There are occasional boats from Tamatave to Isle St Marie and from Diego Suarez to Moroni in the Comores Islands.

Flights

To/From Kenya Both Air Madagascar and Air Tanzania fly twice weekly to Madagascar from Nairobi (Nairobi-Tananarive). A 21-day excursion ticket costs 1906 Kenyan Sh (£150).

To/From Tanzania Air Tanzania fly from Dar to Tananarive once weekly.

Air Madagascar fly the same route twice weekly but are more reliable than Air Tanzania. The latter have no office in Dar so you have to buy your ticket through Air Tanzania which means you have to wait a few days for confirmation as they have to telex Tananarive. There are usually no problems as there's not much traffic on this route. A 21-day excursion ticket with either airline costs 1527 Tanzanian Sh (£95). There is a Malagasy Embassy in Dar es Salaam.

If you'd like to see the Comores Islands, the cheapest flights available are those from Majunga to Moroni. Tananarive to Fort Dauphin costs 16,100 Fr.

Madeira

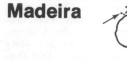

A Portuguese island since the 13th century, Madeira lies north of the Canary Islands off the north-west coast of Africa. Funchal, the capital, has a population of about 100,000 and remains fairly peaceful and unaffected by tourism. There are plenty of bars and cheap cafes and an excellent market for fruit and vegetables. Buses are cheap and efficient and cover the whole of the island though most of the roads keep to the coast. The countryside is very mountainous, villages are small and cafes are scarce — most people are fishermen or farmers so there's little call for cafes. The climate is near perfect with a noticeable drop in temperature at night though it can get very cool in the mountains, some of which are over 2000 metres high. Sandy beaches are very rare but pools formed in the rocky coast make swimming very pleasant. The ocean temperature is often the same as the air temperature. The other smaller island of Porto Santo has sandy beaches and is about as far off the beaten track as you could get. A ferry connects the island with Funchal. Very few travellers come this way unless they're heading for the Azores and South America as there's no way you can get from Madeira to the African mainland except by very expensive boat. We include it for the sake of completeness.

VISAS
The regulations are the same as for Portugal. Visas are required by nationals of Austria, Israel, New Zealand and South Africa.

CURRENCY
The unit of currency is the Escudo = 100 centavos. Import/export of local currency is allowed up to 5000 Escudos. Exchange rate:

£1	=	106 Escudos
US$1	=	46 Escudos
A$1	=	53 Escudos

TRANSPORT
There is a daily (in either direction) inter-island ferry between Madeira and Porto Santo. Journey time is approximately three hours. Departs Funchal at 8 am (summer and winter) and Porto Santo at 4 pm (winter) and 5 pm (summer). One way fare is 160 Escudos (winter) and 190 Escudos (summer). The operator is Organizacao Nautica Amigos do Mar, rua Dr Fernao de Ornelas 7-2, 900 Funchal, Madeira.

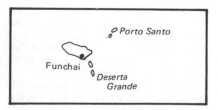

Porto Santo

Funchal

Deserta Grande

Malawi

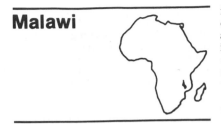

Formerly the British Protectorate of Nyasaland, Malawi gained its independence in 1964. Dr Hastings Banda, president since independence, rapidly became the favourite African leader of the white supremacist regimes in Rhodesia and South Africa since, although in his public statements he condemned them and said he would have no diplomatic dealings with them, his attitude towards them in other respects contradicted the rhetoric. As a result, South Africa made a loan of eight million Rand for the construction of the new capital at Lilongwe and made more money available for the extension of the Nacala railway.

His attitude towards his fellow African leaders was also shot through with ambivalence. Only a few years after independence he described their attitudes to South Africa as 'illogical, hypocritical, dishonest and unfair' since, in his books, if the Europeans had to get out of South Africa then the same should apply to the Arabs in the north of the continent. There were also attempts to claim half of Lake Nyasa and four other territories within Tanzania as well as districts within Zambia. Naturally, these actions made him unpopular with the leaders of neighbouring states and his repressive policies towards those who opposed him prompted a group of Malawian exiles to launch an assassination attempt from Tanzania in 1967. Somewhat miraculously he has managed to survive in power though the cost to his countrymen can be measured to some extent by the large number of political prisoners languishing in his jails and the fact that it's virtually impossible to discuss politics with a Malawian — they're always looking over their shoulders for informers and some pretty hairy stories do the rounds from time to time which are a great contrast to the outward peace and friendliness of the country.

The other aspect of Banda's foreign policy is an open commitment to the west particularly towards Britain, Israel, the USA and Taiwan and the encouragement of private and government investment in the tea and tobacco estates. He was, for many years, bitterly hostile towards China and Egypt though with recent events there this may soon change.

Though Banda's regime is pretty repressive we hope you won't be put off going there. It's an incredibly beautiful country!

FACTS
Malawi is a very poor country and at any one time ¼ million of the 2.8 million inhabitants are working in the mines in northern Zimbabwe and South Africa or on the tobacco farms of southern Zimbabwe. About 20% of the country is composed of Lake Nyasa, situated in a deep rift valley. It's the only lake in Africa which is free from bilharzia except around Karonga where the water is really murky. Most of the land is cultivated and about 95% of the population is involved in agriculture. The climate varies from one part to another but is generally sub-tropical with rainy seasons from December to March in the south and October to April in the north.

VISAS
Required by all except nationals of the Commonwealth countries, Western Europe (except Austria, France, Italy, Spain and Switzerland), South Africa, USA and Zimbabwe.

The official blurb on visas also says 'Female passengers will not be permitted to enter the country if wearing short

179

dresses or trouser-suits except in transit or at Lake holiday resorts or National Parks. Skirts and dresses must cover the knees to conform with Government regulations. The entry of 'hippies' and male persons with long hair and flared trousers is forbidden'. His Excellency, the Life President Ngawzi Kisumi Hastings Banda (as he likes to be addressed) is obviously out of touch with current trends in fashion and the economic realities of overland travel through Africa.

At the Chitipa border with Zambia, they're generally pretty easy-going except about hair length. It must be in line with your mouth — and they mean it! You might be dealt with by one of the 'Young Pioneers', Banda's adaptation of the Hitler Youth, who are like overgrown schoolkids in their approach to

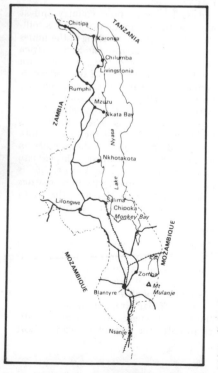

authority. They've been programmed to be up-tight about 'communism' so if you're asked, you've never, of course, been to any communist country and you've never heard of Karl Marx.

The borders with Tanzania may still be closed to overland traffic in which case you'll have to enter or leave the country via Chitipa and Zambia. This generally presents no problems since most travellers heading south take the Iringa-Mbeya-Mpika-Lusaka road anyway. The borders with Mozambique are closed to foreigners.

South African Visas Very easy to obtain in Lilongwe. They are free and issued the same day. If you're planning on going there by air, you have to have an onward ticket before the visa will be issued.

CURRENCY
The unit of currency is the Kwacha = 100 tambala. Import/export of local currency is allowed up to 20 Kwacha.

Exchange rate:

£1	=	1.80 Kwacha
US$1	=	0.78 Kwacha
A$1	=	0.90 Kwacha

You have to fill in a currency declaration form on entry. There is a small blackmarket in Blantyre where you can get up to 10% more than in the banks. Note that District Commissioners Treasury offices give better rates than the banks but they don't always know what the rate is so check with the banks first.

Airport tax for international flights is 4 Kwacha.

LANGUAGE
The national language is Chichewa but English is widely spoken. There are also a number of local languages.

ACCOMMODATION
In almost every town there's either a

Government or a District Rest House. The District Rest Houses are cheaper but more crowded and cost 25 tambala per night or 5 tambala for a piece of floor. They're clean. The Government Rest Houses are plusher and cost Kw 3 a single or Kw 4 a double including breakfast in your room. They're very clean. An extra bed can be moved into a single room, if there's one to spare. In some of the larger Government Rest Houses (eg Blantyre and Nkhotakota) there are dormitories for 50 tambala which includes the use of the toilets and hot baths and you can have your own food cooked for you. At these places there's usually someone who'll do your laundry for you for a small charge and, generally, the cook will bake bread for you if you provide her with the ingredients.

Blantyre

A modern, largeish town with a lot of charm. It stretches for about 20 km but everything necessary is within walking distance of the *Rest House*. The restaurant there has a fantastic-looking menu but stocks only an eighth of what's on it but it's worth eating there as there's an old man who often sits in and plays some incredible rhythms on a couple of old drums. Cheap food can also be found at the *Mt Soche Hotel* coffee shop which serves excellent vegetable curry for 75 tambala, and at the *Hong Kong Restaurant* if you order carefully. There are cheap cafes down the road next to the bus terminals.

Both the British Council and the United States Information Service have excellent reading rooms/libraries which are good for sussing out information and for meeting expatriates. The people at the LEPRA Mission are generally happy to meet travellers and talk about their work if your interests lie in this direction. The Poste Restante service is very good as is the market — ebony, soapstone, baskets, mats, etc. It's possible to find some very good bargains. There's a swop-shop opposite the Central Bookshop which has cheap secondhand and new books. Bluet Gaz stoves and cartridges can be bought in Blantyre for about Kw 1.

Chitipa

Located near the Malawi-Zambian border and the most frequent point of entry. The *Rest House* here is excellent.

Lilongwe

The new capital. It's still being built but is already the centre for the embassies and many Government departments. It isn't particularly inspired so there's very little to see. The *Council Rest House* costs Kw 2 a single and Kw 4 a double or you can sleep on the grass outside for 25 tambala. Camping is possible on the Golf course.

Livingstonia

Situated 1300 metres up at the top of the Livingstone Escarpment with incredible views, waterfalls and beautiful old red-brick buildings. Many Irish Presbyterians work here and are generally very helpful people particularly with lifts into town (there's no public transport). There is a camp site overlooking the lake.

Karonga

The *Rest House* is situated about 10 minutes from the lake. Very friendly management who will provide food but there are no dormitories. There are several good bars nearby where dancing goes on virtually all night. They are about 20 minutes from the Rest House.

Mzimba

The only accommodation available is the *Rest House* for Kw 4/bed.

Mzuzu

Cheap food available here at *Bota's Res-*

taurant. There's also a good bookshop.

Nkata Bay

There is a *Government Rest House* for the usual Kw 4 and a *Provincial Rest House* for 10 tambala on the floor. You can camp at these places for 50 tambala. If you want something in between try the *Heart Hotel* for 50 tambala per bed. They only have three rooms but a good cafe. Camping also possible here for Kw 1 per night.

All the stores and bars are arranged around a central 'meeting place'. Dancing goes on all the time in the bars — people just wander in and out. You can buy fish at dusk when the boats come in. The Rest House cook will fix it for you. If you need to change money, a Barclay's Bank Land-Rover arrives on certain days of the week. There is a beautiful and practically deserted beach about 20 minutes from the Rest House.

Nkhotakota

Reputedly one of the oldest African market towns complete with a large Chinese agricultural mission where you may be invited in for a Chinese meal. The *Rest House* is right next to the lake where the boat docks. The dormitory costs 25 tambala and meals are available. The town itself is about a km from the lake and the post office, money change places and other government buildings are about a km further. There are plenty of cheap cafes and several good shops for fabrics. Buses (mostly for Lilongwe) depart two to three times per day from the market but they're always full. There's no ticket office in town so pay on the bus. If you're heading south for Salima make sure you get dropped off at the junction four to five hours out of Nkhotakota and hitch trucks to Salima from there. Note that it's not advisable to swim in the lake here as there's a bilharzia risk.

Monkey Bay

The *District Rest House* is situated in town quite near the port. Good meals available for 75 tambala. The *Government Rest House* costs Kw 1.50 per bed. Meals are available or you can cook your own. For camping there's the *Government Rest House* for 50 tambala or the grounds of the *Monkey Bay Hotel*. Monkey Bay is a watering hole for expatriates and if you're lucky you may be invited to stay with someone. The beach isn't very attractive and the place is famed for its mosquitos. If it's a beach you want to stay on then you'd be better going to Cape Maclear about six km from Monkey Bay. It's much quieter there and you can rent a beach hut or camp on the beach but take your own provisions as there are no shops.

Rumphi

The *Rest House* is situated about a km from the market. There is no electricity or meals but hot baths are available. This is a good place to try for lifts to the Chelinda Game Park on the Nyika Plateau (entrance fee is 50 tambala). Lots of deer, antelope and leopards. There are some beautiful walks in the woods and plenty of trout in the rivers and streams if you're into fishing. The lodge complex at Chelinda consists of one large building with four double bedrooms and four seperate bungalows. Everything costs Kw 3 per person and includes baths, a cook and as much wood as you need, but you should take your own food as there's very little there. It's quite high up and therefore cool. You can change money there and people are friendly and helpful. Don't pick the flowers! Chelinda is totally different from the Game Parks further north — rolling hills and mountains, pine forests (man-made) and jungle-type forests (natural).

Salima

The town is about 15 km from the lake and is where most people stay. If heading for the lake, stop in Salima to pick up provisions as the stores at the lake hardly stock anything that's edible. The *Grand Beach Hotel* at the lake is very un-grand but has a very good camp site with showers and toilets for 75 tambala including firewood. The hotel bar is nothing special and the food there is expensive. The beach is pleasant and you can hire boats there for around Kw 1 per hour. Fish can be bought at certain times of the day. You can change money and buy postage stamps, etc, from the Grand Beach Hotel. About two km from the village of Salima Bay there is an excellent ivory carver who lives in a small rush hut and will carve anything to order — local kids will take you to him. Worth a visit.

Zomba

The old capital of Malawi with a large vegetable market. The *Government Rest House* is situated about an hour's walk from town down the mountainside. Costs 50 tambala in the dormitory. The Zomba Plateau is worth a visit for the amazing views and for Chingwe's Hole which is so deep no-one has ever measured it. Free camping available with running water, toilets and hot showers but bring your own food as the hotel meals are very expensive.

TRANSPORT

Hitching is OK in the south but very slow in the north as there's hardly any traffic. There is a metalled road from Lilongwe to the Zambian border at Mchinji/Chipata but very few others. The roads in the centre and north of the country are usually in an atrocious condition. Note that if you take the coast road and want to stop off to visit Livingstonia you'll have to walk up the escarpment to the town as it's too steep for the buses.

Buses Some examples of fares — Nkhata Bay-Mzuzu: costs 50 tambala, the road is surfaced. Mzuzu-Mzimba: costs Kw 1.56. Mzimba-Lilongwe: costs Kw 2.86, two buses daily. Lilongwe-Chipate: daily buses in either direction. The road is surfaced.

If you're coming in from the north via Chitipa and Karonga note that the buses along this stretch only operate in the dry season. At other times you may well have to wait days for a connection from Chitipa. Most people walk and you might as well do the same. There are buses all year from Kambwe to Karonga but by the time you get there you're almost at Karonga anyway. If you're travelling to Zambia and Tanzania via this route you'll probably have to walk nine km from Chitipa to the Zambian customs — follow local people who are going this way. Allow two to three days to get from Chitipa to Nakonde. A transit visa for Zambia is needed by some nationals but you can do without Zambian currency if you're heading straight for Tanzania. Zambian customs are very thorough even though you're only going to be there for a few hours.

Trains Slow and cheap. They connect Limbe, Blantyre, Nsanje, Chipoka and Salima with a branch to Zomba. Malawian Railways are connected to the Mozambique system (a) via Novo Freixo in the east, and (b) via Sena in the south. The latter branch terminates in Beira on the Mozambique coast and from there you can get to Salisbury in Zimbabwe. With the very recent independence of Zimbabwe, and Mozambique making friendly overtures to South Africa, this line may well become very useful for travellers. Trains to Beira from Nsanje depart daily at 6.10 am and arrive 24 hours later. The Friday service has a 2nd class and is quicker. The fares are Kw 8.35 in 2nd class and Kw 4 in 3rd class.

From Blantyre to Chipoka, there is a daily train at 5.30 am. It takes 11 hours and costs Kw 1.50.

Lake Nyasa Steamers There are two boats — *Illala* and *Chauncy Maples* — operated by Malawi Railways Ltd. The *Chauncy Maples* has only 2nd and 3rd classes and 2nd is very crowded and not worth the extra. They're very strict about you staying in the class which you bought a ticket for so don't expect to be able to wander around. Food is available on the boats but otherwise you can buy fish, eggs and fruit from people who come out to the boat to sell these things. There are occasionally some nasty storms on the lake so watch out. Tickets for the *Chauncy Maples* are only sold when the boat appears so queuing tends to start about a day before the boat is due (it's often late) but there's no question of anyone being refused — it just gets filled up ...... and up ...... and up. In Kambwe (the port of Karonga) the only way to find anything positive out about the *Illala* is to go to the harbour master. The trouble is, he's hardly ever there but his wife is friendly and makes excellent cookies.

The schedules below should be taken as approximate, especially for the *Chauncy Maples.*

Ilala schedule

Port	Northbound arrive	depart	Southbound arrive	depart
Monkey Bay	—	08.00 Fri	12.00 Thu	—
Chipoka	11.00	21.00	00.30 Thu	09.00
Nkhotakota	04.30 Sat	05.30	16.00	17.00
Likoma Island	11.30	13.30	08.00	10.00
Chisumulu	15.00	16.45	06.00	06.30
Nkhata Bay	20.00	04.00 Sun	17.00	02.30 Wed
Usisya	06.45	08.30	13.00	14.00
Ruarwe	09.30	10.30	11.00	12.00
Mlowe	12.30	14.00	08.00	09.00
Chitimba	15.00	16.00	06.00	07.00
Chirumba	17.30	01.30 Mon	16.00	04.30 Tue
Kambwe (Karonga)	05.30 Mon	—	12.00 Mon	—

Chauncy Maples schedule*

Monkey Bay	—	14.00 Tue	10.00 Mon	—
Chipoka	17.00	03.00 Wed	18.00	07.00 Mon
Nkhotakota	20.00	01.30 Thu	18.00	01.00 Sun
Nkhata Bay	17.00	04.05 Fri	19.15	02.30 Sat
Usisya	09.00	10.30	14.00	15.00
Ruarwe	11.30 Fri	—	13.00 Fri	—

*also stop at other smaller, intermediate places.

Fares (first class):
    Chipoka to Nkhata Bay: Kw 19.58
    Chipoka to Chirumba: Kw 29.75

OTHER INFORMATION

Climbing If you're interested in climbing Mt Mulanje contact Mt Mulanje Mountain Club, Blantyre for hut bookings. They go up every weekend.

Markets Virtually every town has a market though most sell only vegetables rice, peanuts, fruit and dried fish though some have old clothes, utensils and crafts. Around Salima it's possible to pick up beautiful mats and baskets for Kw 2.50 and Kw 1.50 on average. Some markets have ebony bracelets for around Kw 1 and large strings of carved ivory beads for around Kw 20. The best markets for bargains are in the north of the country; further south things get a little more expensive. Market traders don't hike their prices, as a rule, for travellers and although it's possible in some places, bargaining secures little reduction in the first asked price.

Dope .... which is, of course, illegal, as you might expect, as you're not even allowed to wear flared trousers. Most Malawians are very secretive about it given the number of informers and the general level of police activity but there is some excellent grass to be had (called 'chamba') for around Kw 2 for a 20 cm long, 10 cm wide cob wrapped in maize leaf.

Clothes Tailors will make up virtually anything to order and make it well too. Material is more expensive than in Tanzania and Kenya but there are some beautiful prints available. Charges for labour are outrageously low. Want a nice outfit for the customs' people?

Mali

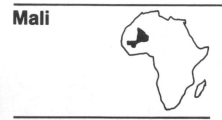

The area occupied by the modern states of Mali, and to some extent, Niger and Senegal, was, during medieval times, one of the most important trading centres of the entire Islamic world stretching from Spain and Morocco to Western China. The reputation of some of its trading cities — like Jenne, Timbuktu and Gao, as centres of wealth and cultural brilliance became world-famous and surrounded by a mystique which has endured through the centuries right up to the present day. Others, famous in their day, like Kumbi and Audagost, remain only as heaps of ruins on the edge of the Sahara. The development of these places owed much to the spread of Islam which became the religion of trade in those days though the religion itself made little impact on the peoples of the Sahel, except in so far as it was commercially convenient, until the 15th and 16th centuries. Throughout this time the traditional beliefs continued to be of paramount importance and still survive even today among peoples like the Dogon and Songhay.

The wealth of these trading cities was based primarily on the taxes levied on the transport of West African gold to North Africa and the Middle East and salt from the Saharan oases to West Africa. It was further encouraged by the demand for gold by the expanding cities of southern Europe in the 12th century. So important was West African gold in those days that there would have been no general use of the metal as a medium of exchange in medieval times otherwise. Monarchs as far away as England struck their coins in gold which had originated in West Africa. The long series of powerful medieval empires which grew up and collapsed in this part of the world from the 9th to the 16th century only finally came to an end following invasion from Morocco and the breaking of the Moslem monopoly on trade in Africa and the Indian Ocean by the European maritime nations.

Berber traders who plied the trans-Saharan routes west from Morocco through Mauritania and south through the Fezzan to the Middle Niger and Lake Chad had been important during Phoenician and Roman times but for a long time after this trade was disrupted by the invasions of the Vandals, Goths, and Visigoths and was not to be revived until the advent of Islam. Islam brought with it an accepted system of law and order which enabled trade to thrive once again. Ghana, the first empire to spring up among the Soninke people in the area of the Upper Niger and Senegal Rivers, came into being in the 9th century. By that time they had come to dominate all the important relay stations along the western trade routes and had their capital at Kumbi, 200 km north of modern Bamako. Like all the empires which were to grow up in this part of the world their wealth was principally based on the movement of gold and ivory from West Africa to the Mediterranean and Middle East and the movement of salt from the Saharan oases to West Africa but it also encompassed copper and cotton, fine tools and swords initially from Arabia and later from Italy and Germany, horses from Morocco and Egypt and kola nuts and slaves from southern West Africa. The empire of Ghana was, like most early medieval empires, based almost exclusively on the personal rule of the king and his immediate companions. There was no system of bureaucracy or civil service as was to be developed by the later empires of Mali and Songhay. None of Ghana's kings converted to Islam but retained their traditional beliefs based on a community of the ancestors, the living, and the still-to-be-born.

After nearly 500 years of existence, Ghana was finally destroyed by the invading Muslim Berber armies of the Almoravids from the plains of Mauritania in 1076 — the same people who also took possession of Moorish Spain. The Almoravids were unable to hold on to power, being restless raiders, and what was left of Ghana struggled on until 1230 when the capital, Kumbi, was taken by people from the Tekrur area in northernmost Senegal. Shortly afterwards a new empire arose among the Mandinka under the leadership of Sundiata Keita who converted to Islam as a gesture of friendship to the trading partners to the north but also to take advantage of the efficiency and organisation which allegiance to Islam brought with it. Nevertheless Sundiata owed his political success as much to the exploitation of traditional religion as to Islam, and also to the fact that the Mandinka were the most successful cultivators of rice and other foods in the hinterland of Gambia and Casamance Rivers. This new empire of Mali with its capital at Niani reached its greatest extent under Mansa Musa (1312-1332) when it reached from the Atlantic to the borders of present-day Nigeria. It was about this time that trans-Saharan trade reached its

peak and so wealthy was the empire under Mansa Musa that when he passed through Egypt on his pilgrimage to Mecca he ruined the value of the Egyptian gold-based dinar for several years by his lavish gifts of the precious metal.

Musa's reign was a period of stability and prosperity and it is from this time that Timbuktu and Jenne's long career of scholarship and cultural brilliance begins. Musa brought back architects from Arabia to construct new mosques in these cities and improved his administration by making it more methodical and literate but the advent of an actual civil service had to await the rise of Songhay.

The Songhay still survive as a group of some ¾ million people living as farmers, fishermen and traders along the banks of the Niger River, stretching from the borders of Nigeria to the lake region west of Timbuktu, and it is their villages, especially around Bandiagara near Mopti, which are the major attraction for travellers in Mali other than the old trading cities of Gao, Timbuktu and Jenne. Though originally vassals of Mansa Musa, by 1375 the Songhay had founded a strong city-state based on Gao and were able to throw off Malian overlordship and make a bid for empire themselves. By 1400 they were strong enough to even raid the Malian capital of Niani and in 1464, under the leadership of Sunni Ali finally embarked on a systematic conquest of the Sahel which was to eclipse the Malian empire. The final collapse of Mali came under Ali's successor, Askia Mohamed Ture, who came back from Mecca with the authority to act as Caliph of Islam in West Sudan. Ture pushed his armies west towards the Atlantic coast and east as far as Kano overrunning the Hausa states in the process. Following these successes the armies turned north to take the Tuareg stronghold of the oases of Air establishing a community of Songhay settlers there whose descendants still survive today.

Like the rulers of Mali, those of Songhay converted to Islam but took care to preserve and respect the traditional beliefs of the peasants of the countryside. Where Songhay excelled over Mali was in the creation of a civil service controlled by provincial governors on long-term appointments, a professional army and the beginnings of a professional navy on the Niger River. The sympathies and power base of the early rulers of Songhay lay in the peasants of the countryside but gradually this was transferred to the Muslim dominated trading cities. In this transfer and the consequent alienation of the countryside peasants lay the basic weakness of the empires in this region. Such an arrangement was fine as long as the rulers could rely on the Islamic system of beliefs and government for promoting centralised rule, long-distance trade and credit but in times of crisis these town-based empires were an easy prey to collapse and this was the main reason why Songhay was rapidly eclipsed in 1591, following an invasion from Morocco and the ensuing internal revolt of subject people. On the other hand, even had Songhay been able to withstand the invasion from Morocco it's doubtful that the prosperity of the Niger trading cities would have lasted long once the European maritime nations had found a means of circumventing their middleman role by trading directly with the primary producers along the West African coast and further south. With the rise of European naval hegemony, the trans-Saharan trading routes lapsed into relative obscurity though even as late as the 1950's caravans consisting of thousands of camels were still transporting salt from the Saharan oasis of Bilma (in Niger) south to Nigeria.

In the 19th century, Mali became part of the French colony of Soudan and gained its independence in 1960. The present military regime came to power in 1968 after overthrowing the government of President Modibo Keita in a coup. Keita, along with many of his ministers was incarcerated in the notorious salt mines at Taoudenni for many years afterwards. The coup, however, brought no instant solution to the economic stagnation of the country nor the discontent among many sections of the population. Desperate measures have been resorted to, such as repression of the Tuareg and even an attempted military occupation of neighbouring Upper Volta, but all to no avail. Links with France, though better maintained than in Guinea, were loosened early after independence, precipitating the withdrawal of the French from their bases in 1961 and 1962 and the creation of a Malian currency outside the French-controlled Franc Zone in the latter year. Since then, the government has pursued a policy of liberalising the economy despite opposition from students and labour unions.

Mali was one of the countries which suffered disastrously from the Sahelian drought in the early 70's. This drought turned enormous areas of once marginal grazing and crop-raising land into desert and resulted in massive losses of crops and livestock and spelled the end of a centuries-old way of life for many desert nomads who now crowd the cities of the Niger as refugees.

FACTS

Only in the extreme south is rainfall high enough to permit cultivation without irrigation. Bamako, for instance, receives about 110 cm per annum but the amounts decrease rapidly further north. The cultivation of crops depends chiefly on the flooding of the Niger and its tributaries and upon irrigation but rearing livestock is the chief occupation in Mali. Available resources are so limited that many workers migrate seasonally to Senegal and Gambia to help with groundnut cultivation while other mig-

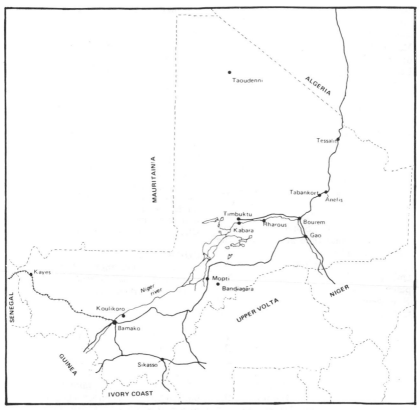

rants find work in the plantations of Guinea and the Ivory Coast.

A dam has been constructed at Bamako which makes possible the irrigation of a large area by a barrage at Sansanding which has raised the level of water in the river by four metres. Water can now be led by former tributaries and other channels over a wide area. Two thirds of the annual crop is now rice while cotton and sugar cane are also grown. Below Timbuktu, millet and rice are grown while in uplands during the short rainy season millet, cotton and ground nuts can be cultivated. The River Niger is a rich source for fishing, which is carried out on a commercial scale with the surplus being exported to Ghana.

Timbuktu, once an important and thriving caravan crossroads as well as a cultural centre, has lost much of its former grandeur although it has benefited from the recent revival of interest by travellers.

VISAS

Required by all except nationals of France. Visas, from the very few Malian Embassies around the world, are generally issued for a stay of one week but if you keep checking in with police — unavoidable — you can effectively stay as long as you like. In Dakar, Senegal, the Malian Embassy is on Avenue Lamine

Gueye. Visas there cost 2500 CFA and take 24 hours to issue. In Accra, Ghana, visas cost 10.50 Cedi. Note there are no Malian Embassies in Niger, Upper Volta or any of the coastal countries east of Ghana. The only other place where there is a Malian Embassy is Abidjan, Ivory Coast. French Embassies cannot issue Mali visas.

If you are bringing a car from Algeria to Mali via Jessalit make sure you have a visa. If you don't have one the border guards will refuse entry. Since you won't have enough petrol/deisel to get back to Adrar you'll be forced to sell the car — and guess who to? After you have sold the car to him, he'll allow you to continue on to Gao. It pays to remember that the Sahelian countries have always made their money from the trans-Saharan routes.

Mali once acquired a reputation among travellers as one of the worst places on earth for bureaucracy as far as visas were concerned. Formalities could take days. They've eased up a lot now, though if you're taking the train from Bamako to Dakar (Senegal) you still have to get an exit permit from the Police Speciale along the railway track near the station before you can buy a ticket. It's free but can take hours so don't leave it too late. Coming in the opposite direction from Dakar, the train stops at Kayes — the first town over the border — for a couple of hours to give everyone time to go through immigration.

If you're coming by air visas can be issued on arrival. Yazbecks or Air Mali will notify the Immigration authorities a few days before you arrive. On arrival you have to surrender your passport, fill in a form, collect MFr 2500 worth of fiscal stamps from Tresoir (near the Hotel Majestic) or the Post Office, and provide one photo. The visa (valid for a week's stay) is issued in an hour or so.

As far as arriving at an overland border without a visa is concerned, a recent traveller had this to say:

'At last Mali has eased up on the visa situation ……. not knowing this, and not wanting to trek down to expensive Abidjan for a visa, we crept up to the border above Odienne without visas, rehearsing tales of the road to Abidjan being blocked by rain, etc — then the young guard didn't even look for a visa, just stamped us in! On arrival in Bamako we went straight to the Immigration Office, again with stories at the ready. We were given a form to fill, asked for 2500 francs worth of fiscal stamps from Tresoir plus one photo and told to come back in an hour for the visa. It was given for one week and could have been extended at the end of that time. I left with it expired and no-one noticed....'

One week visa extensions cost MFr 100.

CURRENCY

The unit of currency is the Mali Franc (MFr). There is no restriction on the Import/export of local currency.

Exchange rate:

£1	=	MFr 930
US$1	=	MFr 404
A$1	=	MFr 455

Although the Mali Franc is no longer part of the CFA zone, recent reports indicate that CFAs (of, say, Ivory Coast, Senegal, etc) are acceptable legal tender in Mali. Mali Francs are acceptable in Senegal but not usually elsewhere so get rid of them before you leave if you're not going that way.

Airport tax on domestic flights is MFr 1000. For flights to other African countries it's MFr 3000 and for other international flights it is MFr 5000.

LANGUAGES

French and many local languages.

ACCOMMODATION

Hotel accommodation is generally very

expensive and it's worth looking around for alternatives. It's sometimes possible to stay with the Peace Corps — though not in their hostels. Catholic Missions are worth checking out as they sometimes have cheap places to stay. 'Campements' (Government Rest Houses) all cost about the same at MFR 5000/ double including breakfast and meals for MFr 1800. They sometimes allow camping in the grounds for a small fee.

Bamako

Foyer d'Accueil, rue Ousmane Bagayoko has floor space for MFr 1000. *Maison de Jeunes* costs MFr 1500 per night and is clean and friendly but you can only stay there as long as there is no youth activity going on at the time. *Le Paysan Hotel*, costs MFr 2000 per person. *Bar Mali*, near the Vox Cinema, is popular with travellers and costs MFr 2500/ single and MFr 3000/double. It also serves cheap and reasonably good food. Keep an eye on your gear there. *Hotel de la Gare*, opposite the railway station, costs MFr 2400/single. *Hotel Majestic* costs MFr 4000/double and has good facilities. They often allow more than two people to share a double room.

The Catholic Mission is opposite the cathedral in the centre of town — worth checking out — as too is the Croix Rouge in Les Enfants Jardine in the main square if you're looking for floor space. Ask for Zan who may let you sleep there for free but you have to be out very early in the morning before the children arrive. Showers available there.

The Peace Corps tend to hang around *Le Berry Bar* though their office is on El Hadja Samba Kone, Quartier Niarella (tel 24 479). They cannot put you up at the hostel but they may take you up with them to the villages in which they work. Could be very interesting.

For food, other than the Bar Mali or the Berry Bar, try the *Chez Jean Restaurant* situated near the large market (it isn't called that anymore but people still know it as Chez Jean). Other cafes for reasonably cheap, good food, are the *Restaurant Centrale*, first turn right past the *Printania* supermarket; *Le Gondole*, Avenue de la Nation, which has French and Lebanese food, and the *Patisserie Venus* which has good ice creams, cakes, beer, fresh milk and yogurt. The average price of a meal in these places is around MFr 800-1000.

The Post Restante in Bamako is very good. Taxis cost MFr 100 around town. They run on fixed rates.

Bandiagara

Situated in the Sangha country east of Mopti. A visit here is an absolute must and probably one of the main reasons you have come to Mali. Incredible views, life style, and a very interesting and unique people.

Le Conseil costs MFr 1150, it's clean, friendly and fairly new. *Le Campement* costs MFr 4000/single but it's not the best place to stay. There is an hotel with no name which you get to by going past the Campement and turning right at the river bank. It costs MFr 1100. Pink drapes and lukewarm beers. The owner knows a lot of interesting walks you can do in the region. Other than these you could stay with people in Dini Village. To get there, go past the Campement and the American Mission and then ask for Dini Village. When you get there ask for Ogo (Ogotemelon Dolo) or his younger brother Amatigue Dolo. They will put you up — usually on the roof — cook for you and act as guides etc. Arrange a price with them that's within your budget — say MFr 5000 for a week's stay. They've helped many travellers in the past, and are far, far cheaper than any offical tours. If you ask any officials in Bandiagara where anything is you will just get an expensive, official tour laid on you.

In nearby Sangha village (45 km from Bandiagara) where a fascinating market is held every five days, ask

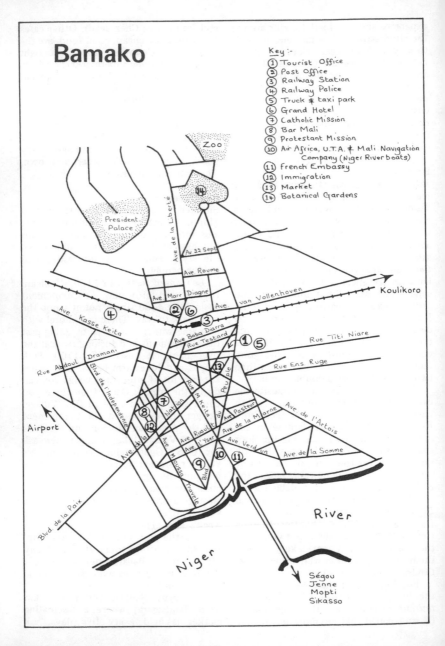

Bamako

Key :-
1. Tourist Office
2. Post Office
3. Railway Station
4. Railway Palice
5. Truck ★ taxi park
6. Grand Hotel
7. Catholic Mission
8. Bar Mali
9. Protestant Mission
10. Air Africa, U.T.A. ★ Mali Navigation Company (Niger River boats)
11. French Embassy
12. Immigration
13. Market
14. Botanical Gardens

Zoo

President Palace

Ave de la Liberté

Av. 22 Sept

Ave. Roume

Ave Marr Diagne

Ave van Vollenhoven → Koulikoro

Ave Kasse Keita

Rue Baba Diarra

Rue Testard

Rue Titi Niare

Rue Abdoul Dramani

Blvd de l'Indépendance

Rue Ens. Ruge

Rue M Keita

Rue du Peuple

Nathon

Ave Pasteur

Ave de la Marne

Ave de l'Artois

Airport

Ave de la

Ave Riaul

Ave l'Yser

Ave Verdun

Ave de la Somme

Blvd Moussa Travéle

Blvd de la Paix

River

Niger

Ségou
Jenne
Mopti
Sikasso

around for local accommodation otherwise there is *Le Campement* for MFr 6075/double, MFr 4300/single but you are obliged to eat there too at MFr 1970 per meal. Showers available for a further charge.

Note that if you intend to take photographs in the Sangha country you need a permit for this from the police station near the Campement in Bandiagara. It's important to have this.

Djenne (Jenne)
There is a *Campement* here at the usual rates.

Gao
Le Village has local-style huts for MFr 1000 per night. *Chez Yarga* offers dormitory type rooms and rooftop space for MFr 1000 per person. The *Hotel Atlantide* has cheap and nasty rooms for MFr 750 per night. Use it as a last resort if there's nowhere else.

Cheap, good food is available from the *Blackpool (!) Cafe.*

Mopti
The most popular place here is the *Hotel Bar Mali*, recommended for its desert atmosphere but have a candle handy as the electricity supply tends to be erratic. Costs MFr 1500-2000/room or MFr 300 on the roof. Good food available. *Le Campement* costs MFr 4000/single but dinner there is obligatory and this costs an extra MFr 1000.

If you would like something more ethnic, there are river boats at certain times of the year where you can rent a bed in a four-bunk cabin for around MFr 3000. You need your own bedding and some of the boats are very decrepit. Choose one that looks like it will still be afloat in the morning. The cabins on the river side are cooler.

Very basic accommodation is sometimes available for around MFr 300-400 in the taxi park.

For food try the *Bar Mali* or the *Bozo Restaurant*. The latter is situated at the end of the harbour, and has good, cheap food. The *Welcome Bar* is good for a touch of fading French culture — wine and cheese portions. Taxis anywhere in town for MFr 100 but piroques will take you virtually anywhere for MFr 10-30.

Segou
Le Campement costs MFr 5000 for both doubles and singles.

Timbuktu
Ask Baba at *Baba's Restaurant*. He'll show you a nice house where you can stay the night for around MFr 500. Baba does cheap food for MFr 100-150 a meal. Note that there's no bank in Timbuktu. There are many Tuaregs here who are worth a visit.

TRANSPORT
Most roads in Mali are pretty rough at the best of times and when it rains often get washed out completely. Barriers are generally erected when there is flooding. The road from Bamako to Senegal is hardly used at all — most passengers and goods go on the twice-weekly train. It's possible to pick up occasional free lifts but generally you will have to pay a more or less standard charge for these. There are plenty of trucks and Peugeots in addition to buses but rides to Gao can be difficult to find and involve a lot of waiting. During February it's extremely difficult to get a ride between Gao and Timbuktu.

There are occasional border skirmishes between Mali and Upper Volta usually engineered by the Mali authorities in a vain attempt to divert attention away from internal problems and as a result the border between the two countries is often closed.

Trucks, Buses & Taxis
Some examples of lift prices and fares are as follows:

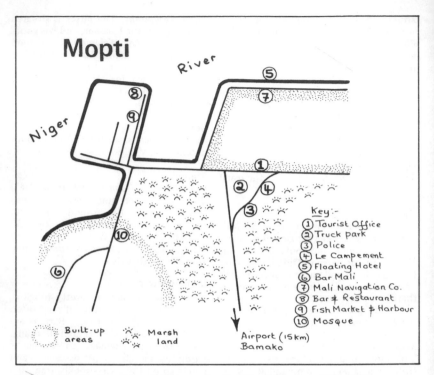

Mopti

Key:-
① Tourist Office
② Truck park
③ Police
④ Le Campement
⑤ Floating Hotel
⑥ Bar Mali
⑦ Mali Navigation Co.
⑧ Bar & Restaurant
⑨ Fish Market & Harbour
⑩ Mosque

Built-up areas

Marsh land

Airport (15km)
Bamako

Bamako-Mopti: Trucks, pick-ups and taxis leave every morning from the truck park in Bamako but you must get there early if you want a truck. Trucks cost about MFr 4000, pick-ups MFr 5000 and Peugeot taxis MFr 6000. The journey takes about 10 hours.

Mopti-Djenne (Jenne): By truck this costs MFr 1750 and by taxi MFr 2000. The journey takes all day and access to the town is quite difficult as it's situated in the swamp area south-west of Mopti on the River Bani which joins the Niger at Mopti. There is a ferry which operates most of the year but is suspended in the middle of the dry season as the river gets too low.

Djenne-San: costs MFr 2000

San-Koutiala; costs MFr 2000

Koutiala-Sikasso: costs MFr 2000, bad road.

Mopti-Gao: Finding a truck going this way can take a long time and you should allow two to three days. They cost on average MFr 8000.

Gao-Niamey (Niger): Truck lifts cost around MFr 4000 and pick-ups MFr 5000-5500. There is also a once-weekly SNTN bus in either direction. If you are coming from Niamey, it departs on Tuesday from the truck park. The bus costs MFr 3000 and takes a day and a half — quite a lot of time is taken up with border formalities.

Gao-Adrar (Algerian): Truck lifts will cost around MFr 15,000. You need to put in a lot of leg-work to find a lift going this way. Takes four to five days.

Bamako-Bouake (Ivory Coast): Trucks cost MFr 8610. Many police check points along this route and they all have sticky fingers. Expect to have to pay MFr 500 extra as bribes.

Mopti-Bouake: Trucks cost MFr 1100. Lifts to Ferkessedougou are also possible for the same price.

Sikasso-Bouake: costs MFr 7000 but expect to have to pay an extra MFr 500 as bribes to the police.

Bougouni-Ivory Coast border: Trucks cost MFr 2500.

There used to be a twice-weekly bus in either direction between Bamako and Abidjan (capital of Ivory Coast) but it doesn't seem to run any more. If you need to do the journey quickly it might be a good idea to enquire if it's running again. It's a fairly rapid journey as the roads are good in Ivory Coast and it's an easy hitch once you get there as there are police checkpoints every five to 10 km where you can enlist their help in finding lifts. There's an alternative route through Odienne from where there's the choice of continuing on to either Monrovia (Liberia) or Abidjan — see the Ivory Coast chapter for details.

Sangha/Dogon country: If you don't want to spend a fortune going there avoid organised tours in Land Rovers from Mopti or Bandiagara which will cost upwards of MFr 35,000 shared between three people. It is sometimes possible to get a lift (share expenses) with travellers who have their own transport — enquire at the Campement in Mopti or Bandiagara. Alternatively get a truck or pick-up from Mopti to Bandiagara for MFr 1000 and another from there to Sangha Village for MFr 1000. You may be able to find one going all the way for around MFr 1500 in which case they stay overnight in Bandiagara and continue onto Sangha

the next day for the market which is held there every five days. The road is pretty rough and rocky. If you are thinking of staying in Sangha, get there before the market as accommodation is difficult on the day. Also, if you stay after the market you may have to wait another six days for a lift back to Bandiagara. It is a fascinating place and one of the highlights of any visit to Mali.

The trans-Saharan route from Timbuktu/Gao (Route du Tanezrouft) to Tamanrasset in Algeria is covered in the Algerian chapter.

Trains The only rail link is between Bamako and Dakar (Senegal) via Kayes and Tambacounda. There are two trains per week on Tuesdays and Saturdays from Bamako. The journey takes about 30 hours. The trains depart Bamako at 8 am but you need to sleep at the station overnight if you plan on getting a seat. The train arrives at 4 am and is packed out with people who will offer you their seat for around MFr 200 — often worth paying. The train is always crowded and you should take your own food and drink. Before you can buy a ticket you must get an Exit Permit from the Police Speciale a little way along the railway track from the station in Bamako. It's free. There used to be student concessions available in both directions but they seem to have been discontinued if you are going *from* Mali to Senegal. Check this out with the station master in Bamako. Bamako to Dakar costs MFr 19,000 in 1st class and MFr 12,575 in 2nd class plus a reservation fee of MFr 250 Bamako to Tambacounda costs MFr 7420 in 2nd class. A sleeping berth in 1st class costs an extra MFr 10,000 over and above the fare. If the Police Speciale is closed in Bamako, buy a ticket to Kayes, go through immigration there and then buy another ticket from there to Dakar.

Riverboats Two boats, the *Mali* and

Soumare, ply between Mopti, Timbuktu and Gao between August and late December. When the river is high enough they also go as far as Koulikoro near Bamako. The boats depart Mopti on Thursdays when they are running. The trip to Timbuktu from Mopti takes two days and from there to Gao another two days. If you don't want to stay in Timbuktu for several days (while the boat returns from Gao), you just have time to visit by taxi while the boat docks for a few hours at Kabara. Note that Kabara, 11 km from Timbuktu, is the port for that town. A taxi between the two will cost MFr 50. Koulikoro is the boat terminal for Bamako. A taxi between the two will cost you MFr 500. You can either take your own food and drink or rely on what's for sale at each stop along the way — usually little more than bread and peanuts. There are four classes of accommodation on the boats. 4th class is OK on the *Mali* but atrocious on the *Soumare*. If you want anything approaching some degree of comfort you will have to go 2nd class. The fares are as follows:-

Mopti-Gao: 1st class costs MFr 26,415 (2 berth cabins including food); 2nd class costs MFr 17,680 (4 berth cabins including food); 3rd class costs MFr 11,756 (8 berth cabin including food); 4th class costs MFr 3,630 (deck space only, no food).

The food in third class doesn't compare with that in second and first classes. If you are travelling fourth class, it's possible to go and sit in the first class bar during the heat of the day. If you are interested in entomology you will love this boat trip!

In addition to the riverboats there are piroques (native dug-outs) without motors which ply between the same places. Enquire down at the riverboat terminals. If you are thinking of going by piroque you need *plenty* of time. The journey from Mopti to Gao by piroque can take four weeks.

Mauritania

A largely dry and inhospitable country which exists almost entirely on its exports of iron ore, dates and herd animals. Though ethnically a part of Mahgreb in that the majority of its population are either Berbers or Tuareg, it was, for many centuries, bypassed by the many empires which grew up and declined in the Western Sudan and Morocco. It became a French colony in 1904 and acquired a sort of self-government under the Loi Cadre in 1957 with full independence in 1960, under the presidency of Mukhtar Ould Daddah. Daddah built up his political power base with French Colonial assistance and maintained it for years with the help of French troops against opposition from people in the north of the country who favoured union with Morocco and others in the south who feared Arab domination.

Agitation in the trade unions, in particular among the teachers, led to strikes and anti-government riots in the mid-60s over the issue of language and in 1968 the Constitution was amended to make Arabic, along with French, an official language. In line with this there has been a re-orientation of foreign policy towards the Arab world and away from Black Africa much to the disappointment of the Negro population in the south. The event which caused most unrest, however, and led to the overthrow of Ould Daddah, was the war with the Saouarhis of the Western Sahara. In the late '70s, Spain unwilling to get embroiled in a war of liberation in what was then known as the Spanish Sahara, agreed to hand over the colony to Morocco and Mauritania against the wishes of the indigenous Saouarhis. The Mauritanians took the southern half and the Moroccans the phosphate-rich northern half. Both countries immediately found themselves fighting a war with the guerillas of the Saouarhi POLISARIO Front which was supported by Algeria, Libya and Cuba. The guerillas were so successful that they virtually wrecked the Mauritanian economy by blowing up the mining installations at F'Derik, the railway line between there and Nouadhibou, and the port facilities at Nouadhibou. The small Mauritanian army was no match for these guerillas and unrest came to a head in a coup which toppled Ould Daddah and led to the withdrawal of Mauritania from the Western Sahara. Though the situation inside the country has now settled down, Morocco's annexation of the whole of the Western Sahara means that a war is still going on in this area and that the trans-Saharan route (Route du Mauritaine) from Algeria to Mauritania and Senegal is still off the overland map. Even if you were prepared to take the risk of a Moroccan Air Force raid along this route, it is very unlikely that the Algerian authorities would allow you to go this way.

The only way to get to Mauritania at present, unless you are taking the fortnightly Polish Ocean Lines ship from Santa Cruz de Tenerife in the Canary Islands to Nouadhibou, is from Senegal. As a result, very few travellers have been there for years and the information which we have will undoubtedly be somewhat out of date especially regarding prices. We are going to include what we knew from before the war but warn you to treat it as a guide only.

VISAS
Required by all except nationals of France and Italy. The nearest Mauritanian Embassies are Dakar, Rabat and Madrid. There is a Vice-Consulate in Las Palmas in the Canary Islands located at 'Pecheurs Mauritaine' in a poorly marked office in Calle Raffael Cabrera and although you can get a visa here it takes about a month as your passport has to be sent to Madrid. The visas cost 250 pesetas and two photos.

It is sometimes possible to get a visa on arrival at the border but don't count on it. Sometimes they turn you back. Visas can be extended at any Commissaire de Police inside the country.

Senegal Visas These are obtainable at the Rosso border free. No photos are required and there is no hassle.

CURRENCY
The unit of currency is the Ouguiya = 5 khoums. Import/export of local currency is allowed up to 1000 Oug.

Exchange rate:

£1	=	95 Oug
US$1	=	42 Oug
A$1	=	48 Oug

Currency declaration forms are issued on arrival and the authorities are very keen about them. You may well be stopped by police inside Mauritania and searched. If they find you have more foreign currency than you declared on the form on arrival they confiscate the extra. Take this seriously — many people have been caught out. The customs post between Atar and Nouakchott at Akjoujit is very thorough — boots off, etc, so watch it.

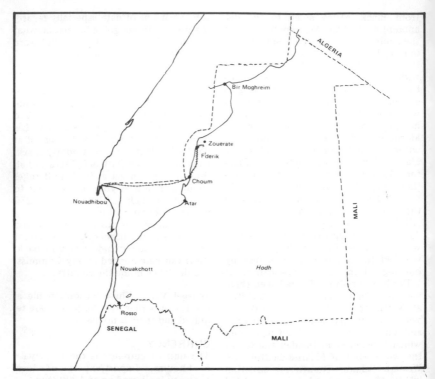

There are two banks at Nouadhibou, BALM which charges hefty commissions for changing travellers cheques, and BIMA which doesn't. There is a bank at Rosso on the Mauritanian side of the river where Ouguiya can be obtained if you are coming from Senegal. It is closed between 12.30 and 3 pm. If you are buying CFA with Ouguiya there is a commission of 3 Oug for every 100 changed.

ACCOMMODATION
Atar
A beautiful oasis town with a camel market. You can sleep free on the roof of the police station or have a mat on the floor of the *Restaurant Keur Noflaye* for 40 Oug. The owner is often to be found at the nearby bar, *Chez Aicha*.

This bar is also a good place to look for a lift. There a number of small, cheap cafes near where the taxis and trucks stop.

Nouadhibou
You can sleep at the *Catholic Mission* free and the priest's friend, the French doctor, will buy any whisky you have brought with you at a good price. If you can't get in at the Mission, there are hotels with rooms for around 400 Oug. There are also two bars/cafes where you can often meet Senegalese and Gambians who, if they take a liking to you, may offer you a place to stay for the night or a lift the next day. The cafes are the *Cad Blanc* and the *Chez Diallo Samba Apollo VIII*. In the latter you can get rice and fish for 50 Oug. The

alternative to all this is to go to Port Mineralier, a few kilometres from town, and sleep on the sand dunes. At the port you might well meet with a welcome from bored crews from western Europe who will treat you to a drunken weekend and might even fix you up with a lift back to Europe or further south.

Nouakchott

You can sleep at the *Catholic Mission* free. They are very friendly, sincere people. The Mission is an 10 Oug taxi ride from town. It is also possible to stay with Peace Corps volunteers — contact the PC office, BP 222, Nouakchott, for addresses. It is also possible to sleep on the beach which is a 15 Oug taxi ride from town plus 15 Oug for your baggage. Other than these there are three hotels in town but they are all pretty expensive — expect to pay around 600 Oug for a double room. The *Hotel Oasis* charges 600 Oug/single and 750 Oug/double. The cheapest restaurant in town is the *Restaurant de la Serenite*. The Poste Restante is very good.

TRANSPORT

Road Transport NB The trans-Saharan route (Route du Mauritaine) from Algeria. to Senegal via Mauritania is effectively closed to overland traffic at present due to the war in Western Sahara and Morocco.

There are only two roads in Mauritania (a) Rosso (Senegal border) to Nouadhibou via Nouakchott, (b) Nouakchott to Bir Moghreim via Atar, Choum, F 'Derik, Zouerate. Truck prices along this route are as follows —
Bir Moghreim-Zouerate: Trucks cost 300 Oug and taxis 500 Oug. Note there are no banks in Bir Moghreim and you can only change money at the Post Office (no commission to change French Francs).
Zouerate-Choum: Trucks cost 300 Oug or you can take the free ore train

(see under 'Trains' below).
Choum-Nouakchott: Trucks cost 600 Oug but the drivers start at 1000 Oug and you have to do some bargaining. The trip can take 24 hours and you will be expected to lend a hand where there are punctures or you get stuck in sand/dust.
If there are no hold-ups it is possible you will get there in less time.
Atar-Nouakchott: Trucks cost 600 Oug and take all day. If you want to get there quicker, take a taxi for 700 Oug which takes around six hours. Note that all the trucks and taxis go to La Gare Routier, a suburb of Nouakchott. There are no banks in Atar and you have to change money at the Post Office.
Nouakchott-Rosso (Senegal border): Trucks cost 250 Oug and taxis 300 Oug plus 25 Oug for each bag you are carrying. Arriving at Rosso, if you want to carry on to Senegal, ask to be put down at the 'frontera' otherwise you will have to walk back three km from the centre of Rosso instead of 200 metres. The ferry across the Senegal River costs 5 Oug or 50 CFA. It is also possible to go across by canoe for slightly less. Senegalese visas are obtainable at the border free, no photos, no questions asked. There are buses from Rosso to the first Senegalese town of St Louis for 350 CFA and taxis for 500 CFA. Fast and comfortable.

Trains The only railway in the country runs from Nouadhibou to Zouerate via Choum and F'Derik. It is an iron ore train and the longest in the world — often three km long! As you might expect, it is open-topped, filthy, makes no concessions to comfort and is slow. But it is free. Simply choose your wagon. It runs two to three times daily in either direction. In Nouadhibou you have to catch it from Pont Centrale, a 30 Oug taxi ride from town. The train takes 12 hours to cover the 540 km of Saharan landscape and is a bone-shattering experience. It doesn't stop until it gets to Choum but there is no chance of you missing this 15 minute stop as it is quite impossible to sleep on the train. Take the night train if you want to miss the heat of the day — leaves Nouadhibou at 6 pm but be there by 4.30 as it sometimes leaves early. Try to get into a wagon towards the front of the train. That way there is less dust to contend with. If you are getting off in Choum, you need the right hand side of the train for the cafes, taxis etc. Take food and water with you and, if you are going during the day, something to cover your head with. If you want a more interesting ride, it is worth trying to chat up the driver on the train (there are four diesel engines which pull the train) he might invite you on board. The difference in comfort and the standard of refreshments is incomparable. There is also a baggage wagon right at the end of the train which is somewhat more luxurious than the ore wagons but you have to pay to ride in this.

Boats The only regular ships with some passenger accommodation which call at Mauritania are those of the Polish Ocean Lines. They operate a fortnightly service, which, on the outward journey, calls at Santa Cruz de Tenerife/Las Palmas, Nouadhibou, Dakar, Banjul, Freetown, Monrovia, Abidjan, Tema, Lome, Cotonou, Douala, etc. Their fares are relatively expensive and we have never heard of anyone using this boat. If you are interested, contact their agent in Britain: Stelp and Leighton Agencies Ltd, 238 City Road, London EC1.

Flights There is a daily flight in either direction between Nouadhibou and Nouakchott.

Mauritius

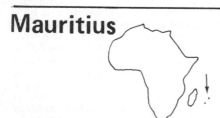

An independent island group east of Madagascar consisting of Mauritius, Rodrigues and two much smaller groups of islands and reefs to the north and north-east. All the islands are volcanic in origin, are surrounded by coral reefs and have a sub-tropical climate. Mauritius, the largest island, is 61 km long by 47 km wide and has a multi-racial population of 800,000 with the largest ethnic group consisting of Indians (both Hindus and Moslems). Rodrigues is a much smaller island east of Mauritius with a population of around 23,000. Mauritius was once the home of several flightless birds, the best known being the dodo. All are now extinct.

The island of Mauritius was known to Arab and Swahili traders as early as the 10th century though no attempt was made to settle it. It was next visited by the Portuguese at the beginning of the 16th century but it was the Dutch who attempted to colonise it on two separate occasions between 1638-58 and between 1664-1710. After the Dutch abandoned the island it became a haunt of pirates for a while until taken by the French East India Company in 1721. The French used Mauritius and their neighbouring colony of Reunion as bases to attack the British in India and in the late 18th century the two islands became vital way-stations for French, Danish and American ships. Following the French Revolution and the attempt to abolish slavery, the French settlers on the island of Mauritius broke away from France but in 1810 it was taken by the

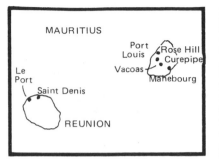

British and declared a colony.

Following British annexation, a plantation economy was introduced and slaves imported from East Africa and Madagascar. With the abolition of slavery in 1835, most of the former slaves left the plantations and settled in the coastal towns to be replaced by Indian indentured labourers most of whom stayed on the island rather than return to India, and gave rise to the largest ethnic group on the islands. The sugar plantations thrived until competition from European-grown sugar beet led to decline though, even today, the economy is heavily reliant on the sale of sugar. Another factor which led to a decline in the importance of Mauritius was the opening of the Suez Canal which enabled ships to by-pass the long journey via the Cape of Good Hope.

Independence came in 1968 though the government is having an uphill battle trying to cope with the fragile sugar-based economy and the relatively high rate of unemployment. A demand, endorsed by the OAU, was recently made for the return of Diego Garcia, the British-American military base in the middle of the Indian Ocean, which was detached from Mauritius just before independence and its 1200 inhabitants shipped to Mauritius in exchange for 'compensation'. With the present obsession in the west about Russian expansionism in Asia it seems unlikely that anything will come of this demand.

FACTS

Probably the only way you'll get to see Mauritius if you're a budget traveller is on a stop-over flight between Africa and Australia or between Africa and India but if you do get the opportunity it's well worth the effort. The climate is similar to that of Fiji. The geography of the island ranges from the low plain of the north, through the plateau in the centre to the mountainous area in the south. The hot season stretches from November to April and the cool season from May to October. Heavy rain and cyclones are a common feature of the hot season. The actual amount of rainfall varies depending on the location but on the central plateau it averages 200 inches per year.

VISAS

Required by all except nationals of Commonwealth countries, European Common market countries and South Africa. 'Onward tickets' are an entry requirement.

CURRENCY

The unit of currency is the Mauritian Rupee.

Exchange rate:

£1	=	Rs17.00
US$1	=	Rs 7.40
A$1	=	Rs 8.50

There is no blackmarket (the Rupee was devalued in October 1979). Airport tax is Rs 20 on all departures. In addition, there is a 10% tax on all airline tickets bought in Mauritius.

ACCOMMODATION

There is a 10% Government tax on all accommodation and restaurant bills so make sure this is included in the quoted prices. Most mid-range tourist hotels will cost between A$25-50 for bed and breakfast per person. Two of the cheapest places available are:-

Blue Lagoon Situated in Mahebourg is a small family-run, beach hotel fairly close to the airport but without air-conditioning. Bed and breakfast costs A$10 per day. They also offer several modest bungalows for rent having two, four or six beds for between A$8.50 and A$16 per day.

Falbaire Campment Situated at Point d' Esney, Mahebourg, offers eight pension-type rooms near the bar at A$6.50 to A$11.50 per day for bed and breakfast.

TRANSPORT

Local buses are available around the island. Fares are very reasonable. Note that if you take a taxi from the airport the driver is entitled to charge you for the return journey even if you're not going both ways. Also there are no meters so bargaining is a must. Check out with Government Tourist Office staff (recognisable by their uniforms) on arrival regarding average charges.

Morocco

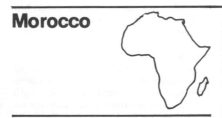

Morocco, unlike other North African countries, is still largely populated by the descendants of its original Berber settlers who came to this area thousands of years ago and at one time controlled all of the land between Morocco and Egypt. They were never united except for brief periods when expediency dictated such an arrangement to face a threat from a common enemy and even today the various tribes in Morocco jealously guard their independence. Berber society is based on the clan and village, each village being autonomous and ruled by a council of adult males. Sometimes villages will come together in a loose kind of confederation to better administer something of mutual concern but the autonomy of each village is always respected. This entrenched unwillingness to forfeit their independence has muted the effects of various conquerors who have come and gone over the centuries and resulted in one of Africa's

most fascinating and colourful cultures being preserved into the 20th century. It has understandably been a travellers' Mecca for many years though excessive tourism is beginning to spoil many of its unique features.

The Berbers speak a different language to the Arabs who began arriving here in the wake of the Moslem expansion after the death of the Prophet, Mohammed, and have their own script. Arab horsemen failed to penetrate the mountains of the Rif and Atlas with the result that these areas remain firmly Berber though a considerable amount of

intermixing has gone on in the cities and on the plains. Examples of the art and buildings left by the many brilliant cultures and empires which have grown up here can still be seen today, ranging from the Roman city of Volubilis to the Moslem kingdoms which had their capitals variously at Marrakesh, Fez, Meknes and Rabat.

The Berbers first come into recorded history as the merchants who traded with the Phoenician coastal cities by virtue of their control of the trans-Saharan gold and ivory trade. They were never much influenced by the urban culture of the Phoenicians though they sometimes allied with them to fight the Romans if it paid in terms of trade. Likewise, when the Romans finally established themselves here, the Berbers were willing to trade with them — even fight for them if it paid — but were unwilling to give up their independence so that Roman rule was at best tenuous in this part of North Africa. All the same, Roman rule ushered in a long period of peace and prosperity during which many cities were founded and Berbers of the coastal plains became city dwellers. Christianity arrived in the 3rd century AD yet even here the Berbers asserted their traditional dislike of centralised authority by taking advantage of doctrinal differences and adopting the heretical Donatist line like the Copts of Egypt.

The Roman Empire began to disintegrate in the 5th century with the arrival of the Vandals from Spain but the end came slowly and the invaders were unable to graft themselves on to the urban culture and relaunch it under new management. Their principal effect was to disrupt the agriculture of the coastal plains and the trans-Saharan trade routes which were not to recover until the arrival of Islam. This came in the 7th century as the Arab armies swept out of Arabia taking Byzantine Egypt and then moving west to conquer the whole of the North African coast and eventually much of Spain too. Their lightning success was probably as much to do with the chaos and provincialisation which followed the collapse of the Roman Empire as it was to the attraction of an idea of universal brotherhood in which all men, regardless of the circumstances of their birth, could (at least in theory) be members of a new and broad community based on equal dignity and worth. In this respect the Arab conquest was markedly different from that of the Romans, but although they couldn't have been as successful as they were without delivering some of the goods, the reality was a long way from the Utopia and once the initial flush of enthusiasm had subsided the basic tribal divisions and animosities began to reappear. As with the Christians, there grew up doctrinal differences based on the interpretation of Mohammed's teaching and disputes over where power should reside in the Islamic community. It is from this time that the basic schism between Sunnis and Shi'ites dates.

The Berber tribes were not slow in seeing these schisms as a convenient way of expressing their independence while at the same time remaining Moslems and they were to develop their own brand of Shi'ism known as Kharijism. The Kharijite brotherhood was essentially a puritanical movement of the oases and distant plains which denounced the decadent and easy-going tendencies of the cities and, while rejected by Islam as a whole, it attracted many followers especially around Sigilmasa — the great caravan centre in southern Morocco — and Tahert in what is now Algeria. These Kharijite communities were able to carve out successful kingdoms for themselves during the 8th and 9th centuries in the Western Mahgreb and that of the Idrisids with its capital at Fez was to sow the seed which would later germinate into the idea of a united Moroccan kingdom.

In the 11th century another fundamentalist movement got under way among the Berbers of the plains of Mauritania and Morocco which was enthusiastically supported by the peasant people of this area. The Almoravids, as they became known, quickly overran Morocco, Moslem Andalusia and then turned south to destroy the power of the kingdom of Ghana, in the Western Sudan, which had expanded to a point where it had succeeded in imposing tribute on Audaghost, the principal southern trading centre of the Berbers. The Almoravids went on to found Marrakesh and build a rich and prosperous empire over the western half of the Mahgreb but in doing this they gradually lost the simple faith, military energy and cohesion of their desert days. A revolt among the tribes of the Moroccan Atlas Mountains led to their overthrow and replacement by another dynasty, the Almohads. Under these new rulers a professional civil service was set up and the cities of Fez, Marrakesh, Tlemcen and Rabat reached the peak of their cultural development. To pay for all this as well as a professional army and navy, the Almohads had the land throughout their empire surveyed and taxes levied according to its productivity. In doing this they came up against the age-old problem of tribal rivalries by intensifying an already apparent distinction between the confederation which had overthrown the Almoravids, and who were now the rulers, and the rest. Discontent spread among the 'excluded' tribes which, together with the threats posed by the Christian armies in Spain and the advancing Bedouin from the east, forced the Almohads to divide their administration. One of these — the Hafsids of Tunis — became so successful that, after defeating the Bedouin, they declared themselves independent of Marrakesh and began trading directly with European nations. Some time after this, Almohad prestige suffered a drastic

set-back with the resounding Christian victory of Las Nevas de Tolosa in Spain and the empire began to disintegrate into its constituent tribal parts. During the confusion the Bedouin seized the opportunity of over-running much of what is now Tunisia and Algeria. Morocco itself continued to be held together after a fashion by a succession of small kingdoms but gradually lost Spain to the Christian armies in the 15th century. Nevertheless, neither the victorious Spaniards nor the Ottoman Turks, who conquered the rest of North Africa in the 16th century, were able to take Morocco and in time a new period of cultural brilliance was born under the Sa'did dynasty from which the present ruler, King Hassan is descended.

The Sa'dids reached the peak of their power after victories over the Turks and Portuguese in the late 16th/early 17th centuries and thereafter took advantage of dissensions within the empire of Songhay in the Western Sudan to attack that too. Though the attack on Songhay was successful and led to its disintegration, the Sa'dids were unable to govern what they had taken and there was chaos on the trans-Saharan commercial routes as well as in the cities of Timbuctu, Gao and Jenne. These trading cities of the Western Sudan were never to recover from this blow and the primary trading routes were shifted further east leaving Morocco as a commercial backwater.

Morocco managed to retain its independence throughout the 19th century as Tunisia and Algeria became French colonies though less through any effort on its own part than the mutual jealousies of the European nations and it was not until 1911 that it was partitioned between Spain and France. The fiercely independent mountain tribes, however, were not fully 'pacified' until the mid-30s. During its brief period as a French colony, many French went to settle there as farmers but when independence came in 1956 all but 90,000 of the 400,000 who had gone there abruptly returned to France dealing a severe blow to the country's economy which it has taken many years to recover from. The Spanish renounced their Moroccan possessions shortly after the departure of the French but hung on to Ifni in the south and the Mediterranean ports of Cueta and Melilla. Ifni was handed back to the Moroccans in 1969 but the two Mediterranean ports remain Spanish to this day.

King Hassan II, the present ruler, has several times been threatened with attempted coups but he remains, to all intents and purposes, a despotic ruler with all the prerogatives attached to absolute monarchy. There is a lot of political repression within the country designed to keep things that way with troops and police very much in evidence along main roads and in towns. The former leader of the opposition party, Ben Barka, was abducted and murdered whilst living in exile in Paris in 1965 following his alleged complicity in the conspiracy against Hassan in 1963. Subsequent French investigations into his murder led to the issue of arrest warrants for several high-ranking members of Hassan's government including the Minister of the Interior. This led to a temporary break in diplomatic relations with the French.

Recalling Morocco's historical claims to the Western Sahara, Hassan organised several hundred thousand men, women and children to walk over the border into Spanish Sahara in 1975 in an attempt to force Spain to hand over the territory. There was a great deal of diplomatic and military sabre rattling at the time but in the end Spain, unwilling to get embroiled in a colonial war, agreed to hand over the territory to Morocco and Mauritania for partition between the two — much against the wishes of the indigenous Saouarhis who wanted independence. The result was a guerilla war fought by the Saouhari POLISARIO Front, supported by Algeria, Libya and Cuba, against Mauritania and Morocco which has on several occasions brought Morocco and Algeria very close to war. The Mauritanians eventually withdrew having had their economy virtually wrecked by the activities of the POLISARIO Front but Morocco refuses to budge an inch and has taken over the part vacated by the Mauritanians. There is little doubt that one of the reasons underlying Morocco's interest in the Western Sahara is based on the fact that the territory contains the world's largest deposits of phosphate ore. Morocco is already a major supplier of this mineral, generally used as a fertilizer, so with control over the Saharan deposits they will secure a virtual monopoly. The war is still being fought and its effects on travellers has been to put a large part of southern Morocco and the trans-Saharan Route du Mauritaine out of bounds for the while. The continuing bad relations between Algeria and Morocco means that only the overland crossing between Oujda and Tlemcen is presently available and even that is sometimes closed. Keep your eye on the political situation if you're going that way.

FACTS

The principle crops are cereals, dates, olives, citrus fruits and grapes and there is a good deal of market gardening for vegetables — principally tomatoes. In the mountains large flocks of goats and sheep are reared.

A prominent characteristic of rural life is the weekly market or souk, normally held on a traditional site and located about 30-50 km from each so that tribesmen can visit the nearest one and return home within a single day. The traditional means of travel is on foot though buses and cars have changed this pattern somewhat in the last few years. Local produce is exchanged for imported or manufactured articles such as household hardware, tea, coffee and cloth, while the services of tradesmen and skilled workers such as cobblers, bankers, tinkers and blacksmiths are available. There is also an itinerant 'doctor' who treats minor ailments.

Native Moroccan towns are generally overgrown villages and three distinct functional sectors are commonly discernible; the Medina — the traditional huddle of houses comparable to the villages; the Mellah — mainly occupied by the Jews who have long been active in the commercial life of Morocco and the rest of the Maghreb; and the Kasbah — the Arab quarter. In some cases a fourth has been added — the European quarter or the Ville Nouvelle, situated a short distance away from the main town and more spaciously laid out.

VISAS
Required by all except nationals of Western Europe (excluding West Germany and Portugal), the Commonwealth countries, Japan and the USA. If you are one of those few nationals who need visas, note that the Moroccan Embassies may refuse to issue a visa if you already have an Algerian visa. A lot depends on the current state of political tension between the two.

Nationals of Israel and South Africa are not admitted.

If you intend to stay more than three months you must make an application to the police within 15 days of arrival. Nationals of France and Spain are allowed unlimited stay if they report to the police within three months of arrival.

Note that the official blurb says that visitors who don't comply with requirements regarding general appearance and dress (eg 'hippies') may be refused entry even if they have sufficient funds, a return ticket or a visa. In fact the hassle over hair length has cooled off in recent years. Tangier used to be really heavy but the spotlight has apparently shifted

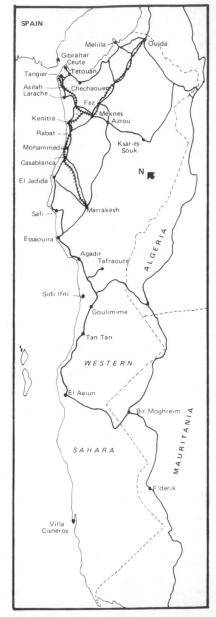

to the Ceuta/Moroccan border which used to be no trouble. On the other hand this border is very busy and it's also unlikely you'll be refused entry unless you're outrageously hairy. The one thing the authorities are very heavy on is dope. Give it a miss in this part of the world, there are too many travellers rotting in Moroccan, Algerian and Spanish jails already.

Algerian Visas When the embassy in Rabat is open, visas cost Dr 16 and take one week to issue but it's better to get them at the consulate in Oujda where they take two hours to issue and cost the same. If the embassies and consulates are closed, you have to get your visa from the United Arab Emirates Embassy in Rabat in which case they cost Dr 16, four photos and take 24 hours to issue.

Cameroon Visas Obtainable from the French Embassy in Rabat. Cost Dr 13.50 and four photos for a 10-day visa.

Egyptian Visas These cost Dr 30 take two days to issue and they demand to see that you have 'sufficient' funds.

Mauritanian Visas These cost Dr 36 and are issued on the spot. No questions asked.

Niger Visas Obtainable from the French Embassy (or consulates). A one month visa costs Dr 28, three photos and takes 24 hours to issue. Transit visas cost Dr 16.

Tunisian Visas These cost Dr 25 and take half an hour to issue.

CURRENCY
The unit of currency is the Dirham = 100 centimes. Import/export of local currency is prohibited.

Exchange rate:

£1	=	8.50 Dirhams
US$1	=	3.70 Dirhams
A$1	=	4.25 Dirhams

There is a currency blackmarket but in most places you should be very careful as rip-offs are common with all the usual tricks employed. It's very open and reasonably safe in Oujda with plenty of money-changers doing the rounds. The rates for Algerian Dinar here are much better than those prevailing inside Algeria. The money-changers will take Moroccan, Spanish and French money. If you're not keen on street deals, you can change Moroccan Dirham into Algerian Dinar at the bus station or the Tourist Office in Oujda at the rate of Dr 1 = 1.20-1.30 Dinar or US$1 = 6 Dinar (official rate is US$1 = 4 Dinar).

Don't change too much money into Dirhams as it's very difficult to get banks to reconvert even into Spanish pesetas.

Banks are open from 8.30 am to 11.30 am and from 3 pm to 5.30 pm Monday through Friday.

Note that the advent of package tours from North America and Europe has put costs up considerably in recent years. The prices of a few staples are as follows — kous-kous and vegetables: 2.50 Dr, kous-kous with meat: 4 Dr, loaf of bread: 0.55 Dr, yogurt: 0.60 Dr, coffee: 1 Dr, mint tea: 0.60 Dr.

LANGUAGE
Moorish, Arabic, French and Spanish are the main languages. English is spoken in some places. Spanish is more common in the north, French in the remainder.

ACCOMMODATION
Campsites It's legal to camp anywhere so long as you have the permission of the owner. Tourist Offices have lists of official camp sites.

Youth Hostels If you're travelling alone, these are the cheapest places to stay at but if you are a couple you might as well rent a cheap hotel as men and women are segregated and you will have to split up. Youth Hostels (called Auberge de Jeunesse) costs Dr 5 per night. Meals are not usually available and hot showers generally cost extra (cold showers free). You need an International Youth Hostel Card to stay there but if you haven't got one they will sell you one for Dr 25. There are YHs in Asni, Asrou, Casablanca, Fez, Ifrane, Marrakesh, Meknes, Mohammadia and Rabat. Where there is no Youth Hostel there is often a Centre de Sportif et Jeunesse where basic accommodation can usually be found for a small fee (bargain madly!). Sometimes they offer floor space, other times a bed but they are the cheapest around other than the mat-on-the-floor Berber-style hotels.

Cheap hotels These cost on average around Dr 10.

Agadir

The town was rebuilt after an earthquake in 1960 and is now madly expensive and no longer so interesting. There's a luxurious camp site just out of town on the Essaouira road which costs Dr 4. Another camp is located at Paradise Plage, 27 km from town on the road to Safi. Open all year.

American Express is at Voyages Schwartz, rue de Hotel Deville, Immeuble 'Freres'. The Tourist Office is at Immeuble 'A, Avenue du Prince Heritier Sidi Mohammed (tel 28 94).

Asni

The *YH* is on the Route d'Amliyt and has 40 beds.

Azrou

The *YH* is on the Route de Midelt and also has 40 beds.

Casablanca

Camp site at *Camping Oasis* near Beause Jours. From Casaport railway station the No 30 bus takes you straight there. Open all year with facilities at the nearby restaurant. The *YH* is at 6 Place Admiral Philbert (tel 74301). Large hos-

tel, comfortable and clean.

American Express is at Voyages Schwartz, 112 Avenue du Prince, Moulay Abdallah (tel 222946). The Tourist Office is at Places des Nations-Unies (tel 209-09).

Chechaouen

The town is also known as Xuan and Chouan. *Pension Rashidi* costs Dr 6 per night. The Ibn Batouta in the Medina used to be a popular place with travellers but may now be closed. There's also a beautiful camp site at this place.

Erfoud

Hotel Ziz costs Dr 10/single.

Essaouira

Camp site near the beach open all year. Running water, toilets, cooking facilities. Costs Dr 1 per night plus Dr 2 if you need a tent. *Des Amis Hotel* costs Dr 15/double and is popular with travellers. *Hotel Majestic* costs the same. Somewhat cheaper and more basic accommodation can be found at *Hotel du Sud* for Dr 5/single and at *Hotel Tangaro* a kilometre and a half walk south along the sand dunes, which costs Dr 3/single and is very peaceful. Near the Tangaro it's sometimes possible to rent a beach hut for Dr 15/month but they are often full.

For food in town, the cheapest places are the Berber cafes just off the main street — there's a whole row of them. The Tourist Office is at Sahaat Moulay Abdallah.

Fez

Excellent camping site at Parc Moulay Slimane which is enclosed and secure, with water and toilets nearby. Costs Dr 1 per tent and Dr 2 per person. The camp shop is expensive but the market is nearby. *Hotel Croissant*, near the palace in the old city, costs Dr 15/double; clean. *Hotel Mauritania* costs Dr 15/double including hot showers. *Hotel du*

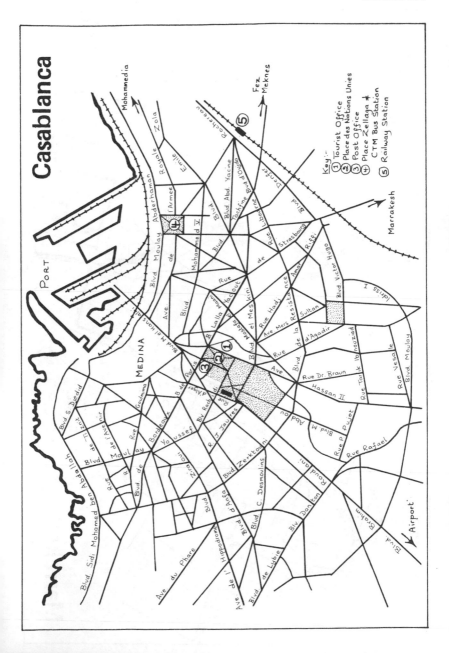

Casablanca

Key:-
① Tourist Office
② Place des Nations Unies
③ Post Office
✛ Place Zellaga
⑤ Railway Station
CTM Bus Station

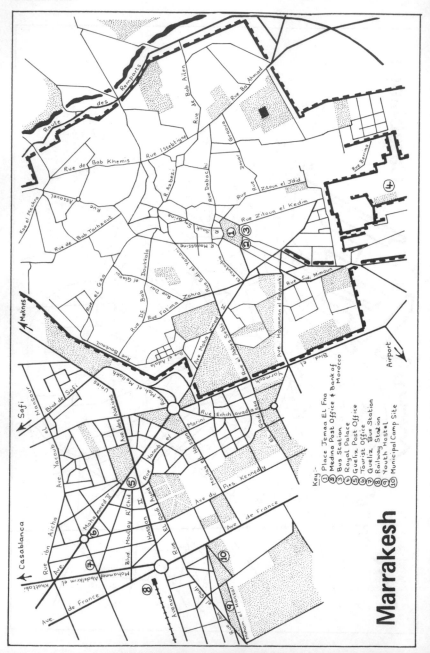

Marrakesh

Key:-
1. Place Jemaa El Fna
2. Medina Post Office & Bank of Morocco
3. Bus Station
4. Royal Palace
5. Gueliz Post Office
6. Tourist Office
7. Gueliz Bus Station
8. Railway Station
9. Youth Hostel
10. Municipal Camp Site

Pacha costs Dr 20/double and is highly recommended. The Tourist Office is at Boulevard Hassan II (tel 234-60).

Goulimime

Annual camel fair here in July but every week caravans depart for the Sahara. The weekly market is on Saturdays. Good camp site here for Dr 1 per tent and Dr 1 per person. It is also possible to find cheap accommodation on the roofs of cafes.

Ifni

El Fatah Hotel costs Dr 5/single. *Hotel Ifni*, near the cinema costs Dr 10 per room. Latter has showers but the water is only turned on for two hours in the morning and evening.

Marrakesh

Though still a fascinating place full of palaces and fortresses and an incredible souk, Marrakesh has been raped by tourism and recent travellers report some heavy resentment against foreigners. All the same, don't miss this city. Life starts and ends around the Djemaa El Fna, the main square, where both the CTM and SATAS buses have their terminals and where many budget hotels are located.

The YH is inconveniently situated well out of town at Terrain de Camping Gueliz in the Quartier Industrielle and the warden is renowned for being incapable of keeing his hands off women. You'd be far better renting a cheap room off Djemaa El Fna — average price is around Dr 15/double. *Hotel Afrique*, near CTM bus terminal, costs Dr 20/double and Dr 25/room for three people. *Hotel Agdal* and *Hotel de France* both cost Dr 15/double. There are plenty of other cheap hotels near the *Hotel Essaouira* which is situated on the street second right off the main square from the bus station and follow the signs from there. There is a camp site along Avenue de France next to the racecourse.

For food the best place to eat in the evenings is the Djemaa El Fna which comes alive every evening with food stalls and cafes. Nearby is the *Snack Hippy* which serves somewhat expensive omelettes, chips, salad and yogurt. Similar food is available from the *Cafe Oriental*.

The Tourist Office is at Place Abdelmoumen Ben Ali (tel 302-58). American Express is at Voyages Schwartz, rue Mauritania, Immeuble Mouataouakil No 1 (tel 333-21).

Taxis around town cost Dr 0.35 minimum plus whatever is on the meter. Buses vary according to distance from Dr 0.15 to Dr 0.40.

Meknes

Camp site in the centre of town at *Camping Esplanade*. Costs Dr 1 per person plus Dr 1 if you want a hot shower. The YH is at Stade Municipal and has 25 beds. Cooking facilities available. *Hotel Victoria*, near the medina costs Dr 10/double bed or Dr 15/double room. The *Metropolitan Hotel* has rooms for Dr 12 with attached bath.

The Tourist Office is at 12 rue Bouameur (tel 305-08). Taxis within town costs Dr 0.30 per person. A taxi from Meknes to Volubilis (the Roman ruins) via Moulay Idriss costs Dr 30 return.

Oujda

Camp site at Parc Lalla Aicha but the facilities are primitive. *Hotel Majestic* costs Dr 12/double. *Hotel du Peuple* costs Dr 6/single. *Hotel Menhara* costs Dr 10/double. *Hotel Royal* costs Dr 10/double and is clean.

This is the last place to get an Algerian visa (where required) if you are heading that way. It's also the only border crossing open at present. Note that the train from Oujda to Tlemcen no longer runs due to tension between Morocco and Algeria over the Western Sahara.

Rabat

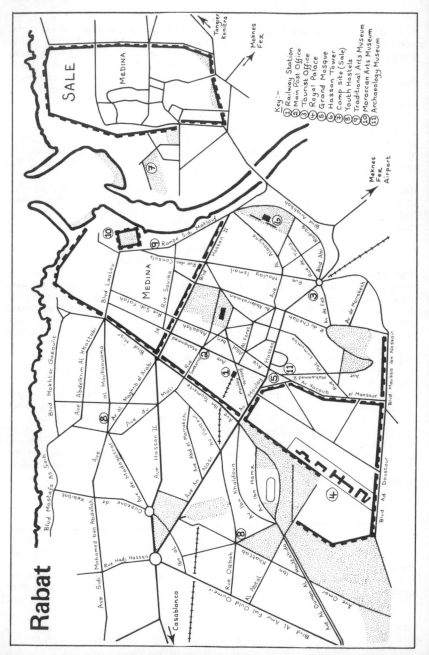

Key:-
① Railway Station
② Main Post Office
③ Tourist Office
④ Royal Palace
⑤ Grand Mosque
⑥ Hassan Tower
⑦ Camp site (Sale)
⑧ Youth Hostels
⑨ Traditional Arts Museum
⑩ Moroccan Arts Museum
⑪ Archaeology Museum

Rabat

Camp site at Sale Beach open all year. Running water and toilets, provisions available at camp shop. The *YH* is situated on Avenue Al Moukaouama near the Place de Russie. It's described as dirty and uncomfortable complete with rats but the cheapest place to stay if you are travelling alone. *Hotel France* opposite CTM bus station inside the medina walls, costs Dr 15/double and is clean and comfortable. *Hotel Casbah*, in the medina — sign in Arabic only — costs Dr 10/double. *Hotel Maroc* costs Dr 10 plus extra Dr 1 for a hot shower. For food, the *Restaurant de Jeunesse* has been recommended for good, reasonably priced food.

The Tourist Office is at 22 Avenue d' Alger (tel 212-52). The CTM bus station is at Avenue Hassan II (tel 215-21). Royal Air Maroc is at Avenue Mohammed V (tel 322-96).

Taghazout

An amazingly beautiful little fishing village 15 km north of Agadir with a population consisting of about 150 locals and up to 200 tourists which one traveller described as 'an exclusive clientele of hippies'. You can rent a room/small house here for Dr 50 per week or even cheaper if you are planning on staying longer. The town is said to be a garbage dump.

Tangier

There are several cheap pensions along the rule de la Plage (also called the rue de Portugal) which cost on average Dr 20-25/double. In the medina there are the *Hotel Chouan* for Dr 4-5 'if you want to share a room with 16 others or the roof with up to 40 others', and the *Pension Monaco* for Dr 5 per person. Latter is quite pleasant and clean. Other cheap hotels are the *Hotel Marrakesh* (Dr 15/double) and the *Hotel Miami* (Dr 5 in shared room, clean and friendly).

Tourist Office is at 29 Boulevard Pasteur (tel 394-53). American Express is at Voyages Schwartz, 76 Avenue Mohammed V (tel 334-59). The Transmediterranea Ferries office is at 31 rue Quevedo (tel 341-01). Limadet Ferries Office is at 13 rue Prince Moulay Abdellah (tel 336-21). Royal Air Maroc is at Place de France (tel 215-01).

Tetuan

Pension Marrakesh, Calle Meca No 4, costs Dr 20/double. *Pension Seville*, costs Dr 15/double. *Pension Navarra* costs Dr 15/double. There are also a lot of Berber-style hotels which you can recognise by the soup plates on a table outside a single-door entrance. Inside you will find tables with tea and tajins. Ask in here — speak French or Spanish. For food, the *Restaurant Moderne* has been recommended.

TRANSPORT

Road Transport Due to the war, police have numerous road blocks and checkpoints — twice out of every main city and then every 40-50 km. They search vehicles for arms. Foreign-registered cars get lighter treatment.

Hitching is reported to be OK and although the many police checkpoints along all main roads can be a hassle, you can't altogether avoid these even on buses. Note that because of the war with the POLISARIO guerillas and the tension between Morocco and Algeria, Goulimime is the furthest south that it is now possible to go by road though a plane is available if you want to go as far as Tantan. Also, because of the above, the only overland crossing possible at present between Morocco and Algeria is via Oujda and Tlemcen. For the more intrepid, it's possible to buy a camel in Goulimime for around US$100 at the weekly camel market there.

Buses There is a very good and frequent network of buses all over the country

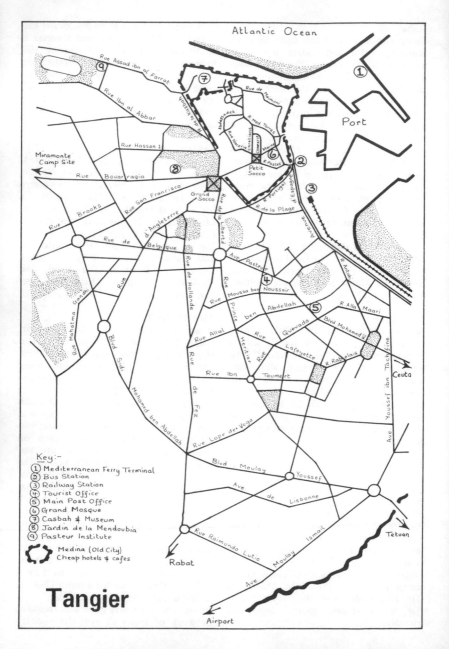

Tangier

Key:-
1. Mediterranean Ferry Terminal
2. Bus Station
3. Railway Station
4. Tourist Office
5. Main Post Office
6. Grand Mosque
7. Casbah & Museum
8. Jardin de la Mendoubia
9. Pasteur Institute

Medina (Old City)
Cheap hotels & cafes

and on most you can book a seat in advance. CTM are the most luxurious but they cost on average Dr 10 per 100 km which is about 50% more expensive than the other bus companies such as SATAS. SATAS are just as fast and just as reliable as CTM but you have to pay a small fee for 'registration' of your baggage. Departure times and prices are chalked up at every bus terminal. Note that if your baggage has to be put on the roof the driver's companion who organises all this will charge you Dr 2 for the effort.

Some examples of bus fares and journey times follow — Tetuan-Cueta costs Dr 3, Tetuan-Chaouen costs Dr 5, Tetuan-Casablanca costs Dr 25 and departs at 7.30 am, Casablanca-Essaouira costs Dr 18.50 (on SATAS) and takes six hours. Casablanca-Agadir costs Dr 20 and goes via Taghazout. Chaoun-Fez costs Dr 14.60, Casablanca-Marrakesh costs Dr 18.50, Fez-Marrakesh costs Dr 25 (on CTM) and takes 10 hours. Departs at 6 am and 9.30 am from the new town. Marrakesh-Agadir costs Dr 19.50 (on SATAS) and takes 6½ hours, Marrakesh-Ouarzazate costs Dr 17.80 (on CTM). Agadir-Essaouria costs Dr 11.50 and takes 3½ hours, many departures every day. Agadir-Taroudant costs Dr 5.
Trains These are very slow but cheaper than the buses if you travel 3rd class. There are three classes — 1st, 2nd and 'classe economique' so if you have to change trains what otherwise might have been a short journey can turn into a long one. 'Classe economique' is quite an experience — something like travelling in a farmyard.

Some examples of the fares follow — Fez-Meknes-Casablanca-Marrakesh costs Dr 40 and takes 10 hours if there are no delays. Tangier-Rabat costs Dr 14 in classe economique. The journey normally takes four hours but has been known to take 24 hours! Rabat-Fez costs Dr 9.40 in classe economique. Fez-Meknes costs Dr 2.20 (classe econ) Meknes-Rabat costs Dr 9.60 (classe econ). Casablanca-Marrakesh costs Dr 13.00 (class econ).

Note that the through trains to Algeria have all been suspended including the Oujda to Tlemcen train.
Flights Air Maroc offer 40% discounts for anyone 26 years old or under. Casablanca-Nouakchott (Mauritania) by Air Maroc costs US$200. It is cheaper from Agadir but you have to book in advance from there.

Going to Algeria
The Oujda-Tlemcen crossing is the only overland route open at present. From Oujda there are several buses daily to the border costing Dr 1.50. From there you have to take another Algerian bus to Tlemcen. There are many money-changers in Oujda who offer Algerian Dinar at much better rates than you will find inside the country — see under 'Currency' for further details. Note that at the Algeria border post there may only be a cursory baggage search but a little way into Algeria the bus you are on may well be stopped again by gendarmes who make a thorough search of your baggage.

OTHER INFORMATION
If you are carrying maps of the Moroccan-Algerian border area (eg Michelin map No 153) the Moroccan customs will confiscate them so hide them well and have a Tourist Office map handy for confiscation. If you are driving your own Land Rover you may well have a lot of hassles leaving Morocco for Algeria as these are what the POLISARIO are using to attack Moroccan positions inside Western Sahara and southern Morocco and they reckon you could well sell the vehicle to these guerilla fighters.

Mozambique

Although the Portuguese first arrived here in the late 15th century their early activities were restricted to building a number of coastal forts and trading with the interior. It was not until the 18th century that colonisation was begun in earnest and it was only in the late 19th century that the borders of the country were defined during the European scramble for African colonies. Mozambique won its independence in 1975 following a 10 year war of liberation waged by the Front for the Liberation of Mozambique led by Samora Machel. The war left the country in a shambles from which it is only just beginning to recover and the dissatisfaction which spread among the Portuguese armed forces who were fighting not only this war but also others in Angola and Guinea led to the coup which toppled the Caetano regime in Portugal itself. Like the other former Portuguese colonies, Mozambique is committed to a policy of radical social change. Since independence all private and church schools have been nationalised as well as mission hospitals, private medical practices and law firms abolished, and the judicial and educational systems reorganised.

Much of the early effort had to go into reconstructing communications systems which were destroyed in the war and expanding the medical services particularly in the rural areas — after the exodus of the Portuguese community there remained only a hundred doctors in the country to service a population of about 9 million. The reconstruction is being aided by loans, grants and technical assistance mainly from the socialist countries and the United Nations is financing a major vaccination campaign against smallpox, measles and tuberculosis.

Early on the new government took a firm stand against the minority regimes in South Africa and Rhodesia and provided training grounds and bases for Robert Mugabe's Rhodesian guerilla forces which resulted in many devastating 'hot pursuit' raids and even invasions into Tete province by the Rhodesian armed forces. For many years, Machel acted in concert with the other Front Line Presidents of Angola, Zambia and Tanzania in trying to force Smith to concede a majority government in Rhodesia. Nevertheless, despite the many changes which have taken place inside Mozambique since independence progress has been slow and only recently Machel announced a major shift in policy aimed at encouraging a mixed economy and some degree of co-operation with South Africa.

Since the reconstruction effort facing the new government was so vast, Mozambique has not encouraged tourism and for many years the area was off the overland map. We have not heard from any travellers who have been there and

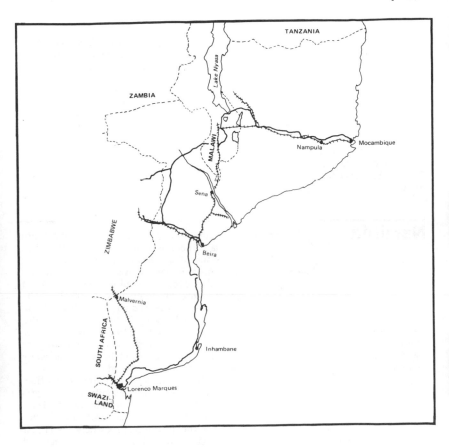

visas are still quite difficult to come by but with the recent softening of the government's attitude towards western countries it may be that travel will become possible there.

VISAS
Required by all. Applications for visas must be submitted through the Mozambique embassies in Tanzania, Portugal and the USA or through the Ministerio de Negocias Estrangeiros, CP 290, Maputo, Mozambique, or the Direccao Nacional de Migraco, CP 1296, Maputo Mozambique. Applications must be made well in advance of any intended visit and if approved will be issued on arrival at a cost of 200 Mozambique Escudos. You need an official application form and three photos to apply for a visa.

CURRENCY
The unit of currency is the Mozambique Escudo = 100 centavos. Import/export of local currency is prohibited.

Exchange rate:

£1	=	65 Escudos
US$1	=	28 Escudos
A$1	=	33 Escudos

On arrival you are required to change into Mozambique currency the equivalent of 1000 Escudos in hard currency. Airport tax for domestic flights is 10 Escudos, for international flights it is 50 Escudos. There is also a 'Protection Tax' of 100 Escudos in addition to the above.

LANGUAGES
Portuguese and many African languages such as Ronga, Shangaan, Muchope, etc. Some English is spoken.

ACCOMMODATION & TRANSPORT
Since we have not heard from anyone going there we have no details of these. If you manage to get into the country, please write us a letter and let us know what is available.

Namibia

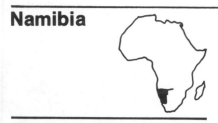

During the carve up of Africa at the Berlin Conference in 1884, Namibia became a German Colony — except for the British enclave of Walvis Bay — and remained so until after WW I when the League of Nations gave the mandate to South Africa. South Africa tried on a number of occasions to get the League's permission to incorporate the territory into the Republic but was always refused yet the country remains under the direct control of South Africa and is administered as a virtual 5th province despite the recent setting-up of a semi-independent government. The United Nations has passed many resolutions demanding that the country be handed over to a government elected by universal franchise but these continue to be ignored by South Africa which is afraid of having yet another antagonistic regime on its doorstep.

It is rich in copper and diamonds which are mined by South African and international companies. Half of Namibia's income comes from mining but none of the profits go to black Namibians and every year a third of all Namibia's income from all sources is exported to foreign companies as profit. The mines are manned largely by black Namibians who work in near slavery conditions, earn only a fraction of the wages of white mining works and are not allowed to prospect in the areas where minerals may be found.

With a small population of less than one million, most Namibians are segregated in reserves and allowed to leave only for work in the 'white areas'. Outside the northern areas where the largest reserves are situated, areas designated for Africans are small and far apart and under close supervision by white officials. In many cases a single tribe has been broken up into widely separated reserves in order to facilitate white settlement. Movement in and out of the reserves is rigorously controlled and Africans must have passes to travel outside their home areas, to buy a railway ticket, to travel within the Police Zone and to remain on a reserve other than their own for more than 48 hours or in an urban area for more than 72.

Only 46% of African children attend school, compared to 100% of white chil-

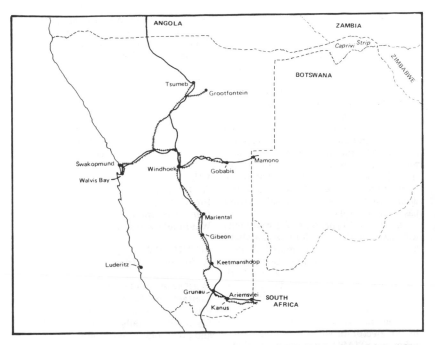

dren, and of those 90% are in the first four grades. The medical and other services are similarly orientated towards the white population. Existing trade unions are all white and there is no provision for the registration of African unions or the arbitration of disputes with management. In addition to the income from mining, fishing brings in over $10 million a year and pelts, cattle, goats and dairy produce bring in Rand 14 million. Again, the white colonisers are the chief beneficiaries.

The South West Africa People's Organisation of Namibia (SWAPO) has been fighting a political and guerilla war for over 15 years now and although, in the beginning, its effect was small activities have been stepped up in recent years with a series of hard-hitting attacks on South African regular troops along the Namibia-Angola border. There have been widespread arrests and de-

tention of SWAPO leaders and members of the 350,000-strong black Lutheran Church and there is evidence of the torture of Namibian detainees who are held under the provisions of the Terrorism Act and the Suppression of Communism Act. At his own trial in 1975, SWAPO National Chairman, David Merero, gave extensive details of his own torture at the hands of the South African police during his five month detention in solitary confinement. He was later forced to flee the country for fear of renewed arrest.

During the civil war in Angola in 1975-6 South Africa invaded the southern part of that country. The invasion was defended on the grounds of 'protecting' the Kunene hydro-electric scheme, which was partially financed by South Africa and designed to provide power for the lucrative foreign-owned Namibian mining industry, but it was also used to wipe out SWAPO guerilla camps over the border. Since then, many Namibian tribespeople living along the border and in the Caprivi Strip have been forcibly moved, their villages burnt down, and a 'free fire zone' created in an attempt to prevent the infiltration of SWAPO guerillas from Angola.

The political strategy of the South African regime is one of keeping the Namibian population divided along ethnic lines in order to maintain white supremacy. Their main tactic is to win over the chiefs of the minority tribes by playing on their fears of alleged Ovambo domination in any political system based on majority rule.

A Transkei-type of self government was attempted in 1973 in Ovamboland headed by the most prominent supporter of the Pretoria regime, Chief Elifas who was Ovamboland's Chief Councillor. It was he who was responsible for the public flogging of several hundred SWAPO detainees in the aftermath of the 'elections' that year when only 2.8% of the electorate voted following a campaign by SWAPO for a boycott of the elections. The attempt collapsed when Elifas was shot a little while later but his assassination provided a convenient pretext for South African and tribal police to clamp down on political opponents and impose a reign of terror throughout the area which led to the flight of several thousand SWAPO members across the border into Angola.

More recently, SWAPO has called for the recognition of Namibia's territorial integrity and the establishment of a republic. There would be provision for the protection of minorities along the lines drawn up by the UN Bill of Rights and other conventions and membership of the Commonwealth is favourably considered but ethnic regionalism and proportional representation has been firmly ruled out. SWAPO has also said that the future territory must include Walvis Bay and the Caprivi Strip, the former being essential for any post-independence economy since over 90% of Namibia's mineral, fish and agricultural exports are shipped out via this port. Given South Africa's intransigence, however, and the capital invested in the Kunene hydro-electric scheme and mining operations, an early settlement seems unlikely though with Zimbabwe's independence under a black majority government change may very well come sooner rather than later.

VISAS
As for South Africa. Permits necessary for visiting the Homelands — available from the Ministry of Bantu Affairs, Windhoek, without any fuss.

CURRENCY
As for South Africa.

ACCOMMODATION
Contact the South Africa Tourist Offices or the Tourist Office in Windhoek for further details. Some youth hostels and government rest houses.

Asab Box 2084, Mariental on the main road to Keetmanshoop, costs Rand 2.50 for B&B.
Goageb Konkiep, PO Box Goageb (tel 3122), costs Rand 2.50.
Gobabis *The Central*, Box 7, Voortrekker Road, Gobabis (tel 11) costs Rand 2.50-4.
Kalkfield *The Kleiber*, Box 5, Kalkfield (tel 10) costs Rand 2.50.
Rehoboth *The Rehoboth*, Strand 56, Box 19, Rehoboth, costs Rand 2.
Seeheim *The Seeheim* PO Seeheim, (tel 12-440), costs Rand 2-3.
Walvis Bay *The Desert Inn*, Strand 307, Narraville, Box 8044 (tel 2827) costs Rand 2-3.50.
Windhoek *The South West Star*, Chrysler Road, Box 8061, (tel 4689), costs Rand 2. The Anglican Church Hall also sometimes puts people up — ask permission from the Minister.

TRANSPORT

Travel within Namibia is complicated by the necessity to have special permits for many areas which include Oranjemund, the diamond mining areas around Luderitz, Ovamboland, the African homelands and the African and Coloured townships. Both the Caprivi Strip and the area around the Kunene Dam, along the Angolan border, are security areas and 'out of bounds'. The permit for Oranjemund can be obtained in Port Nolloth just south of the border on the South African-Atlantic coast. The other permits are obtainable from the tourist office in Windhoek. There are no restrictions coming over the border at the Orange River.

There are several possible points of entry; along the Cape Town, Springbok, Windhoek road at Noordoewar; along the Upington, Karasburg road at Ariamsvlei; along the Ghanzi, Gobabis, Windhoek road at Mamuno from Botswana.

There is very little traffic but the main roads are good and cars with room generally stop. Otherwise try trucks on which you usually have to pay. Often possible to get lifts all round tourist sites (eg Etosha, Petrified Forest, White Lady, Cape Cross, Seal Colony, Swakopmund, Namib Desert, Fish River Canyon).

There is quite an extensive network of railway lines. From the Republic the line goes from Upington via Karasburg and Keetmanshoop to Windhoek with a branch to Luderitz. From Windhoek the line runs to Walvis Bay with a branch north to Otjiwarongo and Grootfontein. There's also a line from Windhoek to Gobabis.

OTHER INFORMATION

If you would like more information on the social and political aspects of Namibia get hold of copies of the *Namibia News*, *Alternative Press Digest* and the *Namibia File*. Excellent tourist literature at Tourist Office and the AA in Windhoek.

Niger

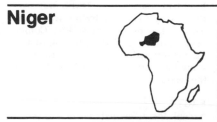

Niger is one of those incongruous legacies of late 19th century European colonialism which might well have been better divided up between its neighbouring republics. Ethnically it straddles territories which were once part of the empires of Songhay and Kanem-Bornu in the Western Sudan and others to the north which are populated by the Tuareg. Few countries are more dependent on the good will of their neighbours and upon foreign aid than land-locked Niger

with over two-thirds of the country being desert. The Sahel drought in the early '70s had a disastrous effect and brought the country to the brink of total ruin from which it is only just beginning to recover. Groundnuts, which used to provide 50% of the country's income, were virtually wiped out and the losses of cattle and sheep stood at 50% and 24% respectively. Thousands of nomadic Tuareg were forced to abandon their centuries-old way of life and seek refuge in the cities and towns.

The only thing which saved Niger from economic disaster was the discovery of uranium deposits at Arlit, north of Agadez. Concessions to work these deposits were granted to the French, West Germans and Italians with the French holding the largest stake. Production started in 1971 and reached a figure of 950 tons in 1973 when exports of the mineral were valued at 5 billion CFA. The total deposits are estimated at 100,000 tons. A search for oil was undertaken by Texaco in the early '70s since the country lies between the rich oil fields of Libya and Nigeria but nothing was found.

Like Mali, Niger lies at the crossroads of the trans-Saharan trade routes which, during medieval days, used to be of vital importance to the Mediterranean and coastal West African states. Though these eastern routes which ran north through the Fezzan to Tripoli and Cairo and east through Darfur to the cities of the Nile Valley were not as important as those further west which ran through Jenne, Timbuktu and Gao to Morocco and Algeria because of the sparcity of gold available in what is now Nigeria to the south, they were important enough to support an empire in the grasslands east, west and north of Lake Chad. This was the empire of Kanem-Bornu which appeared in the 9th century at approximately the same time as the empire of Ghana arose much further west in the area of the present Senegal-Mali border. Unlike the empires further west — Ghana, Mali and Songhay — Kanem-Bornu was to last right into the middle of the 19th century and even today its effect lingers on in eastern Niger and northern Nigeria. Originally its wealth was based on trading salt and copper from the oasis of Bilma in north-east Niger for the fine cotton goods and food of coastal West Africa, but following the destruction of the empire of Songhay by the Moroccans in the late 16th century, Kanem-Bornu began to inherit much of the gold and ivory trade which had previously passed along the more westerly routes.

The old empire of Kanem-Bornu was based to the east of Lake Chad and had converted to Islam in the 11th century. Though an overall system of law and order had been established — a necessary prerequisite for profitable trade to take place — the empire collapsed into its constituent parts in the 15th century with a rebellion of subject peoples, notably the Bulala. After many years of civil war, a new empire was established this time west of Lake Chad and during the 16th century the empire produced its greatest ruler, Idris Alooma, who united the whole of the grassland area from the borders of Darfur in the east to Hausaland in the west. Diplomatic missions were maintained in Tripoli and Cairo and there were even contacts with the Ottoman Sultan in Constantinople.

With the breaking of the trans-Saharan trade monopoly by the European maritime powers, however, the wealth associated with these routes diminished gradually. It hasn't quite ceased even today and until very recently annual caravans consisting of thousands of camels were still loading up with salt at the oasis of Bilma and heading south for Nigeria and Cameroon.

Niger became a French colony in the 19th century and gained its independence in 1960. Until 1974 it was ruled by President Hamani Diori who was overthrown in that year by an army coup led by the present president, Colonel Seyni Kountche. The latter announced his determination to hang on to power some time ago and has refused to allow the release of Diori.

FACTS

Except for a few patches of mountain, Niger is a huge plain with an average height of 300 metres. The climate, except in the south-west, is very hot and dry. The heaviest rains come in August, if they come at all — and at this time tornadoes can also occur. November and January are the coolest months when the Harmattan blows off the desert.

VISAS

Required by all except nationals of Belgium, Denmark, Finland, France, West

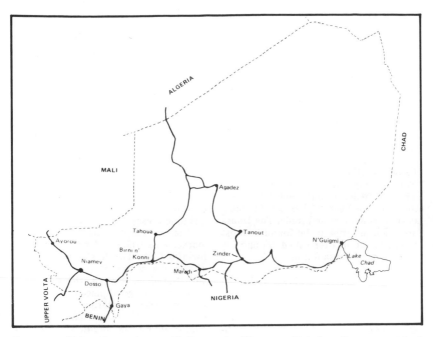

Germany, Italy, Luxembourg, Netherlands, Norway, Sweden and the UK.

Note that Niger Embassies are few and far between so if you are heading this way bear this fact in mind. French embassies are sometimes empowered to issue Niger visas where there is no Niger representation but this isn't true of all French embassies. In Freetown, Sierra Leone, the Ivory Coast embassy will issue visas for Niger which cost Leone 3. There are Niger embassies in Algeria (Algiers) and Nigeria (Lagos).

You are supposed to report to the police in each town you arrive at in Niger but if you want any pages left in your passport you are advised to overlook this except in Agadez. Before you are allowed to leave Niger you have to have an Exit Permit from Immigration in Niamey. Two photos are required for this permit.

Benin Visas Available from the embassy in Niamey which is quite a way out of town. They cost 300 CFA plus two photos for a three day visa. It is almost impossible to get anything other than a three day visa but it is worth a try.

Togo Visas Obtainable from the French embassy in Niamey (there is no Togo embassy).

Upper Volta Visas Obtainable from the French embassy. Costs 750 CFA and takes 24 hours. The visas are valid for 90 days. (There is no Upper Volta embassy).

CURRENCY
The unit of currency is the CFA. Import/export of local currency is allowed up to 25,000 CFA.

Exchange rate:

£1	=	473 CFA
US$1	=	208 CFA
A$1	=	237 CFA

French Francs are the best currency to carry in Niger as they can be changed anywhere at any time.

MAIL
If you're collecting mail in Niamey make sure you check both of the main post offices — the one at the Hotel des Postes, near the Surete National, and the larger, older General Post Office. There is a charge of 80 CFA for each letter collected.

LANGUAGES
French, very little English is spoken. Though French is very useful for dealings with bureaucracy, Hausa is the language of commerce and trade. The Hausa are a Muslim tribe to be found in most towns in the quarter called 'Zongo'. A few words of Hausa follow:

Numerals: 1-gudda, 2-biuw, 3-uku, 4-fuddu, 5-byarr, 6-shidda, 7-bokwei, 8-tokos, 9-tara, 10-goma.

Thank you — nagodi; yes — yay; good morning — ina kwana (reply: lafi-ya lau); good evening — ina wuni.

ACCOMMODATION
In most towns you can find *Maison de Jeunes* where you can often sleep free or for a small charge — usually between 300-500 CFA. As in most other ex-French colonies there are also *Campements* (Government Rest Houses) but they are expensive though if you have a tent it is often possible to camp in the grounds for much less. Note that many bars are expensive so check out prices before you eat or drink.

Agadez
Rooms at *Hotel Sahara* for 3000 CFA, less on the roof but bargain hard. At *Hotel L'Air* 600 CFA to sleep on the terrace, rooms are more expensive. At *Hotel Atlantide* you can sleep on the roof for 500 CFA — or singles/1000 CFA, doubles/2000 CFA. Clean and pleasant with showers, a bar and restaurant.

If you are really short of money you can sleep free at the Gare Routiere where the truckies heading for Tamanrasset, Zinder and Niamey stay. Local children will offer accommodation in private houses for between 200-500 CFA — a bargain if you find a pleasant place to stay. There is a *Youth Hostel* of sorts but is often not worth the trouble of finding as it is usually full of permanent residents. The camp site is eight km from town but situated on a beautiful site which was formally known as 'Joyce's Garden'. It costs 500 CFA per night and has a swimming pool but food is expensive there.

There are many small cafes in the market area which offer rice and sauce for 100 CFA. The *Restaurant Senegalaise* in the centre of town is popular with travellers. It has a friendly, young crowd and is a good place to ask around for lifts. Other watering holes include the *Bar l'Ombre du Plaisirs* and the *Family House Restaurant*. The former is a good place to hang around in the evenings — local musicians play all night and cheap quinine/maize beer is available.

The bank in Agadez (and the one in Arlit where the uranium is mined) give good rates of exchange especially for French Francs but they won't change Algerian Dinar and generally charge a 250 CFA commission on exchanges.

You must register with the police on arrival in Agadez. If you neglect to do this you will get a lot of hassle later.

If you would like to take a camel trip to the Air Mountains or the hot springs at Tafadek, ask for Musa, a silversmith ('forgeron') who arranges these trips. To find his house take the main road from the post office to the police station, go past the mission and then ask. The trips cost about 3200 CFA per day including camel and guide per person. Many travellers have said it is really worth while but others have

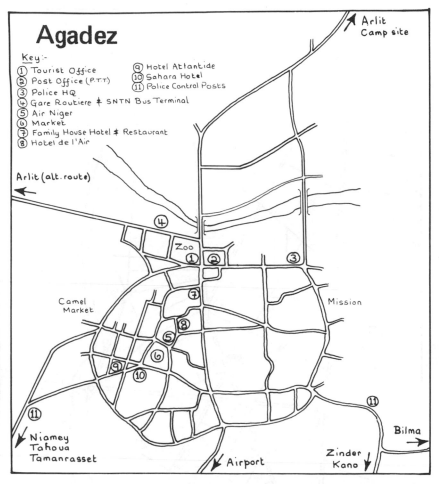

said that Musa is something of a rip-off merchant. Check him out for yourself. His trips are certainly cheaper than most of those you will be offered.

Niamey

Maison de Jeunes costs 300 CFA if you can persuade them to let you sleep there — the director is very unpredictable. Tell him the hotels are full but don't go too early. *Hotel Domino* costs 1800 CFA/single; 2100 CFA/double and 2700 CFA/triple. Double and triple rooms often have attached showers. *Hamani's Auberge* is situated behind the Peace Corps office (not the same as the hostel) past the Arbre de Liberte. It costs 2100 CFA per night, has showers and is very clean. *Chez Moustache* has rooms for 2500 CFA/double. Other places to stay which have been recommended are *L'Elephant Blanc* and the

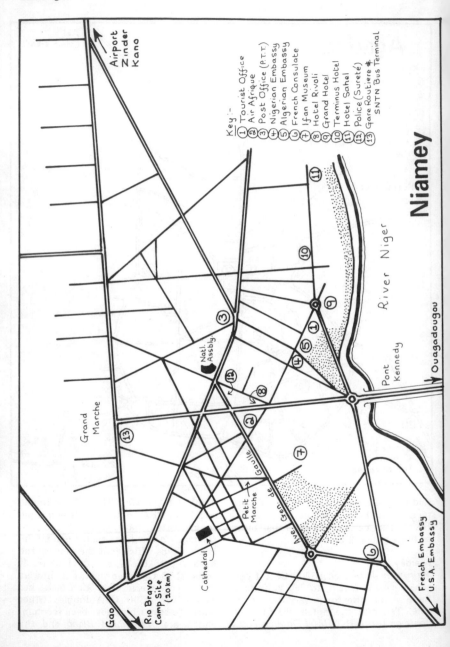

Niamey

Key:-
1. Tourist Office
2. Air Afrique
3. Post Office (P.T.T)
4. Nigerian Embassy
5. Algerian Embassy
6. French Consulate
7. Ifan Museum
8. Hotel Rivoli
9. Grand Hotel
10. Terminus Hotel
11. Hotel Sahel
12. Police (Sureté)
13. Gare Routière / SNTN Bus Terminal

Airport
Zinder
Kano

Grand Marche

Natl. Assbly.

Petit Marche

Cathedral

Gao

Rio Bravo Camp Site (20 km)

French Embassy
U.S.A. Embassy

Pont Kennedy

Ouagadougou

River Niger

Hotel Nigerienne.

Note that the *Peace Corps Hostel* situated between the Grande Marche and rue Salaman will no longer take travellers but they may allow you to sleep on the lawn if you are lucky. Otherwise, if you are short of money, it is possible to sleep outside the Commisariat de Police next to the Grande Marche. They are friendly people and it is safe. Another place where you can sometimes sleep free, is in the school opposite the Hotel Nigerienne but you have to leave early in the morning before the children arrive.

There are two camp sites, a new one which is four km from town at Yantala and which costs 750 CFA per night. It is clean. The older camp site, known as 'Rio Bravo' is 28 km from town and run by two Germans. It also costs 750 CFA and is situated on the banks of the Niger River and has a small zoo.

The *Islam* opposite the Grande Marche serves meals for 300 CFA. The bar in the *Hotel Domino* is a good place to meet other travellers.

There are swimming pools at the *Hotel Terminus* and *Grand Hotel* which you can use for 300 CFA. There is also another at the *Hotel Rivoli* uphill from the Place de Kennedy opposite the Canadian Embassy and, although there are a lot of overland vehicles parked outside as a rule, it is an expensive place. The American Recreation Centre also has a swimming pool. The American Cultural Centre Library near the market is open to all.

The Tourist Office is situated near the Nigerian Embassy. It has maps of Niamey for 200 CFA. The Ifan Museum has some spectacular displays and is well worth a visit. It costs 200 CFA and is closed on Mondays.

Taxis around town cost 100 CFA per journey. A taxi to the airport (about five km out of town) costs 500 CFA but you can do it cheaper in a shared Peugeot cab. Bicycles can be rented in Niamey at many places for 150 CFA per day.

Birni N'Konni
Le Campement costs 750 CFA. It is very comfortable and has cold beers. There are hotels nearby for 500 CFA. Mosquito nets are provided but the hotels are not very clean.

Tahoua
Camping in the grounds of *Le Campement* costs 150 CFA per person, otherwise camp free at the *Maison de Jeunes.*

Zinder
The *Peace Corps Hostels* and missions will no longer take travellers. *Hotel Central* costs 1000 CFA/double. This is a good place to sell unwanted gear that you needed to cross the Sahara. The hotel at the back of the *Africa Restaurant* opposite the market on the way to the BP station, offers double rooms for 500 CFA but there are no beds. On the other hand it does sell the cheapest beers in Niger.

The *Gare Routiere* has cheap food. The *Restaurant Senegalaise* offers meals for 100 CFA. Another cafe which has been recommended is the *La Liberte* — excellent cheap food.

Don't miss the beautiful, large market at Zinder!

TRANSPORT
Road Transport If you are hoping to find free rides or, at least, rides you can afford, you will be in for some long waits but it is still possible. As in other Sahelian countries, the prices for lifts on trucks are more or less fixed, although bargaining can reduce them a little. Note that when you are making arrangements for lifts, never hand any money across (even for a 'deposit') until you are on the truck. This includes giving money to people who are touting for passengers. There are a number of

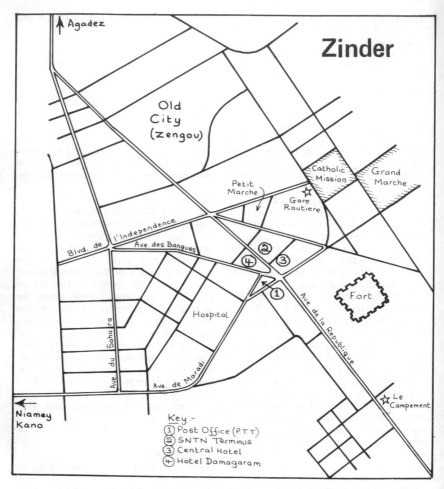

buses which connect Niamey, Tahoua, Birni N'Konni, Maradi, Zinder and Agadez which are often cheaper than trucks but very crowded. For the more intrepid it is possible to buy a horse in many of the villages and towns along the Niger River and to ride down to the coast where you can usually re-sell at a small profit. Feed the horse on millet and grass which are cheap. Keep your horse off the roads as they are used to scrub and get freaked out by trucks hurtling past. Customs officials are often enthused by this form of transport and welcome you. Whatever form of transport you are on remember that the roads are all very rough. In view of this, it is better to get a ride on a loaded truck rather than an empty one as the latter bounce around a lot and will leave you bruised for days afterwards.

Some examples of transport costs and journey times are:

Agadez-Zinder: Trucks cost between 7000 and 8000 CFA (the local people pay 5000 CFA but as a foreigner you won't get it for this). They leave early in the morning and arrive about the same time next day. The trucks stop during the night so that everyone can catch some sleep. The road is one of the worst in Africa. There is also an irregular bus doing this run which costs 2000 CFA.

Agadez-Niamey: Trucks cost 7000 CFA sometimes cheaper on empty trucks); Peugeot cars 8000 CFA and taxis 10,000 CFA. The journey takes two days on average. Note that if you are taking a taxi, make sure it is taking you right into Niamey. Some travellers have been dumped 80 km from Niamey and had to pay extra for another taxi from there.

Zinder-Niamey: There is an 'express' bus on Tuesdays, Wednesdays and Thursdays at 8 am which costs 5750 CFA. A cheaper bus costing 3500 CFA runs on Mondays and Fridays. A Peugeot car costs 4000 CFA (shared). Note that it is almost impossible to hitch along this stretch because of military and police checkpoints (they're not keen on hitchhikers). The journey takes two days. There are also daily trucks doing this run which leave from the small market in Zinder.

Niamey-Tahoua: Bus on Tuesdays and Fridays in the early morning. Costs 2200 CFA and stops overnight in Birni N'Konni where you have to change buses.

Tahoua-Agadez: Trucks most days of the week throughout the dry season. Costs 3000 CFA.

Niamey-Maradi: Daily bus at midday which leaves from the main truck park and arrives Maradi at dawn the next day. Costs 3000 CFA.

Maradi-Zinder: Costs 4000 CFA by truck and takes one day.

Niamey-Dosso: Costs 600 by truck.

Dosso-Arlit: Costs 7000 CFA by truck.

Niamey-Gaya (on the Niger/Benin border): Costs 1200 CFA by truck.

River transport Motorised piroques (dug-outs) can be found for hire at Pont Kennedy in Niamey. They are excellent for visiting small villages along the Niger River. Beautiful countryside, friendly villages, fish and dates available but take water purifying tablets with you and when you get back have a check up for amoebic dysentery at a hospital. It is endemic in these villages. A three-day trip for three people should cost around 5500 CFA. Food is extra but is very cheap and interesting in the villages.

It is also possible to pick up motorised piroques going to Benin or Nigeria but you might have to hang around for a few days playing cards and peeling manioc before you locate one. Niamey to Gaya on the Niger-Benin border will cost about 1200 CFA or 3000 CFA to Melanville in Benin. The trip takes three to four days. If you are heading for Benin, make sure you have a visa (if necessary). We had a letter recently from some travellers who were dumped in Benin because the piroque owner didn't want to go any further. They found themselves stuck in the customs house at Melanville for a week until a diplomatic commerical attache happened to pass through and got a message back to the Canadian Embassy in Niamey. They sent someone down who managed to persuade the Benin authorities to allow them to return to Niger. They have no idea how long they would have been held there otherwise.

Routes to & from Niger
(a) Niger-Algeria (Route du Hoggar)
There are no buses along this route and you will have to arrange a lift with a truck going from Agadez to Taman-

rasset. It's probable that you will find yourself in the company of several other travellers who are all going this way so you may well have some bargaining power. All the trucks charge the same price (it's effectively government controlled these days) which is an outrageous 12,000-15,000 CFA! Unfortunately there's no alternative. Flight prices are even more outrageous. The price generally includes food and water provided by the truckie but you should confirm this. The journey takes four to five days and you stop for about three hours every day during the hottest period. Bread is cooked directly in the sand which is an indication of how hot it gets. If you are lucky enough to find a lift in a Land-Rover the journey will take about 3½ days. Note that if food and water are not included in the price

the only place you can get water along the route is at In Guezzam on the border. If you are a woman or two women travelling alone, make sure you get on a truck in Agadez which is also taking several other male travellers. We have had several letters about the customs officials on the Algerian border who make themselves thoroughly obnoxious and who could possible be dangerous (they get drunk all the time as there is nothing else to do). Sexual hassles and pistol waving have been mentioned. You should also choose a truck which looks like it is going to make the journey as this route is littered with vehicles that simply died.

(b) **Niger-Nigeria** Zinder to Kano by truck costs 1500 CFA as a rule but can be as much as 3000 CFA (depends on the truckie). The best days to find a truck are Thursdays and Friday mornings as at least 30 trucks do this run at that time having bought supplies in Zinder market. Sometimes it is even possible to get a free ride. The journey takes a day. There is also another possible route from Niamey to Dosso, Gaya and Kamba. A truck from Niamey to Dosso costs 600 CFA and from there to Gaya costs a further 600 CFA. The border with Nigeria is no hassle and customs officials are usually friendly but make sure you have either a visa or entry permit (see under 'Nigeria').

(c) Niger-Upper Volta Niamey to Ouag-adougou costs 2500 CFA by truck or bus and takes 1½ days. The buses leave three times a week but only go when full so there is no definite departure time. If you are coming in the opposite direction it will cost you 3500 CFA! The roads are really rough.

(d) Niger-Mali SNTN bus once per week in either direction between Niamey and Gao. Departs Niamey on Tuesdays from the truck park and costs 1500 CFA. The journey takes 1½ days (delays on the border). There are also trucks which do this run but they generally take about two days.

Nigeria

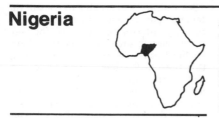

Nigeria is one of Africa's largest, most populous, and, since the discovery of oil, wealthiest states. It also has one of Africa's most intractible identity problems since it is a polyglot of different peoples, cultures, histories and religions, which were never united at any period in the past except in name only during the relatively brief time that it was a British colony. Though it is this great diversity of cultures and social forms which make it a fascinating country to visit, the rivalries between the various groups and regions have bedevilled politics since independence in 1960 and led to much bloodshed on more than one occasion, the most devastating being the attempted secession of Biafra in eastern Nigeria during the years 1967 to 1970.

Most of the ethnic groups living in Nigeria today appear to have originated far to the west in the Tekrur area which straddles the borders of Mali, Senegal and Guinea. Various migrations to the east took place from the 9th century onwards, often due to pressures exerted by the empires of Ghana, Mali and Songhay which held sway over the Western Sudan from the 9th to the 16th century during the heyday of the trans-Saharan trade routes. While the urban cultures of some of these migrants, especially those of Benin and the Yoruba, can be traced back to the 10th and 11th centuries, others, like the Fulani and Hausa, remained for a long time nomadic pastoralists who managed their own affairs independently of the people among which they lived. Throughout the centuries that these migrations were taking place and civilizations like those of Benin and Oyo developing, the empire of Kanem-Bornu at the cross-roads of the eastern trans-Saharan trade routes held sway over large parts of northern Nigeria, Niger and Chad. This empire was destroyed in the mid-19th century under the onslaught of the Fulani and Hausa but in the 16th century was one of the most powerful states in Africa and one whose influence still lingers on in that part of Nigeria.

The first of the Yoruba empires which grew up in western Nigeria was that of Benin and by the time the Portuguese arrived in this part of the world Benin City was a large, well-planned metropolis whose products and those of the areas under its control were much in demand in Morocco and other Islamic Mediterranean states. Unlike the empires in the Western Sudan, Benin retained its traditional pagan religions and customs and Islam made little headway here until the late 18th century. Benin continued to prosper and trade with the European maritime nations until the limelight was taken by the emerging power of Oyo further north — another Yoruba state — in the 16th century. The Alafins of Oyo set up a strong state which was to survive virtually without serious challenge for more than two centuries amd was only finally destroyed by the Fulani in the mid-19th century.

While all this was taking place in the west, the Hausa in the north were gradually becoming urbanised and Islamised, founding a number of city-states in the process. Of these the most important were Zaria, Katsina and Kano with Kano eventually surfacing as the most influential and acquiring in the 16th century a reputation throughout North and West Africa as a centre of trade, scholarship and effective government. These city-states of the Hausa never established anything more than a loose federation, sometimes of partners, at other times of rivals, until the 19th century when the Fulani conquest united the greater part of the Hausa lands under the single authority of the Sultan of Sokoto.

The destruction of Oyo led to a period of anarchy and intense rivalry which the British, with their colonial policy of divide and rule, found very convenient in the late 19th century as they advanced further and further into Nigeria in an effort to forestall the French who were sweeping across the Western Sudan towards Lake Chad. The British colonial period also had a more indirect effect — that of the conversion of large numbers

of Ibo in eastern Nigeria to Christianity. This was a factor which would further complicate inter-tribal relations following independence.

At independence the country was divided up into three administrative regions which largely corresponded to the three major traditional tribal and cultural areas — the north, largest of the three with half the seats in the federal assembly with its Hausa/Fulani population ruled by conservative and traditionalist Muslim emirs; the west with its largely Yoruba population and the east, the traditional homeland of the Christian Ibos. The north, looking back on the successes of the Fulani conquests in the 19th century and seeking to control the federal government, first arranged a marriage of convenience with the Ibos of the east in order to make this effective but this broke up in 1964. Following this the north attempted to impose its will on the Yoruba of the west but this led to a breakdown of law and order and discontent among the army and civil service many officers of which were Ibo. In 1966 a group of young army officers, led by Generals Ojukwu and Ironsi both of whom were Ibos, assassinated the Sardauna of Sokota together with a number of his agents including the prime minister, Sir Abubakar Tafawa Balewa, who was a northerner. A military administration was set up with Ironsi at its head, civil disorder brought under control and the country split up into 12 administrative divisions in an attempt to control regional rivalry. The arrangement, however, was not to the liking of the bulk of the troops, most of whom were northerners, nor to the surviving leaders of the north and six months later Ironsi and many leading Ibo officers were killed in a coup led by a Christian northerner, General Gowon.

The tribal animosity which had surfaced during the coup, however, shackled Gowon from the start and led to difficulties with the Ibos, many of whom were prominent in the administration, technical services and commerce. As matters came to a head many thousand Ibo were massacred throughout the country and up to a million refugees poured back into the already overcrowded Ibo heartland of the east. Here lay the seeds of the Biafra conflict which erupted six months later with General Ojukwu's announcement of the east's secession from the republic as the independent state of Biafra. The Biafran forces, hoping to arouse the Yoruba of the west to their cause against the north, struck out for Lagos but support failed to materialise and all but a handful of African countries refused to accord Biafra diplomatic recognition. Ojukwu's forces were soon thrown back into the Ibo heartland but the civil war was to drag on for another 2½ years as the Ibo forces fought tooth and claw for every inch of land which the federal army took. By late 1969 a disastrous food shortage had developed inside Biafra and the Ibo forces were forced to capitulate.

Gowon arranged a relatively generous settlement but was overthrown in 1971 by Brigadier Mohammed while Gowan was attending an OAU meeting in Kampala. Gowon subsequently enrolled at Warwick University in England as a student of Politics and International Affairs — a somewhat curious direction to take! Demands were made for his extradition to face charges of treason but they came to nothing despite threats of an economic blockade of Britain by Nigeria and Brigadier Mohammed was himself assasinated soon after.

The country is presently moving towards a return to civilian government and although this might be a welcome change it is unlikely that the rivalries which have plagued the country for so many years are anywhere nearer to compromise now than they have ever been, though in an attempt to break up large power blocks even further the country has been divided into even more administrative units. Nigerians remain very sceptical as any glance at a newspaper will demonstrate.

FACTS

Despite the revenue from oil (which is still increasing) agriculture is still by far the most important economic mainstay of Nigeria with 70 to 80% of all male workers directly dependant on it. The crops of the north are mainly annuals (groundnuts, cotton, some tobacco, sugar cane, rice and wheat) reflecting the comparatively short rainy season and the use made of riverine lands flooded during the rains. In the south they are predominantly root and tree crops (cocoa, rubber, palm oil, kola nuts) reflecting conditions prevailing in the rain forests of this area. From the central region comes beniseed, ginger and yams. The Fulani of the north keep large herds of cattle, goats and sheep. While oil revenues have considerably bettered the economy of the country as a whole, Nigeria, like Libya, has been discovering that the sudden accession of wealth on a narrow front like this does not benefit the inhabitants of the country generally. The comparatively high wages paid in the oil sector and in the towns has encouraged people to leave the countryside so that less food is likely to be produced. At the same time urban workers are prepared and able to pay more for foodstuffs and as a result food prices have risen sharply with hardship being experienced in turn by agricultural workers. Many problems have been created by this kind of inflation.

The climate is hot and dry in the north and hot and wet in the south. The rainy seasons are: April to September in the north and March to November in the south. A long dry season stretches from December to March when the Harmattan blows off the desert to the north. The coast is an almost unbroken

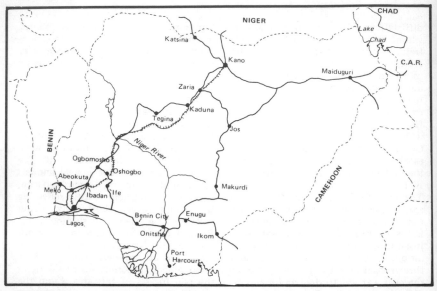

line of sandy beaches and lagoons running back to creeks and mangrove swamps. Inland the country rises in richly planted hillsides before giving way to savannah with Sahelian plains in the north.

VISAS

Required by all. They can not be issued at the border and if you enter on a tourist visa then, officially, you are supposed to have an onward ticket, but we have not heard of anyone entering overland being hassled about this. Transit visas are usually for seven days and cannot be extended.

In Accra, Ghana, visas are free and issued the same day. In Niamey, Niger they are free but take 48 hours to issue. In Cotonou, Benin, they are free, take 24 hours to issue and you need three photos.

If you enter Nigeria via Ketou and Meko on the Benin/Nigerian border in the south there is no customs post there and you will be taken under police escort to Abeokuta — they are after illegal immigrants into which category you fall

if you have no visa — but after a few questions the traditional Nigerian hospitality generally surfaces and some people have even been given their fare to Lagos where you must apply for a visa if you don't have one.

Try not to overstay your visa as Immigration Control is computerised and border officials are liable to get shirty.

Benin Visas These take two to three days to process and allow for a stay of 24 hours only! Also, you must pay a bribe of 2 Naira to get it. This is a typical Benin absurdity.

Cameroon Visas These cost 5.60 Naira, three photos and take 24 hours to issue but they are also available at the border — see the 'Cameroon' chapter. The embassy address is 4 Elsi Fermi Pearse Street, Victoria Island, Lagos.

Central African Republic Visas These cost 5 Naira for a one month visa but it takes quite a bit of effort to get them to issue you with one. They have a tendency to refer you to Yaounde in Cameroon. The embassy address is 108

Awolowo Road, Ikoyi Island, Lagos.

Ghana Visas These cost 1.45 Naira or 50 kobo for a Commonwealth Entry Permit. They take one or two days to issue and they demand photographers' photos (not photo kiosk ones).

Ivory Coast Visas These cost 5 Naira for a 90-day visa and are issued the same day if you get there early.

Kenya visas These cost 2.50 Naira, one photo and take 24 hours to issue.

Niger & Upper Volta Visas Both are available from the Niger Embassy. They are free, issued while you wait, and allow for a stay of one week.

Senegal Visas These cost 3.30 Naira for a 90-day visa and are issued the same day.

Tanzanian Visas These cost 2.50 Naira, three photos and take 24 hours to issue. Commonwealth Entry Permits are free. The Embassy address is 45 Ademola Street, Ikoyi Island, Lagos.

Zaire Visas These cost 5.60 Naira, three photos and take 24 hours to issue.

CURRENCY

The unit of currency is the Naira = 100 kobo. Import/export of local currency is allowed up to 50 Naira.

Exchange rate:

£1	=	1.26 Naira
US$1	=	0.55 Naira
A$1	=	0.63 Naira

Despite the fact that Nigeria is a major oil exporter, there is a flourishing currency blackmarket offering up to 80% more than the official rate of exchange. Kano, Maidguri and Lome (Togo) are the best places to buy Naira. In Lagos the rates are somewhat less. Average blackmarket rates are as follows:

£1	=	2 Naira
US$1	=	1 Naira
200 CFA	=	1 Naira

Because of the oil boom, inflation in Nigeria has hit the roof. It is now one of Africa's most expensive countries. Nothing is cheap. If you stay for any length of time have a fortune handy. Corruption too, is rife. If you have to have any dealings with the police or the bureaucracy expect to have to pay a bribe.

Banks tend to charge heavy commissions for changing travellers cheques. Especially avoid those in Oyo. Airport tax for international departures is 5 Naira.

LANGUAGES

English is the official language of government and commerce but there are many local languages such as Hausa, Yoruba and Ibo.

DRIVING LICENCES

If you are driving your own vehicle, you need a Nigerian Licence which you can get by producing your own national driver's licence or an International Driving Permit. You need two photos. Insurance is compulsory and cheap — enquire at Barclays.

Note that in Lagos you can only drive on alternate days according to the first number on your licence plate. Odd numbers can drive on Mondays, Wednesdays and Fridays and even numbers on Tuesdays and Thursdays between the hours of 6 am and 6 pm. Outside these hours and at weekends there are no restrictions other than the insane, bumper-to-bonnet, 24 hour non-stop traffic jam, that makes Lagos a totally impossible city to live in. If you are crazy, do not miss this place.

ACCOMMODATION

Hotel accommodation is ridiculously expensive — up to 20 Naira in the coastal areas and up to 12 Naira elsewhere for 'budget accommodation'. Even a beer will set you back 1.50 Naira in most places. The same applies to meals

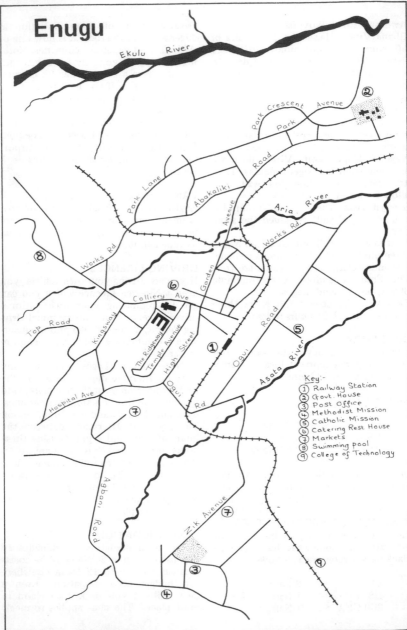

Enugu

served in cafes. In view of this it is hardly surprising that many travellers try to get in on the expatriate, university and construction circuits in the hope of meeting people who might offer to put them up for the night and possibly even pass them on to friends elsewhere in the country. The construction industry people are probably the most friendly and many of them are really pleased to see a face from home and have a long rap, etc. These people hang out in such places as the Ikoyi Club, Lagos; The Plateau Club, Jos; The Kano Club, Kano; University Staff Club, Ibadan University, and the Institute of Tropical Agriculture about 11 km north of Lagos (which is like an enclave of the USA). If you are offered this sort of hospitality remember than these peoples' overheads are very high so make a contribution.

Other possibilities include the VSO and Peace Corps Volunteers and religious missions. Many of these places will offer you basic accommodation (often just floor space) for around 2 Naira a night. During university vacations accommodation is possible at the universities of Lagos, Ibadan, Kano, Zaria, Ife and Enugu for 1 Naira if you have a student card. Enquire at the Student Affairs Office. Some travellers find Nigerians very friendly and hospitable especially off the main roads, but others have had exactly the opposite experience. The effects of inflation on things like food prices may well have a lot to do with any unfriendly responses you meet with. On the other hand we have heard from many travellers who have been overwhelmed with hospitality all the way through Nigeria. We wish you luck.

Somewhat less expensive than hotels (but still expensive) are the Catering Rest Houses which are the equivalent of Campements in the ex-French colonies. Any Nigerian Tourist Office will supply you with a list.

Benin City

Try the Catholic Mission first. Otherwise there is the *Hotel Crispo* for 4 Naira/single and the *Seven Sisters Hotel* for 4 Naira/single and 7 Naira/double. The latter is fairly primitive but has character. Food is available and clothes can be laundered.

The Oba's Palace and the Museum here are fascinating and two of the biggest attractions in Nigeria. Don't miss them! The bronze and brass-smiths on Igun Street are also worth a visit.

Enugu

St Helens Guest House has rooms for 6 Naira. *Palm Beach Hotel* costs 10 Naira/single.

Ife

The *Chinese Restaurant* near the university offers accommodation for 12 Naira.

Jos

The *ECWA* and *Cociwa Guest House* both cost 11 Naira per person.

Ibadan

The *Rem Hotel* costs 7 Naira per person. The *Palace Guest House*, situated very close to the truck park in the Molette area on the road to Lagos, costs 5 Naira per person. There are other cheap hotels in the vicinity.

You could also try the *Institute of Church and Society Guest House*. Meals are also available here. There is a swimming pool at the *Premiere Hotel* which non-residents can use for 50 kobo.

Kaduna

The *YMCA* opposite the Polytechnic, costs 4 Naira per night. For food, one of the best and cheapest places is *Nanette Restaurant* on Ahmadu Belloway opposite Levantis Stores. There is an excellent museum in this city.

Kano

Try contacting VSOs or ex-VSOs at the

Ibadan

Key:-
1. Railway Station
2. Truck Parks
3. Post Office
4. Catholic Mission
5. Catering Rest House

Kaduna

Key:-
① Railway Station
② Post Office
③ Kaduna Club
④ Swimming Pool
⑤ Technical College

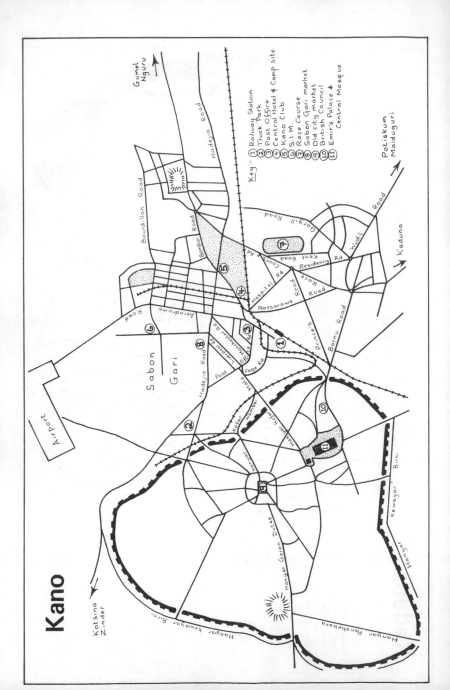

Kano Club and ask if they know of anywhere to stay. The trouble with this is that these days it costs 25 Naira for a week's temporary membership and you cannot get this on a weekend anymore. On the other hand, if you would like to stay here for a while it might well be worth it. The club also has good food at reasonable prices, a bar, swimming pool and cinema. If you haven't got 25 Naira spare, try the *Central Hotel* which is a popular drinking spot with expatriates. Note that the British Council has lists of hotels and their prices, details about places to go and see and an excellent VSO handout which is packed with information. Get hold of a copy.

Otherwise there are the following: *Wapa Hotel* costs 5 Naira per person. *Challenge Guest House* is located in the Sabon Gari area, costs 6 Naira/night. Other cheap hotels include the *SIM Guest House* (near the SIM Eye Hospital on Zaria Avenue off Aerodrome Road); *Sheku Usman Memorial Guest House* and *Green Valley Lodge*, 86 Ballat Hughes, Sabon Gari.

There is a new camp site behind the Race Course but it lacks water, toilets, shade, quiet, safety and cleanliness. Some travellers say it is simply dangerous. It costs 1 Naira per night but you also have to pay the nightwatchman — or else! There is another camp site between the Central Hotel and the Kano Club down a turning marked Motor Vehicle Registry Office, past the Law Courts. Again you must pay the guard and keep an eye on your belongings otherwise they walk.

Kano is a fascinating place that will take you many days to see properly. It is an old, walled city that dates back many centuries. The Emir's Palace, Gidon Makama market (leather, gold and silver), Sabon Gari market, the Grand Mosque and the dye pits are all well worth visiting.

If you need to change money see the changers who hang around the Central Hotel.

An excellent place to visit near Kano is the Yankari Game Reserve. It's best in the dry season as the game has to go to the water holes. The Wikki warm springs there are unbelievable if you have just come across the desert.

Katsina

Central Hotel costs 5 Naira. It is just about the only place there is to stay. Like Kano, Katsina is an ancient walled town.

Lagos

Most travellers describe Lagos as a 'Hellhole' which isn't too far from the truth. Even the Nigerians agree! It is also extremely expensive, humid, and supercongested between the hours of 8 and 9 am and 3.30 and 5 pm. Whatever else you do, don't get caught in the rush hours but even outside these hours it can take half a day to get across the city in any form of transport. Most travellers are to be found at the far end of Bar Beach on Victoria Island about two miles past the Federal Palace Hotel. To get there take bus No 84 from Racecourse. It costs 10 kobo.

YMCA: 77 Awolowo Road, Ikoyi Island. Costs 3 Naira for the first night and 2 Naira for subsequent nights.

YWCA: King George V Street, Lagos Island. Costs 5 Naira including breakfast.

St Helens Rest House: Aninwede Street, off Edinburgh Road. Costs 5 Naira/double and has a good cafe attached.

Hotel City: Sometimes has cheap accommodation for 3 Naira per person.

Jubilee Hotel: Near Hotel Bobby, costs 12 Naira/double.

King's College Hotel: Near the Racecourse, costs 5 Naira per night.

For food, the canteens attached to government offices in the centre of

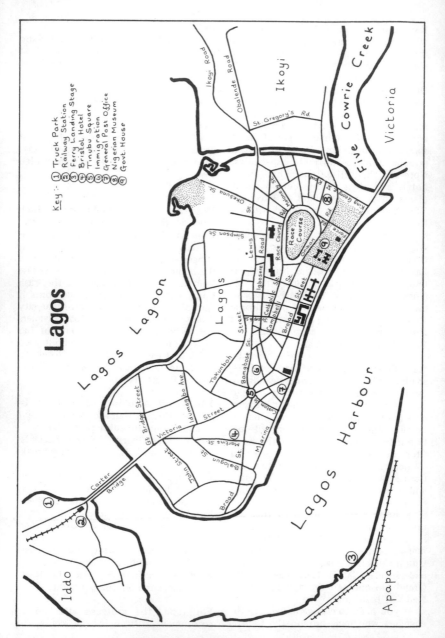

Lagos

Key:
① Truck Park
② Railway Station
②a Ferry Landing Stage
④ Bristol Hotel
⑤ Tinubu Square
⑥ Immigration
⑦ General Post Office
⑧ Nigerian Museum
⑨ Govt. House

town are cheap places to eat.

If you need to change money, the centre for street deals is the *Bristol Hotel* — they will find you. American Express is at Scantravel Ltd, Unity House, 37 Marina, PO Box 1897 (tel 50635). The Tourist Office and bookshops stock *Guide to Lagos* which costs 2 Naira. Contains maps, plenty of info, etc, and is worth getting hold of.

On Lagos Island buses cost either 5 or 10 kobo depending on distance. Taxis cost 50 kobo for a short run and 1 Naira anywhere else. The use of the meter is compulsory — make sure that it is being used and that the dial is on zero before you start.

Maiduguri

There is a free camp site at the zoo situated at the Kano end of town. Take the first turn on the right after the 'Welcome' sign. *Borno Guest House* costs 5 Naira/night.

Note that the truck park here is situated about 8 km out of town at the fish market and customs post. Possible to get trucks from here to Cameroon.

Onitsha

Cheap rooms available during vacations at Christ the King College. *Star Hotel Extension* costs 10 Naira/double. *Major Hotel* costs 8 Naira.

Sokoto

Government Rest House costs 10 Naira. *Good Food Hotel* costs 5 Naira per person. The *SIM Mission Guest House* has also been highly recommended.

Zaria

Try the university during vacations otherwise there is the University Conference Centre which offers accommodation for 6 Naira and has a swimming pool. Like Kano and Katsina, Zaria is an ancient walled city with a palace, mosque and dye pits which are all worth visiting.

TRANSPORT

Roads are very good and most are sealed so journeys tend to be relatively short (in comparison to neighbouring countries). Hitching is excellent as Nigerian people are generally hospitable. Car drivers are reluctant to stop between towns but vans and trucks will do so. On the other hand, many travellers have said they rarely felt safe on the roads of Nigeria as drivers — especially those driving oil tankers — are often reckless and careless and the roads are littered with burnt-out wrecks. With luck, you will rarely be asked to pay for lifts especially in the north but if you do have to pay, trucks and cars generally charge less than 1 kobo/mile in the north and 1 kobo/km in the south. You must bargain.

As elsewhere, there are truck parks in most cities and towns. From these places you can also pick up 'passenger transport cars' — often Ford Transit vans which are crammed full with about 16 people and their baggage. They have no schedule and leave when full. It is best to enquire what other passengers are paying before you get on otherwise you will be paying double. They cost on average 1-2 Naira/100 km (somewhat cheaper in the north). In rural areas you may still come across 'mammy wagons' which are any kind of utility vehicle used to transport local people, their animals and market produce over short distances. They were once part of the local colour and always good for a story to friends back home but they have become a thing of the past now in the cities and the more prosperous areas.

Buses Most of the federal states are supposed to operate their own Greyhound-type bus lines connecting other major cities in Nigeria but many of them seem to go through phases when the service collapses so you will have to take things as you find them. The services operated by Kano, Mid-West and

Benue-Plateau have so far managed to avoid collapse. The buses are fast, comfortable and relatively expensive. They tend to leave when full and to hell with the timetable, so get there early. Some sample fares and journey times — Lagos-Kano: Mid-West Line, costs 15 Naira and takes 18 hours. There are one or two daily in either direction. Officially they depart Lagos at 12 noon and Kano at 10.30 am. It is also possible to pick up this bus at Ibadan, two hours out of Lagos. Lagos-Ibadan: Mid-West Line, costs 3 Naira and takes two hours.

Mid-West Line has ticket offices near the Palmgrove Estate, Irorodu Road, Lagos; behind the Main Post Office in Kano, and next to the Premier Hotel in Ibadan.

Kano-Ibadan: Kano Express Line, costs 11 Naira and takes 16 hours. Kano-Lagos: Kano Express Line, costs 14 Naira and takes 18 hours. Kano-Sok-Sokoto: Kano Express Line, costs 6 Naira. Kano-Jos: Kano Express Line, costs 3.50 Naira and takes five hours. Ibadan-Kaduna costs 10 Naira. Kano-Kaduna costs 3 Naira. Lagos-Onitsha costs 5 Naira. Onitsha-Owerri costs 1 Naira. Onitsha-Enugu by Ford Transit costs 1 Naira. Enugu-Jos: Oriental Bus Line costs 5.50 Naira. If you are starting from Jos the bus departs from opposite the City Hotel. Jos-Maiduguri: North-East State Bus Line, costs 7.40 Naira. Maiduguri-Kano: North-East State Bus Line, costs 7.40 Naira and takes nine hours. Maiduguri-Cameroon border in a Ford Transit van costs 4 Naira.

Trains Two lines run north, one from Lagos to Kano via Ibadan, Ogbomosho, Kaduna, Zaria, Kaura Namoda, and the other from Port Harcourt to Maiduguri via Enugu, Makurdi, Kaduan and Jos. In third class they're cheaper than the bus lines but third class is very crowded. Kano-Lagos costs 7.50 Naira in third class. Port Harcourt-Kano costs 7.50 Naira in third class.

Trips to Lake Chad If you would like to go there it is worth enquiring at the Lake Chad Club in Maiduguri as they organise trips fairly frequently. Alternatively you can make your own way there by taking a taxi from Maiduguri to Baga (costs 3 Naira one way) followed by a Land-Rover across the dried-up part of the lake for 50 kobo per person each way. If you would like to go on a boat trip through the reeds to the open part of the lake you will have to hire a guide and boat at a fishing village. Bargain for the fare which should cost around 1.50-2 Naira for up to three people. If you go via Baga and need somewhere to stay there contact Samuel Adura at the Police Station. He likes visitors and will put you up in the cells overnight.

Routes to & from Nigeria
(a) Nigeria-Niger There are two routes, one leading from Kano to Zinder and the other from Lagos to Niamey via Kamba and Gaya at the point where the borders of Niger, Nigeria and Benin meet.

Between Kano and Zinder there are buses for 1.50 Naira, fast vans for 1.25 Naira and lifts on trucks for about 1 Naira. The best days to hitch from Kano to Zinder are Tuesdays and early Wednesdays as at least 30 trucks do the run to pick up produce from the Zinder market on Thursdays. Free lifts are a definite possibility.

If heading for Niamey, make your way to the border village of Kamba via Birnin Kebbi and then cross over the border to the first Niger village — Gaya. From there a taxi to Dosso costs 600 CFA and a taxi from there to Niamey costs another 600 CFA. Hitching along this stretch is not recommended as there is very little traffic.

(b) Nigeria-Benin & Togo A Peugeot taxi from Lagos to Lome (Togo) costs 8 Naira plus a charge for baggage. Taxis doing this run leave from Lagos Island at the end of Carter Bridge. A taxi to Cotonou (Benin) costs 4 Naira plus a baggage charge. Many travellers, on the other hand, use the Abeokuta-Meko-Ketou-Zagnanado route. This isn't an official border crossing as there is no customs post so make sure your passport is in order with any necessary visas. Note that the Nigeria-Benin border is sometimes closed abruptly for a day or two for real or imagined reasons best known to the Benin authorities.

(c) **Nigeria-Cameroon** There are three main routes — (a) Maiduguri-Maroua in northern Cameroon is little used. (b) Enugu/Calabar-Ikom-Mamfe is the most popular route. Calabar-Ikom by Peugeot taxi costs 2.50 Naira. Ikom-border by taxi costs 50 kobo (the Nigerian border village is called Mfum). From the Nigerian side of the border it is a kilometre walk to the Cameroon border village of Ekok. From Ekok there are taxis to Mamfe for 700 CFA. Mamfe to Bamenda costs 1200 CFA by taxi and Mamfe to Kumba by taxi costs 1000 CFA. There are several army/police checkpoints between the border and Mamfe where you and your baggage will be searched.

(d) **Port Harcourt-Idua Oron-Victoria** There is a ferry which runs from Idua Oron (on the opposite bank of the river from Calaber) to Victoria which costs 5.25 Naira or 2500 CFA. You are supposed to go to Calabar for an exit stamp before leaving on this boat. If you have to go to Calabar there is a ferry from Oron which costs 50 kobo and takes 1½ to two hours. The federal government boat is the fastest. Both Nigerian and Cameroon boats do the Idua Oron-Victoria run but the Cameroon boat is the best if you want something stolen! If you need a visa for Cameroon and are taking this boat, get your visa before you set off.

OTHER INFORMATION
Some recommended books for background reading on Nigeria (and other West African countries) include:

Military Regimes in Africa, W Gutteridge (Methuen)
An Economic History of Nigeria R Ekundare (Faber)
An Economic History of West Africa A Hopkins (Longman)
How Europe Underdeveloped Africa W Rodney
History of West Africa J Fage
The Story of Nigeria M Crowder (Faber)
Nigeria J Coleman

The VSO put out *Guide to Nigeria* principally for the use of its volunteers but it is possible for others to get hold of a copy at British Council offices in Lagos, Kano, Ibadan, and Freetown (Sierra Leone). It is very detailed and has plans of all the major towns.

Rwanda

A tiny country with a dense population but one which, like its neighbour Burundi, has a history as an independent kingdom which can be traced back over 400-500 years. It consists of three tribes — the Tutsi (14% of the population) who were the feudal overlords for many centuries; the Hutu (84% of the population) who were the peasants and artisans, and the Twa or pygmies (about 2% of the population).

At the turn of the century, Rwanda became a German colony and, after WW I a Belgian Mandated Territory administered from the Congo, until independence in 1962. Following independence, resentment over the Tutsi monopoly of power boiled over and led to a series of massacres in which many Tutsi were killed and thousands more forced to flee into neighbouring countries in direct contrast to the situation in Burundi where Hutu rebellions failed to dislodge the ruling Tutsi minority. After the revolt in Rwanda, a Hutu president was elected but in 1973 the army took over in a bloodless coup.

FACTS

The economy is based on the export of coffee and, to a lesser degree, tea, cotton and pyretheum (an organic insecticide extracted from the flowers of a certain species of chrysanthemum). Tin and associated metals are mined between Lakes Tanganyika and Kivu. Almost all the country's exports pass through Uganda which makes Rwanda extremely vulnerable to the passing fancies of that volatile state. There are problems with agriculture because of density of population and the rapid deterioration of the soil due to over-exploitation. Steep forest-clad slopes rise from Lake Kivu to form peaks of over 1000 metres. The rainy seasons are mid-January to mid-May and mid-October to mid-December.

VISAS

Required by all except nationals of West Germany. There are very few Rwanda Embassies around the world. In Africa they are in Addis Ababa (Ethiopia), Bujumbura (Burundi), Dar es Salaam (Tahzania), Kampala (Uganda), and Nairobi (Kenya). If you get your visa in one of these places it will cost about US$4.50 plus two photos but they demand a letter of recommendation from your own embassy (as Zairois Embassies do). On the other hand, visas are obtainable at the border and it is probably much less hassle to get them this way. What you pay for them at the border is the subject of endless speculation. Every traveller has a different story to tell. The following are what people have paid for them recently — 13 Zaires for a three day visa; 20 Zaires for a 10-day visa; 3,000 Rwandan Francs for a one month visa; US$25 for an 'Entry Visa'; US$6 or 26 Zaires for a 'Transit Visa'; 500 Rwandan Francs for a three to eight day visa. Take your pick. Transit visas can be renewed for a further month's stay in Kigali for 1000 Rwandan Francs plus one photo. Immigration is situated next to Air France.

Burundi Visas These cost 1000 Rw Fr plus two photos for a one month visa. They are issued in 24 hours and there is no fuss.

Zaire Visas One letter recently said that the Zaire embassy will only issue visas to Rwandan nationals.

CURRENCY

The unit of currency is the Rwandan Franc = 100 centimes. Import/export of local currency is allowed up to 5000 Rw Fr.

Exchange rate:

£1	=	199 Rw Fr
US$1	=	88 Rw Fr
A$1	=	99 Rw Fr

There is a flourishing blackmarket which offers up to 150 Rw Fr = US$1 but is usually 100 in Gisenye and 120 in Kigali. Rwanda is one of those places where you will wish you had brought some cash if all you have is travellers cheques. The banks here charge 200 Rw Fr commission for changing travellers cheques. It is possible to buy cash dollars (US$) in Kigali if you are prepared

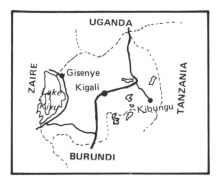

to hassle a lot and not take no for an answer but in view of the blackmarket rate you would be paying a hefty premium on them.

Airport tax on flights to Burundi, Tanzania, Uganda and Zaire is 150 Rw Fr. For other international flights it is 25 Rw Fr.

LANGUAGES
Kinyarwanda, Swahili and French. Very little English is spoken.

FOOD
Here's what you can eat in a Rwandan restaurant: *andazi*, sort of dumpling affair with soup sometimes, Rw Fr 20; *sambusa*, as per Swahili, spicy meat-filled pastry, Rw Fr 20; *umugati*, bread Rw Fr 10; *usize*, margarine, Rw Fr 10; *imineke*, bananas, Rw Fr 2 each; *amata* milk, Rw Fr 30-40; *ibirayi*, potatoes; *ibishyimbo*, beans; *umuceli*, rice; *ibitoki* plantains, combinations of any two of these from Rw Fr 25-35; *inyama*, meat; *inkoka*, chicken, Rw Fr 45; *inka*, beef Rw Fr 25; *melange*, usually rice, potatoes and veg, best value, Rw Fr 35-60; *mushikaki*, shish kebab, Rw Fr 20.

ACCOMMODATION
Gisenye
Hotels are prohibitively expensive. Ask for a friendly Belgian who lives opposite the border post on the corner. He is interested in herbs and bees and will let

you sleep in his garden free.

Kigali
The *Presbyterian Church* 'Auberge', rue des Resume, costs 250 Rw Fr dormitory and 1000 Rw Fr/double. It is not a very friendly place and you have to make an effort to get yourself accepted. They also have single rooms for Rw Fr 550. The *Anglican Mission*, Avenue Paul VI, costs 200 Rw Fr in the dormitory. *Bon Appetit Restaurant* has rooms available for 525 Rw Fr. *Hotel Relais* has rooms for 550 Rw Fr with own shower and toilet. The Catholic Mission have a 'hotel' which they are very reluctant to let you stay in. If you are successful it is a very comfortable place. Costs 250 Rw Fr for bed and huge breakfast.

For food try the *Mabenga Restaurant* which offers omelettes for 30 Rw Fr, beans and rice for 40 Rw Fr and tea for 10 Rw Fr. Also recommended is the *Restaurant Impala* which has brochettes for 40 Rw Fr.

Taxi from/to airport costs Rw Fr 1000. Note that all out-patient treatment and even dentists are free in Kigali which also has a reputation for thefts — keep an eye on your baggage.

Ruhengeri
Centre d'Accueil is situated 100 metres down a dirt road opposite the Prefecture, costs 100 Rw Fr in noisy dorm or 150 Rw Fr in a single room. Meals are available for 50 Rw Fr, or 150 Rw Fr, if you want meat with it. The Catholic Mission also has cheap accommodation available at similar prices to the Centre d'Acceuil.

The Saturday market in Ruhengeri is worth seeing.

TRANSPORT
The road from Kigali to the Tanzanian border is now sealed and there is plenty of traffic along it. If you are hitching from Tanzania a lot of heavy trucks bound for Rwanda leave from the port

of Bukoba on Lake Victoria. The road from Gisenye to Goma in Zaire is also well maintained. It is easy to hitch between Kigali and Butare (a university town) with expatriates — mostly French and Canadians. If you are hitching, watch out for the licence plates which will tell you where vehicles come from: AB for Kigali, CB for Butare, HB for Ruhengeri, and JB for Gisenye.

If you are not hitching there are plenty of buses, trucks and taxis but note that local transport (usually pick-up trucks) are ridiculously overcrowded and relatively expensive — around 2 Rw Fr/km though this is negotiable to some extent. Some examples of bus transport include: Ugandan border-Ruhengeri costs 120 Rw Fr. Ruhengeri-Kigali costs 250 Rw Fr. Ruhengeri-Gisenye costs 150-200 Rw Fr, excellent sealed road, hitching is excellent. Kigali-Gisenye; daily buses at 6 am and 1 pm from Pointe Ronde. They go via the lake road (Lake Kivu) and cost 350 Rw Fr. Kigali-Kibungu; daily buses at 7 am which cost 250 Rw Fr takes about two hours. Kibungu-Tanzanian border (Rusumu); Peugeot taxis for 150 Rw Fr. The Tanzanian border post is a three km walk from the Rawandan customs post. No hassles at the border. Two daily buses on this route — depart at 7 am and mid-day and cost 100 Rw Fr, takes two to three hours.

OTHER INFORMATION

The gorilla sanctuary near Ruhengeri is well worth a visit — there are very few left and you will need to hire a guide otherwise there is very little chance of your seeing any.

The Kagera National Park is worth a day's detour if you are heading for Tanzania. The Rusumo Falls are the main attraction. Entry costs 750 Rw Fr and camping an extra 250 Rw Fr.

Another park worth visiting is the Parc National des Volcans near Ruhengeri. Entry to the park costs 600 Rw Fr (no student concessions) and a guide is pulsory (guides cost 200 Rw Fr per day). You can get free camping tickets from the Bureau de Conservator, 15 km from Ruhengeri near the volcano. It is possible to get a free ride to the park in a government bus from Ruhengeri. Take food and water with you though potatoes can be bought from the office at the entrance to the park. Sabyinyo volcano is one of the most popular climbs and you can sleep in a cabin about half way up despite what they tell you to the contrary in the park office.

If you are looking for a place to hang your boots for a while, Gisenye is a very beautiful lake resort.

Last word: Rwandans greet each other with the word 'Amashyo' (May you have herds) to which the reply is 'Amashongure' (May you have herds of females).

Senegal

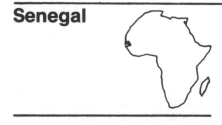

Senegal and, to some extent, the neighbouring Guinea and Western Mali, was the area of origin of many of the people who migrated east, as far as Cameroon, between the 9th and 15th centuries. As far back as the 9th century there grew up here the kingdom of Tekrur which was an important power on the trans-Saharan trade routes from the Guinean coastlands to Morocco. It became Islamised during the 11th cen-

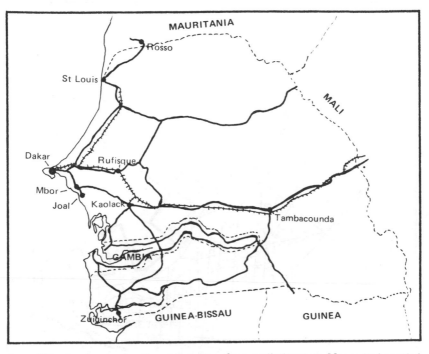

tury. The country is also the oldest of the former French colonies in Africa dating back to the 17th century, when the islands of St Louis in the Senegal estuary and Goree off the Cape Verde peninsula were occupied. Early French attempts to create a plantation economy here failed and so until the middle of the 19th century, St Louis and Dakar were regarded merely as convenient collection points for the slave trade and the products of the Western Sudan.

The expansion of the colony was largely the work of Louis Faidherbe who was appointed governor in 1854 and who undertook the systematic conquest of the Senegal basin and the conversion of the inhabitants into farmers producing crops of value to France — mostly groundnuts. His successor destroyed the rising power of al-Hajj 'Umar, a Tucolor who, on his way back

from a pilgrimage to Mecca, had married one of the daughters of the Sultan of Sokoto and raised a jihad (holy war) against what he considered to be his decadent Islamic neighbours. By 1863, 'Umar had created an empire which stretched from the land occupied by the French to Timbuktu but it was not to last long. The reasons were not entirely due to French expansionism — his forces were as much concerned with plunder as the reform of Islam and the tribes which he had subjected were soon in revolt.

Dakar was built up as the administrative centre and showpiece of France's West African empire and because of this, when independence was granted, in 1960, Senegal inherited one of the best ports in West Africa, a fully functioning university, an international airport and a good road and rail network. There was a

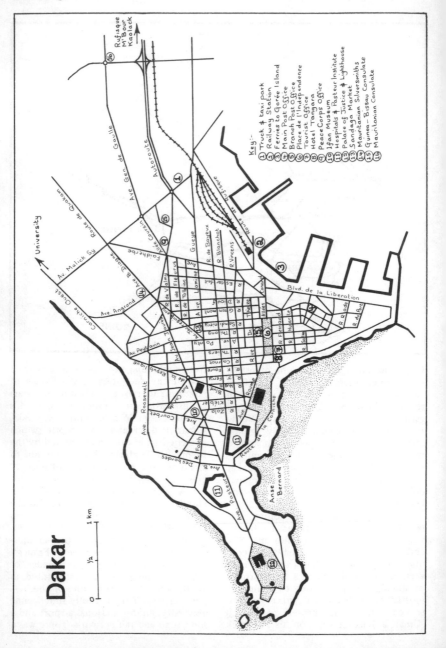

Dakar

Key:-
1. Truck & taxi park
2. Railway Station
3. Ferries to Gorée Island
4. Main Post Office
5. Branch Post Office
6. Place de l'Independence
7. Tourist Office
8. Hotel Tangara
9. Peace Corps Office
10. Ifan Museum
11. Hospitals & Pasteur Institute
12. Palace of Justice & Lighthouse
13. Sandaga Market
14. Mauritanian Silversmiths
15. Guinea-Bissau Consulate
16. Mauritanian Consulate

brief period in 1959 when Senegal attempted a federation with Mali but it was shortlived. The president since independence has been Leopold Senghor, one of Africa's 'moderate' leaders who favours 'dialogue' with South Africa and, before he became president, one of Senegal's most prominent poets.

Student unrest explodes from time to time at Dakar University over what is generally considered the government's too complacent attitude towards imperialism and neo-colonialism and a coup was once attempted by the former prime minister, Mamadou Dia, in 1962. Dia was not released from detention until the mid-70s.

FACTS

The economic prospects for Senegal are pretty bleak. Its main export is groundnuts. North of the Gambia, the territory in the interior is barren and unproductive. Few crops can be grown due to the lack of water except on the flood plain of the River Senegal where millet and groundnuts are grown, though a number of irrigation schemes are under way which will increase the area under cultivation and allow rice to be grown.

Soils have suffered from wind erosion and from increasing salinity — the dry season is very windy as the Harmattan blows off the desert for lengthy periods of time. Rainfall in Dakar is about 60 cm annually whereas in the south of the country it averages 160 cm. The best time for travel is between December and May when it's cool and dry.

An eighth of the population lives in Dakar. Stock rearing is important in the marginal lands in which most of the inhabitants are Hamitic. The main groups include the Wolofs (36% of total population), the Fulani (18%) and the Serer (17%). Nomadic groups include the Moors and the Bassaris. Animals and animal products enter little into the cash economy of the country.

VISAS

Required by all except nationals of Belgium, Denmark, France, West Germany, Irish Republic, Italy, Luxembourg and the Netherlands. Nationals of South Africa are not admitted. Officially all visitors must have an onward ticket but this is rarely enforced.

Visas for Senegal can be obtained from French embassies where there is no Senegalese embassy or consulate. In London visas cost £2.50 plus three photos for a one month visa and take 48 hours to issue. In Banjul, Gambia, they cost 10 Dalasi for a single-entry and 20 Dalasi for a double-entry visa.

It's sometimes possible to enter without a visa (where one is required). This is true of the Mauritanian-Senegalese border at Rosso where they are issued free with no hassles whatsoever. Other travellers have made it from Mali on the Bamako-Dakar train.

Mali Visas These cost 2500 CFA and take 24 hours to issue. They allow for a stay of one week. The embassy is on Avenue Lamine Gueye.

Mauritanian Visas The cheapest visas available are the 72-hour transit visas which cost 750 CFA. Before the embassy will issue a visa they demand a letter of recommendation from your own embassy.

Niger Visas Obtainable from the French embassy. They cost 1250 CFA for a three month visa and 675 CFA for a seven-day visa and take 24 hours to issue.

CURRENCY

The unit of currency is the CFA. Import and export of local currency is allowed up to 20,000 CFA.

Exchange rate:

£1	=	473 CFA
US$1	=	208 CFA
A$1	=	237 CFA

LANGUAGES
French, very little English is spoken.

ACCOMMODATION
Dakar
Hotel du Paradis on rue Vincens, off Ave William Ponty, costs 900 CFA/double with own shower.

Hotel des Artistes, rue G Diouf, near the corner of rue Vincens, costs 500 CFA/single.

Hotel St Louis, 68 rue Felix Faure, costs 1200 CFA/single.

Hotel du Coq Hardi, 34 rue Raffenel, has single rooms for between 700 and 1000 CFA. Excellent food in the restaurant, meals for 400 CFA.

Hotel Mon Logis, rue Blanchot, costs 1000 CFA/single. If the rooms are full ask 'le patron' if you can sleep on the roof. He's very friendly and likes travellers.

Hotel des Princes costs 2500 CFA a double and is friendly. There's a cheap cafe downstairs.

Hotel Oceanique, *Hotel Provencal* and *Hotel Oasis* all cost 1000 CFA/single.

Hotel Le Relais, route de Quikam, five km from the centre of town, costs 2500 CFA for a room which will sleep four people.

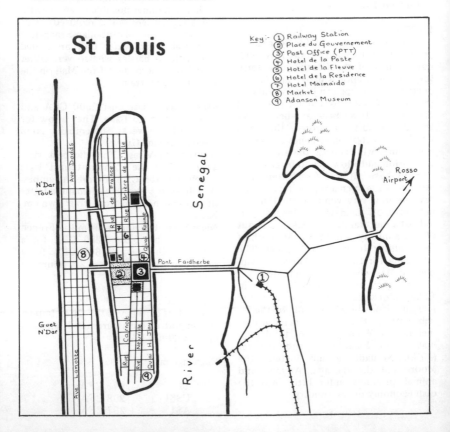

St Louis

Key:- ① Railway Station
② Place du Gouvernement
③ Post Office (PTT)
④ Hotel de la Poste
⑤ Hotel de la Fleuve
⑥ Hotel de la Residence
⑦ Hotel Maimaida
⑧ Market
⑨ Adanson Museum

It's sometimes possible to get a place to stay free during vacations at the Cite Universitaire. Take bus No 7 from the Place de l'Independence to get there. If you're looking for Peace Corps people try their office on Allee Coursin opposite the Grande Mosque. Some travellers sleep on the beach below the Place de l'Independence or at Anse Bernard beach nearby. Doing this is highly unrecommended unless there's a group of you. Muggings and robbery with violence are becoming a little too common to be able to do this in safety except in groups. Because of this you should also avoid offers of boat tickets, lifts and blackmarket money exchanges which involve going back to a house alone or down little alleys. Dakar is a heavy city in some ways. If you do go to Anse Bernard take bus No 9, 13 or 15 from the Place de l'Independence.

Other than the *Coq Hardi* there is the *Keir Ndeye Restaurant*, rue Vincens, which serves superb traditional Senegalese food for 400-500 CFA per meal. Also recommended are the *Chez Nanette* (European food), *Gangotte du Plateau*, rue Felix Faure and the *Gargoutier* (delicious cheap dinners).

There's also an un-named place which is reputed to be the cheapest and best place in Dakar. To get there, stand with your back to the railway station, take the second street on the left, then the first on the right where there's a small door with red and black ribbons. From there the cafe is the second or third on the left. You can eat rice, fish and coffee there for 100 CFA. If you're looking for street food there are stalls in the market near the post office.

The Tourist Office, Place de l'Independence, has maps of the city and a list of all the hotels with current prices. The poste restante charges 80 CFA per letter.

The Ile de Goree is well worth a day trip. There are ferries every two hours from Dakar which cost 300 CFA oneway. Excellent historical museum there, slaves' house, marine zoo and old colonial houses.

Joal

The Catholic mission, five km before Joal on the road from Dakar, offers accommodation or you can sleep on the beach at Joal. Just outside Joal is the village of Fadiouth, a town built of shells with no roads or cars. You have to get there either on foot or by piroque. It is worth a visit.

Kaolack

For accommodation try the Catholic mission or the *Peace Corps Hostel* behind the Dakar taxi rank.

St Louis

Hotel Maimaido costs 1000 CFA a double, good cheap food available. *Hotel St Louis* costs 1600 CFA a double, clean and noisy. Other cheapies include the *Hotel de la Poste* and *Hotel de la Fleuve*.

Tambacounda

The Catholic mission, a half km from the post office, offers very clean, individual rooms with own shower free! Cheap hotels include *Hotel Astor Kebe* and *Hotel de la Gare*. Note that the banks here will only change cash — no travellers' cheques.

Ziguinchor

Hotel Tourisme costs 1250 CFA for a very pleasant double room. *Hotel Balkady*, behind the Grande Marche, costs 700 CFA/single. This is the cheapest hotel you will find and is within walking distance of the truck park. Camping is possible at Cap Skirring on the coast.

TRANSPORT

The main routes through Senegal are south from the Mauritanian border town of Rosso, via St Louis to Dakar and from there via M'Bour to Kaolack. At Kaolack you can either branch off to

Ziguinchor

Key:-
① Hotel Aubert
② Market
③ Post Office (PTT)

Tambacounda and Kayes if heading for Mali or take one of the two routes south to the Gambia. If you are heading for Banjul, the Gambian capital, you take the most westerly route to Barra Point and then the ferry across the Gambia River to Banjul. If heading for Ziguinchor and the Casamance area of Senegal, possibly the most interesting area of this country — then you take the more direct Transgambia highway which bridges the Gambia River further to the east. There are plenty of trucks, pickups and Peugeot taxis between all the main towns as well as regular buses. One traveller we heard from walked all the way through Senegal and met with tremendous hospitality all the way. In the evening he stopped at the nearest village and asked the headman about the possibilities of accommodation. He said he was never refused and was always offered food in addition to somewhere to stay.

Rosso-St Louis, costs 300 CFA in a pick-up with seats or a small bus. Dakar-Ziguinchor, via the Transgambian highway costs 1400 CFA by bus and takes six to seven hours. Dakar-Kaolack by taxi costs 700 CFA or by minibus 500 CFA plus a luggage charge (usually 100 CFA for a backpack). The journey takes five hours. The Dakar to Ziguinchor stretch can be done in stages as follows — Dakar-Rufisque (costs 75 CFA); Rufisque-M'Bour (costs 150 CFA); M'Bour-Kaolack (costs 350 CFA); Kaolack-Gambian border (costs 400 CFA); Gambian border-Ziguinchor (800 CFA).

Kaolack-Barra Point (Gambia) by taxi costs 600 CFA and by truck 500 CFA. The Barra Point-Banjul ferry costs 50 batuts and takes 20 minutes. It goes every two hours throughout the day. Last ferries around 8 pm each night.

Dakar-Tambacounda by a pick-up truck costs 1100 CFA. It is very unlikely that you would take the road through to Bamako (Mali) from Tambacounda. Almost everyone and everything goes by rail along this stretch,

Trains

(a) **St Louis-Dakar** departs every day at 6.30 am, costs 700 CFA in 2nd class and takes seven hours. You need to be there at least an hour before departure if you plan on getting a seat. There's plenty of food and drink at the stations along the way.

(b) **Dakar-Bamako (Mali)** Departs every Tuesday and Friday at 6.30 pm costs 6300 CFA in 2nd class and takes 36 hours. A student reduction is available though this apparently no longer applies if you are coming in the opposite direction. If you have any trouble getting the concession ask to see the Chef du Gare (Station Manager). You must be at the station by at least 2 pm if you want a seat. The train is hot and uncomfortable and in 2nd class, very crowded. You can pick this train up at Tambacounda. Other fares along this line are — Dakar-Kaolack: 600 CFA, Kaolack-Tambacounda: 575 CFA.

Ships Dakar is one of the largest ports in West Africa and there are many cargo ships with some passenger accommodation which call here. The vast majority connect European and North American ports with those on the west coast of Africa. Dakar is often the first port of call on the outward journey and the last on the return journey. However, they are not cheap. Minimum fares to European ports from Dakar start at around £230 (US$495) and to North American ports at around £305 (US$650). In most cases, it is cheaper to fly.

There is also a car ferry operated by Paquet Cruises which connects Dakar with Morocco, the Canary Islands, Spain and France but even the minimum fare from Dakar to Casablanca is about £117 ((US$250 or 55,800 CFA). Here are the details -

Paquet Cruises: HQ 5 Boulevard Malesherbes, Paris 8, France.
Agence Maritime Gaillard 'Le Cygne V', Ave F Roosevelt, 83100 Toulon, France.
Voyages Paquet, 65 Ave de l'Armee Royale, Casablanca, PO Box 60.
Ets Paquet Afrique, Boulevard Hassan II, Agadir, PB 35.
Senegal Tours, 5 Place de l'Independence, Dakar, PB 164.

The ships are *Massalia* and *Azur* and the route is Toulon (France)-Ibiza-Motril-Malaga (Spain)-Casablanca-Agadir (Morocco)-Dakar (Senegal)-Arrecife-Safi-Casablanca (Morocca)-Cadiz (Spain)-Toulon.

The service to Ibiza, Motril and Malaga only operates between January and June inclusive. Ferry departs Toulon once each month, usually on the 8th or 10th of the month and arrives in Dakar six days later. The return journey takes seven days. The journey from Dakar to Casablanca takes four days or three days to Agadir. The return journey from Dakar usually starts in the middle of the month. For exact dates contact the company or its agents. Minimum fares are Dakar-Casablanca: £117 (US$253 or 55,800 CFA), Dakra-Toulon: £153 (US$330 or 72,759 CFA).

If you have any interest in the cargo/passenger boats which connect Dakar with Northern European ports and Dakar with other West African ports contact any of the following:

Polish Ocean Lines (Agents Stelp & Leighton Agencies Ltd, 238 City Road, London, EC1). Service every two weeks on the route — Northern Europe - Canary Islands - Nouadhibou - Dakar - Banjul - Freetown - Monrovia - Abidjan - Tema - Lome - Cotonou - Douala - Owendo - Pointe Noire - Casablanca-Northern Europe.

Nigerian National Shipping Line Ltd (Agents Killick Martin & Co, Eastgate PO Box 115, 53-73 Leman Street, London E1). Service along the route London/Liverpool-Dakar-Banjul - Freetown - Takoradi/Tema-

Lagos-Port Harcourt-Douala-Matadi.

Nautilus Line (Agents Walford Lines Ltd, St Mary Axe House, St Mary Axe, London EC3). Service along the route Italy - France - Spain (various) ports) - Dakar - Freetown - Abidjan-Tema - Lome - Cotonou - Douala - Owendo - Port Gentil - Point Noire-Boma - Matadi - Point Noire-Libreville-Douala - Victoria - Abidjan - Freetown-Casablanca - Spain - France - Italy (various ports).

OTHER INFORMATION

Jobs There's a great demand for English teachers in Senegal and it is a well-paid job, You'll have no difficulty finding work and there are no hassles with work permits or tax. Minimum pay in schools at present is 2000 CFA per hour. If you want a job contact either the American Cultural Centre, the Institute pour le Perfectionement de la Langue Anglaise or the Institute Britannique. All run regular courses and need teachers.

Seychelles

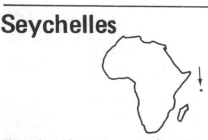

The only mid-oceanic group of granite islands in the world, the Seychelles lie about 1500 km east of the East African coast and about 3000 km west of India. There are 87 islands in all, 38 of them granitic and the remainder coralline. Though they cover a vast expanse of ocean their total land area is little more than 438 square km, Mahe and Praslin being the largest. It used to be possible to get to the Seychelles relatively cheaply on the boats which plied between Bombay and various ports on the east

coast of Africa but these have been discontinued and virtually the only way of getting there at present is on a stopover on a long-distance flight. All the same, it's well worth the effort of getting there as they are some of the most beautiful islands in the world. The vegetation is luxurious; the coastlines are indented with gently curving bays and deep lagoons edged with beaches of white coral sands and, like the other groups of islands in this part of the world, they sport varieties of bird and fish life found nowhere else.

Though sighted by Vasco da Gama at the end of the 15th century and used by pirates during the 16th, it was not until 1756 that they were claimed by the French and settlement attempted. The first settlers arrived in 1770 with their slaves and set up plantations of cinnamon, cloves, nutmeg and pepper but the islands remained French only for a

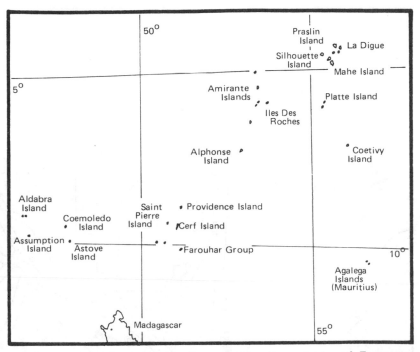

very short period and were taken by the British in 1794. Nevertheless, French influence made a lasting impression on the way of life and even today the lingua franca is a French patois, the religion is predominantly Roman Catholic and the legal system is based on the Code Napoleon. Until 1872 the islands were administered from Mauritius but in 1903 the Seychelles became a Crown Colony. They gained their independence in 1976. The first leader of the country, James Mancham, remained in power for only a very short while and was ousted in a coup while attending a Commonwealth Conference in London. Recently, friendly overtures have been made to the Russians who are looking for a military base in the Indian Ocean.

FACTS

The population is just over 60,000 and consists of a mixture of Europeans, Negroes, Indians, Chinese and Malays. Most of the people depend on agriculture for their livelihood, the chief cash crops being copra, cinnamon, vanilla and patchouli. Many Seychellois augment their incomes by fishing and boat building.

The islands lie only a few degrees below the equator but because they are situated far out in the ocean, weather patterns are unpredictable though, unlike Mauritius, they lie outside the cyclone belt. There are two monsoons — the south-east from May to October and the north-west from December to March. The south-east monsoon is strong, cool and dry, often bringing overcast skies and choppy seas whereas the north-west is calmer though hotter and rainy. In view of these conditions the best time to visit the islands is during May, June

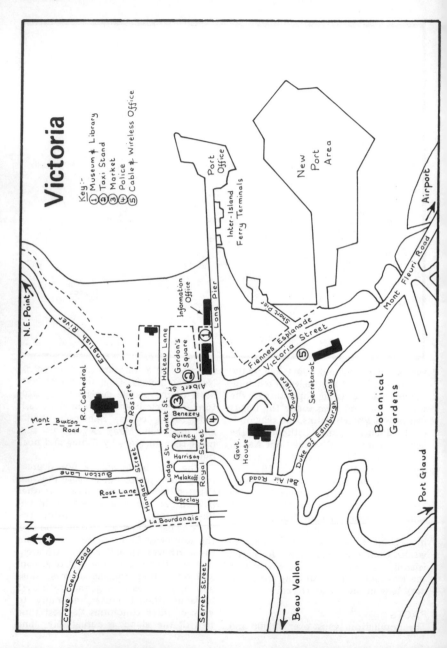

Victoria

Key:-
① Museum & Library
ⓝ Taxi Stand
③ Market
④ Police
⑤ Cable & Wireless Office

or October. Note that the weather on Mahe is conditioned by the central mountains which rise to a height of nearly 1000 metres in parts. This means that it can be calm and sunny on one side of the island and rainy and rough on the other.

VISAS

Not required by anyone. You must, however, have an onward ticket or sufficient funds to buy one. Note that customs are very thorough.

CURRENCY

The unit of currency is the Seychelles Rupee = 100 cents. There are no restrictions on the import of local currency but export is limited to Rs 120. There is no blackmarket for currency.

Exchange rate:

£1	=	Rs 12.86
US$1	=	Rs 5.59
A$1	=	Rs 6.43

LANGUAGE

English, French and Creole.

ACCOMMODATION

Prices are very high and you'll be lucky to come across anything costing less than Rs 70 a single (about US$10) unless you rent a self-catering room on a weekly basis. The cheapest available on Mahe Island are:

Villa Fond des Lianes, situated at North Point. It offers self-catering rooms at Rs 400 per week but has only three rooms available.

Abbeville is a privately-run guest house situated up in the mountains on the way to La Misere pass. Four rooms are available, costing Rs 66/single or Rs 132/double for bed and breakfast. Full board costs Rs 98 and Rs 197 respectively.

Sunset is situated by the sea in the vicin-

ity of Beau Vallon, west of Victoria. This guest house has 12 rooms which cost Rs 70/single and Rs 140/double for bed and breakfast. Full board costs Rs 90 and Rs 180 respectively.

Glacis is in the same area as Sunset and costs Rs 90/single or Rs 160/double for bed and breakfast. There are eight rooms available.

Bel Air is an eight-room guest house about two km from the centre of Victoria. Singles are Rs 100 or doubles Rs 190 for bed and breakfast. Full board is Rs 145 and Rs 260 respectively.

On Praslin Island there is the *Indian Ocean Fishing Lodge* at Grand Anse which costs Rs 100/single and Rs 140/double for bed and breakfast and has six rooms available. Full board costs Rs 130 and Rs 200 respectively.

On La Digue Island the cheapest available are *Choppy's Bungalows* which cost Rs 55/single and Rs 105/double. There are four rooms available.

TRANSPORT

Mahe and Praslin Islands are the only ones with sealed roads. Buses (irregular) and taxis are available as well as cars for hire. The latter start at around Rs 100 per day or Rs 550 per week unlimited mileage. Petrol costs about Rs 9 per gallon.

Inter-Island Transport

Air services between Mahe, Praslin and Bird Islands are operated by Air Mahe and Inter-Island Airways. There is a government ferry service between Mahe, Praslin and La Digue Islands on Mondays, Wednesdays and Fridays departing Victoria, Mahe, at 8 am. The fares are as follows:

	1st class	2nd class
Mahe-Praslin/La Digue	Rs 50	Rs 30
Praslin-La Digue	Rs 20	Rs 10

Travellers who have stayed in the Seychelles report that hitch-hiking is 'a dream come true'.

See the introductory 'Getting There' section for details on airfares to the Seychelles from the UK or Australia.

Sierre Leone

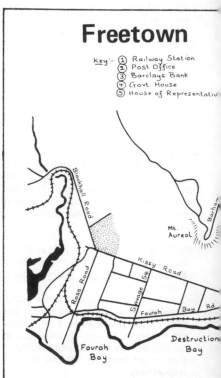

With the intention of finding a home for a few unwanted ex-slaves from Britain and North America, a number of British anti-slavery humanitarians founded a colony around what is today Freetown at the end of the 18th century. The colony survived with difficulty until 1808 when it was taken over by the British government. Between then and 1860 the British Navy's anti-slave patrol liberated about 70,000 Negroes at Freetown but even by the end of the 19th century the colony still only comprised a few square km around Freetown. It did, however, have far more influence over the course of West African events than either of the other two ex-slave colonies of Liberia and Gabon, founded by the Americans and French respectively. Many of those who were landed at Freetown assimilated European ways, especially as a result of educational work undertaken by the Protestant missions who deliberately chose Sierra Leone as their first footing in West Africa. There grew up a community of African traders, priests, doctors, lawyers and administrators some of whom eventually returned to the land of their origin — especially Yorubaland in Nigeria — and thus helped spread their Christian and British influence.

As in Liberia, the Creoles — descend-

Freetown

key:- ① Railway Station
② Post Office
③ Barclays Bank
④ Govt. House
⑤ House of Representativ

ants of the ex-slaves who were landed here, formed a distinct minority of the population as a whole, most being people of indigenous origin from the interior, but tension between the two groups has never reached the same explosive proportions as it has in Liberia. Though a lot of the political and economic power is still held by Creoles, the colonial administrators took care to groom the first of the indigenous members of the population to gain a university education, Milton Margai, for president when independence was granted in 1960.

Margai was removed in a coup in 1967 but a second coup a year later restored the civilian government though under the rule of the former opposition party, the All Peoples' Congress. There is a constant struggle for power between the various factions of the APC which appears to be motivated almost entirely by opportunism and the desire to get rich by gaining control of the country's finances, though there are few ideological differences between them. Maoist China and Cuba have been involved in training rival bands of guerillas for the main factions of the APC but so far Sierra Leone has avoided the sort of bloodbath which recently engulfed Liberia.

FACTS

The economy is based on the export of

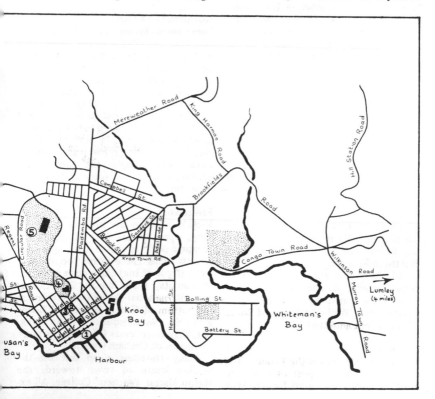

minerals, which bring in 75% of the country's income with diamonds easily the most important of these. There's a great deal of diamond smuggling in spite of government attempts to cut it down and enforce licences on the Africans who flood the miners' hastily built shanty towns.

The leading agricultural exports include palm kernels, coffee, cocoa, kola and ginger, but government interest in agriculture has been lacking and the co-operative system has been allowed to collapse, except for a few large, mechanical prestige projects. Sierra Leone is the world's largest producer of piassava used in brushes and brooms.

The rainy season is long and lasts from April to November or December, though no month is entirely free from rain. The average annual rainfall is 350 cm! Temperatures are constantly in the 30°Cs and the humidity hovers around 90%. It's an ordeal if you're used to a temperate climate.

VISAS

Entry permits are required by nationals of the Commonwealth countries, Belgium, Denmark, Iceland, Irish Republic, Italy, Luxembourg, Netherlands, Norway, Spain and Sweden. These are issued free of charge. The authorities are fairly lax about possession of entry permits and, if you haven't got one on arrival, they tell you to report to immigration on Wellington St, Freetown, the next day. Entry permits allow for a stay of one month, extendable to three months in Freetown.

All those not entitled to an entry permit require a visa. These cost 5 Leone for a tourist visa and 2 Leone for a transit visa. 'White' nationals of South Africa are not admitted.

CURRENCY

The unit of currency is the Leone = 100 cents. The import/export of local currency is allowed up to 20 Leone. Also, officially, you are not allowed to export Sterling currency notes in excess of £10 or other foreign currency notes in excess of the equivalent of 20 Leone but we've not heard of anyone having currency notes confiscated.

Exchange rate:

£1	=	Leone 1.94
US$1	=	Leone 0.84
A$1	=	Leone 0.97

Airport tax for international flights is 3 Leone.

LANGUAGE
English and local languages.

ACCOMMODATION
There are no hotels outside of Freetown and Bo. The Peace Corps often have hostels (eg at Bo and Kenema) where you might be able to stay for a small charge if they have a spare room. Otherwise there are teachers and other volunteers who are often willing to put you up if you're prepared to help out and contribute to your keep in the following places: Bonthe, Kabala, Kailahun, Kambia, Pujehon and Segbwema. In smaller towns and villages ask around for accommodation — somebody always helps out.

Freetown
Vicki's, next to the brothel and curio shop, opposite the City Hotel, is the cheapest place to stay but she apparently only takes Peace Corps people these days. If you manage to persuade her to let you stay there it costs 2.50 Leone. The *International Travel Inn*, situated at the bottom of George St, costs 4 Leone a double. No mosquito nets or breakfast. *City Hotel* costs 6 Leone, the place has shades of Graham Greene.

Many travellers sleep out on the beaches south of town towards the Milton Margai Teachers' College. All except Lumley Beach are unspoilt by tourism or day trippers and even Lumley is barely touched. Take bus No 3 to get there but they're irregular so ask at the bus station.

For food, try the Q Cafe in the Quadrangle behind McCarthy Square, a good clean place to eat and they do breakfasts too.

Sulima

If you're looking for a relatively deserted beach to live on for a while head for this place. Miles of sand, a few fishermen and lagoons. Take food with you as there's very little available locally. We heard recently that the president was constructing a summer palace here, so things may change when this is completed.

TRANSPORT

Hitching is possible along the main routes but slow if you're looking for free lifts. There are many police and army checkpoints on the roads of Sierra Leone where they'll want to see your papers and search your baggage. There is a good government bus service between Freetown and all the larger provincial centres such as Bo, Kenema, Makeni and Sefadu. They're fast and cost about 1 Leone/100 km but be there well before the buses are due to leave if you want to be sure of getting on. Pay for your fare on the bus.

Some examples of bus transport are:

Freetown-Kenema costs 6 Leone. Kenema-Segbwema costs 1 Leone. Segbwema-Pendembu costs 1.50 Leone. Pendembu-Kailahun costs 80 cents. Kailahun-Koinda costs 2 Leone. Koindu-Foya (Liberia) costs 1 Leone.

In addition to buses there are Passenger Transport Cars called 'poda poda' which are the main means of transport apart from the buses. They are very crowded, uncomfortable and, at times, somewhat hazardous. They cram about 24 people into a VW-sized minibus or Toyota pickup. There are also cheap taxi services between Bo and Kenema and good internal taxi services in Freetown, Bo, Sefadu, etc. If you're heading for the airport at Lungi in Freetown, there is a cheaper bus which departs from outside the Paramount Hotel.

If you're heading for Guinea, there is now a twice weekly bus service between Freetown and Conakry.

In addition to the route to Liberia, outlined above in the bus routes, there is a shorter, though less scenic route via Pujehun and Zimmi. If you're going via Kaiahun and Koindu (not to be confused with the diamond mining town of Koidu), it's best to go on Sunday morning as there's a lot of market traffic on that day from Guinea, Liberia and Sierra Leone. Freetown in Monrovia can be done in a day if you keep moving.

Flights Freetown-Banjul (Gambia) costs 87 Leone (about US$81).

Somalia

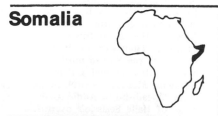

The Somali coast once formed part of the extensive Arab controlled trans-Indian Ocean trading network and its ports of Mogadishu and Brava were part of the East African chain which stretched through Malindi, Mombasa, Zanzibar and Kilwa as far as Sofala in Mozambique. The prosperity of these ports and indeed the trading network itself were

largely destroyed by the Portuguese in the early 16th century following the latter's discovery of a sea route to India and beyond via the Cape of Good Hope. From that time until the 19th century, Somalia lapsed into obscurity being ignored by European traders because of its lack of exploitable resources.

In the 19th century much of the Ogaden Desert — ethnically a part of Somalia — was annexed by the empire of Ethiopia during Menelik I's reign. This loss has never been accepted by the Somalis and has not only poisoned Somali-Ethiopian relations for over half a century but has led to war on more than

one occasion. Throughout the '70s Somali guerilla organisations dedicated to recovering the Ogaden were supported by the Somali government and at one point had succeeded in not only throwing back regular Ethiopian Army troops from the desert area but in taking Jijiga and almost capturing Harrar and Dire Dawa — the major towns in southern Ethiopia. They were eventually thrown back over the Somali border only with massive Russian and Cuban assistance following Moscow's switch of allegiance from Mogadishu to Addis Ababa in the wake of Haile Selassie's overthrow and

Somalia 265

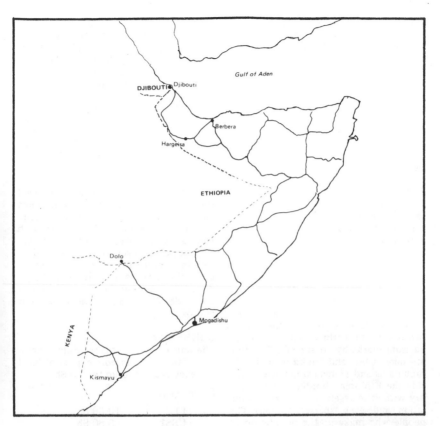

the Marxist take-over in Ethiopia. Somalia also claims parts of northern Kenya which were detached during the late 19th century by the British though these claims are on a much lower key than those relating to the Ogaden.

At the turn of the century, Somalia was divided between the British, who took the northern part opposite the South Yemen, and the Italians, who took the southern part alongside the Indian Ocean, but the two parts were reunited when independence was gained in 1960. Nine years later a military coup brought the current President, Mohamed Said Barre, to power on a ticket of radical socialism which has resulted in great changes in Somalian society. The government places great emphasis on self-reliance and the use of team work and many roads, houses, hospitals and agricultural projects have been created by such methods, paralleling similar developments in Maoist China. As a result of the coup which brought Barre to power, the USA withdrew the Peace Corps and in 1970 imposed a trade embargo on the country following news that Somalia was trading with North Vietnam. The USSR immediately stepped into the vacuum with economic and military aid and several years later

Somali's armed forces became one of the best-equipped and best-trained in the whole continent. The honeymoon, however, came to an end when Russia stepped in to support Mengistu's Marxist regime in Ethiopia, Somali's traditional arch-enemy. The Russians were summarily ordered to leave Somalia in the late '70s and since then there has been a rapprochement with the west, including even a recent offer of the use of the Soviet-built port facilities at Berbera for the American Navy.

FACTS

Severe droughts are a continuing problem in this part of the world and the one which struck in the mid-70s had a devastating effect on the people living in the Ogaden area and demanded large-scale relocation to more favourable areas. As we go to press another drought is forcing hundreds of thousands of traditionally desert and scrub dwellers to flee to the more fertile coastal plains.

The coastline has some of the longest beaches in the world which are protected from sharks by coral reefs. The climate here is hot and humid while in the mountains and plateau which rise alongside the Ethiopian border it is hot and dry with little vegetation, a sparse population and even sparser rainfall. The people who make up the population of 4½ million are perhaps some of the most beautiful in the world — tall, aquiline features, ebony-black skin, long flowing robes. They are quiet and dignified and tend to ignore strangers although those who have learned to speak English are quite ready to talk unless they are politically suspicious of you. Mogadishu, the capital, is well known for its beautiful, gleaming white, Hammawein quarter which goes back centuries and for its Bonadir weavers and old mosques.

Very few travellers went to Somalia during the '70s because of the unpredictable military activities which were taking place there and the difficulty of getting a visa but from the few letters we have received it is well worth the effort and getting easier all the time. The cost of living is low — far lower than in neighbouring Kenya — and you are unlikely to meet any other travellers there. If you get to Kenya, why not make a detour up the coast and experience one of Africa's previously most inaccessible countries, totally unspoiled by tourism?

VISAS

Required by all. It is now possible to get tourist visas in Nairobi without much hassle. The same applies if you are coming through Djibouti. The borders with Djibouti and Kenya are open but that with Ethiopia closed. You need to apply well in advance for visas since applications still have to be OK'ed in Mogadishu. They are on the expensive side at £8 (US$17) — and you need four photos.

CURRENCY

The unit of currency is the Somali Shilling = 100 cents. Import/export of local currency is allowed up to 100 Sh.

Exchange rate:

£1	=	13.30 Sh
US$1	=	5.80 Sh
A$1	=	6.65 Sh

Blackmarket rate in Nairobi is approximately double the offical rate. Currency declaration forms are issued on arrival but ignored on departure. Airport tax for international flights is 10 Sh.

LANGUAGES

Somali is the official language. Arabic, Italian and English are also spoken in the cities.

ACCOMMODATION

There are a few hotels as such outside

the main cities of Kismayu, Mogadishu, Hargeisa and Berbera but costs are low.

Mogadishu
Savoy Hotel costs 10 Sh for a bed. A taxi from the airport costs 1 Sh.

TRANSPORT
There are very few buses but plenty of trucks. As in other African countries where trucks are the main form of transport, the price of lifts is more or less fixed. You have to have your passport stamped in most of the towns through which you pass or stay in. If you have a camera with you, get permission from people before taking pictures — they are very suspicious of cameras which is not surprising in view of the recent confrontation with Ethiopia.

Arab dhows ply between the ports of South Yemen, Mogadishu, Kismayu and the Kenyan ports of Lamu and Malindi. This is probably the easiest way of getting to Somalia from Kenya.

We regret we have no more details since we have not heard from anyone who has been there for years. Please send us some information if you go there!

South Africa

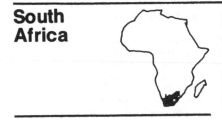

The Cape of Good Hope had been known to Europe since the early Portuguese voyages of discovery towards the end of the 15th century but it was not until 1652 that any attention was paid to this area of Africa. In that year the Dutch, having displaced the Portuguese from their dominant position on the Indian Ocean trade routes, landed a small group of settlers there with orders to grow fresh vegetables and meat for the Dutch East India Company's ships on their way to and from the East Indies. For the first few years the group all but starved to death until the local African tribes were enslaved to provide the menial labour — something which these early settlers and their descendants regarded as a God-given right and which was to grow into the policy of 'apartheid' on which the modern state is based. Colonisation of the interior was a slow process and by the time the Napoleonic Wars were over in Europe there were still only 15,000 Dutch settlers in Cape Province.

Further east the much more fertile lands between the Drakensberg Mountains and the coast had been settled by the Bantu-speaking people from the 13th century onwards. These people were in touch with the Indian Ocean merchants a century before the arrival of the Portuguese but were ignored by the latter since there were no rich coastal cities worthy of plunder. The Bantu prospered and multiplied to such an extent that by the 18th century new land for settlement was in short supply. The Bantu's traditional solution to this problem had been to hive off junior groups and send them off in search of new lands elsewhere. In this process they had clashed with the original Hottentot and Bushmen settlers and pushed them further south and west but their ability to do this became more and more limited as the insatiable Dutch demand for more land and free labour spread its wings further into the interior. By 1760 the Dutch had already crossed the Orange River and a confrontation became inevitable. It culminated in the first Bantu war of 1779 — the first of many bitter wars which would be fought by the two groups. The event which gave most impetus to further Dutch expansion, however, was the annexation of Cape Province by the British during the Napoleonic Wars and the antipathy of the Dutch settlers to the anti-slavery colonial policies of the British.

In an attempt to get away from these restrictions the Dutch, who were gradually coming to see themselves as a new nation and had in fact declared two small republics in 1795, pushed further and further inland, culminating with the 'Great Trek' across the Orange and Fish Rivers in 1834, following the outlawing of slavery by the British. The pressure on the Bantu tribes had by this time become intolerable and was to lead to profound political changes among those of the more populous Natal area. The change was initiated by Dingiswayo a chief of the Mtetwa, who reorganised and unified his tribe into a military nation on European lines. The man whom he placed in charge of his regiments — Shaka — undertook a military revolution doing away with the traditional Bantu methods of conducting warfare based on ritualised single-combat and the ransom of fallen champions and substituting hard-trained soldiers who fought in formation and who were intent on anihilating their rivals. Shaka's own clan, the Zulu, soon became dominant in Natal having killed, subdued or driven out their rivals. These grim years of inter-tribal warfare left a scene of carnage and devastation hitherto unknown in this part of Africa and created an impression in the minds of Europeans who arrived shortly afterwards that this was the normal state of affairs between the tribes — an impression which has lingered on to the present day despite its inaccuracy. It also led to the migration and dispersal of many defeated tribes. One such migration, led by Mzilikazi, even got as far as the shores of Lake Tanganyika, destroying in the process the effete Karanga empire based on Great Zimbabwe and Khami in present-day Zimbabwe. Other groups fled south and west over the northern foothills of the Drakensberg Mountains clashing there with other settled tribes and leaving a similar scene of devastation. In this latter process a group of clans rallied under the leadership of Mosheshwe on the table top mountain of Thaba Bosiu and were able to settle there in relative safety forming the nucleus of what was to become the Basuto nation. The Basuto successfully resisted attacks by the troops of Mzilikazi, the Boers (which the Dutch had become known as) and the British until the area was declared a British Protectorate.

Into this scene of forced migration, devastation and fanatical Zulu militancy came the Boers in search of new lands and, not far behind them, the British who were settling in ever increasing numbers in Cape Province and Natal. War between the Bantu and the Boers on the one hand and between the Bantu and the British on the other was a more or less constant feature throughout much of the 19th century and was to result in the alienation of the most fertile lands from the Bantu by the time the two Boer republics of the Orange Free State and Transvaal and the two British colonies of Cape Province and Natal were established. Never at any time were relations good between the British and the Boers, though when gold was discovered on the Rand and the Boers needed to attract British capital in order to be able to exploit the deposits, British workers were allowed into the Transvaal and Orange Free State, though denied citizenship and heavily taxed. Naturally this situation was not to the liking of the British (anymore than it is to the 'gastarbeiters' in present day Germany and Holland) and provided a pretext to interfere more and more in the internal affairs of those republics. Friction between the two communities reached flashpoint and resulted in the Boer wars of 1890 and 1899-1902 which were finally brought to an end by the Treaty of Vereniging in which both Boers and British were recognised as equal partners. The rights of the Bantu were not even considered. In 1910, the Union of South Africa was created with dominion status within the British Empire (and later, the Commonwealth). This arrangement lasted until 1961 when South Africa was thrown out of the Commonwealth for its hated 'apartheid policy'. Political estrangement however, did not lead to economic ostracism and western capital investment in South Africa has continued apace.

The population of the Republic stands at around 25 million composed of approximately 16% whites, 12% 'coloureds' mostly of Indian origin, and 72% blacks. The blacks are concentrated mostly in the densely populated eastern parts of the country though there are other groups, like the Bechuana in the more sparsely populated central areas and the Hottentots in the western and remoter areas of the south and west, though most were driven into their present home on the fringes of the Kalahari Desert by the advancing Bantu. Of the white element the Boers enjoy an overall numerical superiority (60% of white use Afrikaans as their native language and only 36% English) and are concentrated on the open veldt while the descendants of the English settlers are found mostly in the provinces of Natal and Cape. The Boers are, on the whole, conservative and it is from them that the government receives its greatest support for its 'apartheid' policy. The descendants of the English settlers tend to be less in favour of it. Most of the 'coloured' people are descendants of indentured plantation labourers who were brought over from India by the British in the latter part of the 19th century.

Neither the blacks nor the 'coloureds' have any access to political power, are subject to arbitrary arrest and detention without trial and are only permitted to settle and practise agriculture in the 'Homelands' which comprise about 13% of the total land area of the Republic. Although many of the 'Homelands' lie in the better-watered parts of the Republic most are too mountainous or rugged to support agriculture and none of them, of course, lie in areas where there is appreciable mineral wealth (from which South Africa derives the bulk of its income). As any agriculture which is possible in the 'Homelands' is largely on a subsistence basis only, many blacks are forced to work in factories and mines situated in 'White' areas far from their 'Homelands' where they are joined by thousands of other black migrant workers recruited from Swaziland, Lesotho, Botswana, Malawi and even Zaire. The disruption and misery which this causes among African families is incalculable and the conditions under which these black labourers are forced to work and the wages which they are paid is nothing less than scandalous. In the early '70s the wage gap between white and black workers stood at 20 to 1 and, although this provoked an international outcry in the press and other media, which resulted in a few desultory changes, the situation remains essentially unchanged. This abundant supply of what is virtually slave-labour explains why there are more than 500 British companies alone which own subsidiaries in South Africa with a total investment well over the £1000 million mark. Equally, Carter's much-lauded human rights policy hasn't resulted in a noticeable drop in US investment here either. As with most countries which rake in the profits from this vast pool of human misery it's simply a lot of hot air while business proceeds as usual.

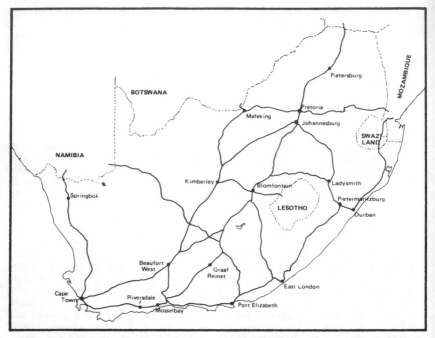

The resentment which this racist system generates broods like a time-bomb just beneath the surface and, since Zimbabwe's independence, could explode at any moment. Unfortunately the situation will not be resolved without a bloodbath. The South African government's reaction to protest and opposition, however reasonably presented, has always been ferocious and totally uncompromising, ranging from the Sharpeville massacre of 20 years ago through the shooting of unarmed demonstrating schoolchildren in Soweto in the late '70s to the torture and murder, while in police custody, of political activists like Steve Biko. So-called·reforms, like the repeal of the hated 'pass laws' which required all non-whites to carry ID whilst in 'white designated' areas on pain of imprisonment, have so far been merely cosmetic. The victories of the African liberation struggles in

Angola, Mozambique and recently in Zimbabwe, have pressed the South African government's back ever more firmly against the wall and contributed to·a war psychosis which has resulted in higher and higher 'defence' budgets and the development of a nuclear capacity with the assistance of the West Germans.

In an attempt to hive off black political activity from the 'white' areas the government has recently pursued a policy of granting 'independence' to a number of Bantu 'Homelands', the first being that of the Transkei in late October 1976. Others have followed since that time but this blatant exercise in window-dressing has been universally recognised for what it is and diplomatic recognition of these puppet states has been withheld by even those African countries, like Malawi and the Central African Republic, which maintain good relations with South Africa. In order to maintain its 'independence' the Transkei depends on South Africa for 75% of its income, has up to 55% of its adult male population working as migrant labour in the Republic at any one time, retains such pillars of apartheid as the Mixed Marriages Act and the Immorality Act (which outlaws sexual relations and marriage between whites and blacks), and maintains separate schools for the 11,000 whites remaining there. The 'independent' homelands thus provide South Africa with a convenient pool of cheap labour which can, in the eyes of the Republic, be legitimately denied citizenship rights. They are also a way of channelling the opportunism of various petty chiefs into maintaining inter-tribal animosities.

But all is not well even among the white political leadership. South Africa was recently rocked by one of the biggest scandals ever to surface when it was disclosed that tens of millions of dollars had been pumped into a secret propaganda scheme to improve South Africa's image abroad by bribing western newspapers and other media controllers and attempting to acquire majority interests in various influential publications. The disclosures led to the enforced resignations of Drs Vorster (Prime Minister), Mulder (Minister of Information) and Diederichs (Minister of Finance) as well as lesser figures. Like Watergate in America, the full truth never came out and the present leaders have yet to rid themselves of the suspicion that they too were a party to the conspiracy.

That such a bunch of narrow-minded psychotics should continue to fuel racial hatred around the world and to deny the majority of their countrymen even basic human rights let alone the franchise is intolerable. South Africa is a beautiful country with a diversity of peoples and cultures with few parallels elsewhere in the world. The writing is on the wall and the sooner it leaps off and strangles these cretins, the better. Please

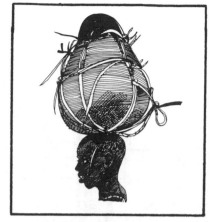

go there and spread the news, the papers are censored.

VISAS

Required by all except nationals of the Irish Republic, Switzerland and the UK. If you're one those nationals which require a visa and intend to visit neighbouring countries (such as Lesotho and Swaziland) and then to return to South Africa, make sure you apply for a multiple-entry visa. Most people are given a three-month, triple-entry visa which allows you to visit Lesotho and Swaziland without further visa hassles.

Before you're allowed to enter South Africa you must have an onward ticket and 'sufficient' funds to maintain yourself while you're there. And they mean it! If you haven't got an onward ticket, border officials insist on a bond of Rand 600 (about US$600) in CASH there and then. It's returnable on departure but they won't accept travellers' cheques or letters from a bank confirming that you have sufficient funds held in reserve in case of emergency. Customs officials are also entitled to demand that you furnish proof that you've never been refused entry into or deported from the Republic or from Namibia (which they call

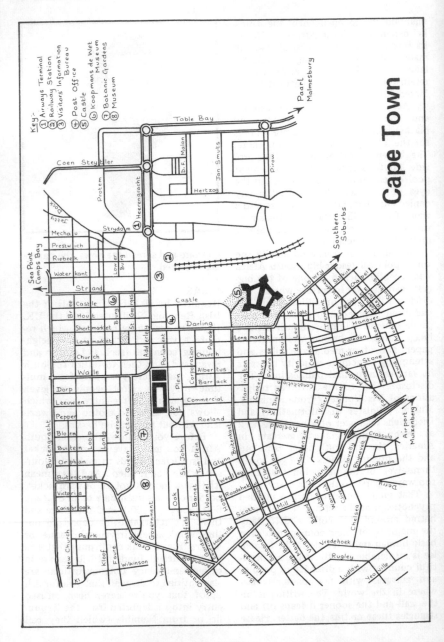

Cape Town

Key:-
1. Airways Terminal
2. Railway Station
3. Visitors' Information Bureau
4. Post Office
5. Castle
6. Koopmans de Wet Museum
7. Botanic Gardens
8. Museum

South West Africa), that you've never been convicted of any crime in any country and that you're not suffering from any contagious disease or any other mental or physical deficiency. Before you throw up your hands in despair or disbelief you should know that, in practice, they only put you through this bullshit on the Zimbabwean frontier. On the Botswana border it's unlikely you'll be asked to show either an onward ticket or money. On the other hand, since Zimbabwean independence, things may change so have that Rand 600 handy in case. The latest news is that it is still very easy-going at Ramathlabha on the Botswana-South Africa border, especially if you were entering by passenger train.

Note that South African stamps in your passport can bring you a lot of hassles further north. Zambian and Tanzanian officials, in particular, don't get off on them and may refuse you entry or at least keep you waiting all day while they glare at you with revolutionary disgust.

CURRENCY
The unit of currency is the Rand = 100 cents. Import of local currency is limited to Rand 50. Export is limited to Rand 20.

Exchange rate:

£1	=	Rand 1.74
US$1	=	Rand 0.76
A$1	=	Rand 0.87

ACCOMMODATION
Despite the political climate of the country, or perhaps because of it, white South Africans can be very hospitable to white travellers and you may find that, if you fall into this category, you will rarely have to use hotels and campsites, etc. Because of the apartheid regulations you cannot use African hotels and the 'white' hotels, are naturally, far more expensive. There is, however a network of inexpensive Youth Hostels which average Rand 1 per night and Youth Centres which average Rand 2.50 per night (sometimes less). Camp sites often have 'rondavels' which are small huts with beds. YMCAs cost Rand 2.50 for bed and breakfast. Food tends to be cheap by European standards.

Cape Province
Youth Hostels available in Cape Province are as follows:

Stan's Halt, The Glen, Camps Bay, Cape Town, situated next to the Round House Restaurant (tel 48 9037), costs Rand 1.20 per night and has hot water and laundry facilities. It is popular with travellers.

Port Rex Youth Hostel, 128 Moore Street, East London (tel 25151), costs Rand 1 per night and has hot water. 'Run by a tyrannical old lady who underneath it all has a heart of gold'.

Abe Bailey Youth Hostel corner of Maynard and Westbury Roads, Muizenberg, Cape Town (tel 88 4283) costs Rand 1.20 and has hot water and laundry facilities.

Lanhern Youth Hostel, Beach Road, PO Box 766, port Elizabeth (tel 27739), costs Rand 1.20 per night for bed and breakfast and has hot water and laundry facilities. Run by a young couple who are quite free and easy. It is best to ring before turning up as it is a popular place for school parties.

Cape Town
The following budget hotels are all located in the central area.

Cafe Royal, 23 Church Street (tel 22-9047), costs Rand 4.50-5.50 per bed, restaurant attached.

Castle, 42 Canterbury Street (tel 22-9227), costs Rand 3.50 per bed or Rand 4.50 for bed and breakfast.

City Hall, 50 Darling Street (tel 22-

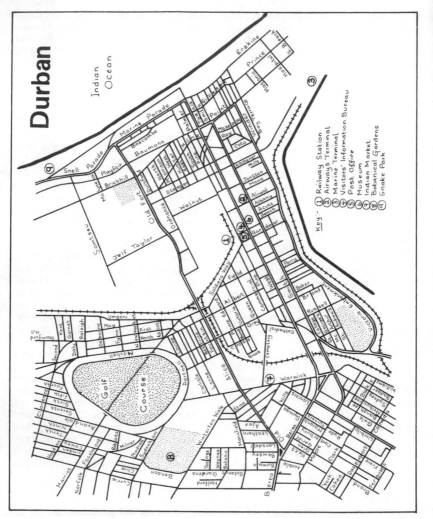

Durban

Indian Ocean

Key:- ① Railway Station ② Airways Terminal ③ Marine Terminal ④ Visitors' Information Bureau ⑤ Post Office ⑥ Museum ⑦ Indian Market ⑧ Botanical Gardens ⑨ Snake Park

3771), costs Rand 4.50-5.50 for bed and breakfast.

Good Hope, 87 Loop Street (tel 22-3369), costs Rand 4-6 per bed or Rand 5-8 for bed and breakfast.

Green Hansom, 85 Long Street (tel 22-6667), costs Rand 5 per bed or Rand 7 for bed and breakfast.

Oranje, Union Street (tel 41 0525), costs Rand 5.25-6.25 per bed or Rand 7.25 to 8.30 for bed and breakfast.

Red Lion, 111 Longmarket Street (tel 22 0427), costs Rand 6.50-7.25 for bed and breakfast.

Stag's Head 71 Hope Street (tel 45-

4918), costs Rand 4-6 per bed or Rand 5-7 for bed and breakfast.

Tudor Greenmarket Square (tel 41-0196), costs Rand 7-8 for bed and breakfast.

The Tourist Office is 3rd Floor, Broadway Centre, Heerengracht. American Express; Greenmarket Place, Greenmarket Square, PO Box 2337, Capetown, 8000, tel 228581.

Beaufort West

Donkin House Donkin Street (tel 4287) costs Rand 3.75 per bed and is popular with travellers. It is a good place to pick up lifts going elsewhere.

Royal, 20 Donkin Street (tel 3241/2), costs Rand 4 per bed or Rand 8.50-10.50 for bed and breakfast.

Park Rooms, Danie Theron Street (tel 3878) costs Rand 4 per bed, meals are available.

Young's Halfway House, 143 Donkin Street (tel 3878), costs Rand 4.50 per bed, meals are available.

Safari Tourist Rooms, Pritchard Street (tel 2439), costs Rand 4.50 per bed.

Graaf Reinet

Mrs M Nel, 106 Caledon Street (tel 2456) costs Rand 4 per bed.

Mrs F van der Merwe, 100 Caledon Street (tel 3749) costs Rand 7.50 per person, meals are available.

Caledon Chambers, Caledon Street (tel 3670) costs Rand 5 per bed.

Urquhart Tourist Camp, PO Box 71 (tel 2121 & 3796), situated 2½ km out of town on the Murraysburg road, costs Rand 3 per day per person, plenty of facilities.

Vryburg

Afrikaaner Boarding House, costs Rand 3 per night for bed and breakfast.

Natal Province
Durban

Youth Hostel, 22 Leventhal Road, (tel 359 321), costs Rand 1.20 per night. Other than the Youth Hostel there are many small boarding houses and holiday flatlets around the Gillespie Road area which can be found for between Rand 3 and 6 per person per day. Some of those available are:

Casa Mia, 17 Cato Street (tel 32 0920) costs Rand 4 per day, meals are available.

Blenheim, 37 Gillespie Street (tel 37-4060), costs from Rand 5 per day.

White House, 51 Marine Parade (tel 37-8231), costs Rand 4.75-6.75 for bed and breakfast.

Hilton Heights Holiday Flats, 5 Gillespie Street (tel 37 1535), self-contained flatlets for between Rand 6-15 per day.

Killarney, 21 Brickhill Road (tel 37-4281), costs Rand 5.15-8.85 per day for bed and breakfast.

Sea Breeze Hotel, 55 Gillespie Street (tel 37 8696) costs Rand 25/double per week for bed and breakfast, recommended by quite a few travellers.

Springbok Hotel, Gillespie Street, costs Rand 3 per bed.

The Tourist Office is at 320 West Street, PO Box 2516, Durban 4000. American Express is at Denor House, 1st Floor, Cnr Smith and Field Streets (PO Box 2558). Durban 4000 (tel 323491).

Pietermaritzburg

Youth Centre; ask local people for directions. It costs Rand 2.50 per night but they generally accept less if you are on a tight budget.

Cosy, 456 Church Street (tel 2 3279) costs Rand 5.50 for a bed and Rand 6.50 for bed and breakfast.

New Watson, cnr Church & West Streets (tel 2 1604), costs Rand 5.70-6.85 per bed and Rand 7.45-8.60 for bed and breakfast.

Norfolk 23 Church Street (tel 2 6501/2), costs Rand 7-9 for bed and breakfast.

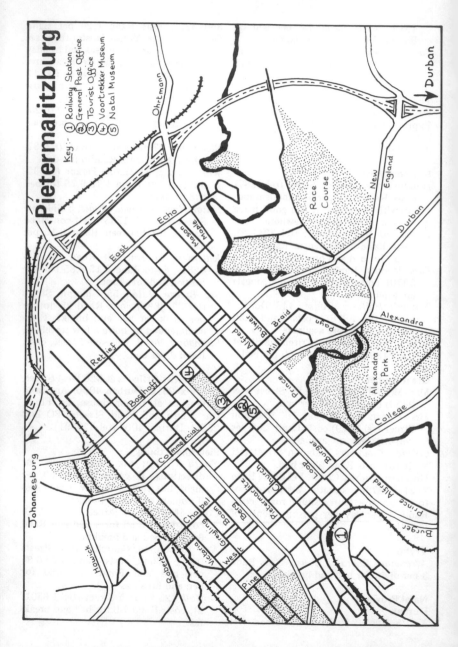

Pietermaritzburg

Key :-
① Railway Station
② General Post Office
③ Tourist Office
④ Voortrekker Museum
⑤ Natal Museum

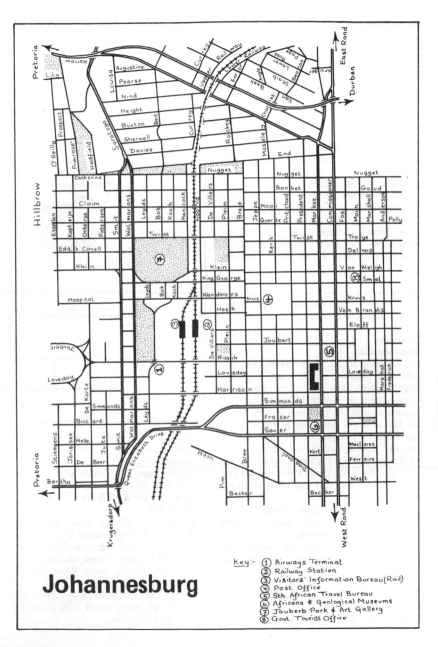

Johannesburg

Key:-
1. Airways Terminal
2. Railway Station
3. Visitors' Information Bureau (Rail)
4. Post Office
5. Sth. African Travel Bureau
6. Africana & Geological Museums
7. Jouberb Park & Art Gallery
8. Govt. Tourist Office

St Michael's-on-Sea

Mountjoy, 12 Crown Road (tel 5 1306), costs Rand 6.50-8.50 including all meals. Another recommended place to stay is the NHF Holiday Camp *Resthaven*, Surf Bay near St Michael's (tel 38).

Orange Free State
Bloemfontein

Capitol, 126a Maitland Street (tel 7-7711), costs Rand 6.75-9.75 per bed.

Oranje, 62 St Andrews Street (tel 7-9849), costs Rand 8-9 for bed and breakfast.

The Tourist Office is on the Ground Floor of the FVB Centre, Maitland Street, (PO Box 3515), Bloemfontein 9300.

Stellenboch

Lanzarac Hotel, costs Rand 8 per night and is 'incredible value'.

Transvaal
Johannesburg

Youth Hostel, 32 Main Street, Townsville (tel 268051), costs Rand 1.20 per night. There are no meals available. Other than the Youth Hostel, most travellers stay in the Hillbrow area of town or the adjacent Berea area where there are many budget hotels and guest houses. Here are some examples:

Kolping House, 4 Fife Avenue, Berea (tel 643 1213), costs Rand 4.50 per night for bed and breakfast or Rand 30 per week.

Hawthorne, 45 Olivia Road, Berea (tel 642 5915), costs Rand 5.75 per bed, meals are available.

Ambassador, 52A Pretoria Street (tel 642 5051), costs Rand 7.50-11 for bed and breakfast.

Chelsea, Catherine Avenue, Berea (tel 642 4541) costs Rand 5.50-7.75 for bed and breakfast.

Constantia, 35 Quartz Street, Joubert

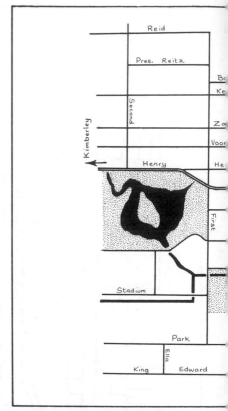

Park (tel 725 1046), costs Rand 6.50 per bed or Rand 7.50 for bed and breakfast.

Cosmopolitan, 285 Commissioner Street (tel 614 3315), costs Rand 6.50 per bed or Rand 8-9.50 for bed and breakfast.

East London, 54 Loveday Street (tel 836 5862), costs Rand 6 per bed or Rand 7 for bed and breakfast.

Europa, 63 Claim Street, Joubert Park (tel 725 5321), costs Rand 5-6 per bed.

Federal, 181 Commissioner Street (tel 22 8846), costs Rand 5.25-10.50 for bed and breakfast.

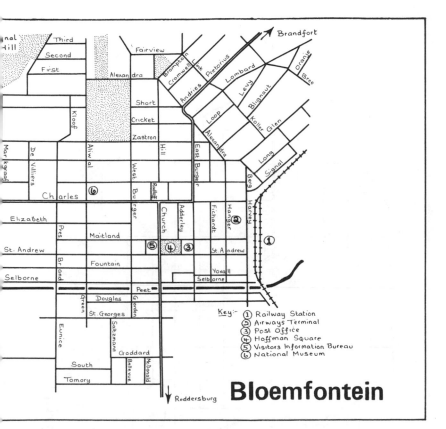

Bloemfontein

Key:-
1. Railway Station
2. Airways Terminal
3. Post Office
4. Hoffman Square
5. Visitors Information Bureau
6. National Museum

Gresham, 13 Loveday Street (tel 834 5641) costs Rand 4.50 per bed or Rand 6.50 for bed and breakfast.

Rondebosch, 24 Edith Cavell Street, Hillbrow (tel 724 4151), costs Rand 3.75-5.20 per bed and Rand 6-7 for bed and breakfast.

Whitehall, 8 Abel Road, Berea (tel 643 4911), costs Rand 6.50 per bed or Rand 7.50 for bed and breakfast.

The Odyssey (8 Lily Lane near Soper (Road) and the *Alexandra Boarding* (Soper Street) have also been recommended as good value.

For meals the cheapest places include *Mark H* in the Hillbrow area. If you buy several meal tickets at once they cost Rand 1.50 each for enormous seven-course dinners. Another good place is the *Rich Man Poor Man*, again in the Hillbrow area. Meals here cost Rand 1 but it's a 'whites only' place. A good multi-racial night club is the *Las Vegas* on Commissioner Street. Entrance is Rand 1, a good place for contacts.

The Tourist Office is at Suite 4611, Carlton Centre (PO Box 1094), Johannesburg 2000. American Express is at Merbrook 123, Commissioner Street (PO Box 9395), Johannesburg 2000 (tel 37 4000).

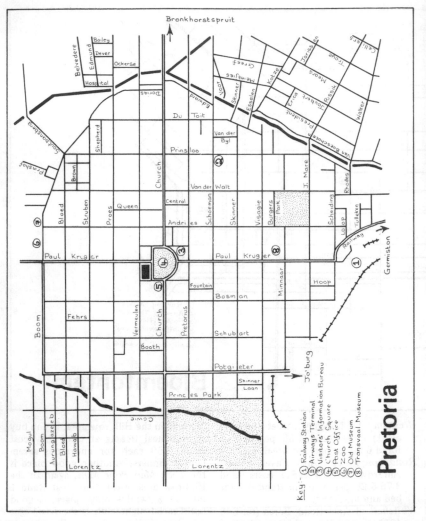

Pretoria

Belgrave, 22 Railway Street (tel 3 5578), costs Rand 6.76-7.30 for bed and breakfast.

Louis, 599 Schoeman Street (tel 44 4238), costs Rand 5 for a bed or Rand 7 for bed and breakfast.

Pretoria, 611 Schoeman Street (tel 42 5062), costs Rand 6.50-9 per bed or Rand 7.50-10 for bed and breakfast.

Republique, 47 Schoeman Street (tel 3 2025), costs Rand 6-7 per bed or Rand 7.25-8.25 for bed and breakfast.

The Tourist Office is on the third floor,

Frans du Toit Building, Schoeman Street, Pretoria 0001. American Express is at the SAAU Building, 308 Andries Street (PO Box 3592), Pretoria 0001 (tel 29182).

TRANSPORT

Hitching is easy on the main roads — so easy in fact that most travellers rarely use the bus or train networks but you must get out of the towns and cities proper before you start (most sprawl for miles). It's not advisable to try to hitch over the border into South Africa as customs and passport formalities will then take all day, (they assume you are impecunious). On the other hand, if you are hitching, be prepared for long, boring, bigoted lectures about apartheid and about Africans being animals, etc, etc, though many of the people who pick you up can be extremely generous and hospitable — after all you must be human if you're white. Ignore silly stories about the dangers of hitching in the Homelands where they say you will be murdered. We have had many letters from travellers who were told this but hitched there anyway and met with nothing less than friendship and hospitality. The accident rate on South African roads is one of the highest in the world. Hitching from Johannesburg to Durban takes a day. From Johannesburg to Cape Town takes about three days. The latter may involve long waits for lifts.

Visiting the Homelands

We recently had this letter from a traveller who spent five weeks working in Bophuthatswana, the Homeland adjacent to the Botswana border. It speaks for itself:

Virtually all I saw of South Africa was Johannesburg — a very unfriendly place (very sterile). The apartheid signs have come down but everyone knows the rules and it is just as horrible as most people imagine.

Bophuthatswana was quite different. The most incredible friendly people I have met anywhere, although it takes a bit of time to break down the old black-white barriers, and the people are pretty suspicious of you at first. I certainly can't imagine being murdered whilst hitching there. Maybe I was treated differently because I went there to help sick people, but I don't think so — people are dying for a chance to be friendly and invite you into their homes and feed you (even though they are incredibly poor), they're just a bit scared you will push them around like most of the Afrikaaners do.

There's really no-where to stay in Bophuthatswana except in people's homes or camping. A few of the larger villages have an Afrikaaner hotel but they are very dreary and the atmosphere is incredibly heavy apartheid. There is not much to see there anyway apart from the huge mealie (maize) plantations run by Afrikaaner farmers and lots of squalid little settlements where the Tswana people from Jo'burg and Cape Town were dumped after the homeland was created in 1976. Infectious diseases are rife in these places but no-one in any position of authority really cares so life becomes even more of a stuggle for the Tswana.

In contrast to the basic friendliness of the Africans, the Afrikaaners are quite unfriendly and incredibly bigoted and paranoid and they try to convince you that the Africans are absolute morons or animals — it's a very funny and very sad story all at the same time. The English South Africans are somewhere in between — they welcome you enthusiastically and really turn on a great time for you, but a lot of them tend to think a bit along Afrikaaner lines (although not nearly so extreme — at worst they treat the Africans like children). However, many English South Africans mix socially with Africans, or at least as much as the laws and their spying Afrikaaner neighbours permit. (I'm serious they call the police and cry 'communist/revolution'!)

Interestingly, the South African male has the highest incidence of heart disease, a stress (paranoia?) related illness, in the world. Hence, excellent heart surgeons!! Also South Africa has the world's highest suicide rate and the country is riddled with huge psychiatric institutions!'

OTHER INFORMATION

Jobs These are fairly easy to get if you are a tradesman or secretary. Wages are higher in Jo'burg than in Durban or Cape Town but Jo'burg is a concrete jungle. There is a Gasol (coal liquifaction project) plant about 75 km from Jo'burg which always needs pipefitters. There is a three-week training course during which you will be paid Rand 300

per month. After that you get Rand 600 per month. Food and accommodation are provided. If you don't fit into any of these categories, try Modern Technical Services and TTS which are employment services situated in the Trust Bank Building, Elaff St in downtown Jo'burg. They are situated on the 2nd and 6th floor respectively. These agencies specialise in placing travellers in jobs. Note that the Government is tightening up on work permits and usually insists that you get one before you start a job. They are rarely granted unless you have a skill which is much in demand.

Spanish North Africa

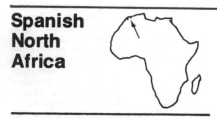

All that now remains of the Spanish Colonies in Africa are the two tiny enclaves of Ceuta and Melilla on the north Moroccan coast and the tiny islands of Alhucemas, Chafarinas and Penon de la Gomera just off the coast. Ceuta and Melilla are two intensely Andalusian cities which came under Spanish control in the 15th century at a time when the Moslem armies were gradually being pushed out of Spain and Portugal. They remained under Spanish control when Morocco gained its independence in 1956. Both are administered as city provinces of Spain. 90% of the inhabitants are Spanish and the cities' main function is to supply the Spanish troops stationed there and to service the NATO base and other calling ships. Fishing and the export of iron ore from the Rif Mountains are the other main activities. The Moroccan Government occasionally

campaigns for their return to Morocco.

The main interest of these places to the traveller is that the cheapest ferries to and from Morocco and Spain operate through there and customs formalities tend to be easier going than at Tangier.

VISAS
As for Spain.

CURRENCY
As for Spain.
Exchange rate:

£1	=	144 pesetas
US$1	=	63 pesetas
A$1	=	72 pesetas

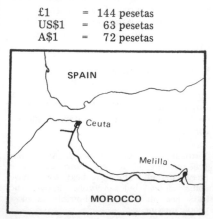

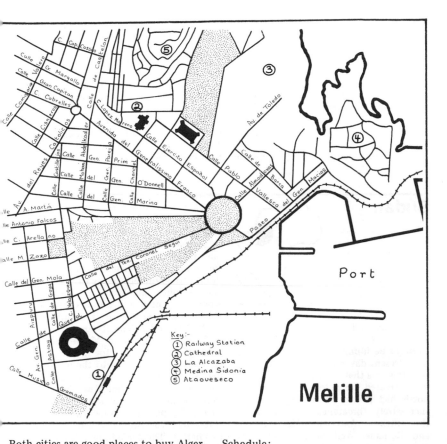

Key:-
1 Railway Station
2 Cathedral
3 La Alcazaba
4 Medina Sidonia
5 Ataoveseco

Melille

Both cities are good places to buy Algerian Dinar. Better rates of exchange than
in Algeria itself. See the 'Algeria' chapter for further details.

TRANSPORT
Ferries The ferries from the southern
Spanish ports of Algeciras, Malaga and
Almeria to Ceuta and Melilla are cover-
ed in the 'Mediterranean Ferries' section
in the introduction.

Ceuta-Melilla Ferries
Operator: Compania Transmediterranea.
Car ferries.

Schedule:

Port	Arrive	Depart
Ceuta		23.30 Mon
Penon de Velez	07.00 Tue	08.00 Tue
Alhucemas Is	11.00 Tue	11.30 Tue
Melilla	16.00 Tue	08.00 Thu*
Chafarinas Is	11.00 Thu *	
Chafarinas Is		15.00 Thu*
Melilla	18.00 Thu*	23.15 Thu
Alhucemas Is	07.00 Fri	08.00 Fri
Penon de Velez	11.00 Fri	12.00 Fri
Ceuta	18.00 Fri	

* denotes that the ferry service between Melilla and Chafarinas Is only operates on alternate weeks.

Minimum Fares

Ceuta to:

Penon de Velez	240 pesetas
Alhucemas Island	240 pesetas
Melilla	308 pesetas

Melilla to:

Alhucemas Island	270 pesetas
Penon de Velez	270 pesetas
Chafarinas Island	170 pesetas

OTHER INFORMATION

Petrol is duty free in Ceuta and Melilla so if you are travelling in your own vehicle stock up here whether you are going to Spain or Morocco.

These are possibly the cheapest places in Africa for film. Kodachrome 135-36 with processing costs 550 pesetas which is less than in Spain or France.

Sudan

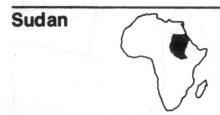

The world-wide fame of Egypt's ancient monuments and those of its later Islamic period has tended to overshadow those to be found further south in Nubia — present day northern Sudan. Yet it is to this area that the Egyptian civilization retreated once the empire to the north had passed its heyday and was successively threatened or invaded by the Hittites, Assyrians, Macedonians, and Romans. Well before 1000 BC, Nubia, between the first and third cataracts on the Nile, had been made into an Egyptian colony and was the empire's most important source of gold, producing an estimated 40,000 kg per year. Further south in the Kush lay a whole series of Egyptian towns including an offshoot of the Amon Temple at Jebel Barkal. Out of the latter grew the independent kingdom of Kush around 1000 BC whose rulers conquered Egypt in the 9th century BC and made Napata, their capital between the third and fourth cataracts, the centre of the ancient world for a while. Following the sack of Thebes by the Assyrians in 666 BC, the Pharoahs retreated south into Kush where their Egyptianised kingdom was to survive through the centuries of Persian, Greek and Roman occupation of lower Egypt. The frontiers of this kingdom were gradually pushed further and further south into what was then well-wooded country and a new capital established at Meroe near the confluence of the Nile and Atbara Rivers.

The move south to Meroe was not entirely in response to threats from the north but also due to the over-grazing which had taken place around Napata and the fact that Kush had both iron ore and fuel in abundance. Of the latter, Egypt had none and though Nubia had iron ore there was little fuel to smelt it. The technique of iron smelting had been introduced by the Assyrians and if the slag heaps around many of the ancient sites along the Kushitic Nile are anything to go by, Meroe must have been the Birmingham of the Middle East and Africa at the time.

The city prospered for many centuries through the export of ivory, slaves, rare skins and ebony and its buildings show influences from as far afield as India but decline set in during the first century AD due to the rise of the rival trading state of Axum in Ethiopia. Meroe's end came in the fourth century AD when it was sacked by the then

Christian rulers of Axum and recent excavations suggest that Meroe's rulers fled west to Kordofan and Darfur and set up a successor state there. During the many centuries when the Egyptian kingdom was pushed south and then west, the original Caucasoid population became gradually mixed with Negro blood until, when Meroe was at its height, it became an almost entirely Negro state. Its influences — particularly those surrounding the idea of divine kingship and the marriage of the king with his sister — spread far and wide through Africa and have been traced as far as the Zimbabwean Monomatapa empire which only came to an end in the early 19th century.

After the sack of Meroe by Axum, a Christian kingdom eventually grew up in Nubia with its centre at Dongola and was sufficiently powerful to stop the advance of the Arab Islam armies which overran Egypt in 639 AD. Islam made no further inroads here until Dongola collapsed in the 14th century.

Little of note was to happen from then until the early part of the 19th century when Muhammed Ali, the Khedive of Egypt, invaded the Sudan and overthrew the Moslem sultan of Sennar. The main object of the invasion was to ensure a constant supply of Negro slaves as recruits for the Egyptian army. Ali's armies pushed to the borders of modern-day Uganda though the procurement of slaves gradually became the business of private individuals from Khartoum, the new capital. Later on in the 19th century, when Britain became the de facto ruler of Egypt, Muhammed Ali's descendants employed the explorer Baker and General Gordon as Governors of the Sudan. Gordon pushed the frontiers of Sudan to their present limits but failed to bring the Ugandan kingdoms of Buganda and Bunyoro under Egyptian rule. Aware that his lines of communication to the north were impossibly long, Gordon even initiated an attempted

occupation of Kismayu on the Somali coast but the Egyptian forces were persuaded to withdraw by the British who were then in the process of trying to get the Sultan of Zanzibar to curtail the slave trade (Kismayu was part of the Sultan's domain). Gordon was murdered in 1881 in Khartoum during the Mahdist revolution and, for a while, Egyptian rule there came to an end.

The reconquest of the Sudan did not take place until 1896 and was prompted by news that the French had pushed through to Fashoda from Gabon. Anxious to be in control of the sea route to India, the British Government ordered the Egyptian Army, commanded by Kitchener, to move south. Two years later Khartoum was taken after the battle of Omdurman but the campaign cost the lives of 20,000 Sudanese and, after Kitchener confronted the French at Fashoda with a vastly superior force, brought France and Britain almost to the point of war. In 1899, Sudan became an Anglo-Egyptian condominium but in 1924 as a result of the assassination of Sir Lee Stack, the Governor-General of Sudan and Commander-in-Chief of the Egyptian Army, Britain banned Egypt from any responsibility for the government of Sudan. From this time on Sudan began to take its own course into the modern world. The foundations of a modern economy were laid with the irrigation of the Gezira and the cultivation there of a viable cotton crop and the growth of education began to produce a professional class with nationalist aspirations.

The overthrow of the effete King Faruq in Egypt in 1953 led to an agreement between Egypt and Britain whereby the Sudanese would be allowed to decide their own future after a three-year transitional period of self-government. When the time came, Sudan voted to become an independent republic. The early years were clouded with an open revolt by the pagan and Christian Negroes of the south who feared domination by the essentially Arab Moslem government in Khartoum and in 1958 the Army took over. Their attempt to subdue the south by force proved disastrous and led to the flight of much of the population into the bush or over the border into neighbouring countries so, that by 1964, with no settlement in sight, the country was returned to parliamentary government. When this produced no better result power was seized by a group of young officers led by Colonel Numeiry, the present head of state. Like the previous military government, Numeiry at first attempted to subdue the south by force but eventually bowed to mounting international criticism, especially from Christian churches both within and outside Africa, and agreed to grant autonomy to southern Sudan. The reconciliation of north and south has been Numeiry's greatest achievement though the concessions he has made have not pleased some of the more radical Moslem states like Libya which constantly attempts to interfere in Sudan's affairs and to underwrite coups — none of which have so far been successful.

FACTS

The Sudan, with a population of about 15 million, is one of Africa's poorest and least developed countries. To the north and west are vast areas of desert which support little life while in the east is the semi-desert of Nubia, alongside the Red Sea. Rain hardly ever falls in these areas and when it does creates raging torrents in the wadis (dry river courses) which can cut communications for days on end. In the summer months there are frequent dust storms. The only areas which support crops of any size are the Gezira — between the Blue and White Niles south of Khartoum — and a small area south of Suakin on the Red Sea coast but for most people life centres around the date palm, camels and stock rearing. Further south, the desert

eventually gives way to the rain forest on the borders of Zaire and Uganda. Very few tarred roads exist and communication is largely over desert tracks or via the Nile steamers or the railways. But although travel can be slow and unpredictable it is more than compensated for by the incredible hospitality that is to be found everywhere — and not just from the common people but from officials, including the police too. This is something which every traveller experiences and we have had countless letters which rave on about the friendliness and welcome which is to be found in this country. Don't miss it, it's unique!

Sudan is presently engaged in one of the largest irrigation projects ever attempted in Africa centred on the vast swamp area of the Sudd. These swamps, which provide a natural habitat for large herds of buffalo, elephant and hippopotami and are essential for the cattle-rearing activities of the indigenous tribes, were first proposed as a source of water for irrigation by the British over 80 years ago but had the original plan been carried out would have resulted in the destruction of the ecology of this 6500 square km area. The new proposals, which are being undertaken jointly by the Sudanese and Egyptian governments and monitored by a United Nations ecology unit, envisage taking 20 million cubic metres of water per day from the Sudd via the Jonglai Canal. In this way it is hoped to maintain the seasonal fluctuations in the water level, while improving navigation on the White Nile and reducing the mosquito population (and therefore the incidence of malaria).

VISAS

Required by all. Nationals of South Africa are not admitted. In Cairo, visas are issued the same day, cost E£5.10 and two photos. Before you apply for a visa you must have a 'letter of recommend-

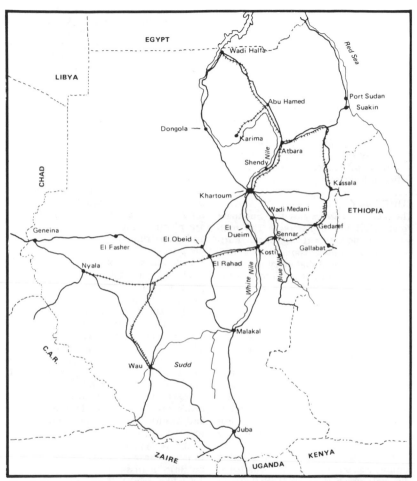

ation' from your own embassy but, other than this, there are no problems. 'Letters of recommendation' are generally put together in a few minutes and issued free of charge. The Sudanese Embassy is situated on Shari Latin America opposite the Canadian Embassy in Garden City. Don't apply for your visa in London — it will cost you £15!!

Visa extensions can be obtained from the Ministry of the Interior, Khartoum, for S£5. They take three days.

Special permits are required to travel anywhere west, south or east of Khartoum (you don't need one to take the train from Khartoum to Wadi Halfa). These are obtainable from the Ministry of the Interior in Khartoum or from the police if you enter Sudan through anywhere other than Khartoum. The permit to travel to Juba takes a 'regulation' three days to come through. Note that if you are travelling from Wau to Juba in southern Sudan it is worth calling in at police stations along the way to let them see your permit as they can be very helpful with accommodation and lifts. Very friendly and helpful people.

If you are bringing a car into Sudan and intend to drive it through to the Central African Republic, Zaire, or Kenya expect to run into a mountain of bureaucracy which can take a long time and a lot of money to sort out.

A permit is also required if you have a camera and intend to take photographs anywhere in the Sudan. Obtainable free of charge from the Tourist Office in Khartoum.

CURRENCY

The unit of currency is the Sudanese Pound (S£) = 100 piastres = 100 milliemes. Import/export of local currency is prohibited though it is (unofficially) accepted that everyone brings in some Sudanese currency from Egypt.

Exchange rate:

			(Tourist)
£1	=	S£1.10	S£1.84
US$1	=	S£0.48	S£0.80
A$1	=	S£0.55	S£0.91

There is a thriving blackmarket where the rates are: £1 = S£1.30-1.50 and US$1 = S£0.60-0.80 with the best rates being obtainable in Juba. Travellers' cheques naturally change hands for less than cash. US dollars and £ sterling are the preferred hard currencies. In Khartoum try the camera shop off United Nations Square (opposite the Khartoum Mosque) which gives US$1=S£0.60. In Juba hang around the Greek Club or try the Greek owner of the Africa Hotel who offers US$1=S£0.72 and £1= S£1.30.

Banks charge 75 piastres for every travellers cheque transaction though a smaller commission for changing cash. Currency Declaration Forms are issued on arrival so make sure you get at least one bank stamp on it before you leave. Forms are not checked thorough-

ly on leaving, especially at Wadi Halfa where it is generally chaos, so change the minimum in the banks. Sudan is an expensive country. Jeans and watches fetch good prices in Sudan if you need to supplement your funds. A US$50 cassette player will sell for US$120-140.

Airport tax for domestic flights is S£1, for international flights it is S£3.

LANGUAGES
Arabic and English.

FOOD
Local food is mainly 'fool' (a bean stew) served with bread and 'dura' (cooked maize or millet). Dates, figs and bananas are plentiful and cheap as are tomatoes and grapefruit in the south. Some sample prices:

Khartoum: tea 2 pt; coffee 33 pt; meat sandwich 9 pt; salad 5 pt; grapefruit 8 pt; guava milk shake 15 pt; 'fool' 15 pt; 'farsulia' 15 pt; meat dish 35 pt. *Wau*: 'shai laban' 2 ot; 'jabana' 5 pt; 'fool' with yogurt 10 pt; 'karkade' 5 pt; bowl of meat, lentils, 'farsulia' or an omelette 15 pt. *Juba*: tea 3 pt; 'gahwa' 5 pt; 'fool' 15 pt; 'kibla' 35 pt. If you are thinking of having a feast, a sheep will cost you S£30 or a camel S£200.

Each district has its own intoxicating drink (even Moslems like a drink now and again). They include 'duma' (a fermented concoction of honey and millet); 'aragi' (a type of whiskey made by distilling cassava — costs about 50 pt a bottle); 'marissa' (a brown and fizzy cider-like drink). If you are looking for a beer, Zairois and Kenyan brands are recommended.

ACCOMMODATION
Remember that the Sudanese people are extremely hospitable and it is very difficult to avoid being offered food and a place to sleep even in the large towns so you may find you hardly have to use this section at all. An offer of money as a contribution towards your

keep will probably be politely refused and may even offend. It is against the grain and spirit of Moslem hospitality. A thoughtful gift on the other hand goes down very well and is the least you can do. There are very few places left like the Sudan.

Atbara

The *Hotels Atbara* and *Astoria* have been recommended. They cost S£1 per person. The latter is situated about 500 metres from the railway station. If you are short of money, enquire at the Police HQ where you will be given a bed and where cheap meals, iced water and table tennis are available. Bicycles can be hired here for 35 pt/day.

El Obeid

Hotel Liban, located by the petrol station where the lorries fill up for the trip to Omdurman, costs 35 pt per night, but takes men only. *Shaharazad Hotel* costs 65 pt per person. *Hotel John* costs S£1.50 for a good room with fan.

Don't miss the 'fool' (bean) place where everyone seems to go in the evening on the north side of the souk. Entertainment plus 'fool' for 6 pt. The souk itself is also well worth a visit.

Juba

Hotel Africa costs 82½ pt for a bed or 30 pt on the floor. Clean and popular with travellers, it serves good meals for 50 pt but it is not the cheapest place to eat. If you are short of money you can sleep on the floor of the Police Station at Malakia two miles from the town centre. If you stay at the latter you will be regaled with a dawn bugle call — useful if you want to be in time for that lift.

For food, the cheapest place is the *People's Restaurant* where you can get a meal for 20 pt. Otherwise you can eat at the *Hotel Africa* or the *Greek Club*. A meal at the latter costs between 55 and 80 pt depending on what you have.

On arrival in Juba you must register with the police — costs 10 pt for a revenue stamp. If you are heading for Zaire (not always possible), Uganda or Kenya, you must obtain an exit permit before setting off. These are obtainable from the Immigration Department (in the same buildings as the police station) for 25 pt. It is a good idea to get this permit before looking for a lift.

Malakia, two miles from Juba town centre, is where much of the actual life of Juba seems to take place. It is a traditional village with a huge market. Good handicrafts are available here especially from the Dinka tribespeople.

Juba is full of international aid agencies which are worth checking out if you are heading for Uganda or Kenya. It is sometimes possible to get free lifts. If you have to hang around in Juba for a while until your lift south is ready to go, it's a good idea to spend the time visiting the nearby villages of Yei, Torit or Gilo. The latter, 50 km from the Ugandan border in the Imetong Mountains at 2000 metres, is highly recommended. It used to be a hill station during British colonial days. It also has the added attraction that there are no mosquitos or tsetse flies, and it's cool. Stay at the *Gilo Guest House* there which, although it was looted during the civil war, still retains a lot of charm. During the wet season the road there is often impassable (like many others in this area).

If you need some cash US dollars you can get them at the airport by buying something at the duty free shop with a travellers' cheque and getting the change in cash.

Kapoeta

Free accommodation at the police check post.

Kassala

Bahrain Hotel costs 50 pt per night. The

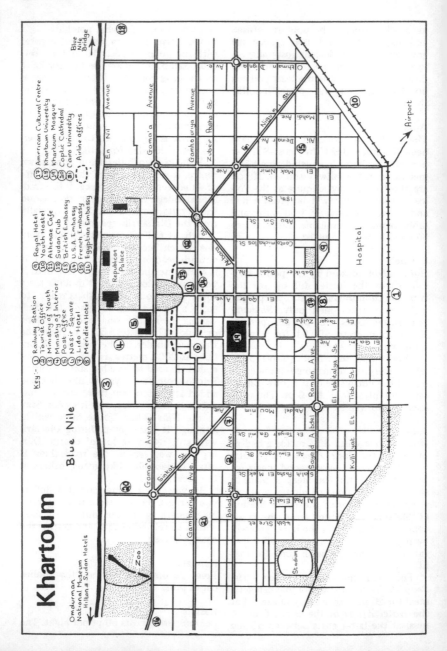

Khartoum

Key:-
1. Railway Station
2. Tourist Office
3. Ministry of Youth
4. Ministry of Interior
5. Post Office
6. Nasir Square
7. Lido Hotel
8. Meridien Hotel

9. Royal Hotel
10. Youth Hostel
11. Athenae Cafe
12. Sudan Club
13. British Embassy
14. U.S.A. Embassy
15. French Embassy
16. Egyptian Embassy

17. American Cultural Centre
18. Khartoum University
19. Khartoum Mosque
20. Coptic Cathedral
21. Cairo University
   Airline offices

El Watania Hotel (near the market and Shell garage), *Hotel Shark* (near the Ethiopian Consulate), the *Hotel Abu-Tayara* and the *Hotel Africa* all cost S£1 per night. They're all very much of a similar standard. There is also a *Youth Hostel*, situated beside the railway tracks about a km from the station, costs 50 pt per night.

Khartoum

The *Youth Hostel* costs 50 pt per night and is the cheapest place in Khartoum. It's open all day, is clean, has cold showers and is easy-going — but watch your gear. No food available. *Hotel Royal* costs 70 pt per night, rooms have fans and showers. Friendly place and popular with travellers. *El Nahrein Hotel*, El Nahrein Street, costs 80 pt per night. *Port Sudan Hotel*, Killiyet At Tibb Street, five minutes from the station, is cheap, airy and has comfortable rooms. *Asia Hotel*, near the bus station, costs S£4/double room. *Hotel Lido* costs S£4.70/double room.

Others which have been recommended include the *El Khalil Hotel* (opposite the bus station). It's cheap, clean and a good place to meet students. *Hotel Arkwett*, near the Hotel Meridien, is also cheap.

For food try the cafe downhill from the *Juice Shop*, near the Youth Hostel and hospital (excellent 'fool' and yogurt), the police canteen opposite the Youth Hostel, the *El Khalil Hotel* or the snack bar across from the American Embassy. A popular meeting place is the *Athenae Cafe* in the little square behind the British Embassy. Many travellers go there. If you'd like a game of bridge, snooker or squash or a swim or just a glimpse of how the other half live, try that bastion of the British Empire, the Sudan Club. A week's temporary membership costs S£2.50 per person. It's possible to meet friendly VSOs here who might put you on to friends up-country. There are free films at the American Cultural Centre.

It's quite easy to hitch to Khartoum and the person who gives you a lift will probably take you to your destination. Otherwise shared Toyota taxis cost 6 pt for any distance along their route. Buses for Omdurman leave from Sinkat Street and cost 5 pt. There are also shared taxis from United Nations Square to Omdurman for 6 pt. The journey to Omdurman takes 10 minutes. If you're staying in Omdurman try the *Hotel Abir* next to the post office. Costs 60 pt for a bed in a double room. Many of the rooms have fans, balconies and showers (cold water only). Don't miss the Dervish dancing every Friday afternoon in Omdurman.

Nyala

Hotel Darfur costs 25 pt per night, cold showers and interesting toilets. The Souk in this interesting town is well worth a visit.

Port Sudan

An expensive town which is also very crowded at the height of the pilgrimage season to Mecca (the last boats leave in November). The cheapest places are the *Hotel Sinkat*, *Hotel Africa* and the *Hotel Olympia Park* which all cost S£1 per night for a single room.

The Red Sea Club, on the seaward end of the main street, costs 25 pt per day for temporary membership and has a swimming pool, bar and incredibly torn snooker table. The Tourist Office here is incredibly helpful and will even issue student concession rail tickets. The coral reefs are worth a visit here, if only to see the variety of fish which live amongst them.

Suakin

This used to be the old Red Sea port of Sudan. It was abandoned by the British in the 1930s and is full of decaying old coral houses. Many people find it a fascinating place to visit. Hardly anyone comes here anymore. The *Government Rest House* costs S£1 per night but you can get cheaper places by asking around.

Torit

Free huts are available near the police station or you could try the Norwegian Church Relief (!) organisation who have put travellers up in the past.

Wadi Halfa

If you're only staying overnight you can sleep at the police station free of charge. Otherwise there's a very basic hotel opposite the railway station for 25 pt per night. Cold showers and tea and 'fool' are also available. There is a bank here.

Wau

Sleep free in the yard of the police station and meet some interesting 'criminals' but the mosquitoes are bad and there's no water. The Catholic mission also sometimes offers a free place to stay. Otherwise the cheapest place is the *Youth Hostel* which costs 30 pt per night if you have an International YH Card. If you haven't got one of these it tends to cost a lot more. No meals available. Hotel accommodation is somewhat expensive. *El Nilein Hotel* costs S£1.50 per bed in a room with four beds and the *Riverside Hotel* costs S£1.98.

The best place to eat is the *Unity Restaurant*. 'Jo Souk' at the far end of town has some excellent wooden handicrafts. Lifts from here are arranged in the shop at the side of the Catholic mission but you can also wait outside the police station as all trucks have to register here before leaving. It's also worth enquiring at UNICEF, FAO, government departments and the Sudanese Council of Churches for the occasional free lift.

Wadi Medani

Hotel Gezira costs S£2 a double room.

Yei

The Agricultural Research Station offers free places to stay.

TRANSPORT

Whichever route you take through Sudan you'll end up having used an interesting combination of trucks, riverboats, trains, international aid agency jeeps, mail vans and perhaps even the occasional free flight in a light aircraft. Apart from flights, all travel is slow and many routes are impassable in the rainy season from June to September so allow plenty of time to get through this country. In the south it can take up to a week to find a truck or jeep going in the direction you want to go, especially from Wau to Juba and from Juba south to either Uganda or Kenya. In the north there are usually daily connections between the major centres. Remember that to travel anywhere west, south or east of Khartoum you need a special permit either from the Ministry of the Interior in Khartoum or from the local police if you entered Sudan other than along the Wadi Halfa-Khartoum route. These permits are just a formality and you won't experience any difficulty in getting them, but they do take, on average, three days to come through, so plan ahead.

There are very few metalled roads (Khartoum-Wadi Medani being one). Most 'roads' are just a set of tyre tracks in the sand or a dirt track through the forest. Trucks frequently get bogged down in sand/dust (or mud in the south) and everyone has to get off and start digging. This can be immense fun and an excellent way of getting to know local travelling companions. You certainly won't be lacking for stories to tell when you get home! Many roads in the south are closed for around nine months of the year as they get washed out in the rains so if you want to go to Juba by road the best time to travel is between February and April (the Kosti-Juba road is closed during the rest of the year). Protect yourself from the sun when travelling on the top of trucks otherwise you may end up with sunstroke. In the desert, you are strongly advised to take water with you otherwise you will end up having to rely on water holes and will probably come down with hepatitis or dysentery later on. Free lifts are a rarity but rates are more or less standardised and you are unlikely to be overcharged. It is sometimes possible to travel in the cab of the truck but this generally costs twice as much as on the top. Arrange lifts before departure — the day before in the north; whenever you can in the south. As in most other African countries, trucks leave either from the market place or truck park in the early mornings. Note that in Khartoum there are two truck parks — one in Khartoum North and the other in Omdurman. Trucks heading west generally depart from Omdurman.

Routes through the Sudan
Even the most direct route from north to south from Wadi Halfa to Kosti will take you at least 15 days (including the three days it takes to get the travel permit for the Khartoum-Juba trip) *if* you make all the connections. If you just miss the fortnightly river steamer connection at Kosti during the nine months of the year when the road from Kosti to Juba is closed it could take you a month. If you are short of time (or money) you may well have to take a flight over part of the route if you miss the steamer connection. While this route is interesting it's possibly not the *most* interesting and many travellers with plenty of time at their disposal prefer to take the more roundabout route from

Khartoum to Juba via either Nyala or Wau using a combination of train and truck. If you're very lucky this might take you three weeks but if you have to hang around waiting for lifts, it could well take at least a month. This latter route is not possible during the wet season as the roads between Nyala/Wau and Juba get washed out. The overland route from Juba to Kenya takes about four days at the best of times though you should allow a week. In addition you may have to wait around in Juba/Torit/Kapoeta for at least a week before you find a lift. The alternative is to fly.

The direct route Wadi Halfa-Khartoum-Kosti-Juba
Aswan-Wadi Halfa Lake Nasser Steamer see 'Egypt' chapter for further details.
Wadi Halfa-Khartoum   Train. From Wadi Halfa the trains connect with the Lake Nasser steamers but the exact departure time varies (though they do wait for the steamer to empty). When it goes you get two minutes warning. From Khartoum the train departs at 6.45 am on Thursdays and Sundays. It's very crowded and dusty so expect to arrive looking like a piece of desert and if you are travelling in either fourth or third class take something to sit on — slatted wood benches. Many people travel on the roof. Steam engine enthusiasts can ride on the footplate till their teeth rattle out. Food is available at all the stations from Abu Hamed to Khartoum. Fares are — fourth class: S£3.18, third class: S£5.54, second class is approximately twice the third class fare and first class about four times the third class fare.

Student reductions (with an International Card or letter from your embassy) of about 50% are available on the above fares. Authorisation for the reduction is obtained from the Ministry of Youth in Khartoum. There is no place in Wadi

Halfa, however, to get authorisation for the reduction. Some travellers have got around this by getting on without a ticket and giving their passport to the ticket inspector when he comes around. On arrival in Khartoum they then go to the Ministry of Youth for authorisation, buy a reduced price ticket for the journey and collect their passport. Others have paid the full fare from Wadi Halfa then, on arrival in Khartoum, gone to the Ministry of Youth and got authorisation for free tickets as far as Wau, Nyala or Juba on the strength of having paid full fare on the previous journey. The latest rumour, however, is that this somewhat more ingenious method is no longer possible. The journey from Wadi Halfa to Khartoum takes about 35 hours if there are no breakdowns.

If you are interested in visiting the antiquities between Dongola and Abu Hamed along this route you have to take a truck from Wadi Halfa to Dongola (rough as hell) or get off the train at Abu Hamed and take the branch line to Karima. From Karima there is a Nile steamer to Dongola. There are regular trucks between Dongola and Omdurman.

If you would like to visit Port Sudan, Suakin or Kassala, get off the train at Atbara. From here there are trains to both Port Sudan and Kassala. Student reductions are available from the Area Controller's office in the station. Alternatively, take a truck from Atbara to either Port Sudan or Kassala. The former costs S£2 and the latter S£1. Suakin to Kassala costs S£2 and takes about two days. Kassala to Khartoum costs S£1.25 and takes about 18 hours. There is also a once weekly train in either direction between Kassala and Khartoum which departs Khartoum at 1.30 pm on Tuesdays. If you are entitled to a student concession, it is slightly cheaper than the truck fare. There is also a bus from Khartoum to Kassala which is much quicker than the trucks but costs

S£2.50. Departs from the truck park in Khartoum North.

Khartoum-Kosti Train, costs S£1.44 in third class with student concession. Remember that you need the travel permit from the Ministry of the Interior before applying for student concession authorisation from the Ministry of Youth. In Kosti, student concessions are available from the Area Controller's office across the street from the station. The journey takes about 12 hours. You can also do this journey in stages by bus or truck from Khartoum to Wadi Medani and from there to Kosti by truck.

Kosti-Juba Nile River Steamer, this 'steamer' is half a dozen old barges roped together and pushed by a paddle steamer. Fortnightly service in either direction departing Kosti at about 10 am on Wednesdays and Juba at about 5 am on Fridays. The journey upstream takes nine days on average but can take 11 depending on the strength of the current and eight days downstream. The fares are — third class: S£10.805, second class (cabin with bunks): S£28.770, first class (own cabin): S£43.170.

Student concessions of 50% are available on the above fares. Authorisation from the Ministry of Youth in Khartoum or from the Ministry of Information in Juba. Again, remember that you need a travel permit from the Ministry of the Interior in Khartoum or from the Ministry of Information in Juba before applying for student concession authorisation. You're advised to take your own food on this boat trip and, if possible, a small stove to cook it on. This is what all the locals do. If you have no stove, make friends with those who have on the boat. The last place to stock up on food is Malakal. A mosquito net wouldn't go amiss either. Nor would some grass — it's a long, slow journey! There is plenty of wild life to be seen (the river goes through the Sudd swamps) and tribal villages along the way. The boat is often very crowded.

If you are short of time or you have missed the boat connection at Kosti there are flights between Khartoum and Juba. It's apparently possible to qualify for a 50% student reduction (with an International Card) plus a 50% youth fare reduction (if you are 26 years old or under) on the remainder making this fare ¼ of the usual amount. We have only ever heard from one traveller who accomplished this amazing double reduction so though it's 'possible' we suggest you count on 50% reduction.

Khartoum-Juba via Nyala or Wau

Khartoum-Nyala Nyala is the railhead in Darfur Province. This is the place you pass through on your way to the Central African Republic (and Chad if the civil war ever ends there). For its own sake travellers come here to explore Jebel Marra, Sudan's second highest mountain. You can either get here direct by train from Khartoum or by truck. If coming by truck you pick up lifts in Omdurman. Omdurman to El Obeid costs S£4 and takes two days — a very rough journey. From El Obeid to Nyala costs S£7 and takes four to five days.

In Nyala get a truck from the souk to Nyertete at the base of Jebel Marra (over 3000 metres). Costs S£2 and takes eight hours. The last four hours of the journey are incredibly rough! In Nyertete you can buy a donkey for around S£18 and wander around the mountains. Those who have done this trip rave on about the most incredible hospitality they have been offered everywhere. People virtually drag you into their houses and insist you eat with them. Finding your way is no problem — people you meet along the way will put you right or go out of their way to put you on the right track and then insist that you eat with them. You can only buy food in the souks — mangoes, grapefruit and oranges are grown everywhere and cost virtually nothing if people don't actually give them to you.

Water is available everywhere in the mountains and incredible views. You can re-sell your donkey in Nyala usually for the same price you paid for it.

Khartoum-Wau Train. Same railway line as the above as far as Babanusa where you must change for the connection to Wau. The change can take an hour or a day — it depends what delays have been experienced further down the line. Whatever time of year you go this is a very slow train with many long inexplicable delays and breakdowns. It also often arrives at the station in Khartoum for the outward journey packed out so don't count on getting a seat immediately. The journey takes five days on average and costs S£3.23 with student concession in third class. Most of the time you spend in relative luxury on the roof or in the buffet car.

Wau-Juba Two road routes are possible (no trains):

(a) Wau-Rumbek-Juba. This is the shorter but rougher road which passes through Dinka country. The total cost of lifts along this route works out about S£6. The route is impassable during the wet season.

(b) Wau-Tambura-Yambio-Maridi-Juba. The longer though better of the two possible routes. It's little used though open during the wet season (with difficulty). There are amazing views to be had along the Maridi-Yei-Juba section of the Congo and Nile basins. The total cost of lifts along this route works out at about S£8-10.

Which route you take will depend largely on what season it is and how long it takes you to find a lift. A week's wait in Wau for a lift along the southern route is not unusual with similar waits at other places along the way unless you get a lift right through to Juba. For lifts first try the various international agencies like UNICEF, FAO, etc and the government department and Sudanese Council of Churches. It's sometimes possible to get free lifts to Juba. If no luck, there is a mail truck which leaves Wau for Juba every Monday and costs S£6 for the three to five day journey. Competition for a place can sometimes be steep. Otherwise there are quite a few commercial trucks which cover the route. Some other prices include: Yambio-Maridi for S£1.50, Nzara-Yambio for S£0.30 by Toyoto cab.

Juba-Uganda/Kenya You need an exit stamp and a 'letter of exit' from the Sudanese police to do this journey. The best road south from Juba goes through Nimule into Uganda and this is the best route preferred by truckies but the route can be closed for long periods because of repeated emergencies in Uganda. Don't count on it. The other route goes direct into Kenya from Juba via Torit, Kapoeta, Lokichoggio and Lodwar and is the one you will probably have to use. The road as such ends in Kapoeta. After that it is a track through the bush across deep river beds avoiding fallen trees, treacherous patches of mud and overhanging thorn trees (if you're lucky). The route is out of the question during the rainy season and for a while after there's very little traffic. Waiting for rides in Juba, Torit and Kapoeta often takes up more time than the journey itself which can be done in three or four days (Kapoeta-Kitale). Check out with international aid agencies or missions·to see if they are going that way (they often go to Kenya to pick up various supplies). Commerical truck companies which cover this route include 'Interfreight' and 'Sharaf Sudfreight'. Before setting out for Kapoeta you need a travel permit from the Ministry of Immigration in Juba — issued free of charge. Trucks leave Juba daily for Torit from the Nile Bridge which is 45-60 minutes walk from the centre of town. Costs S£1. The Kapoeta customs/police are not interested in the Currency Declaration Form.

If you don't want to spend two weeks doing this leg of the journey then you will have to fly. Before you buy a ticket on a commercial airline it is worth checking out with the various international aid and missions planes which fly to Nairobi regularly for supplies (they go there empty and come back full). Try ACROSS (Aid Committee for the Rehabilitation of Southern Sudan) and·ask for 'Jim' — the pilot. He will take you to Nairobi free but expect a 'donation'. Otherwise the commercial airlines fly regularly to Nairobi from Juba. The fare is S£40.40 (US$105) or S£30.55 with a student reduction. If you want the student reduction you have to buy your ticket in Khartoum. It is apparently not possible to get it in Juba. In addition to the national airlines operating between Juba and Nairobi there is a private Nairobi based charter company called 'Sunbird' which flies twice weekly in either direction between Juba and Nairobi and costs US$105 (no reductions available).

OTHER TRANSPORT INFORMATION
Sudan-Ethiopia
The borders with Ethiopia are presently closed and overland entry not possible. The only way to get in is to fly from Khartoum to Addis Ababa.

Sudan-Saudi Arabia
You need an 'onward ticket' before a Saudi visa will be issued. The air fares tend to be cheaper than the boat fares if you qualify for the 50% Youth Fare reduction. Otherwise there is the following boat operated by the Mohamed Sadaka Establishment. The route is Jeddah-Port Sudan and the Ship is the *Saudi Golden Arrow*. It is a weekly service, minimum fare (third class) costs 270 Saudi Riyals (about US$80). The ship is a car ferry.

OTHER INFORMATION
Medical The Civil Hospital in Khartoum

is free and very good. Drugs are free too (prescribed ones). If you go to a private clinic a consultation will cost you S£1.

Jobs Teaching jobs are available in secondary schools. Usually 15 hours per week in 40 minute classes. Accommodation usually provided or, if not, allowed for in the wages which are about S£1000 per year or S£80 per month. Contact the Ministry of Education if interested. They demand proof of degree before giving you a job.

Grass Known locally as 'bango'. It grows abundantly in the south and is cheap. A half kilo costs S£4-5 in Wau; S£6-10 in Nyala (better quality). In Khartoum this quantity will cost you S£35-50. Don't get caught!

Camping gas Gas cartridges for camping stoves can be bought from the duty free shop at Khartoum airport. Otherwise impossible to find.

Swaziland

Like Lesotho, Swaziland had its origins in the Zulu militancy of the early years of the 19th century. In both places, unusually able chiefs were able to merge refugees from the Zulu wars with their own people into new nations which were able to withstand Zulu pressure. In Swaziland's case, the chief was Sobhuza from whom the present ruler, King Sobhuza II is descended. Following the Boer War, at the turn of the century, when the terms of Union were being argued out between the political leaders of Cape Colony, Natal, the Orange Free State and the Transvaal, the Cape failed to persuade the rest to adopt its tradition of voting rights for all races subect to income and property qualifications. One consequence of this was that the three British Protectorates of Basutoland (now Lesotho), Bechuanaland (now Botswana) and Swaziland remained outside the Union of South Africa and hence eventually became independent countries.

Swaziland became independent in 1967 but, like Lesotho, it remains very much an economic hostage of South Africa. The ruler, King Sobhuza II, started out as a constitutional monarch but in 1973 dissolved parliament and banned all political parties following an overwhelming victory by the party of his Prime Minister, Prince Makhosini, at the 1972 elections. The country is now governed by ethnic assemblies where the affairs of state are decided in the traditional manner in the Royal Cattle Kraal. The king and his ministers sit, in traditional dress, on the ground in the Kraal facing the sacred hills across the valley while the audience, regardless of rank, sit in front of the king while measures are debated and the king issues decrees. Critics of this ancient form of government are answered with the claim that direct rule by the monarchy has resulted in Swaziland being one of Africa's most

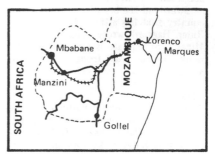

stable states. While this is undoubtedly true, there have been indications of student and labour unrest in recent years. The revolutionary government in Mozambique has condemned the Swazi system which it regards as western-orientated and capitalist based and there was a time when tension was running high between the two countries. This seriously worried the Swazi elite since, in order to maintain some degree of independence from South Africa, they need the co-operation of Mozambique. The railway line from Mbabane, the capital, to Maputo in Mozambique carries a large proportion of Swaziland's exports to the outside world. The Swazis also depend on access to the port facilities in Maputo.

Although the smallest of the former ex-High Commission Territories, Swaziland is the richest and is being developed with skill. The Japanese built the railway line from Mbabane to Maputo in 1964 to carry the iron ore mined in Swaziland — the line carries 80% of the country's exports. Pineapple orchards have been established and large areas irrigated for the cultivation of citrus fruits, rice, sugar cane and bananas. The South African company of De Beers discovered diamonds there in the early '70s and have pumped a large amount of capital into prospecting for them. Much of the best farming land is owned by an influential minority of white South Africans — 9000 compared with half a million Swazis.

Swaziland is a beautiful mountainous country that has attracted people since Rider Haggard wrote *King Solomon's Mines*. The climate is tropical and the rainy season lasts from October to March.

VISAS
Required by all except nationals of the Commonwealth countries, Belgium, Denmark, Finland, Iceland, Irish Republic, Israel, Italy, Luxembourg, Nether-lands, Norway, Portugal, South Africa, Sweden and the USA.

If you intend to stay there for more than two months you have to get a Temporary Residence Permit from the Chief Immigration Officer, Box 372, Mbabane.

CURRENCY
The unit of currency is the Lilangeni = 100 .cents. Import of local currency is allowed up to 50 Lilangeni. Export is limited to 20 Lilangeni. The exchange rate is on a par with the South African Rand. South African Rand are legal tender in Swaziland. Swaziland is a cheaper place than South Africa but still relatively expensive.

LANGUAGES
English and Swazi.

ACCOMMODATION
Manzini
Paradise Camp Site is just outside town on the main road to Mbabane. Costs Rand 1.

Mbabane
A small, pleasant city though very South African-influenced. South Africans come here at weekends to see the films banned by their own censors and to visit the brothels and gambling casino at the Holiday Inn. Manzini gets invaded in the same way for the same reasons. Because of this, all hotel accommodation is geared to SA weekenders and it's impossible to find anywhere cheap to stay unless someone from the Peace Corps, for instance, offers to put you up. If you have a tent, go to the *Timbali Caravan Camp*, 11 km out of Mbabane near the Holiday Inn. Costs Rand 1 per tent but they also have rondavels which cost Rand 5/night and sleep two people (two beds). For food, the *Holiday Inn* is recommended for huge breakfasts which cost Rand 2. They are available up to 10 am.

The Swazi Market is well worth a visit and has lots of interesting stuff for sale — mats, baskets, etc. The Tourist Office, opposite the Tavern Hotel, gives out a free booklet which is worth getting hold of. Plenty of good suggestions for walks, things to see, hot springs, waterfalls, etc.

TRANSPORT

The only regular bus service is between Mbabane and Manzini. There are occasional buses between Mbabane and the Mlilwane Game Sanctuary but don't count on the latter. Hitching is very good between Mbabane and Manzini and between Mbabane and the nearest South African town of Carolina. Note that many of the 'frontiers' with South Africa are non-existent in the sense that there are no customs/police posts on the Swazi side. The South Africans, on the other hand, have a security check at every crossing point where you'll be held up while they check to see if you're a prohibited person. The crossing point at Lavumisa on the Zululand (Natal) frontier has no Swazi checkpoint and there's very little truck traffic along this route. On the other hand, when a truck comes along, they'll stop and give you a lift and try to fix you up with another when they drop you — very friendly people. As mentioned above, there is a railway line between Mbabane and Maputo but it carries freight only. If you're heading for Maputo, speak with the driver or the guard — some people have managed to get lifts.

OTHER INFORMATION

Mlilwane Game Sanctuary Admission costs Rand 1 but you don't really see much game without a guide, who costs Rand 2 per hour to hire. It's a beautiful, peaceful place and well worth visiting. Ask around in Mbabane among holiday-makers for a ride there as, although there are occasional buses, they're unrel-

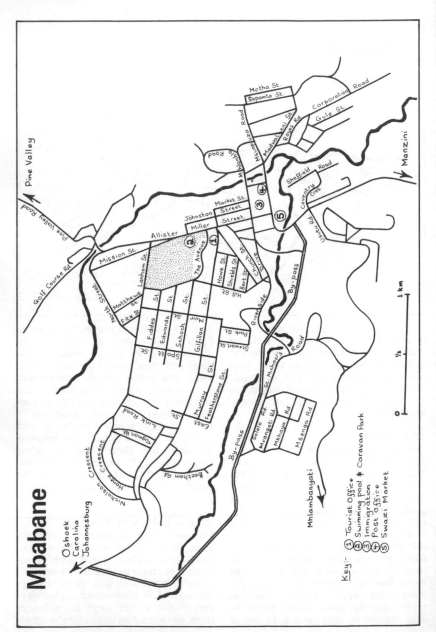

Mbabane

Oshoek
Carolina
Johannesburg

Pine Valley

Manzini

Golf Course Rd

Pine Valley Road

Mission St.

North Street

Nicholson Crescent

Carolina Crescent

Honey Crescent

Beetham Rd

Link Road

Tugman Rd

Matthews St.

Fitz St.

Fiddes St.

Edwards St.

Schoch St.

Gilfillan St.

Spofforth St.

Murray St.

Featherstone St.

East St.

St. Michael's Road

By-pass

Mlhambangati

Selelo Rd.

Myangati Rd.

Mkhaya Rd.

Msenga Rd.

Allister

Lanham St.

The Avenue

Market St. Street

Johnston Street

Miller Street

Howe St.

Shields St.

Bert Street

Hill St.

Muir St.

Park St.

Stewart St.

River Side

Church St.

By-pass

Uswini Road

Mhlonho Road

Msunduza Road

Motha St.

Sepamta St.

Rones Rd.

Madwaleni St.

Corporation Road

Gule St.

Sheffield Road

Coventry Cres.

0   ½   1 km

Key:-
① Tourist Office
② Swimming pool
③ Immigration
④ Caravan Park
⑤ Post Office
⑥ Swazi Market

iable. There is a camp site in the sanctuary but you should take food with you as the camp shop stocks very little. There's plenty of wood around for fires or you can buy charcoal for 60 cents/bag.

Pigg's Peak This is another trip which the Tourist Office recommends. It's nothing special when you get there but the journey takes you through some amazing countryside.

Small Enterprises Development This is an interesting collection of projects designed to utilise local raw materials and industrial by-products with the maximum use of local labour and resources.

It's a kind of 'appropriate technology' development. The one you might be most interested in as a traveller is the handicrafts unit in Mbabane but all are open to visitors and, if you're interested, they'll arrange a free guided tour for you. Further information from SEDCO and SEPO, PO Box 451, Mbabane (tel 2141).

Dope Instead of getting busted in the Republic, where the penalties are as draconian as the apartheid laws, save it till you get here. An 'arm' (that's what it looks like!) costs Rand 5. Easy to locate and the police turn a blind eye.

Tanzania

Tanzania came into existence as a result of political union between mainland Tanganyika and the offshore islands of Zanzibar and Pemba. The mainland became a German colony in the late 19th century but after WW I was administered by the British, first under a League of Nations mandate and then under a United Nations mandate, until independence in 1962. Zanzibar, which was ruled by sultans of Omani extraction and was once the centre of the East African slave trade, became a British colony, again in the late 19th century, and was granted independence in 1963. A year after independence the Sultan of Zanzibar was deposed and soon after this the union with Tanganyika arranged. The country is a one-party state headed by Julius Nyerere — the president since independence and undoubtedly one of Africa's most sincere and inspiring leaders. His

popularity was confirmed in the presidential elections of 1975 with a 92% vote in his favour despite an honest presentation of the hardships and difficulties which lay ahead instead of a welter of rash promises which couldn't be fulfilled such as is heard from most politicians.

Nyerere is perhaps known for his individual brand of socialism based on the Ujamaa village — collective agricultural villages run along traditional African communal lines and incorporating the basic elements of African family life. They were intended to be socialist organisations created by the people and governed by those who lived and worked in them. Basic goods and tools were to be held in common and shared among members while each individual had the obligation to work on the land. Nyerere's proposals for education were seen as an essential part of this scheme and were designed to foster and encourage constructive attitudes to co-operative endeavour, to stress the concepts of social equality and responsibility for service and to counter the temptation among educated to intellectual arrogance towards those whose abilities were non-academic. Nyerere also sought to ensure that those in political power did not develop into an exploitative class through stipulating that all government ministers and others in powerful positions in the national party (and their wives) had also to be farmers or workers and could not hold shares or be directors in any company, were not allowed to receive more than one salary and were prohibited from owning houses for rent. Obviously, all has not been plain sailing and opposition sometimes surfaces, usually from the wealthy or from those in power, yet the country remains one of the most politically honest in the world.

A number of false starts were made with the Ujamaa scheme such as encouraging progressive farmers to expand in the hope that other peasants would follow their lead, but this had little impact on rural poverty and resulted only in producing a few rich farmers. This was abandoned and the government took upon itself the tasks of planning, organising and resettling peasants into well-planned villages with the object of modernising and monetising the agricultural sector of the economy. The settlement schemes were well provided with all the necessary requirements for healthy living and modern husbandry such as clean water supplies, rural health schemes and educational facilities as well as fertilisers, high-yielding seeds, and where possible, irrigation. Again, this failed. Many peasants were hostile to what they regarded as compulsory resettlement and the lack of consultation in the decision-making process and the scheme proved far too expensive for a poor country like Tanzania to sustain (Tanzania is one of the world's 25 poorest countries). Prior to independence, Tanzania's economy was one of subsistence with only sisal and groundnuts of any export significance. 95% of the 4½ million hectares under cultivation were worked by hand tools with only 5% under tractor or animal-drawn mechanisation. Droughts, poor harvests and massive increases in the price of oil have also had a devastating effect on the country throughout the '70s.

Following the failure of the above attempts a new direction was embarked on which involved persuading peasants to amalgamate their smallholdings into communally-owned large-scale farms with economic incentives and handing over the functions of planning, decision making and implementation to the peasants right from the start. Thus the emphasis was shifted onto self-reliance where the benefits enjoyed by an Ujamaa settlement were a direct reflection of the dedication of its individual members. This scheme has been quite successful, despite its critics, and agricultural production on Ujamaa farms is well above the national average. Indeed the scheme was so successful that several years later the government adopted a policy of compulsory villagisation of the entire rural area of the country since only by doing this and so boosting agricultural output could the country avoid building up a massive foreign debt. By 1977 this process had been completed though not all of the villages had adopted Ujamaa in the strict sense of the word.

Tanzania has been foremost in supporting the southern African liberation movements, especially those which led to the independence of Mozambique and Zimbabwe. Nyerere, along with the other so-called Front Line Presidents of Botswana, Zambia and Mozambique, played a large part in gradually forcing the Smith regime in Rhodesia to accept the inevitable and concede a black majority government in that country. His influence on the Zimbabwean guerilla leaders, Nkomo and Mugabe, has also been considerable and has doubtless contributed to their moderation in dealing with the white population now that independence has been achieved in that

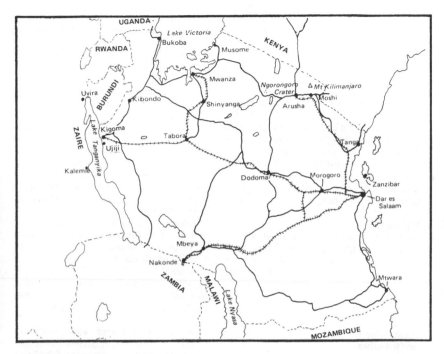

country. Tanzania maintains excellent relations with the Chinese People's Republic and it was they who financed and built the TANZAM railway from Dar es Salaam to Kapiri Mposhi in Zambia. This railway was of vital importance to Zambia during the years of armed struggle in Zimbabwe.

The most dramatic development involving Tanzania was the invasion of Uganda by the Tanzanian army and the ousting of Idi Amin — an event which was greeted with almost universal applause. The Tanzanian action was prompted by an early Ugandan invasion of the Kagera district of Tanzania west of Lake Victoria and the bombing of the ports of Bukoba and Mwanza. Though it took several weeks to rout the remnants of Amin's army which gradually retreated further and further north, the extent of Amin's unpopular-

ity in the country became clear with the wholesale desertions among his troops. Amin now lives in exile in Saudi Arabia, after a spell in Libya, courtesy of Gaddafi, who supplied the bulk of the hardware for Amin's army. Administration of Uganda has been handed over to a civilian government and elections are planned for later this year (1980). 10,000 Tanzanian troops still remain inside Uganda where they are helping to train a new Ugandan army and helping to maintain law and order. Though Nyerere has been criticised for this by neighbouring Kenya, his stated intention is to see a civilian government elected there and to withdraw his troops as soon as is practicable.

FACTS

Because of the large variation in altitude the climate ranges from the languorous tropical heat of the coastal area to the cool of the highlands. The long rainy season is between April and May with another, shorter, season between November and December. The best time to visit the National Parks of Arusha, Lake Manyara, Ngorogoro, Serengeti and Tarangire is between January and March and between June and October. As for the National Parks of Mikumi and Ruaha, the best time is between July and November. Mt Kilimanjaro can be climbed in almost any month except during the long rainy season but the best months are January, February, September and October.

VISAS

Required by all except nationals of the Commonwealth countries, Denmark, Finalnd, Irish Republic, Norway and Sweden. Nationals of South Africa are not admitted. South African stamps in your passport can create a lot of hassle on the border and may result in your being refused entry. If you are one of those who need a visa you can turn up on the Rwanda/Tanzania border without one when you will be given three to seven days to get to Mwanza on Lake Victoria where you can buy a visa. All visitors have to get a 'Visitor's Pass' which is issued free at the border. If you think you might have trouble getting in (eg if you have South African stamps in your passport) get hold of one of these 'Visitor's Passes' at a Tanzanian Embassy before arriving at the border.

The border between Kenya and Tanzania is officially closed and you cannot cross it without special permission. If coming from Kenya you must get this from the Tanzanian High Commission in Nairobi. If going from Tanzania to Kenya permission has to be obtained from the Ministry of Home Affairs near the UMCA in Dar es Salaam (it's no longer possible to get it in Moshi). You have to present this document to the Chief of Police in Arusha who will then issue you

with another form which allows you to cross the border at Namanga. Getting permission to cross the border is more or less just a formality these days but if coming from Kenya you may have to shell out up to Sh 100 in back handers to the border guards. On the other hand we have had several letters from travellers who managed to cross at border points other than Namanga (eg on the main road from Kisumu to Mwanza) without having got permission and encountered very little hassle. Negotiations are in progress between the two countries with a view to normalising relations between them but nothing has been settled yet.

Customs officials on the border may well ask you for proof that you intend to leave the country (eg an 'onward ticket') or demand to see at least the equivalent of Sh 5000 (US$760) in hard currency or travellers cheques. We did, however, hear from someone who had neither and they let him in anyway.

Some useful Embassy addresses: (All in Dar es Salaam) — Burundi: Lugalo Road (tel 29281); Rwanda: 32 Upanga Road (tel 237110; Sudan: Albarakat Building, 64 Upanga Road (tel 22786); Zaire: 438 Malik Road (tel 24181).

Burundi Visas At the Embassy in Dar es Salaam these cost Sh 50 and take 24 hours to issue. They allow for a stay of 14 days.
Zaire Visas Note that the Zaire Embassy demands a letter of recommendation from your own embassy before they will issue a visa. If you are British and haven't got hold of a Zairois visa elsewhere this is bad news as the British High Commission in Dar flatly refuse to provide you with one of these and will refuse to co-operate even if you get the Zairois Embassy to ring them up. Why this should be so we haven't a clue — you don't get this trouble at other British embassies/high commissions. Maybe

a few suitably sardonic letters to the British Foreign Office are called for.

CURRENCY

The unit of currency is the Tanzanian Shilling = 100 cents. Import/Export of local currency is prohibited though, in practice, up to Sh 100 seems to be acceptable if coming from either Kenya or Uganda.

Exchange rate:

£1	=	Sh 18.85
US$1	=	Sh 8.20
A$1	=	Sh 9.45

There is a thriving blackmarket on which you can get up to double the official rate. For example there is a certain hairdresser on Independence Ave in Dar who will give US$1=Sh 17. Outside of Dar expect to get somewhat less than this. In Mwanza you can use Kenyan Shillings to buy Tanzanian Shillings at the rate Ken Sh 1 = Tan Sh 2.50 — again, an excellent rate of exchange.

Currency Declaration Forms are issued on arrival. There are no hassles with these forms if you leave the country via Namanga on the Kenyan border but if you are visiting the Game Parks — especially Ngorogoro Crater — make sure you have one or two bank stamps on this form as you may well be asked to produce this form. Any excess you have over and above what is marked on this form will be confiscated so hide the excess well.

Tanzania is a fairly expensive country if you are changing your money in banks. Airport Tax for international flights is Sh 40.

LANGUAGES

Swahili and English.

MEDICAL

Medical treatment and all prescribed drugs are free even for visitors. The vaccination centre in Dar es Salaam is open from 8 am to 11.30 am. If your International Health Certificate is running out, get it up-dated here.

FOOD

A list of local foods/drinks and their approximate prices in the cheapest cafes follow:

Chai ya maziwa (tea with milk) 50c; Mandazi madogo (a kind of pancake) Sh 1.50; Andazi Kubwa (a kind of doughnut) 50c; Sconsi hafkeki (rock cake) 70c; Maziwa (milk) Sh 1; Chapati Sh 1; Yai la Kutchemshwa (poached egg) Sh 1; Kukaanga (fried egg) Sh 1.30; Wali (rice) Sh 2; Mbuzi (goatmeat) Sh 4; Njegere (peas) Sh 3.25; Maharagwe (beans) Sh 1; Pilao Sh 3.50; Biriani Sh 6; Karanga (antelope meat) Sh 4; Supu (soup) Sh 2; Mchicha (spinach) 60c; Ugali (a very dry and starchy bread) Sh 1; Slesi (slice of bread) 25 c; Siagi (sugar) 75 c; Omelette Sh 3.50; orange or passion fruit juice Sh 2½; egg chop (scotch egg) Sh 3; meat chop Sh 3; Viazi (potato stew) Sh 3.50; Ndizi (banana stew) Sh 3.50; Dengu (lentils) Sh 4; Choroko (small peas) Sh 3; Maini (liver) Sh 6; Coffee Sh 2; Sambusa Sh 1; Mtindi (buttermilk) Sh 1.50; Bhajia (spicy vegetable balls) Sh 2 for a plate of five.

ACCOMMODATION

Hotels are expensive in Tanzania, especially in Dar es Salaam, though it's generally acceptable for two people to share a single room (one sleeps on the floor). Remember that 'hotel' generally signifies a restaurant so you must ask for 'lodgings'. Many Sikh Temples will take travellers — some are free, others make a small charge. If it's free a donation is much appreciated and keeps the ground sweet for those coming after you. Don't turn up too late at these places or they won't take you in. There are many camp sites around the country, especially in the National Parks, but they are relatively expensive for the facilities which they offer. Watch out for 'camp sites' which are just a patch of parched earth with no facilities but which cost the same as the others. Camp sites are rarely full even in the tourist season.

Arusha

The Sikh Temples here won't take people anymore. Most hotels cost Sh 60 for a room with three beds. *Arusha Central Hotel*, beside the market, costs Sh 15 per bed. *Amigo Guest House* costs Sh 40 for a double room. *Flamingo Hotel* costs Sh 30/single room. *Tinga Guest House* costs Sh 30/single room. *Greenland Hotel* costs Sh 20/single room but is noisy.

Other cheapies include *Mt Meru Guest House; Continental Hotel* (behind the market on the first floor); *Medro Meru Lodge; Ruby Guest House* and the *Salamu Lodge* (just past the pink and grey mosque). The *YMCA* costs Sh 80/single room with full board.

You can camp either at the site on Bomba Road near the city centre (beware of theft even though the site is 'guarded') or beside the Equator Hotel near the Clock Tower.

In the Arusha National Park there are several camp sites on both sides of Mt Meru and at Momela Lake (book by phoning Arusha 2335). There's also a site at Lake Duluti, 13 km from Arusha on the south side of the Moshi road which you can book c/o A Czerny, Box 609, Arusha. Beware of thieves at the latter.

A good place to eat in Arusha is the *Co-operative Union Building* ('Ushirika' in Swahili). Serves European style food.

Dar es Salaam

The Sikh Temples still take people here. The best one is on the corner of Livingstone and Nkrumah Roads and costs Sh 10.

Royal Guest House, Mosque Street, costs Sh 20 per bed.

Zahir Guest House, Mshimiri Street, costs Sh 20 per bed.

City Guest House, costs Sh 40 for a double room.

New Dar Guest House, Chagga Street off Jamhuri Street, costs Sh 30/single and Sh 40/double but often only has doubles available.

Florida Inn, Jamhuri Street, costs Sh 40 for bed and breakfast.

Windsor Hotel, very close to the Clock Tower and popular with travellers, costs Sh 45 per bed or Sh 60 for a double room. The rooms are small and stuffy and the plumbing goes on strike from time to time. Nevertheless, many travellers recommend it! Often full.

Clocktower Hotel costs Sh 40 per bed. Very similar to the Windsor and often full.

Salvation Army Hostel costs Sh 40 for bed and breakfast.

Al Mustapha Hotel, Mtaa wa Sewa St, costs Sh 30/single.

Holiday Hotel, costs Sh 56/double room.

YMCA, behind the new Post Office, costs Sh 50 for bed and breakfast. Like a first class hotel, takes women too. It is possible for one person to rent a room and to fit two others on the floor — no one checks. If you are discreet, you can use the facilities (swimming pool) there if you are not a resident.

Luther House, luxury you can't afford at Sh 112.

Almost all the cheap hotels and guest houses are permanently full so you may well have to do a fair amount of legwork to find a room or bed.

For food, try the *Co-operative Bar and Restaurant*. Other cheap cafes opposite the Windsor Hotel and in Kariakoo Market.

Outside of Dar you can camp at Oyster Bay but it is described as 'risky'. If you do go there, meals are available at the *New Africa Hotel*. It is also possible to camp at *Silver Sands* (a beach hotel)

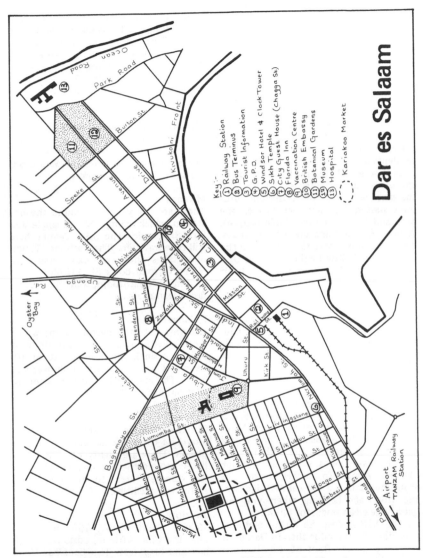

Dar es Salaam

Key:-
1. Railway Station
2. Bus Terminus
3. Tourist Information
4. G.P.O.
5. Windsor Hotel & Clock Tower
6. Sikh Temple
7. City Guest House (chagga St)
8. Florida Inn
9. Vaccination Centre
10. British Embassy
11. Botanical Gardens
12. Museum
13. Hospital
○ Kariakoo Market

for Sh 10 per night which includes the use of the showers. To get there take the Bahari Beach bus from Kariakoo Market in Dar — infrequent service.

The Tourist Office is at the Matasal-amat Building, Independence Avenue — free maps, etc. The American Cultural Centre has good reading material.

The airport bus is No 67. The airlines also run a bus but it costs Sh 40. A taxi to the airport costs Sh 70 but you can share.

Kigoma

Kigoma Community Centre costs Sh 15 a night in shared room. Located 150 metres on the left as you leave the station. Get there first if you arrive by train or ferry as it fills up quickly. The *Kigoma Hotel* costs Sh 55 per bed and serves the best food in town at reasonable prices — the restaurant is open to non-residents too.

Just south of Kigoma is Ujini, one of the oldest market villages in Africa and the place where all the 'I presume' business started (Stanley met Livingstone here and there's the inevitable plaque). A taxi from Kigoma costs a few cents. There are also 'water taxis' between the two places. A little further on from Ujiji is where the fishermen bring in their catch.

Mbeya

Moravian Church Youth Hostel near the radio tower, costs Sh 24 per person including breakfast. Cheap evening meals are available. *Ally's Guest House* costs Sh 30/double or Sh 15 per bed.

Moshi

Most of the cheap guesthouses are near the market. *Amani Guest House*, Kiusa Street, costs Sh 40/double room. *Njaci Hotel* costs Sh 35/double. *Tafia Hotel* on the same street as the Sikh Temple (which takes Sikhs only), is another cheapie. About 75 metres further on from the Tafia is a red-painted sign saying 'Hotel and Lodging' where you can get a large clean single for Sh 35.

The *YMCA* costs Sh 40 for bed and breakfast. Better value than in Dar. You can sleep on the floor of the *Mwariko Art Gallery* for Sh 10 per night but you need an air mattress or a bulky sleeping bag as the floor is concrete. *Family Lodge* near the bus station, costs Sh 38/double room. Both the *Lutherans* (opp-osite the Post Office) and the *Anglican Guest House* offer accommodation for Sh 30. The latter is very good value.

The camp site is about two km out of town on the main road to Arusha and adjacent to the playing fields, costs Sh 10. Good site with showers, etc.

Musoma

The *Mennonite Centre* costs Sh 15 but is a long way from the boat terminal. *Sensera Hotel* costs Sh 20/single. Information is available from the Majira Bus Service office in the market.

Mwanza

There are many hotels around the bus station which charge Sh 32/single and Sh 48/ double. The Sikh Temple here will take travellers. The Catholic Mission only takes those of like persuasion. *Hotel Victoria* costs Sh 115/double including own bathroom, toilet and breakfast. Clean rooms.

Rulenge

Lodgings near the petrol pumps which are labelled, not so informatively 'post office'. A single room there costs Sh 10. Basic but has electricity, a shower and basin. The mission here offers accommodation for Sh 20 per person.

Tanga

The Sikh Temple still takes people. The *Mombasa Guest House* costs Sh 25 per person. There are plenty of other cheap hotels around the bus station. There's a free camp site next to the *Palm Beach Hotel* with facilities.

Zanzibar

Malindi Guest House, 100 metres behind the Cine Afrique, costs Sh 40 for bed and breakfast. The *Zanzibar Hotel* costs Sh 50 per person. *Africa House*, costs Sh 50 per night, it is very good value. *Hotel Uwanjani* is another cheapie at Sh 35 per bed including breakfast but it is hard to get to and so works out almost as expensive as Africa House.

The museum and the old fort are well worth a visit. Costs Sh 2.50 entry.

TRANSPORT
Road Transport There's a severe petrol shortage in Tanzania which is likely to continue as long as Tanzanian troops remain in Uganda — as we go to press there are still 10,000 there. This had made road transport in Tanzania somewhat unreliable because of long queues for petrol. Until the situation improves you should take bus schedules as approximate only. Roads are brilliant after Zaire but poor after Kenya. There is an excellent road from Dar to Moshi and Arusha and the all-weather road from Dar to Tunduma on the Zambian border is now complete. If you want information about road conditions and routes, contact the Automobile Association of East Africa, Cargen House, Azikiwe Street, Dar es Salaam (tel 21965). These people have a reciprocal arrangement with the British Automobile Association and provide an excellent service.

Truck 'fares' at present average Sh 1 per eight km, which works out cheaper than the buses. Buses are usually faster than the trains but tend to be crowded. Note that if you're going to be travelling from Arusha to Iringa there are two possible routes: (a) via Dodoma and (b) via Morogoro. The road via Dodoma is in an atrocious condition and whatever sort of vehicle you're on is likely to break down at least once. The road via Morogoro is somewhat longer but it is surfaced. Also note that Dodoma is a transport bottleneck and if you get off a bus here it may be three or four days before you find a seat on another as they're booked up well in advance. Some examples of bus prices and journey times follow:

Dar es Salaam-Moshi, daily buses in either direction, costs Sh 60 and takes 11 to 12 hours.

Moshi-Arusha, daily buses in either direction, costs Sh 9.

Arusha-Namanga (Tanzanian/Kenyan border), daily buses cost Sh 20, a taxi costs Sh 25.

Namanga-Nairobi, buses cost Ken Sh 18 or you can take a taxi for Sh 25.

Arusha-Musoma, United Bus Services, bus goes via the Serengeti National Park but don't count on seeing too much wildlife. Costs Sh 52 and takes 15 hours plus Sh 30 National Park entrance fee. If you're coming from Musoma the bus departs daily at 7 am.

Arusha-Singida costs Sh 40 — it works out cheaper than going by truck.

Musoma-Mwanza costs Sh 23 and takes six hours.

Mwanza-Nzega costs Sh 23 and takes six hours.

Mwanza-Biharamulo costs Sh 32, the ferry crossing which is necessary along this route is free. Most buses take 10 hours but there is a faster one which takes seven hours and costs Sh 37.

Mwanza-Bukoba costs Sh 45 and takes 24 hours. Note that if you're heading ing for Rwanda and don't want to take the Rulenge crossing, there is a direct bus service from Bukoba to Kigali operated by Rahemtula Bus Service on Kitekene Road, Bukoba.

Mwanza-Rulenge (Rwanda Border) costs Sh 50. If coming from Rulenge the bus leaves every Monday, Wednesday and Friday.

Geita-Rulenge costs Sh 40 which is very expensive considering that the Rulenge-Mwanza bus is only Sh 50.

Railways There are three main routes:
(1) Dar es Salaam to Moshi and Arusha with a branch line to Tanga on the coast. Departs Dar on Tuesdays, Thursdays and Saturdays at 3 pm and takes 18 hours to Moshi. The train from Tanga to Moshi departs on the same days as above at 7 pm.

Fares are Dar-Moshi Sh 25.30 in third class, Dar-Tanga Sh 17.90 in third class and Sh 38.40 in second class, Tanga-Moshi Sh 36.40 in second class.

(2) Dar es Salaam to Kigoma (Lake Tanganyika) with a branch line from Tabora to Mwanza. Daily train in either direction between Dar and Mwanza which departs Mwanza at 8 pm. The journey takes 36 hours. Daily train in either direction between Dar and Kigoma. The journey takes 18 hours and the train tends to be packed out, so get there early. Fares are Dar-Mwanza Sh 53 in third class and Sh 130 in second class, Mwanza-Tabora Sh 18 in third class, Dar-Kigoma Sh 54.60 in third class, Dar-Dodoma Sh 21.70 in third class, Dar-Tabora Sh 37.70 in third class.

(3) TANZAM Railway, Dar es Salaam to Kapiri Mposhi (Zambia). Note that the station for this line is on Pugu Road, Dar, about four km out of town. Take bus No 6 to get there. There are two express trains and two ordinary trains weekly. By taking the express train you go through many interesting areas only at night. If you take the ordinary train you go through the Selaus Game Park during the day and see lots of wildlife.

The express train takes 36 hours and departs Dar on Tuesdays and Fridays at 4.20 pm, arriving in Kapiri Mposhi at 5 am on Thursdays and Sundays respectively.

The ordinary train takes 48 hours and departs Dar on Wednesdays and Sundays at 9.20 am, arriving in Kapiri Mposhi at 3.30 pm on Fridays and Tuesdays respectively.

The express train departs Kapiri Mposhi on Tuesdays and Fridays at 10 pm. The ordinary train departs Kapiri Mposhi on Mondays and Wednesdays at 10.35 am.

Fares are Dar-Kapiri Mposhi Sh 82.80 in third class, Sh 170 in second class and Sh 300 in first class. Bedding for the two nights you spend on the train is available for hire for an extra Sh 9. First class has four bunks per compartment, second class has six bunks per compartment and third class consists of upright wooden seats. A buffet car is attached to the express train.

You can change Tanzanian money into Zambian money on the train by asking the cabin attendant to do it for you — and at a good rate. The Zambian border guards will also change travellers' cheques into Zambian money at the official rate and unless you buy Kwacha from them you're not (officially) allowed to have any Zambian money on you on entry.

There are often a number of undercover agents on the train who sometimes make a nuisance of themselves. Be very careful about photography. If you want to take pictures (eg of wildlife) go into the police compartment and explain what you want to do. If you don't, the chances are that the film will be confiscated and you'll be given a hard time about it. This sort of sensitivity is very much a reflection of the guerilla war in Zimbabwe and the tense relations between Tanzania and Uganda during Idi Amin's reign. Now that both problems are out of the way, things may ease up.

Student reductions of 50% are available on the railways if you have both an International Student Card and a confirmatory letter from the college/university specified on the card. They won't let you have them without the letter. Even with both of these it's extremely difficult to get concession tickets in Mwanza.

Boats
Lake Tanganyika Steamers
The schedule is as follows:

Kalemie (Zaire)	*Kigoma (Tanzania)*	*Kalundu (Zaire)*
Dep Wed at 16.00	Arr Thu at 07.00	Arr Fri at 07.00
	Dep Thu at 14.00	Dep Fri at 09.00

Bujumbura (Burundi)
Arr Fri at 10.00

Bujumbura	*Kalunda*	*Kigoma*
Dep Fri at 12.00	Arr Fri at 13.00	Arr Sat at 07.00
	Dep Fri at 16.00	Dep Sat at 16.00

Kalemie
Arr Sun at 07.00

	first class	*third class*
Fares Kigoma-Kalundu	Sh 79	Sh 29
Kigoma-Bujumbura	Sh 79	Sh 29
Kigoma-Kalemie	Sh 59	Sh 22

Tanzania Coastal Service
Operator is Tanzania Coastal Shipping Line Ltd, City Drive, Dar es Salaam (tel 25329). Ships are the *Lindi* and *Mtwara*, they're passenger ships operating along the route Dar es Salaam-Kilindoni (Mafia Island)-Kilwa-Lindi-Mtwara. They sail once every two to three weeks. Fares from Dar es Salaam are Sh 15 to Kilindoni, Sh 23 to Kilwa, Sh 33 to Lindi and Sh 36 to Mtwara.

Boats to Zanzibar
Probably the most enjoyable way to get there is by Arab dhow. If you can't find one which is going there from Dar, take a dhow to Bagamoyo, about 65 km up the coast from Dar and directly opposite Zanzibar Island. Dar to Bagamoyo will cost Sh 38 one-way and can take a few hours or a few days depending on the wind. Take your own .food and drink.

There are regular ferries to Zanzibar from Dar. The most expensive is the *Mapinduzi* which costs Sh 59 one-way plus Sh 10 for the harbour ride out to the ship. There is a cheaper ferry which does the run once every two weeks and costs Sh 30. Book the latter at the corner of Mission Street and City Drive in Dar. The ferry takes five hours.

If you're pushed for time and there's no ferry immediately available there are daily flights from Dar which cost Sh 180 return plus Sh 40 airport tax at either end.

There are no boats to India from Tanzania any long and no regular passenger ferries connecting Tanzanian ports on Lake Victoria with those in Kenya and Uganda.

NATIONAL PARKS & GAME PARKS
The entrance fee to all game parks is now Sh 30 and there are no student concessions available. If you want to camp inside the game parks this costs an extra Sh 30-40 per night. As in Kenya, organised tours work out very expen-

sive. If you want to keep the costs down contact Mr N Thakar, PO Box 1099, Arusha. He lives in Dodoma House, near the bus station and hires out VW Kombis with drivers to visit the national parks (Manyara, Ngorogoro and Serengeti) cheaper than anyone else. Get a bunch of six people together. Alternatively, try Tanzania Tours Ltd in Dar es Salaam who arrange share-expenses rides through Serengeti.

Ngorogoro Crater
Probably the most famous of Tanzania's wildlife parks and rightfully so. It contains the most amazing variety and quantity of wild life you are likely to see anywhere. Even if you have to give the others a miss, don't miss this place.

The cheapest way to get there is local daily bus from Arusha. This costs Sh 25 and takes eight hours and departs 9 am though you have to be there at 7 am for a compulsory seat. Remember you will also have to pay Sh 30 entrance fee for the park.

Only four-wheel drive vehicles are allowed to go down to the crater bottom. These are for hire at Crater Village and cost, on average, Sh 500. They take up to seven people so get a group together. A guide is compulsory and you may well be asked for your Currency Declaration Form before being allowed to hire a vehicle so make sure it has at least one bank stamp on it otherwise you could be in for a hassle. If, for any reason, you can't hire a four-wheel drive, tour buses leave Crater Village every morning about 8 am arriving on the crater floor about half an hour later.

For accommodation, you can either camp at Crater Rim, about two km from Crater Lodge for Sh 30 or use one of the hotels. Camping equipment can be hired in Arusha or Moshi. Remember that it's pretty cold at nights and very damp in the mornings so prepare accordingly. Rooms are available in Crater

Village where the guides and drivers stay for around Sh 40 in rooms with two beds — ask first at the *Ushirika Co-op Restaurant*, which also does cheap food. One such place is the *Workers' Quarters* which costs Sh 44 for a double room. You can also buy a meal of rice and meat here for Sh 7. A *Youth Hostel* was being built there and may now be complete. Other than these places there is the *Forest Lodge*, five km from Crater Village, which costs Sh 107 per person for full board, Sh 70 for bed and breakfast, and Sh 40 for camping with use of shower and cooker. There is also the very flash *Crater Lodge* which costs a swingeing Sh 300 per person including full board but has a tremendous site. You need to book in advance as it caters for package tours from Europe and the States.

Serengeti National Park
Much the same as the Ngorogoro Crater but not as spectacular. The best time to see the wildebeeste and zebra is from December to May when they mass on the plains in the southern part of the park. From then on, they move away to the north and east where there is permanent water. When the short rains come in November they head back south.

There are a number of camping sites such as the ones at *Klein's Camp* in the north and Kdakaba in the west which are recommended. You have to book in advance for these via Tanzanian National Parks, PO Box 3134, Arusha. The sites cost Sh 50 per night. If you don't want to camp/haven't got the equipment, there is a lodge in Seronera Village Settlement on the main Musoma-Arusha road which costs Sh 30 per night but you must bring your own food.

Lake Manyara National Park
One of the smallest and most beautiful of the parks. Wading birds, elephants, etc. The best time to go is around

Christmas when it's packed out with wild life.

There are several camp sites near the entrance to the park which you must book in advance through Tanzania National Parks, PO Box 3134 Arusha, but the best camp site is up on the plateau near the *Manyara Hotel*. Costs Sh 30 though as it is inside the national park you will have to pay the daily entrance fee of Sh 30 as well. There is a *Youth Hostel* just outside the park gates which is very comfortable and costs Sh 40 per night. Other than this there is a hotel in the nearby village of Mto Wa Mbu which works out cheaper than camping in the Park.

There is a bus from the YMCA in Moshi to Lake Manyara when there is sufficient demand.

Mount Kilimanjaro (5896 metres)
Climbing this mountain is not easy but it is not tough either. You just need to be reasonably fit. The path is well-trodden and easy to follow and there are a series of huts where you can sleep or rest but you need to take all your food and bear in mind that, past the second hut, there's no water. A portable cooker is very useful as it is next to impossible to hire one. You will need to hire gloves, boots, a woolly hat and, if you are going up into the snow, snow goggles. You can get all these in Arusha. Remember that the higher reaches of the mountain are shrouded in cloud after about 9-10 am. If you don't want to go with a group you could tag discreetly along behind an organised tour. The entrance fee to the park is now Sh 180.

If you are looking for an organised tour the cheapest way to do it is to ask around in the hotels at Marangu near Moshi. Assuming you have a group together it should cost Sh 150 for a five-day trek plus Sh 30 'rescue fee,' Sh 40 per night for any huts you use plus Sh 340 for a guide and Sh 290 for each porter. Otherwise you can book trips through the YMCA in Moshi which cost Sh 530 (includes a guide and the use of huts for the five day trek) or through the Kibo hotel for Sh 800-plus. The YMCA prices excludes food whereas the Kibo trek includes this item.

Olduvai Gorge
Situated about three km off the road to Ngorogoro and the place where Dr Leakey discovered the world's earliest known bone fragments of man. There are a number of tourist buses which do a whirlwind tour of the diggings lasting a couple of hours but the guides are very ill-informed by all accounts and if you are interested it might be better to go there yourself and speak with the people who are working there.

OTHER INFORMATION
Makonde Carvings Best places to buy them are in the Kariakoo market or on the corner of Mkunhuni and Nyamwesi Streets in Dar es Salaam, near the new market place and Post Office. Or get bus No 5 from the old Post Office (on harbour front) and ask conductor to tell you when to get off. They sit and carve them by the side of the road. Supposed to be better than bargaining in Kariakoo Market. Prices from Sh 5-25.

Togo

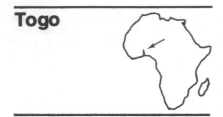

Like Gambia, further to the west, Togo is another idiosyncratic legacy of European colonialism. In the early 1880s Togoland became a German colony and remained so until after WW I when it was divided between Britain and France and administered first under a mandate from the League of Nations and later under a similar arrangement from the United Nations. The British portion was incorporated into Ghana, which gained its independence in 1955. The French portion became independent in 1962 under the presidency of Sylvanus Olympia. He was overthrown in an army coup in 1967 led by Etienne Eyadema who has been the ruler ever since though he attempted to hand power back to a civilian government in 1972 much to the consternation of the bulk of the population, which feared another outbreak of rivalry between the north and south.

The country's foreign policy is dominated by its larger neighbour Ghana and by its relations with France, the main supplier of aid. The country very nearly became a part of Ghana four years after independence when the electorate voted for integration with that country but this was blocked by Olympia, who no doubt feared political eclipse by the charismatic Nkrumah. Apart from aid from France, Germany and the USA have provided loans for development.

VISAS
Required by all except nationals of Belgium, Denmark, France, West Germany, Italy, Luxembourg, Netherlands, Norway and Sweden. Nationals of South Africa are not admitted. Joint passports are not acceptable, you must have your own.

At the embassy in Porto Novo (Benin) visas are valid for a stay of one month. Everywhere else they're valid for only 48 hours. In Ghana visas cost Cedi 3.90, two photos and take 24 hours to issue. Visas from the French Embassy in Freetown, Sierra Leone, cost Le 5.45.

You can extend your visa in Lome but the bureaucracy is incredible and, unless you're staying in a very expensive hotel, takes four to six days to come through.

You need an exit visa if you stay more than 48 hours — obtainable from Surete National in Lome. You also have to give 48 hours notice of your intention to leave the country, which is of course the epitome of bureaucratic silliness if you come in on a 48 hour visa and don't intend to stay longer than that.

If you get a Ghanian visa here you are required to buy Cedi Vouchers. Visas for Benin cannot be obtained in Lome — get it elsewhere if you're going that way.

CURRENCY
The unit of currency is the CFA. Import or export of local currency is allowed up to 50,000 CFA.

Exchange rate:

£1	=	473 CFA
US$1	=	207 CFA
A$1	=	237 CFA

Lome is the currency blackmarket capital of West Africa. It's a good place to buy Cedis (Ghana) and Naira (Nigeria). The average rates are 1000 CFA = Cedi 45 or Naira 4.80.

Airport tax for domestic flights is 200 CFA, for flights to Nigeria or Zaire

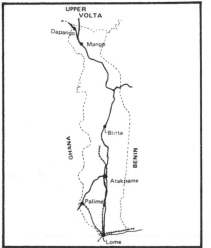

it's 600 CFA and for other international flights it's 1500 CFA.

LANGUAGE
French, some English is also spoken.

ACCOMMODATION
Atakpame
Liberty Bar costs 800 CFA a double; pretty dingy place but the cheapest in town. The *Relais du Sorad*, situated on the road into town, costs 1500 CFA a double, a very pleasant place to stay.

Lome
Most of the cheap hotels are located around the central market but they are not the only cheap places to stay at.

Hotel de la Plage, junction of Boulevard Circulaire and Boulevard de la Republique, right on the sea front, costs 2000 CFA/double.

Centre Communitaire de Tokoin, located on rue Missim, near the market, costs 450 CFA per person and is recommended. There's another Centre Communitaire on the outskirts of town.

Bar Ramatou, rue Anecho on the beach, past the port, costs 250 CFA per person. It's very friendly. Otherwise you can sleep on the beach.

Foyer de Jeunes Filles Protestante, in the town centre, takes both men and women and costs 500 CFA per person for students and volunteers. For others it's 800 CFA per person. The *Foyer de Jeunes Filles* which is attached to the university is not as good as this place.

Hotel Paloma, centrally located, costs 1200 CFA.

Hotel Continental, situated in the Automotive, costs 1600 CFA/double.

Good meals at *Sous le Manguier* near the Centre Communitaire de Tokoin. *Bar Tabac* on rue d'Atakpame near the Hotel Continental serves good cheap food. Two restaurants on the rue Grand Marche are also very good and cheap. They are the *Amitie* and the *Pajar*. A beer costs 40 CFA and a meal 100 CFA.

Taxis around town cost 100 CFA.

Palime
Delima Bar costs 850 CFA a double, a good place. You could also try getting in touch with ASTOVOCT (Association Togolaise de Voluntaires Chietiens au Travail), an active group of Togolese students involved in various grass-roots projects. They've very welcoming to travellers and might well put you up or allow you to eat in their canteen. If they put you up give them a contribution to your keep as they work on a shoestring.

Togoville
Centre of the fetish cult located on the north side of Lac Togo. The Catholic mission will let you stay there free but they're unfriendly. OK if you're a Jesuit! On the opposite side of the lake at Agbodrafo you can camp on the beach or in the huts that are no longer used by

the Barracuda Club. Watch out for kids who tend to walk off with your belongings.

Elsewhere in Togo ask for the village chief. People are very friendly in the small villages and you'll often be provided with accommodation and food. It's customary to give a little money in return.

TRANSPORT
Except in the north roads are very good and open throughout the year. Hitching is OK and there are plenty of trucks and Peugeot taxis. The border with Benin is occasionally closed because of recurrent and often fictional national emergencies in Benin. Lome-Atakpame costs 600 CFA in a Peugeot taxi, Atakpame-Sokode also costs 600 CFA.

There is a railway which runs north to Sokode via Atakpame from Lome and a branch line which runs from Lome to Palime. There is also a coastal line which links Lome with Porto Novo in Benin. We have no current details of schedules and fares.

OTHER INFORMATION
Camping Gaz cylinders are available in Togo (also in Benin and Upper Volta though not in Ghana or Nigeria).

Tunisia

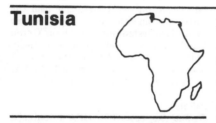

The smallest of the three Maghreb states Tunisia has a rich cultural and social heritage stemming from the many empires which have come and gone in this part of the world ranging from the Phoenicians through the Romans, Byzantines, Arabs and Ottoman Turks to the French. In addition, there have been substantial numbers of immigrants from Spain, Italy and Malta and many Jews are still numbered among the population. Because of the thoroughness of the Arab invasions, the original Berber population now forms only 1% of the total, confined mainly to the dry and inhospitable south of the country. In this respect Tunisia differs from the other Maghreb states of Algeria and Morocco which still have very substantial Berber populations.

Phoenician staging posts were estab-

lished very early on throughout the length and breadth of the Mediterranean but remained relatively unimportant until the mother cities along the Syrian coast lost their independence in the 6th century BC and Greek colonies began to be planted in Cyrenaica (eastern Libya) from the 7th century BC onwards. As a result of these events, Carthage, a few km from Tunis, grew rapidly into the metropolis of the Phoenician world and, at its height, had a population of about a half million people. The Phoenicians, who were principally maritime traders, had a profound effect on the native Berbers by introducing them to advanced agricultural methods and urban living. The Jews too, many of whom were involved in trade, helped spread the idea of a montheistic religion among these pagan tribes.

Carthage eventually fell to the Romans, who literally ploughed the city into the ground, but were quick to appreciate the value of the settled Tunisian plains as a granary for the empire and began to erect their own cities here. The remains of many of these cities stand today and are one of the country's principal attractions, though

Roman Carthage itself is somewhat of a disappointment, much of its stone having been carted away to erect the later Arab cities. The greatest Roman contribution to this part of Africa, however, was largely incidental — that of opening up North Africa to the spread of Christianity. In the centuries following the Roman conquest, Carthage became the greatest of Christian centres second only to Alexandria and produced one of that religion's greatest figures — St Agustine who was a Libyan Berber educated in Carthage. Roman rule here was never popular and opposition to it found expression in religious doctrinal differences and the adoption of Donatism, regarded by the orthodox Byzantine Church as a heresy. Persecutions launched by Byzantium as a result alienated much of the population but the many centuries of influence, first of Judaism and then of Christianity, paved the way for the rapid adoption of Islam which had the advantage of not being associated with the imposition of foreign rule.

The Arabs first arrived here in 670 AD and established a base at Kairouan but they lost this after a disastrous attempt to conquer the lands further west and were not able to establish their control here until the end of the century when the Byzantine navy had been defeated and could not cut the Arab's lines of supply to Egypt by landing troops in Libya. Even then they had to contend with a confederacy of marauding tribes, led by a woman leader, Kahina, which swept down from the Aures Mountains in eastern Algeria. This sort of resistance from the Berber tribes was to continue for many centuries and even after Islam had been adopted was to find expression in the Kharijite schism as it had in Donatism during the Christian era. (Kharijism was a puritanical form of Shi'ism which stemmed from the disagreements in the Islamic hierarchy as to whether the companions or the blood relations of the Prophet should succeed to the Caliphate).

After the political fragmentation of the Arab Empire, Tunisia became part of the Moroccan Empire of the Almohads and remained so until the dual threats of the Christian armies in Spain and the Bedouin in the central Maghreb forced the Moroccan rulers to divide their administration and appoint the Hafsid family as governors of the eastern half of the empire in Tunis. The Hafsids were spectacularly successful in defeating the Bedouin but in doing so intensified the destruction of the central Maghreb and so effectively cut Tunisia off from Morocco. In the years which followed, Tunisia became an island of stability and prosperity and in 1230 created its own independent Hafsid monarchy, which began trading on its

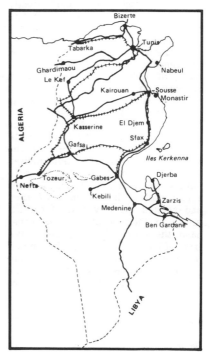

own account with European states. The Hafsids remained in power until 1574 when Tunisia was conquered by the Ottoman Turks. Ottoman rule here, however, soon became merely nominal after the defeat of the Turkish fleet by the Christians at Lepanto and power in Tunis, as also in Algiers, came to reside in self-perpetuating cliques descended from the Greek corsairs and Anatolian janissaries who had accomplished the conquest. (The janissaries were the professional elite of the Ottoman armies and were composed of forcibly recruited Christian youths within the Ottoman Empire who were subjected to a rigorous military and Moslem training). In time, the conquerors merged with the local people and by the 18th century had produced their own national monarchy, the Husainid Beys, who revised the Hafsid practice of training directly with the European states and the Sudan, despite being still nominally part of the Ottoman Empire.

In the late 19th century, the Turks, frightened of losing their grip on yet more of their North African lands, attempted to re-assert their authority over Algeria and Tunisia but were prevented from doing so by the French Navy which annexed Algiers. Tunisia itself was spared colonisation until much later since its Beys, aware of the growing power of the industrialised European nations, had taken steps to outlaw piracy and to westernise their administration. Indeed, in 1857 they had granted the very first of constitutions to their people. On the other hand, the continued extravagance of the Beys of Tunis — like that of Muhammed Ali in Egypt — led to more and more European interference until in 1881 the French declared a 'protectorate' over Tunisia.

In the 1930s a movement for national liberation — the Neo-Destour — grew up with Habib Bourguiba as its leader. Its activities soon became a threat to continued French domination and four years later Bourguiba was imprisoned and the movement proscribed but when Tunis was briefly occupied by the Germans during WW II Bourguiba was released and the Beys again allowed to appoint ministers from among the Neo-Destour. When this came to an end with the Allied victories in North Africa, Bourguiba went into exile in Egypt where he organised propaganda and resistance against the French which led to two years of guerilla warfare and forced the French to grant autonomy to Tunisia in 1955. Bourguiba returned to head the new government and a year later, following the example of Morocco, Tunisia was granted independence. In 1957 the Bey was deposed and Tunisia became a republic with Bourguiba as President.

Since independence Tunisia has been one of the most stable and moderate of the Arab countries and, as such, its friendship has been cultivated by the USA and West Germany which supply the bulk of the foreign aid. A union with Libya came into existence after a number of hurried negotiations between Gaddafi and Bourguiba some years ago but it collapsed almost as soon as it had been announced. There were strained relations between Tunisia and France and Italy in the '60s due to the expropriation of European-owned farms, but this was eventually patched up with the offer of compensation. The country is rapidly becoming one of the major Mediterranean tourist attractions which yearly draws millions of northern Europeans to its shores and so is now a fairly expensive country for the budget traveller.

VISAS
Required by all except nationals of Western European countries, Canada, USA and Japan. Nationals of Israel and South Africa are not admitted.

Libyan Visas Before you apply for a visa you must have your passport details translated into Arabic — they won't entertain you otherwise. If you didn't have this done when your passport was issued your own embassy in Tunis will generally do it. If they won't, you will have to go to a travel agent. However, the forms for the visa are printed in French as well as Arabic so you shouldn't be completely at sea. Visas cost 2.80 Dinar and take about five days to issue. The Libyan Embassy is at 48 rue du Ier Juin, Tunis.

Egyptian Visas The embassy is at 16 rue Es Souyouti El Menzah, Tunis.

CURRENCY

The unit of currency is the Dinar = 1000 millimes. Import/Export of local currency is prohibited.

Exchange rate:

£1	=	0.94 Dinar
US$1	=	0.41 Dinar
A$1	=	0.47 Dinar

You can re-exchange up to 30% of the foreign currency you changed into Tunisian Dinar on departure up to a limit of 100 Dinar. There is a blackmarket for currency but you have to be Tunisian to find it. Banks don't charge commission. On the Algerian side of the border at Ghardimou, the customs officials will offer to change any spare Tunisian currency you have into Algerian Dinar but at a poor rate. If you have to do this, make sure you do it before you fill in the Currency Declaration Form otherwise they will have to change them at the official rate — which is even worse. Note that Algerian banks won't accept Tunisian currency.

LANGUAGE

Arabic and French are main languages though a little English, German and Italian is spoken.

ACCOMMODATION

There are few camp sites with any facilities worth talking about. Most travellers use the *Youth Hostels* which are the cheapest accommodation available and cost 500 millimes per night. They are usually modern purpose-built places with good facilities like showers and a meal service. There are also a number of *Centre de Jeunesse* where you can usually sleep on the floor for about 100-200 millimes. Many travellers sleep on the beaches which are superb. Remember that the Youth Hostels are closed at certain times of the year (varies from one to the next) so you should get hold of an International Youth Hostel Handbook and check these out.

Bizerte

The *Youth Hostel* is situated on Route de la Corniche (tel 02-31608).

Djerba

The *Youth Hostel* is at Houmt-Souk near the Municipalite off Avenue Habib Bourguiba just before the harbour.

Gabes

The *Youth Hostel* is opposite the railway station on the main street. There is a camp site at the *Centre de Formation de Jeunesse*. To get there take the road from the main market down past the Agip garage opposite the Marche Detail then over the bridge and through the iron gates on the left hand side. Costs 100 millimes per night. If you want a cheap hotel, try the *Hotel de la Gare*.

Kibili

The cheapest hotel in town is the *Hotel Nifzaoun* at the end of the main street.

Nabeul

The *Youth Hostel* is situated right on the beach about two km from the centre of town. Nearby is the *Hotel Riadh* which costs 1350 millimes including breakfast and dinner.

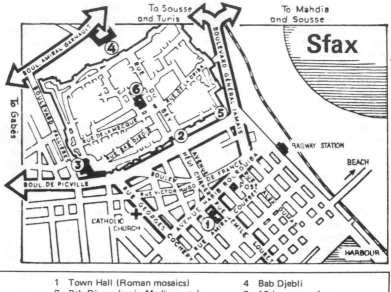

1	Town Hall (Roman mosaics)	4	Bab Djebli
2	Bab Diwan (main Medina gate)	5	12th century fort
3	Kasbah	6	Great Mosque

Sfax

A *Maison de Jeune* is available here. One of the cheapest hotels is the *Hotel Maghreb* in the Medina by the main gate. Ask to sleep on the roof if you want somewhere cheap.

Sousse

The *Youth Hostel* is situated on Plage Boujaafer which is a short walk from the centre of town.

Tabarka

The cheapest hotel is the *Hotel Corail* which costs 1 Dinar per night. Note this town has music festivals at weekends throughout the summer months which attracts many well-heeled tourists so prices are high at this time.

Tozeur

There is a camp site at Belvedere in the oasis but there are no facilities. Beautiful site though! *Hotel Essada* is one of the cheapest at 1 Dinar/single.

Tunis

Hotel du Lion, 6 rue El Karamed is the cheapest in town and very popular with travellers. Costs 800 millimes for a bed in the dormitory; 1 Dinar for a single room and 1.40 Dinar for a double room. It's clean and friendly but there are no showers. *Hotel Savoie*, 13 rue de Boucher, costs 1 Dinar/single. Clean.

Other cheapies include the *Hotel de la Republique* (rue de Maroc); *Oukala des Voyages* (rue de Boucher); *Hotel de Milano* (just inside the Medina); *Hotel Sahara* and the *Hotel Tranquilite*. The *Youth Hostel* is situated in the Maison de Jeunes de Rades at Tunis-Rades which is a long way out of town and so very inconvenient if you have got a lot to do/see there.

The Tourist Office is on Avenue Mohammed V. American Express is at

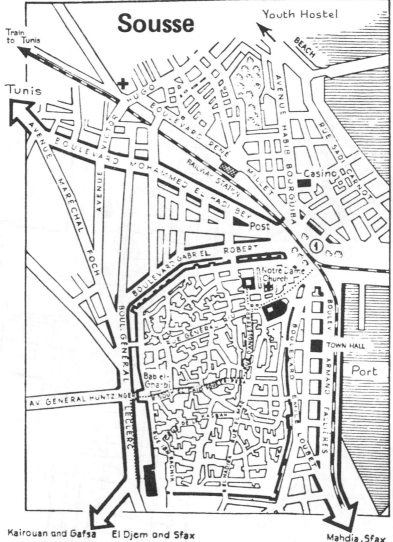

Sousse

Youth Hostel

Train to Tunis

Tunis

BEACH

Casino

Post

Notre Dame Church

Bab el-Gha-bi

AV. GENERAL HUNTZINGER

TOWN HALL

Port

Kairouan and Gafsa   El Djem and Sfax

Mahdia, Sfax

Tourafric, 52 Ave Habib Bourguiba (tel 245 066). If you arrive by air, take blue bus No 35 from the airport to the city centre. Service every half an hour.

| 1 | Square Farhad Hached & long-distance bus station & taxi rank ('louages') |

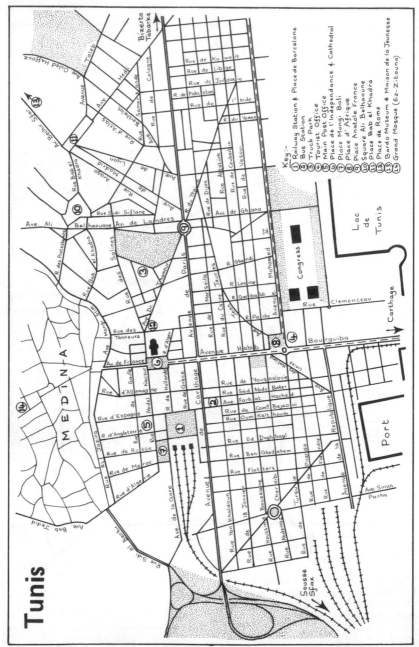

Tunis

Key:-
1. Railway Station ‡ Place de Barcelone
2. Bus Station
3. Truck Park
4. Tourist Office
5. Main Post Office
6. Place de l'Independance ‡ Cathedral
7. Place Mong: Bali
8. Place d'Afrique
9. Place Anatole France
10. Square Ali Belhaoune
11. Place Bab el Khadra
12. Place de Rome
13. Bardo Museum ‡ Maison de la Jeunesse
14. Grand Mosque (Ez-Zitouna)

TRANSPORT

Hitching Fairly easy in the north and down the coast through to Libya. More difficult on the minor roads and in the south where there will be long waits between lifts as there is very little traffic. It's especially difficult to hitch the stretch between the Tunisian and Algerian borders between Gardimaou and Souk Ahras — might be better to take the daily train from Jendouba to Souk Ahras which leaves at 4 pm and costs 1.64 Dinar. Don't attempt to hitch during the festival of 'L'Aide' (late December) as all life stops around then.

Buses Regular and cheap services throughout the country — costs on average 550 mill/100 km. There are two to three departures per day from major population centres to others. An alternative form of transport is the 'louage' — large taxis with seats for five passengers. They leave key points in the town to each destination and don't go until they are full. Fares are slightly higher than trains and buses, eg Tabarka-Tunis costs 0.92 Dinar.

Trains Network of rail connections between all major centres together with two lines to Algeria. Furthest point south the lines go is Gabes and Tozeur. There is no railway to Libya.

Boats

Sfax-Iles Kerkenna Off the coast of Tunisia about half way down. Depart every day from Sfax at 7 am to 10 am and 1 pm. Coming from the islands to Sfax they depart at 8.30 am, 11.30 am, and 2.30 pm. Costs 120 mill one way. Beautiful quiet place and very friendly people but there are no cheap hotels and very, very few restaurants. *Hotel Cercinna* 800 mill/single; *Hotel Kerkenna* 1 Dinar/single. Also there are houses to rent on a monthly basis during the winter for 4 Dinar/month.

Mainland (Dhorf-Djerba Island)

Ferry every 20 minutes from 5 am to 7 pm. Costs 50 millimes. As an alternative you can cross via the Roman causeway between Zarsis and Djerba.

Routes to & from Tunisia

Tunisia-Italy Ferries See under 'Mediterranean Ferries' in the Introduction.

Tunisia-Algeria There are three main border crossings but many others are available — look at a map.

(a) Tabarka-Annaba via Le Calle (El Kala). The most northerly route along the coast. There is very little traffic along this road so be prepared to walk the 15-20 km between the border posts. Beautiful countryside but local people are reported to be none too friendly. There are buses linking Le Calle with Tabarka. Last bus from Le Calle leaves at 6 pm.

(b) Gardimaou-Souk Ahras Difficult to hitch by all accounts because of the lack of villages between the two towns — therefore very little local traffic. You have to pick up someone who is going a long way. Again there is a 20 km walk between border posts if you get stuck. There is a daily train linking Souk Ahras with Tunis. Cost from Jendouba — Souk Ahras is 1.64 Dinar.

(c) Gafsa-Nefta-El Oued A little used route. Very little local traffic so hitching is very slow. There is a bus twice weekly.

Tunisia-Libya Almost without exception travellers follow the coast route via Gabes, Medenine to Tripoli. Border is at Ras Gedir. It is usually fairly easy to hitch this stretch — most hitch-hikers seem to score really long lifts on this road which takes them at least as far as Tripoli and often as far as Benghazi. There are buses from Tunis to Tripoli twice per week (Mondays and Thursdays) at 6.30 am. Takes two days.

There are an infinite variety of stories circulating about Libya. You will be

To Tunis

CEMETRY

To Sbeïtla and Maktar

Kasbah

BOUL. SADIKI

RUE DE LA GRANDE MOSQUE

SUKS

RUE SAUSSIER

BOULEVARD CORREARD

SQUARE CARNOT

RUE DE SFAX

PLACE PODUMARE

RUE BREARD

AV. PICHON

CHURCH

Post

To Sousse

RAILWAY STATION

AV. DE LA GARE

Kairouan

0   1   2   3   4   500 M.

1	Bab el Djeladine	4	Djama Amor Abbada Mosque
2	Zaouia Sidi Abid el Ghariani	5	Zaouia Sidi Sahab Mosque
3	Bir Barouta	6	Great Mosque

told you can't get across the land border and that there are no buses (even the Tourist Office will tell you this but what is even more amazing is that the customs people at Ben Gardane will deny there is any public transport). The facts are that there are taxis every day to the frontier for 600 mill. The Libyan Customs is 150 metres walk from Ben Gardane.

PLACES TO SEE

From Easter onwards the eastern coast gets crowded with tourists although there are many beautiful spots especially on the Island of Djerba. The beaches on the northern coast are much less popular with tourists and relatively unspoilt and there is beautiful mountain scenery along the Algerian border. The oases around Tozeur are worth visiting. At Douz between Gabes and Tozeur there is a yearly Sahara Camel Festival between 26—29th December when there are camel races, folk songs, displays of crafts and dances. Transport from Gabes every day by mini-bus at noon arriving at Douz at 2.30 pm costing 800 mill. Or bus every day from Gabes to Tozeur, changing at Kibili for Douz. Depart Gabes at 5 pm and arrive four hours later costing 700 mill. The people at Douz are very friendly, hospitable and poor. There is every possibility you will be offered accommodation by a local family — try to contribute if you are offered this.

Underground houses at Matmata near Gabes are worth a visit. The Medina at Tunis and Sfax are quite touristy these days but there is still the possibility of bargains in local crafts and the like. Roman ruins and Carthaginian ruins at Carthage very near Tunis and at El Djem where there is a magnificently preserved colosseum as large as that at Rome. Kairouan is a traditional holy city and university centre. Plenty of beautiful mosques. Famed for its dates as it's built on an oasis. The Bardo Museum in

Tunis is well worth a visit — large collection of mosaics housed in the former Bey's palace. Many different periods of history displayed. There is also the National Museum of Islamic Arts, Dar Hussein, 4 Place du Chateau, Tunis and the Regional Museum of Folk Arts and Traditions, Dar Ben Abdallah, rue Ben Abdallah, Tunis. This latter has branches in the following places: Dar Jelloali, 5 rue Sidi Ali Nouri (Medina), Sfax — housed in 18th century mansion with clothing, jewellery and household objects from the 18th century — at Houmt-Souk, Djerba — clothing, pottery, jewellery from Djerba. The entrance fee for museums is 100 mill except the Folk Museum which is 50 mill. On Sundays and Fridays it's half-price in the 100 mill-museums. They are open 9 am to 12 noon and 2 pm to 5.30 pm in winter and 3 pm to 6.30 pm in summer.

At Nabeul there is really good pottery and earthenware drums. (Underground mosaics at Bulla Regia near Jendouba. Tunisian folk music in the concert hall of the open court yard of the Rachidia in the Tunis Medina.

There is an old man at Tozeur who has a small garden-cum-zoo called 'le Paradis'. He makes syrups from roses, violets, crab apples, bananas and pistachio nuts — an excellent drink.

OTHER INFORMATION

Taking your own vehicle No carnet is needed for Tunisia. A temporary importation licence valid for three months is issued on arrival. This can be renewed for a further three months on payment of certain taxes. You need your registration book, a driver's licence (a national licence is sufficient) and an international insurance certificate (third party insurance is compulsory). You can also buy third party insurance on the border or at the port of entry. A good route advisory service is provided by the Automobile Club de Tunisie, 29 Avenue

Habib Bourguiba, Tunis (tel 243 921).

If you are planning on driving in the desert you first have to contact the National Park Post in Medinine or the Sahara Centre in Gabes with a plan of your proposed itinerary. Usually you have to travel in convoy and have a suitable vehicle (eg four-wheel drive).

Uganda

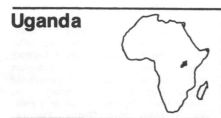

There is evidence of organised states being in existence in what is today Uganda as far back as the 8th and 9th centuries AD but, until quite rencelty, they remained isolated from the outside world. Even during the heyday of the Arab dominated Indian Ocean trade routes, when cities like Malindi, Mombasa and Kilwa were thriving, there is no evidence that there were any trade routes between the Ugandan interior and the coast. It's been suggested that the reason for this lay in the fact that between the Great Lakes region and the coast lies a wide belt of the driest and least cultivable land in East Africa which was, at that time, inhabited by warrior tribes who had neither the inclination nor the organisation to supply or protect caravans. It seems a somewhat spurious reason in view of the existence of the much longer trade routes across the Sahara which existed at this time. All the same, it was not until the 18th century when the Bantu of western Tanzania began to move into this area and begin cultivation, that trade routes were at last established between the interior and the coast.

The establishment of these routes saw the rise of the traditional Ugandan kingdoms of Buganda, Bunyoro, Karagwe, Ankole and Toro. The Buganda, who became the most powerful group, used their armies to raid the Soga to the east and the small Haya states to the south and procure slaves for sale to the Arabs. They traded these and ivory for cloth and arms from the coast. It was with arms like these that they successfully resisted Gordon's Egyptian armies when an attempt was made to subdue them during Gordon's period as Governor-General of the Sudan in the late 1880s.

In the carve-up of Africa into colonies by the European nations towards the end of the 19th century, Uganda became a British colony. In the run-up to independence, three parties — the Democratic Party, the Kabaka Yekka Party and the Uganda People's Congress wrestled for control. Milton Obote's Uganda's People's Congress, based on the less developed northern part of the country, entered a coalition with the Kabaka Yekka party of the leading Buganda tribe. After the coalition had won independence in 1962, Obote set about winning over members of the opposition and by 1965 had been successful enough in this venture to turn the tables on his former allies and establish a one-party state. This was followed by the arrest of a number of cabinet ministers on charges of conspiracy and an army attack on the Kabaka's palace. The Kabaka fled the country and Obote then turned on the other three traditional Ugandan kingdoms of Bunyoro, Ankole and Toro thus alienating any support he previously enjoyed in the south of the country and relying more and more on the support of the army which was recruited principally from the north. As Obote's rule became more and more erratic, the inevitable happened, and he was deposed by his army commander, Idi Amin, who had led the attack on the Kabaka's palace several years previously.

Unfortunately, Amin had even less idea about how to constructively govern a country than Obote and was soon resorting to cheap popularity campaigns to maintain support for his imbecilic regime. The most dramatic of these was the expulsion of the Asian community in 1972 for allegedly sabotaging the economy. Another was his transparent switch of religious affinities when he became a Moslem, thus ensuring the support of that other idiosyncratic, but powerful ruler, Gaddafi in Libya. None of these moves gained him any more than fleeting support so that eventually his main activity became the conducting of savage vendettas and pogroms against any group or individual, whether civil or military, that he even suspected of denying him the devotion he demanded. These years of violence and torture will be remembered for a long time in Uganda.

Amin eventually took things too far by invading northern Tanzania and bombing the Lake Victoria ports of Bukoba and Musoma. Tanzania reacted by invading Uganda and pursuing Amin's forces until they had been routed and Amin had fled to Libya and later Saudi Arabia. Though the Tanzanian action was criticised by other African countries at the time, most breathed a sigh of relief that this cretin had finally been removed from power. Tanzanian troops are still in the country helping to train a new Ugandan army and maintain law and order and elections for a civilian government are planned for later in 1980. Even with the best will in the world it will be difficult for any new administration to put the country back on its feet again. They inherit a bankrupt economy and a legacy of bitterness and

suspicion which will take a long time to put right. Even now, as we go to press, a major power struggle has surfaced between the President, Binaisa, and the new army chief, Brigadier Ojuk. Binaisa fears that Ojuk, who is a personal friend of Obote, may stage a coup in the latter's favour, and has attempted to remove him from his post though both Nyerere and Obote are committed to free elections rather than a military-backed government.

FACTS

Uganda lies beside Lake Victoria. The White Nile which passes through it makes it one of the best watered areas of Africa. The country ranges from the lush and fertile areas around the northern shores of the lake to the snow-covered Ruwenzori Mountains in the west (the so-called Mountains of the Moon). The tropical heat is tempered by the altitude which averages over 1000 metres. The rainy season is from March to May and from October to November.

VISAS

Required by all except nationals of the Commonwealth countries, Denmark, Finland, Germany (West), Iceland, Irish Republic, Italy, Norway, Spain, and Sweden. Officially, everyone has to get a visitor's pass before arrival either from a Ugandan embassy/consulate or from immigration in Entebbe, Malaba or Tororo. In practice this is only enforced if you are coming from Kenya. If you are coming from Sudan along the Juba to Nimule road, a Sudanese permit for travel in the south is acceptable to the Ugandan/Tanzanian border guards. From there you have to go to immigration in Kampala and get a visa or visitor's pass (valid for a stay of one month).

Note that you might be refused entry unless you are reasonably smartly dressed — the tourist blurb drones on about 'hippies' and other lesser sentient

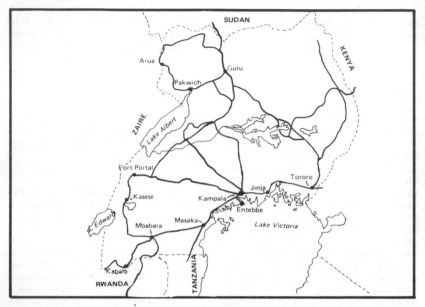

beings. Uganda is a good place at present to get visas for other countries in this part of Africa because of the amazing blackmarket rate for hard currency.

CURRENCY

The unit of currency is the Ugandan Shilling = 100 cents. Import/export of local currency is prohibited.

Exchange rate:

£1	=	Sh 16.70
US$1	=	Sh 7.25
A$1	=	Sh 8.35

The blackmarket here is incredible and it is possible to get a rate of US$1 = Sh 90.00!! On the other hand, some of the prices have been adjusted to reflect the blackmarket rate — such as food (a bun costs Sh 10 and imported Kenyan beers cost Sh 125). But other costs like telephone calls, postal services, game park fees and accommodation (government-run) and transport haven't gone up by

anywhere near as much so, while it lasts here is your chance to go on an African safari without having to fork out a fortune or call up your friends across the other side of the globe and have a rap (a three minute call to the USA costs just over Sh 100).

This situation won't last long however as the IMF is currently putting pressure on Uganda to devalue as a precondition for a massive loan. Currency declaration forms are issued on arrival but are no problem on leaving the country.

LANGUAGE

English, Swahili and many local languages.

ACCOMMODATION

Note that many places were damaged or destroyed in the war so don't expect too much at present even in the relatively expensive hotels. It's often difficult to find a room in a hotel in Kampala due to the fact that many government officials have taken up permanent residence in these places but the hotel owners are getting very choked-off by these non-paying, voucher-signing guests so things many change soon.

Kampala

There are several cheap places to stay on the left hand side as you leave the station such as the *New Star Shelly Apartments, 3 Star Hotel*, etc. They charge on average Sh 200/single and Sh 300/double. Keep an eye on your gear — things develop legs. The expensive hotels — *International, Speke, Imperial*, etc — are all in the same price bracket but the International may well give you some hassles regarding your currency declaration form. Not even the expensive hotels are in good shape and none of them have constant running water due, mainly, to looting by Amin's troops.

For food try the *International* or *Speke* hotels where you can get a three course meal with coffee/tea for Sh 90-120 or the *Seroun Hotel and Restaurant*, Dastur Street near the market, which has steak dinners for Sh 90. There's also good food at the *YMCA* (beans, 'matoke' and chappati). The latter is very cheap and friendly.

The best places to change money are the shops near the market and the curio shops around the corner from the Imperial Hotel (they offer $1 = Sh 90 for cash and Sh 85 for travellers cheques). If you have DM, they offer Sh 45 for cash or travellers cheques).

Tourist Office (Uganda Tourist Development Corporation) is situated off Kampala Road. It has plenty of maps, info on safari lodges, timetables, etc. Pretty helpful people. Note that if you can't find a hotel room for the night you can stay free at the police station.

It is recommended that you make a visit to Entebbe (a bus costs Sh 10 and a shared taxi Sh 30) where the Israelis rescued the hostages held by Amin. There is also a beautiful botanical garden there and a zoo worth visiting.

Chobe

Located in the Murchison Falls/Kabale area, a beautiful position overlooking the Nile. Costs Sh 300-340 a double with meals for Sh 90-110 (three courses). This is probably the best place to see wild life — amazing numbers of buffalo, hippos, elephants, warthog, giraffe, crocodile, etc. Ranger vehicles are cheap to rent and probably the most convenient way of seeing the animals though you can sometimes pick up private cars. River trips down to the falls are still possible.

Mweya

Situated in the Ruwenzori National Park overlooking the former 'Lake Amin' (did the man's vanity know no limits?!) Costs Sh 300-240 for a double and three-course meals for Sh 90-110. You may well come in for some hassle with your currency declaration form here but a slight 'fee' (about US$1) and a brief friendly discussion solves any 'problems'. The wild-life in this park suffered more than most during the war but there are still plenty of lions around.

Kabale

White House Inn Located in beautiful terraced hillsides where much of Uganda's vegetables and fruits are grown. Costs Sh 240 for a double.

TRANSPORT

There are buses and taxis almost everywhere and because of the present incredible exchange rate they work out very cheap. Here are some examples: Gulu-Kampala by shared taxi costs Sh 250. Kabale-Kampala by shared taxi costs Sh 300. Gulu-Kampala by bus costs Sh 80. Kampala-Kasese by train costs Sh 90. It's an overnight journey but don't expect to get much sleep! Kampala-Kenyan border by train this costs Sh 100 but there are no through trains to Nairobi and you have to change at the border.

Flights work out very cheap and you don't have to show your currency declaration form to buy tickets though normally you have to give the travel agent a back-hander. Entebbe to Nairobi presently costs Sh 900.

OTHER INFORMATION

During Amin's regime the wildlife suffered catastrophically at the hands of his troops. Armed with modern automatic weapons they systematically exterminated elephants, rhinos and other big game for the money to oe made out of their ivory horns and skins. In the 10 years since Amin came to power the country's herd of 40,000 elephants was reduced to just 1500! In the Kabalega Falls Park rhinos, including the rare white rhino, have ceased to exist. The story is much the same in the Ruwenzori Park which is littered with the carcasses and bones of elephants which were gunned down in groups of up to 10 at a time, with automatic rifles. The game wardens have been able to do little about this until recently as they are starved of funds and equipment. A little has been given by the World Wildlife Fund and Frankfurt Zoology Society but so far nothing more has been forthcoming. The slaughter of the animals continues and unless cash and equipment are forthcoming it will soon be too late. Try to do what you can to prevent this happening. One of the ways you can help is to visit the parks since it is the revenue from park entrance fees etc which goes towards facilities for the wardens and their staff. Another thing — don't buy ivory.

Upper Volta

The history of Upper Volta is essentially that of the country's chief tribe, the two million-strong Mossi, though there are substantial numbers of Hausa and Fulani in the northern parts of the country. Under their rulers — known as Moro Naba, the present holder of which is the 35th — the strongly disciplined Mossi set up a small but enduring kingdom whose roots can be traced back to the 13th century. This kingdom was never incorporated into the Sudanic empires of Mali and Songhay which held sway to the north during the heyday of the trans-Saharan trade routes but they effectively limited Mossi activity on the latter's northern frontier. The Mossi alone resisted the spread of Islam south and so provided a cover for the largely animist peoples further south in what is today Ghana, the Ivory Coast, Togo and Benin.

The country became a French colony in the late 19th century and although the Moro Naba was stripped of his temporal powers in line with normal French policy in their colonies, he retained his religious authority. Independence was granted in 1960 under a government headed by Maurice Yameogo. Yameogo was re-elected as president in 1965 but deposed by the army two months later in a coup headed by Lieutenant Colonel (now General) Lumizana whilst he was in Brazil on an expensive honeymoon having only just announced austerity measures.

The country is desperately poor and the new military government was faced with the task of implementing Yameogo's austerity measures but they have had very little success. There are few mineral resources and very little industry. Some 94% of the population are employed in largely subsistence agriculture though it does manage to export some cotton and groundnuts. The long rail link to Abidjan on the Ivory Coast is a major obstacle to the development of an export market. Though none of the country is actual desert it does suffer from a water shortage and there are numerous small dams on the Volta River which help spread water out over the year and provide fish to supplement the normal high-starch diet of most of the people. The country is heavily dependent on French financial and administrative assistance as well as various forms of aid and assistance from many international aid agencies.

FACTS
The rainy season is from June to October and the climate hot and very humid in the south. In the north it is generally hot and dry.

VISAS
Required by all except nationals of Belgium, France, West Germany, Italy, Luxembourg and the Netherlands. Visit visas are valid for a stay of eight days from the date of entry. There are very few Upper Volta embassies (Abidjan, Ivory Coast, being one), but where there is no representation, visas can be obtained from the French Embassy though the latter won't always issue the full eight-day visa. The French Embassy in Algiers issues only two-day visas (two photos required and take 24 hours to issue). Transit visas are not required if you intend to pass through the country within 24 hours but you can't count on this. Transport can be very slow.

Ghanaian Visas   The embassy is 200 metres south of the Centre d'Accueil, Ougadougou. Entry permits cost 200 CFA and take 24 hours to issue. This is the best place to get the entry permit as there are no hassles about buying Cedi Vouchers.

Benin Visas   Available from the French embassy, Ougadougou. A two-day visa

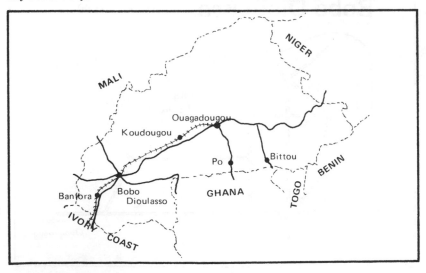

costs 550 CFA and a three-day visa 750 CFA.

Ivory Coast Visas Available from the French Embassy. They cost 750 CFA, two photos and take 24 hours to issue. No hassles.

If you are bringing your own vehicle into Upper Volta note that on some of the border crossings a carnet is accepted but at others you will be forced to buy a 'laissez passe' for 200 CFA.

CURRENCY
The unit of currency is the CFA. Import/export of local currency is limited to 50,000 CFA.

Exchange rate:

£1	=	473 CFA
US$1	=	208 CFA
A$1	=	237 CFA

The Upper Volta CFA is accepted as legal tender in Mali.

LANGUAGE
French and local languages. Very little English is spoken.

ACCOMMODATION
Banfora
A really beautiful area — don't miss the 'Cascades' about 15 km from town. You can stay at the *Maison de Jeunes* or camp at the *Cascades*. Bicycles can be hired for 500-750 CFA per day.

Bobo Dioulasso
Foyer de Scouts, located in the Quartier Coco, costs 300 CFA per person in a room with four bunk beds. This is the cheapest place to stay. A taxi there from the market costs 50 CFA. From the railway station a taxi costs 150 CFA. *Mission Protestante* near the Cathedral, sometimes has places to stay for 1000 CFA/double room.

Koudougou
Relais de la Gare, near the railway stat-

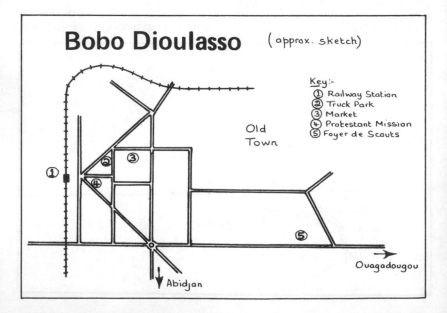

Bobo Dioulasso (approx. sketch)

Key:-
① Railway Station
② Truck Park
③ Market
④ Protestant Mission
⑤ Foyer de Scouts

Old Town

Ouagadougou

Abidjan

ion, costs 1000 CFA/double room.

Ouagadougou

Hotel La Refuge, Avenue Yennenga near the large mosque and about 1½ km from the railway station, costs 1000 CFA/double room. One traveller described it as 'filthy' but another said it was 'clean, friendly, has showers and serves cheap food'. You can't get more contradictory than that!

Pavilion Vert costs 800-1500 CFA per person. *Hotel Royal*, opposite the Grand Mosque, costs 1500 CFA/double room. Quite pleasant. *Hotel Ouidi* costs 2500 CFA a double. *Centre d'Accueil* is part of the Maison de Jeunes near the Hotel de Ville. You can stay here for free but you're supposed to have authorisation from various offices although there's little hassle if you haven't. The *Peace Corps Hostel* in the Quartier Ouidi, near the Bar Apollo, is said to be closed these days.

L'Eau Vive has good steak and chips, it's run by nuns. *Don Camillo* does steak and vegetables for 500 CFA. *Wend Yamn Restaurant*, Avenue Pompidou in the Quartier Tienpalago, serves good cheap food. Also try the *Hotel la Refuge* and the *Hotel de la Marche*.

The Tourist Office is in the foyer of the Hotel Independence. Entrance charge to the Ethnographic Museum is 100 CFA. It has a very good collection.

Ouahigouya

Le Campement costs 1000 CFA a double. Steak, salad and rice (enough for two people) costs 450 CFA — a cheap meal!

TRANSPORT

Hitching is slow and the roads are pretty poor but there are all-weather roads linking Upper Volta with Mali and the Ivory Coast. The road south to Ghana via Po is also reasonably good. In the dry season there are regular buses linking all the major towns and also plenty of Peugeot taxis (shared) with more or less standardised prices. Some examples of transport prices and journey times are:

Ougadougou-Niamey (Niger) by daily trucks for 3100 CFA. Takes 16 hours in the dry season but can take up to six days (!) in the wet, when a system of rain barriers are erected after heavy rain to let the road dry out before traffic is allowed to pass. It's a rough ride. There are also buses run by SVTR which depart on Monday, Wednesday and Friday at about 11.30 am. Book well in advance as seats are limited.

Bobo Dioulasso-Mopti (Mali) costs 3500 CFA by bus or 4700 CFA by taxi. There are many police checkpoints along this road and you may well be asked to chip in for bribing the customs people not to search the vehicle. This seems to be an accepted part of the price for the ride so you should allow a further 500 CFA as bribe money.

Ouahigouya-Bandiagara (Mali) — this is a very difficult road and should not be attempted without four-wheel drive.

Bobo Dioulasso-Bamako (Mali) by bus costs 3500 CFA and takes 24 hours. It's a good road.

Trains The line runs from Ouagadougou to Abidjan via Koudougou, Bobo Dioulasso. Daily trains depart Ougadougou at 5.40 am. Ouagadougou to Bobo takes six hours and Bobo to Bouake takes 12 hours. Sample fares are: Ouagadougou-Abidjan is 5800 CFA in second class; Ouagadougou-Bobo is 1795 CFA in second; Bobo-Banfora is 625 CFA in second.

OTHER INFORMATION

The Pan-African Film Festival takes place in Ouagadougou in early March every year. The films tend to be entirely

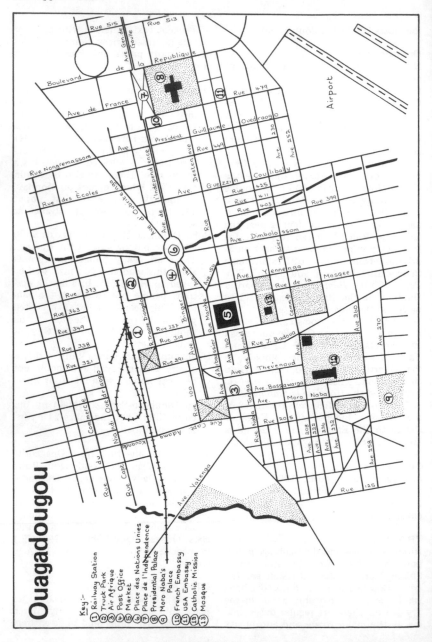

Ouagadougou

Key:-
1. Railway Station
2. Truck Park
3. Air Afrique
4. Post Office
5. Market
6. Place des Nations Unies
7. Place de l'Independence
8. Presidential Palace
9. Moro Naba's Palace
10. French Embassy
11. USA Embassy
12. Catholic Mission
13. Mosque

French-language ones from the former French colonies.

If you are going to visit the Parc National de l'Arly in the far east of the country you have to buy a permit, valid for 12 months, for 2000 CFA.

Beware of the common simulium fly in the Gourma swamp area. Their bite can lead to blindness. There are also quite a few tsetse flies here which, of course, spread sleeping sickness.

Zaire

This vast country epitomises everyone's archetypal image of Africa — endless jungles, enormous rivers, wild animals, wild people, mountains, volcanoes and the most diabolical transport system (system !?) you will come across anywhere in the world. Any traveller who has been there will entertain you for hours with the most improbable stories about the place and fall over backwards to recommend it to you. Although, politically, it's a very screwed-up country, village people are very hospitable and easy going but it does take a long time to get through, whichever route you take. It's impossible to plan anything but its fascination is endless. You'll love it! If you get the chance before you go, try reading Livingstone's *Missionary Travels and Researches*. The country hasn't changed much since then.

The existence of organised states here has been traced back as far as the 8th century AD when copper was being mined and forged on the banks of the Lualaba (the upper reaches of the Zaire River) in Katanga though no royal tombs or capital city sites have yet been found. When the Portuguese arrived off the west coast in the late 15th century they came into contact with two powerful 'Sudanic' states located near the

mouth of the Congo River (now called the Zaire River). The most important of these was that of the Bakongo who were a Bantu people formed from an offshoot of the older Luba civilization centred on Katanga and north-eastern Angola. In order to promote trade and Christianity the Portuguese sent missionaries and craftsmen to this kingdom and shipped many sons of the ruling hierarchy back to Portugal to be educated there. In this venture they were initially successful and the rulers of the kingdom remained, at least nominally, Christian until the early 17th century but the rot set in when the Portuguese demand for slaves for its Brazilian colony outstripped the numbers which could be supplied by traditional methods. Though relations with the Bakongo remained peaceful for quite some time it was not long before Portuguese-trained raiding parties further south in Angola began to encroach on the southern extremities of the Bakongo lands. Various kings of the Bakongo attempted to bring these activities under control by addressing appeals to the Popes in Rome and, for a time, stern letters passed between Rome and Lisbon though the Portuguese naturally pretended they had no control over their subjects in that part of the world. Exasperated by these efforts, the Bakongo resorted to war in 1660 but were disastrously beaten by the Portuguese and their kingdom rapidly disintegrated.

Further east, another kingdom came into being among the Luba and Lunda peoples which, by the middle of the 17th century, controlled large areas of present-day southern Zaire, northern Zambia and Angola. Their kings — known as Mwata Yamvo — established indirect commercial links with the Portuguese in which ivory and slaves were exchanged for firearms, cloth and other luxuries from the outside world. With the arms thus acquired, an offshoot of this kingdom — the Kazembes — established another state further south, in the 18th century, around the shores of Lake Mweru, which grew rich through trade with Portuguese stations on the Zambesi River and with the east coast cities via the Nyamwezi people of Tanzania, who were renowned for their porterage capabilities.

Despite all these trade links with European powers there was no direct penetration of the interior of this part of Africa until the advent of the explorers and missionaries in the 19th century. Livingstone was the first of these to explore this part of the continent from coast to coast and his chronicles were to fire the imagination of mid-19th century Europe and lead to many government and Church-funded expeditions. Livingstone was soon followed by the American newspaper reporter, Stanley, and the two were to meet in the now-famous encounter on Lake Tanganyika at Ujiji. Stanley's reports were followed with great interest by various European governments and when he landed at Marseille after one such trip was met by representatives of King Leopold of the Belgians with whom he took service in 1879. Over the next five years Stanley established a practicable land and water transportation system from the Congo estuary to the falls (later called Stanley Falls) near Kisangani, 1500 km upstream. Leopold had in mind a personal empire encompassing the whole of the Congo basin and because of the mutual rivalries and suspicions between the various European powers was spectacularly successful in getting them to recognise his claim over this area. But this success

more than any other development, was to unleash the late 19th century scramble to carve up the rest of Africa into colonies.

The 'Congo Free State' did not last long, however, as Leopold's personal empire. Unable to provide the necessary funds which other European governments did to administer their more conventional colonies, his rule there sank to appalling depths of maladministration with funds being raised by ill-trained and barbarous native soldiers who levied arbitrary amounts of tribute on rubber and ivory. When news of the worst atrocities leaked out to the outside world they raised a storm of protest and Leopold was forced to surrender his empire to the Belgian Government in 1908. The Belgian government's rule followed closely that of Leopold's in being rigidly paternalistic, denying political rights not only to the white settler population in the copper belt but also to the black population. It did, however encourage black workers in the mining industries to bring their families with them and thus create a stable labour force in contrast to the situation in neighbouring Rhodesia and South Africa where the white trade unions, afraid that Africans would acquire skills and training sufficient to challenge the white monopoly, discouraged a stable labour force.

The years following the depression in the '30s saw a phenomenal economic boom in the country, which underwrote a large part of the war effort during WW II, but no political advance whatsoever. After 1955, when many African countries were gaining their independence, the Belgians were forced to relax their rigid paternalism and allow a number of African political parties to emerge. Yet the change came too suddenly and too late for any unity to be forged between the many disparate tribal and regional groups in this vast territory. This lack of any sense of unity or nationalism has plagued Zairois politics ever since and is still a long way from resolution.

The demand for independence was led by Patrice Lumumba who attended the All African Peoples Conference at Accra, Ghana, in 1958 and secured immediate recognition for his radical ideas. Mounting disturbances in the Congo over the next two years forced the Belgians to precipitously grant independence in 1960, hoping thereby to retain their economic interests there. Lumumba was elected as the country's first leader but he was only able to govern with the support of other politicians of very different persuasions and relied very heavily on the Belgian-manned civil service and the Belgian-led army. African officers in this army, despairing of every having control over their own affairs, encouraged a mutiny which toppled the government and led to many years of civil war. In the thick of this, the Governor of Katanga Province, Moise Tshombe, declared that province's secession from the Congo. Lumumba was, naturally, unwilling to see the loss of the country's most economically important province (at the time it supplied the world with 8% of its copper and 60% of its cobalt among other things) and appealed to the UN for military assistance to crush the secession. On his return from the UN, Lumumba was dismissed as prime minister by the president, Joseph Kasavubu. Lumumba reacted by dismissing Kasavubu. Various manoeuvres followed ending in victory for Kasavubu and the imprisonment of Lumumba who shortly afterwards, under the eyes of United Nations troops who were ordered not to intervene, was delivered into the hands of his arch-rival, Moise Tshombe and there murdered.

The Katangan secession was eventually crushed by United Nations troops but the financing of the operation almost wrecked the UN itself and led to bitter wrangling about what constituted 'legitimate' intervention in another country's affairs. With Katanga returned to the fold, Kasavubu was faced with armed resistence on many fronts ranging from Lumumbists through dissident tribesmen and gangsters to would-be war lords. His solution to the problem was to invite the arch-dissident Tshombe back from exile to be prime minister. Though Tshombe was able to secure western financial aid and military assistance (including white mercenary troops) to establish a crude control over virtually all the Congo, neither he nor Kasavubu inspired political confidence so that when a bloody revolt sprung up among the Simba tribespeople in the north-east and east of the country, were swept from power in a coup led by General Mobutu in 1965. Tshombe went into exile for a second time but in 1967 a chartered plane carrying him was forced to land in Algeria. There, two years later in an undisclosed prison it was announced he had died of heart failure.

Mobutu has ruled Zaire since the coup in 1965 and although his regime has brought relative stability he has only achieved it by continuing the old pattern of murdering political opponents — whether judicially or otherwise. So-called 'amnesties' are periodically announced for rebel leaders in exile. Those foolish enough to take up these offers are sooner or later brought to trial on some pretext or other, found guilty, and then either incarcerated or executed. One of these Pierre Mulele — was actually murdered at the reception arranged to welcome him back to Zaire. The government of the country is almost entirely in the hands of the elite 'Binza' group named after the suburb of Kinshasa where most of them live. Strategically placed men in the army and government form a tough elite who manipulate their followings and local party organisations in

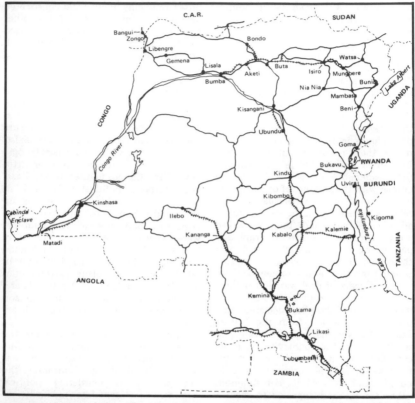

support of Mobutu's continued rule but corruption, incompetence and tyranny continue to be widespread.

Opposition to Mobutu's regime continues to surface, particularly in the eastern part of the country, but the most serious threat to his regime recently came from the invasion of Katanga (now called Shaba Province) by 5000 Angolan-supported guerillas of the Congo National Liberation Front in early 1977. They got as far as the important mining town of Kolwesi in a lightning campaign during which there were many desertions from the Zairois army and evidence (naturally suppressed) that whole units had gone over to the rebel side. Two months later the guerilla army was driven back over the Angolan border but not before Mobutu had secured the assistance of 1500 regular Moroccan troops and military hardware, US$15 million worth of military aid from the USA, and smaller amounts of similar aid from West Germany, Belgium, South Korea, China, Egypt and the Sudan. Relations with Angola remain very sour.

FACTS

The greater part of the country, especially in the centre and north-west, forms a huge flat basin averaging 300 to 500 metres high filled with lakes, marshes, rivers and rain-forest, ringed on all sides by mountains except along the Atlantic littoral. The average temperature is around 27°C and humidity is high at all times. The best time to visit is between June and September south of the Equator, and between November and March north of the Equator, which roughly corresponds to the 'dry' season.

VISAS

Required by all. Don't get your visa in Europe or America before setting off otherwise it will cost £8 (US$17.50) or the equivalent and involve you in complications regarding money and 'onward tickets' and will probably be valid only for entry and exit via Kinshasa. (Embassies in Western countries will tell you that entry and exit can only be made through Kinshasa which is bullshit and designed to make sure that those who don't know otherwise spend the maximum amount of money getting there.)

Except in Bangui, Central African Republic, (where you can sometimes get it without), you need a 'letter of introduction' from your own embassy before applying for a Zairois visa. They won't consider you without this. If you are on a British passport, note that the British High Commission in Dar es Salaam, Tanzania, will refuse to issue you with one of these so arrange your visa elsewhere. In Bangui, Zaire visas cost 1130 CFA for one month. They take 24 hours to issue and there's no fuss about money-showing or 'onward tickets'. You should specify on the application form that you want a three month visa with multiple entry. If you don't, you will be issued with a one month, single entry. The cost is the same for both types.

You can have your visa renewed up to a maximum of three months. In Kisangani apply at the Centre Nationale de Documentation on the old airport road. Extensions are free, require two photos, take 24-48 hours to issue and there's no fuss about money or onward

tickets. In Bukavu, three month, multiple entry visas cost Z3 and take three to four days to issue.

If you want to visit the diamond-mining areas of Kasai Oriental and Kasai Occidental (Kananga, Tshikapa, Mbuji-Mayi) you need special authorisation from the Secretariat General de la Presidence in Kinshasa and a very good reason why you want to go there. Foreigners are not allowed to visit the mining areas of Shaba Province.

You may occasionally encounter trouble with government officials (eg customs, army, police, post office, etc). If you do, remember that they probably haven't been paid for the last three to six months (this happens frequently). A Z1-5 backhander usually solves any problems.

Rwanda Visas At Goma these cost Z25 or Rw Fr 500 or US$6 for either three or six days. If you want longer they cost Rw Fr 3000 so try to get your visa elsewhere.

CURRENCY

The unit of currency is the Zaire (Z)= 100 makutas. Import/export of local currency is prohibited.

Exchange rate:

£1	=	Z4.54
US$1	=	Z1.97
A$1	=	Z2.27

Despite the 50% devaluation of the Zaire in early 1978, there is still a flourishing blackmarket but the rates vary a lot from one place to the next. It is generally true to say that the blackmarket rate improves from west to east with the best rates being available in the cities on Great Lakes. US dollars are the preferred currency. French Francs are the least preferred. There is a lot of paranoia associated with the blackmarket, so you will have to feel your way around. Try Pakistani shops in Kisangi. A selection of recent rates follows:

Kisangani: US$1 = Z2.50
CAR Border (Zongo): £1 = Z2.50
Kundu: £1 = Z5.50
Bukavu: £1 = Z4.50
Goma: US$1 = Z3.00

Currency declaration forms are issued at some points of entry — such as Kinshasa airport — but not on most land crossings. If you leave Kinshasa by air you will be expected to prove that you have exchanged at least Z20 in foreign currency for every day you have spent in Zaire (Z30 for a married couple). The average minimum daily expenditure you can expect in Zaire at present is US$8-10. Airport tax for international departures is Z1.00

LANGUAGE

French is the official language and is more or less indispensable. Very little English is spoken. There are numerous local languages however, the main ones being Lingala (spoken in the north-east) and Swahili (spoken in the east). For a short Swahili vocabulary see the 'Kenya' chapter. A short vocabulary of Lingala follows:

Mai: water, **Mbote**: hello, **Songo**: manioc, **Makemba**: bananas, **Biloko yakolia**: things to eat, **Makasi**: strong, **Musika**: very far, **Nazondo**: market, **Loso**: rice, **Madeso**: beans, **Makaibo**: salted fish, **Mbisi**: fish, **Niama**: meat, **Lobi**: tomorrow, **Wapi**: where?, **Mbwa**: dog, **Malam**: OK, thanks, **Sango**: new, **Sangonini**: what's new? (greeting), **Sangote**: nothing new (reply), **Kolia**: eat (infinitive), **Komela**: drink (infinitive), **Mingi**: a lot, **Kokende**: depart, **Okeyi wapi**: where are?, **Nake**: go, **Ponanini**: why?, **Ndako**: house, **Mboka**: home.

MAIL

Letters to or from America, Europe or Australasia, take a long time to get to their destination. One month to Europe is quite normal (air mail).

FOOD

There are chronic food shortages and prices vary enormously even over short distances of about 20 km because of problems with distribution (eg a bottle of beer which sells for Z1 in Kisangani goes for Z5 by the time it gets to Beni). Always go for what grows locally. Here are some sample prices for staples in various locations:
(B=Beni; E=Epulu; I=Isiro; N=Nyakunda; W=Watsa):
orange: 10-20 makutas; can of pilchards: Z4; Italian tomato puree: 70 makutas; Loso makaibo: Z1.50 (I); Loso niama: Z3 (I & E); Loso mbisi: Z2.50 (I); Loso pondu: Z1.50 (I), Z2.50 (E); Loso madeso: Z1.50(I), Z3 (E&B); egg: 50 makutas (I) 30 makutas (N); tomato omelette: Z3 (B); bottle of Primus beer: Z5 (B); tin of margarine: Z5 (B); coffee or tea without sugar: 10 makutas (W) 25 makutas (I) 50 makutas (E); same with milk: 50 makutas (W) 60 makutas (B) Z1.20 (E); Baigne: 5 makutas (W) 10 makutas (I,E & N); sardines: Z1.50; three bananas: 3 makutas (W) 10 makutas (B,E,I & N); bottle of Skol: 60 makutas to Z1 (I); pineapple: 50 makutas (E, I & W) Z1 (N); bread: 50 makutas to Z2 depending on the size of the loaf; Argentinian corned beef: Z3.

ACCOMMODATION

Hotels are very expensive except in the smaller towns where they are often really filthy. Kinshasha itself is attempting to be the Las Vegas of Africa and prices are outrageous. It's got all the usual reminders of bored and aimless urban living plus night-time muggings and is about as far removed from life in the rest of Zaire as you can get. It's suggested you avoid the place. Most travellers stay with various Christian missions or with local people — hospital-

clue where to stay or there doesn't appear to be anywhere, ask the Chef du Localite/Chef de la Collective/Chef de Village or even the Chef des Postes. Make sure they understand that you are prepared to sleep on the floor and eat local food otherwise they often assume that you're not. In many places you will get VIP treatment. Apart from this there are the missions run by the Catholic Church and the various Protestant Churches where you can often get cheap or even free accommodation. It all depends on the priest and locality. Sometimes the missions are issued directives from the Ministry of Tourism in Kinshasa telling them not to accommodate low-budget travellers and to send them them to the nearest hotel where they can contribute to the national economy (ho, ho). On the other hand, it's gradually becoming official Catholic policy not to accommodate travellers any more except where purpose-built accommodation is available — the Catholic Mission in Kisangani won't take you any more for instance.

Awitcha
You can sleep on the floor of the *Protestant Mission and Hospital* free or have a bed for Z3 with sheets and washing facilities though the Police Commandant would rather you stay at the hotel where there are rooms for Z8 and Z12. No food at the Mission.

Bayenga
You can stay at the Catholic mission which is run by a Dutch Father. Otherwise there is a Belgian businessman next door who always puts up travellers.

Beni
Hotel Beni costs Z11/single but you can have as many people in a room as you like. The hotel buys hard currency (cheques or cash) for excellent rates. For a cheap breakfast try the cafe behind the boulangerie. For a larger meal

ity can be incredible. If you're offered food and a roof over your head, be generous with a contribution towards your keep — most people are very poor. Some travellers have suggested that hooks and fishing lines are excellent gifts to bring with you in exchange for accommodation. Though we've extracted some of the more regular places to stay for inclusion in this section, a great deal will depend on your own efforts especially in the more remote areas but to get a more comprehensive idea of what's available and how to find it we're including several extracts from travellers letters later on in this chapter.

If you arrive in a place and haven't a

there is a cheap restaurant in the market. If you are planning on climbing the nearby peak of Mutwanga in the Ruwenzori range, guides are obligatory and cost around Z100.

Bukavu
There are several cheap hotels averaging Z5 per person near the 'Mama Mobutu' market otherwise you can stay at the school situated on the hill above the Revolutionary Monument for Z2. Meals are available. Camping is allowed there too. Follow the signs for the school.

Epulu
Clean rooms available for around Z4 if you look hard up or you can camp at the Station de Capture for Z1. Some people sleep there free without a tent.

Gemena
The Catholic Mission in town won't put you up but there is another about three km from town where you can stay free. If no luck, the soap factory will put you up and arrange rides for you.

Goma
Camp at the *Centre Sportif* free or rent a double room for Z2. *Hotel Haute Zaire*, situated behind the market, costs Z13 for a room with a single and a double bed. Good food available. There are other more basic hotels near the main street for Z3-4. Good tea and omelettes from the *Restaurant Stade des Volcans* between the market and the Hotel Haute Zaire.

Isiro
The *Tennis Club* is situated near the airport and guarded at night. You can sleep free on the verandah or camp there. There is a swimming pool you can use free of charge, a private bar where you can get ice-cold Skol for 60 makuta but there is no food available. In addition to this place there are a number of missions but note that the Catholic Mission won't even give you a drink of water let alone offer you accommodation.

Lisala
The Catholic Mission has rooms for 50 makuta regardless of numbers sharing and showers. Free camping at the Protestant Mission, *Hotel Montaigne* has rooms for Z3.50-7.

Lolwa
The Protestant Mission is a very friendly place. Described by one traveller as 'just like home!' Be prepared to 'see the light' overnight.

Lubero
A ghost town with one truckies' hotel for Z6/single and Z10/double. Meals are available for Z5 or you can buy tea and an omelette for Z1.50.

Lubutu
The Catholic Mission here is friendly.

Kabalo
The *Hotel du Parti* is the cheapest in town, costs Z5/single.

Kalundu
This is the port for Uvira on Lake Tanganyika. You can sleep on the porch of the Maritime Commission free of charge.

Kinshasa
Protestant Mission, Ave Kalemie, has accommodation available for Z9. Also try the Salvation Army but forget about the Catholic Missions. If you are looking for some light entertainment, the British Embassy Club has films on Tuesdays and Thursdays at 8 pm, costs Z2. On the same days of the week the US Embassy Club also has films but at 6.30 pm. Costs Z1.50 and food is available.

Kisangani
Two of the cheapest hotels are the

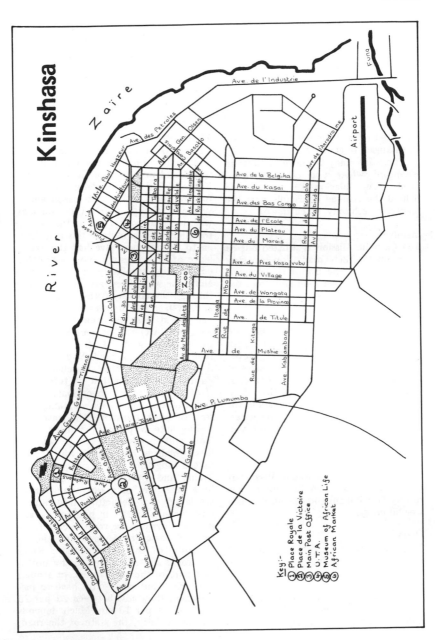

Kinshasa

Key:-
1 Place Royale
2 Place de la Victoire
3 Main Post Office
4 U.T.A.
5 Museum of African Life
6 African Market

Olympia Hotel (but expensive food) and the *Boyoma Hotel* (in the Quartier des Musiciens). You could also try the *French Cultural Centre* for a cheap place to stay. The American Consul here is very helpful. Many travellers camp or sleep out at Tshopo River where there are pavilions to sleep under and a bar on the hill adjacent to the small zoo. You will need a taxi from the central market in Kisangani to get there.

There are many Greek restaurants in Kisangani where you can buy good meals. The blackmarket is located behind the Banque du Peuple near the market — cash only, no cheques.

Mambasa
The Catholic Mission is situated out of town on the Beni road. You can stay here and have the use of the showers but bring your own food and don't expect any favours.

Mt Hoyo
Auberge is the only place to stay and it's expensive. Camping costs Z5 with hot water laid on, incredible views. Meals are excellent though expensive at Z5 for breakfast and Z11 for dinner. If you can't afford this, stay in the village below overnight. If you are heading for the waterfalls or 'grottes' it's suggested you hire a guide otherwise you will probably get lost.

Nia Nia
You can stay at the Catholic Mission if you are lucky and they have room. It is run by two Italians and the old Pere is a wee bit crazy.

Uvira
You can always stay at the Catholic Mission. Very friendly.

Wamba
You can sometimes stay at the Catholic Mission, if you approach them in the right manner and only stay one night. They are reluctant to let you stay at first, but once accepted they really look after you — meals, good bed and showers.

Zongo
Many travellers stay at the Catholic Mission but watch your gear.

TRANSPORT
Zaire is Africa's wildest country. The 'roads' are some of the worst in the world and nothing runs on time. Ever. You can find yourself waiting for weeks for transport in the wet season and if you are relying on free lifts you may well have to walk a lot of the way — travellers who have done this and written to us say they have had the experience of their lives and have been offered amazing hospitality in every village along the way. There are no quick ways through the country (other than flying) and, even in the dry season, you should plan on at least six weeks to get from Bangui (CAR) to Goma or Bukavu on the Rwanda border. In the wet season there is no way of predicting how long it will take you. Most travellers cross Zaire by a combination of truck lifts (free or otherwise), river-boats, trains and the occasional bus or taxi. Any sort of road transport will leave you feeling like a piece of bruised jelly. You will need to rest up between lifts which is one reason why it will take a long time to cross this country. Trains and riverboats, like buses, do have schedules of a sort though they are largely for decorating tidy-minded civil servants' desks. In practice departures and arrivals are very much a function of passenger demand and the inclination of the driver/captain. Rides on trucks are often free in the northeast part of the country except around Lake Kivu but where you have to pay for them they cost between Z1 per 25 km and Z1 per 10 km. Much depends on the locality, the state of the road,

and the driver.

Routes

Because of the political colour of Zaire's Atlantic neighbours, Angola and Congo-Brazzaville, the only practicable land crossing in the western part of the country is Bangui (CAR)-Zongo (Zaire). In the eastern part on the other hand, crossings are possible all the way from Sudan to Zambia via Uganda, Rwanda, Burundi and Tanzania. So the main routes through the country start from various points along the long eastern frontier and converge on Lisala and Zongo across the province of Haut-Zaire. Since the journey from Bangui to Lisala on the River Zaire is common to all routes we start from Bangui and move east.

(1) Bangui/Zongo-Lisala via Gemena The ferry across the Ubangi River from Bangui to Zongo costs 50 CFA when it isn't broken down — which happens from time to time. If it's out of commission there are motor boats and piroques which will take you across. Avoid the latter if possible as they're expensive. Stock up with Zairois currency in Bangui as there are no banks at Zongo or Lisala. There are banks at Gemena and Bumba. The Zaire customs at Zongo are usually easy going but they sometimes demand you change a certain amount of money into Zaires (most people wriggle out of this one way or another). Cameras have to be declared and are sealed by the customs. Currency declaration forms are not issued here.

There is no regular transport between here and Lisala and you will have to rely on lifts with trucks. The journey to Lisala generally takes between five days and a week. Expect to have to wait a day or two for lifts at various points en route.

At Lisala you have the option of either continuing by road to Bumba (about a day's ride) or taking the Zaire

River steamer to Kisangani via Bumba and Basoko. If you are in a 'hurry' or you are heading for Rwanda, Burundi or Tanzania, take the steamer. If you are heading for Sudan or want to explore northern Haut-Zaire, carry on to Bumba and branch off from there to Aketi and Buta.

(2) Lisala-Kisangani Zaire River steamer once weekly in either direction along the route Kinshasa-Bolobo-Mbandaka-Lisala-Bumba-Basoko-Kisangani. Kinshasa to Kisangani takes nine days upstream and five days downstream. The boat usually departs Lisala on the upstream journey on Sunday afternoon or Monday morning.

Fares are as follows: Lisala-Kisangani, first class is Z58.46 including three meals per day; second class is Z20.24 including two meals per day, third class is Z15.00, no meals included.

There is not much to choose between third and second class. First class is pretty good if you can afford the extra. Note that it's very difficult to conceal extra people in a first class cabin if you are thinking of trying to share the cost. Third and second class tends to be already full by the time the boat reaches Lisala in which case you will have to pay the extra for first class or wait for the next boat in a week's time. There is a canteen on board but it is best to buy fruit from the dug-out canoes which come alongside. Food served on board is usually fiery corned beef, mountains of maggoty rice and beans full of weevils!

(3) Bumba to the Sudanese or Ugandan border via Aketi, Buta, Isiro, etc. The precise route you take to the eastern frontier will largely depend on the availability of transport and the season, though most people initially take the railway from Aketi to Isiro or Mungbere (the rail head). A truck from Bumba to Aketi takes a day. The train from Aketi to Isiro is a glorified freight train — metal goods wagons with sliding doors but no windows — and it goes when there are enough people to fill it. This may mean sleeping at the station for up to two days. It's an incredibly slow train and takes about 48 hours to get to Isiro. If you are lucky there may be a connection to Mungbere but it doesn't always turn up so plan on hitching rides from Isiro. The only 'regular' transport as such in this part of Zaire is a twice weekly bus service from Faradje to Bunia run by a mining company. It's apparently free. On the other hand, since foreigners are a novelty in this part, you may well get a lot of free lifts.

If you are heading for Sudan, take the Watsa-Faradje-Aba road through to Yei (Sudan) and from there to Juba. There is an occasional bus between Watsa, Faradje and Aba called the 'Tulla Tulla' — aptly named since in Lingala this means 'couldn't care less' — but otherwise it's an excellent trek and highly recommended.

(4) Kisangani to Beni, Goma & Bukavu via Nia Nia & Mambasa There are plenty of trucks along this route and there's a 50:50 chance that you will get free rides. On the other hand, don't expect free rides between Bunia and Bukavu. Travellers are no longer a novelty in that part of Zaire. The journey from Kisangani to Goma takes on average four days in the dry season (though it can be done in two days). In the wet season it can take 10 days to two weeks though we did hear from one incredibly lucky individual who made it from Kisangani to Beni in 2½ days during the rains. The roads between Nia Nia and Adusa are good but there are some very bad parts between Adusa and Mambasa so expect delays. A lot of improvement has gone into the roads between Beni and Bukavu over the last few years but the stretch from Kamande to Beni is a disaster area with holes up to three

metres deep! It has been known for travellers to take two weeks to cover this stretch alone though this is exceptional. Some of the most amazing countryside in Africa is to be seen between Beni and Goma — the road goes between two volcanoes, one of which only erupted a couple of years back, and over a 2000 metre pass. East of Beni are the Ruwenzori Mountains.

Some examples of lift prices are: Goma-Rutshuru for Z6, Goma-Lubero Z45 by bus, Goma-Butembo Z35 (bus along this route costs Z40 to Z60 and takes two days). Butembo-Beni Z5, Beni-Kasindi Z10.

Lake Kivu Steamers These connect Goma with Bukavu and call at many remote missions en route. The luxury steamer departs six days per week in either direction and takes three to seven hours depending on the number of calls it makes. The fare is Z10 in first class and Z3.50 in second class. You may need to book two days in advance. There is also an older boat which runs less regularly, costs Z1.50 and takes up to 17 hours.

(5) Kisangani to Burundi & Tanzania There are three possible routes here:
(a) Kisangani to Bukavu overland. From Bukavu you can either head north to Goma and from there to Rwanda via Gisenye or south to Uvira on Lake Tanganyika and from there take the Lake Tanganyika steamer to either Bujumbura (Burundi) or Kigoma (Tanzania).
(b) Kisangani to Kindu by Zaire riverboat and from there overland to Bukavu.
(c) Kisangani to Kindu by riverboat, railway from Kindu to Kabalo and then railway from Kabalo to Kalemie on Lake Tanganyika. From Kalemie you can take the Lake Tanganyika steamer to Kigoma (Tanzania), Bujumbura (Burundi) or Uvira (Zaire).

(a) This is a straightforward hitch with journey times similar to those in (4) above. If you're in a hurry options (b) or (c) are quicker.

(b) Kisangani-Kundu — for the first leg you take the train from Kisangani to Ubundu. It runs twice weekly on Fridays and Sundays departing Kisangani at about 8 am and connects with the riverboat going south from there. The journey takes about 10 hours and costs Z1 (there's only one class on the train — 'economique'). It's a fascinating ride through the jungle and the wood-burning engine stops every 20 km or so to take on wood and/or water. Food is sold at stops along the way and on the train (groundnuts, rice and corn and beer). It's quite a social occasion.

The river steamer from Ubundu to Kindu takes about three days. Third class costs Z1 (entitles you to an iron-slatted bunk with no mattress). Organisation is virtually non-existent on the boat so grab a bunk and argue about the fare afterwards. Good food is available in the first class dining room but the boat stops frequently at wayside ports and you can buy rice, manoie, cakes, nuts, oranges and bananas there. From Kindu it's a straight hitch through to Bukavu.

(c) Kisangani-Tanzania — follow the route in (b) as far as Kindu then take a train through to Kabalo where the line branches. One goes south to Lumumbashi and the other goes east to Kalemie on Lake Tanganyika. It's a slow train so make sure you get the 'special' train which has an attached restaurant with a bar. Helps to pass the time.

At Kalemie you take the Lake Tanganyika steamer which connects Kalemie with Kigoma (Tanzania), Kalundu (Zaire) and Bujumbura (Burundi). The schedule is as follows

Kalemie	*Kigoma*	*Kalundu*	*Bujumbura*
dep 16.00 Wed	arr 07.00 Thu	arr 07.00 Fri	arr 10.00 Fri
	dep 14.00 Thu	dep 09.00 Fri	

Bujumbura	*Kalundu*	*Kigoma*	*Kalemie*
dep 12.00 Fri	arr 13.00 Fri	arr 07.00 Sat	arr 07.00 Sun
	dep 16.00 Fri	dep 16.00 Sat	

Fares:

	first class	*second class*		*first class*	*second class*
Kalemie to:			Kalundu to:		
Kigoma	Z12.79	Z4.72	Bujumbura	Z 5.34	Z2.13
Kalundu	Z25.84	Z9.26	Kigoma	Z17.14	Z6.24
Bujumbura	Z25.84	Z9.26			

For the fares between Tanzania and Zaire/Burundi and between Burundi and Zaire/Tanzania see the 'Tanzania' and 'Burundi' sections.

Other Regular Transport

Flights Freight planes fly regularly between all the major airports and some travellers have managed to get very cheap flights by hanging around the airport and speaking with the pilots. It's worth a try, especially in the rainy season. Otherwise there are regular scheduled flights which you can pay for using Zaires bought on the blackmarket which makes the flights quite cheap but avoid the Air Zaire office in Kisangani. If you ask for the student fare there they demand evidence that you are a resident. Naturally you can't prove this so they demand you pay in hard currency for the ticket. Avoid this hassle by buying your tickets through travel agents. The only other Air Zaire office where you will encounter this problem is in Kinshasa. Anywhere else they don't give a tinkers'. Some sample fares are — Kisangani-Goma Z69, Kisangani-Bukavu Z72.

TRAVEL EXPERIENCES

Since each traveller's experience of crossing Zaire will be unique and since it is impossible to generalise too much about road transport (or any other sort of transport for that matter) we're including extracts from letters which travellers have sent us. We hope they'll supplement the transport section and encourage you to go there.

Steve Fuhramann 'We managed to hitch as far as Bumba. It took one day from Zongo to Libenge where we crashed on a mission porch. Libenge to Lisala took two days and Lisala to Bumba one day. Due to a combination of terrible roads and crazy drivers we arrived in Bumba pretty fucked-up and covered in bruises and since we had managed to avoid public transport to date we decided to treat ourselves to a train ride. By taking the train as far as Mungbere near Isiro we'd save ourselves 1000 km hitching and double that number of bruises. The train goes (incredibly slowly) when there's enough people to fill it. This necessitated crashing a couple of days at the station. The carriages are metal goods wagons with sliding doors and no windows, packed with jabbering women who fight violently for space and then deposit their umpteen kids in a large circle around them and immediately start stuffing manioc and sardines into their faces. Add to this the huge piles of pots and pans and other such shit plus dozens of squawking chickens buried underneath the luggage and a couple of goats plus half a dozen leg-less Zairois men all trying to crash out on top of one another and two squashed, bewildered, and stoned hippies and away we went!

Aketi to Isiro took 40 hours. After three days waiting at Isiro they eventually realised that no train was coming and put us on a bus. Altogether quite an experience. The only food available was groundnuts, gorgeous pineapples, South African (!) sardines and, of course, manioc.

In Mungbere the manager of the CV Zaire Transport Company told his drivers not to give us a lift so after a week of waiting we set off walking to Bunia since the road to Mambasa was impassable at the time. It took us 30 days to get from Mungbere to Bunia due to the fact that there was hardly any transport and also a couple of bridges collapsed when we were in Arebi so nothing could get through and we had no choice but to walk. We had an amazing time staying in little villages, eating local food, sleeping in mud huts and sharing many a smoke with Pygmies. We stayed on a coffee plantation for a week and in all this time no-one allowed us to spend a penny and we never ate so much in our lives. After Bunia, travel became a little easier and once we got to Kamande we started picking up Kisangani traffic. From Kamande to Beni the lorry drivers were asking too much but after only an hour we got a free ride in a little Ford pick-up which had no less than ten punctures before it finally pegged-out leaving us a seven km moonlit walk through the forest to a small village called Eringeti where we crashed at the school having spent several hours trying to push our vehicle out of nightmare ruts. Amazing scenery all the way ...... Everyone seemed amazed that we hitch-hiked at all but it's relatively easy so long as you're relaxed and have a little patience. Some times you have to wait for days for a lift but people will always put you up if you ask ....'

Esther & Amin Mawan Got lift from Zongo to Gemena. Arrived late in the evening and a soldier took us to the Officers' Club where they let us cook on our stove and then told us we should sleep inside in case it rained. Should mention here that Amin, my husband, was born and brought up in Kenya and speaks fluent Swahili which is probably why the soldiers were so hospitable as we met travellers who'd had the oppos-ite reception from the military. No transport all the next day. Day after that we got a truck to Akula. A white nurse gave us a lift to the mission in Binga where we got rooms as an Austral-ian guy we'd run into had a touch of sun-stroke and was running a fever. Belgian priest there, one of the nicest we'd met gave us iced water and wouldn't take any money for rooms. He ran us into town in the morning for a lift. Soon got truck to Lisala .... Had to wait five days for a boat but we didn't want to go by road. If you're there on Sunday go to Mass. It's like nothing I've ever seen. Very beautiful with drums and women dancing, etc. From Kisangani, a truck to Kamande cost Z5. Took two weeks from Kamande to Goma. Trucks piled up for days because of large holes in the roads.

Chris Corry I hitched to Kampala then to Murchison Falls Park before making my way to Kasese in western Uganda. I left Kasese and then hitched to the bor-der town of Bwera (Mbewera). I believe it's possible to get a bus from Mbewara to Kasese. At Mbewera I stayed at a guest house and ate cheaply and well at local restaurants. The next day a lorry took me through to the customs post at Mpondwe about two miles further up the road and then all the way up to

Mbwera. We reached the Zaire entry post at Kasindi and got into the country without difficulty. The road was shock-ing! Then on to Nia Nia and Kisangani. A lot of traffic goes from Bukavu, Goma and Beni to Bunia but again the road is bad. Passes through jungle all the way with many villages along the way. There was a long wait at Kamande then a lorry to Nia Nia (thunder storms plus a couple of hours of non-stop lightning forced us to stop for the night and rest huddled together in a small roadside shelter).... The next day we stopped at Epulu and then onto Nia Nia and from there a ride to the bridge 92 km from Kisangani which was broken and closed to traffic. It rained most of the time and was hot and steamy. Finally got another ride to Kisangani.

Roger Northridge I spent a little over four weeks walking and hitching in the north from Aba to Isiro and from Isiro to Nia Nia, Epulu, Mambasa, Nyakunde and Beni. I walked 200-300 km and didn't try very hard to get lifts but I never had to pay for a lift. When you get to Beni though everything changes: the people have some experience of tourists, prices are double what they are in the north, and everyone expects to be paid for transport. Further north in little towns like Watsa and Wamba foreigners are still a novelty. From Beni to Butembo the standard rate in someone else's vehicle was Z15 but he wasn't put out when I only paid Z10. From Butembo to Goma there is a coach service for Z60 taking two days or so. Lubero to Goma on the same coach is Z45. Butembo to Lubero is Z10 by truck but I only paid Z5. Rutshuru to Goma is Z10 (72 km). A note on the state of the roads in Feb/March: Aba-Faradje-Watsa was good; Watsa-Gombari quite bad, with some very narrow bits and a lot of boulders, but Mungbere to Isiro is quite good. Isiro to Nia Nia is very good. Nia Nia to Adusa is good but Adusa to Epulu has some really bad parts if it rains. All this is excellent for walking except for a bit of 'grand foret' 20 km south of Bayenda ('Matete' on old maps) which goes on for 25 km — sans habitation! From Epulu to Mambasa there are great gaping holes in places. Lolwa to Nyakunde is not bad in the dry season as the ground is higher. From Kamande to Beni is a disaster area! When I passed there were 60 trucks waiting to get through a series of holes which stretched about three miles and were sometimes 10 feet deep. Some were waiting four days to get through. Beni to Goma is quite good on the other hand and improves at the Goma end.

Bob Bell We entered the Congo at Ishash near Rutshuru about 60 miles further south of Masindi. Hitched a lorry to Beni which took 1½ days along a good dirt road that wound round up and down through beautiful green hills. Next day caught a truck going to Mambasa and then Kisangani — normally takes three to four days in the dry season, several weeks in the wet season.

Bob & Gayle Cuddy Good road to Mambasa, wretched after that ... but the most gorgeous scenery in Africa. From Nia Nia to Kamande you pass through rain forest. Near Beni you can climb one of the Ruwenzori peaks — there is also a grotto around what used to be the film set for *King Solomon's Mines* and a steep waterfall known as Venus' Staircase. The road itself winds down a magnificent ridge with neatly spaced white houses forming villages on the slopes. Finally you come to Kabasha Escarpment and begin an hour long descent into Virunga National Park. We saw elephants, hippos, buffalo, antelope, warthogs — all from the main road. Others saw lions. The whole journey should take about 10 days from Kisangani to Goma. Near Goma there's an extinct volcano you can climb.

Kisangani-Goma. Six of us hitch-hiked alone — took about the same time from Kisangani to Beni excluding time off for visiting the pygmies — nine days on average, eg Kisangani-Komanda, 1½ days on one truck, four days on another. The women didn't have to pay, the men paid about Z30 each. Roads generally are

much better than the descriptions in the guide, but a bridge was out somewhere between Lubero and Goma so we who were on trucks went on a very bad road which must be what all the roads used to be like — eg my truck took two days to do the last 60 km to Goma. There are two routes to Goma — the truck route doesn't go all through the park because there is a barge with a two-ton limit. Those of us who had rides in tourist cars missed the bad road, eg one took five hours driving time from Lubero to Goma. Truck route takes three to four days! (Park entrance fee Z12.) Many of the small towns the trucks stop in have hotels with rooms for Z1.50-2. Generally no windows or electricity but they provide gas lamps, a bed, and no cockroaches or bedbugs. No complaints!

OTHER INFORMATION

National Parks The Virunga National Park between Beni and Goma alongside Lake Edward is highly recommended and includes some of the most beautiful countryside in Africa. Rain forests, snow-capped mountains and volcanoes. The main attractions are the two volcanoes — Nyiragongo and Nyamulgira — both of which can be climbed. Nyiragongo can be climbed in a day but most people spend the night on the rim of the volcano and return the next day. This way you get to see the molten lava in the crater after mists clear in the early evening. The sight is nowhere near as spectacular during the day. There is a hut just below the crater rim where you can stay the night. Treks up Nyiragongo start from Kibati, 13 km north of Goma. There is a small cafe here where you can arrange a guide and porter. Entrance to the National Park costs Z12 and the fee for a porter and guide will be about US$10 for each 24 hours. It's a good idea to take charcoal with you if you are thinking of staying on the crater rim overnight. A flashlamp is also more or less essential if you don't want to break your leg climbing down from the crater rim to the hut after dark. All treks have to begin by 1 pm at the latest. Nyamulgira is a three-day trek and you have to take all your own supplies with you as nothing can be bought along the way. Though Nyamulgira has no boiling lava like Nyiragongo the views over the steaming rain forests below are unforgettable and it's well worth the effort to go on this trek. The entrance fee to the park entitles you to visit both volcanoes. The best time to visit these volcanoes is between December and January or in June. At other times of the year they tend to be shrouded in mist and cloud.

Kahuzi Biega National Park is about 35 km north-west of Bukavu and is one of the last sanctuaries of the gorilla. There are very few of them left because of hunting and capture for zoos so if you want to see any you will have to hire guides. Treks are arranged at the Park Warden's office in Bukavu located on the main street. He also collects the entrance fee of Z12.

Smokables Congolese grass is world famous and needs no further comment. You buy it in small banana leaf rolls. A small roll in Kisangani will cost about 10 makutas. The Pygmies make beautiful pipes to smoke it from.

Selling things If you can get to Kolwezi in Shaba Province in the extreme south of the country (at present foreigners are not allowed to visit the mining areas of Shaba) you can buy small pieces of carved malachite (a copper ore). You can re-sell these to any jeweller in Johannesburg (such as the ones in the Carlton Centre) for a handsome profit.

Zambia

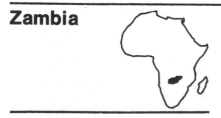

This strangely-shaped country came together as a result of Cecil Rhodes' activities in the late 19th century, out of what was left of central southern Africa after all the neighbouring areas had been claimed variously by the Belgians, Germans, and Portuguese. Like many other countries on the continent its borders are a legacy of colonialism and correspond neither to any single or complete tribal area nor to the boundaries of any kingdom which existed here before the arrival of the Europeans. Because of this it has been hard for Zambia's leaders to generate a strong sense of national unity among the many different sections of the population though the president, Kenneth Kaunda, like Nyerere of Tanzania, is one of those few African leaders who have managed to retain a high degree of sincerity and integrity about their regime despite all odds.

When the Portuguese arrived in Mozambique at the end of the 15th century they encountered an empire which ruled all the land from the Zambesi estuary to the Kariba gorge on the borders of what is today Zambia and Zimbabwe. This was the Monomatapa empire, called this by the Portuguese from the title of its ruler, the Mwenemutapa. These people were the successors to the Great Zimbabwe civilisation which flourished between the 11th and 15th centuries on the Rhodesian plateau and had been forced to move north due to the exhaustion of salt supplies in that area. The Portuguese quickly took over the Zambezi River ports of Sena and Tete from the Arab and Swahili traders and thus established themselves only four to five days march from the Monomatapa capital, 250 km north of modern Salisbury. Missionaries were sent to the ruler of this kingdom who agreed to be baptised but then had the missionaries murdered at the instigation of his advisors. The murders led to a series of military expeditions over the next 15 years resulting in a treaty favouring the Portuguese.

A peaceful trading partnership continued between the two until the 17th century when the Monomatapas were forced to appeal to the Portuguese for military assistance to combat the growing threat from the expanding Changamires further to the south. This new force, however, proved too powerful for either and eventually drove both the Monomatapas and the Portuguese off the plateau. This defeat signalled the end of the Monomatapas and by the 18th century it had shrunk to a tiny area between the river ports of Tete and Zumbo in Mozambique. The Changamires themselves were later destroyed in devastating raids by migrating Zulu warriors from Natal in the early 19th century.

In 1890, Cecil Rhodes, seeking to encircle the Boer Republics of Transvaal and the Orange Free State and thus make them more amenable to British pressure and influence, sent a column of British pioneers north to occupy Shona tribal territory east and north-east of Matabeleland. As a result of their efforts they carved out what was shortly to become Northern Rhodesia though not before they had been forced to conquer a Matabele nation resentful of their presence and subsequently put down a rising among the Matabele and Shona caused by the settlers' demands for land and labour. Economic development of this land, however, was slow due to the lack of roads and railways which made the export of mineral resources very costly. Even today Zambia suffers from the lack of an adequate transportation system so that when the border between the country and Rhodesia was closed during Ian Smith's regime there, the action all but bankrupted the Zambian economy since the bulk of mineral exports had to be sent through Rhodesia to Mozambican and South African ports. The Benguela rail link between the Angolan port of the same name and Zambia via southern Zaire proved to be too unreliable and congested to adequately substitute for the rail link through Rhodesia though matters improved when the TANZAM railway, linking Lusaka with Dar es Salaam, was completed in the mid-70s.

Zambia gained its independence from Britain in 1964, gollowing the break-up of the Federation of Rhodesia and Nyasaland which had become dominated by right-wing white politicians bent on preserving white supremacy. The man who led the struggle against this and has been president since independence is Kenneth Kaunda, an ex-farmer and teacher and son of a Church of Scotland missionary. He is similar in many ways to Nyerere of Tanzania in his passionate desire to see Zambia develop into a just and equitable society and frequently weeps publicly when things don't go right as a result of sloth and lack of commitment. On many occasions he has berated Zambians for being a nation of drunkards and threatened to resign. At the same time he has been one of the foremost supporters of African Liberation movements and is much respected for putting principle before cost. He provided a base for Mozambican FRELIMO guerillas during the '60s and '70s in their struggle with the Portuguese colonial authorities and in the late '70s a base for the Zimbabwean guerillas of Joshua Nkomo. Along with the other so-called Front Line Presidents, he lent his weight to the many initiatives which attempted to force Smith to concede a black majority government in Rhodesia (now Zimbabwe).

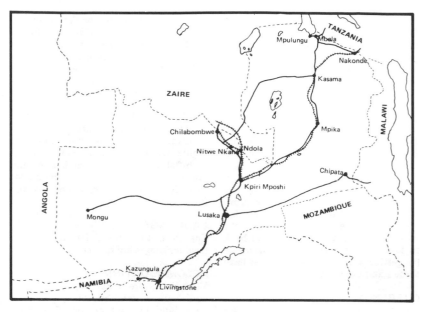

FACTS

The country is made up largely of the former 'native reserve' of Barotseland, large areas of which were virtually depopulated during the era of the Arab slave trade — a fact which is reflected in the relatively small 4½ million population. Its main source of wealth and almost its only export is copper from the vast deposits north of Lusaka near the Zairois border. Reliance on this one source of income has, however, created serious problems in the last few years, which, until electric power became available from the Kariba Dam (jointly owned by Zambia and Zimbabwe), were compounded by the need to import coal from the Wankie collieries to fuel the copper smelting industry. And all this during the many years of confrontation with the white regime in Salisbury.

The state controlled agricultural boards have displayed an abysmal performance in a nation which could be the breadbasket of southern Africa and massive food imports are necessary. This is one of the reasons why many foodstuffs are in short supply in this country. Meanwhile the drift from the land continues and if present trends are maintained 40% of the population will soon be living in urban areas while millions of hectares of cultivable land remain untouched. Of the total of 116 million hectares, only one million are cultivated in any continuous fashion and a few hundred commercial farmers are responsible for nearly all of Zambia's maise requirements — the staple food for both people and cattle. Hopefully with the independence of Zimbabwe, many of the drains on the country's resources will have now been removed and a mild degree of prosperity looked forward to.

VISAS

Required by all except nationals of the Commonwealth countries and the Irish Republic. Those who require visas can generally get them on arrival at the border. If you have a South African stamp in your passport which shows that you spent more than 24 hours there, you will have to buy a visa (regardless of nationality). These cost Kw 2.25. If you do have such a stamp in your passport, it is advisable to get the visa before arrival.

Tanzanian visas From the High Commission, Woodgate House, Lusaka. A visitor's pass needs two photos and takes 24 hours to issue. Look clean and tidy. The Tanzanians are even less keen on South African stamps than the Zambians and if you arrive on the Tanzanian border with one of these stamps in your passport they may well send you back to Lusaka to get a visa. Avoid this hassle by getting a visa in Lusaka if you have these stamps in your passport.

CURRENCY
The unit of currency is the Kwacha (Kw) = 100 ngwee. Import or export of local currency is allowed up to 10 Kwacha.

Exchange rate:

£1	=	Kw 1.73
US$1	=	Kw 0.76
A$1	=	Kw 0.87

There is a thriving blackmarket where you can get up to US$1 = Kw 3. In Lusaka try the following places for changing money: Barbeque Place, five km from the centre of Lusaka (ask for Tony), the photo studios on the main street in Lusaka (US$1 = Kw 2.50) or Chako's Industries, Freedon Road, behind the Lusaka Hotel.

Currency declaration forms are issued on arrival but are seldom collected when leaving. All the same, make sure it's in order as they sometimes have purges and can get very strict.

If you're coming from Botswana or Zimbabwe, the nearest bank is at Livingstone. If the bank is closed go to the North Western Hotel about four km from the railway station. It's an expatriate hang-out and someone will change for you if you ask around.

You can pay for flight tickets (domestic and international) in Kwacha, which makes them quite cheap if you're changing on the blackmarket.

Airport tax is Kw 2 for domestic flights, Kw 4 for international flights.

Inflation is fierce in Zambia and any prices quoted here will soon be out of date. It's a very expensive country and food is scarce.

LANGUAGE
English is the official language. Many local languages are spoken.

ACCOMMODATION
Most hotels are pretty expensive and if you're on a tight budget they'll eat a large hole in your pocket. Somewhat cheaper are the Government Rest Houses of which there are quite a number. The Tourist Offices in Lusaka, Ndola and Livingstone will provide you with a full list as well as a useful free map of Zambia. The main ones you're likely to use are in Chipata, Livingstone, Lusaka, Kasama and Mbala. Some missions offer accommodation to travellers or at least a place where you can camp. There's also the possibility of staying in secondary schools during the vacations.

In the National Parks there are a series of Catering and Non-Catering Lodges. Some are open all year whereas others are only open during the dry season. Again the Tourist Offices will provide you with a full list.

Chipata
The *Government Rest House* here is opposite the bus station. It costs Kw 1.35 per person. Other than this there is the *Crystal Spring Hotel*.

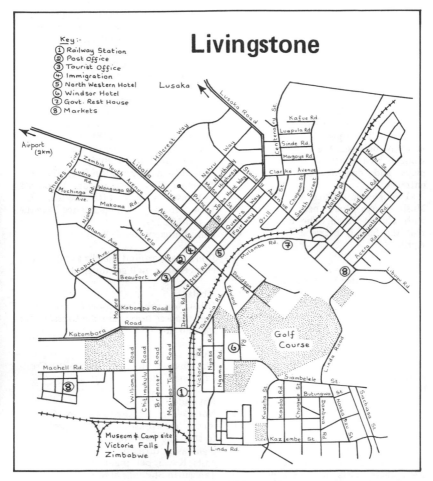

Map key:

Key:-
1. Railway Station
2. Post Office
3. Tourist Office
4. Immigration
5. North Western Hotel
6. Windsor Hotel
7. Govt. Rest House
8. Markets

Livingstone

Kapiri Mposhi

The only hotel here is the *Kapiri Mposhi Inn*. It's only got 12 beds so if you're going to stay there, be early.

Kasama

The only hotel here is the *Kwacha Relax Hotel* (30 beds). There is also a *Government Rest House* for Kw 1.35 per person.

Livingstone

Situated very close to Victoria Falls. Other than the *Government Rest House*, the cheapest hotel is the *Windsor Hotel* which is where most travellers stay. It costs Kw 6 per person. If you have a tent you can camp either at the official camp site a km from the falls for Kw 2 per tent or at the hotel at the falls themselves for Kw 2. Excellent facilities. This hotel also has rondavels for Kw 8-9 a double including breakfast. Good meals can be bought in the hotel's restaurant for Kw 5.

For night time action try the *North-Western Hotel* bar, which is an expat hang-out. Otherwise there is a buffet and African dancing for Kw 5 at the *Musi-O-Tunya Intercontinental Hotel* which has been recommended by several travellers. The open-air cultural centre half-way between the falls and Livingstone is well worth a visit for the displays and dancing. Costs Kw 0.25 entrance.

The Tourist Office is situated on Mosi-o-Tunya Road, near the junction with Mutelo Road. The best time to visit the falls is between October and April.

Lusaka

The Sikh Temple has beds and will put you up free but it's often full. The cheapest hotels are the *Bwacha Hotel* (near Chachacha Street); *Annexe Hotel; College Hotel* (Kw 15 a triple with full board); *Zani Muone Hotel* and the *Hill Top Hotel.* The *YMCA* is opposite the hospital but is expensive. The camp site is at Makeyi, about seven km south of town on the Livingstone road, next to an Italian restaurant. If you're really stuck, try the teachers' hostel. The *Dutch Volunteer Hostel* ("the Dutch farm") is run by a Zambian called Alex, a very nice place but 10 km out of town (a taxi there costs Kw 4-5). Accommodation there costs Kw 5.50 including breakfast. Lunch costs Kw 1.50 and dinner Kw 3.

Useful addresses:

Tourist Office, Block 26, Independence Avenue (tel 50188).
Automobile Association of Zambia, Dedan Kimathi Road (tel 75311).
Zambia Airways, Haile Selassie Avenue, (tel 74213).
Air Malawi, Heroes Place, Woodgate House, Cairo Road (tel 72541).
East African. Airways, Chester House, Cairo Road (tel 75891).

Embassies & High Commissions:
Botswana High Commission, 2647 Haile Selassie Avenue (tel 50804).
British High Commission, Independence Avenue (tel 51122).
French Embassy, Unity House, Katunjila Road/Freedom Way (tel 75283).
Kenya High Commission, Kafue House, Cairo Road (tel 75897).
Malawi High Commission (tel 75997).
Tanzania High Commission, Woodgate House, Cairo Road (tel 51300).
USA Embassy, Independence Avenue (tel 50222).
Zaire Embassy (tel 77232).

Don't walk around Lusaka at night. The chances are you'll get mugged.

Mbala

Other than the *Government Rest House*, the cheapest hotels are the *Grasshopper Inn* and the *Arms Hotel.*

Mpika

The cheapest hotel in town is the *Crested Crane Hotel.*

Nakonde

Not a very pleasant town. The *Government Rest House* is the cheapest place to stay but you won't get much sleep at night as it turns into a brothel. A bed costs Kw 3 per night. Good rates for Tanzanian Shillings here.

Ndola

The cheapest hotels are the *Rutland Hotel, Jacaranda Hotel* and the *Hotel Victory.* If you want something a little more salubrious than these, try the *Falcon Hotel.*

TRANSPORT

Hitching·is relatively easy but beware of drunken drivers — you'll see many cars and trucks stoved in at the side of the road. Drunkenness is a real problem in Zambia. Many of the truckies are Somalis. Some charge for lifts; others don't. In addition to the above there are buses between all the major towns daily. Departure times tend to be erratic so you'll have to play it by ear.

Some examples are Kapiri Mposhi-Lusaka costs Kw 4.45 by luxury express bus. There are cheap ordinary buses but they stop at every mango tree. Lusaka-Chipata costs Kw 6.30. Lusaka-Livingstone takes 10 hours (but often more) and costs Kw 6. There are daily buses at 7 and 11 am. Lusaka-Nakonde costs Kw 8.40 and takes two days. The daily bus departs at 4 pm.

The Zambian-Zimbabwe border is now open so road and rail links with Zimbabwe will again be available. Since Zimbabwe only gained its independence as this was being typed we have no details of these as yet. If you go there, please drop us a line with more details.

Trains
The TANZAM Railway from Kapiri Mposhi to Dar es Salam (Tanzania) — the express train departs Kapiri Mposhi on Tuesdays and Fridays at 10 pm. The ordinary train departs on Wednesdays, Thursdays and Saturdays at 10.35 am. 50% reductions are available for International Student Card holders. The booking office in Lusaka is situated next to the GPO. For more details about this train and the fares see the 'Tanzania' chapter.

From Lusaka to Livingstone the 'Kabue Express' departs Lusaka daily at 4.20 and 7.40 am. The train departs Livingstone daily at 8 am. The journey takes nine hours and the fare is Kw 8 in standard class and Kw 5.50 in economy class. There are 50% student reductions available on these fares except on Saturdays and Sundays.

Slower, cheaper trains also operate on this route but they involve travelling at night.

Although the Zambian railway system connects with the Zairois system it's strictly for freight and there are no passenger services.

Boats There are no regular passenger boats connecting Zambian ports on Lake Tanganyika with Tanzania, Zaire or Burundi but there is a once weekly cement carrying freighter called the *Independence* which leaves from Mpulungu (near Mbala) and goes to Bujumbura (Burundi). It's a three day trip but it's free. You must take your own food. If interested ask around for the captain who's called Georgolidis.

Flights There are daily flights (often several daily) between Lusaka and all the major towns in Zambia. In addition Zambian airways connects Lusaka with Francistown and Gaberone (Botswana), Maputo (Mozambique), Blantyre (Malawi), Dar es Salaam (Tanzania), Nairobi (Kenya), Mauritius and Matsapa (Swaziland) usually on a once-daily schedule in either direction. Student reductions are available on these flights to International Student Card holders.

Other Routes
Zambia to Botswana direct When the border between Zambia and Zimbabwe was closed the tiny strip of common border between Zambia and Botswana at Kazangula on the Zambezi was the only way you could get from Zambia to the rest of southern Africa and even this was out of the question for a while after the Rhodesian Air Force had sunk the ferry. It's again possible to go this way and there's now a good all-weather road between Kazangula and Francistown in Botswana (called the BOTZAM road) but since the border between Zambia and Zimbabwe is again open, following Zimbabwean independence, it's probable that most travellers will prefer to

use the better transport facilities through Zimbabwe and enter Botswana via either the road or rail between Bulawayo and Francistown. Whichever route you want to take, both options are now open.

OTHER INFORMATION
National Parks Zambia has some 15 Game Parks/National Parks varying in size from the huge Kafue National Park to the tiny Blue Lagoon National Park. Most of these parks have a selection of Catering and Non-Catering Lodges run by the government. Some of them are open all year but others are only open from June to October/November (the dry season). For a full list of these and a free map marking their locations, contact any Zambian Tourist Office. The entrance fee to the parks is Kw 0.50 plus Kw 2 if you take a vehicle in.

Zimbabwe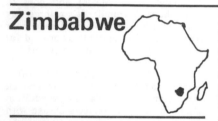

Zimbabwe became Africa's most recent independent nation in April 1980 under an internationally-recognised black majority government headed by Robert Mugabe, thus ending 15 years of rebellion by the white supremacist regime of Ian Smith and many years of bitter guerilla warfare. The settlement came about as a result of a long conference in London in late 1979 between the main contenders in the struggle — the two guerilla leaders of the Patriotic Front, Robert Mugabe and Joshua Nkomo; the Prime Minister of the short-lived Zimbabwe-Rhodesia, Rev Muzorewa, and Ian Smith, leader of the white Rhodesian Front party. This conference succeeded where many others in the past had failed largely due to the recent escalation in guerilla activities operating from bases within Mozambique and Zambia. Attempts to contain this threat first by the Ian Smith regime and then by the Muzorewa Government, had begun to place an intolerable strain on the Rhodesian economy — already hard-pressed by international sanctions — and led to increasing emigration by white settlers. The gradual withdrawal of essential South African military, economic and diplomatic support and the efforts of the so-called Front Line Presidents of Botswana, Mozambique, Zambia and Tanzania also went a long way to ensure that a settlement was reached.

The settlement set aside 20 seats in the 100-member Parliament for the white settlers (all taken by Ian Smith's Rhodesian Front party) with the rest allocated to the black section of the population. In the elections for these latter seats Robert Mugabe's Zimbabwe African National Union Patriotic Front party swept up a resounding 57 of the total leaving Nkomo's party with 20 and Bishop Muzorewa's party with three. Since coming to power, Mugabe, a committed socialist and Marxist-orientated thinker, has acted with remarkable restraint in his dealings with the white community and has been doing his best to persuade them to stay and help rebuild a new multi-racial society. He has even included two whites in his Cabinet as Ministers of Commerce and Industry and Mines. Nevertheless, he has a hard task ahead of him, if only because of the high expectations which have been raised among the blacks and the difficulty of delivering the goods at a pace which will maintain support for his government. A considerable amount of aid has already been pledged by various countries, notably Britain and the USA, but it is still well short of that considered necessary to rebuild an economy ravaged by so many years of guerilla warfare and international economic sanctions. Mugabe's election came as a shock to the South African regime which had expected Muzorewa to pick up the bulk of the black seats and had assisted him in his election campaign. The failure of their protege now leaves South Africa even more vulnerable to the change which must inevitably come there sooner or later though for the moment the advantage remains on their side of the fence.

After the break-up of the white-dominated Federation of Rhodesia and Nyasaland which led to the independence of Zambia and Malawi in 1964, the comparatively large white settler population of Southern Rhodesia, numbering about 250,000, attempted to retrench themselves there and deny power to the five million blacks. When it became clear that Britain would refuse to grant independence to the country without evidence of at least substantial and continuing progress towards true majority rule, the new Prime Minister, Ian Smith with the majority of white settlers firmly behind him, unilaterally declared independence. Though the Southern Rhodesian regime had during the '50s been multi-racial in outlook it gradually became almost indistinguishable from its South African neighbour in all but name. International sanctions against trade with Rhodesia were agreed to by member states of the UN in an attempt to bring the illegal regime to heel but while Rhodesia had free access to the ports of Mozambique and South Africa and the governments of these countries were sympathetic to her, these remained largely ineffective. There were also many instances of clandestine sanctions-busting operations by European and other nations, including British oil companies, eager for the profits to be made from trading with mineral-rich Rhodesia.

Black resistance to white supremacy was beset with fratricidal quarrels and opportunism for many years — a point not lost on Smith who was able to manipulate each and every one of these to his own advantage in delaying any serious consideration of majority rule and as an excuse to jail the various black leaders from time to time. The turning point came with the victory of FRELIMO in Mozambique and the ending of Portuguese colonial rule there. The new regime closed the border with Rhodesia stopped Rhodesian access to its rail and port network and began to assist Robert Mugabe's efforts to raise a guerila army. As the incursions of this army into eastern and southern Rhodesia began to get more and more serious and led to increasing emigration by the white settlers Smith started to court Nkomo, Ndabaningi Sitole and Muzorewa. They were plied with offers of negotiations which would lead to black majority rule though with the whites retaining the power of veto and control over the security forces.

The only one to take the carrot was Muzorewa and, as a result of elections in which the Patriotic Front were banned from participating, Zimbabwe-Rhodesia came into being with Muzorewa as Prime Minister. Diplomatic recognition of the new regime was withheld by most countries in the world and Nkomo went into exile in Zambia, there to raise a second guerila army. The two armies were eventually united under the banner of the Patriotic Front after pressure from the Front Line Presidents who were supporting the armed struggle and could see that only by presenting a united front could an effective campaign be launched. Mozambique took the brunt of reprisals by the Rhodesian security forces which launched several thinly-disguised invasions of that country in an attempt to wipe out guerilla bases there. Nevertheless, the war continued unabated and the attempt to contain the dual threat from Zambia and Mozambique eventually placed such a strain on the economy, and on the human resources which the white settlers could muster, that they were forced to accept the offer of mediation by the British, and the conference which paved the way for true majority rule.

Zimbabwe has a long history of settled civilization as witnessed by the massive stone structures at Great Zimbabwe, Khami and Dhlo Dhlo among others. By 1000 AD, trade and production for trade were already making an impact on the stratification of society and leading to cultural changes. It was about this time that states based on divine kingship emerged and the first stone structures built on the Rhodesian plateau. Over the next few centuries these states prospered through trade in gold and viory with the Arab and Swahili traders from the East Coast ports and this eventually led to the rise of the Monomatapa empire in the 1400s. By 1440, the Karanga King, Mutota, had welded the whole of the Rhodesian plateau between the Zambezi and Limpopo Rivers and the Zambezi River valley down to the sea into one empire though not long afterwards it was torn apart by internal rivalries with one group, the Changamires, moving south-west to establish a new state around modern Bulawayo and the

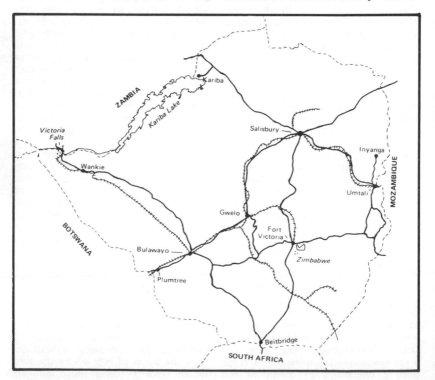

rest moving north to continue the empire there.

The arrival of the Portuguese in the early 16th century considerably altered the balance of power. With the advantage of superior arms they were partially successful in imposing their military and political authority over the Monomatapa empire and, after defeating the latter in battle in 1628, in displacing the ruler of that empire with a nominee of their own. This Portuguese intervention ruined the Monomatapa system of government, trade and production and led to its rapid decline. Their success, however, was short-lived and in 1690 they too were driven off the plateau by the Changamires never to return.

The period between the end of Portuguese interference on the plateau and the beginning of the 19th century was one of peace and prosperity and it was during this time that the centres of Great Zimbabwe, Khami and Dhlo Dhlo received their greatest enlargement. Since there were few threats from outside to the existence of this culture, none of these sites show anything more than a mere hint of fortification and were probably exclusively palaces and temples. The end came swiftly in the early years of the 19th century as these people and their culture was smashed to pieces by northward-moving Zulu warriors from Natal who had themselves been forced out of southern Africa by a combination of Boer and British demand for land and the activities of Shaka's highly disciplined Zulu troops. Some of these Zulu warriors eventually settled in the ravaged lands around Great Zimbabwe only to be followed there 50 years later by Cecil Rhodes' bands of British pioneers.

VISAS
Required by all except nationals of the Commonwealth countries, Austria, Belgium, Denmark, Iceland, Irish Republic, Italy, Luxembourg, Netherlands, Norway, Portugal, South Africa, Sweden, Switzerland, and the USA. Note that there may be a number of changes to the above list once the new Zimbabwe Government gets into its stride so check this out before turning up.

An 'onward ticket' and sufficient funds — or, alternatively, plenty of money are necessary before you will be allowed in. Customs can be very strict. You should also look as clean and tidy as possible when crossing the border.

CURRENCY
The unit of currency is the Rhodesian Dollar (R$) = 100 cents. Import/export of local currency is limited to R$20.

Exchange rate:

£1	=	R$1.43 (approx).
US$1	=	R$0.62
A$1	=	R$0.72

LANGUAGE
English and various local languages.

ACCOMMODATION
Very few travellers (or any other tourists for that matter) have been going to Zimbabwe for some time now because of the very real dangers posed by the escalating guerilla war but with this now settled, things should ease up considerably. Also the borders with Zambia and Mozambique, which were closed for a number of years, will again be open. Because of the above, we have very little current information, so much will depend on your own initiative. If you go there, please let us know some details about accommodation and transport.

Bulawayo
Youth Hostel: Situated on 11th Avenue between Lobegula and Basch Streets, five minutes walk from the railway station.

Inyanga

Tsanga Lodge is located on the Trout-beck-World's End View road. It is primarily intended for school parties so check whether there is room before going there.

Salisbury

The best contact point for travellers used to be 161 Union Ave where you could get a bed and snacks for less than R$1. There was also 81 Livingstone Ave which is a big old house opposite a park. Similar to Union Ave. There is a *Youth Hostel* at 6 Montagu Ave, about 15-20 minutes' walk from the centre. Very clean with a friendly warden but you need an International YH Card to stay there.

Victoria Falls

You can once again visit these falls both from the Zambian and Zimbabwean sides without having to make a long detour through Botswana but the facilities on the Zimbabwean side may be somewhat run-down since the hotel there was bombed during the guerilla war. Best time to visit is during the rainy season.

Zimbabwe

The stone ruins of the Monomatapa and later Changamires are located near Fort Victoria and are well worth a visit. The *Zimbabwe Ruins Hotel* at the site has a camp site as well as a 'hitch-hikers' bedroom' which will accommodate two people at very reasonable rates. Friendly management.

TRANSPORT

There is a very good network of roads and railways and hitching is very good. Most people who pick you up are very friendly and helpful. Unfortunately we have no current details of regular scheduled transport. If you go there, please send us some!

Update Supplement

Visas

A suggestion has been sent in which may help you to get through Africa without having to renew your passport due to stamp-happy customs authorities and police (Mali, for instance, demands nine blank pages!!!). This is to staple blank note-paper into the middle of your passport. Most embassies of African countries will accept this except French embassies acting for their former colonies (eg the French embassy in Ougadougou, Upper Volta, which issues visas for Togo).

Selling Things

A bottle of brandy bought for about £1 (US$2.25) in Spain or at Ceuta or Melilla is still fetching the equivalent of £15 in local currency in Algeria with no bargaining necessary.

Health

Hepatitis A 500 mg shot of gamma globulin is now accepted within the medical profession as giving adequate protection against infectious hepatitis (known as 'Type A'). Gamma globulin does not protect you against serum hepatitis (known as 'Type B') and you should be aware that, on average, more than 10% of the population of most Third World countries are healthy carriers of this virus. Prostitutes have a particularly high carriage rate and serum hepatitis can be transmitted sexually. As far as infectious hepatitis is concerned it's now been confirmed that food or water must be contaminated by human faecal matter to be infective (it isn't apparently transmitted by mucus droplets).

Polio A doctor has written to us to ask us to stress the need to have a polio vaccination before you go (unless you've already been immunised). If you catch it it may result in permanent deformity and disability and can be fatal.

Dysentery Note that a mistake was made under this section in the main part of the guide. 'Flagyl' (metronidazole) has no effect on amoebic dysentry. It's an antibiotic and antibiotics have no effect on amoebic dysentry.

For bacillic dysentry the best thing to use for slowing down intestinal movements is codeine phosphate (30 mg tablets — take two, once every four hours). It's much more effective than Lomotil or Imodium and cheaper.

To make water safe for drinking you can use five drops of 2% tincture of iodine (the sort used for cuts) to each litre of clear water or 10 drops for cloudy water. Leave it for 30 minutes before use. The water will taste quite strongly of iodine so you may need to flavour it to make it palatable.

Malaria If you're pregnant, proguanil ('Paludrine') is the recommended drug for malaria prophylaxis.

Vaccination Centres If you're in Liverpool, UK, you can get all the vaccinations from the Liverpool School of Tropical Medicine, Pembroke Place, Liverpool, 3.

EUROPE TO AFRICA

A selection of recent flight prices from London to Africa: To Accra, Ghana

(£350-355); Athens (£82-90); Cairo (£190-195); Dar es Salaam, Tanzania (£330); Johannesburg (£385); Khartoum, Sudan (£360); Marrakesh (£170); Nairobi (£265-290); Tangier (£155); Tunis (£180). All the above are return fares.

If you want to take the hovercraft across the English Channel special offers are available from Hoverlloyd: London-Paris (£16.50); London-Calais (£12.25); London-Brussels (£14); London-Amsterdam (£16.50).

Magic Bus is presently offering bus connections between London and Athens and London and Tangier for £38 and £52 respectively. Another bus company which offers a service to Athens for £34 is European Express Super-coaches.

Check the above in *Time Out* (weekly at bookshops and newsagents throughout the London area).

ALGERIA

Along the road in the north-east you will see scores of children selling live desert foxes. These animals are fast becoming extinct because of the market tourist have created for them. Don't buy them, even if you plan to let them go, it will only increase the demand for them.

Tamanrasset Very little food to stock up on here. If you plan to buy in the market get there early in the morning because things go fast! The bakery next to the supermarket has a surprising variety of pastries if you feel like a splurge before crossing the desert. The supermarket has almost nothing — tinned jam and olives is literally all there was. A near riot erupted at the arrival of powdered milk.

EGYPT

The information on travel between Israel and Egypt was supplied by Janene Madgwick, a New Zealander who is doing a lot of travelling in that area.

Look for the new and comprehensive guidebook to Egypt by Michael von Haag titled *Guide to Egypt*. It's available from Lonely Planet in Australia.

Visas

In Israel Egyptian visas can be obtained from the Egyptian Consulate (tel 03-224151/2) at 54 Rehov Basel, Tel Aviv. The consulate is open from Sunday through Thursday from 9 to 11 am except for Moslem holidays. Visas cost US$2 plus I£64.50 (about US$12 in total) for Australians and New Zealanders. In London they cost US$6. Visas are valid for a one month stay. Two photographs are required and the visa takes three days to issue. Note there are long queues at the consulate after Moslem holidays.

In Athens visas cost 270 drachs, one photo and take 24 hours to issue. They can be renewed easily in Cairo.

Currency

The official bank rate for tourists is now US$1 = 69 pt and £1 = E£1.63. The blackmarket rates are about 77 pt and E£1.80 respectively. Best rates and most hassle-free exchange can still be done with the money changer at the Golden Hotel in Cairo where conversions into Sudanese pounds can also be made. Banking hours are during the morning from Saturday through Thursday but 24 hour facilities are available at the Nile Hilton, the Sheraton and other large hotels.

The compulsory money-changing requirement on entry is still going on and in a completely arbitrary fashion. One traveller recently managed to avoid changing all but a very small amount by hiding most of his travellers' cheques and saying that the small remainder was all he had. He commented that the most important point about the whole affair is to have the stamp from the money-changers on the back of the embarkation card (which you get no matter how much you change). The official who stamps your passport doesn't care *how much* you've changed and wouldn't know if you didn't tell him. All he wants to see is the stamp.

Accommodation

Alexandria   Outside of the city the *Costa Blanca Hotel* at Agami Beach costs E£7.60 for four people without breakfast.

Aswan   *Rosewan Hotel*, near the railway station, has triple rooms at 87 pt per person. It's good value and there is a water-cooler downstairs. The manager will change travellers' cheques giving E£1.70 = S£1. *Continental Hotel* now costs E£1.10 a double and 55 pt in the dormitory.

For food the small cafe opposite the *Youth Hostel* is highly recommended and excellent value. For 60 pt you can have a two-egg omelette, yoghurt, honey, bread, butter, jam, tomato salad or tahina, orange or banana juice and tea or coffee!

A four-hour felucca trip to visit Elephantine Island and the Tomb of the Aga Khan will cost E£6. You need to get a group together to do it for that price as you have to hire the whole boat. The local ferry to Elephantine Island costs 5 pt only. The boat to Philae Island costs E£1 per person plus the entrance charge of E£2. Note that it's still possible to get to the above places free if you can get on the Oberoi launch but you have to be very confident about it as they're quite sharp. The Nubian dancing at the Cultural Centre, Nile St, is still excellent value at E£1 with student reduction (the normal charge is E£3).

Asyut   *Zamzam Hotel* costs E£1 per person in a double room.

Cairo   *Golden Hotel*, 13 Talaat Harb, is still very popular with travellers and one of the best places for picking up travel information if you're heading south but it is getting pricey. It now costs E£1.25 for a dormitory bed and E£5 a double room with shower, toilet and hot water. Some of the rooms are definitely in need of redecorating and some maintenance. The place is still run by 80-year old Mr Fez who is the life and soul of the place and George, the money-changer, is still there. He's giving US$1 = E£0.80 and E£1.80 = S£1 which is more or less what you get on the street but he doesn't like travellers' cheques (which are easily changed on the street). Mr Fez will lock up your excess gear free of charge whilst you go off elsewhere. The Golden is also organising shared taxis to El Arish on the Israeli/Egyptian border for E£4.50 per person.

Pension Roma now costs E£3.65 a double including a continental breakfast. *Plaza Hotel*, 8th Floor, Kasr El Nil St, costs E£2.50 per person including breakfast and has been recommended. *Pension Oxford*, like the Golden, is still popular with travellers and another good place to pick up information. It now costs E£1 per bed. *Hotel Minerva*, 39 Talaat Harb, has comfortable double rooms for E£5.70 including hot water and own bathroom. *Hotel Omayad*, 22 26th July St (corner of Talaat Harb), has single rooms with own shower and bathroom for E£1.38. *Hotel Select*, 19 Adli Pasha St, costs E£5.50 a triple for bed and breakfast.

The Tourist Police are at 5 Adli Pasha St. Free maps of the city are available on the 2nd floor. If you need a doctor there is a medical service at the Nile Hilton — enquire at the reception. Consultation fee is E£10 plus the cost of medication if needed.

The Egyptian Museum now charges E£1 entrance per person plus the same for entrance to the Mummy Room. The Giza pyramids now cost E£2 per person entrance. Many travellers have complained about how touristy they've become (was there ever a time when they weren't?) and that the activities of the baksheesh brigade have become unbearable. Admission to the Sakkara pyramid and ruins of Memphis is now E£1.10 per person (without student reduction). The train to El Badrshein now costs 3½ pt and the local bus from the station to Sakkara is now 10 pt.

El Minya The *Palace Hotel* is probably the best place to stay here. It's an amazing French colonial style place, incredibly clean, with massive rooms, balconies and even four-poster beds! It costs E£1 per person. Rooms have their own washbasin and the showers and bathrooms have hot and cold water. Highly recommended.

To get to Beni Hassan and the Hatsheput Temple nearby take the local bus to Abu Qurqas then walk three km to the Nile. From here you cross the Nile by local ferry (5 pt) and then walk another three km to the tombs.

Hurghada This holiday resort on the Red Sea coast is becoming quite popular and many travellers seem to be going there. Captain Mohamed Awad's *Hurghada Happy House*, El Dhar Mosque Square, has been recommended as probably the best place to stay (though there are others). Rooms here cost E£1.50 per person. Mask, fins and snorkel are available for hire. Trips to the 'House of Sharks' and to the nearby islands by boat are offered. The latter costs E£5 per person for the day including a meal.

Idfu *Samin Amis Hotel* on the main road into town costs E£2.50 a triple room. It's very basic but as good as the other hotel nearby.

The Horus Temple nearby is well worth visiting. Entrance costs E£1.10 with student reduction.

Luxor A new *Youth Hostel* has been built here which, though very clean, is said to be very unwelcoming. It costs E£1 for members and E£1.50 for non-members.

Salah El Din Hotel, a short way from the railway station on the road parallel with the Nile road, costs E£1 per person in a double room. It's clean, relatively new and serves breakfast in the rooftop restaurant. Breakfast here (two-egg omelette, bread, butter, jam, cheese, tea or coffee) costs 70 pt.

Seti Gorden Hotel now costs E£1.50 per person including breakfast. It's still good value and travellers continue to recommend it. The hotel rents out bicycles for 75 pt a day. *New Karnak Hotel* now costs E£1 per person in a double room. *Radwan Hotel*, round the corner from the New Karnak, costs E£2 per person including breakfast. It's good value and has a very friendly manager.

There's also another hotel in an unlikely place opposite the Colossi of Memnon which costs E£1.50 per person but it's often booked up and, at present, you have to go into Luxor for drinking water.

For food, the *New Karnak* is very popular with travellers. It has a menu and individual prices which many of the others don't. Breakfast here costs 60 pt. The prices of food from street stalls and small cafes is 5-10 pt for falafels (depending on size); 10-15 pt for a glass of carcade, and E£1 for sheesh kebab, salad and bread (the meat is often very stringy!)

Visiting the various archaeological sites can burn a large hole in your pocket and many travellers have complained recently that the whole town is geared up to take as much money as possible from you. Current entrance fees to the sites are: Luxor Temple (E£1); Karnak Temple (E£2); Luxor Museum (E£1); Valley of the Queens (50 pt — note there are only two tombs open); Valley of the Nobles (E£1); Valley of the Kings (E£2); Ramesseum (E£1); Dair el Bahari (E£1). Shared taxis to the Valley of the Kings cost E£6 (rumour has it that local people pay 15 pt per person!! which gives some indication of the mark-up).

Qena *El Salam Hotel*, behind the school opposite the GPO, costs E£1 per person and has been recommended as good value. It's a new place, has baths on each floor with hot and cold water available.

Places to See
Abu Simbel The boat from Aswan leaves on Saturdays only and costs E£3.25 one way. The return journey takes three days.

Aswan High Dam If you take a taxi it costs E£0.60 per person to cross the top of the dam. Restrictions have been lifted on the Philae Temples and the only cost now involved is the boat fare which is usually E£1. If you're with a large group it can be slightly less.

Luxor Bicycle hire in Luxor now costs E£1 per day. If you're heading for the Valley of the Kings, donkey hire costs 75 piastres per day. You will also have to hire a donkey for your guide and negotiate a price for his time. The entrance fee to the Valley of the Kings is E£2 or E£1 on production of a Student Card. Most of the other tombs cost E£1 entrance fee. If you also plan to visit the Valley of the Nobles ask first how many tombs are open since unless you're travelling in the tourist season you may find that most of them are closed. Not even all the tombs in the

Valley of the Kings are open outside the tourist season.

Giza Entrance to the funerary chambers in the middle of the Cheops Pyramid now costs E£2 (this is an extortionate price to pay since there's precious little to see in there). Note, too, that although they're officially open until 5 pm, they tend to be closed early. The English-language Son et Lumiere now costs E£2 and is on Saturday nights starting at 7.30 pm.

Transport
Egypt-Israel Between Israel and Egypt you can go by shared taxi ('sherut') which takes seven passengers or by bus. By taxi the total cost is about US$15 per person and the route is as follows:

Jaffa Clock Tower-border: costs I£140 per person and takes two hours.
El Arish-Suez Canal: costs E£2 per person and takes 2½ hours. The Suez Canal crossing is a regular free service which takes a few minutes. It's a very short walk from the pier to El Qantara but locals will direct you if not escort you personally.
El Qantara-Cairo: costs E£2 per person and takes 2½ hours. For this fare the taxi driver should be prepared to take you to a specific address in Cairo.

By bus there are two possibilities. An Egged bus 362 leaves Tel Aviv on Sunday through Thursday at 11 am and arrives at the border about 3 pm. You continue to Cairo by sherut taxi.

VIP Tours (tel 03-242181-2) runs an air-con bus once or twice per week to and from Cairo. You should book in advance and the fare is US$34 one-way. VIP's opposite number in Cairo is Emeco Tours located opposite Pan Am in a 3rd floor office on Talat Harb near Tahrir Square, Cairo. If you're booking a bus with them to Israel you can pay for the fare in Egyptian currency so long as you can produce bank receipts for foreign exchange totalling US$150.

At the Israeli border all you need is your passport, Between the Israeli and the Egyptian border you have to take a bus for a short distance which costs I£4. At the Egyptian border passports are collected and distributed between the two banks on a 50:50 basis and each person is required to change the equivalent of US$150 regardless of intended length of stay. It's difficult to get away with changing less than this amount though you may well find that some bank clerks are more flexible. Janene Madgwick managed US$100. Changing from your allotted line to another (for instance, because a bank clerk in another queue is more flexible) leads to all hell breaking loose.

If you intend buying an onward ticket in Egypt in Egyptian currency (considerably cheaper than buying one in Israel) then you need to have changed US$150 anyway and the rates in El Arish compare well with anywhere else.

After you've changed your money the bank receipt, visa and immigration card are checked. Passports are collected and the biggest delay is waiting for them to be returned. Expect these formalities to take at least two hours. There is also a minimal baggage check. Note that the border closes at 4 pm and a late arrival on Thursday will mean a long wait until Sunday. When you leave again for Israel there is a border crossing tax of E£3. You have to report to the passport office for registration within seven days of arrival. In Cairo the office is open from 3 to 9 pm.

You should be aware of the logistics of travelling between Israel and Arab countries. Coming from Jordan you can enter Israel (via the 'occupied west bank') and then return to Jordan or continue to Egypt. You cannot enter Jordan from Israel if you've not come

from Jordan in the first place. Thus if you are visiting Egypt, Israel and Jordan the order has to be Jordan-Israel-Egypt unless you plan to fly.

Trains Cairo-Aswan costs E£7 in 1st class with a student card and provides you with a large, comfortable, reclining seat and air-conditioning (very cool!). If the air-con doesn't work you're entitled to a refund at the other end. The journey takes 17 hours, in 2nd class the fare without student reduction is E£4.20.

Cairo-Luxor costs E£3.46 in 2nd class without student reduction. Trains to Luxor depart at 7.30, 8 and 8.30 pm. El Balyana-Asyut costs 42½ pt in 3rd class, 87 pt in 2nd.

Note that a student card or youth hostel card gets you half price on rail tickets and museum entrance fees.

Buses Aswan-Idfu costs 70 pt in a non air-con bus and takes three hours. Idfu-Qena costs E£1.30 in a non air-con bus. Cairo-Hurghada costs E£5 in an air-con bus. Departures are at 7.30 am daily and you arrive at 4 pm. Book the day before at the terminus on Ramses Square near the railway station. From Hurghada to Cairo the buses depart daily at 4.30 am and arrive at 1 pm. Book the day before at the bus station near the mosque.

Taxis Share taxis cost E£2 per person for Luxor-Aswan; E£1.50 per person for the five hour trip Qena-Hurghada; E£3 for Hurghada-Suez and E£1.50 for Suez-Cairo.

Local taxi meter fares are very cheap, in fact so cheap that most drivers won't use the meter. Tahrir Square to Ramses Square would be only 25-30 pt on the meter. Therefore it's wise to get an idea of what the fare should be before using taxis. Local people are happy to give this kind of information. Tip accordingly. Obviously most drivers will attempt to charge as much as they think you will pay.

GHANA

The people in the Abidjan Ghana Embassy are helpful and co-operative — if you already have cedi vouchers and decide *not* to go to Ghana the only way to get a refund is at the embassy where you bought them! Takes three to eight days.

IVORY COAST

Abidjan *Hotel Palymre* is being renovated and prices now range from 6000 CFA to 8000 CFA. *Hotel Atlantide*, near Palmyre, starts at 3600 CFA. *Le Prince* on 20th Avenue near Palmyre has very clean and recently renovated air-con rooms with showers and sinks from 3800 CFA. *Restaurant Senegalais* on 21st Avenue, one block from Le Prince, has good cheap food and friendly people. A bowl of soup with buttered bread is 100 CFA, omelette 175 CFA, beef and peas for 350 CFA.

City buses from Boulevard de la Republique to Treichville are 5 or 25, cost 75 CFA. Buses 6 and 18 go to the airport. The number 6 is more direct but both cost 100 CFA.

Man The *Mission Catholique Guest House* (Centre Bethani) is very nice and in a beautiful location but costs 4500 CFA. *Hotel Les Montagnes* has rooms from 2500 CFA to 4000 CFA, all with showers, some with air-con rather than fan. It's a bit dingy but better than Hotel Mont Dent.

Taxis around town cost 75 CFA for locals, at least twice that for tourists. Buses and taxis to Abidjan leave from the lorry park on the same street as the supermarket. Buses cost 3800 CFA, taxis 5000 CFA, both include baggage. A good taxi with a semi-suicidal driver will make the trip in about 6½ hours. The fact that the majority of locals were willing to pay the extra 1200 CFA to go by taxi should indicate how long the bus will take!

Odienne This is where the tarmac ends if you're heading for Bamako. *Le Campement* is newly renovated and very clean. A double with shower, sink, flush toilet and fan is 3000 CFA, with air-con it's 4000 CFA. *La Bonne Auberge*, across from the Grand Marche, has rice and sauce for 150 CFA and steak and french fries for 450 CFA. The bus to Man leaves between 6 and 10 am, depending on when it's full, from the lorry park next to the SNTMVCI (National Transport Office). Costs 2750 CFA plus 20% for one bag and takes around seven hours.

KENYA
Visas

The border between Kenya and Tanzania is still officially closed and likely to remain so for some time. To cross it you need permission from both the Kenyan and Tanzanian authorities. This is considerably harder to obtain if you are going from Kenya to Tanzania rather than in the opposite direction. If going from Kenya you need to write a letter (or telex, if possible) to the High Commissioner of Police, Ministry of Home Affairs, PO Box 9141, Ghana Avenue, Dar es Salaam, Tanzania, asking for authority. Give as many reasons as possible why you need to go overland and specify that you will not be working in Tanzania. You also need to telephone or call the Chief Police Officer at Police Headquarters, Nairobi (tel 335124) to get his permission. All this can take time so set the wheels in motion as soon as you get to Kenya. It's well worth doing as the air fares even on Ethiopian Air or Air Zambia can be as high as US$400 one way!

If you simply haven't the time to do this or it all seems too complicated there is now an alternative which is to go to Tanzania via Uganda. Ugandan Entry Permits are easy to obtain in Nairobi for all nationalities and travelling in that country is now relatively safe and likely to be increasingly so.

Ethiopian visas in Nairobi require possession of an air ticket into and out of the country plus US$500 per person minimum. It's now possible to get permission to cross the border into Ethiopia for a day at Moyale but it's unlikely you'll get any longer.
Somali visas in Nairobi cost 200 Sh, two photographs and take about one month to issue. Note there is friction between the Kenyan and Somali governments at present due to a secession movement among ethnic Somalis living along the north-east border region of Kenya.
Sudan visas in Nairobi cost 20 Sh and require three photographs. They may ask to see an air ticket into Sudan but with some perseverance you can get a visa without one of these.
Ugandan & Tanzanian Entry Permits are easily obtained while you wait from the Immigration Dempartment, Harambee Avenue, Nairobi. The Ugandan Permit costs 22.50 Sh and the Tanzanian Permit 25 Sh. No photos are required.

Currency
The blackmarket for Kenyan Shillings is now virtually defunct.

Accommodation
Kisumu Note that *Sam's Hotel* has now turned into an expensive brothel.

Kitale The *Executive Lodge*, near the Museum, is clean, comfortable, safe and quiet at 46/95 Sh for singles/doubles.

Lamu The general price of most lodges has now increased to 15 Sh a night. *Mama Nawili's* is now very popular with travellers. She's a local woman who owns an old rustic Lamu house with a thatched roof kitchen. Beds cost 10 Sh per night or 5 Sh on the roof. Cold showers are available. If you want to stay in Lamu for a while the best accommodation deal is to get a group together and rent a house. They cost around 300 a month and can be found by asking around the restaurants.

For food the *Pumuwani Hotel* just before the Zinj theatre has been recommended and the *Yogurt Shop* continues to be very popular with travellers. The latter has western-style food and excellent taped music but is somewhat more expensive than the other restaurants.

A connoisseur of local brews has informed us that the only decent palm wine is to be found at Matondoni village near Lamu where the school chairman offers accommodation, food and palm wine for a very reasonable price. Note that the dreaded weed is hard to come by at Lamu so if you want a smoke, bring your own.

The best time to visit Lamu is outside of the tourist season. Between November and March it's 'full of safari-suited, camera-toting Europeans'.

Mombasa If you're looking for a mid-range hotel here the *Castle Hotel*, Moi Avenue (Kilindini Rd) has been recommended. It costs US$20-plus per night but is a beautiful old place.

For food, the *Hotel Splendid* serves

excellent meals and the *Taj Hotel*, near the Hydro on a road branching off left from Digo Rd leaving town beyond the Mobil garage, serves huge vegetarian curries and parotha for 20 Sh.

If you're looking for some action, try the garden restaurant on the 1st floor of the *Hotel New Bristol* which has good live bands on Thursday and Friday evenings. The *Rainbow Hotel* has also been recommended for more basic distractions.

Nairobi The *YWCA* offers excellent monthly rates at 900 Sh including full board. On a shorter term basis bed and breakfast costs 76 Sh a day plus there are a variety of lesser rates for doubles and some 'remarkably crowded' dormitories. On the other hand, the YWCA is reluctant to take short-term visitors. The food they serve is nothing special. Supper costs 12 Sh for 'stringy meat and boiled-to-death vegetables in the best English tradition'. The *Youth Hostel* is now on Ralph Bunche Rd and costs 20 Sh a night. It's pleasant and comfortable. The *Sunset Lodge*, Latema Rd, costs 45 Sh a single. It's a brothel, somewhat dingy but centrally located.

Princess Hotel on Tom Mboya St is 75 Sh a double. The toilet and bathroom is dirty but the beds are clean. It's a bit noisy from the nightclub next door. The *Embassy Hotel* at the market costs 152 Sh for a double with your own toilet and bathroom. It's clean and comfortable (hot water and even a bathtub) and breakfast is included in the price. *Chiromo* is very comfortable at 124 Sh a double — there's even a swimming pool but it's a bit loud due to the disco in the evening. *Iqbal Hotel* on Datema Rd is 46 Sh a double — noisy and dirty. The *New Kenya Lodge* on River Rd/Laterna Rd is safe and good value at 60 Sh a double.

For food try the *Sarker Indian Restaurant*, Moi Avenue, near the junction with Latema Rd, which has good cheap vegetarian food. One visitor reported that things to see in Nairobi, apart from the mosque, market, National Museum, Central Park and Uluru Park include the manager of *Giorgio's Italian Restaurant*. He 'positively dances and glides around the place and is absolutely fantastic'!

There is an information and hotel booking centre in a kiosk opposite the Hilton Hotel. Note that the Kenya Airlines airport bus which costs 20 Sh is willing to drop you at any named hotel in Nairobi and not just the downtown depot. Non-profit handicraft shops can be found in the Vohumi Building, Aga Khan Walk. If you need to stock up on film buy it in Nairobi where prices are very competitive. A reel of Kodak 135 colour print, 24 exposures, costs 30-48 Sh.

Nakuru *Amigo's*, near the market by the roundabout, is clean and friendly and costs 35 Sh a bed. For food try the *Skyways* cafe which is good and cheap.

Nanyuki The hotel near the Standard Bank costs 35 Sh a double and was described by one traveller as 'the cleanest place in Africa'.

Nyeri There are many cheap hotels down the dirt road opposite a restaurant 500 metres from the market. The third one you come to — the *GK* — costs 20 Sh a night and is very clean.

Transport
Flights The cheapest flights to India (Bombay) are offered by Global Travel Muindi Mbingu St, Nairobi (tel 333624). The flights are by Ethiopian Airways via Addis Ababa. Although the normal price of a ticket is 3700 Sh Global Travel will sell you one at 2900 Sh

(some say 2600 Sh) so long as you provide them with bank receipts totalling 3700 Sh. This firm has been recommended by many travellers.

Boats *There are no passenger boats to India and no chance of getting work on a boat going there. The same applies to Tanzania.* Many travellers still come to Mombasa expecting to find a cheap ship passage to India. There are none. You must fly.

Nairobi Airport A taxi from the airport to the railway station will cost about 120 Sh, a Kenya Airways bus will be 25 Sh.

Trains Nairobi to Mombasa on the 7 pm train costs 175 Sh in 1st, 75 Sh in 2nd, 39 Sh in 3rd. In 2nd and 3rd men and women are put in different wagons.

Buses Akamba Bus Service (near the Fire Station in Nairobi) is uncomfortable and slow but cheap and reliable. Nairobi-Sotik (via Kericho) is 60 Sh. There's a bus at 9 am and another in the afternoon. Kericho-Nairobi departures are at 11.30 am and 2.30 pm and the fare is 51 Sh.

MPS (Mombasa Peugeot Service) have a bus service from the Nairobi River Rd/Latema Rd junction. They're fast, comfortable, reliable but expensive. Nairobi-Eldoret is 110 Sh, departures at 8.30 am and 2.30 pm. Kericho-Nairobi is also 110 Sh.

Kitale to Lodwar by lorry is 50 Sh and takes six to eight hours in the dry but two days when it's wet, despite which it's a fantastic trip. From Lodwar you can get lorries to Sudan. Ask the manager of the Mombasa Bar in Lodwar. He has good information and fantastic rock and reggae tapes!

Nairobi-Namanga (Tanzanian border) costs 24 Sh by bus or 40 Sh in a shared taxi. Nairobi-Eldoret is 50 Sh on a cheaper bus. Mombasa-Lamu is 50 Sh, Mombasa-Nairobi is 70 Sh or 90 Sh by Peugeot taxi.

Hitching is reported to still be easy with no more than a two hour wait for a lift.

Things to Buy
Good stone carvings are made at Tabaka, near Kisi on Lake Victoria. You can see them being made, the people are friendly and prices are low.

Game Parks
Mt Kenya Most people tend to rush this trek and end up suffering from altitude sickness. Two days is insufficient time for acclimatisation. It's suggested you first take one of the three-four day walks around the lower slopes before attempting to climb. Two good guides for these treks are, *Mountains of Kenya* and *A Rockclimbers Guide to Mt Kenya & Kilimanjaro.* The latter is very good for non-climbers too as it has good maps and details of the around the mountain walks mentioned above. They're both readily available and published by the Mountain Climbing Club which has a club house at Wilson Airport.

One traveller suggested that a good place to see animals is on the road south of Narok on the way to the Masai-Mara Game Park. You may see more animals there than in the park itself (except hippos).

MALAWI
Visas
Do not attempt to cross into Tanzania or vice versa through Kaporo/Songwe River/Kyera from the northern tip of Malawi. The route is used by local people and Malawi and Tanzanian officials may encourage you to use it too but it's not an official entry/exit

point for white foreigners and you will be turned back.

Accommodation
Government Rest Houses are now Kw 7 a single and Kw 11 a double. *District Rest Houses* are now Kw 2 a single and you're no longer allowed to rent a piece of floor — you must hire a mattress.

Livingstonia The Rest House here is the best in Malawi. It costs Kw 2.50 a night. There are no luxuries but the caretaker is a very friendly woman who will cook for you either in an official capacity (you buy the food and she charges Kw 1 for the service) or she'll let you use all the equipment free of charge and give you a hand doing it.

Nkhata Bay The Government Rest House here charges the standard rates but is often empty. The District Rest House costs Kw 2.50 but is not very clean and the sanitation is appalling.

Transport
Note that a second 'Illala' went into service in October 1980. It appears that 2nd and 3rd Classes are no longer separated so you might as well buy 3rd Class tickets. Good food is available on board (rice and cabbage, for instance) for 40 tambala — provide your own bowl/plate. Monkey Bay to Nkhata Bay costs Kw 4 (3rd Class) and Kw 8 (2nd Class).

The Chauncey Maples is presently out of service.

Other Information
The main Poste Restante is still at Blantyre (it hasn't yet moved to Lilongwe).

MALI
Bandiagara 'I would agree that the Sangha country is an 'absolute must' but I sure wouldn't say that about Bandiagara' said Sam Terry. 'It seems to be getting spoiled fast. I would rate the locals here as among the most obnoxious I've seen this trip. In the market the kids insist that you can't buy anything without them to bargain for you. They refuse to go away and won't let you bargain without them. The women in the stalls go along with it because these kids make sure you don't get a good price on anything. Everywhere else, the kids crowd around and demand gifts. One kid came up and demanded 100 MFA. When I said no he spat at me! This town was quite a shock after meeting nothing but warm, friendly people everywhere else I'd been.'

Gao *Blackpool* is hard to find but good omelettes are available for 300 MFA or steak for 400 MFA at the *Oasis.*

Mopti Beware of the tourist board here. If they see you in a private vehicle with camping gear they will threaten to impound the vehicle if you don't pay a 10,000 MFA per person 'tourist fee'. It seems you're not welcome in Mali unless you're spending money. Also each district requires a photo permit which takes one picture of yourself and around 1000 MFA (depending on the district) to get one from the police. If caught without they are said to take away your film and possibly your camera. *Lebozo* (one word) is still a great place for cheap food and beer with a view of the harbour, much better than *Bar Mali.*

Timbuktu It seems to be gearing up for a tourist boom. There is now a supermarket and bank (open 8.30 to 11 am) and a 40 room hotel under construction.

NIGER
Visas
In Monrovia (Liberia) Niger visas are available at the Ivory Coast embassy, they cost $5 and take overnight.

Agadez *Joyce's Garden* is now *L'Oasis* and run by Tuaregs but it's still very nice with a pool and ice cold beer or orange drink for 250 CFA — twice what it costs in town.

Arlit Don't get your hopes up for a cold beer here, the one bar on the main street that sells beer has a broken fridge, same as it was four years ago.

Niamey You can get Mali visas from an obscure office near Gran Marche. Type written paper on the door is the only clue to its whereabouts. The best way to find it is to take a taxi which costs 100 CFA anywhere in town. Visas take 24 hours or less and cost 2500 CFA.

The campsite at Rio Bravo has become very run down — one glance at the loo and you'll see no reason not to camp in the bush instead! The campground four km from town at Yantala is still very clean and has showers — 750 CFA per person. There is good, semi-cheap food at the *Domino Hotel*.

The swimming pool at the *Grand Hotel* now costs 500 CFA and may not be open much longer due to abuse by travellers — one person paying, three swimming and so on. The American Recreation Centre is only open to Americans who have paid a 500 CFA membership fee. That also entitles them to a third discount on the snack bar and drinks.

NIGERIA
Visas
Many travellers are having hassles getting a visa for Nigeria. It's suggested you don't apply for one in the UK as they stamp 'Visa applied for' in your passport when they reject your application making it difficult to get one elsewhere without some official-looking rubber stamp work to obliterate the words. Morocco is presently a good place to apply for a visa.

Another traveller said that unless you can be vouched for by a Nigerian citizen on your application for a visa they demand to see the equivalent of £30 (US$60) per day in funds, an onward ticket and all relevant vaccination cards.

A visa for Nigeria is required even if you just step off one plane and on to another at the airport. They cannot be issued at the airport.

Accommodation
Note that Nigeria is now ridiculously expensive. Hotels are often N40 a night in most places and in Lagos often N100 a night! The pollution and noise in many Nigerian cities has now reached overwhelming proportions.

Transport
Note that the Kano area buses have collapsed. If you're hitching you may well be asked to pay outrageous prices for lifts so check beforehand. One of the best forms of road transport is the 'passenger transport cars' (shared taxis) which are fast and efficient. Kaduna to Jos, for example, costs N6. For local transport use 'white microbuses' which are often full but cheaper than taxis.

Trains are still the cheapest form of transport though quite slow. They leave on time. Kano to Kaduna will take about five hours.

SOUTH AFRICA

Visas

If you enter via Beit Bridge (Zimbabwe/
South Africa border) the border
officials will insert a loose card into
your passport with the entry stamps
on it if you explain that you will be
going to Tanzania later.

Similarly, if you're going to the
Transkei Republic and apply for your
visa at the consulate in Durban, the visa
can be issued on a separate form but
note that if you enter near Kei Bridge
the officials there will insist on stamp-
ing your passport proper (it's said that
they never check cars for extra passengers so you could risk it and stay in the
car). If you leave/enter via Kokstad
(which is legal) there is no border post.

Accommodation

In the Transkei Republic We've had a
very pleasant letter from the night
manager of the *Grosvenor Hotel*,
Umtata, which, on his initiative, now
offers a reduction for hitchhikers in
that hotel. Accommodation here costs
R4 per person including morning coffee
though if you're really strapped for
funds he might let you sleep on the
floor of his room free. He's also been
busy compiling a list of cheap places
to stay in Southern Africa which will
include a network of people who are
willing to offer somewhere to sleep for
overseas hitch-hikers even if it's just a
place on the floor. He also says that
many commercial travellers stay at the
Grosvenor and that many of them are
more than willing to offer lifts from
Umtata to places like East London,
Durban and Port St Johns. Peace Corps
people on vacation also frequently stay
at the Grosvenor.

He also mentioned that there are
many beautiful places to stay in the
Transkei, particularly along the coast,
which are very cheap. At Port St Johns
rondavels are available for Rs 3 consisting of a mattress, table and chair and
a place to hang clothes. The rondavels
sleep two people. Larger rondavels are
available. There are other places along
the coast where rondavels are available
for as little as R2.50 and sleep up to
eight people especially in the nature
reserves. Permits are needed to visit
these reserves and they're available free
in Umtata.

Transport

A selected list of train schedules and fares follows. Note that the schedules are
abbreviated — we indicate only the main stations. For a comprehensive timetable
you should get hold of a copy (free) of the South African Railways Timetable
from any office of the SA Railway Travel Bureau. The addresses of the main
offices are:

Bloemfontein: FVB Centre, Shop 29, 40 Maitland St (tel 7-6352)
Cape Town: Travel Centre, Station Building, Adderley St (tel 218-2391/2282)
Durban: Trust Bank Centre, 475 Smith St (tel 310-3376/3363/3371)
East London: Southern Trident House, 56-58 Terminus St (tel 2-3952)
Johannesburg: North City Building, Cr Plein & Klein Sts (tel 713-5541/4941/4163/
5441)
Pietermaritzburg: Capital Towers, Cr Commercial Rd & Prince Edward St (tel 55-
2461/2)
Port Elizabeth: Fleming Building, Market Square (tel 2-2922/2233)
Pretoria: African Eagle Life Centre, 236 Vermuelen St (tel 294-2222/3/4)

Pretoria-Johannesburg-Bloemfontein-Cape Town (31¼ hours)

Station	Frequency	Station	Frequency
	Daily except Mon		
Pretoria	7.18 pm	Cape Town	9.00 pm
Johannesburg	8.30 pm	De Aar	4.20 pm
Kroonstad	12.35 am	Noupoort	7.10 pm
Bloemfontein	5.05 am	Springfontein	10.30 pm
Springfontein	7.41 am	Bloemfontein	3.30 am
Noupoort	11.45 am	Kroonstad	7.20 am
De Aar	2.45 pm	Johannesburg	11.19 am
Cape Town	8.30 am	Pretoria	12.28 pm

Only 1st & 2nd class compartments are available between De Aar and Cape Town and vice versa. On Sundays the train departs from Pretoria at 7.25 pm. There is also a train from Bloemfontein to Pretoria at 7 am daily which arrives in Pretoria at 6.35 pm (change at Johannesburg).

Pretoria-Johannesburg-Kimberley-Cape Town (20-24¼ hours)

Station	Frequency		
	'Trans-Karoo' Daily except Mon & Wed	'Blue Train' Mon, Wed & Fri	Daily
Pretoria	8.35 am	10.00 am	8.15 pm
Johannesburg	10.30 am	11.30 am	10.00 pm
Klerksdorp	1.51 pm	2.39 pm	2.18 am
Kimberley	6.47 pm	7.11 pm	8.35 am
De Aar	11.06 pm	10.21 pm	2.45 pm
Beaufort West	3.43 am	2.39 am	7.21 pm
Cape Town	2.35 pm	12 noon	8.30 am

The 'Trans-Karoo' takes only 1st & 2nd class passengers. This train will not take passengers getting off at intermediate stations between Pretoria and De Aar. The 'Blue Train' consists of special de-luxe saloons with air-conditioning only. A different scale of fares applies to this train (see later). 'Blue Train' does not operate year round. The ordinary daily train conveys only 1st & 2nd class passengers between Pretoria and Kimberley and De Aar to Cape Town. In addition to the above trains there are the following which cover part of the route: From Kimberley 'Orange Express' (from Natal) at 1.50 pm on Tuesdays and Fridays. 1st & 2nd Class only. Arrive Cape Town at 8.50 am next day. Ordinary train (from Zimbabwe) at 3.28 pm on Fridays 1st & 2nd class only. Arrive Cape Town at 11 am next day. From De Aar ordinary train at 5.30 pm daily. Arrive Cape Town at 1.40 pm next day.

Station	Frequency		
	'Trans-Karoo' Daily except Mon & Wed	'Blue Train' Mon, Wed & Fri	Daily
Cape Town	9.45 am	12 noon	9.00 pm
Beaufort West	8.36 pm	9.44 pm	9.30 am
De Aar	1.45 am	1.39 am	3.30 pm
Kimberley	5.46 am	5.19 am	9.00 pm
Klerksdorp	10.29 am	9.20 am	2.27 am
Johannesburg	2.50 pm	12.50 pm	6.30 am
Pretoria	3.57 pm	2.00 pm	8.02 am

The 'Trans-Karoo' takes only 1st & 2nd Class passengers. This train will not take passengers getting off at intermediate stations between Cape Town and Kimberley. The 'Blue Train' does not operate year round. The ordinary daily train conveys only 1st & 2nd class passengers between Cape Town and De Aar. In addition to the above trains there are the following which cover part of the route: To Kimberley the 'Orange Express' (to Natal), departs Cape Town 6 pm on Mondays and Fridays and arrives Kimberley at 1.10 pm next day. 1st & 2nd class only. Ordinary train (to Zimbabwe) departs Cape Town at 2.30 pm on Mondays and arrives at Kimberley 9.38 am next day.

Pretoria-Johannesburg-Bloemfontein-Port Elizabeth

Station	Frequency	
	Tues, Thur, Fri & Sun	Daily except Mon
Pretoria	12 noon	7.18 pm
Johannesburg	2.00 pm	8.30 pm (change trains)
Kroonstad	5.43 pm	12.35 am
Bloemfontein	10.25 pm	5.05 am
Springfontein	1.03 am	7.41 am
Noupoort	4.25 am	7.30 pm
Port Elizabeth	1.10 pm	7.30 am

Journey time is 25 hours (12 noon train) or 36 hours (7.18 pm train). The 12 noon train does not convey 3rd class passengers between Johannesburg and Bloemfontein.

Station	Frequency	
	Mon, Wed, Fri & Sat	Daily
Port Elizabeth	5.00 pm	8.30 pm
Noupoort	1.35 am	10.10 am
Springfontein	4.30 am	3.15 pm
Bloemfontein	8.10 am	8.30 pm
Kroonstad	11.40 am	1.15 am
Johannesburg	3.00 pm	6.12 am (change trains)
Pretoria	4.32 pm	7.25 am

Pretoria-Johannesburg-Bloemfontein-East London (24½ hours)

Station	Frequency	Station	Frequency
	Tues, Thurs, Fri & Sun		Mon, Wed, Fri & Sat
Pretoria	12 noon	East London	11.15 am
Johannesburg	2.00 pm	Bloemfontein	11.40 pm
Kroonstad	5.43 pm	Kroonstad	7.15 am
Bloemfontein	9.45 pm	Johannesburg	11.20 am
East London	12.35 pm	Pretoria	12.28 pm

The train does not convey 3rd class passengers between Johannesburg and Bloemfontein.

Pretoria-Johannesburg-Pietermaritzburg-Durban (15 to 22½ hours)

Station	Frequency			
	Daily	'Drakensberg' Fri only	Daily	'Trans-Natal' Daily
Pretoria	8.35 am	—	—	5.45 pm
Johannesburg	10.15 am	5.45 pm	6.05 pm	6.30 pm
Volksrust	4.58 pm	10.32 pm	11.33 pm	10.57 pm
Ladysmith	10.40 pm	2.17 am	3.51 am	2.40 am
Pietermaritzburg	4.00 am	6.08 am	7.31 am	6.38 am
Durban	7.00 am	8.45 am	10.15 am	9.15 am

Station		Frequency		
	Daily	'Drakensberg' Sun only	'Trans-Natal Daily	Daily
Durban	9.30 am	5.45 pm	6.00 pm	8.00 pm
Pietermaritzburg	12.15 pm	8.14 pm	8.28 pm	10.49 pm
Ladysmith	5.21 pm	11.30 pm	11.47 pm	4.17 am
Volksrust	11.21 pm	3.17 am	3.45 am	9.35 am
Johannesburg	5.50 am	7.35 am	8.30 am	4.00 pm
Pretoria	6.34 am	—	9.23 am	—

On the 8.35 am daily from Pretoria and the 9.30 am daily from Durban you must change trains at Johannesburg. The 'Drakensburg' consists of special de luxe saloons with air-conditioning only. Fares on this train are equivalent to 1st class plus 15%. The 'Trans-Natal' has only 1st & 2nd classes. It does not convey intermediate passengers between Johannesburg and Mooirivier or between Durban and Standerton.

Cape Town-Worcester-Mosselbay-Port Elizabeth (38 hours)

Station	Frequency	Station	Frequency
	Daily		Daily
Cape Town	3.45 pm	Port Elizabeth	6.40 pm
Worcester	7.43 pm	Mosselbay	4.05 am
Moselbay	9.05 am	Worcester	3.45 am
Port Elizabeth	6.15 am	Cape Town	8.40 am

Cape Town-De Aar-Noupoort-Queenstown-East London (34½ hours)

Stations	Frequency	Station	Frequency
	Tues, Thur & Sun		Tues, Thur & Sat
Cape Town	6.15 pm	East London	3.55 pm
Beaufort West	7.31 am	Queenstown	11.06 pm
De Aar	2.25 pm	Noupoort	7.55 am
Noupoort	5.25 pm	De Aar	2.45 pm
Queenstown	3.45 am	Beaufort West	7.21 am
East London	10.45 am	Cape Town	8.30 am

The 3.55 pm train from East London conveys only 1st & 2nd class passengers between De Aar and Cape Town.

Cape Town-Bloemfontein-Kroonstad-Ladysmith-Pietermaritzburg-Durban (40½ to 53 hours)

Stations	Frequency		Stations	Frequency	
	'Orange Express' Mon & Fri	Daily expt Fri		'Orange Express' Mon & Thur	Daily expt Sat
Cape Town	6.00 pm	9.00 pm	Durban	4.00 pm	7.30 pm
De Aar	8.55 am	4.20 pm	Pietermaritzburg	6.22 pm	9.53 pm
Kimberley	1.10 pm	—	Ladysmith	10.27 pm	2.25 am
Noupoort	—	7.10 pm	Kroonstad	6.00 am	—
Bloemfontein	4.55 pm	9.00 am	Bloemfontein	10.10 am	10.10 pm
Kroonstad	8.55 pm	—	Kimberley	1.50 pm	8.35 am
Ladysmith	4.08 am	12.37 am	De Aar	5.45 pm	2.15 pm
Pietermaritzburg	7.50 am	8.00 am	Worcester	5.37 am	4.25 am
Durban	10.30 am	8.00 am	Cape Town	8.50 am	8.30 am

The 'Orange Express' has only 1st & 2nd classes. It does not convey intermediate passengers between Cape Town and Kimberley. It does convey intermediate passengers between Bloemfontein and Cape Town. The ordinary daily train has only 1st & 2nd classes between Cape Town and De Aar.

Pretoria-Johannesburg/Cape Town/Port Elizabeth/East London to Mafeking Botswana and Zimbabwe

There are two trains per week to Bulawayo, Zimbabwe, via Botswana from Mafeking. The train from Pretoria and Johannesburg connects with the Thursday train from Mafeking. The trains from Cape Town, Port Elizabeth and East London connect with the Tuesday train from there. The schedule is as follows:

Pretoria-Johannesburg-Mafeking (9¾ hours)

Station	Frequency	Station	Frequency
	Thur only		Wed only
Pretoria	10.30 am	Mafeking	6.10 am
Johannesburg	12.30 pm	Johannesburg	2.45 pm
Mafeking	8.15 pm	Pretoria	3.57 pm

1st & 2nd classes only between Johannesburg and Mafeking.

Cape Town-De Aar-Kimberley-Mafeking (29½ hours)

Station	Frequency	Station	Frequency
	Mon only		Fri only
Cape Town	2.30 pm	Mafeking	6.15 am
De Aar	5.50 am	Kimberley	3.28 pm
Kimberley	10.15 am	De Aar	7.28 pm
Mafeking	8.10 pm	Cape Town	11.00 am

1st & 2nd classes only.

Port Elizabeth-Noupoort-Kimberley-Mafeking (27 hours)

Station	Frequency	Station	Frequency
	Mon only		Fri only
Port Elizabeth	5.00 pm	Mafeking	6.15 am
Noupoort	2.45 am	Kimberley	4.00 pm
De Aar	5.50 am	Bloemfontein	10.25 pm
Kimberley	10.15 am	Noupoort	4.25 am
Mafeking	8.10 pm	Port Elizabeth	1.10 pm

1st & 2nd classes only

East London-Bloemfontein-Kimberley-Mafeking (33½ hours)

Station	Frequency	Station	Frequency
	Mon only		Fri only
East London	11.15 am	Mafeking	6.15 am
Bloemfontein	5.20 am	Kimberley	4.00 pm
Kimberley	10.15 am	Bloemfontein	9.45 pm
Mafeking	8.10 pm	East London	12.35 pm

1st & 2nd classes only.

Mafeking-Botswana-Zimbabwe (17 hours)

Station	Frequency Tues & Thur	Station	Frequency Tues & Thur
Mafeking	9.00 pm	Bulawayo (Zim)	11.45 am
Lobatse (Bot)	10.44 pm	Plumtree	2.19 pm
Gaborone	12.29 am	Francistown (Bot)	4.03 pm
Pilane	1.17 am	Palapye	7.10 pm
Artesia	2.45 am	Mahalapye	8.45 pm
Mahalapye	5.15 am	Artesia	11.22 pm
Palapye	6.33 am	Pilane	12.19 am
Francistown	9.56 am	Gaborone	1.27 am
Plumtree (Zim)	12.10 pm	Lobatse	3.29 am
Bulawayo	2.10 pm	Mafeking	5.30 am

1st & 2nd classes only.

Johannesburg-Pretoria-Pieteresbrg-Messina-Beitbridge (17 hours)

Station	Frequency Daily	Station	Frequency Daily expt Sun
Johannesburg	7.05 pm	Beitbridge	1.00 pm
Pretoria	8.30 pm	Messina	1.40 pm (change trains)

Station	Frequency	Station	Frequency Daily expt Sun	Sun only
Pietersburg	3.05 am	Messina	3.30 pm	3.30 pm
Louis Trichardt	7.10 am	Louis Trichardt	7.51 pm	7.23 pm
Messina	10.46 am (change trains)	Pietersburg	12.51 am	11.45 pm
Messina	11.30 am	Pretoria	7.06 am (change trains)	5.37 pm
Beitbridge	12.12 pm	Johannesburg	8.50 am	7.10 am

Johannesburg-Pretoria-Middleburg-Nelspruit-Komatipoort-Mozambique (16¾ hours)

Station	Frequency Daily	Station	Frequency Daily
Johannesburg	6.15 pm	Maputo (Moz)	4.35 pm
Pretoria	7.53 pm	Komatipoort	9.34 pm
Middleburg	11.23 pm	Nelspruit	12.05 am
Nelspruit	4.15 am	Middleburg	4.18 am
Komatipoort	7.35 am	Pretoria	8.05 am
Maputo (Moz)	11.05 am	Johannesburg	9.30 am

1st & 2nd classes only between Maputo (Moz) and Komatipoort.

De Aar-Prieska-Upington-Namibia (32½ to 36¾ hours)

Station	Frequency Wed only	Fri only	Daily expt Sat
De Aar	2.30 am	8.00 pm	8.45 pm
Prieska	6.02 am	11.32 pm	12.50 am
Upington	10.51 am	4.22 am	6.40 am
Karasburg (Nam)	5.37 pm	10.47 am	1.53 pm
Keetmanshoop	10.52 pm	5.00 pm	8.17 pm
Windhoek	11.00 am	6.00 am	9.25 am

Station	Frequency Fri only	Mon only	Daily expt Fri
Windhoek (Nam)	10.00 pm	2.30 pm	9.00 pm
Keetmanshoop	10.45 am	1.15 am	9.50 am
Karasburg	5.25 pm	6.25 am	4.05 pm
Upington	12.25 am	12.55 pm	11.10 pm
Prieska	6.10 am	5.45 pm	5.20 am
De Aar	10.00 am	9.30 pm	10.00 am

Intermediate passengers getting on or off between Windhoek and De Aar on the 2.30 pm from Windhoek must arrange for the train to stop in advance.

SOUTH AFRICAN RAILWAYS FARE TABLE

Station	Bloemfontein			Cape Town			Durban			East London		
	1st	2nd	3rd	1st	2nd	3rd	1st	2nd	3rd	1st	2nd	3rd
Beaufort West	34.05	22.70	10.40	28.50	19.00	8.70	70.55	47.05	21.50	44.40	29.60	13.55
Bloemfontein	–	–	–	59.35	39.55	18.10	40.50	27.00	12.35	32.05	21.35	9.75
Cape Town	59.35	39.55	18.10	–	–	–	86.90	57.95	26.50	68.30	45.55	20.85
De Aar	20.95	13.95	6.40	41.50	27.65	12.65	58.45	39.00	17.85	32.05	21.35	9.75
Durban	40.50	27.00	12.35	86.90	57.95	26.50	–	–	–	67.55	45.05	20.60
East London	32.05	21.35	9.75	68.30	45.55	20.85	67.55	45.05	20.60	–	–	–
Johannesburg	21.45	14.30	6.55	72.70	48.50	22.20	37.55	25.05	11.45	52.20	34.80	15.90
Kimberley	8.95	6.00	2.75	52.20	34.80	15.90	49.65	33.10	15.15	40.50	27.00	12.35
Ladysmith	26.05	17.40	7.95	78.10	52.05	23.80	14.95	10.00	4.55	55.85	37.20	17.05
Mafeking	28.00	18.65	8.55	67.55	45.05	20.60	52.20	34.80	15.90	57.60	38.40	17.55
Maputo (Moz)	53.00	35.65	15.95	95.40	63.90	28.90	67.25	45.15	20.30	78.90	52.95	23.90
Maseru (Leso)	7.40	4.95	2.25	65.20	43.45	19.19	36.05	24.05	11.00	39.05	26.00	11.90
Messina	51.25	34.20	15.65	91.80	61.20	28.00	65.20	43.45	19.90	76.15	50.75	23.20
Mosselbay	49.15	32.80	15.00	26.95	17.95	8.20	79.95	53.30	24.40	52.20	34.80	15.90
East London	32.05	21.35	9.78	68.30	45.55	20.85	67.55	45.05	20.60	–	–	–
Pietermaritzburg	35.05	23.35	10.70	84.70	56.45	25.85	–	–	–	63.55	42.35	19.40
Port Elizabeth	36.55	24.35	11.15	54.00	36.00	16.50	71.30	47.55	21.75	24.80	16.50	7.55
Pretoria	23.50	15.65	7.15	74.80	49.85	22.80	39.50	26.35	12.05	54.00	36.00	16.50
Ramatlhabama	29.00	19.35	8.85	69.05	46.05	21.05	53.10	35.40	16.20	58.45	39.00	17.85
Windhoek (Nam)	81.80	54.55	24.95	93.05	62.05	28.40	102.75	68.50	31.35	87.85	58.60	26.80

	Johannesburg			Kimberley			Port Elizabeth			Pretoria		
	1st	2nd	3rd	1st	2nd	3rd	1st	2nd	3rd	1st	2nd	3rd
Beaufort West	50.10	33.40	15.30	25.80	17.20	7.85	40.50	27.00	12.35	53.10	35.40	16.20
Bloemfontein	21.45	14.30	6.55	8.95	6.00	2.75	36.55	24.35	11.15	23.50	15.65	7.15
Cape Town	72.70	48.50	22.20	52.20	34.80	15.90	54.00	36.00	16.50	74.80	49.85	22.80
De Aar	37.55	25.05	11.45	12.35	8.25	3.75	27.45	18.30	8.40	41.00	27.35	12.50
Durban	37.55	25.05	11.45	48.70	32.45	14.85	71.30	47.55	21.75	39.50	26.35	12.05
East London	52.20	34.80	15.90	40.50	27.00	12.35	24.80	16.50	7.55	54.00	36.00	16.50
Johannesburg	—	—	—	25.80	17.20	7.85	55.85	37.20	17.05	—	—	—
Kimberley	25.80	17.20	7.85	—	—	—	39.50	26.35	12.05	29.50	19.65	9.00
Ladysmith	23.00	15.35	7.00	34.55	23.05	10.55	60.20	40.15	18.35	25.05	16.70	7.65
Mafeking	16.00	10.65	4.90	19.10	12.75	5.85	68.30	45.55	20.85	19.65	13.10	6.00
Maputo (Moz)	34.20	23.10	10.25	58.40	39.25	17.60	82.35	55.20	24.90	30.75	20.80	9.20
Maseru (Leso)	28.50	19.00	8.70	16.25	10.85	4.95	43.45	28.95	13.25	29.50	19.65	9.00
Messina	33.05	22.05	10.10	56.70	37.80	17.30	78.75	52.50	24.00	29.50	19.65	9.00
Mosselbay	66.75	44.50	20.35	52.20	34.80	15.90	30.00	20.00	9.15	68.30	45.55	20.85
East London	52.20	34.80	15.90	43.45	28.95	13.25	24.80	16.50	7.55	54.00	36.00	16.50
Pietermaritzburg	32.05	21.35	9.75	43.45	28.95	13.25	67.55	45.05	20.60	34.05	22.70	10.40
Port Elizabeth	55.85	37.20	17.05	39.50	26.35	12.05	—	—	—	57.60	38.40	17.55
Pretoria	—	—	—	29.50	19.65	9.00	57.60	38.40	17.55	20.95	13.95	6.40
Ramatlhabama	17.30	11.55	5.30	20.40	13.60	6.25	57.60	38.40	17.55	20.95	13.95	6.40
Windhoek	90.50	60.35	27.60	76.80	51.20	23.40	85.80	57.20	26.15	93.05	62.05	28.40

TABLE OF FARES FROM RAMATLHABAMA (SA/BOTSWANA BORDER) TO BOTSWANA & ZIMBABWE

Station	Bulawayo			Francistown			Salisbury			Victoria Falls		
	1st	2nd	3rd	1st	2nd	3rd	1st	2nd	3rd	1st	2nd	3rd
Ramatlhabama	38.25	26.66	13.91	35.69	25.62	12.81	62.40	43.49	22.69	62.40	43.49	22.69

NB All the fares in the above tables are in South African Rand.
Beds and mattresses can be hired on trains on overnight journeys.

SUDAN

Visas

Note that it's near impossible to get into the countryside near the Sudan-Ethiopian border as you have to have special permits from National Security headquarters in Khartoum.

Currency

Inflation is running high in Sudan and in Khartoum they have stopped using coins. This means that the 25 piastre note is the smallest unit you can use. The blackmarket rate has increased considerably and now hovers between S£2.1-2.2 = UK£1. As a result of the above, most of the prices quoted in the main part of the guide are now out of date. This applies particularly to food. With luck you will be able to get an Ethiopian-style meal of wat and injera for S£1 and an inferior Sudanese meal for a little less.

Transport

The Khartoum-Wadi Medhani-Gedaref-Kassala-Port Sudan road is now metalled all the way.

TANZANIA

Visas

If you're planning on going to Tanzania or applying for a visa avoid having South African stamps in your passport and note that any evidence in it that you have *worked* in that country will bar you from entry and ensure that your visa application is rejected.

The border between Tanzania and Kenya is officially closed and likely to remain so for some time. To cross it you need permission both from the Kenyan and Tanzanian authorities. This is relatively easy to obtain in Tanzania but considerably more difficult in Kenya. First obtain permission from the Tanzanian authorities by writing a letter to the High Commissioner of Police, Ministry of Home Affairs, PO Box 9141, Ghana Avenue, Dar es Salaam, and deliver it yourself. Note that permission is granted in a very arbitrary fashion so give as many reasons as possible why you need to go overland (tourist, limited funds, etc) and specify that you're not going to Kenya to work and that you will not be returning to Tanzania. Collect your answer in two day's time from the Department of Home Affairs (Porter's Office) near the YWCA. On your way to Namanga you must have the permit confirmed by the police in Arusha. Having written the letter to the Tanzanian authorities you must also telex or phone the Chief Police Officer at the Police Headquarters in Nairobi (tel 335124) to get his permission too. Don't write a letter as it takes weeks to get a reply. You can, if you like, phone from Arusha or Namanga. If you phone from Namanga permission comes through to the border within half a day as a rule. It's a good idea to have the name of the current Chief of Police in Nairobi when phoning up. Your embassy in Dar will know his name.

If the above seems too complicated or you haven't the time to spare then the alternative is to go to Kenya via Uganda. Entry Permits for Uganda are easy to obtain for all nationalities and travel in that country is now relatively safe and likely to be increasingly so. Permits are free and obtainable from the Uganda Liaison Office, 10th Floor, Maktabu St, Dar es Salaam.

Currency

The blackmarket is still thriving. Current rates are 25 Sh = US$1 and 50 Sh =£1. The African operators around the Askari monument in the centre of Dar give the best rates but be very careful as there are police stooges. It's safer to change with the Indian traders but they often demand that you change a lot of money and have it in large denomination bills.

Tanzanian border posts are still very hot on Currency Declaration Forms.

Accommodation

Arusha *Christchurch Anglican Guest House*, near the Clock Tower, has excellent accommodation available. It costs 30 Sh per person for a self-contained flat (bedroom, well-equipped kitchen and bathroom). It tends to be booked up in advance so ring Rev C Stott if possible before arrival (tel Arusha 2476 or 3097). The *Lutheran Centre*, also near the Clock Tower, has rooms for 40 Sh a single and 70 Sh a double. It's very clean and westernised. One of the cheapest hotels in Arusha is the *Beach Hotel* near the bus stand which costs 30 Sh a single. It's clean.

For food try the *Naars* near the Clock Tower. They serve good cheap food.

Bagamoyo The *Badeco Beach Hotel* right on the beach costs 60 Sh a double and is the same price as other hotels in town. The water supply is erratic.

Dar es Salaam The Sikh Temple on Livingstone St off Nkrumah Rd still apparently takes some people free of charge though normally it charges a deposit of 100 Sh. Although this deposit is returnable it's been suggested that if you can afford it and you've stayed there for a few days to leave it as a donation. The place is clean and has fans. The *YWCA* is excellent value for women at 55 Sh per person in double room or 70 Sh a single. Book in advance if possible. Cheap meals are available here (the lunches are particularly good) for an average of 16 Sh. The *YMCA* now costs 120 Sh per person for bed and breakfast.

Moshi The *Mwariko Art Gallery* now charges 20 Sh to sleep and 10 Sh to look around. The *Njaci Hotel* is still one of the cheapest in town but now costs 55 Sh a double. It's recommended by many travellers and is clean. The *YMCA* costs 77 Sh a single and 120 Sh a double for bed and breakfast. The swimming pool is open to non-residents and costs 10 Sh. Excellent food is available here (cooked by catering students) for 35 Sh (three courses).

The *KUC Hotel* near the Clock Tower offers expensive accommodation but good cheap food in the canteen on the top floor. Vegetarian curry and rice costs 20 Sh.

Zanzibar Cheap *Government Guest Houses* are one of the best deals at 130 Sh a night but they're fairly primitive and usually have no electricity or cooking facilities though primus stoves can be hired. Water usually comes from a well.

Transport

Flights Bukoba-Mwanza costs 200 Sh. Good views of Lake Victoria en route. Dar es Salaam-Zanzibar daily flights costs 146 Sh one way.

Trains Note that student discounts have been discontinued on Tanzanian railways. The TANZAM railway is now more expensive than long-distance buses and said to be less reliable. Mwanza-Kigoma (on Lake Tanganyika) via Tabora costs 90 Sh.

Road Transport Hitching is reported to be easy except between Mbeya and Dar es Salaam. Money is rarely accepted. Trucks are not keen to give lifts.

Mbeya-Dar es Salaam: Bus costs 136 Sh and can take over 20 hours. It departs daily at 10 pm from Mbeya and goes via Mukumi Game Park.

Arusha-Moshi: Bus costs 13 Sh and takes two hours. There are hourly departures. Arusha-Namanga (Tanzanian/ Kenya border): Peugeot 404 taxis depart for the frontier when full and cost 35 Sh. There is a bus from Namanga to Nairobi at 7.30 am which costs 24 Sh. A shared taxi over this route costs 40 Sh.

Boats *There are no passenger boats to India and no chance of getting work on a boat going there. The same applies to Kenya.* The only way to get there is to fly (see Kenyan up-date section for cheapest fares).
Dar es Salaam-Zanzibar Once weekly boat on Sunday at 12 noon which costs 110 Sh one way. You do not need to book in advance if you get there early (around 8 am). It is now impossible to get a dhow from either Dar es Salaam or Bagamoyo to Zanzibar as the government has made this illegal for foreigners and the captains are observing this ban.
Lake Tanganyika boat There is now a boat called the *MV Liemba* which does a once-weekly run from Bujumbura (Burundi) to Mpulungu (Zambia) calling at Kigoma, Katumbi, Kibwesa, Karema, Kipili and Kasanga (all in Tanzania). The fare from Kigoma to Mpulungu costs 250 Sh in 3rd Class.

Game Parks
Note that the entrance fee to all national parks in Tanzania is now 40 Sh per person per day.

Kilimanjaro The cheapest *organised* tours are offered by the YMCA and cost about 1600 Sh but the cheapest way to go there is to make your own way to the park entrance and make arrangements there. The best accommodation available here is the *YMCA* which has a really good hostel at the foot of the mountain with a swimming pool. Rooms cost 80 Sh including an excellent breakfast.

Lake Manyara Note that to really see this park you need your own transport as you're not allowed to walk and there is no public transport within the park.

Ngorogoro Crater The cheapest way to see this is to take the local bus from Arusha to the crater. This costs 30 Sh, takes eight hours and is very hot and dusty. The bus stops at the park village where you can find accommodation for 25 Sh a bed and food for around 13 Sh. You then need to get a group together to hore a Land-Rover (private cars are not allowed in the crater). Land-Rovers cost 1000 Sh a day and will take you down into the crater and to Olduvai Gorge in the afternoon. It's still expensive but a fraction of what is being asked for organised tours in Arusha.

Kolo Rock Paintings Kolo is located between Arusha and Dodoma. These are worth a visit if you're passing through there. It's been suggested that your own vehicle would be an advantage here.

Other Information
Ujamaa Villages If you'd like to visit one of these or get off the beaten track in any way you must apply for permission from the Ministry of Information and Broadcasting in Dar es Salaam. The committee meets approximately once every month to consider applications so you need to apply well in advance.

TUNISIA
Tunis *Hotel du Lyon*, reported by one traveller to be cheap but infested by bed bugs. For not much more there are considerably better places he thought. For example *Hotel Sabra* (tel 494 875) at 83 Rue Tourbet El Bey, is clean, central and very friendly. 'On several occasions I was asked by the management to join

them for a meal at no extra cost'. Nightly cost is 1.30 Dinar. It's in the Medina but difficult to find via the Medina. It's easier to start at the post office in Rue Charles de Gaulle and follow it to its end at Rue el Algerie. Turn right and continue into Ave Bab Djedid (continuation of Algerie). The hotel sign is on the right about half a km along. You pass beneath an arch into a small lane where there are two hotels, one immediately after the turn and Sabra 100 metres along on the right. Ave Bab Djedid is an easily located road.

UGANDA

The political situation in Uganda has now cooled down and it's once again safe to visit the country. We've had several letters from travellers recently who've been very impressed both by the beauty of the country and by the friendliness of its people. Not all the services are back to normal yet due to the effects of the war but it's pretty easy to get from one place to another. Note that Mbarara and Masaka west of Lake Victoria were flattened by the Tanzanians so it will be some time before reconstruction is completed. Uganda is also the link between Kenya and Tanzania if you don't have the time or inclination to arrange an overland border permit between those two countries.

Visas

In Nairobi, Kenya, Ugandan Entry Permits are easily obtained while you wait from the Immigration Department, Harambee Avenue. They cost 22.50 Sh and no photos are required. In Dar es Salaam, Tanzania, Ugandan Entry Permits are free and obtainable from the Ugandan Liaison Office, 10th Floor, Maktabu St.

Currency

The official rate of exchange is still on a par with the Kenyan Shilling and if this is how you change your money you will find the country incredibly expensive. There is, however, a thriving blackmarket which in Feb '81 was offering US$1 = 110 Sh and £1 = 250 Sh. You can change Kenyan currency at the border for 1 Ken Sh = 10 Ug Sh (the rate is worse further into Uganda). This unusual exchange rate will undoubtedly drop as the new government gets to grips with the economy.

Accommodation

If you have a tent try enquiring at the local police station or at the Gombolola Headquarters for a place to camp. Two travellers who were there recently said they were always allowed to camp at one or the other in every place they went and on many occasions were offered a room and bathing facilities.

Kampala A cheap place to stay is on the roof of the *Tourist Lodge*, Kampala Rd, just round the corner from the station.

Kasese The cheapest place to stay is the *Highway Hotel*, next door to the Valley Hotel. The best place to eat here is the *Valley Hotel*, Margret St. If you ask to speak to Kalanzi he'll fix you up some excellent food.

Ruwenzori Mountains These are well worth a visit but if you're thinking of climbing them remember that it's a long trek from Ibanda, the last village, and that you will definitely need a guide and porters or you'll get hopelessly lost. It's advisable to write to John Matte, PO Box 276, Kilembe, Uganda, beforehand if you're thinking of doing a trek. He's been recommended as a very friendly and helpful person.

Transport

Hitching is still difficult because of the scarcity of cars and petrol. One traveller said that if you're really broke the buses will take you free of charge. There is still no train which crosses the border into Kenya from Uganda. There is now a bus which runs from Kampala to Bukoba (Tanzania). The baggage search at this border is very cursory.

Other Information

Your own vehicle Note that carnets are not accepted. If you want to drive through you have to leave a cash deposit at the border which (they say) is refundable when you leave — but only in Kampala and only in Ugandan currency. In other words, you don't get it back so it's best to come to some arrangement with the border guards. Bargain hard!

ZAIRE

When you apply for a Zaire visa the application form may state 'Entry through Kinshasa only' but this isn't stamped on your visa so no worries. If you're entering Zaire via the ferryboat across the River Zaire from Brazzaville, you need a 'laissez-passer' as well as a visa. The former can be obtained at the Zairois embassy in Brazzaville if you show them an onward ticket. If you have to buy this onward ticket in Brazzaville you can buy a Yaounde-Kinshasa return flight ticket and then cancel it after you've got the 'laissez-passer' at a loss of about US$7. The 'laissez-passer' costs CFA 1000.

There's no fuss at the ferry customs entering Zaire and baggage is checked cursorily. You're advised to hide well any Zairois currency obtained outside the country all the same.

If you intend to travel through the provinces of Kasai Occidental or Oriental then you officially need a 'laissez-passer' but recent travellers have had no problems without one. Your Zaire visa usually satisfies the authorities. Entry into Shaba province is no longer a problem.

Note that corruption in Zaire has now reached an incredible level.

Currency

Rate of exchange:
  US$1 = Z3
  Blackmarket = Z7.1

If you're coming in from Brazzaville you can change money there next to the warehouse 'Monoprix' or down near the ferry to Kinshasa. The rate there is CFA 35 = Z1. It's virtually impossible to find the blackmarket in Kinshasa. Outside Kinshasa try American volunteers or missionaries if you want to change money. You're obliged to change some foreign currency on arrival. It's negotiable so try to change as little as possible (eg Z70) and tell the customs people you intend to change the rest at another bank. Currency Declaration Forms are issued on arrival. If you're worried about problems with these at the border when leaving Zaire simply change the amount on the form. Note that it's almost impossible to change Zairois currency outside the country. It's said there are only two 'approved' banks in the whole country (at Kinshasa and Kisangani) where you can change money officially!

Mail

The poste restante in Kinshasa is very efficient.

Accommodation & Transport

Kinshasa You can find reasonable rooms outside the centre for about Z15 but note that sometimes you have to pay double if you intend to use the room during the daytime. Check this out before taking a hotel. Reasonable food (breakfast and lunch) at *Nicoise's* opposite the GPO but it's not very cheap.

The ferry between Kinshasa and Brazzaville operates on an hourly basis in either direction between 8 am and 6 pm except at 1 pm. It costs CFA 1500 one way.

Kinshasa-Kibombo & Kalemie via Kikwit & Kananga There are buses to Kikwit (and Matadi if you're heading west) by the 'Compagnie Sotraz' from the depot next to the GPO, Kinshasa. They're luxury buses and depart daily at 7 and 8 am. Kinshasa to Kikwit costs Z100 plus extra for your luggage (Z5 for a rucksack). Buy your ticket the day before between 7 am and 12 noon and 3 and 6 pm. The road is metalled all the way to Kitwit.

Hotels are available at reasonable prices in the centre (Kikwit cite).

Trucks depart daily to Idiofa at around 6 am from Kikwit Ville at the 'barriere'.

At Idiofa there is a hotel opposite the 'carrefour' (where the trucks park) for Z25 a room. Good food available here too.

At Mapangu (previously called Brabanta) ask for the *Maison de la Passage* owned by PLZ (Plantations Lever Zaire). It's a rest house for employees of PLZ travelling through Mapangu but seldom used. You can get accommodation here for Z15 per person. Good meals are also available. There are regular trucks from here (often PLZ trucks) to Ilebo and other places. There are also occasional river boats going in the direction of Lusambo.

At Ilebo there is a train to Kananga on Wednesdays which takes two days and costs Z32. Trucks are more expensive but often faster even though it's a gravel road.

Kananga is said to be the world's largest city still without running water and electricity. It has half a million inhabitants and is Zaire's second largest city. Accommodation is available at *Hotel Musube* for Z45 a triple room and at the *Hotel Palace* for Z29 a triple room. Good meals are available (breakfast, lunch and dinner) at reasonable prices at the *Pax Restaurant* (also called the Restaurant Lavick). Accommodation can also sometimes be found with the Protestant Missions (there are two) and the Peace Corps. You can find interesting wooden statuettes for sale on the road between Ilebo and Kananga but the best examples (for sale) are to be found at the museum in Kananga (costs Z1 entrance). If you buy any and want to export them it's useful to have an 'Autorisation de sortie d'Arte Moderne' to show at the border. These can be bought for Z2. There's also a good market in Kananga.

Transport further eastwards is poorly developed. There is a train on Saturdays to Kamina. From there you can take the train to Kalemie on Lake Tanganyika. There are trucks to Mbuji-Mayi, Lodja, Kamina and other destinations. The road to Lusambo is seldom used. Weekly service by MAS from Kananga to Lusambo costs Z46. It's very difficult to find transport going east from Lusambo — there are trucks approximately once per month only — so you may well have to fly from Kananga (see below). Lusambo has a colonial air about it (built by the Belgians) and is worth a visit. The weekly MAS service to Kananga leaves on Thursdays or Fridays.

There are flights from Kananga by Air Zaire to Mbuji-Mayi, Kinshasa, Lumumbashi, Kalemie, Kindu and Goma. The Kananga-Goma flight leaves on Saturdays and costs Z111 with student reduction. Note that student reductions on Air Zaire are 75% which makes flying cheaper than going overland. It's useful to have a confirmatory letter from a college/university as well as a student card to get the reduction but many travellers have got it without the letter. You must be under 26 years old. Book well in advance for flights — weeks rather than days — and note that you may have to grease a palm or two to get on the flight you booked for. A ticket is no guarantee of getting on the flight.

At present, trucks will cost Z20 per 100 km if you're hitching.

Central African Republic to Eastern Zaire If you have your own vehicle you have to hire the whole ferry to cross from Bangue to Zongo. And that isn't all, since the engine on the ferry doesn't work you also have to hire a tug! Each group has to pay the full amount even if there are several vehicles at once. Hire of the ferry costs CFA 3500 and hire of the tug costs CFA 3850.

At Lisala, ask for the Portuguese compound where you can find accommodation, discreetly change money and get cheap government petrol (if you have your own vehicle). Note there is no crane to load cars onto the Bumba ferry here.

ZAMBIA

Visas
Recent travellers confirm that visas can be bought on the border for Kw 2.25.

Currency
Zambia is a very expensive country — one traveller said more so than Germany. It's suggested that you don't declare all your money on entry — especially cash — so you can exchange on the blackmarket. Don't change more than you need as it's impossible to change Kwachas outside the country or to reconvert within Zambia (you can only take out up to Kw 10). Note the mistake in the main guide under Lusaka — the place for changing money is the Barbeque Inn not the Barbeque Place. The rate is presently Kw 2 = US$1.

Accommodation
Kitwe There are three hotels here. The *Ekane* near the centre of town costs about US$14 a night and the *Buchi Hotel* about six km out of town costs about US$7 a night.

Lusaka Note that many hotels in Lusaka are often booked out and so you could be in for a long taxi ride. If you're arriving at Lusaka Airport only taxis are available to take you into town. You should not pay more than Kw 10.

Accommodation is available from a farming family near Lusaka in exchange for some help on the farm. They might also try to take you to church on Sunday! They are Mr & Mrs Bland, Yieldingtree Farm, Botha's Rust Rd, Lusaka. The farm is about 10 km out of Lusaka going south on the road to the satellite station.

Victoria Falls On the Zambia side the *Rainbow Hotel* has been recommended. It's a very pleasant hotel with very simple but adequate rondavels for Kw 120 a double. Food, as elsewhere in Zambia, is expensive and limited in variety.

Game Parks These are probably the most interesting part of a visit to Zambia. Two which have been recommended are *Luangwe* near the Malawi border (at least six places to stay, all of them with catering facilities) and *Kafue* west of Lusaka.

Transport
Hitching is slow from Mbala to Lusaka. A bus along this stretch will cost Kw 10. Note that the Zambian/Zimbabwean border at Victoria Falls is now open and there are no problems crossing it. The border is open from 7.15 am and at about 8 am there is a bus to Wankie/

Bulawayo. If you miss the bus you can walk about 1.5 km to the railway station and get a train to Bulawayo. The bus costs Z$5.

ZIMBABWE

A great deal has changed here since Mugabe came to power and travellers are once again visiting the country in increasing numbers. Though it's still politically unstable because of tension between the two rival former guerilla armies and between the blacks and whites, most areas are now safe to visit though there are some places, including attractive wilderness areas such as Mono Pools, which are closed because they are controlled by bored and angry guerillas. The situation changes constantly so travellers should seek up-to-date information locally.

Martin Rothman, who worked there for four months as a radiographer, recently sent us a long report. Some of his comments about the situation in general included:

'. . . the local tourist industry has greatly revived since the end of the war — nearly all the hotels which existed before the war have now reopened. Most of the 'tourists' are whites and include a sizeable proportion of South Africans who, after all, are barred from most nearby countries . . . . The political situation is unstable and dangerous. Zimbabwe is destined to have a one-party dictatorship ruled by a strong man but there are two main tribes — the Shona and Ndebele — and each has a large army. 'Reconciliation' and building a single national army collapsed in late October 1980. The writing is on the wall and the whites are getting out faster than ever before. In Bulawayo in November (1980) between 300 and 500 died in fighting (not the 60 claimed by the press) adding another convincing argument. No one wants a civil war but most view it as likely — both black and white . . . . Mugabe granted big wage increases creating a consumer boom and expansion of the money supply —

inflation to follow. Skilled labour is leaving which will bring big problems and the white farmers are being forced off the land — I worked in five hospitals and they're collapsing fast. White doctors, technicians and nurses are leaving en masse. I worked often in casualty and you would be shocked by the high level of violence — bar fights, wife-beating, and also grenade and gun-shot wounds. Never seen anything like it. The pattern of disease among the Africans is like Europe 150 years ago. TB, typhoid, cholera, measles as a child killer, whooping cough, scarlet fever, osteomyelitis, malnutrition and, of course, tropical parasitic diseases. Even some of the black nurses go to witch doctors . . . . Don't get ill.'

Visas

Mozambique visas Note that the land border is still closed. You are only allowed to fly in. Visas can be obtained in Salisbury *but only for Maputo* and preferably through Musgrove and Watson who operate a single beach holiday package (about Z$300 for one week) to a beach near Maputo. Martin Rothman said he got the distinct impression that no-one goes to Mozambique and that you could easily disappear there. He said there are ambushes on the Umtali-Beira road and that the country is only for those who like to flirt with danger.

CURRENCY

Import/export of Zimbabwean currency is allowed up to Z$20. There's no restriction on the import of foreign currency so long as it is declared on arrival.

Banking hours are: 8.30 am to 2 pm on Monday, Tuesday, Thursday and Friday; 8.30 am to 12 noon on Thursday and 8.30 am to 11 am on Saturday.

ACCOMMODATION

Hotels in the cities cost between Z$10 and Z$25. The quality is high. There is a government tax on hotels charging more than Z$2 per person per night. This is 10c for ungraded hotels, 20c for one-star hotels, 30c for two-star hotels, 40c for three-star hotels, 50c for four-star hotels and 60c for five-star hotels.

Bulawayo Tourist Information is at Bulawayo & District Publicity Association, City Hall, Selbourne Avenue (tel 60867).

Hotel Cecil, Fife St/Third Ave (tel 60295) costs Z$8.67 with own bath and TV; Z$7.92 with own bath and Z$7.42 without own bath. The hotel has a restaurant and laundry service. At *Grey's Inn*, 73 Grey St (tel 60121), bed and breakfast costs Z$6-7.50. The hotel has a restaurant and swimming pool.

New Royal Hotel, 6th Ave/Rhodes St (tel 65764/5) has bed and breakfast and own bath or Z$6.25 without own bath. The hotel has a restaurant, swimming pool, garden and snack bar. *Bee Gee Hotel*, Reynolds Drive/Stanley Ave (tel 35452) costs Z$10 a double with breakfast and own bathroom; Z$11.60 a double with dinner, breakfast and own bath and Z$12.80 a double for full board and own bath.

At *Plaza Hotel*, 14th Ave/Abercorn St (tel 64281) bed and breakfast with own bath costs Z$7.50 or Z$5.75 without own bath. Dinner, bed and breakfast with own bath costs Z$8.50 or Z$7.75 without own bath. *Waverly Hotel*, 133 Lobengula St/12th Ave (tel 60033/60036). Rooms here cost Z$4. There is a restaurant at the hotel. *Youth Hostel*, Cnr 11th Ave/Lobengula St (tel 70899). Dormitory accommodation for men and women at Z$1 per head for members and Z$1.50 for non-members. Cooking facilities, utensils and crockery is provided.

Fort Victoria

Tourist Information is at Fort Victoria/ Zimbabwe Publicity Association, Allen Wilson St (tel 2643). Fort Victoria is the nearest urban centre to the Great Zimbabwe ruins.

Chevron Hotel, (tel 2054/5), costs Z$10.75 a single and Z$20 a double including breakfast. Air-conditioning costs 50c extra per person. The hotel has a restaurant, grill room, two bars and a swimming pool. *Flamboyant Hotel*, (tel 2005/6) costs Z$8 a single without breakfast; Z$9.50 a single with breakfast, and Z$16.50 a double. If you occupy a double room on a single basis this costs Z$10. All rooms have their own bathroom and the hotel has a restaurant and swimming pool.

Zimbabwe Ruins Hotel, (tel 2274) is located at the Zimbabwe ruins. Bed and breakfast here costs Z$8 per person. All rooms have their own bath, radio and phone. The hotel has its own restaurant, swimming pool and organises daily tours of the ruins. Cars can also be rented here. *Kyle View Chalets and Caravan Park* (tel 223822) is six km from the Zimbabwe ruins on Lake Kyle. The furnished chalets are equipped with shower, toilet, kitchenettes (including linen and crockery) and cost Z$4 per person per night. There is a food and liquor store and swimming on the site and boats can be hired for use on the lake.

Gwelo Tourist Information is at Gwelo Publicity Association, Civic Theatre, Livingstone Ave (tel 2226).

Midlands Hotel, Main St (tel 2581) has rooms facing the front of the hotel for Z$11 a single and Z$18 a double. In the side wing rooms cost Z$9 a single and Z$18 a double. In the side wing rooms cost Z$9 a single and Z$15.20 a double. All the rooms have their own bath, TV and air-conditioning and the charges include breakfast. The hotel has its own restaurant. *Cecil Hotel*, Moffat

Ave (tel 2862/3) costs Z$9 per person for bed and breakfast in an air-conditioned room with own bath. The hotel has its own restaurant, swimming pool, sauna and library.

You can camp at the *Gwelo Caravan Park*, Livingstone Ave (tel 2929), for Z$1 per night. It's a well-equipped site with laundry facilities, swimming pool, squash, tennis, TV room and bar.

Inyanga This is the centre for exploring the Inyanga National Park and Mt Inyanga. It's a large area in the extreme north-east with red-leaved Msasa trees, rocky hills, wildlife and waterfalls and the popular 'World's View' where you can see amazing sunsets. Mt Inyanga (2595 metres and the highest point in Zimbabwe) can be climbed in about 1½ hours. From the top you can look out far into Mozambique and along the enscarpment as it drops precipitously. The area was previously controlled by guerillas and has only recently been opened up again.

The *National Park Lodges* here cost Z$5 per person per night including good food and firewood — book in advance. *Holiday Hotel*, PO Box 19 (tel 336) has 14 double rooms and six family rooms all with their own bath and radio. Full board costs Z$6 per person. There are two swimming pools and a games room. *Rhodes Inyanga Hotel*, Private Bag 8024N, Rusape (tel Inyanga 377) is located in the Inyanga National Park outside of Inyanga town, rooms here cost from Z$9.50 a single with own bath in the main block; from Z$8.50 per person for a room in a cottage; from Z$8 for a room in the annexe and from Z$7 for a rondavel. Single people occupying a double room are charged Z$1 extra.

Warning Here, as in many other places, it's inadvisable to stray from safe paths as you may step on a land mine. This warning will apply for many years.

Kariba Kariba is the local substitute for the sea shore. It's a huge, beautiful, blue lake with good views, plenty of wildlife and lake cruises. Fishing (for tiger fish) is expensive. You need a car to get around. There is a crocodile farm here which has a giant that has reputedly eaten eight people! Note that Lake Kariba is 260 km long and the resorts at the eastern and western ends are not directly connected by road or boat services. Kariba East includes the town of Kariba itself which has grown up around the dam wall and power station and Bumi Hills furthest west. Kariba is connected by tarred road to Salisbury. Kariba West includes Binga, Mlibizi and Msuna Mouth which are reached by turn-offs from the Bulawayo-Victoria Falls highway.

The cheapest hotel here is the *Kariba Heights Hotel* which costs Z$13 per night. *Binga Rest Camp*, PO Box 9, Binga (tel Binga 11) consists of three chalets (each with four beds and a bath) and six rooms. The chalets cost Z$7 person for bed and breakfast and the rooms Z$6. There is a restaurant, bar, store, warm spring swimming pool, boats for hire and even a crocodile farm on the site. Camping is allowed and costs 60c per person per day including use of facilities.

Bumi Hills Safari Lodge, PO Box 41, Kariba (tel 353) is 50 km uplake from Kariba, the Lodge offers a range of accommodation from a luxury lodge with private game-viewing platform from Z$19, through a room in the Fish Eagle Lodge from Z$17, to a traditional cottage from Z$12.50. The rates include breakfast and dinner. All rooms have their own bath, phone and fans and the lodge has its own restaurant. Transport to the Lodge is by launch or float plane from Kariba. Game viewing and foot safaris are organised by the Lodge.

Kariba Heights Cottages is ½ km from Kariba. There are two-bedroom cottages fully equipped and serviced but without linen. They cost Z$3 per person per day and must be booked in advance through PO Box 5, Salisbury (tel 21537).

Salisbury Tourist Information is at Salisbury Publicity Association, Cecil Square, Second St/Stanley Ave (tel 705085).

Elizabeth Hotel, Kingsway/Manica Rd (tel 708591/2) has bed and breakfast for Z$5.10-6.10 a single and Z$9.20-10.20 a double. The higher priced rooms have their own shower. The hotel has its own restaurant and disco. *Federal Hotel*, 9 Salisbury St (tel 706118) costs Z$3.50 per person for bed and breakfast. The hotel offers live music and dancing every day. *Earlside Hotel*, 5th St/Selous Ave (tel 21101) costs Z$4 per person for bed and breakfast; dinner, bed and breakfast is Z$4.50 per person and full board Z$5 per person. The hotel has a swimming pool and garden.

Casamia Hotel, Third St/Central Ave (tel 790066/7) costs Z$4.95 for bed and breakfast; dinner, bed and breakfast is Z$5.75 per person. Single and double rooms and family flats are available. *Bronte Hotel*, 132 Baines Ave (tel 21999/21768) has rooms with breakfast for Z$5 a single and Z$9.50 a double. Full board costs Z$7 a single and Z$14 a double. Most of the rooms have their own bath and verandah. *Caves Hotel*, 131 Baines Ave (tel 27641/2/3) costs Z$4.50 per person for bed only; Z$5.25 for bed and breakfast and Z$6.25 for dinner, bed and breakfast. *Cloisters Hotel*, 121 Baines Ave (tel 791143/4) costs Z$7 a single and Z$12 a double including breakfast. Dinner, bed and breakfast costs Z$8 a single and Z$14.50 a double. All the rooms have their own bath and the hotel has its own restaurant.

The *Youth Hostel*, 6 Montagu Ave, Causeway (tel 26990) has separate dormitory accommodation for both men and women at Z$1 per person for members and Z$1.50 per person for non-members. Members are given preference. The hostel has cooking facilities and cutlery and crockery are provided. The hostel is closed between 10 am and 5 pm.

Umtali Tourist Information is at Manicaland Development and Publicity Association, Market Square, Milner Ave (tel 64711).

City Centre Hotel, Main St, Paulington, Umtali (tel 62441) costs Z$7.50 per person for bed and breakfast. All rooms have their own bath or shower and the hotel has its own restaurant.

Victoria Falls Tourist Information is at Victoria Falls Publicity Association, Park Way (tel 202).

Victoria Falls Motel (tel 344/5) costs Z$8 per person for bed and breakfast plus 5% service charge. All rooms have their own shower, bath, radio and air-conditioning. There is a restaurant, swimming pool, a live band each night and transport available to the centre of town.

Accommodation in the immediate area of the Falls includes the 'colonial' *Victoria Falls Hotel* at around Z$22 per night and a number of cheaper hotels down to Z$12 per night. There is also a camping site which costs Z$2 per night. The best place to stay, however, is the *National Park Lodge* located about four km upriver from the falls. This costs Z$8 for a lodge which will sleep up to five people. The lodges consist of two bedrooms, a living room, kitchen (with fridge and cooker) and a servant is provided for every two lodges. The lodges are sited right out in the bush along the Zambesi where crocodiles crawl up on the banks and hippos can be seen in the river. In addition to these, baboons, vervet monkeys, deer, mongooses, wart hogs, guinea fowl and a wide range of birds and insects can be observed at close hand. You can rent a bicycle in Victoria Falls town from one of the petrol stations for Z$4 a day to get to the lodges though hitching the four km stretch is easy.

Vumba This is an outstandingly beautiful area north of Umtali with deep jungle, tea, coffee and banana plantations. You need a car to get there. Views into Mozambique can be had from here.

Leopard Rock Hotel (tel 2176-10) is 32 km from Umtali. Full board costs Z$15-Z$18 per person. All rooms have their own bath. There is a restaurant, swimming pool and outdoor and indoor games facilities. *The Mountain Lodge* (tel Umtali 2185-20) is a half-timbered old English style lodge 32 km from Umtali located in a beautiful setting and offering things like log fires in the evenings, etc. Full board costs Z$9.50 in a room without its own bath and Z$10.50 for room with own bath. The hotel also has its own swimming pool.

Zimbabwe Ruins There is no longer a hitch-hikers dormitory at the *Zimbabwe Ruins Hotel* but you can still leave your pack there while you explore the ruins.

Accommodation in National Parks

One of the best ways of seeing Zimbabwe is to use the National Park Lodges. The only drawback here is that to get to the National Parks in the first place you need a car. Local transport is very limited and doesn't go to the parks. The National Park Lodges, cabins and campsites are cheap but they must be booked and paid for in advance in Salisbury. You would be very lucky to turn up at one of their facilities and find something.

There are over 250 chalets, cottages and lodges located in the various National Parks of Zimbabwe. They're all equipped with basic furniture, refrigerators, bedding and lighting (kerosine pressure lamps, gas or electricity). Firewood has to be purchased from the park authorities. Some of these lodges are only open seasonally and opening and closing times are liable to change depending on road conditions.

Charges for the various types of accommodation are for the complete lodge, chalet or cottage on the basis of two people per bedroom. If more than two people wish to occupy a room this has to be arranged in advance. There are one or two bedroom chalets with cooking facilities and utensils and communal showers and toilets (hot and cold water). Guests must supply their own cutlery and crockery. A one-bedroom unit costs Z$3.50 per night and a two-bedroom unit Z$4-5 per night. Cottages are much the same as a chalet except that each unit has its own bathroom and toilet. Again, guests must supply their own cutlery and crockery. A one-bedroom unit costs Z$4.50 per night and a two-bedroom unit Z$6.75 per night. Lodges consist of two or more rooms including kitchen, bathroom and toilet, bedding for two to four people, cooking utensils, cutlery and crockery. They cost Z$4.50-5.50 per night for a one-bedroom unit and Z$6.50-8.50 per night for a two-bedroom unit. There are also a number of camping sites with shower and toilet facilities which cost Z$1.50 per night for up to six people.

The above accommodation must be booked in advance at the Travel Centre, Stanley Avenue, Salisbury (tel 706077). If you're booking from abroad the postal address is PO Box 8151, Causeway, Salisbury. You must report to the Park Office on arrival even if you have confirmed bookings. Note that the accommodation charges do not include entrance fees to the National Parks.

Brief detals of the National Parks are as follows:

Charara Safari Area (Private Bag 2002, Kariba) (tel 2327) — 28 km from Kariba, camping available.

Chimanimani National Park (Private

Bag 2063, Melsetter) (tel Melsetter 03322) — at the foot of the mountains 21 km from Melsetter, camping and chalets available.

Chizarira National Park (Private Bag 6020, Gokwe) (tel Victoria Falls 310) — located 50 km south-east of Binga. Special permission must be obtained to visit this park. The entrance fee is Z$3 for seven days.

Gonarezhou National Park — the park is divided into two areas — the Chipinda Pools area and the Mabalauta area. There is no road link between the two sections and at present the park is closed. It may open again soon in which case the entrance fee is Z$3 per person for seven days.

Kyle Recreational Park (Private Bag 9136, Fort Victoria) (tel 2913) — located 32 km east of Fort Victoria. Lodges and camping available. The entrance fee to the park is Z$1 for seven days.

Matusadona National Park — on the southern shore of Lake Kariba, 13 km from Bumi Hills and 48 km from Kariba by boat or 268 km from Karoi by road, camping and lodges available. Entrance fee to the park is Z$3 for seven days unless you arrive by boat and stay on the lake shore in which case it's free.

Mushandike Sanctuary (Private Bag 9036, Fort Victoria) (tel 294525) — 40 km from Fort Victoria, camping available. Entrance to the park costs Z$1.

Ngezi Recreational Park (Private Bag 207, Featherstone) (tel Umtali 426) — 63 km from Featherstone and 67 km from Battlefields. Lodges and camping available. Entrance fee to the park is Z$1.

Rhodes Inyanga National Park (Private Bag T7901, Umtali) (tel 274) — lodges and camping available.

Rhodes Matopos National Park (Private Bag K5142, Bulawayo) (tel Matopos 0-1913) — there are four sites within

the park — Maleme, Mtshelele, Mpopoma and Toghwana, lodges and camping at each site. Maleme, the first site is 54 km from Bulawayo. Entrance fee to the park is Z$1.

Robert McIlwaine Recreational Park (Private Bag 962, Norton) (tel Norton 229) — 40 km west of Salisbury on the Bulawayo road, chalets, lodges and camping available. Entrance fee to the park is Z$1.

Sebakwe Recreational Park (PO Box 636, Que Que) (tel Que Que 2476-15) — 54 km from Que Que on the Umvuma road, lodges and camping available. Entrance fee to the park is Z$!.

Sinoia Caves Recreational Park (PO Box 193, Sinoia) (tel 2550) — located eight km north of Sinoia, camping available. Entrance fee to the park is Z$1.

Zambesi and Victoria Falls National Park (Private Bag 5920, Victoria Falls) (tel 222) — located six km upstream from the falls, lodges available. The park is open from 1st May-31st October and costs Z$1 entrance fee.

Vumba Botanical Reserve (Private Bag V7472, Umtali) (tel Umtali 2127-22) — 32 km from Umtali on a steep winding road, camping available. Entrance to the park costs 20c.

Wankei National Park (Private Bag DT 5776, Dett) (tel Dett 64) — there are three main areas here — Main Camp, Sinamatella Camp and Robins Camp, lodges, chalets, cottages and camping available. Entrance to the park costs Z$3 for seven days.

Transport

Road transport is a problem since all the whites own cars and there is only one good bus service — the 'Express Motorways'. These buses are fairly cheap (eg Salisbury-Umtali costs Z$9) but infrequent, often booked up and run only between main towns. They do not serve the National Parks. There is also the local, African bus service. These are slow, crowded, very cheap and run from township to township. Their schedules are very approximate and while they are fine to use during the daylight hours you should avoid using them at night. Martin Rothman commented about these buses saying that a white face in many black townships after dark, unaccompanied by a local, is unknown. He said you could easily get killed in circumstances like that.

If you are hitch-hiking make an effort to look like a tourist — hang a camera around your neck. Local people are very suspicious of whites who are too poor to have their own car! Rides are fairly easily got but traffic is sparse off the main routes.

Car rental is expensive though no more so than anywhere else and you need one to get to the National Parks. Roads are generally good including many high quality gravel roads.

Buses-Express Express Motorways Africa (Central) Ltd — the head office of this company is at 109 Belvedere Rd, Salisbury (tel 702121) and the booking office is at Rezende St, Salisbury (tel 20392). They operate buses along the following routes:
Salisbury-Gwelo-Bulawayo — departs Salisbury on Monday, Wednesday and Friday at 7.45 am arriving Gwelo at 11.40 am and Bulawayo at 2 pm. In the opposite direction they depart Bulawayo on Tuesday, Thursday and Saturday at 7.45 am arriving Gwelo at 10.30 am and Salisbury at 2 pm. Salisbury - Gwelo - Bulawayo - Johannesburg — departs Salisbury on Tuesday and Friday and 6 am arriving Gwelo at 10 am and Bulawayo at 12.30 pm the same day and Johannesburg at 3.30 am the following day. In the opposite direction they depart Johannesburg on Wednesday and Saturday at 9 pm arriving Bulawayo at 12.45 pm,

Gwelo at 2.35 pm and Salisbury at 6.45 pm all on the following day. Salisbury-Umtali — depart Salisbury daily except Sunday at 8 am and arrive at Umtali at 11.40 am. In the opposite direction they depart Umtali daily except Saturday at 2.30 pm and arrive Salisbury at 6.15 pm. Salisbury-Kariba — depart Salisbury on Friday only at 6 am and arrive at Kariba at 11.05 am. In the opposite direction they depart Kariba on Sunday only at 1.15 pm and arrive Salisbury at 6.45 pm.

Buses — Local Bulawayo-Victoria Falls: The 'Wankie Express' operated by F Pullen & Co departs from the bus station at the end of 6th Avenue extension at 9 am daily and arrives at Victoria Falls at 3.30 pm the same day. In the opposite direction the bus departs from the African township in Victoria Falls at 7.30 am daily and arrives at Bulawayo at 2 pm. The fare is Z$4.80. This bus can be taken if you're heading for Wankie National Park.

Flights There is a daily flight from Victoria Falls to Wankie National Park at 2.50 pm. The flight takes 30 minutes and costs Z$20.30 one way. The UTC bus from the airport to Main Camp costs Z$3.50. Note that there is no direct flight from Bulawayo to Wankie National Park.

Salisbury-Beira (Mozambique): twice weekly, costs Z$95. Salisbury-Maputo (Mozambique): once weekly, costs Z$208. Note that Air Mozambique recently announced a 50% price hike but at the time of writing it hadn't gone into effect.

Trains Railway Travel Bureaux are situated at Mercury House, (tel 70-2456) Salisbury and Africa House, (tel 6-8541/2) Cnr Fife St & Tenth Avenue Bulawayo.

The following trains connect Bulawayo

with Salisbury, Victoria Falls and South
Africa (latter via Mafeking):

Station	Depart	Comments	Depart	Comments
Bulawayo	8.00 pm	daily, all classes	7.30 pm	On Fri, Sat,
Gwelo	12.45 am	except Fri, Sat, Sun,	11.55 pm	Sun, 3rd & 4th
Gatooma	3.50 am	1st & 2nd classes	2.55 am	classes only
Hartley	4.35 am	only on Fri, Sat,	3.37 am	
Salisbury	7.00 am	Sun	6.00 am	
Salisbury	8.00 pm	daily, all classes	7.30 pm	On Fri, Sat,
Hartley	10.38 pm	except Fri, Sat, Sun	9.52 pm	Sun, 3rd &
Gatooma	11.15 pm	1st & 2nd Classes	10.41 pm	4th Classes
Gwelo	3.05 am	only on Fri, Sat, Sun	2.15 am	only
Bulawayo	7.00 am		6.00 am	
Bulawayo	7.00 pm	daily, all classes		
Wankie	3.44 am			
Thomson Junction	4.05 am			
Victoria Falls	7.45 am			
Victoria Falls	6.30 pm	daily, all classes		
Thomson Junction	10.15 pm			
Wankie	10.38 pm			
Bulawayo	8.00 am			
Bulawayo	11.45 am	Tues & Thurs only		
Plumtree	2.19 pm			
Francistown	4.03 pm			
Palapye	7.10 pm			
Mahalapye	8.28 pm			
Artesia	11.22 pm			
Pilane	12.19 am			
Gaborone	1.27 am			
Lobatse	3.29 am			
Ramatlhabama	5.00 am			
Mafeking	5.30 am			

Station	Depart	Comments	Station	Depart	Comments
Salisbury	9.30 pm	daily, 2nd,	Umtali	9.00 pm	daily, 2nd,
Marandellas	11.45 pm	3rd & 4th	Rusapi	12.15 am	3rd & 4th
Headlands	2.20 am	classes	Headlands	1.25 am	classes
Rusapi	3.15 am		Marandellas	4.10 am	
Umtali	6.00 am		Salisbury	6.00 am	

There are connections from Mafeking to Johannesburg and Pretoria at 6.10 am on Wednesdays;
to Cape Town, Port Elizabeth and East London at 6.15 am on Fridays, and, to Durban at 6.15
am on Wednesdays.

Mafeking	9.00 pm	Tues & Thurs only,
Lobatse	10.44 pm	1st & 2nd classes
Gaborone	12.29 am	only
Pilane	1.17 am	

Artesia	2.45 am
Mahalapye	4.55 am
Palapye	6.33 am
Francistown	9.56 am
Plumtree	12.10 pm
Bulawayo	2.10 pm

Working

Martin Rothman commented: 'Only for skilled workers and the need is growing. At present, Temporary Employment Permits can be gotten within. It used to be that any white face was snapped up. Not any more. The Government doesn't want whites and the doors are closing but, like in Malawi and Zambia, they will probably be forced to offer fat expatriate contracts to keep the place running. Wages are slightly above those in England but the cost of living is less.'

PEOPLE WHO HELPED WITH INFORMATION

Christoria Hoffman (West Germany); Dr B E Juel-Jensen (UK); Andreas Falk (West Germany); W Aldridge (Australia), Cedric Yoshimoto (Kenya); Jonnie & Alison Wolf (Sri Lanka); Hans de Vries (Netherlands); Ray Swanepoel (Transkei, Southern Africa); Janene Madgwick (New Zealand); Martin Rothman (UK); Chas Porter (Zimbabwe); Alicen Baker (Australia?); Kathleen Darby (UK); Dave & Sally Hillebrandt (UK); Don Hammersley (Australia); Roger Smith (Australia); Roberto Paloscia (Italy); Frank Carter (Australia); Sam Terry (USA).

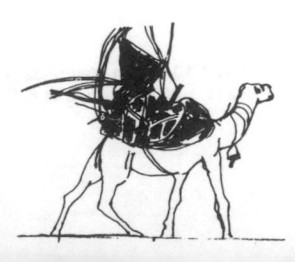

LONELY PLANET NEWSLETTER

We collect an enormous amount of information here at Lonely Planet. Apart from our research we also get a steady stream of letters from people out on the road — some of them are just one line on a postcard, others go on for pages. Plus we always have an ear to the ground for the latest on cheap airfares, new visa regulations, borders opening and closing. A lot of this information goes into our new editions or 'update supplements' in reprints. But we'd like to make better use of this information so, starting in November '81, we're going to produce a quarterly newsletter packed full of the latest news from out on the road. It will appear in February, May, August and November of each year. If you'd like an airmailed copy of the most recent newsletter just send us A$1.50 (A$1 within Australia) or A$5 (A$4 in Australia) for a year's subscription.

Africa on the Cheap
Australia — a travel survival kit
Burma — a travel survival kit
Central Asia on a Shoestring*
Europe — a travel survival kit**
Hong Kong, Macau & Canton
India — a travel survival kit
Israel & the Occupied Territories
Japan — a travel survival kit
Kashmir, Ladakh & Zanskar
Kathmandu & the Kingdom of Nepal
New Zealand — a travel survival kit
Pakistan — a travel survival kit
Papua New Guinea — a travel
   survival kit
The Philippines — a travel survival kit
South America on a Shoestring
South-East Asia on a Shoestring
Sri Lanka — a travel survival kit
Trekking in the Himalayas
USA West

Forthcoming Titles:
   North-East Asia on a Shoestring
   Singapore & Malaysia — a travel
      survival kit
   Thailand — a travel survival kit

* earlier editions were titled *Across*
   Asia on the Cheap
** available only in Australasia

Lonely Planet travel guides are available around the world. If you can't find them, ask your bookshop to order them from one of the distributors listed below. For countries not listed or if you would like a free copy of our latest booklist write to Lonely Planet in Australia.

Australia — Lonely Planet Publications Pty Ltd, PO Box 88, South Yarra, Victoria 3141.
Canada — Milestone Publications, Box 6006, Victoria, British Columbia, V8P 5L4.
Hong Kong — The Book Society, GPO Box 7804, Hong Kong.
India — UBS Distributors, 5 Ansari Rd, New Delhi, 110002.
Japan — Intercontinental Marketing Corp, IPO Box 5056, Tokyo 100-31.
Malaysia — see Singapore
Nepal — see India
Netherlands — Nilsson & Lamm bv, Postbus 195, Pampuslaan 212, 1680 AD Weesp.
New Zealand — Caveman Press, PO Box 1458, Dunedin.
Papua New Guinea — Gordon & Gotch (PNG), PO Box 3395, Port Moresby.
Philippines — see Singapore
Singapore — MPH Distributors (S) Pte Ltd, 71-77 Stamford Rd, Singapore 0617
Thailand — Chalermnit, 1-2 Erawan Arcade, Bangkok
UK — Roger Lascelles, 16 Holland Park Gardens, London, W14 8DY.
USA (West) — Bookpeople, 2940 Seventh St, Berkeley, CA 94710.
USA (East) — Hippocrene Books, 171 Madison Ave, New York, NY 10016.
West Germany — Buchvertrieb Gerda Schettler, Postfach 64, D-3415 Hattorf a H.